THE MASKS OF GOD: OCCIDENTAL MYTHOLOGY

Joseph Campbell has been interested in mythology since his childhood in New York, when he read books about American Indians, frequently visited the American Museum of Natural History, and was fascinated by the museum's collection of totem poles. He earned his B.A. and M.A. degrees at Columbia in 1925 and 1927 and went on to study medieval French and Sanskrit at the universities of Paris and Munich. After a period in California, where he encountered John Steinbeck and the biologist Ed Ricketts, he taught at the Canterbury School, then, in 1934, joined the literature department at Sarah Lawrence College, a post he retained for many years. During the 1940s and '50s, he helped Swami Nikhilananda to translate the Upanishads and *The Gospel of Sri Ramakrishna*. The many books by Professor Campbell include *The Hero with a Thousand Faces, Myths to Live By, The Flight of the Wild Gander,* and *The Mythic Image*. He has edited *The Portable Arabian Nights, The Portable Jung,* and other works.

JOSEPH CAMPBELL

THE
MASKS OF GOD:
OCCIDENTAL
MYTHOLOGY

PENGUIN BOOKS

Penguin Books Ltd, Harmondsworth,
Middlesex, England
Penguin Books, 625 Madison Avenue, New York,
New York 10022, U.S.A.
Penguin Books Australia Ltd, Ringwood,
Victoria, Australia
Penguin Books Canada Limited, 2801 John Street,
Markham, Ontario, Canada L3R 1B4
Penguin Books (N.Z.) Ltd, 182–190 Wairau Road,
Auckland 10, New Zealand

First published in the United States of America by
The Viking Press 1964
Viking Compass Edition published 1970
Reprinted 1971 (twice), 1972, 1974 (twice), 1975
Published in Penguin Books 1976
Reprinted 1977, 1978, 1980, 1981, 1982

LIBRARY OF CONGRESS CATALOGING IN PUBLICATION DATA
Campbell, Joseph, 1904—
Occidental mythology.
(His The Masks of God; v. 3)
Includes bibliographical references and index.
1. Mythology. I. Title. II. Series.
[BL311.c276] 291'.13 76-23179
ISBN 0 14 00.4306 3

Printed in the United States of America by
Offset Paperback Mfrs., Inc., Dallas, Pennsylvania
Set in Linotype Times Roman

The Scripture quotations in this publication are from the
Revised Standard Version of the Bible, copyrighted 1946 and 1952
by the Division of Christian Education, National Council of
Churches, and used by permission

*The author wishes to acknowledge with gratitude the generous
support of his researches by the Bollingen Foundation.*

CONTENTS

++

ILLUSTRATIONS

Sketches for Figures 8, 13, 15, 16, 17, 20, 21,
27, 28, 30, 31, 32, are by John L. Mackey.

THE MASKS OF GOD:
OCCIDENTAL MYTHOLOGY

ON COMPLETION OF

The Masks of God

Looking back today over the twelve delightful years that I spent on this richly rewarding enterprise, I find that its main result for me has been its confirmation of a thought I have long and faithfully entertained: of the unity of the race of man, not only in its biology but also in its spiritual history, which has everywhere unfolded in the manner of a single symphony, with its themes announced, developed, amplified and turned about, distorted, reasserted, and, today, in a grand *fortissimo* of all sections sounding together, irresistibly advancing to some kind of mighty climax, out of which the next great movement will emerge. And I can see no reason why anyone should suppose that in the future the same motifs already heard will not be sounding still—in new relationships indeed, but ever the same motifs. They are all given here, in these volumes, with many clues, besides, suggesting ways in which they might be put to use by reasonable men to reasonable ends—or by poets to poetic ends—or by madmen to nonsense and disaster. For, as in the words of James Joyce in *Finnegans Wake:* "utterly impossible as are all these events they are probably as like those which may have taken place as any others which never took person at all are ever likely to be."

THE AGE
OF THE GODDESS

✦✦

Myth and Ritual: East and West

The geographical divide between the Oriental and Occidental ranges of myth and ritual is the tableland of Iran. Eastward are the two spiritual provinces of India and the Far East; westward, Europe and the Levant.

Throughout the Orient the idea prevails that the ultimate ground of being transcends thought, imaging, and definition. It cannot be qualified. Hence, to argue that God, Man, or Nature is good, just, merciful, or benign, is to fall short of the question. One could as appropriately—or inappropriately—have argued, evil, unjust, merciless, or malignant. All such anthropomorphic predications screen or mask the actual enigma, which is absolutely beyond rational consideration; and yet, according to this view, precisely that enigma is the ultimate ground of being of each and every one of us—and of all things.

The supreme aim of Oriental mythology, consequently, is not to establish as substantial any of its divinities or associated rites, but to render by means of these an experience that goes beyond: of identity with that Being of beings which is both immanent and transcendent; yet neither is nor is not. Prayers and chants, images, temples, gods, sages, definitions, and cosmologies are but ferries to a shore of experience beyond the categories of thought, to be abandoned on arrival; for, as the Indian Kena Upanishad states: "To know is not to know, not to know is to know"; [1] * and the Chinese Tao Te Ching: "Those who know are still." [2]

"Thou art that," declares the Vedic sage; [3] and the Japanese: "It is your true self." [4]

"O thou," states a basic Buddhist text, "who art gone, who art

* Numbered reference notes begin on page 527.

3

gone, who art gone to the yonder shore, who at the yonder shore hast disembarked: Enlightenment! Hail!" [5]

In the Western ranges of mythological thought and imagery, on the other hand, whether in Europe or in the Levant, the ground of being is normally personified as a Creator, of whom Man is the creature, and the two are not the same; so that here the function of myth and ritual cannot be to catalyze an experience of ineffable identity. Man alone, turned inward, according to this view can experience only his own creaturely soul, which may or may not be properly related to its Creator. The high function of Occidental myth and ritual, consequently, is to establish a means of relationship—of God to Man and Man to God. Such means are furnished, furthermore, by institutions, the rules of which cannot be learned through any scrutiny of nature, whether inward or without. Supernaturally revealed, these have come from God himself, as the myth of each institution tells; and they are administered by his clergy, in the spirit of the myth.

However, certain exclusively Occidental complications result from the fact that, where two such contradictory final terms as God and Man stand against each other, the individual cannot attach his allegiance wholly to both. On the one hand, as in the Book of Job, he may renounce his human judgment in the face of what he takes to be the majesty of God: "Behold, I am of small account; what shall I answer thee?" [6] Or, on the other hand, as in the manner of the Greeks, he may stand by his human values and judge, according to these, the character of his gods. The first type of piety we term religious and recognize in all traditions of the Levant: Zoroastrianism, Judaism, Christianity, and Islam. The other we term, in the broadest sense, humanistic, and recognize in the native mythologies of Europe: the Greek, Roman, Celtic, and Germanic.

By and large, the recent history of Occidental mythology can be described in terms of a grandiose interplay of these two contrary pieties; specifically, a violent tidal seesaw of exchanges, East to West, West to East, East to West, and West to East again, commencing with the first serious Persian attempt against Greece in 490 B.C. Alexander's conquest of the Levant turned the Levantine tide and was followed by the victories of Rome. However, even in the earliest Roman period, a counter-current of Levantine mythologies flowing west had begun to make itself felt. During the Carthaginian wars, in 204 B.C., the cult of the Phrygian Magna Mater was introduced formally to the city. Stoicism also carried a Levantine-Oriental strain, and at the height of Roman power, in the period of the Antonines, the Persian syncretic cult of Mithra became the chief religion of the empire. Christianity followed, after which the European empire fell, and Levantine Byzantium assumed both its name and its role as the New or Second Rome. Next, Mohammed's revelation burst upon the world, in 622 A.D., and through the following millennium bade fair to become the ultimate religion of mankind—until, once again, the tide turned. For as Persia had been stopped at Marathon (490 B.C.), so at Poitiers (732 A.D.) was Islam; and thereafter the stirring desert cry of the muezzin to communal prayer was year by year forced back. Within Christianized Europe itself, furthermore, the absolute authority of the One Church was dissolved through the irresistible return to force of the native European principles of individual judgment and the worth of rational man. The Reformation, Renaissance, Enlightenment, and present Age of Science followed, culminating, as of now, in the European spiritual conquest of the world—with, however, the next Levantine tide already on the rise.

Much of the complexity and vitality of the Occidental heritage must be attributed to the conflicting claims—both of which are accepted—on the one hand, of the advocates of what is offered as the Word of God, and, on the other, of the rational individual. Nothing quite of the kind has ever seriously troubled the mentality of the Orient east of Iran, where the old hieratic Bronze Age cosmology of the ever-circling eons—static yet turning ever, in a round of mathematical impersonality, from everlasting to everlasting—endures to this day as the last word on the universe and the place of man within it. All, according to this vision, though in apparent tumult, is harmony at root, as a manifestation of the all-supporting, all-suffusing mystery of being, which transcends thought, imaging, and definition; that is to say, transcends the search of science. Like a jewel, ever turning facets to the light, apparently in change but actually unchanging, this Bronze Age image of the cosmos, still intact in the Orient, renders a fixed world of fixed duties, roles, and possibilities: not a process, but a state; and the individual, whether man or god, is but a flash among the facets. There is no concept, or even sense, of either will or mind as a creative force. And when the Westerner exhibits these, the sage Oriental simply gazes, baffled, yet with the consoling sense of watching only a devil at work whose time will surely be short, and of himself, meanwhile, as securely rooted in all that is eternally true in man, society, the universe, and the ultimate secret of being. All of which he knows, or at least believes he knows, out of the old, old store of wisdom that both he and we inherit from the Age of Bronze.

For on a deeper level of the past than that of the shuttleplay of Persia, Greece, Rome, Byzantium, Islam, and, later, Europe, the legacy of the Bronze Age supplied many of the basic motifs of Occidental, as well as of Oriental, mythological thought. Moreover, the origins of this legacy were neither in India, as many still suppose, nor in China, but in the Near East, the Levant, where the spades of recent archaeological investigation have uncovered a background of preparation going back to c. 7500 B.C. At about that time, in the high, protected mountain valleys of Asia Minor, Syria, northern Iraq, and Iran, the arts of agriculture and stock-breeding were developed, and these produced an epochal mutation in both the character of human existence and its potentialities for development. Whereas earlier mankind had lived only precariously by food-collection (the hunt and vegetable-gathering), men now became substantial tillers of the earth. Self-sustaining villages appeared, and their number, steadily increasing, spread in a broad band eastward and westward, arriving simultaneously at both oceans, about 2500 B.C. Meanwhile, in the developed zone of origin, the nuclear Near East, a second epochal mutation occurred c. 3500 B.C., when in the river land of Mesopotamia the fundamental arts of all high civilization were invented: writing, mathematics, monumental architecture, systematic scientific observation (of the heavens), temple worship, and, dominating all, the kingly art of government. The knowledge and application of these reached Egypt with the first pharaohs of Dynasty I, c. 2850 B.C., Crete and the Indus Valley, c. 2500 B.C., China, c. 1500 B.C., and c. 1000–500 B.C. passed to Mexico and Peru.

Now in the neolithic village stage of this development and dispersal, the focal figure of all mythology and worship was the bountiful goddess Earth, as the mother and nourisher of life and receiver of the dead for rebirth. In the earliest period of her cult (perhaps c. 7500–3500 B.C. in the Levant) such a mother-goddess may have been thought of only as a local patroness of fertility, as many anthropologists suppose. However, in the temples even of the first of the higher civilizations (Sumer, c. 3500–2350 B.C.), the Great Goddess of highest concern was certainly much more than that. She was already, as she is now in the Orient, a metaphysical symbol: the arch personification of the power of Space, Time, and Matter, within whose bound all beings arise and die: the substance of their bodies, configurator of their lives and thoughts, and receiver of their dead. And everything having form or name—including God personified as good or evil, merciful or wrathful—was her child, within her womb.*

Toward the close of the Age of Bronze and, more strongly, with the dawn of the Age of Iron (c. 1250 B.C. in the Levant), the old cosmology and mythologies of the goddess mother were radically transformed, reinterpreted, and in large measure even suppressed, by those suddenly intrusive patriarchal warrior tribesmen whose traditions have come down to us chiefly in the Old and New Testaments and in the myths of Greece. Two extensive geographical matrices were the source lands of these insurgent warrior waves: for the Semites, the Syro-Arabian deserts, where, as ranging nomads, they herded sheep and goats and later mastered the camel; and, for the Hellenic-Aryan stems, the broad plains of Europe and south Russia, where they had grazed their herds of cattle and early mastered the horse.

In the following chapters, it will be our pleasure, first, to remark the ubiquity of the goddess, even in myths in which she is not sup-

* Compare Figures 31 and 32, infra, pp. 512 and 513.

posed to be playing any part, or indeed even to exist (Chapter 1); next, to glance back for a moment to the period of her dominance (Chapter 2); and then (Chapters 3 to 9), to make a systematic progress down the richly studded vale where stand the temples of the godly visions of the chief creative peoples of the Western World.

THE SERPENT'S BRIDE

++

I. The Mother Goddess Eve

No one familiar with the mythologies of the goddess of the primitive, ancient, and Oriental worlds can turn to the Bible without recognizing counterparts on every page, transformed, however, to render an argument contrary to the older faiths. In Eve's scene at the tree, for example, nothing is said to indicate that the serpent who appeared and spoke to her was a deity in his own right, who had been revered in the Levant for at least seven thousand years before the composition of the Book of Genesis. There is in the Louvre a carved green steatite vase, inscribed c. 2025 B.C. by King Gudea of Lagash, dedicated to a late Sumerian manifestation of this consort of the goddess, under his title Ningizzida, "Lord of the Tree of Truth." Two copulating vipers, entwined along a staff in the manner of the caduceus of the Greek god of mystic knowledge and rebirth, Hermes, are displayed through a pair of opening doors, drawn back by two winged dragons of a type known as the lion-bird (Figure 1).[1]

The wonderful ability of the serpent to slough its skin and so renew its youth has earned for it throughout the world the character of the master of the mystery of rebirth—of which the moon, waxing and waning, sloughing its shadow and again waxing, is the celestial sign. The moon is the lord and measure of the life-creating rhythm of the womb, and therewith of time, through which beings come and go: lord of the mystery of birth and equally of death—which two, in sum, are aspects of one state of being. The moon is

9

the lord of tides and of the dew that falls at night to refresh the verdure on which cattle graze. But the serpent, too, is a lord of waters. Dwelling in the earth, among the roots of trees, frequenting springs, marshes, and water courses, it glides with a motion of waves; or it ascends like a liana into branches, there to hang like some fruit of death. The phallic suggestion is immediate, and, as

Figure 1. The Serpent Lord

swallower, the female organ also is suggested; so that a dual image is rendered, which works implicitly on the sentiments. Likewise a dual association of fire and water attaches to the lightning of its strike, the forked darting of its active tongue, and the lethal burning of its poison. When imagined as biting its tail, as the mythological uroboros, it suggests the waters that in all archaic cosmologies surround—as well as lie beneath and permeate—the floating circular island Earth.

Figure 2, from an Elamite painted bowl of the late Sassanian period (226–641 A.D.), shows again the ancient guardian of the World Tree, up the trunk of which it coils.[2] In this form the dangerous, warning aspect of the presence is apparent. However, like the serpent in the Garden, Ningizzida is generally favorable to those who, with due respect, approach the boon of his sanctuary. Figure

Figure 2. The World Tree

3, from an early Akkadian seal of c. 2350–2150 B.C., displays the deity in human form, enthroned, with his caduceus emblem behind and a fire altar before.[3] Being conducted into his presence by a crowned divinity is a devotee, the owner of the seal, followed by a figure bearing a pail, with a serpent dangling from his head, who is an attendant of the god enthroned and corresponds to the lion-bird porters of Gudea's cup. The moon, the source of the waters of life, hangs above the cup elevated in the god's hand, whence the introduced initiate is now to imbibe.

Here an association of the serpent lord, the cup of immortality, and the moon is obvious; equally so a motif common to all antique

Figure 3. The Serpent Lord Enthroned

mythologies, namely, the multiple appearance of a god simultaneously in higher and lower aspects. For the porter at the gate, admitting or excluding aspirants, is a reduced manifestation of the power of the deity itself. He is the aspect first experienced by anyone approaching the presence; or, phrased another way, the testing aspect of the god. Moreover, the god—and his testing aspect, too—may appear in any one or more of a number of forms together: anthropomorphic, theriomorphic, vegetal, heavenly, or elemental; as, in the present instance: man, snake, tree, moon, and the water of life—which are to be recognized as aspects of a single polymorphous principle, symbolized in, yet beyond, all.

A series of three further seals will suffice to bring these symbols into relationship with the Bible. The first is the elegant Syro-Hittite example of Figure 4,[4] which shows the Mesopotamian hero Gil-

Figure 4. *Axis Mundi*

gamesh in dual manifestation, serving as the guardian of a sanctuary, in the way of the lion-birds of Gudea's cup. But what we find within this sanctuary is of neither human, animal, nor vegetal form; it is a column made of serpent-circles, bearing on its top a symbol of the sun. Such a pole or perch is symbolic of the pivotal point around which all things turn (the *axis mundi*), and so is a counterpart of the Buddhist Tree of Enlightenment in the "Immovable Spot" at the center of the world.[5] Around the symbol of the sun, atop the column, four little circles are to be seen. These, we are told, symbolize the four rivers that flow to the quarters of the world.[6] (Compare the Book of Genesis 2:10–14.) Approaching from the left is the owner of the seal, conducted by a lion-bird (or cherub, as such apparitions are termed in the Bible) bearing in its left hand a pail and in its right an elevated branch. A goddess follows in the role of the mystic mother of rebirth, and below is a guilloche—a labyrinthine device that in this art corresponds to the caduceus. So that, again, we recognize the usual symbols of the mythic garden of life, where the serpent, the tree, the world axis, sun eternal, and ever-living waters radiate grace to all quarters—and toward which the mortal individual is guided, by one divine manifestation or another, to the knowledge of his own immortality.

In the next seal, Figure 5, where the bounty of the mythic

Figure 5. The Garden of Immortality

garden is shown, all the personages are of the female sex. The two attending the tree are identified as a dual apparition of the underworld divinity Gula-Bau, whose classical counterparts are Demeter and Persephone.[7] The moon is directly above the fruit being offered, as in Figure 3 above the cup. And the recipient of the boon, who is already holding one branch of fruit in her right hand, is a mortal woman.

Thus we perceive that in this early mythic system of the nuclear Near East—in contrast to the later, strictly patriarchal system of the Bible—divinity could be represented as well under feminine as under masculine form, the qualifying form itself being merely the mask of an ultimately unqualified principle, beyond, yet inhabiting, all names and forms.

Nor is there any sign of divine wrath or danger to be found in these seals. There is no theme of guilt connected with the garden.

The boon of the knowledge of life is there, in the sanctuary of the world, to be culled. And it is yielded willingly to any mortal, male or female, who reaches for it with the proper will and readiness to receive.

Hence the early Sumerian seal of Figure 6 [8] cannot possibly be,

Figure 6. The Goddess of the Tree

as some scholars have supposed, the representation of a lost Sumerian version of the Fall of Adam and Eve.[9] Its spirit is that of the idyll in the much earlier, Bronze Age view of the garden of innocence, where the two desirable fruits of the mythic date palm are to be culled: the fruit of enlightenment and the fruit of immortal life. The female figure at the left, before the serpent, is almost certainly the goddess Gula-Bau (a counterpart, as we have said, of Demeter and Persephone), while the male on the right, who is not mortal but a god, as we know from his horned lunar crown, is no less surely her beloved son-husband Dumuzi, "Son of the Abyss: Lord of the Tree of Life," the ever-dying, ever-resurrected Sumerian god who is the archetype of incarnate being.

A fitting comparison would be with the Greco-Roman relief shown in Figure 7,[10] where the goddess of the Eleusinian mysteries, Demeter, is seen with her divine child Ploutos, or Plutus,* of whom the poet Hesiod wrote:

Happy, happy is the mortal who doth meet him as he goes,
For his hands are full of blessings and his treasure overflows.[11]

Plutus, on one plane of reference, personifies the wealth of the earth, but in a broader sense is a counterpart of the god of mys-

---

* Not the same as Plouton or Pluto, god of the netherworld, though frequently identified with him by assimilation of the names.

Figure 7. Demeter

teries, Dionysus. In *Primitive Mythology* and *Oriental Mythology*
I have discussed a number of such deities who are at once the con-
sorts and sons of the Great Goddess of the Universe. Returning to
her bosom in death (or, according to another image, in marriage),
the god is reborn—as the moon sloughing its shadow or the serpent
sloughing its skin. Accordingly, in those rites of initiation with
which such symbols were associated (as in the mysteries of Eleusis),
the initiate, returning in contemplation to the goddess mother of the
mysteries, became detached reflectively from the fate of his mortal
frame (symbolically, the son, who dies), and identified with the
principle that is ever reborn, the Being of all beings (the serpent
father): whereupon, in the world where only sorrow and death
had been seen, the rapture was recognized of an everlasting becoming.

Compare the legend of the Buddha. When he placed himself on
the Immovable Spot beneath the Tree of Enlightenment, the Creator
of the World Illusion, Kama-Mara, "Life-Desire and Fear of Death,"
approached to threaten his position. But he touched the earth with
the fingers of his right hand and, as the legend tells, "The mighty
Goddess Earth thundered with a hundred, a thousand, a hundred
thousand roars, declaring: 'I bear you witness!'; and the demon
fled." [12] The Blessed One that night achieved Enlightenment, and
for seven times seven days remained absorbed in rapture, during

which time a tremendous tempest arose. "And a mighty serpent king named Muchalinda," we then read,

> emerging from his place beneath the earth, enveloped the body of The Blessed One seven times with its folds, spreading his great hood above his head, saying "Let neither cold nor heat, nor gnats, flies, wind, sunshine, nor creeping creatures come near The Blessed One!" Whereafter, when seven days had elapsed and Muchalinda knew that the storm had broken up, the clouds having dispersed, he unwound his coils from the body of The Blessed One and, assuming human form, with joined hands to forehead, did reverence to The Blessed One.[13]

In the lore and legend of the Buddha the idea of release from death received a new, psychological interpretation, which, however, did not violate the spirit of its earlier mythic representations. The old motifs were carried to an advanced statement and given fresh immediacy through association with an actual historical character who had illustrated their meaning in his life; yet the sense of accord remained between the questing hero and the powers of the living world, who, like himself, were ultimately but transformations of the one mystery of being. Thus in the Buddha legend, as in the old Near Eastern seals, an atmosphere of substantial accord prevails at the cosmic tree, where the goddess and her serpent spouse give support to their worthy son's quest for release from the bondages of birth, disease, old age, and death.

In the Garden of Eden, on the other hand, a different mood prevails. For the Lord God (the written Hebrew name is Yahweh) cursed the serpent when he knew that Adam had eaten the fruit of the tree of the knowledge of good and evil; and he said to his angels: " 'Behold, the man has become like one of us, knowing good and evil; and now, lest he put forth his hand and take also of the tree of life, and eat, and live for ever'—therefore Yahweh sent him forth from the garden of Eden, to till the ground from which he was taken. He drove out the man; and at the east of the garden of Eden he placed the cherubim [i.e., lion-birds], and a flaming sword which turned every way, to guard the way to the tree of life." [14]

The first point that emerges from this contrast, and will be demonstrated further in numerous mythic scenes to come, is that in the context of the patriarchy of the Iron Age Hebrews of the first millennium B.C., the mythology adopted from the earlier neolithic and Bronze Age civilizations of the lands they occupied and for a time ruled became inverted, to render an argument just the opposite to that of its origin. And a second point, corollary to the first, is that there is consequently an ambivalence inherent in many of the basic symbols of the Bible that no amount of rhetorical stress on the patriarchal interpretation can suppress. They address a pictorial message to the heart that exactly reverses the verbal message addressed to the brain; and this nervous discord inhabits both Christianity and Islam as well as Judaism, since they too share in the legacy of the Old Testament.

However, the Bible is not the only source in the West of such ambivalence of teaching. There is a like inversion of sense in the legacy of Greece.

II. The Gorgon's Blood

Jane Ellen Harrison demonstrated over half a century ago that in the field festivals and mystery cults of Greece numerous vestiges survived of a pre-Homeric mythology in which the place of honor was held, not by the male gods of the sunny Olympic pantheon, but by a goddess, darkly ominous, who might appear as one, two, three, or many, and was the mother of both the living and the dead. Her consort was typically in serpent form; and her rites were not characterized by the blithe spirit of manly athletic games, humanistic art, social enjoyment, feasting and theater that the modern mind associates with Classical Greece, but were in spirit dark and full of dread. The offerings were not of cattle, gracefully garlanded, but of pigs and human beings; directed downward, not upward to the light; and rendered not in polished marble temples, radiant at the hour of rosy-fingered dawn, but in twilight groves and fields, over trenches through which the fresh blood poured into the bottomless abyss. "The beings worshiped," Miss Harrison wrote, "were not rational human, law-abiding *gods*, but vague, irrational, mainly malevolent δαίμονες, spirit-things, ghosts and bogeys and the like, not yet formulated and enclosed into god-head." [15] The atmosphere of the rituals, furthermore, was not of a shared feast, in the simple spirit of *do ut des,* "I give, so that thou shouldst give," but of riddance: *do ut abeas,* "I give, so that thou shouldst depart"; to which, however, there was always joined the idea that if the negative aspect of the daemon were dispelled, health and well-being, fertility and fruit, would issue of themselves from their natural source.

Figure 8 is from a votive tablet found in the Piraeus, dedicated

Figure 8. Zeus Meilichios

to a form of Olympian Zeus known as Zeus Meilichios.[16] But that heavenly Zeus—of all gods!—should have assumed the form of a serpent is amazing; for, as Miss Harrison points out: "Zeus is one of the few Greek gods who never appear attended by a snake." [17] Her explanation of the anomaly is that both the name and the figure belonged originally to a local daemon, the son-husband of the mother-goddess Earth, whose cult site in the Piraeus was taken over by the conquering high god of the Aryan pantheon from the north. To Zeus's name that of the local earth-spirit then was added as an epithet. And the annual spring rites of the daemon's cult also were assumed, together with their un-Olympian type of sacrifice—a holocaust of pigs—carried out, as one Greek commentator observed, "with a certain element of chilly gloom." [18]

Chilly gloom, however, is not the atmosphere that one associates with the Bronze Age civilizations of pre-Homeric, Minoan Crete and the contemporary Cycladic Isles, from which most of these un-Hellenic cults appear to have been derived. The atmosphere suggested in their lovely works of art, on the contrary, is of a graceful accord with the majesty of the cosmic process. Nor can it be claimed that even in later Classical times the old mother-goddess, amid her entourage of serpents, lions, fishponds, dovecotes, turtles, squids, goats, and bulls, was always a personage feared and abhorred. Sir James G. Frazer, in *The Golden Bough,* it is true, has shown that her cult in the now famous grove at Lake Nemi, near Rome, was indeed dark and ominous enough.

"In this sacred grove," as he has described the site in the opening pages of his great work,

> there grew a certain tree round which at any time of the day, and probably far into the night, a grim figure might be seen to prowl. In his hand he carried a drawn sword, and he kept peering warily about him as if at every instant he expected to be set upon by an enemy. He was a priest and a murderer; and the man for whom he looked was sooner or later to murder him and hold the priesthood in his stead. Such was the rule of the sanctuary. A candidate for the priesthood could only succeed to office by slaying the priest, and having slain him, he retained office till he was himself slain by a stronger or a craftier. The post which he held by this precarious tenure carried with it the title of king; but surely no crowned head ever lay uneasier, or was visited by more evil dreams, than his. For year in, year out, in summer and winter, in fair weather and in foul, he had to keep his lonely watch, and whenever he snatched a troubled slumber it was at the peril of his life.[19]

A somber scene, indeed! And we have others too from the annals of Greece and Rome that produce the same atmosphere of dread: the oft-told tale, for example, of Queen Pasiphaë of Crete, her love for a bull from the sea; and their child, the terrible Minotaur, pacing to and fro in the labyrinth built to cage him. However, still other pre-Hellenic ritual scenes suggest an idyll, rather, of harmony and peace, wisdom and a power of prophecy, for those in whose heart there is no fear of spooks. In a treatise "On the Nature of Animals" the Roman author Aelian (d. 222 A.D.) described a serpent sanctuary at Epirus that was said in his time to be of the god Apollo, but was actually—like the serpent shrine of Zeus Meilichios—the vestige of an earlier, pre-Hellenic Aegean mythology.

> The people of Epirus sacrifice in general to Apollo, and on one day of the year they celebrate to him their chief feast, a feast of great magnificence, much reputed. There is a grove dedicated to the god, with a circular enclosure, within which are snakes—playthings, surely, for the god. And they are approached only by the maiden priestess. She is naked, and she brings to the snakes their food. These snakes are declared by the people of Epirus to be descended from the Python at Delphi. And now, if when the priestess approaches them the snakes are seen to be gentle, and if they take to their food kindly, that is said to mean that there will be a plentiful year and free from disease; but if they frighten her and do not take the honey cakes she offers, they portend the reverse.[20]

Or let us regard the vase painting of Figure 9, which, in essentially the same spirit, shows the mythic tree of the golden apples in the sunset-land of the Hesperides.[21] An immense horned snake coils up around the tree, and from a cave in the earth at its root water wells from a spring with double mouth, while the lovely Hesperides themselves—a family of nymphs known to antiquity as daughters born without father to the cosmic goddess Night [22]—are in attendance round about. And all is precisely as things would have remained in Eden, too, if the recently installed patriarch of the estate (who was developing his colorable claim to priority not only of ownership but even of being) had not taken umbrage when he learned what things were going on.

For it is now perfectly clear that before the violent entry of the late Bronze and early Iron Age nomadic Aryan cattle-herders from the north and Semitic sheep-and-goat-herders from the south into the old cult sites of the ancient world, there had prevailed in that world an essentially organic, vegetal, non-heroic view of the nature and necessities of life that was completely repugnant to those lion hearts for whom not the patient toil of earth but the battle spear and its plunder were the source of both wealth and joy. In the older

Figure 9. The Tree of the Hesperides

mother myths and rites the light and darker aspects of the mixed thing that is life had been honored equally and together, whereas in the later, male-oriented, patriarchal myths, all that is good and noble was attributed to the new, heroic master gods, leaving to the native nature powers the character only of darkness—to which, also, a negative moral judgment now was added. For, as a great body of evidence shows, the social as well as mythic orders of the two contrasting ways of life were opposed. Where the goddess had been venerated as the giver and supporter of life as well as consumer of the dead, women as her representatives had been accorded a paramount position in society as well as in cult. Such an order of female-dominated social and cultic custom is termed, in a broad and general way, the order of Mother Right. And opposed to such, without quarter, is the order of the Patriarchy, with an ardor of righteous eloquence and a fury of fire and sword.

Hence, the early Iron Age literatures both of Aryan Greece and Rome and of the neighboring Semitic Levant are alive with variants of the conquest by a shining hero of the dark and—for one reason or another—disparaged monster of the earlier order of godhood, from whose coils some treasure was to be won: a fair land, a maid, a boon of gold, or simply freedom from the tyranny of the impugned monster itself.

The chief biblical example was Yahweh's victory over the serpent of the cosmic sea, Leviathan, of which he boasted to Job. "Can you draw Leviathan out with a fishhook, or press down his tongue with a cord? Can you put a rope into his nose, or pierce his jaw with a hook? Will he make many supplications to you? Will he speak to you soft words? Will he make a covenant with you to take him for your serpent for ever? Will you play with him as with a bird, or will you put him on leash for your maidens? Will traders bargain over him? Will they divide him up among the merchants? Can you fill his skin with harpoons, or his head with fishing spears? Lay hands on him; think of the battle; you will not do it again." [23]

The counterpart for the Greeks was the victory of Zeus over Typhon, the youngest child of Gaea, the goddess Earth—by which deed the reign of the patriarchal gods of Mount Olympus was secured over the earlier Titan broods of the great goddess mother. The Titan's form, half man, half snake, we are told, was enormous. He was so large that his head often knocked against the stars and his arms could extend from sunrise to sunset (Figure 10). From his shoulders, according to Hesiod's account, there reared a hundred serpent heads, all flashing fiery tongues, while flames darted from the many eyes. Within could be heard voices, sending out sounds the gods could understand; but also bellowing like bulls, roaring

Figure 10. Zeus against Typhon

like lions, baying like dogs, or hissing, so loudly that the mountains echoed. And this terrible thing would have become the master of creation had not Zeus gone against him in combat.

Beneath the feet of the father of the gods Olympus shook as he moved, the earth groaned; and from the lightning of his bolt, as well as from the eyes and breath of his antagonist, fire was bursting over the dark sea. The ocean boiled; towering waves beat upon all promontories of the coast; the ground quaked; Hades, lord of the dead, trembled; and even Zeus himself, for a time, was unstrung. But when he had summoned again his strength, gripping his terrific weapon, the great hero sprang from his mountain and, hurling the bolt, set fire to all those flashing, bellowing, roaring, baying, hissing heads. The monster crashed to earth, and the earth-goddess Gaea groaned beneath her child. Flames went out from him, and these ran along the steep mountain forests, roaring, so hot that much of the earth dissolved, like iron in the flaming forge within the earth of the lame craftsman of the gods, Hephaestus. And then the mighty king of the gods, Zeus, prodigious in storming wrath, heaved the flaming victim into gaping Tartarus—whence to this day there pour forth from his titan form all those winds that blow terribly across seas and bring to mortal men distress, scatter shipping, drown sailors, and ruin the beloved works of dwellers on the land with storm and dust.[24]

The resemblance of this victory to that of Indra, king of the Vedic pantheon, over the cosmic serpent Vritra is beyond question.[25] The two myths are variants of a single archetype. Furthermore, in each the role of the anti-god has been assigned to a figure from an earlier mythology—in Greece, of the Pelasgians, in India, of the Dravidians—daemons that formerly had symbolized the force of the cosmic order itself, the dark mystery of time, which licks up hero deeds like dust: the force of the never-dying serpent, sloughing lives like skins, which, pressing on, ever turning in its circle of eternal return, is to continue in this manner forever, as it has already cycled from all eternity, getting absolutely nowhere.

Against the symbol of this undying power the warrior principle of the great deed of the individual who matters flung its bolt, and for a period the old order of belief—as well as of civilization—fell apart. The empire of Minoan Crete disintegrated, just as in India the civilization of the Dravidian twin cities, Harappa and Mohenjo-daro. However, in India the old mythology of the serpent power presently recovered strength, until, by the middle of the first millennium B.C., it had absorbed the entire pantheon and spirit of the Vedic gods—Indra, Mitra, Vayu, and the rest—transforming all into mere agents of the processes of its own, still circling round of eternal return.[26] In the West, on the other hand, the principle of indeterminacy represented by the freely willing, historically effective hero not only gained but held the field, and has retained it to the present. Moreover, this victory of the principle of free will, together with its moral corollary of individual responsibility, establishes the first distinguishing characteristic of specifically Occidental myth: and here I mean to include not only the myths of Aryan Europe (the Greeks, Romans, Celts, and Germans), but also those of both the Semitic and Aryan peoples of the Levant (Semitic Akkadians, Babylonians, Phoenicians, Hebrews, and Arabs; Aryan Persians, Armenians, Phrygians, Thraco-Illyrians, and Slavs). For whether we think of the victories of Zeus and Apollo, Theseus, Perseus, Jason, and the rest, over the dragons of the Golden Age, or turn to that of Yahweh over Leviathan, the lesson is equally of a self-moving power greater than the force of any earthbound serpent destiny. All stand (to use Miss Harrison's phrase) "first and foremost as a protest against the worship of Earth and the daimones of the fertility of Earth."

"A worship of the powers of fertility which includes all plant and animal life is broad enough to be sound and healthy," she adds, "but as man's attention centers more and more on his own humanity, such a worship is an obvious source of danger and disease." [27]

Well, so it is! And yet, one cannot help feeling that there is something forced and finally unconvincing about all the manly moral attitudes of the shining righteous deedsmen, whether of the biblical or of the Greco-Roman schools; for, in revenge or compensation, the ultimate life, and therewith spiritual depth and interest, of the myths in which they figure continues to rest with the dark presences of the cursed yet gravid earth, which, though defeated and subdued, are with their powers never totally absorbed. A residue of mystery remains to them; and this, throughout the history of the West, has ever lurked within, and emanated from, the archaic symbols of the later, "higher" systems—as though speaking silently, to say, "But do you not hear the deeper song?"

In the legend of Medusa, for instance, though it is told from the point of view of the classic Olympian patriarchal system, the older message can be heard. The hair of Medusa, Queen of Gorgons, was of hissing serpents; the look of her eyes turned men to stone: Perseus slew her by device and escaped with her head in his wallet, which Athene then affixed to her shield. But from the Gorgon's severed neck the winged steed Pegasus sprang forth, who had been begotten by the god Poseidon and now is hitched before the chariot of Zeus. And through the ministry of Athene, Asclepius, the god of healing, secured the blood from the veins of Medusa, both from her left side and from her right. With the former he slays, but with the latter he cures and brings back to life.

Thus in Medusa the same two powers coexisted as in the black goddess Kali of India, who with her right hand bestows boons and in her left holds a raised sword. Kali gives birth to all beings of the universe, yet her tongue is lolling long and red to lick up their living blood. She wears a necklace of skulls; her kilt is of severed arms and legs. She is Black Time, both the life and the death of all beings, the womb and tomb of the world: the primal, one and only, ultimate reality of nature, of whom the gods themselves are but the functioning agents.

Or let us take the curious legend of the blind sage Tiresias, to whom even Zeus and Hera turned once for a judgment. "I insist," the king of the gods had playfully said to his spouse, "you women have more joy in making love than men do." She denied it. And so they called upon Tiresias; for, in consequence of a strange adventure, he had experienced both sides of love.

"One day, while in the green wood," as Ovid tells the tale,

> Tiresias offended with a stroke of his stick two immense serpents, mating, and (O wonder!) was changed from man to woman. Thus he lived for seven years. In the eighth, he saw the same two again and said: "If in striking you there be such virtue that the doer of the deed is changed into his opposite, then I shall now strike once more"; which he did, and his former shape returned, so that again he had the gender of his birth.[28]

When required to resolve the quarrel of the father of the gods and his queen, therefore, Tiresias knew the answer—and he took the part of Zeus. The goddess, in a pique, struck him blind; but the god, in compensation, bestowed on him the gift of prophecy.

In this tale the mating serpents, like those of the caduceus, are the sign of the world-generating force that plays through all pairs of opposites, male and female, birth and death. Into their mystery Tiresias blundered as he wandered in the green wood of the secrets of the ever-living goddess Earth. His impulsive stroke placed him between the two, like the middle staff (*axis mundi*) of Figure 1; and he was thereupon flashed to the other side for seven years—a week of years, a little life—the side of which he formerly had had no knowledge. Whence, with intent, he again touched the living symbol of the two that are in nature one, and, returning to his proper form, was thereafter the one who was in knowledge both: in wisdom greater than either Zeus, the god who was merely male, or his goddess, who was merely female.

The patriarchal point of view is distinguished from the earlier archaic view by its setting apart of all pairs-of-opposites—male and

female, life and death, true and false, good and evil—as though
they were absolutes in themselves and not merely aspects of the
larger entity of life. This we may liken to a solar, as opposed to
lunar, mythic view, since darkness flees from the sun as its opposite,
but in the moon dark and light interact in the one sphere. The blinding of Tiresias was an effect, then, a communication to him of lunar
wisdom. It was a blindness merely to the sunlight world, where all
pairs of opposites appear to be distinct. And the gift of prophecy
was the correlative vision of the inward eye, which penetrates the
darkness of existence. Hence Tiresias comes like a visitant from
the deepest subliminal stratum of the Greek heritage, to move as a
mysterious presence among the characters of the upper, secondary
sphere of those gods and myths of Olympus by which the other had
been overcast—yet not entirely suppressed.

For have we not already seen the serpent Zeus Meilichios? And
was it not in such a form that Zeus had intercourse with his daughter Persephone when the earth-goddess Demeter, of whom she had
been born, left her in a cave in Crete, guarded by the two serpents
normally harnessed to her chariot?

The reader recalls, perhaps, the Orphic legend cited in *Primitive
Mythology*,[29] of how, while the maiden goddess sat there, peacefully weaving a mantle of wool on which there was to be a representation of the universe, her mother contrived that Zeus should
learn of her presence; he approached in the form of an immense
snake. And the virgin conceived the ever-dying, ever-living god of
bread and wine, Dionysus, who was born and nurtured in that cave,
torn to death as a babe, and resurrected.

Comparably, in the Christian legend, derived from the same
archaic background, God the Holy Ghost in the form of a dove approached the Virgin Mary and she—through the ear—conceived
God the Son, who was born in a cave, died and was resurrected, and
is present hypostatically in the bread and wine of the Mass. For the
dove, no less than the serpent, was an attribute and companion of
the Great Goddess of the pre-Homeric, pre-Mosaic East. In
Figure 11 she is seen as Aphrodite, surrounded by worshiping
Erotes, holding a dove in her left hand.[30] Thus, in the world pano-

Figure 11. Aphrodite with Erotes

rama of mythology, God the Father of the Christian Trinity, the father-creator of Mary, God the Holy Ghost, her spouse, and God the Son, her slain and resurrected child, reproduce for a later age the Orphic mystery of Zeus in the form of a serpent begetting on his own daughter Persephone his incarnate son Dionysus.

The victory of the patriarchal deities over the earlier matriarchal ones was not as decisive in the Greco-Roman sphere as in the myths of the Old Testament; for, as Jane Harrison has shown, the earlier gods survived, not only peripherally in such aberrant forms as Zeus Meilichios, but also in the rites of the popular field and women's cults, and particularly in the mysteries of Demeter and the Orphics, whence numerous elements of the heritage were passed on to Christianity—most obviously in the myths and rites of the Virgin and the Mass. For in Greece the patriarchal gods did not exterminate, but married, the goddesses of the land, and these succeeded ultimately in regaining influence, whereas in biblical mythology all the goddesses were exterminated—or, at least, were supposed to have been.

However, as we read in every chapter of the books of Samuel and Kings, the old fertility cults continued to be honored throughout Israel, both by the people and by the majority of their rulers. And in the very text of the Pentateuch itself the signs remain, carried silently in symbols, of the wisdom of the old earth mother and her serpent spouse.

> The Lord Yahweh said to the woman, "What is this that you have done?" The woman said, "The serpent beguiled me and I ate." Yahweh said to the serpent, "Because you have done this, cursed are you above all cattle and above all beasts of the field. Upon your belly you shall go, and you shall eat dust all the days of your life. I will put enmity between you and the woman, and between your seed and her seed; he shall bruise your head and you shall bruise his heel."

Thus Yahweh cursed the woman to bring forth in pain and be subject to her spouse—which set the seal of the patriarchy on the new age. And he cursed, also, the man who had come to the tree and eaten of the fruit that she presented. "In the sweat of your face, you shall eat bread," he said, "till you return to the ground; for out of it you were taken; you are dust, and to dust you shall return" (Genesis 3:13–19).

But the ground, the dust, out of which the punished couple had been taken, was, of course, the goddess Earth, deprived of her anthropomorphic features, yet retaining in her elemental aspect her function of furnishing the substance into which the new spouse, Yahweh, had breathed the breath of her children's life. And they were to return to her, not to the father, in death. Out of her they had been taken, and to her they would return.

Like the Titans of the older faith, Adam and Eve were thus the children of the mother-goddess Earth. They had been one at first, as Adam; then split in two, as Adam and Eve. And the man, rebuked, replied to Yahweh's challenge in a way entirely appropriate to his Titan character. "The man," we read, "called his wife's name

Eve, because she was the mother of all living." As the mother of all living, Eve herself, then, must be recognized as the missing anthropomorphic aspect of the mother-goddess. And Adam, therefore, must have been her son as well as spouse: for the legend of the rib is clearly a patriarchal inversion (giving precedence to the male) of the earlier myth of the hero born from the goddess Earth, who returns to her to be reborn. See again Figures 6 and 7.

Moreover, as in the early Bronze Age seals of Ningizzida and his serpent porter, we have clear and adequate evidence throughout the biblical text that the Lord Yahweh was himself an aspect of the serpent power, and so himself properly the serpent spouse of the serpent goddess of the caduceus, Mother Earth. Let us recall, first, the magical serpent rod by which Moses was to frighten Pharaoh. Yahweh said to him, "What is that in your hand?" And Moses said, "A rod." Yahweh said, "Cast it on the ground." So he cast it on the ground and it became a serpent; and Moses fled from it. But Yahweh said to Moses, "Put out your hand and take it by the tail." So he put out his hand and caught it, and it became a rod in his hand.[31] The same rod later produced water from the rock in the desert.[32] And when the people in the desert presently murmured against Yahweh, as we read:

> Yahweh sent fiery serpents among the people, and they bit the people, so that many people of Israel died. . . . So Moses prayed for the people. And Yahweh said to Moses, "Make a fiery serpent, and set it on a pole; and every one who is bitten, when he sees it, shall live." So Moses made a bronze serpent, and set it on a pole; and if a serpent bit any man, he would look at the bronze serpent and live.[33]

We are informed in II Kings that the people continued to revere this bronze serpent idol in Jerusalem until the time of King Hezekiah (719–691 B.C.), who, as we are told, "broke in pieces the bronze serpent that Moses had made, for until those days the people of Israel had burned incense to it: it was called Nehushtan." [34]

Shall we be astonished, then, to learn that the name of the priestly tribe of Levi, the chief protagonists of Yahweh, was derived from the same verbal root as the word Leviathan? [35] or that when pictures did at last appear of the unpicturable god, his form was of a god with serpent legs? *

III. Ultima Thule

We turn now to Ireland, where the magic of the goddess of the land of youth survives in fairy lore to this day. In the Middle Ages the mystic spell of her people of the fairy hills poured over Europe in the legends of the Table Round of King Arthur, where Gawain, Tristan, and Merlin brought the old Celtic Fianna and Knights of the Red Branch to life again in the armor of the Crusades. And a bit further back in time, in a period little studied, c. 375–950 A.D., the epic narratives themselves from which those heroes came were fashioned from mythic tales already old.

The first inhabitants of Ireland of whom trace remains arrived on its beaches during that obscure prehistoric time between the Old Stone Age and the New that is known as the mesolithic. The glaciers had retreated; but a chill, dank, misty air remained, through which gulls flew across gray-green waters whereon icebergs sailed like ships: and the life therein was of the seal, the walrus, and the whale. The great age of the paleolithic hunt was already of the long past, when the wonderful painted caves of southern France and northern Spain had been the chief religious sanctuaries of the world. There had been nothing in their time, anywhere on earth, to match or even to approach them: c. 30,000–15,000 B.C. But as the ice continued to retreat during the final stages of the Würm glaciation, there had ensued an irreversible deterioration of the conditions of the hunt. The semi-arctic tundra landscape, which had supported the woolly mammoth and rhinoceros, musk ox, and reindeer, gave way at first to grassy plain on which immense herds of bison, wild cattle, horses, and antelope ran; but then the plains gave way to forest, and the meat supply decreased dramatically. Many of the hunting folk followed their quarry northward, to become in time, as their province decreased in wealth, ancestors of those scattered hunting and fishing tribes that still populate thinly the farthest north. Others, however, remained to cull sustenance not only from

* See Figures 25 and 26, infra, pp. 274–75.

the forest but also from the sea and shores. Already in the Magdalenian period, during the final prosperous millenniums, the fishing spear, fishhook, and harpoon had appeared among the weaponries of the chase, and the pursuit of the whale, the walrus, and the seal, in perilous coracles, had been developed—which has continued to the present among the last cultural inheritors, the Eskimos. But in the sequel both man's zeal for life and the conditions of the European field so declined that the area became merely an outland of grubbing, residual forest folk.

The vital centers of cultural life had shifted south and to the southeast, where the grazing plains of North Africa and Southwest Asia, which today are largely desert, still supported mighty herds. A world of action flourished there that is vividly depicted in the rock paintings (not in caves now, but on the surfaces of cliffs) of the Capsian style of North Africa and southern Spain. The bow and arrow appear for the first time in this art, together with the dog as a companion of the hunt. And whereas the paintings of the earlier north had been primarily of beasts, those of this later Capsian art, c. 10,000–4000 B.C., were largely of human scenes, in a vigorously fluent narrative style. Moreover, the life depicted in these scenes was at first of hunters but then of herding tribes. For it was during the final stages of this terminal phase of the paleolithic that the arts of cattle-breeding and agriculture were developed in that Levantine part of its broad range that is known to historians today as the nuclear Near East.

Leo Frobenius was the first to use the terms West-East Pendulation and East-West Pendulation to represent the two successive trends of diffusion, respectively, of the paleolithic (hunting) and neolithic (agricultural) ages. "We can say," he wrote in his inexhaustibly suggestive little book, *Monumenta Terrarum,*

> that, by and large, the pendulation of the transfer of culture in prehistoric times proceeded in the paleolithic from a starting point in Western Europe, along the southern shore of the Mediterranean, eastward, across Egypt, to Asia. In the Old Stone Age, that is to say, the tide of culture moved from West to East, south of the regions formerly covered by the great

glaciers. Then followed [in Europe] a cultural hiatus—until, presently, from eastward, there came the tide of a High Bronze Age, infinitely richer than anything before. This arrived both overland, through eastern Europe, and by sea, along the northern Mediterranean shores. From Asia Minor it came across the Aegean (Greek culture) to Italy (Rome); whence, faring westward still, it flowered in the Gothic (in France, Belgium, and Spain), culminating at its western extreme (in rationalistic England) with the preparation of the present age of world economy. In other words: separated from the earlier West-East Pendulation by a hiatus, a later East-West Pendulation brought the tide of the higher cultures.[36]

And in a subsequent work on Africa Frobenius pressed the observation further.

Geographically as well as historically [he wrote], the Mediterranean Sea is divided by the land bridge of Italy and Sicily into a western and an eastern basin. Assigning to each of these the name of the large island in its midst, we may term them, respectively, the Sardinian Sea and the Cretan. The destiny of Northwest Africa has been determined, both from inward necessity and from without, by events in the regions around the Sardinian Sea, while the destiny of Levantine Africa has been shaped by those of the lands around the Cretan. . . . During the late paleolithic period the center of gravity of European culture was in the west: Spain during the Capsian period stood in close relationship to Northwest Africa, while in the greatly earlier Chellean age Northwest Africa and all of Western Europe constituted a single immense culture zone.—And now, in exactly the same way, the dependency can be noted of Levantine, Northeast Africa upon events around the Cretan Sea; so that, as the Sardinian to Western Europe, the Cretan Sea was related to Western Asia.[37]

In sum, therefore: Throughout the almost endless period of the paleolithic hunt, Northwest Africa and Western Europe were a single immense culture province—the paleolithic fountainhead, as Frobenius termed it—whence a broad West-to-East pendulation carried the arts of Old Stone Age man to Asia; whereas in the later, much briefer period of rapid cultural transformation that we know as the neolithic or New Stone Age, Southwest Asia and Northeast

Africa became the creative culture hearths, and the tide flowed back to Europe, East-to-West. Furthermore, whereas the earliest European mythological records of importance date from the paleolithic caves of c. 30,000–15,000 B.C., those of the Levant are of the neolithic age, c. 7500–3500 B.C. In the European spirit the structuring force lives on of the long building of its races to the activities of the hunt, and therewith the virtues of individual judgment and independent excellence; while, in contrast, in the younger, yet culturally far more complex, Near East the virtues of group living and submission to authority have been the ideals bred into the individual—who, in such a world, is actually no individual at all, in the European sense, but the constituent of a group. And, as we are to see, throughout the troubled history of the interplay of these two culture worlds in their alternating pendulations, the irresoluble conflict of the principles of the paleolithic individual and the neolithic sanctified group has created and maintained even to the present day a situation of both creative reciprocity and mutual disdain.

But to return to Ireland.

IV. Mother Right

The particular force and character of the contributions of Ireland to the early development of the West derived from the fact that, although throughout the paleolithic period the island had been uninhabited, at the very start of the West European Age of Bronze, c. 2500 B.C., it became suddenly—and for good reason—one of the most productive fountainheads of the Occidental scene. Britain during paleolithic times had been of a piece with the mainland, but Ireland, not. Hence, it was only when the dangerous, late paleolithic adventure of the sea hunt of the walrus, seal, and whale developed that the island could be reached at all. But even then no permanent settlement was achieved.

The only remains from that remote time are those already mentioned, of the mesolithic age. They were discovered along the northeast Antrim coast, on "raised beaches" (now some twenty-five feet above the sea), notably at Larne, Kilroot, and Portrush, and on Island Magee. And what is already strange is the fact that, whereas

the artifacts of the first three sites exhibit affinities with the mesolithic cultures of the Baltic and North Seas, those of Island Magee,
which is within sight of Larne, are linked rather with the industries
of northern Spain. These contrary associations were to continue
to contribute to the destiny of the island. However, the early mesolithic visitors were not themselves in any sense the founders of that
destiny. Who they were, what brought them to Ireland, when, or
how—or why they disappeared—we do not know. In the words of
Professor R. A. S. Macalister, of University College, Dublin, for
many years President of the Royal Irish Academy and of the Royal
Society of Antiquities of Ireland, "their memorial has perished
with them. Their lives, their loves, their hates, their speech, their
manners, customs, and scheme of society, their deaths, their gods,
all have faded as in a dream." [38] The dating of their ephemeral
settlements can be reckoned only vaguely, as somewhere—anywhere—between the end of the glacial ages in the north, c. 7800
B.C., and the appearance, c. 2500 B.C., of the earliest Copper and
Bronze Age remains, with which the high history not of Ireland
alone, but of the entire northwest of Europe, properly begins.

The motive force of this sudden Bronze Age development is to
be seen in what Professor Macalister has termed the chief "impulsive," as distinct from "expulsive," cause of the colonization of a
land so difficult of access. "There are," he states, "impulsive as
well as expulsive reasons for colonization. Expulsive causes are
those which make the original home temporarily or permanently
uninhabitable—the pressure of an inrush of enemies, of adverse
climatic conditions, or what not. Impulsive causes are those which
make the new home attractive; and undoubtedly gold, of which
Ireland was understood to possess great stores, was the chief attrac-
tion which the country offered to invaders or to settlers." [39] Gold
lay twinkling in the beds of the rivers, much as in the days of pan-
ning gold in our own American Wild West. "The large collection of
gold ornaments in the National Museum," Professor Macalister
continues, "shows that the gold of the river-gravels was industri-
ously collected: in fact, the Bronze Age goldsmiths seem to have
exhausted the supply." [40] Stores of copper, too, were to be found

in many parts of the island, and this was a metal likewise of incalculable value. Tin, however, the other ingredient of bronze, was not at first available, the nearest resource being in neighboring British Cornwall. But this was presently discovered and mined by the Irish. So that even in the period of the flowering of Babylon, Middle Kingdom Egypt, Troy, and Minoan Crete, there was a remote secondary hearth, beyond the wilderness of the farthest northwest, from which flowed an export of lunate ornaments of gold, a particular type of flat copper ax and, later, when the tin had been discovered, a characteristic bronze halberd.

But the point of particular interest for the student of mythology, and of continuing force for the importance of Ireland in all the later developments of European mythic and legendary lore, is that the period of this foundation of the culture style of the island was intermediate in time between the twilight of the great European paleolithic ages and dawn of the still greater patriarchal ages of the Aryan Celts, Romans, and Germans. The culture was of a radically different order from either of the two between which it arose. Nor was its period brief, for it endured from c. 2500 to as late as c. 500–200 B.C., when the first of the iron-bearing Celtic tribes arrived, of whose religious lore the druids were the masters. Its order of mythology and morality was of the Bronze Age, of the mother-goddess and Mother Right, and its relationship to the later, patriarchal, Celtic system was about the same as that of the early Creto-Aegean to the classic Olympian of Greece.

In fact, even in the late Celtic legends many startling traits are revealed of brazen dames who preserved the customs of that age up to early Christian times. They were in no sense wives in the patriarchal style. For even at the height of the Celtic heroic age, c. 200 B.C. to c. 450 A.D., many of the most noted Irish noblewomen still were of pre-Celtic stock; and these bore themselves in the imperious manner of the matriarchs of yore.

There is, for example, the episode of the pillow colloquy of Queen Meave of Connaught with her Celtic spouse, Ailill of Leinster, in the bizarre epic known as "The Cattle Raid of Cooley."

The couple were at peace in their fort of Cruachan, having just spread the royal couch, when "Woman," said Ailill, "it is true indeed, the saying that a good man's wife is good." She replied, "Yes; but of what relevance to you?" He answered, "Because you are a better woman now than you were the day I married you." She said, "I was good before ever I saw you." "Curious, then," he responded, "that we never heard anything of the kind, but only that you placed trust in your woman's wiles, whereas the enemies on your borders were freely plundering you of your plunder and your prey."

And then it was that Meave gave the retort of a true queen matriarch, no bartered bride of any man, but the mistress of her own realm—and of the king himself, besides, with all the rights reserved to herself that in the patriarchy belong to males.

"I was not as you declare," she told him, "but I dwelt with my father Eochaid, King of Ireland, who had six daughters, and the noblest and most worshiped of us all was I. For as regards largess, I was the best; and as regards battle, strife, and combat, again I was the best. I had before and around me twice fifteen hundred royal mercenaries, all chieftains' sons; with ten men for each, and for each of these, eight men; for each of these, seven; for each of these, six; for each of these, five; for each of these, four; for each of these, three; for each of these, two; and for each of these, one. These I had to my standing household; for which reason, my father gave me one of his provinces of Ireland; namely this of Cruachan, wherein we are now; whence I am known by the designation, Meave of Cruachan."

That Queen Meave was a mistress not only of her own castle but also of the Irish art of poetic magnification appears from the fact, as Professor Macalister has pointed out, that the retinue here specified amounts to 40,478,703,000 persons, "or rather more than three times the whole population of modern Dublin crowded upon every single square mile of Ireland." [41] Having made this point, the Queen continued.

"Thereupon," she said to her spouse, "there came an embassage to sue for me from Finn mac Rosa Rua, King of Leinster; another from Cairpre Niafer mac Rosa, King of Tara; one from the King of Ulidia, Conachar mac Fachtna; and yet another from Eochu Beg. But I rejected them; for I was she that required a strange bride gift, such as no woman had ever demanded from any man of the men of Erin; namely that my husband should be a man not the least niggardly, without jealousy, and without fear.

"For should the man that I had be niggardly, that were not well, since I should outdo him in liberality. And were he timorous, that were not well, since I alone should have the victory in battles, contests, and affrays. And were he jealous, neither would that be well; for I have never been without one man in the shadow of another. And I have gotten myself, indeed, just such a husband, namely yourself: Ailill mac Rosa Rua of Leinster. For you are not niggardly, jealous, or a coward. Moreover, I presented you with wedding gifts of such worth as become a woman; to wit, cloth for the raiment of twelve men, a battle car of the value of three times seven slave girls, your face's width of ruddy gold, and white bronze to the weight of your left forearm. So that if anyone should disparage, maim, or cheat you, there is no insurance or compensation for your damaged honor, but what is mine: for a petticoat pensioner is what you are." [42]

One of the foremost of the generation of pioneer Celtic scholars of the late nineteenth century, Professor H. Zimmer, Senior,* points out in his discussion of this tirade of Queen Meave, that, among the Celts of the British Isles, a bride was "compensated for her violated honor" by a "morning gift" from her husband,[43] and that for a king the compensation for violated honor was "a platter of gold as broad as his face"—which would have been caused to redden for shame.[44] Consequently, the sharp point of Meave's final thrust resided—as Dr. Zimmer observes—in its "complete reversal of the conditions that prevail under an uncorrupted system of Father Right."

> Meave [he writes further] takes to herself a spouse, not at
> all as under the patriarchy a maiden accepts her husband; and

---

* H. Zimmer (1851–1910), not to be confused with his son of the same name, the distinguished Sanskritist, Heinrich Zimmer (1890–1943), whom I have cited in *Oriental Mythology*. To prevent confusion, I designate the elder as H. Zimmer and the younger as Heinrich Zimmer.

he is not a mere good for nothing either . . . but a king's son, a brother of kings, whose possessions are not, in fact, inferior to her own. She counts out the stipulated marriage donation; bestows on him the morning gift as *Pretium virginitatis;* and just as the man under the patriarchy reserves to himself the right to take concubines, so does Meave claim as her right, and as condition to her marriage contract, "House-friends": one man in the shadow of another. What her words represent is not an exaggeration uttered in the heat of argument, but a proclamation of the ground rules, openly understood on her part, tacitly recognized by Ailill, and clearly illustrated in her acts [45]

—as we are now to see.

For when Ailill had been thus abused, he called for a comparative count of properties, and before the eyes of the two there were paraded, first, their mugs and vats, iron vessels, urns, brewers' troughs and chests; rings and bangles, various clasped ornaments, thumb-rings and apparel, as well crimson, blue, black, and green, as yellow, checkered, and buff, pale-colored, pied, and striped. Then all their numerous flocks of sheep were driven in from the greens, lawns, and open country, found to be in number equal, and dismissed: likewise their steeds; likewise their herds of grunting swine. However, when the cattle lumbered past, it was noticed that, though they were in multitude the same, there was among those of the king a certain bull named The White-horned, which had been a calf among Meave's cows but, not desiring to be governed by a woman, had departed and taken his place among the cattle of the king. His match for size and majesty could not be discovered among the master bulls of her lot, and when this inequality came to light the queen felt as though she did not possess a pebble's worth of stock.

Queen Meave inquired of her herald, Mac Roth, whether in any province of Ireland there was a bull of worth equivalent to The White-horned; and "Why, indeed!" he answered; "a fellow in double measure better and more excellent I know; namely, of Daire mac Fachtna's herd in Cooley, which is known as The Brown of Cooley."

"Be off," then ordered Meave; "and of Daire crave for me one year's loan of that bull; at the end of which year the loan fee to be paid to him shall be, besides The Brown of Cooley himself, fifty heifers; and if any of that country should think ill of giving up even for a time that extraordinarily precious thing, well, then let Daire come along with his bull and I shall settle on him an estate of a size equal to that of his present land, besides a chariot of the value of three times seven slave girls, and he shall have, in addition, the friendship of my own upper thighs."

An embassy of nine, therefore, with Mac Roth crossed the island from Connaught in the west to Cooley in the northeast, and when Daire was told that if he arrived with the bull he would have an estate of a size equal to his own now in Cooley, besides a chariot worth twenty-one slave girls, and the friendship, moreover, of Meave's own upper thighs, "he was so well pleased," we read, "that he threw himself in such wise that the seams of the mattresses beneath him burst asunder." [46]

The rest of the tale can wait; for the only point to be made now is that both the archaeology and the ancient literature of Ireland demonstrate that the patriarchal, iron-bearing Celts, who gained the mastery during the last three or four centuries B.C., overcame but did not extinguish an earlier, Bronze Age civilization of Mother Right. The circumstance resembled that of the overthrow by the iron-bearing Dorian Greeks of the Bronze Age order of the Cretan-Aegean world—the myths and rites of which, however, lingered on. And as the work of Miss Harrison, already cited, has disclosed, not only were many of the best-known Homeric myths actually fragments of pre-Homeric mythology reinterpreted, but also in the field festivals, women's rites, and mystery cults of the Classic world there survived beneath (and even not far beneath) the sunny Olympian surfaces a dark, and to us even appalling, stratum of archaic ritual and custom. Comparably, in the epics of ancient Ireland, the Celtic warrior kings and their brilliant chariot fighters move in a landscape beset with invisible fairy forts, wherein abide a race of beings of an earlier mythological age: the wonderful Tuatha De Danann, children of the Goddess Dana, who retired,

when defeated, into wizard hills of glass. And these are the very
people of the *sidhe* or Shee, the Fairy Host, the Fairy Cavalcade,
of the Irish peasantry to this day.

"Who are they?" asks the poet Yeats. And he gives a trilogy of
answers: " 'Fallen angels who were not good enough to be saved,
nor bad enough to be lost,' say the peasantry. 'The gods of the
earth,' says the Book of Armagh. 'The gods of pagan Ireland,' say
the antiquarians, 'the *Tuatha De Danān,* who, when no longer worshiped and fed with offerings, dwindled away in the popular imagination, and now are only a few spans high.' " But he adds: "Do not
think the fairies are always little. Everything is capricious about
them, even their size." [47]

THE CONSORT OF THE BULL

✦✦

I. The Mother of God

Can Notre Dame de Chartres be the same as Nuestra Señora de Guadalupe? No Catholic would hesitate to kneel and pray before either image: "Holy Mary, Mother of God, pray for us sinners, now, and at the hour of our death." Yet the usual anthropologist, arriving as it were from Mars, for whom theories of diffusion are anathema and all cross-cultural comparisons methodologically beneath contempt, would be in danger of returning to his planet of pure thought with two exquisitely separate monographs: the one treating of a local French, the other of a local Mexican goddess, functionally serving two entirely different social orders; Our Lady of Chartres, furthermore, showing the influence of a Gallo-Roman Venus shrine, of which the evidence appears in the cult of the Black Madonna observed in the crypt of the present (twelfth to sixteenth century) cathedral, whereas Our Lady of Guadalupe is clearly of Amerindian origin, having appeared in vision (or so it is alleged by all native informants) hardly a decade after the overthrow of Montezuma, on the site of a native shrine, probably of the great serpent-goddess Coatlicue. All of which, of course, would be true, and yet, not true enough.

Let us press the question further: Can the Virgin Mary be the same as Venus-Aphrodite, or as Cybele, Hathor, Ishtar, and the rest? We think of the words of the goddess Isis addressed to her initiate Apuleius, c. 150 A.D., which are cited at the opening of *Primitive Mythology*:

I am she that is the natural mother of all things, mistress and governess of all the elements, the initial progeny of worlds, chief of the powers divine, queen of all that are in hell, the principal of them that dwell in heaven, manifested alone and under one form of all the gods and goddesses. At my will the planets of the sky, the wholesome winds of the seas, and the lamentable silences of hell are disposed; my name, my divinity is adored throughout the world, in divers manners, in variable customs, and by many names.

For the Phrygians that are the first of all men call me the Mother of the gods of Pessinus; the Athenians, which are sprung from their own soil, Cecropian Minerva; the Cyprians, which are girt about by the sea, Paphian Venus; the Cretans, which bear arrows, Dictynian Diana; the Sicilians, which speak three tongues, infernal Proserpine; the Eleusinians, their ancient goddess Ceres; some Juno, others Bellona, others Hecate, others Ramnusie, and principally both sort of the Ethiopians, which dwell in the Orient and are enlightened by the morning rays of the sun; and the Egyptians, which are excellent in all kind of ancient doctrine, and by their proper ceremonies accustomed to worship me, do call me by my true name, Queen Isis.[1]

No good Catholic would kneel before an image of Isis if he knew that it was she. Yet every one of the mythic motifs now dogmatically attributed to Mary as a historic human being belongs also—and belonged in the period and place of the development of her cult—to that goddess mother of all things, of whom both Mary and Isis were local manifestations: the mother-bride of the dead and resurrected god, whose earliest known representations now must be assigned to a date as early, at least, as c. 5500 B.C.*

It is often customary in devotional cults to limit the view of the devotee to a single local manifestation, which then is honored either as unique or as the primary, "truest," form of the divinity repre-

* Since the publication of *Primitive Mythology,* a dramatic breakthrough has occurred in the archaeology of southwest Anatolia (Turkey), where a developed neolithic village culture dating from c. 7000 B.C. has been established at Hacilar. Ceramic wares, including a vivid series of naturalistic statuettes of the mother-goddess, appear there in a stratum dated c. 5700–5400 B.C. See James Mellaart, "Excavations at Hacilar: Fourth Preliminary Report, 1960," *Anatolian Studies,* Vol. 11 (1961); also Mellaart, "Hacilar: A Neolithic Village Site," *Scientific American,* Vol. 205, No. 2, August 1961.

sented. Even in India, from the lips of a leading teacher of the
unity of religions, Ramakrishna (1836–1886), we read the following words of advice to a devotee: "You should undoubtedly bow
before all views. But there is a thing called unswerving devotion to
one ideal. True, you should salute everyone. But you must love one
ideal with your whole soul. That is unswerving devotion." And he
gave as illustration a case from the lore of Krishna and the Gopis.[2]
"The Gopis had such single-minded devotion to the cowherd
Krishna of Vrindavan," he said, "that they did not care to see the
turbaned Krishna of Dwaraka." [3]

However, one has to recognize a distinction between the ends
and means of devotion and of science; and in relation to the latter
there is no reason to fear a demonstration of the derivation of local
from more general forms. It is simply a fact—deal with it how
you will—that the mythology of the mother of the dead and resurrected god has been known for millenniums to the neolithic and
post-neolithic Levant. Its relation to the earlier, paleolithic cult of
the naked goddess of the age of the mammoth hunt is unclear; [4]
but there is no question concerning the obvious continuity from the
nuclear Near East c. 5500 B.C., to Guadalupe, 1531 A.D. The entire
ancient world, from Asia Minor to the Nile and from Greece to the
Indus Valley, abounds in figurines of the naked female form, in
various attitudes, of the all-supporting, all-including goddess: her
two hands offering her breasts; her left pointing to her genitals and
the right offering her left breast; nursing or fondling a male child;
standing upright among beasts; arms extended, holding tokens—
stalks, flowers, serpents, doves, or other signs. Such figurines are
demonstrably related, furthermore, to the well-known Bronze Age
myths and cults of the Great Goddess of many names, one of whose
most celebrated temples stood precisely at Ephesus, where, in the
year 431 A.D., the dogma of Mary as Theotokos, "Mother of God,"
was in Council proclaimed. At that time the pagan religions of the
Roman Empire were being implacably suppressed: temples closed
and destroyed; priests, philosophers, and teachers, banished and
executed. And so it came to pass that, in the end and to our day,
Mary, Queen of Martyrs, became the sole inheritor of all the names

and forms, sorrows, joys, and consolations of the goddess-mother in the Western World: Seat of Wisdom . . . Vessel of Honor . . . Mystical Rose . . . House of Gold . . . Gate of Heaven . . . Morning Star . . . Refuge of Sinners . . . Queen of Angels . . . Queen of Peace.[5]

II. The Two Queens

The vision of a goddess shown in Figure 12 is from a Cretan sealing of c. 1500 B.C., found by Sir Arthur Evans amid the ruins of the labyrinthine palace of Knossos. The ancient civilization of

Figure 12. The Goddess of the World Mountain

Crete is of especial importance to our study, since it represents the earliest high center of developed Bronze Age forms within the European sphere. The island, as Frobenius noted, is in the zone of Levantine influence, and the high period of its palaces, c. 2500– c. 1250 B.C., was exactly that of the Indus Valley cities of Harappa and Mohenjo-daro.[6]

In the sealing, the goddess, spear in hand, stands on a mountain flanked by lions. Behind her is a building bearing on its architraves the characteristic "horns of consecration" of all Cretan shrines, and before her, in a posture known from other images to signify adoration, stands a young male, who is possibly a god (her dead and resurrected son and spouse), possibly the young Cretan king (who, if Frazer is correct,[7] was sacrificed, either actually or symbolically, at the end of each Venus-solar cycle of eight years),* or, possibly, simply a devotee.

Sir Arthur Evans, to whose labors during the first quarter of this century we owe the rediscovery of Cretan civilization, maintains throughout the six volumes of his monumental work, *The Palace of Minos*,[8] that the numerous goddess images discovered in the course of his excavations represent, to quote his own words, "the same Great Mother with her Child or Consort whose worship under various names and titles extended over a large part of Asia Minor and the Syrian regions beyond."[9] Professor Martin P. Nilsson of Lund, on the other hand, whose *History of Greek Religion* is today the unmatched masterwork in its field,[10] rejects Evans' view, advising caution.

The goddess with spear in hand, who stands on the mountain symmetrically flanked by two lions [he writes] indeed resembles the beweaponed Lady of the Beasts. Moreover, the representation of the mountain compellingly suggests the μήτηρ ὀρεία, "the Mountain Mother," Cybele of Asia Minor, accompanied by lions, while the identification of Cybele with Rhea, who gave birth to Zeus in Crete, would seem to support her association with this island. The goddess of the seal has therefore been identified unhesitatingly with the Great Mother of Asia Minor. Yet a fact to be borne in mind is that many centuries (indeed, but for Hesiod, a full thousand years) extend between this picture and our stories of the Great Mother. Without prejudice to the possible, or probable, ethnic connection between Minoan Crete and Asia Minor, it would be more prudent not to attribute to the Minoan goddess traits of the Great Mother first known to us from the historic period, but simply to confine ourselves to the observation that our sealing shows a nature goddess like or related to that of Asia Minor; for in the intervening centuries the character of the latter can have developed or altered.[11]

* Venus requires 584 days to complete one cycle of phases (one synodic period). Five such ($584 \times 5 = 2920$ days) amount to eight years ($365 \times 8 = 2920$ days). Hence Venus requires eight years to return to the same point of the zodiac while at greatest brilliancy.

It would seem to be only prudent to heed such a warning. However, in the years since the writing of Professor Nilsson's paragraph, a new light has been cast across the entire theater of antiquity, and in its flare the position of Sir Arthur would seem to be the one that has been reinforced. Specifically, in 1953 a young British architect, the late Michael Ventris, deciphered the Cretan Linear B script, and what he found was that the language was an early Greek.[12] Further, although the writings proved to be merely accountants' notes, recording, among other matters, offerings made in temples, the gods to whom the offerings were addressed were those that in the classic Greek tradition are associated with Crete. For instance:

"To Dictaean Zeus, oil."

"To the Daidaleion, oil."

"To the Lady of the Labyrinth, a jar of honey."

Moreover, at a site on the Greek mainland now identified as Pylos, the Mycenaean palace-city of King Nestor of the *Iliad,* a second store of Linear B notations has turned up, which tells of a large number of gifts to the Greek sea-god Poseidon, "the Lord (*posei*) of the earth-goddess (*dās*),"[13] including cattle, rams, sheepskins, wheat, flour and wine, cheeses, honey and unguent, gold, and even human beings.[14] We learn of a divine triad called "the Two Queens and Poseidon"; further, of "the Two Queens and the King."[15] We find, also, that the city of King Nestor was near the sanctuary of a goddess known as Potnia, "the Lady," and that there the king had a large temenos or estate.[16]

Scholars have recalled in this connection the words of Nausicaa, the daughter of King Alcinous of the seafaring Phaeacians, in the *Odyssey.* "You will find," she told Odysseus, "a lovely poplar grove to Athena near the road. A spring wells forth therein. A meadow lies all about. And there is the temenos of my father, and his fruitful orchard."[17]

But now what can have been the relation of Potnia to the king; or of "the Two Queens" to the king; or of "the Two Queens" to the god Poseidon? And what bearing will all this have upon our concept of the role of the Goddess in Crete, and through Crete to Classical Greece and beyond?

There is an ivory plaque from the ruins of Mycenae, showing two women seated with a child (Figure 13).[18] The triad is now interpreted, in the light of what has been learned from the texts of Linear B, as representing the Two Queens and the King, or the Two Queens and the Young God. "The plaque from Mycenae," states Professor Leonard Palmer, who worked with Ventris in the reading of the script, "is widely regarded as a most beautiful repre-

Figure 13. The Two Queens and the King

sentation of the Mycenaean 'divine family.' But there is other evidence of a more schematic kind. A number of terra-cotta figures are known which show two women joined together like Siamese twins and with a child seated on their common shoulder. These too have been interpreted as representations of the Twin Goddess with the Young God." [19]

In the earliest recorded mythology of Sumer, the dead and resurrected god Dumuzi-absu, "the Faithful Son of the Abyss," was in destiny involved with two mighty goddesses; or, better, one goddess in dual form. She was, on one hand, goddess of the living, and, on the other, goddess of the dead. As the former, she was

Inanna, Queen of Heaven, who became, in later Classical mythology, Aphrodite; and, as the latter, she was the dreadful Queen of the Underworld, Ereshkigal, who became in Classical myth Persephone. And the god who in death dwelt with the latter, but in life was the lover of the former, was in the Greek tradition Adonis. We note that in our figure the child is passing from one goddess to the other. Almost certainly, in the old Sumerian system, such a triad as that of this Mycenaean plaque would have represented Inanna and

Figure 14. Demeter, Triptolemus, and Persephone

Ereshkigal with Dumuzi, or his counterpart, the king in whom his spirit was incarnate; while in Classical Greece they would have suggested the great triad of the mysteries of Eleusis: Demeter (the mother-goddess Earth), Persephone (Queen of the Underworld), and the young god, their foster child Triptolemos (once a local king),[20] who is said to have brought Demeter's gift of grain into the world and, as the fosterling of Persephone, to reign now in the land of the dead.[21]

For comparison, Figure 14 is an illustration of the Greek triad, from an early red-figured cup discovered in the precincts of Eleusis.[22] Demeter, at our left, is handing grain to her fosterling,

Triptolemus, who is holding his "crooked plow" in a way that suggests a basic plow-phallus analogy; while behind him stands Persephone, with two torches in her hands that denote her queenship of
the Underworld. (Compare, now, Figure 7.) "Mother and Maid in
the picture are clearly distinguished," Jane Harrison states; "but not
infrequently," she adds, "when both appear together, it is impossible to say which is which." "Demeter and Kore [Persephone] are
two persons though one god." [23]

Thus a reasonably firm continuity appears to have been established between the two Sumerian goddesses of the myth of the dead
and resurrected god, the Two Queens of the late Cretan Linear B
accounts, and the well-known Mother and Maid, Demeter and
Persephone, of the Greek Mysteries of Eleusis of which Socrates
speaks in the Gorgias.[24] In other words, Sir Arthur Evans' view of
the continuity of the mythology of the Great Goddess, from the
nuclear Near East to Minoan Crete, and from Minoan to Classical
times, seems to have been confirmed; and with this in mind we may
now proceed with Evans to a deeper view of the symbolism of the
Cretan-Mycenaean dual goddess.

There is, fortunately, an eloquent, though silent, document in the
beautiful "Ring of Nestor" found by a peasant in a large beehive
tomb at Pylos (Figure 15): a ring of solid gold, of 31.5 grams, of
which the date, according to Evans, should be c. 1550–1500 B.C.

> The field of the design [he writes] is divided into zones
> . . . by the trunk and horizontally spreading boughs of a
> great tree . . . old, gnarled, and leafless. It stands with
> spreading roots on the top of a mound or hillock with its
> trunk rising in the center of the field and with wide-stretching
> horizontal boughs. . . . The scenes that its branches thus
> divide belong, in fact, not to the terrestrial sphere, but to the
> Minoan After-World. An obvious analogy is suggested with
> Yggdrasil, the Ash of Odin's steed and the old Scandinavian
> "Tree of the World."
> *Upper left:*
> In the first compartment of the tree may be recognized the
> Minoan Goddess, seated in animated conversation with her
> wonted companion, while above her head there flutter two
> butterflies. The symbolic significance of these, moreover, is

emphasized by the appearance above them of two small objects showing traces of heads at the tip and with hook-like
projections at the side, in which we may reasonably recognize
the two corresponding chrysalises. . . . Placed as they are
here in connection with their pupal forms, it is difficult to
explain them otherwise than as an allusion to the resurgence of
the human spirit after death.

It can hardly be doubted, moreover, that they apply to the
two youthful figures who appear beside them on the ring, and

Figure 15. The Tree of Eternal Life

must be taken to be symbolic of their reanimation with new
life.

The youth, with long Minoan locks, standing behind the
Goddess, raises the lower part of his right arm, while the short-
skirted damsel who faces him with her back to the trunk,
shows her surprise at the meeting by holding up both hands.
. . . We see here, reunited by the life-giving power of the
Goddess and symbolized by the chrysalises and butterflies, a
young couple whom Death had parted. The meeting indeed
may, in view of the scene of initiation depicted below, be
interpreted as the permanent reunion of a wedded pair in the
Land of the Blest.

Upper right:
In the next compartment, right of the trunk, the sacred

Lion of the Goddess crouches in an attitude of vigilant repose on a kind of bench, tended by two girl figures (though in men's dress) in whom we recognize the frequently recurring representations of her two little handmaidens. The Lion of the Goddess would naturally keep watch and ward over the realms below.

The religious character of the scene is further enhanced by the bough . . . the "sacred ivy" that springs from the trunk. (. . . The plant, the shoots of which spring forth from the trunk of the Tree of the World to give shade to the lion guardian of the realms below, must be identified with the same "Sacral Ivy" that climbs the rock steeps in the cycle of wall paintings. The heart-shaped leaves and even the double terminal tufts of flowers are distinctly indicated. . . . It is impossible not to recall the Golden Bough, which, when plucked by Aeneas, opened for him the passage to Avernus [*Aeneid* VI. 136 ff.]. But ever, as one was torn away, another branch of gleaming gold sprang in its place. . . .)

Lower left and right:

The lower zone on either side of the trunk, beneath the spreading branches, unfolds one continuous scene, the whole of which seems to depict the initiatory examination of those entering the Halls of the Just in the Griffin's Court. In the left compartment the young couple reappear, treading, as it were, the measure of a dance and beckoned forward by a "griffin lady," right of the trunk, while another warns off a youth on the extreme left, as a profane intruder. Right of the trunk, beyond the first, two more "griffin ladies"—dressed in the usual short-skirted fashion of the early part of the New Era [c. 1550 B.C.] with hands upraised in adoration—head the procession to the presiding figure of the tribunal. This is a winged griffin of the milder, peacock-plumed variety, seated on a high stool or throne, while behind stands another female personage, in whom we may recognize a repetition of the Goddess herself. A pre-eminent characteristic of the griffin—eagle-headed in his origin on Cretan soil—is his piercing sight, which qualifies him here for his post as Chief Inquisitor. Below, on the mound at the foot of the Tree, amidst shoots that seem to stand for herbage, is couched a dog-like monster, the forerunner of Cerberus, but who may also be compared in a broader aspect with the dragon— the loathly Nidhogger—at the foot of Yggdrasil.[25]

The lesson is clear enough. And the image of a life beyond death represented in this scene differs *toto coelo* from the dismal Hades of the later, epic period, while suggesting, on the other hand, the more genial Classical images of the Islands of the Blessed and Elysian Plain. We think of Virgil's Fortunate Woodlands:

> *Largior hic campos aether et lumine vestit*
> *Purpureo, solemque suum, sua sidera norunt.**

We think, also, of the old Sumerian island paradise, Dilmun, in the midst of the primeval sea, where, as an ancient cuneiform text of c. 2050 B.C. relates:

> The lion does not kill,
> The wolf snatches not the lamb. . . .
>
> Its old woman says not "I am an old woman,"
> Its old man says not "I am an old man." [26]

It is a view of that "Elysian Plain and the world's end," described by the old sea god Proteus to the spouse of Helen, Menelaus, in the fourth book of the *Odyssey*, "where," as he declares, "is Rhadamathus of the fair hair, where life is easiest for men. No snow is there, nor yet great storm, nor any rain; but always Ocean sendeth forth the breeze of the shrill West to blow cool on men." [27]

"The Greek religion of the historic period," Professor Nilsson states, "developed from the fusion of the religions of two populations of differing race—of both of which we know unfortunately all too little. Still, the deeply rooted difference can be sensed between the emotional religion of the pre-Greek population, which seems to have been impressed with a mystic tendency, and the temperate religion of the Indo-Germanic invaders, who entrusted the protection of the unwritten laws of their patriarchal order to their gods." [28]

I want to make a large point of this remark, as announcing what is to remain, throughout the breadth and length of the history of religions in the West, the chief occasion for a sordid, sorry chronicle of collision, vituperation, coercion, and spilled blood. For in the Levantine sphere, as well as in the Greek, a deeply

---

* "Here an ampler sky invests the fields with purple light, and their own sun they know, their own stars" (*Aeneid* VI. 640–41).

rooted contrast prevails between the pre-Semitic, pre-Aryan mystic-emotional religion of the agrarian neolithic and Bronze Age populations, and, on the other hand, "the temperate religion" (let us call it so, for the time being) of the various invading warrior folk, "who entrusted the protection of the unwritten [later, written] laws of their patriarchal order to their gods." Indeed, we do not merely "sense," we experience acutely in our souls, and have documented for every period of our culture, the force that holds apart in us these contrary trends. But the one point to be stressed in the present portion of our chapter is simply that neither to the patriarchal Aryans nor to the patriarchal Semites belong the genial, mystic, poetic themes of the lovely world of a paradise neither lost nor regained but ever present in the bosom of the goddess-mother in whose being we have our death, as well as life, without fear.

III. The Mother of the Minotaur

There is in the University Museum, Philadelphia, an important and fascinating terra-cotta plaque from ancient Sumer, c. 2500 B.C. (Figure 16), that shows the ever-dying, ever-living lunar bull, consumed through all time by the lion-headed solar eagle. The victim has fiery signs of divine power flashing from his four limbs; a calmly beatific smile radiates from his human countenance, framed by a great square beard that is characteristic in archaic art (Egyptian as well as Sumerian) of those lordly beasts, usually serpent or bull, that are symbolic of the power that fecundates the earth; and his right foreleg is here placed squarely on the center of a mound symbolic of the summit of the cosmic holy mountain, which, as we know from numerous texts, is the body of the goddess Earth. A prominent device resembling the Cretan "horns of consecration" marks the field of contact between the receptive earth and bestowing god, whose leg and foot are thrust to its center to form with it a sort of trident: and the god, in this view, is above, for it is from the moon above, as it wanes, consumed by the light of the sun, that the life-restoring dews and fertilizing rain descend.

But there is water, also, beneath the earth. The Creto-Mycenaean god Poseidon, whose animal is the bull and whose attribute is the trident, dwells in the sea, in springs, and in the waters beneath the earth. Likewise in India, Shiva, "the Great Lord," whose animal is the bull, whose attribute is the trident, and the name of whose consort, Parvati, means "the Daughter of the Mountain"—her animal, moreover, being the lion—is in one aspect known as dwelling with his goddess on the summit of Mount Kailasa, but at the same time

Figure 16. Moon-Bull and Lion-Bird

is honored chiefly in the symbol of the lingam (phallus), rising from the waters of the abyss and penetrating the yoni (vulva) of the goddess Earth. Shiva as "the Cosmic Dancer" is shown with his right foot planted firmly on the back of a prostrate dwarf named Ignorance and the left lifted in a cross kick. The meaning of this posture is said to be that with the right foot the god of the trident is driving his divine creative energy into the sphere of mortal birth and with the left yielding release from this temporal round. I cannot help wondering whether a similar thought may not have been implied by the posture of the front legs of this bull.

In the royal tombs of Ur, discussed in *Primitive Mythology*, the silver head of a cow was found in the chamber of the buried Queen Shub-ad, while in the tomb complex of her spouse, A-bar-gi, whom she with her whole court had followed in death below ground (suttee theme),* there was the golden head of a bull, with square lapis-lazuli beard, decorating the sounding box and pillar of an elegant little harp.[29] The sound of this harp, I have suggested, was symbolically the summoning song of the moon-bull, bidding Queen Shub-ad to follow her beloved into the realm of the Queen of Death. The myth implied is that of the Two Queens and the King. And the music of the ornamented harp, the bull's voice, was the music of those mysteries in which life and death are known as one.

The following Mesopotamian rite for the replacement of the head of a temple kettledrum, described by Dr. Robert Dyson, Jr., of The University Museum, speaks for both the import of the bull and the function of art in the rites of the ancient world.

> The eligibility of the bull was strictly defined: it had to be unmarked by a goad, to have no white tufts, to have whole horns and hoofs, and to be black as pitch. It was then brought to what was called the *mummu*-house and set on a reed mat with its legs tied with a goat hair rope. After the offering of a sheep, the ritual of "washing the mouth" was performed by whispering an incantation into the bull's ear through a reed and then sprinkling him with cedar resin. He was then purified symbolically in some way with a brazier and torch. Around him a circle of flour was made and, after further recitations by the priest, he was killed with a knife. The heart was burned with cedar, cypress and a special kind of flour in front of the kettledrum. The tendon was removed from the left shoulder for some reason not specified, and the animal was skinned. The body was then wrapped in a red cloth and buried facing west. Elaborate instructions were then given for the preparation of the hide, which would eventually serve as the new drumhead.[30]

The mythic lunar bull, lord of the rhythm of the universe, to whose song all mortality is dancing in a round of birth, death, and

---

* Suttee (*Satī*) was the name of another incarnation of Shiva's eternal consort. For the meaning of the name, see *The Masks of God: Oriental Mythology*, pp. 65–66.

new birth, was called to mind by the sounds of the drum, strings, and reed flutes of the temple orchestras, and those attending were set in accord thereby with the aspect of being that never dies. The beatific, yet impassive, enigmatic Mona Lisa features of the bull slain by the lion-bird suggest the mode of being known to initiates of the wisdom beyond death, beyond changing time. Through his death, which is no death, he is giving life to the creatures of the earth, even while indicating, with his lifted forefoot, the leftward horn of the mythic symbol.

The symbol here seems to represent the plane of juncture of earth and heaven, the goddess and the god, who appear to be two but are in being one. For, as we know from an ancient Sumerian myth, heaven (*An*) and the earth (*Ki*) were in the beginning a single undivided mountain (*Anki*), of which the lower part, the earth, was female, and the upper, heaven, male. But the two were separated (as Adam into Adam and Eve) by their son Enlil (in the Bible by their "creator," Yahweh), whereupon the world of temporality appeared (as it did when Eve ate the apple).[31] The ritual marriage and connubium was to be understood as a reconstruction of the primal undifferentiated state, both in meditation (psychological aspect) for the refreshment of the soul, and in act (magical aspect) for the fertilization and renovation of nature: whereby it was also to be recognized that there is a plane or mode of being where that primal state is ever present, though to the mind and eye of day all seems to be otherwise. The state of the ultimate bull, that is to say, is invisible: black, pitch black.

Thus it can be said that, just as in the Indian symbolic form of the Dancing Shiva, so likewise in this Sumerian terra-cotta plaque, a statement is to be recognized of the archaic Bronze Age philosophy discussed in my earlier volume, which has survived to this hour in the Orient. In its primary, unintended mode, this philosophy is properly comparable to the childlike state of mind termed by Dr. Jean Piaget "indissociation."[32] In its developed, higher forms, however, it has been the most important single creative force in the history of civilization. Its import is experienced immediately in the ultimate mystical rapture of non-duality, or mythic identification, and is symbolized in the various imageries of ancient Egypt's Secret of the Two Partners, China's Tao, India's Nirvana, and Japan's development of the Buddhist doctrine of the Flower Wreath.[33] There is a touch of it, too, in the image of Paradise regained in the oft-cited passage of Isaiah (c. 740–700 B.C.):

> "The wolf shall dwell with the lamb, and the leopard shall lie down with the kid, and the calf and the lion and the fatling together, and a little child shall lead them. The cow and the bear shall feed; their young shall lie down together; and the lion shall eat straw like the ox. The suckling child shall play over the hole of the asp, and the weaned child shall put his hand on the adder's den. They shall not hurt or destroy in all my holy mountain; for the earth shall be full of the knowledge of Yahweh as the waters cover the sea.[34]

Except that here the idyllic situation is postponed to a day to come, whereas in the earlier view it exists now, in this world as it is, and is recognized as so through spiritual initiation. It is the vision represented in our plaque of the lunar bull and solar lion-bird; but it is represented on the plane of earth as well: by the living bull and lion who in Mother Nature's heart dwell in ever-lasting peace, even now, as they enact their monstrous mystery play of life, which is called "Now You Eat Me."

The enigmatically blissful, impassive expression of the bull on the terra-cotta plaque appears again, *mutatis mutandis,* on the masklike features of the Indian dancing Shiva. The god holds a drum in his lifted right hand, the drumbeat of time, the beat of creation, while on the palm of his left is the fire of the knowledge of immortality by which the bondages of time are destroyed. Shiva emanates flames, as do the four legs of this bull; and in Shiva's hair the skull of death is worn as ornament, alongside the crescent moon of rebirth. Shiva is the Lord of Beasts (*paśupati*); so too is the great Sumerian lord of death and rebirth, Dumuzi-Tammuz-Adonis, whose animal is this beatific bull; so too, furthermore, is the Greek God Dionysus, known—like Shiva—as the Cosmic Dancer, who is both the bull torn apart and the lion tearing:

> Appear, appear, whatso thy shape or name,
> O Mountain Bull, Snake of the Hundred Heads,

> Lion of the Burning Flame!
> O God, Beast, Mystery, come! [35]

It was something of a shock to many when the name Dionysus appeared among the words deciphered from Linear B.[36] And so, let us return with this name to Crete.

In *Oriental Mythology* I have discussed the mythology of the god-king Pharaoh of Egypt, who was called "the bull of his mother";[37] for, when dead within the mound of his tomb (the mound symbolic of the goddess), he was identified with Osiris begetting his son, and when alive, sitting on his throne (likewise symbolic of the goddess), he was the son of Osiris, Horus; and these two, as representing the whole mythic role of the dead yet reembodied King of the Universe, were in substance one. The cosmic cow-goddess Hathor (*hat-hor,* the "house of Horus") stood upon the earth in such a way that her four legs were the pillars of the quarters and her belly was the firmament. The god Horus, symbolized as a golden falcon, the sun, flying east to west, entered her mouth at evening to be born again the next dawn and was thus, indeed, in his night character, the "bull of his mother"; whereas by day, as ruler of the world of light, he was a keen-eyed bird of prey. Moreover, the animal of Osiris, the bull, was incarnate in the sacred Apis bull, which was ceremonially slain every twenty-five years—thus relieving the pharaoh himself of the obligation of a ritual regicide. And it seems to me (though I cannot find that anyone has yet offered the suggestion) that the ritual game of the Cretan bull ring must have served the same function for the young god-kings of Crete.

We have a number of representations of Cretan kings, and they always show a youth of about twenty; there is none of an old man. So there may have been a regicide at the close of each Venus cycle, after all; though the prominence of the bull ring in the ritual art of Crete suggests that a ritual substitution may have been made.

Professor Nilsson regards the bull game as devoid of religious import;[38] but the lively design of Figure 17 seems to me to controvert this view. We see a man-bull—a Minotaur—attacked by a man-lion; and the analogy with the bull and lion-bird of Sumer cannot be denied. Indeed, the dynamics of this masterful little art work even suggest the idea of an ever-turning, never-ending cycle. For as in Sumer, so in Crete: whereas the lion was the animal of the blazing solar heat, which both slays the moon and parches vegetation, the bull was the animal of the moon: the waning and waxing god, by the magic of whose night dew the vegetation is restored; the lord of tides and the productive powers of the earth, the lord of women, lord of the rhythm of the womb.

Figure 17. Minotaur and Man-Lion

In the picture language of mythology the image of the Minotaur equates the idea of the moon-bull with that of the moon-man or moon-king, and so suggests that the king's place may have been taken by a bull in Crete, as it was in Egypt, in the age-old agrarian ritual of the god-king's life-endowing death. Moreover, that the bulls were indeed *ritually* slain in the ring seems to be shown in Figure 18, where a *priestly* matador is dealing the *coup de grâce:* the beast, coursing in full stadium career, is here being ritually slain. The matador and sword, that is to say are performing the same function as the lion-bird of Sumer, while the bull is in its standard role of the ever-dying, ever-living god: the lord, Poseidon, of the goddess Earth.

Thus a prospect of Cretan thought emerges from the ruins that sets it in a well and widely known Bronze Age context; but with a particular accent on the role of the female that sets it apart no less from the great priestly civilizations of the Nile and Tigris-Euphrates than from the later patriarchal Greeks.

Figure 18. The Sacrifice

In spite of the limitations imposed by the nature of the evidence, [Nilsson writes] certain characteristic traits of Minoan religion do emerge in contrast to the Greek. One is the preponderance of goddesses and of female cult officiants. Masculine deities are, in contrast to feminine, very scarce; masculine cult images are lacking altogether; in the cult scenes women appear far more frequently than men; and it is likely that this preponderance of the female sex accounts for the emotional character of the religion, which appears particularly in tree cult scenes. The most clearly recognizable cults are that of the household serpent goddess and the nature cult in its two aspects, that of the Lady and Lord of Beasts and that of Trees. How these relate to the nature sanctuaries that have been discovered is unfortunately unknown. And the observation must finally be added that all reference to sexual life, all phallic symbols, such as abound and are so aggressive in numerous religions—including the historic religion of Greece —are in Minoan art completely missing.[39]

Evans too has remarked the decency and decorum of Minoan art: "from its earliest to its latest phase," he writes, "not one single example has been brought to light of any subject of an indecorous nature." [40]

The culture, as many have noted, was apparently of a matriarchal type. The grace and elegance of the ladies in their beautifully flounced skirts, generous decolleté, pretty coiffures, and gay bandeaux, mixing freely with the men, in the courts, in the bull ring—lovely, vivid, and vivacious, gesticulating, chattering, even donning masculine athletic belts to go somersaulting dangerously over the horns and backs of bulls—represent a civilized refinement that has not been often equaled since: which I would like the present chapter to fix firmly in place, by way of a challenge to the high claims of those proudly phallic moral orders, whether circumcised or uncircumcised, that were to follow.

And a contrast no less evident sets the Cretan world apart from the kingly states of both Sumer and the Nile. Its mythology and culture appear to represent an earlier stage than theirs of Bronze Age civilization: a milder, gentler day, antecedent to the opening of the great course of Eurasian world history that is best dated by the wars and victory monuments of its self-interested kings. There were no walled cities in Crete before the coming of the Greeks. There is little evidence of weapons. Battle scenes of kingly conquest play no role in the setting of the style. The tone is of general luxury and delight, a broad participation by all classes in a genial atmosphere of well-being, and the vast development of a profitable commerce by sea, to every port of the archaic world and even—boldly—to regions far beyond.

The datings of Cretan civilization set up by Sir Arthur Evans have been modified by later scholarship, but the main lines remain, and, with the alterations that later findings have suggested, may be summarized as follows:

	Neolithic Beginnings: perhaps from c. 4000 B.C.	
	Early Minoan	I: to c. 2600 B.C.	
2500 B.C.		II: c. 2600–2300 B.C.	Pre-Palatial
		III: c. 2300–2000 B.C.	
	Middle Minoan	I: c. 2000–1850 B.C.	
		II: c. 1850–1700 B.C.	Early Palatial
		IIIA: c. 1700–1660 B.C.	(Hieroglyphics)
		IIIB: c. 1660–1580 B.C.	
	Late Minoan	IA: c. 1580–1510 B.C.	High Palatial
1500 B.C.		IB: c. 1510–1450 B.C.	(Linear A)
		II: c. 1450–1405 B.C.	
		III: c. 1405–1100 B.C.	Mycenaean Age (Linear B)

(High Period spans from 2500 B.C. to 1500 B.C.)

All authorities agree that the neolithic strata must have derived from Asia Minor. Hence the recent excavations in southwest Anatolia (Turkey) are of especial interest. Their ceramic wares, which have been dated from c. 5500 B.C.,* may be taken to represent the earliest known background of the Cretan goddess cult. They include the statuette of a naked goddess seated upon and fondling leopards; also, one of such a goddess embraced by an adolescent youth; another of the goddess holding a child; and several of female figures alone, lying down or standing—but always handled (to quote the words of their excavator, Professor James Mellaart) "with admirable taste and a mastery of modeling heretofore unknown until late classic times." [41]

Moreover, in the neighboring so-called Taurean corner, where southeast Asia Minor meets northern Syria, an abundant series of female figurines appeared c. 4500–3500 B.C., in association with the beautiful painted Halaf ware of that zone; and here (as shown in *Primitive Mythology*) [42] a number of symbolic forms first appeared that were later to be prominent in Crete: the bull's head (bucranium) viewed from before, the double ax, the beehive tomb, and figures of the dove, as well as of the cow, sheep, goat, and pig.

In *Oriental Mythology* I have shown that the earliest known

* Supra, p. 43, note.

temple compounds in the history of civilization arose in this area c. 4000 B.C. and that by their form they suggested a reference to the female genitalia; specifically, the matrix of the cosmic mother-goddess, Cow. The milk of the sacred cattle raised within their enclosures was equivalent to that of the mother-goddess herself, whose calf was the animal of sacrifice. And when the pastoral-agrarian village culture of which this temple complex was a part spread south to the newly entered Mesopotamian mudlands, c. 4000–3500 B.C., this cattle cult went along.[43] But it also crossed Iran to India, where it appeared in the complex of the Indus Valley civilization, c. 2500 B.C., just about the time of the rise in Crete of Early Minoan II.

An important school of Italian scholarship has recently begun to write of a "Mediterranean culture complex" reaching as far east-ward as the Indus, dominated by the myths and rites of the Great Goddess and her consort.[44] Professor Nilsson writes of this group with a certain scorn.[45] However, it is difficult to imagine how one should otherwise explain the occurrence of a single syndrome of symbolic forms in two landscapes differing as greatly as the island world of the Aegean and the landlocked plains of northern India: the occurrence in both of a goddess who is both benign (as cow) and terrible (as lioness), associated with the growth, nourishment, and death of all beings, and, in particular, vegetation; symbolized in all her aspects by a cosmic tree of life, which is equally of death; and whose male associate is a god whose animal is the bull and token the trident, with whom, furthermore, the waning and waxing of the moon is linked, in a context showing numerous vestiges of a tradition of ritual regicide. My own view is that the two mythol-ogies are clearly extensions of a single system, of which the matrix was the nuclear Near East; the period of diffusion preceded that of the rise of the great Bronze Age Sumero-Egyptian kingly states; and the motive force of the vast expansion was commercial: the exploitation of raw materials, and trade. In India this late neolithic trading style of civilization gradually declined, yielding its contri-butions, first, to the primitive population, and, next, to the high Vedic Aryan development.[46] From Crete, on the other hand, a vigorous commercial expansion followed, which even reached, in the period of the Middle and Late Minoan stages (Middle Minoan I to late Minoan II), as far northwest as the British Isles. For a connection between Britain and the Cretan sphere has now been definitely shown.

A summary view of the British dates and stages, based on the recent archaeological investigation of Stonehenge by Professor R. J. C. Atkinson, can be offered for comparison with the Cretan series:

1. THE WINDMILL HILL CULTURE, C. 2300 B.C.: Earliest neolithic in Britain; derived ultimately from eastern Mediterranean (Frobenius's Cretan Sea), via Switzerland, France, and Iberia; scattered groups on southern shores: farmer-shepherds. Chief remains: large circular enclosures of earthwork, often comprising several concentric rings (e.g., on Windmill Hill, near Avebury), these may have been cattle corrals; also, long barrows, 10 feet or more in height, 100 to 300 feet in length, containing half a dozen or more bodies. Settlements, for the most part temporary.[47]

2. THE MEGALITHIC BUILDERS, C. 2000 B.C.: Remains: vast chambered tombs on western coasts of Britain.[48] Burials, collective but successive, in contrast to those of the Windmill Hill long barrows. (Correlation with Irish chambered tombs and high period of exploitation of Irish gold and copper, dated by Macalister c. 2000–1600 B.C.) [49] The megalithic diffusion seems to have emanated from the western Mediterranean (Frobenius's Sardinian Sea), and to have passed through France, up the Biscay coast, to Brittany and the British Isles. Its relationship to the much later Iron Age megalithic remains of South India, c. 200 B.C. to c. 50 A.D., remains obscure.[50]

2a. *Development in Britain of Secondary Neolithic Cultures:* Local developments resulting from the impact of Windmill Hill and megalithic arrivals upon the native mesolithic-paleolithic population. "Henge" monuments: large, circular, banked enclosures, normally broken by a single entrance, encompassing a ring of pits, with associated cremated burials. For example, Woodhenge: six concentric ovals of post holes suggest the ground plan here of a roofed wooden building; an infant's skeleton with cleft skull was found buried at the center of the ring.[51]

3. STONEHENGE I, C. 1900–1700 B.C.: The first of three successive phases in the building of great Stonehenge: encircling bank and pits; possibly some wooden structure at the center. The pits, it has been supposed, were for offerings addressed to the earth (the poured blood of slaughtered beasts, possibly also of human beings: compare the Woodhenge infant skeleton above).[52]

3a. Arrivals of Corded-Ware Battle-Ax People, c. 1775 B.C.: Aryan complex? Arrivals on northeast British coasts from across the North Sea; points of departure unknown: ultimate source land, the grazing plains from the Rhine to the Russian steppes. Impressed cord-ornamented pottery (compare Japan: Jomon, i.e. "cord-marked," stratum, c. 2500–300 B.C.); [53] perforated stone battle-axes, martial display, and warlike panoply: chieftainship.[54]

3b. Arrivals of Bell-Beaker People, c. 1775 B.C.: Arrivals on southeast British coasts from Rhineland. Individual burials under round barrows. Related cultures widely distributed in Central and Southwest Europe. Circular gold disks ornamented with a cross (solar reference?).[55]

4. STONEHENGE II, C. 1700–1500 B.C.: Second phase in the building of great Stonehenge: a double circle of seventy-six holes in which moderate-sized monoliths of bluestone once stood (the positions of the stones were changed during the building of Stonehenge III, but the evidence of the earlier placement is unquestioned). Size of stones: between about 6 and 13 feet high; weight, up to 6½ tons. Of particular interest: the axial line of the entrance to this circle (marked by an arrangement of six additional stones, making eighty-two in all) is oriented to the midsummer sunrise—which indicates a change from the earth orientation of Stonehenge I (sacrificial pits: earth-goddess cult?) to a skyward orientation (standing stones: sky and solar deities). Furthermore: the bluestone monoliths of this sanctuary had been brought from a sacred mountain 135 miles away, as the crow flies, namely Prescelly Top in Pembrokeshire, Wales—whose "cloud-wrapped summit," Pro-

fessor Atkinson suggests, "must have seemed no less the home of gods than did Mount Ida to a voyager on the Cretan plain." [56] This mountain (1760 feet) was visible to the tradesmen transporting Irish bronze and gold wares across southern Wales and Britain to the Continent. Further elements of this culture complex: local modifications of beaker pottery forms; Irish copper halberds and other effects of warrior gear, suggesting (to cite Professor Atkinson again) "a warrior-aristocracy, intimately involved in the trade in metal products." [57]

5. THE WESSEX CULTURE, C. 1500–1400 B.C.: Circle barrows (notably in the neighborhood of Stonehenge): single burials beneath a round mound, often of considerable height, surrounded by a ditch, containing numerous rich and exotic ornaments and weapons. An aristocratic community of power and wealth: middlemen in the Irish metal trade (gold, copper, and now also bronze wares) to the Continent, both overland and by sea to and from Minoan Crete and Mycenae. Metal imports from Germany and Bohemia. Necklaces of Baltic amber (the Bronze Age Amber Route was now in use, from the Baltic, overland through Central Europe, to the Adriatic). Gold objects from the Mediterranean. Egyptian faïence beads.[58]

5a. Stonehenge III, 1500–1400 B.C.: The great sarsen circle, 100 feet in diameter, of (originally) thirty tremendous stones: they rise to about 18 feet in height, with an average weight of some 26 tons. A lintel ran around the top, affixed by a type of mortice-and-tenon joint used also in the postern gate at Mycenae. Within the circle, a horseshoe of five trilithons opens toward the northeast (Summer Solstice), the tallest 24 feet above ground. And the earlier bluestones are now rearranged in two series, within and complementing the sarsens, namely in a circle and a horseshoe. Carvings on the stones: dagger of a type found in the shaft graves of Mycenae, 1600–1500 B.C.; ax head of a type of Irish bronze import, 1600–1400 B.C.; a rectangle symbolic of the mother-goddess.[59]

The British dates match the Cretan perfectly and, as Professor Atkinson (who is certainly no romanticist, but an extremely cautious scholar) states, the monument is not by any means a primitive work but suggests very strongly an influence from contemporary Mycenae.

> We have seen [he writes] that through trade the necessary contacts with the Mediterranean had been established. The Stonehenge dagger too may be seen, if one wishes, to point more directly at Mycenae itself. We know from Homer that architects, like the poets of whom he himself was one, were homeless men, wandering from city to city. Is it then any more incredible that the architect of Stonehenge should himself have been a Mycenaean, than that the monument should have been designed and erected, with all its unique and sophisticated detail, by mere barbarians?
>
> Let us suppose for a moment that this is more than mere conjecture. Under what circumstances, then, could a man versed in the traditions and skills of Mediterranean architecture find himself working among barbarians in the far cold North? Only, surely, as the skilled servant of some far-voyaging Mycenaean prince, *fortis ante Agamemnona;* or at the behest of a barbarian British king, whose voice and gifts spoke loudly enough to be heard even in the cities of the Mediterranean. . . .
>
> I believe . . . that Stonehenge itself is evidence for the concentration of political power, for a time at least, in the hands of a single man, who alone could create and maintain the conditions necessary for this great undertaking. Who he was, whether native-born or foreign, we shall never know; he remains a figure as shadowy and unsubstantial as King Brutus of the medieval British history. Yet who but he should sleep, like Arthur or Barbarossa, in the quiet darkness of a sarsen vault beneath the mountainous pile of Silbury Hill? And is not Stonehenge itself his memorial? [60]

Not a written word has come to us from that long-forgotten age, when all of Europe was alive with a commerce of brave men, daring voyages of danger, producing ornaments of grace, uniting by threads of trade the worlds of the gray Baltic and North Seas with the brilliant blue of the seaways of the South. Not even Crete, the nuclear isle of all this activity, has let us know through any text what the tales were that were told, the prayers that were chanted in the sanc-

tuaries, or even the languages that were used. The Cretan hieroglyphic script of the Early Palatial period (c. 2000–1660 B.C.:
Middle Minoan I to IIIA: Stonehenge I to early II) is not deciphered. Nor has the Linear A yet yielded up the secret of the great
High Palatial age (c. 1660–1405 B.C.: Middle Minoan III B to Late
Minoan II; Stonehenge, late II and III). The general view at present
appears to be that the language of Linear A, as well as that of the
earlier hieroglyphic script, was probably derived from the Luvian-
Hittite-Aryan sphere of Anatolia; [61] in other words, represented a
later phase of the culture matrix from which the Cretan neolithic
derived. However, a challenge to this view has recently been issued
by Professor Cyrus Gordon of Brandeis University, who believes
he has detected a Syrian, Phoenician-Semitic vocabulary in the
tablets. The issue is still open. But in either case, the general
area of origin would have had to have been the great Taurean culture volcano from which, as we have now seen and seen again,
waves and tides of greatest import and effect flowed in all directions, from as early as the period of the goddess figurines of the art
of Hacilar.

The language of Linear B, on the other hand (c. 1405–1100 B.C.:
Late Minoan III), which, as we now know, was an early form of
Greek, represents a period of invasion from the Europe of the
north: the Mycenaean heroic age of Agamemnon, Menelaus,
Nestor, and Odysseus, the last days of the long, productive world
age of the goddess, and the opening of the world age of the warrior
sons of gods. In the British series, we have already recorded an
appearance of members of this warrior complex as early as c.
1775 B.C., in the corded-ware battle-ax people, and probably, as
well, in the bell-beaker folk—in whose remains there has been
lately recognized a mingling of Aryan with Continental pre-Aryan
strains. [62] We have remarked, also, that in Stonehenge I the evidence
before this date suggests an earthly orientation, with sacrifices for
the fertilization of the goddess; while in Stonehenge II, the address
of the sanctuary is upward, to heaven and the sun, and with reference to a local Mount Olympus (Prescelly Top). It is reasonably
certain, therefore, that in the middle of the second millennium B.C.

a process of fusion of the two mythologies of the goddess and the gods had commenced in northern Europe.

In the Cretan-Mycenaean sphere, on the other hand, the cult of the goddess still was paramount. Comparably in Ireland, where the impact of the Aryan, patriarchal warrior bands was reduced by the filter of Britain, the elder goddess cult survived and even combined in a wildly brilliant manner with the gods, heroes, and mad warrior deeds of her sons.

I am taking pains in this work to place considerable stress upon the world age and symbolic order of the goddess; for the findings both of anthropology and of archaeology now attest not only to a contrast between the mythic and social systems of the goddess and the later gods, but also to the fact that in our own European culture that of the gods overlies and occludes that of the goddess—which is nevertheless effective as a counterplayer, so to say, in the unconscious of the civilization as a whole.

Psychologically and sociologically, the problem is of enormous interest; for, as all schools of psychology agree, the image of the mother and the female affects the psyche differently from that of the father and the male. Sentiments of identity are associated most immediately with the mother; those of dissociation, with the father. Hence, where the mother image preponderates, even the dualism of life and death dissolves in the rapture of her solace; the worlds of nature and the spirit are not separated; the plastic arts flourish eloquently of themselves, without need of discursive elucidation, allegory, or moral tag; and there prevails an implicit confidence in the spontaneity of nature, both in its negative, killing, sacrificial aspect (lion and double ax), and in its productive and reproductive (bull and tree).

To conclude, then: the beautiful Mycenaean seal ring of Figure 19 may stand as our final wayside shrine to this goddess of the early Garden of Innocence, before Nobodaddy made her serpent lover crawl and locked the Tree of Life away for all time. We see at the top the sun and waning crescent moon above a device that resembles that of the lunar bull and lion-bird plaque of Figure 16. It marks the same dividing line between the earthly and celestial, with the same two presences above: the moon declining and the killing sun. Behind the moon is a little figure bearing a staff in the left hand, somewhat in the manner of the lion-goddess of Figure 12. This little personage is covered by a large Mycenaean shield and suggests the warrior aspect of the goddess. For the later Greek Athene is also characterized by a shield (of the later, smaller, circular type carried on the arm), and since the name *A-ta-na Po-ti-ni-ja* (*Athenai Potniai:* "the Lady of Athens") appears among the tablets

Figure 19. The Goddess of the Double Ax

of Linear B, it is at least possible that an early counterpart of Classical Athene is represented here, in the negative, killing aspect of the goddess. Her right hand points to a series of six sacrificial animal heads strewn along the right (our left) margin of the composition, while across the way, in counterpoise, stands the bountifully flourishing Tree of Life, with a little female figure rising in the air to cull its fruit.

The center of the field is dominated by the Cretan double ax, which points two ways: on one hand, toward the sacrifice; on the other, toward its boon, the tree. We think of the great tree of Figure 15, with its large dead trunk but ever-living bough. The lion of the goddess in that case was of a gentle, protective aspect, as death would appear to have been experienced in this culture, as leading to eternal life. So also here: the goddess of the double ax sits benignantly beneath her tree and is approached by two devotees. To the outstretched hand of the first she offers a triad of poppy-seed pods, while with her left she elevates her breasts. The little figure at her knees, without legs but, as it were, emerging from the earth, holds in her left hand a tiny double ax and in her right a blossoming branch, summarizing, thus, the entire theme and representing the mid-point of balance between the small descending figure with the Mycenaean shield and the small ascending one culling fruit.[63] Compare the two powers of the left and right sides of the Gorgon, whose head in Classical art is affixed to Athene's shield.* As viewed in the pre-patriarchal age, this same goddess in whom death and life reside was herself the mythic garden wherein Death and Life—the Two Queens—were one. And to her faithful child, Dumuzi (the Minotaur), whose image of destiny is the lunar cycle, she was Paradise itself.

IV. The Victory of the Sons of Light

The peace and bounty of the goddess, based upon the rites of her temple groves of sacrifice, spread from the nuclear Near East in a broad swathe, eastward and westward, to the shores of the two seas; but many of the arts and benefits of her reign were scattered also among the wild peoples northward and southward, who became not settled farming folk but semi-nomadic herders of cattle, or of sheep and goats. These, by c. 3500 B.C., were becoming dangers to the farming villages and towns, appearing suddenly in raiding bands, plundering and departing, or, more seriously, remaining to enslave. They stemmed, as we have seen, from two great matrices: the broad grasslands of the north and the Syro-Arabian desert. By 3000 B.C. power states were being established by such invaders, and by c. 2500 B.C. the rule in Mesopotamia had passed decisively to a series of strong men from the desert, of whom Sargon of Agade (c. 2350 B.C.) was the first important example and Hammurabi of

* Supra, p. 25.

Babylon (c. 1728–1686 B.C.) the second. These were contemporaries, approximately, of the sea kings of Crete, but with a radically different relationship to the goddess.

"Sargon am I, the mighty king, Monarch of Agade," we read in a celebrated statement of the former of these two.

> My mother was of lowly birth; my father I knew not; the brother of my father is a mountain dweller; and my city, Azupiranu, lies on the bank of the Euphrates.
>
> My lowly mother conceived and bore me in secrecy; placed me in a basket of rushes; sealed it with bitumen, and set me in the river, which, however, did not engulf me. The river bore me up. And it carried me to Akku, the irrigator, who took me from the river, raised me as his son, made of me a gardener: and while I was a gardener, the goddess Ishtar loved me.
>
> Then I ruled the kingdom. . . .[64]

Here the king has taken to himself, or has had applied to him by his chronicler, a legendary biography of a type known throughout the world. The formula is derived from the older mythology of the goddess and her son, but with a transfer of interest to the son—who now is neither a god nor a dedicated sacrifice, but a politically ambitious upstart. The basic motifs in the present example are: 1. a modified virgin birth (father unknown, or deceased), 2. a vestigial suggestion of the father as a mountain god (his brother a mountaineer), 3. exposure on the waters (water-birth: compare Greek Erichthonius, Hindu Vyasa, Hebrew Moses), 4. rescue and fosterage by an irrigator (theme of fosterage by simple folk, frequently by animals, viz. Romulus and Remus: here the water theme is again stressed), 5. hero as a gardener (fructifier of the goddess), 6. beloved of the goddess Ishtar (Semitic counterpart of Inanna, Greek Aphrodite).

In the early days of the psychoanalytic movement, Dr. Otto Rank wrote an important monograph on the Myth of the Birth of the Hero,[65] in which he analyzed and compared some seventy-odd variants of this formula, drawn from Mesopotamia, Egypt, India, China, Japan and Polynesia, Greece and Rome, Iran, the Bible, Celtic and Germanic, Turkish, Esthonian, Finnish, and Christian

European lore. He showed that the pattern was comparable to that of a certain type of neurotic daydream, where the individual dissociates himself from his true parents by imagining for himself: 1. a noble or divine, higher birth, 2. infant exile or exposure, 3. adoption by a family much more lowly than himself (namely that of his actual parents), and 4. a prospect, ultimately, of return to his "true" estate, with a wonderful humbling of those responsible for the exile and a general sense of great achievement all around.

Dr. Rank's analysis suggests very well the appeal that such a legend must have had for ambitious kings and their biographers, but it underestimates the force (or so it seems to me) of the actual derivation of the formula from a cosmological myth. The whole series cited falls well within the range of the world-diffusion of the arts and rites of agrarian life, and consequently cannot be treated as a mere congeries of daydreams independently produced from a certain type of individual state of mind. Indeed, it might be asked whether the morbid state of mind is not a function of the legend rather than its cause; for, as it stands, the legend represents a descent from the cosmological plane to an individual reference. It therefore produces an inferior meditation, namely, instead of an extinction of ego in the image of a god (mythic identification), precisely the opposite: an exaltation of ego in the posture of a god (mythic inflation), which has been a chronic disease of rulers ever since the masters of the art of manipulating men contrived to play the role of incarnate god and yet save their necks from the double ax. The effect of this chicane—as I have shown in *Oriental Mythology* [66]—was to release royalty from the overrule of the priesthood and stars, transform the state from a religious (hieratic) to a political (dynastic) establishment, and open the age when the chief concern of kings might become the conquest not of themselves but of the world.

The inevitable next step was a projection of this type of royal inflation back upon the king of gods, the model of the earthly king, as in the following opening lines of the prelude of the Law Code of Hammurabi, where the destiny of the monarch is linked to that of the young and newly risen god Marduk.

When exalted Anu [god of the firmament], king of the angels, and Bel [god of the world mountain], who is the lord of heaven and earth; when these, who determine the destinies of the land, committed the sovereignty over all people to Marduk [patron god of the city of Babylon], who is the first-born of Ea [god of the watery abyss]; when they made Marduk great among the great gods; when they proclaimed his exalted name to Babylon, made Babylon unsurpassable in the regions of the world, and established for him in its midst an everlasting kingdom whose foundations are as firm as heaven and earth:

At that time Anu and Bel called to me, Hammurabi, the pious prince, worshiper of the gods, summoning me by name, to bring about the rule of righteousness in the land, to wipe out the wicked and evil, to prevent the strong from oppressing the weak, to go forth like the sun over the human race, to illuminate the land, and to further the welfare of mankind.[67]

The formula here is already that of the standard Oriental tyrant state, where the role of the monarch, gained by human means, is represented as a manifestation of the will and grace of the creator and supporter of the universe. Piety, justice, and concern for the welfare of the people guarantee the righteousness of his reign. And the celestial orb to which the monarch is now likened is no longer the silvery moon, which dies and is resurrected and is light yet also dark, but the golden sun, the blaze of which is eternal and before which shadows, demons, enemies, and ambiguities take flight. The new age of the Sun God has dawned, and there is to follow an extremely interesting, mythologically confusing development (known as *solarization*), whereby the entire symbolic system of the earlier age is to be reversed, with the moon and the lunar bull assigned to the mythic sphere of the female, and the lion, the solar principle, to the male.

The best-known mythic statement of this victory of the sun-god over the goddess and her spouse is the Babylonian epic of the victory of Marduk over his great-great-great-grandmother Tiamat, which appears to have been composed either in, or shortly following, the period of Hammurabi himself. The only extant document, however, is from the celebrated library of King Ashurbanipal of

Assyria, a full millennium later (c. 668–630 B.C.), from which royal treasury of learning most of what we now know of Semitic literature before the composition of the Bible has been derived.

> When heaven above had not yet been named, nor the earth beneath; when the primal Apsu, their begetter, together with Mummu [the son and messenger of Apsu and Tiamat] and Tiamat herself, she who gave birth to all, still mingled their waters and no pasture land had yet been formed, nor was there even a reed marsh to be seen; when none of the generation of the gods had yet been brought into being, called by name, or given a destiny: at that time, within Apsu and Tiamat, the great gods were created.

Here is an early version of the formula, already known to most of us through the writings of the Greeks, of an older and a later generation of divinities. Apsu, Tiamat, and their son Mummu (their messenger, the Word),* like the Classical Uranus, Gaea, and their children, the Titans, enjoy a period of unchallenged dominion antecedent to the rise and victory of those warrior gods who are most honored in the prayers and rites of the people. Such a mythology represents an actual historical substitution of cult: in both these instances, that of an intrusive patriarchal over an earlier matriarchal system. And in both cases, too, the main intention of the cosmic genealogy was to effect a refutation of the claims of the earlier theology in favor of the gods and moral order of the later. Hence, we read:

> Lahmu and Lahamu came into being and were called by their names. Even before they had matured and become tall, Anshar and Kishar were created and surpassed them in stature. These lived many days, adding years to days, and their first-born, heir presumptive, was Anu, the rival of his fathers, equaling Anshar. Anu begot his own likeness Ea, the master of his fathers, broad of understanding, greatly wise and mighty in strength, even stronger than Anshar, his grandfather, with no rival among the gods, his brothers.
>
> And these divine brothers troubled and disturbed the inner parts of Tiamat. Moving, running about within their divine abode, they gave Apsu reason for concern. He could not

* Compare supra, p. 56, "the mummu house."

diminish their clamor. And Tiamat remained silent concerning them, though what they were doing gave pain. Their behavior was not good.

Wherefore Apsu, the begetter of the great gods, called his vizier, Mummu, and said to him: "My vizier, Mummu, you who gladden my heart, come, let us go to Tiamat!" Going, they reposed before Tiamat and took counsel concerning the gods, their first-born. Apsu opened his mouth and said in a loud voice to the glistening one, Tiamat: "Their behavior has become an annoyance to me. By day I cannot rest; by night I cannot sleep. I shall destroy them, put an end to their behavior; and when silence has been restored, let us sleep."

But Tiamat, hearing this, became angry, and cried out to her spouse, raging furiously, pondering his evil in her heart. "Why destroy what we ourselves have produced? Their behavior is indeed painful, but let us take it with good will."

Mummu counseled Apsu, giving unfavorable advice. "Yes, Father, put an end to their disorder," he said; "and have rest by day and sleep by night." Whereupon Apsu brightened with a wicked plan against his progeny, the gods, while Mummu embraced his neck, sat on his knee, and kissed him.

But of what they planned in this way, the great gods became aware, and when they had learned of it, they made haste. They took to silence; sat quietly. And Ea, supreme in knowledge, skillful and wise, who understands all things, comprehended the wicked plan. Ea drew a magic circle against it, within which all took protection; then he composed a powerful incantation, which he recited over the water, out of which sleep poured down upon Apsu and Apsu slept. And when Ea had thus put both Apsu and Mummu, his adviser, to sleep, he loosened Apsu's chin strap, tore off his tiara, carried off his splendor, and put it on himself; and when he had thus subdued, he slew him. On Apsu he then built his dwelling place, and Mummu he seized for himself, holding him by a nose rope. . . .

With this we have arrived, indeed, in the field of the psychology of Freud and Rank: the mythic malice of the father, partisanship of the mother, rivalry of siblings (Mummu, the elder, and Ea, the younger son), with finally a patricide and its mythically justified rationalization—behind which it would be unhealthy to explore. Essentially the myth is a transformation of the earlier formula represented in our Figure 16: of the bull, the goddess, and the lion-bird; i.e., the father (Apsu), the mother (Tiamat), and the son (Mummu). In the present instance the waters of these three are undifferentiated. They represent the state of consciousness that is termed in Indian thought "deep dreamless sleep," and in Freud's, "the oceanic feeling": and in fact, as we are told, the peace of sleep was Apsu's sole desire.

In the triad of Apsu, Mummu, and Tiamat (which in the earlier mythic order, by the way, would probably have been presented as Tiamat and Apsu-Mummu), the non-dual state antecedent to creation is symbolized, out of which all forms, both of myth and dream and of daylight reality, are derived. But in the new mythology of the great gods the plane of attention has been shifted to the foreground figures of duality and combat, power, profit and loss, where the mind of the man of action normally dwells. Whereas the aim of the earlier mythology had been to support a state of indifference to the modalities of time and identification with the inhabiting non-dual mystery of all being,* that of the new was just the opposite: to foster action in the field of time, where the subject and object are indeed two, separate and not the same—as A is not B, as death is not life, virtue is not vice, and the slayer is not the slain. It is all so simple, sunny, and straightforward. The virtuous younger son, Ea of many devices, overcomes the wicked father in his own fine Oedipal way and takes the elder, wicked son (the knower and lover of the father) by the nose.

And so what, then, of the destiny of the mother, Tiamat, in this normative tale of the manner of the victories of virtue?

> After Ea had vanquished his enemies, confirmed his victory over his foes, and peacefully occupied his abode, he called his abode the Apsu, established there his chamber, and dwelt in splendor therein with his spouse, Damkina. And it was there, in that chamber of fate, abode of destinies, that the wisest of the wise, most knowing of the gods, the Lord himself, Marduk, was begotten of his father Ea, born of Damkina, his mother, and nursed by the breasts of goddesses. He was filled thereby with awe-inspiring majesty. His figure was en-

---

* Compare supra, pp. 3–4.

ticing, flashing the look of his eyes, manly his going forth. He was a leader from the start. And when Ea, his father, beheld him, he rejoiced and bestowed on him double equality with the gods. Marduk was exalted beyond them in all ways: in all his members marvelously arranged: incomprehensible and difficult to look upon. He had four eyes and as many ears, and when his lips moved, fire blazed forth. Each of the ears grew large; each of the eyes, also, to see all. He was prodigious and was clothed with the radiance of ten gods, with a majesty to inspire fear.

And it was at this season that the god Anu begot the four winds, raising waves upon the surface of the waters of Tiamat. He also filled his hand, and, diving, created dirt, which the waves stirred up. Tiamat became disturbed. Day and night, she moved about. And those around her [whom she had spawned] said to their agitated mother: "When they killed Apsu, your spouse, you did not march at his side. Now the four winds are created. You are agitated within. We cannot rest. . . . We cannot sleep. . . .

The legend now proceeds to an account of the mounting wrath and battle fury of Tiamat. As all-mother—"she who fashions all things"—she gave birth to monster serpents, sharp of tooth and fang, filled with poison instead of blood, ferocious, terrible, and crowned with fear-inspiring glory, such that to look upon them was to perish: the viper, the dragon, the great lion, the mad dog, the scorpion-man and various demons of storm: powerful and irresistible. Altogether eleven sorts of monster were brought forth, and of these the first-born, Kingu by name, Tiamat exalted and made great in their midst. "I have made you great," she said; "I have given you dominion over all the gods, and I make you my unique spouse. May your name become great." She fastened upon his breast the tablet of destinies and said to him: "May your words quell and your overpowering poison overwhelm all opposition." After which, she and her brood made ready for a battle with the gods.

The reader will have recognized here the pattern of the Greek war of the Titans and the gods, the darker brood of the all-mother, produced of her own female power, and the brighter, fairer, secondary sons, produced from her submission to fecundation by the male.

It is an effect of the conquest of a local matriarchal order by invading patriarchal nomads, and their reshaping of the local lore of the productive earth to their own ends. It is an example, also, of the employment of a priestly device of *mythological defamation,* which has been in constant use (chiefly, but not solely, by Western theologians) ever since. It consists simply in terming the gods of other people demons, enlarging one's own counterparts to hegemony over the universe, and then inventing all sorts of both great and little secondary myths to illustrate, on the one hand, the impotence and malice of the demons and, on the other, the majesty and righteousness of the great god or gods. It is used in the present case to validate in mythological terms not only a new social order but also a new psychology—and to this extent must be understood as in a certain sense representative not of sheer fraud but of a new truth: a new structure of human thought and feeling, overinterpreted as of cosmic reach.

The battle that we are about to view, as though of gods against Titans before the beginning of the world, actually was of two aspects of the human psyche at a critical moment of human history, when the light and rational, divisive functions, under the sign of the Heroic Male, overcame (for the Western branch of the great culture province of the high civilizations) the fascination of the dark mystery of the deeper levels of the soul, which has been so beautifully termed in the Tao Te Ching, the Valley Spirit that never dies:

> It is named the Mysterious Female.
> And the Doorway of the Mysterious Female
> Is the base from which Heaven and Earth sprang.
> It is there within us all the while. . . .[68]

Tiamat [as we now read] made ready to engage in battle with the gods, her offspring. She prepared to attack. And when Ea learned of this, he became numb with fear and sat down. He went presently before his father, Anshar, to let him know what Tiamat was doing. Anshar cried out in wrath, summoned Anu, his eldest son, and bade him go stand against Tiamat; who went forth and did so, but, unable to withstand her, returned.

All the gods, therefore, were assembled; but they sat in

silence, full of fear. And Ea, when he saw their case, called his son, Marduk, to his chamber and disclosed to him the secret of his heart. "You are my son," he said. "Hearken to your father. Prepare yourself for battle and stand forth before Anshar, who, when he sees you, will be at rest."

The Lord, Marduk, was pleased at the word of Ea, his father, and, having prepared himself, drew nigh and stood before Anshar, who, when he beheld him, was filled with joy. He kissed his lips. His fear was gone. "I will accomplish," said the Lord Marduk, "all that is in your heart. Tiamat, a woman, is coming at you with arms. Soon you will trample on her neck. But O Lord of the destiny of the great gods, if I am to be your avenger, to slay Tiamat and keep you alive, convene the assembly and proclaim my lot supreme, namely, that not you but I shall henceforth fix the destinies of the gods by utterances and that whatever I create shall remain without change."

A fine affair indeed! We have now entered a theater of myth that the rational, non-mystic mind can comprehend without aid, where the art of politics, the art of gaining power over men, received for all time its celestial model.

Anshar addressed Kaka, his vizier, and bade him assemble the gods. "Let them converse, sit down to a banquet, eat bread, and consume wine. Declare to them that Tiamat, our bearer, hates us; that all the lesser gods have gone over to her side, even those whom we ourselves created; that Tiamat, who fashions all things now has brought forth weapons, serpents, dragons, the great lion, the mad dog, exalting Kingu as her spouse; that I have sent Anu against her, but he failed; and that now Marduk, the wisest of the gods, declares that if he is to be our avenger, whatever his lips command shall not be changed."

The word went out, the gods gathered, kissed one another in the assembly, conversed, sat to a banquet, ate bread, consumed wine, and the wine dispelled their fears; their bodies swelled as they drank, they became carefree and exalted, and for their lord and avenger, Marduk, they set up a lordly throne upon which he took his place, facing the fathers.

"O Lord," they said, "your destiny is to be supreme henceforth among the gods. To raise up or to bring low—these shall be in your hand. Your utterance shall be truth, your command unimpeachable, none among the gods shall transgress your bounds. We grant to you kingship of the universe."

They spread a garment in their midst [the starry garment of the night sky]. "By your word," said they, "let it vanish; by your word again, let it reappear" [as the night sky on the passage of the sun]. Marduk spoke, the garment vanished; again, the garment reappeared. And when the gods beheld this fulfillment of the sign, they rejoiced, did homage, and declared: "Marduk is king!"

The gods then bestowed on Marduk the scepter, throne, royal ring, and irresistible thunderbolt. He made ready his bow, took up his club in his right hand, set lightning before him, filled his body with flame, made a net to enmesh Tiamat, called the winds of the quarters and various hurricanes, mounted his irresistible chariot of storm with four steeds yoked before, whose names were Killer, Pitiless, Trampler, and Flier, their mouths, their lips, and their teeth, bearing poison; he placed Battle-Smiter on his right, Combat on his left, and, clad in terrifying mail, with a fierce turban haloing his head, set his face toward the place of furious Tiamat. A spell was ready in his mouth. An herb against poison was held in his hand. The gods were milling all around him. And he approached to gaze into her heart and to penetrate the plan of Kingu, her spouse.

As Marduk gazed, Kingu became confused; his will faltered, his action ceased; and the wicked gods who were his helpers, marching at his side, beholding him thus, their sight became blurred. But Tiamat, without turning her neck, cried defiant mockery at Marduk. "You advance like the very lord of the gods! Is it in their place they have gathered, or in yours?"

Marduk raised his mighty weapon. "Why," he challenged, "have you risen up like this, plotting in your heart to stir up strife? You have appointed Kingu to be your spouse, Kingu without worth, in the place of Anu. Against Anshar, king of the gods, you are designing evil. Against the gods, my fathers, you have demonstrated your wickedness. Let your army be equipped! Let your weaponry be in order! Stand forth! I and you shall have at each other!"

Hearing this, Tiamat became as one possessed. She lost her reason; uttered wild, piercing screams; trembled; shook to the roots of her limbs; pronounced an incantation; and all the gods of the battle cried out. Then Tiamat advanced; Marduk, as well: they approached each other for the battle. The Lord spread out his net to enmesh her, and when she opened her mouth to its full, let fly into it an evil wind that poured into her belly, so that her courage was taken from her and her jaws remained opened wide. He shot an arrow that tore into her, cut through her inward parts, and pierced her heart. She was undone. He stood upon her carcass and those gods who had marched by her side turned for their lives. He encircled them with his net, destroyed their weapons, made them captive, and they wept.

The poisonous monsters to which Tiamat had given birth and assigned splendor, Marduk flung into fetters, arms bound behind, and trampled underfoot. Kingu, he tied and flung among the rest, depriving him of the Tablet of Destinies, to which that arrogant one had no right. The Victor took this to himself, sealed it with his seal, affixed it to his breast, and, returning to the carcass of Tiamat, mounting upon her hinder quarters, with his merciless mace smashed her skull. He cut the arteries of her blood and caused the north wind to bear it off to parts unknown. And when his fathers saw this, they rejoiced and sent him gifts.

Marduk now paused, gazing upon the dead body, considering the foul thing, to devise an ingenious plan. Whereafter, he split her, like a shellfish, in two halves; set one above, as a heavenly roof, fixed with a crossbar; and assigned guards to watch that her waters above should not escape. He next traversed the heavens, surveyed its quarters, and, over against the Apsu of his father Ea, measured the magnitude of the Deep. He then established upon this a great abode, the Earth, as a canopy above the Apsu. Anu, Enlil, and Ea, he assigned to their various residences [namely, Heaven, Earth, and the Abyss], and the first part of his enterprise therewith had been accomplished.

The rest we need review, here, only briefly. Victorious Marduk defined the year and its zodiac of twelve signs, the days of the year, the various stellar and planetary orders, and the manner of the moon: its waxing to the middle of the month in opposition to the sun, after which, its waning and disappearance, in approach to the station of the sun; and the god's heart then moved him to fashion something else, something really wonderfully ingenious.

"Blood I shall amass," he confided to Ea, his father; "bone I shall frame, and set up a creature. 'Man' shall be his name. Yes, Man! He will be required to serve the gods; and these, then, will be free to repose at ease." *

Marduk explained to his father the way in which his plan was to be accomplished. He would divide the gods in two groups, one good, the other evil, and from the blood and bones of the bad— namely those who had sided with Tiamat—he would fashion the race of mankind.

Ea, however, answered: "Take but one of the wicked gods, to be delivered up, destroyed, and mankind fashioned of his parts. Let the great gods be assembled. Let the one most guilty be delivered up."

Ea's son, Marduk, concurred. The deities were assembled, and the Lord, Marduk, addressed them. "What was promised, has been accomplished. Who was it, however, that caused Tiamat to revolt and prepare for war? Deliver him to me, and I shall make him take his punishment, rest assured!"

To which the gods replied in accord: "Kingu it was, who caused Tiamat to revolt and prepare for war." They bound him, held him before Ea, slashed the arteries of his blood and with his blood created mankind. Ea then imposed upon mankind the service of the gods, and with that, set free the gods from all labor.

Following the accomplishment of this deed of deeds, the gods were assigned to their various cosmic mansions; and they said to their lord, Marduk: "O Lord, who have delivered us from onerous servitude, what shall be the sign of our gratitude? Come, let us make a sanctuary, a dwelling for our nightly rest; let us rest therein; and let there be there, also, a throne, a seat with back support, for

* Compare the earlier Sumerian myth, where the creation of man to be a servant of the gods was attributed to Ea himself and his spouse, the goddess Earth (*The Masks of God: Oriental Mythology*, pp. 108–11). Babylon with its kings had not at that time risen to world supremacy. The present myth, like many soon to come, is an example of *mythological appropriation*, where a later god takes over the role of another, with or without the earlier god's support.

our Lord." And when Marduk heard this, the glory of his countenance shone forth, and he said: "So shall Babylon be, whose con-
struction you have here announced. . . ." [69]

The epic tale goes on to tell of the building and dedication of
the great Babylonian ziggurat and to conclude with a celebration of
the fifty names of praise of its Lord, Marduk, the utterance of whose
mouth no god whatsoever can change: unsearchable, his heart; all-
embracing, his mind; the sinner and transgressor is an abomination
before him; and let mankind, therefore, rejoice in our Lord,
Marduk.

In the literature of scholarship it has been frequently remarked
that the name of the Babylonian mother monster in this epic of
Creation, *ti'amat,* is related etymologically to the Hebrew term
tehom, "the deep," of the second verse of Genesis, and that as the
wind of Anu blew upon the deep and that of Marduk into the face
of Tiamat, so in Genesis 1:2, "the wind [or spirit] of Elohim
hovered [or was blowing] over the face of the waters." Moreover, as
Marduk spread out the upper half of the mother-body as a roof
with the waters of heaven above, so in Genesis 1:7, "Elohim made
the firmament and separated the waters that were under the firmament from those that were above the firmament"; and again, as Ea
conquered Apsu, and Marduk conquered Tiamat, so did Yahweh
the sea monsters Rahab (Job 26:12–13) and Leviathan (Job 41;
Psalm 74:14).

There can be no question but that the imagery of the various
creation stories of the Bible derives from a general fund of Sumero-
Semitic myth, of which the Babylonian epic of Creation is an example; but it also is to be noted—as many have been zealous to
point out—that between the Bible and this particular epic "the
divergences," to quote one authority, "are much more far-reaching
and significant than are the resemblances." [70] The Bible represents
a later stage in the patriarchal development, wherein the female
principle, represented in the earlier Bronze Age by the great goddess-mother of all things and in this epic by a monstrous demoness,
is reduced to its elemental state, *tehom,* and the male deity alone

creates out of himself, as the mother alone had created in the past. The Babylonian epic stands between, along a line that may be logically schematized in four steps:

1. the world born of a goddess without consort;
2. the world born of a goddess fecundated by a consort;
3. the world fashioned from the body of a goddess by a male warrior-god; and
4. the world created by the unaided power of a male god alone.

Remaining, for the present, with the Babylonian text, we note, first, that the god has brought about by violence what the goddess —who is still recognized as "she who fashions all things"—would have brought about spontaneously of herself, if let alone. From the point of view of the goddess, therefore, the god, her child—for all his pomp—is actually nothing but her agent, seeming to bring to pass what is coming to pass. But she lets him feel that he is doing it himself, building his fine house of blocks with his own strength; and so is a good mother, indeed. But, on the other hand, this epic is far from such a realization of the irony of manly deeds. It is a forthright patriarchal document, where the female principle is devaluated, together with its point of view, and, as always happens when a power of nature and the psyche is excluded from its place, it has turned into its negative, as a demoness, dangerous and fierce. And we are going to find, throughout the following history of the orthodox patriarchal systems of the West, that the power of this goddess-mother of the world, whom we have here seen defamed, abused, insulted, and overthrown by her sons, is to remain as an ever-present threat to their castle of reason, which is founded upon a soil that they consider to be dead but is actually alive, breathing, and threatening to shift.

And a second point to be noted is that with this turn from the plane of the mother to that of the sons, the sense of the identity of life and death disappears, together with that of the power of life to bring forth its own good forms, so that all now is strife and effort, defamation of what is alien, pretentiousness, grandiloquence, and a lurking sense of guilt: which is epitomized, finally, in the myth of the origin of mankind from the blood of abominated Kingu, to be subject to, and of service to, the gods—though God knows (as do you and I), that Kingu had actually a greater right to his Tablet of Destinies than the lord Marduk, who had simply might.

And so now, finally: What is the image of man's fate that accompanies this great victory of the world of the gods over that of the goddess-mother of the gods? The famous legend of Gilgamesh tells the tale, which by many has been termed the first great epic of the destiny of man. We need not review it in all detail, for it is already well known. However, certain of its main themes acquire a new poignancy when viewed against the backdrop of the murder of Tiamat.

Gilgamesh was the name of a king of the early Sumerian city of Uruk. "Divine Gilgamesh," he is termed in the old Sumerian king list. "His father was a lillu-demon," we are told. "He was a high priest of the land and reigned 126 years." [71] In that early document, going back to sources from the old Sumerian cities themselves, his name follows that of Divine Dumuzi, whose name we already know as that of the dead and resurrected son and consort of the goddess; and before Divine Dumuzi was Divine Lugalbanda, who reigned 1200 years. Gilgamesh was, in fact, the last of those kings the lengths of whose reigns exceeded normal human years. He was honored as a god-king; hence the title "Divine." However, in the setting of the later, Babylonian epic, his image, along with that of man's destiny, is greatly changed.

He is still described as "two-thirds god and one-third man"; but as a tyrant, "unbridled in arrogance," "who leaves not the son to his father . . . leaves not the maid to her mother." The people prayed to the gods, and the gods hearkened to their plea. They turned to the mother-goddess, whose name now is Aruru. "You created Gilgamesh," the gods said. "Now create his counterpart." And when she heard this, she conceived in her heart a likeness of Anu, the god of heaven; washed her hands, took a piece of clay, cast it on the ground, and so created the valiant Enkidu.

The old mother had not yet lost her old talent, after all. Indeed, as we are to see, she is actually the chief divine figure of this tale— which is a fact to cause no surprise, since Gilgamesh himself derives,

as we have seen, from an age (c. 2500 B.C.) that was antecedent
to her overthrow by her sons.

But now, the strange appearance of her latest child, Enkidu!

The whole of his body was hairy and his locks were like a
woman's, or like the hair of the goddess of grain. Moreover,
he knew nothing of settled fields or of human beings, and was
clothed like a deity of flocks. He ate grass with the gazelles,
jostled the wild beasts at the watering hole, and was content
with the animals there. But then a certain hunter, coming face
to face with Enkidu at the watering place, and beholding him,
the face of that hunter became motionless. He returned in fear
to his father. "My father," he said, "there is a man with the
strength of a god who ranges with the beasts over the hills,
whom I dare not approach. He has torn up the traps that I set
for the animals of the plain." The father advised going to
Gilgamesh for aid, and when Gilgamesh was apprised of the
marvel, "Go, my hunter," he said; "take along with you a
temple prostitute, and when he comes to the watering hole,
with the beasts, let her throw off her clothes, disclose her
nakedness, and when he sees, he will approach her; and the
beasts thereafter will desert him, which grew up with him on
his plain."

The hunter and temple prostitute set forth, and three days
later reached the watering place. One day they sat; two days;
and on the next the beasts arrived, Enkidu among them,
feeding on the grass with the gazelles. The woman saw him.
"There he is," the hunter said. "Make free your breasts; disclose to him your nakedness: that he may take your favors.
Do not fear. Lay hold of his soul. He will see you and draw
near. Put aside your clothes, that he may lie upon you, and
yield to him the rapture of your woman's art. His beasts that
grew on his plain will desert him when he is knowing you in
love."

The woman did as told: made bare her breasts, revealed
her nakedness. Enkidu came and took possession. She was not
afraid, but, having put aside her clothes, welcomed his ardor;
and for six days and seven nights Enkidu remained mating
with that temple maid's abundance—after which he turned
his face and made a move toward the beasts. But on seeing
him, they ran off, and Enkidu was amazed. His body stiffened,
his knees froze—the animals were gone. It was not as before.

Enkidu returned to the woman and, sitting at her feet, gazed up into her face; and, as she spoke, his ears gave heed. "You are beautiful, Enkidu, like a very god," she said to him. "Why do you run with the beasts of the plain? Come, I will take you to the ramparts of Uruk, the holy temple city of Anu and Ishtar, where Gilgamesh dwells, unmatched in might, who, like a wild bull, wields power over men." And as he heard, his heart grew light. He yearned for a friend. "Very well!" he said. "And I shall challenge him. Shouting, I shall cry out in Uruk: 'I am he who is mighty and can change destinies, he who was born mighty on the plains!' "

"Come then," she said. "Come to ramparted Uruk, where every day is a festival, the lads brave, the maidens lovely; and I will show you Gilgamesh, the man of joy and vigor, mightier even than you."

She took in hand her clothing, and with one piece covered Enkidu, with the other covered herself, and, holding then his hand, led him like a mother to Uruk. She taught him there how to eat and drink, anoint himself with oil, become human. The people, gathering, said of him: "He is like Gilgamesh to a hair: shorter in stature but stronger of bone. A fair match for Gilgamesh, the godlike, has appeared."

And, indeed, when the bed of the goddess Ishtar had been prepared and Gilgamesh, by night, approached it, Enkidu, in the street, barred the way. They met. They grappled, locked like bulls. The doorpost of the temple shattered; the wall shook. And, at last, Gilgamesh relented. His fury gone, he turned away. And the two, thereafter, were inseparable friends.*

One readily sees in this strange old tale a wonderful reduction of the old mythic theme of the goddess Inanna-Ishtar and her divine son and spouse Dumuzi-Tammuz to a plane of superhuman legend—two-thirds god and one-third man. The goddess Ishtar in her character as harlot, mother, bride, and guide, is incarnate in her

* An Assyrian rescension of the Gilgamesh epic in twelve tablets (c. 650 B.C.), collated with fragments of an older Akkadian (c. 1750 B.C.?), as well as a fragmentary Hittite translation of the latter, have supplied the chief sources of the modern scholarly reconstruction of the narrative. My rendition follows the authorities cited above, Heidel, Speiser, and King, with the addition of Stephen Herbert Langdon, *Semitic Mythology: The Mythology of All Races*, Vol. V (Boston: Marshall Jones Company, 1931), pp. 234–69.

temple servant, and the wild Enkidu at the waterhole is the old lunar god in his character as lord of beasts. But a new and wonderful humanity has entered into our tale as a result simply of this transfer of plane from the reincarnating aspect of the characters to the mortal. Time, mortality, and the anguish of humanity in a world of personal destiny, basically related to our own, give to this piece the quality of an epic, "with a dramatic movement," as Professor William F. Albright has well said, "quite foreign to the long-winded, liturgical compositions of the earlier Sumerians." [72]

Enkidu and Gilgamesh became inseparable friends, but after a number of grandiose mythological adventures Enkidu died.

Gilgamesh touched his heart, but it did not beat. And like a lion, storming, like a lioness bereaved of her cubs, the great king paced back and forth before the couch, pulled out his hair, strewed it to the quarters, tore off and flung down his ornaments, called for his craftsmen to fashion a statue of his friend, wept bitterly, and lay stretched upon the ground.

"Oh, let me not die like my friend Enkidu," he cried. "Grief has entered into my body; of death I am afraid. I shall go forth. I shall not tarry by the way." And he set forth in quest of a plant of immortality.

It was a long long adventure: a passage over mountains. Lions he beheld and was afraid. He raised his head, prayed to the moon god, and the moon god sent a guiding dream, after which he took his ax and hacked his way past the lions. Then he came to the mountains of the sunset, where the scorpion men guard the gate, whom it is death to behold. Gilgamesh saw them and his face grew dark with fear; the wildness of their aspect robbed him of his senses. One of them, however, opened to him a gate, and he passed into a thick darkness, through which he proceeded to a fair plain where he saw in a great park a wonderful tree. Precious stones it bore as fruit. Its branches were exceedingly beautiful and its top was of lapis lazuli. Its harvest dazzled the eye. But Gilgamesh passed along and at the shore of the sea—the world sea—came to the residence of a mysterious female, Siduri, who received him with the celebrated lines:

O Gilgamesh, whither do you fare?
The life you seek, you will not find.

> When the gods created man,
> They apportioned death to mankind;
> And retained life to themselves.
>
> O Gilgamesh, fill your belly,
> Make merry, day and night;
> Make of each day a festival of joy,
> Dance and play, day and night!
> Let your raiment be kept clean,
> Your head washed, body bathed.
> Pay heed to the little one, holding onto your hand,
> Let your wife delight your heart.
> For in this is the portion of man.

The lesson is one that we have all heard; as, for example, in the words of Ecclesiastes:

> Behold, what I have seen to be good and to be fitting is to eat and drink and find enjoyment in all the toil with which one toils under the sun the few days of his life which God has given him, for this is his lot. . . .
> And I commend enjoyment, for man has no good thing under the sun but to eat, and drink, and enjoy himself, for this will go with him in his toil through the days of life which God gives him under the sun. . . .
> Let your garments be always white; let not oil be lacking on your head. Enjoy life with the wife whom you love, all the days of your vain life which he has given you under the sun, because that is your portion in life and in your toil at which you toil under the sun. . . .[73]

Gilgamesh, however, was of a different hope and purpose: he insisted on his quest; and the woman sent him on to the ferryman of death, who would pole him across the cosmic sea to the isle of the blessed, where the ever-living hero of the Flood—in this version of the old myth, named Ut-napishtim—dwelt, together with his wife, in everlasting bliss. The ageless couple received the voyager, let him sleep for six days and nights, fed him magic food, washed him with healing waters, and told of the plant of immortality at the bottom of the cosmic sea, which he must pluck if he would live, as he desired, forever. And so, once again, in the boat of the ferryman of death, Gilgamesh was voyaging, as no one ever before him, in the contrary direction, coming back to this mortal shore. "The plant is like a buckthorn," Ut-napishtim had told him. "Its thorns will tear your hands; but if your hands can pluck it, you will gain new life."

At a point midway, the boat paused. Gilgamesh tied heavy stones to his feet, which drew him down into the deep. He spied the plant. It tore his hands. But he plucked it, cut away those stones, and returning to the surface, boarded, and made for shore. "I shall take the plant to ramparted Uruk," he told the boatman. "I shall give it to be consumed and shall eat of it myself, and its name shall be Man Becomes Young in Old Age."

But when he had landed and was on his way, he paused by a freshet for the night; and when he went to bathe, a serpent, sniffing the fragrance of the plant, came out of the water, took the plant, returned to its abode and, consuming it, shed its skin. Whereat Gilgamesh—sat down and wept.[74]

And that is why the Serpent Power of Immortal Life, which formerly was known as a property of man, was taken away and now remains apart—in the keep of the cursed serpent and defamed goddess, in the lost paradise of the innocence of fear.

THE AGE OF HEROES

✦✦

GODS AND HEROES OF THE
LEVANT: 1500–500 B.C.

++

1. The Book of the Lord

The world is full of origin myths, and all are factually false. The world is full, also, of great traditional books tracing the history of man (but focused narrowly on the local group) from the age of mythological beginnings, through periods of increasing plausibility, to a time almost within memory, when the chronicles begin to carry the record, with a show of rational factuality, to the present. Furthermore, just as all primitive mythologies serve to validate the customs, systems of sentiments, and political aims of their respective local groups, so do these great traditional books. On the surface they may appear to have been composed as conscientious history. In depth they reveal themselves to have been conceived as myths: poetic readings of the mystery of life from a certain interested point of view. But to read a poem as a chronicle of fact is—to say the least—to miss the point. To say a little more, it is to prove oneself a dolt. And to add to this, the men who put these books together were not dolts but knew precisely what they were doing—as the evidence of their manner of work reveals at every turn.

The first decisive step toward a reading of the Old Testament as a product, like every other piece of ancient literature, not of God's literary talent but of man's, and, as such, not of eternity but of time, and specifically an extremely troubled time, was taken by Wilhelm M. L. de Wette (1780–1849) in his epochal two-volume work,

Contributions Introductory to the Old Testament (1806).[1] There he showed:

1. that the "Book of the Law," described in II Kings as "found" by the priest Hilkiah in the year 621 B.C., during the repairing of Solomon's Temple, was the nucleus of the Book of Deuteronomy;

2. that on the basis of this alleged find, all the earlier historical and mythological material of the Old Testament was later completely reworked; and

3. that the books of Exodus, Leviticus, and Numbers, which are represented as derived from Moses during the years of the wandering in the desert, actually were the end product of a long development: they were the law book of an already thoroughly orthodox priestly tradition, brought from Babylon to Jerusalem by the priest Ezra, c. 400 B.C., and, by virtue of the power invested in him by the Persian emperor Artaxerxes, ceremoniously established as a book of rules binding for all Jews.[2]

The biblical text in question reads as follows:

> In the eighteenth year of King Josiah [i.e., 621 B.C.], the king sent Shaphan the son of Azaliah, son of Mushullam, the secretary, to the house of the Lord, saying, "Go up to Hilkiah the high priest, that he may reckon the amount of the money which has been brought into the house of the Lord, which the keepers of the household have collected from the people; and let it be given into the hand of the workmen who have the oversight of the house of the Lord; and let them give it to the workmen who are at the house of the Lord, repairing the house, that is, to the carpenters, to the builders, and to the masons, as well as for buying timber and quarried stone to repair the house. But no accounting shall be asked from them for the money which is delivered into their hand, for they deal honestly."
>
> And Hilkiah the high priest said to Shaphan the secretary, "I have found the book of the law in the house of the Lord." And Hilkiah gave the book to Shaphan, and he read it. And Shaphan the secretary came to the king, and reported to the king, "Your servants have emptied out the money that was found in the house, and have delivered it into the hand of the workmen who have the oversight of the house of the Lord." Then Shaphan the secretary told the king, "Hilkiah the priest

has given me a book." And Shaphan read it before the king. And when the kind heard the words of the book of the law, he rent his clothes.

And the king commanded the priest, and Ahikam the son of Shaphan, and Achbor the son of Micaiah, and Shaphan the secretary, and Asaiah the king's servant, saying, "Go, inquire of the Lord for me, and for the people, and for all Judah, concerning the words of this book that has been found; for great is the wrath of the Lord that is kindled against us, because our fathers have not obeyed the words of this book, to do all that is written concerning us."

So Hilkiah the priest, and Ahikam, and Achbor, and Shaphan, and Asaiah went to Huldah the prophetess, the wife of Shallum the son of Tikvah, son of Harhas, keeper of the wardrobe (now she dwelt in Jerusalem in the Second Quarter); and they talked with her. And she said to them, "Thus says the Lord, the God of Israel: 'Tell the man who sent you to me, Thus says the Lord, Behold, I will bring evil upon this place and upon its inhabitants, all the words of the book which the king of Judah has read. Because they have forsaken me and have burned incense to other gods, that they might provoke me to anger with all the work of their hands, therefore my wrath will be kindled against this place, and it will not be quenched.' " [3]

It is interesting that, at this juncture of supreme religious crisis, the company was sent neither to a prophet nor to a priest, but to a prophetess to learn the judgment of their god. And still more interesting is the revelation itself, namely, that until this eighteenth year of the reign of Josiah, 621 B.C., no one had even heard of this Book of the Law of Moses, and all had been worshiping false gods. Moreover, the God of Israel now would punish them terribly— as he did, indeed, within thirty-five years, when their holy city was taken, its temple demolished, the people carried into exile, and another people put in their place. But Josiah, the prophetess declared, because of his piety and repentance, having rent his clothes and wept before the Lord, was to be spared the terrible sight: he would die in peace before it occurred.

The company of messengers brought back these words to their king, and when he heard, he undertook a purging of his land that is worth reporting here at length, as the first of an extensive series of such religious exercises throughout the length and breadth of all the great histories of all the great religions that have sprung from this epochal moment in the shaping of the religious spirit of the West.

The king sent [we read], and all the elders of Judah and Jerusalem were gathered to him. And the king went up to the house of the Lord, and with him all the men of Judah and all the inhabitants of Jerusalem, and the priests and the prophets, all the people, both small and great; and he read in their hearing all the words of the book of the covenant which had been found in the house of the Lord. And the king stood by the pillar and made a covenant before the Lord, to walk after the Lord and to keep his commandments and his testimonies and his statutes, with all his heart and all his soul, to perform the words of his covenant that were written in this book; and all the people joined in the covenant.

And the king commanded Hilkiah, the high priest, and the priests of the second order, and the keepers of the threshold, to bring out of the temple of the Lord all the vessels made for Baal, for Asherah [= Ishtar], and for all the host of heaven; he burned them outside Jerusalem in the fields of the Kidron, and carried their ashes to Bethel. And he deposed the idolatrous priests whom the kings of Judah had ordained to burn incense in the high places at the cities of Judah and round about Jerusalem; those also who burned incense to Baal, to the sun, and the moon, and the constellations, and all the host of the heavens. And he brought out the [image of] Asherah from the house of the Lord, outside Jerusalem, to the brook Kidron, and burned it at the brook Kidron, and beat it to dust and cast the dust of it upon the graves of the common people. And he broke down the houses of the cult prostitutes which were in the house of the Lord, where the women wove hangings for the Asherah. And he brought all the priests out of the cities of Judah, and defiled the high places where the priests had burned incense, from Geba to Beersheba; and he broke down the high places of the gates that were at the entrance of the gate of Joshua the governor of the city, which were on one's left at the gate of the city. However, the priests of the high places did not come up to the altar of the Lord in Jerusalem, but they ate unleavened bread among their brethren.

And he defiled Topheth, which is in the valley of the sons of Hinnom, that no one might burn his son or his daughter as an offering to Moloch. And he removed the horses that the kings of Judah had dedicated to the sun, at the entrance to the house of the Lord, by the chamber of Nathanmelech the chamberlain, which was in the precincts; and he burned the chariots of the sun with fire. And the altars on the roof of the upper chamber of Ahaz, which the kings of Judah had made, and the altars which Manasseh had made in the two courts of the house of the Lord, he pulled down and broke in pieces, and cast the dust of them into the brook Kidron. And the king defiled the high places that were east of Jerusalem, to the south of the mount of corruption, which Solomon the king of Israel had built for Ashtoreth the abomination of the Sidonians, and for Chemosh the abomination of Moab, and for Milcom the abomination of the Ammonites. And he broke in pieces the pillars, and cut down the Asherim, and filled their places with the bones of men.

Moreover the altar at Bethel, the high place erected by Jeroboam the son of Nebat, who made Israel to sin, that altar with the high place he pulled down and he broke in pieces its stones, crushing them to dust; also he burned the Asherah. And as Josiah turned, he saw the tombs there on the mount; and he sent and took the bones out of the tombs, and burned them upon the altar, and defiled it, according to the word of the Lord which the man of God proclaimed who had predicted these things. Then he said, "What is yonder monument that I see?" And the men of the city told him, "It is the tomb of the man of God who came from Judah and predicted these things which you have done against the altar at Bethel." And he said, "Let him be; let no man move his bones." So they let his bones alone, with the bones of the prophet who came out of Samaria. And all the shrines also of the high places that were in the cities of Samaria, which kings of Israel had made, provoking the Lord to anger, Josiah removed: he did to them according to all that he had done at Bethel. And he slew all the priests of the high places who were there, upon the altars, and burned the bones of men upon them. Then he returned to Jerusalem.

And the king commanded all the people, "Keep the passover to the Lord your God, as it is written in this book of the covenant." For no such passover had been kept since the days of the judges who judged Israel [five to six hundred years before this date], or during all the days of the kings of Israel or of the kings of Judah [that is to say, for the past three hundred years]; but in the eighteenth year of King Josiah this passover was kept to the Lord in Jerusalem.

Moreover Josiah put away the mediums and the wizards and the teraphim and the idols and all the abominations that were seen in the land of Judah and in Jerusalem, that he might establish the words of the law which were written in the book that Hilkiah the priest found in the house of the Lord. Before him there was no king like him, who turned to the Lord with all his heart and with all his soul and with all his might, according to the law of Moses; nor did any like him arise after him. . . .[4]

It is hard to imagine how it might have been stated more clearly that until the eighteenth year of the reign of King Josiah of Judah neither kings nor people had paid any attention whatsoever to the law of Moses, which, indeed, they had not even known. They had been devoted to the normal deities of the nuclear Near East, with all the usual cults, which are described clearly enough in this passage to be readily recognized. King Solomon himself, the son of David, had built sanctuaries to the gods and had placed their images in his temple. The convent of the cult prostitutes was in the precincts of the temple, and the stable of horses of the sun-god stood at the entrance. So that no matter what the primitive religion of the Hebrews may have been, or what Moses may have taught, the Hebrews, having settled in Israel and Judah, and having become people not of the desert but of the soil, had assumed the normal customs of that time and paid worship to the normal gods. But in this epochal year of 621 B.C. a priest of the temple (who was the father, by the way, of the future prophet Jeremiah) produced a book purporting to be the book of the laws of Moses (who had died, if he had ever lived, at least six hundred years before), and this book of laws then furnished the platform for a thoroughgoing, devastating revolution—the immediate effects of which endured, however, no longer than the lifetime of King Josiah himself. For, as we read, the following four kings "did what was evil in the sight of the Lord." [5] And in the year 586 B.C.,

Nebuzaradan, the captain of the bodyguard, a servant of King Nebuchadnezzar of Babylon, came to Jerusalem. And he burned the house of the Lord, and the king's house and all the houses of Jerusalem; every great house he burned down. And all the army of the Chaldaeans, who were with the captain of the guard, broke down the walls around Jerusalem. And the rest of the people who were left in the city and the deserters who had deserted to the king of Babylon, together with the rest of the multitude, Nebuzaradan the captain of the guard carried into exile.[6]

II. The Mythological Age

The orthodox Hebrew schedule of world ages, culminating in the cataclysm of the Babylonian Exile, may be summarized as follows:

I. The Mythological Cycle
1. The Seven Days of Creation   (Gen. 1:1–2:3)
2. The Garden and the Fall   (Gen. 2:4–3:24)
3. From the Fall to Noah's Flood   (Gen. 4–7)
4. From the Flood to the Tower of Babel   (Gen. 8:1–11:9)

II. The Legendary Cycle
1. Abraham and the Entry into Egypt   (Gen. 11:10–50:26)
2. The Exodus   (Ex. 1:1–15:21)
3. The Desert Years   (Ex. 15:22 through Deut.)
4. The Conquest of Canaan   (Book of Joshua)

III. The Documentary Cycle
1. The Conquest of Canaan   (Book of Judges)
2. The United Monarchy: c. 1025–930   (I & II Sam., I Kings 1–11)
3. Israel and Judah: c. 930–721   (I Kings 12 to II Kings 17)
4. Judah alone: 721–586   (II Kings 18–25)
5. The Babylonian Exile: 586–538

The basic texts from which the Mythological and Legendary Cycles were constructed are five:

1. The so-called Yahwist (J) Text, representing the mythology of the southern kingdom, Judah, in the ninth century B.C. Here the

Creator is Yahweh (always translated "the Lord") and the mountain of the Law is Sinai.

2. The so-called Elohim (E) Text, representing the mythology of the northern kingdom, Israel, in the eighth century B.C. (as adapted, however, to the Yahwist point of view by an editor, apparently of the seventh century B.C., who brought J and E together). Here the mountain of the Law is Horeb and the Creator, Elohim (intensive plural of the word *el,* always translated "God").

3. A ritual code known as the Code of Holiness (H), purporting to have been received by Moses on Sinai, but dating apparently from the seventh century B.C. Preserved in Leviticus 17–26.

4. The ritual code of the Deuteronomists (D), where the mountain of the Law is again Horeb, but the Creator is Yahweh. The nucleus of D was almost certainly the Scroll of the Law of 621 B.C. And finally:

5. The post-Exilic compound of priestly writings known as the Priestly (P) Text, with as nucleus the Law proclaimed in Jerusalem by the priest Ezra, 397 B.C., amplified and reworked until c. 300 B.C. The composite text of the Mythological and Legendary Cycles cannot possibly have been completed earlier than this date.*

Our first task, therefore, must be to separate, according to these findings, the earlier from later elements of the Mythological Cycle. Here two mythologies are distinguished, one from the Yahwist (J) Text of the ninth century B.C., the other from the Priestly (P) of the fourth. Set apart, they are as follows.†

YAHWIST (J) CREATION CYCLE: 9TH CENTURY B.C.

This version commences at Genesis 2:4b.

On the day that Yahweh made the earth and heavens [it begins], when no plant of the field was yet in the earth and no

* For a convenient and thoroughgoing analysis of the elements, dates, and critical theories, cf. W. O. E. Oesterley and Theodore H. Robinson, *An Introduction to the Books of the Old Testament* (New York: Meridian Books, 1958).

† All of the following biblical texts are from the Revised Standard Version, with the names Yahweh and Elohim left untranslated, however, to make clear the contrast of the two cycles, J and E.

herb of the field had yet sprung up—for Yahweh had not caused it to rain upon the earth, and there was no man to till the ground; but a mist went up from the earth and watered the whole face of the ground—then Yahweh formed man of dust from the ground, and breathed into his nostrils the breath of life; and man became a living being. And Yahweh planted a garden in Eden, in the east; and there he put the man whom he had formed. And out of the ground Yahweh made to grow every tree that is pleasant to the sight and good for food, the tree of life also in the midst of the garden, and the tree of the knowledge of good and evil.* A river flowed out of Eden to water the garden, and there it divided and became four rivers. . . . And Yahweh took the man and put him in the garden of Eden to till it and keep it. And Yahweh commanded the man, saying, "you may freely eat of every tree of the garden; but of the tree of the knowledge of good and evil you shall not eat, for in the day that you eat of it you shall die."

It is easy to see why the priestly editors of the fourth century B.C. were unwilling to let this charming fairy tale go, even though it differed in every detail from the version of creation in seven days already given in Genesis Chapter 1. We recognize the old Sumerian garden, but with two trees now instead of one, which the man is appointed to guard and tend. He is to be in the role, apparently, of the Gilgamesh-like personage of Figure 4; and we are reminded that Sargon as a gardener was beloved of the goddess Ishtar. Again as in Figure 4, four rivers flow from the garden. And finally, it is to be remarked that one of the chief characteristics of Levantine mythology here represented is that of man created to be God's slave or servant. In a late Sumerian myth retold in *Oriental Mythology* it is declared that men were created to relieve the gods of the onerous task of tilling their fields. Men were to do that work for them and provide them with food through sacrifice.[7] Marduk, too, created man to serve the gods. And here again we have man created to keep a garden.

The next episode describes the creation of the animals, to be helpers fit for man, which is in striking contrast to the famous seven

* Or possibly, "the tree of the knowledge of all things." Cf. Rabbi J. H. Hertz, *The Pentateuch and Haftorahs* (London: Soncino Press, 5721—1961), p. 8, note 9, and p. 10, note 5.

days of Chapter 1, where the animals were created first. Here we read, on the contrary, that, after God had created Adam, "out of the ground Yahweh formed every beast of the field and every bird of the air, and brought them to the man to see what he would call them; and whatever the man called every living creature, that was its name."

The idyllic scene is reminiscent of the days of Enkidu among the beasts, before he was seduced by the temple prostitute; whereupon the animals departed from him, and the woman, giving him a cloth to cover his nakedness, conducted him to the city of Uruk, where, presently, he died.* In the present variant we read that, no fit companion being found for the man among the beasts, Yahweh caused a deep sleep to fall upon him, "and while he slept took one of his ribs and closed up its place with flesh; and the rib which Yahweh had taken from the man he made into a woman and brought her to the man." After which, as everyone knows, there followed the fall and expulsion from the garden.

The next episode is that of the rivalry of the first couple's two sons. The elder, Cain, was a tiller of the ground; Abel, the younger, a keeper of sheep. "And in the course of time," as we read, "Cain brought to Yahweh an offering of the fruit of the ground, and Abel brought the firstlings of his flock and their fat portions. And Yahweh had regard for Abel and his offering, but for Cain and his offering he had no regard. So Cain was very angry and his countenance fell."

Cain slew his brother, and, in punishment, Yahweh cursed him, as he had already cursed his father Adam. " 'What have you done? The voice of your brother's blood is crying to me from the ground. And now you are cursed from the ground, which has opened its mouth to receive your brother's blood from your hand. When you till the ground, it shall no longer yield to you its strength; you shall be a fugitive and a wanderer on the earth.' " Yahweh placed a mark upon him and Cain "went away from the presence of Yahweh and dwelt in the land of Nod [= "Wandering"], east of Eden." [8]

As a whole, this early Judean myth—which has seared deeply

* Supra, pp. 88–90.

the soul of Western man—is of the general category that I have discussed in *Primitive Mythology* as common to the planting cultures of the tropics, where numerous counterparts have been collected, from Africa and India, Southeast Asia, Melanesia and Polynesia, Mexico, Peru, and Brazil. Typical features of such myths and their associated rites are: 1. the serpent, 2. the woman, 3. a killing of the serpent, of the woman, or of both, 4. the growth of food-bearing plants from the buried head or body of the victim, 5. the coming into existence at that time of death and procreation, and 6. the end, therewith, of the mythological age.

However, there is no Fall, no sense of sin or exile, in the primitive examples. They are affirmative, not critical, of life. Further, as we have already seen in our discussion of the early Mesopotamian seals, during the neolithic and High Bronze Ages the symbolism of the tree was read cosmologically and mystically as the world axis, where all pairs of opposites come together. (See again Figures 1 to 6, 9, 15, and 19.) The ultimate source of the biblical Eden, therefore, cannot have been a mythology of the desert—that is to say, a primitive Hebrew myth—but was the old planting mythology of the peoples of the soil. However, in the biblical retelling, its whole argument has been turned, so to say, one hundred and eighty degrees; to which point, the following innovations are of particular interest.

1. *Cain's murder of Abel:* Here the murder motif does not precede, but follows, the end of the mythological age, in contrast to the sequence in all the primitive myths.[9] Moreover, it has been transformed to render a duplication of the Fall motif. The ground no longer bears to Cain its strength and he is to wander on the face of the earth—which is, of course, just the opposite result to that which the ritual murder of the agricultural myth produced. The myth has been applied, also, to an exaltation of the Hebrews over the older peoples of the land. Cain was an agriculturalist, Abel a keeper of sheep: the people of Canaan were agriculturalists, the Hebrews keepers of sheep. The Hebrew deity therefore prefers the latter, though the other was the elder. In fact, all through the Book of Genesis there is consistently a preference for younger against

elder sons: not only Abel against Cain, but also Isaac against Ishmael, Jacob against Esau, and Joseph against Reuben. The lesson is not far to seek. And as though to give it point, there has recently been found an old Sumerian cuneiform text of c. 2050 B.C., bearing the tale of an argument between a farmer and shepherd for the favor of the goddess Inanna—who prefers, of course, the farmer and takes him to be her spouse. The following is the protest of the shepherd:

> "The farmer more than I, the farmer more than I,
>   The farmer, what has he more than I . . . ?
> If he pours me his first date-wine,
>   I pour him my yellow milk . . .
> If he gives me his good bread,
>   I give him my honey-cheese. . . .
> More than I, the farmer, what has he more than I?"

To which the goddess:

> "The much-possessing shepherd I shall not marry. . . .
>   I, the maid, the farmer I shall marry:
>   The farmer, who makes plants grow abundantly,
>   The farmer, who makes the grain grow abundantly. . . ." [10]

One millennium later, the patriarchal desert nomads arrived, and all judgments were reversed in heaven, as on earth.

2. *The Two Trees:* The principle of mythic dissociation, by which God and his world, immortality and mortality, are set apart in the Bible is expressed in a dissociation of the Tree of Knowledge from the Tree of Immortal Life. The latter has become inaccessible to man through a deliberate act of God, whereas in other mythologies, both of Europe and of the Orient, the Tree of Knowledge is itself the Tree of Immortal Life, and, moreover, still accessible to man.

In *Oriental Mythology* I have discussed a number of variants of the basic Oriental view, which has been generally dismissed by theologians of the West as "pantheistic"—though it is clearly not theistic, since "god" (*theos*), as a personality, is never its final term. Nor is the prefix "pan-" quite proper either, since the reference of the teaching goes beyond the "all" (*pan*) of creation. As we read in the Upanishads:

> It is other, indeed, than the known
> And, moreover, above the unknown.[11]

> His form is not to be beheld.
> No one ever sees him with the eye.[12]

But then, directly, in the same texts:

> Discerning It in every single being, the wise
> On departing from this world, are immortal.[13]

> The wise who perceive Him as standing within themselves:
> They, and no others, know eternal bliss.[14]

Or, in the language of the Chinese Tao Te Ching:

> The ways of men are conditioned by those of earth. The ways of earth, by those of heaven. The ways of heaven, by those of the Tao, and the ways of the Tao by the Self-so. . . . If one looks for the Tao, there is nothing solid to see; if one listens for it, there is nothing loud enough to hear. . . . The Tao never does; yet through it all things are done.[15]

Or again, the Buddhist Japanese verse:

> A long thing is the long body of the Buddha;
> A short thing is the short body of the Buddha.[16]

The reason for the Occidental rejection—or one might perhaps better say, fear of comprehension—of this doctrine is that our notion of religion, as based on the recognition of a Creator distinct from his Creation, is fundamentally threatened by any recognition of divinity, not simply as present in the world but as inherent in its substance. For, to quote again the Upanishad:

> Whoever thus knows, "I am the Imperishable," becomes this universal: and not even the gods can prevent him from becoming so, for he becomes thereby their very self. Hence, whoever worships another divinity thinking "He is one, and I am another"—he knows not. He is like a sacrificial animal for the gods. But if even one animal is taken away, it is unpleasant. What, then, if many? And so it is not pleasing to the gods that men should know this.[17]

Nor was it pleasing to Yahweh. Nor is it pleasant to those who worship any god. For, according to this view, not any envisioned deity, but the individual, in his own reality, is that which is the reality of being:

> You are the dark-blue bird and the green parrot with red eyes.
> You have the lightning as your child. You are the seasons and
>   the seas.
> Having no beginning, you abide with all-pervadingness,
> Wherefrom all beings are born.[18]

Moreover, not only the individual, but all things, are epiphanies of this reality, which has entered into all things "even to the tips of the fingernails, as a razor is hidden in the razor case or as fire in the material from which it blazes." [19] And as a consequence of this all-affirming, mystically poetic point of view, it has been possible for even the highest spiritual teachings of the Orient to unite directly with the simplest. For what in the simple way of popular devotion is addressed as a god outside of oneself, may honestly and sincerely continue to be so addressed—as a manifest aspect, in reflex, of the Self that is the mystery of oneself.

> He holds the handle of the hoe,
> but his hands are empty.[20]

According to our Holy Bible, on the other hand, God and his world are not to be identified with each other. God, as Creator, made the world, but is not in any sense the world itself or any object within it, as A is not in any sense B. There can therefore be no question, in either Jewish, Christian, or Islamic orthodoxy, of seeking God and finding God either in the world or in oneself. That is the way of the repudiated natural religions of the remainder of mankind: the foolish sages of the Orient and wicked priests of Sumer and Akkad, Babylon, Egypt, Canaan, and the rest—no less than the witch doctors and shamans of the jungle and the steppes, "who say to a tree, 'You are my father,' and to a stone, 'You gave me birth'" (Jeremiah 2:27); for, as the prophet Jeremiah has declared: "the customs of the peoples are false" (10:3).

In any comprehensive view of the great and small mythological systems out of which the beliefs of mankind have been drawn, the biblical idea of God must be clearly set apart, as representing a principle nowhere else exclusively affirmed; namely, of the *absolute transcendence* of divinity. In the sacred books of the Orient, the ultimate mystery of being is said to be transcendent, in the sense that it "transcends" (lies above or beyond) human knowledge, thought, sight, and speech. However, since it is explicitly identified with the mystery of our own being, and of all being whatsoever, it is declared to be immanent, as well: in fact, that is the main point of most Oriental, as well as of most pagan, primitive, and mystical initiations. And it seems to me to be the point, also, of Yahweh's fear lest man, in the words of the Upanishad, should come to know "I am the Imperishable!" and himself thus become God's very self. "Behold, the man has become like one of us," Yahweh declared; "and now, lest he put forth his hand and take also of the tree of life, and eat, and live for ever . . ." It is the same mythology, but transformed to other values; namely, toil on earth, not the realization of bliss.

3. *Sin; the Forbidden Fruit:* "Once," said the Indian saint Ramakrishna to an English-educated visitor who had asked how God could be said to dwell in a sinner, "once a man gave me a copy of the Bible. A part of it was read to me, full of that one thing— sin and sin! One must have such faith that one can say: 'I have uttered the name of God; I have repeated the name of Rama or Hari; how can I be a sinner?' One must have faith in the glory of God's name." [21]—Which may or may not be a bit too easy; but it illustrates the idea of the force of divinity within, which requires only the thought and love of God to be effectively awakened, as compared with that of an absolute distinction in being between Creature and Creator, which can be bridged, and even then but precariously, only by man's obedience to a particular, quite specific, schedule of announced rules.

In the case of Adam and Eve the announced rule was of a type very popular in fairy tales, known to folklore students as the One Forbidden Thing; for instance, the One Forbidden Place (forbidden chamber, forbidden door, forbidden road), the One Forbidden

Object (forbidden fruit, forbidden drink), the One Forbidden Time (sacred day, magical hour), etc.[22] The motif has a world distribution. The Orpheus taboo, Not to Look Back, is related.

There is an interesting use of the One Forbidden Road motif in certain primitive monster-slayer myths, where the young hero deliberately violates the taboo, which has been given to protect him, and so enters the field of one or more malignant powers, whom he overcomes, to release mankind from their oppression.[23] One could reread the episode in the Garden from such a point of view and find that it was not God but Adam and Eve to whom we owe the great world of the realities of life. However, it is certain that the ninth- and fourth-century B.C. shapers of this tale had no such adventurous thought in mind—though something similar is implicit in the Roman Catholic idea that "the essence of the Bible story is that the Fall, the disintegration, is permitted in order that a greater good may come." [24] The greater good, according to this view, is, of course, salvation by the cross, the Second Tree. And there is precedent for this view in the great words of Paul: "God has consigned all men to disobedience, that he may have mercy upon all." * The idea is expressed in the words, *O felix culpa!* "O fortunate sin," "O happy fault," of the service, Holy Saturday, at the Blessing of the Paschal Candles: *O certe necessarium Adae peccatum, quod Christi morte deletum est! O felix culpa, quae talem ac tantum meruit habere redemptorem!* [25]

The fact that this theme, developed rhapsodically in *Finnegans Wake,* can so readily be drawn from the myth of the Fall in the Garden illustrates my argument that the mythic imagery of the Bible bears a message of its own that may not always be the one verbalized in the discourse of the text. For this book is a carrier of symbols borrowed from the deep past, which is of many tongues.

We may turn now to the much later priestly myth of Genesis, Chapter 1.

---

* Romans 11:32. This reference, by the way, is the secret sense of the number 1132 that occurs and recurs in all kinds of transformations throughout James Joyce's *Finnegans Wake.*

PRIESTLY (P) CREATION CYCLE:
FOURTH CENTURY B.C.

In the beginning Elohim created the heavens and the earth. The earth was without form and void, and darkness was upon the face of the deep; and the wind of Elohim was moving over the face of the waters. And Elohim said, "Let there be light," and there was light. And Elohim saw that the light was good; and Elohim separated the light from the darkness. Elohim called the light Day, and the darkness he called Night. And there was evening and there was morning, one day.

And Elohim said, "Let there be a firmament in the midst of the waters, and let it separate the waters from the waters." And Elohim made the firmament and separated the waters which were under the firmament from the waters which were above the firmament. And it was so. And Elohim called the firmament Heaven. And there was evening and there was morning, a second day.

The next day it was dry land and the growth of vegetation. The fourth day, sun, moon, and stars were made; the fifth, birds, sea monsters, and fish. The sixth day animals were made, and man. " 'Let us make man in our image, after our likeness,' " Elohim said.

"And let them have domination over the fish of the sea, and over the birds of the air, and over the cattle, and over all the earth, and over every creeping thing that creeps upon the earth." So Elohim created man in his own image, in the image of Elohim he created him; male and female created he them. . . . And Elohim said, "Behold, I have given you every plant yielding seed which is upon the face of all the earth, and every tree with seed in its fruit; you shall have them for food. And to every beast of the earth, and to every bird of the air, and to everything that has the breath of life, I have given every green plant for food." And it was so. . . .[26]

It is not at all easy to understand how people could have supposed for centuries that the Yahwist myth of Paradise, where man was created first and the animals after, was to be read as Chapter 2 of a tale of the opposite sequence, and where the male and female appear, furthermore, together, "in the image of Elohim," not with Eve drawn from Adam's rib only after a companion for him had been sought among the beasts.

Neither is it clear why the myth of Elohim should ever have been thought to be one of creation *ex nihilo,* "out of nothing," when it describes creation from the power of the word, which in primitive thought is far from "nothing," but on the contrary, is the essence of its thing. As early as c. 2850 B.C. there was an Egyptian myth of creation by the power of the word.[27] And as recently as fifty years ago, a youngster, six and a half years old, said to the Swiss psychologist Dr. Jean Piaget, "If there weren't any words it would be very bad; you couldn't make anything. How could things have been made?" [28]

Moreover, in this creation myth there is no forbidden tree.

And finally, if, when made in the image of Elohim, Adam and Eve appeared together, then Elohim must have been not male alone but androgyne, beyond duality—in which case, why should the godhead not be worshiped as properly in a female as in a masculine form?

Love, they say, is blind. In the curiously baffled history of mythological thought in the West, this chapter of Elohim's creation has played a formidable part; for when it was thought to have been a report from the old World Artificer himself, rendered to Moses on the mountaintop, the majesty and simplicity of its lines carried a force that has now departed. We know today that they were set down by a poetizing priestly hand in the century of Aristotle; and to find the form of the universe described in the fourth century B.C. in terms of the imagery of the mythic world of Marduk, fifteen hundred years before, with a firmament separating the waters above, which fall as rain, from those beneath, which pour forth as springs, is, to say the least, disappointing. But even more so is the present custom of communicating all this archaic lore to our children, as God's eternal truth.

I have already discussed the myth of the Flood in *Oriental Mythology,*[29] so that here it need only be added that in Genesis two versions have been combined. The earlier, from the ninth-century

J Text, declares that Yahweh commanded Noah to herd into his ark, "seven pairs of all clean animals, the male and his mate, and a pair of the animals that are not clean, the male and his mate; and seven pairs of the birds of the air also, male and female, to keep their kind alive upon the face of all the earth" (Genesis 7:2–3); while according to the other, from the P Text, Elohim said to Noah: "And of every living thing of all flesh, you shall bring two of every sort into the ark, to keep them alive with you; they shall be male and female. Of the birds according to their kinds, and of the animals according to their kinds, of every creeping thing of the ground according to its kinds, two of every sort shall come in to you, to keep them alive" (Genesis 6:19–20).

The Tower of Babel story is from the J Text, and is original to the Bible. It, of course, reverses the meaning of the ziggurat, which was not meant to storm and threaten heaven, but to provide a means by which the gods of heaven might descend to receive the worship of their slaves on earth.[30] However, one of the glories of the Bible is the eloquence of its damnation of all ways of worship but its own. Furthermore, Yahweh's frustration of the work through a multiplication of the people's languages and scattering of them over the earth (as though until c. 2500 B.C. there had been but one language in the world and no dispersion of peoples) is chiefly valuable as a text to the old Hebrew notion that all languages except Hebrew are secondary. On opening a pleasant little Hebrew primer dated as recently as 1957, the student learns that "this is the language which God spoke." The idea is the same as that which underlies the Indian regard for Sanskrit, namely, that the words of this holy tongue are the "true" names of things; they are the words from which things sprang at the time of creation. The words of this language are antecedent to the universe; they are its spiritual form and support. Hence, in their study one approaches the truth and being, reality and power, of divinity itself.

III. The Age of Abraham

Had there been no Fall, there would be no need for Redemption. The image of the Fall is, therefore, essential to the Christian myth; whereas the rites, festivals, and meditations of the synagogue rest, rather, on the Legend of the Chosen People.

In the usual Christian view, all mankind has inherited from the revolt of the first couple a corruption of nature that has so darkened understanding, weakened the will, and inclined to evil, that without the miracle of God's merciful assumption to himself of the guilt and punishment due to that sin, the human race would have remained forever divorced from its proper end in the knowledge, love, service, and beatitude of its Creator. The optimistic Oriental notion that by introversion one may come, of oneself, to rest in a realization of godhood within (mythic identification) is here absolutely rejected; for there is nothing within, according to this view, but a corrupt creaturely soul, neither godly in itself, nor capable of achieving, of itself, any relationship with God (mythic dissociation) —who, in forgiveness, on the other hand, has proffered a way, a path, a light, back to himself, in the person of his Son, whose cross, Holy Rood, has countervailed the Tree (mythic restoration). And the meaning of the Legend of the Chosen People, in this Christian view, is that through Abraham and his seed there was prepared a people of God fit to participate with God in the miracle of the Redemption by rendering the flesh, the womb, the manhood of the Son, who was to be True Man as well as True God (therein the miracle). At his death, however, the veil of the temple in Jerusalem was torn asunder (Matthew 27:51, Mark 15:38, Luke 23:45), and the Mosaic ritual law, which up to that time had been the vehicle of God's purpose in this world, ceased to be so. The sacramental system of the church became the only vehicle of God's will and grace on earth, and the symbols of Fall and Redemption, Tree and Cross, shall now remain, world without end, the ultimate terms of the ontology of man.

In the view, on the other hand, of the continuing synagogue, the Christian doctrine of original sin is rejected. As we read in the words of the late Chief Rabbi of the British Empire, J. H. Hertz:

> Man was mortal from the first, and death did not enter the world through the transgression of Eve. . . . There is no loss of the God-likeness of man, nor of man's ability to do right in

the eyes of God; and no such loss has been transmitted to his latest descendants.

Although a few of the Rabbis occasionally lament Eve's share in the poisoning of the human race by the Serpent [Rabbi Hertz continues], even they declare that the antidote to such poison has been found at Sinai; rightly holding that the Law of God is the bulwark against the devastations of animalism and godlessness. The Psalmist often speaks of sin and guilt; but never is there a reference . . . to what Christian theology calls "The Fall." One searches in vain the Prayer Book, of even the Days of Penitence, for the slightest echo of the doctrine of the Fall of man. "My God, the soul which Thou hast given me is pure," is the Jew's daily morning prayer. "Even as the soul is pure when entering upon its earthly career, so can man return it pure to his Maker" (Midrash). . . .

Mankind descending from Adam became hopelessly corrupt and was swept away by the Deluge. Noah alone was spared. But before many generations pass away, mankind once again becomes arrogant and impious, and moral darkness overspreads the earth. "And God said, *Let Abraham be*—and there was light," is the profound saying of the Midrash.[31]

"Now Yahweh said to Abram," we read in the opening lines of this fundamental legend, not only of Judaism but also of Christianity and Islam, " 'Go from your country and your kindred and your father's house to the land that I will show you. And I will make of you a great nation, and I will bless you, and make your name great, so that you will be a blessing. I will bless those who bless you, and him who curses you I will curse; and by you all the families of the earth will bless themselves.' So Abram went, as Yahweh had told him. . . ."[32]

The text is from the ninth-century J document, about a millennium later in date than the incident itself, which, however, no one is quite able to place in the chronology of historical time. For many years it was customary among certain Bible readers to assign a date of c. 1996 B.C. to Abraham,[33] who was born, as the Book of Genesis declares, in "Ur of the Chaldeans," which he left, together with his wife, father, and nephew, to go into the land of Canaan, where he paused a while in Haran.[34] This date falls within the period of the brief restoration and flowering of Sumerian culture that took place during the reign of the pious King Gudea of Lagash (c. 2000 B.C.), whose vision of Ningizzida was the inspiration of our Figure 1. The great Semitic monarch Sargon of Agade (c. 2350 B.C.), whose birth story we have read, had been succeeded by a dynasty of ten descendants, which, however, was overthrown c. 2150 B.C. by an incursion of barbarians from the northeast. "The dragons from the mountains," they were called, "who ravished the wife from her spouse, children from their parents, and the kingdom from the land of Sumer." Their racial affinities are unknown; their kings called themselves "the Kings of the Guti and the Four Quarters"; and their reign was for a hundred years: c. 2150–2050 B.C.[35]

This baneful disaster was followed by an impressive and promising, yet pitifully brief, restoration of the old Sumerian culture forms under the native Sumerian Third Dynasty of Ur (c. 2050–1950 B.C.) and our pious King Gudea of Lagash. Numerous cuneiform tablets from this period have preserved to us all that we know of the old Sumerian epics; and there was a veritable burgeoning of new, enormous ziggurats.

"Viewing the vast extent and complex organization of the area of such a sanctuary," writes Professor Moortgat of the ruins of the ziggurat of Ur, which was constructed at this time, "and considering thereby that the magnitude of Ur was far less than, for instance, that of the much greater temple city of the goddess Inanna at Uruk, we begin to have some sense of the still fundamentally theocratic character of the late Sumerian social order, which was in the truest sense a community of temple builders, comparable to the medieval Christian communities. But then we realize, too, with regret," he adds, "how far from a deep and real understanding is our comprehension of that world." [36]

Such towering ziggurats, city after city, then, may be thought of as having marked the landscape through which the patriarch Abraham wandered with his family and flock.

"With Abraham," states Rabbi Hertz, "the nature of the Book of Genesis changes. Hitherto, in its first eleven chapters, it has given an account of the dawn of the world of human society. The remainder of the Book is the story of the founders of the People whose destiny, in the light of God's purpose, forms the main theme of Scripture. . . . With the Patriarchs, we leave the dim, Primeval world and enter the full daylight of historical times." [37]

To some it may seem a little strange to read of the period of Sumer and Akkad and of the great Egyptian pyramids as a "dim, Primeval world" and to be told in a work published 1961 that with Abraham, whose date cannot be fixed within a margin of four centuries, we have entered into full daylight. However, if Abraham lived, as he may have lived, c. 1996 B.C., a little daylight will perhaps be thrown upon his life by what we know of one of the builders of the ziggurats of that time, who might actually have been seen by him on some notable state occasion, namely, King Gudea of the not too distant city of Lagash.

There is a precious account of the building of Gudea's ziggurat to the god Ningirsu of his city, which may serve to communicate a sense of the piety of the people of that day—whose gods, in contrast to the god of Abraham, were not of a promised future, but already of the fading past, and so may represent to us in requiem the old heritage about to be dismembered and passed on.

The river Tigris having failed to rise, flood, and fertilize the fields, Gudea proceeded to the temple of the god Ningirsu of his city, and there learned the will of that god through a dream, which, however, he could not interpret. So he turned, next, to the neighboring temple of his goddess-mother, Gatumdug; and here we read his prayer to her for help:

"O my Queen, Daughter of Purest Heaven, whose counsel is of profit, occupier of the highest celestial place, who make the land to live: Queen, Mother and Foundress of Lagash! Those whom you favor know the wealth of strength; those whom you regard, the wealth of years. I have no mother, you are my mother; no father, you are my father. In the sanctuary you bore me. O my Goddess, Gatumdug, yours is the wisdom of all goodness. Mother, let me tell you my dream.

"There was in my dream the figure of a man whose stature filled the sky, whose stature filled the earth. The crown upon his head proclaimed him a god, and at his side was the

Imdugud bird.* Storm was at his feet. To right and left two lions lay. And he ordered me to build for him his house. But who he was, I did not know.

"Thereupon the sun rose from the earth before me. A woman appeared—Who was she? Who was she not?—In her hand she had a pure stylus; in the other a clay tablet on which celestial constellations were displayed. She was rapt, as it were, in thought. And there appeared in that dream a second man, a warrior, holding a lapis lazuli tablet on which he drew the diagram of a house. A litter was set before me: upon it, a brick-mold of gold, and in the mold, the brick of destiny. And at the right of my king stood a laden ass."

"My Shepherd," said the goddess, "I shall read for you your dream. The man whose stature filled sky and earth, whose crown proclaimed him a god, and at whose side was the Imdugud bird; storm at his feet, and to right and left two lions, was the god, my brother, Ningirsu. His command to you was to build his temple Eninnu. Now, the sun that rose from the earth before you was your guardian god, Ningizzida: like a sun, his serpent form rises from the earth. The woman holding a stylus and tablet of constellations, rapt as it were in thought, was the goddess, my sister, Nisaba, showing to you the auspicious star for your building of the temple. The second man, a warrior, with lapis lazuli tablet, was the god Nin-dub, designing for you the temple's structure. And the ass, laden, at the right of the king; that was yourself, ready for your task."

Gudea caused a wagon of precious wood to be made, ornamented with gems; spanned before it an ass; placed upon it both the emblem of his city, with his name inscribed upon it, and the lyre of his delight, the celebrated tones of which were his thought and peace; then he came with this gift to the temple of his city, and day and night offered up prayer. Also in the sanctuary of awe, the temple of the blood sacrifice, where the deity Ningirsu dominates his realm, Gudea offered sacrificial beasts, burned aromatic woods, and flung himself before his god in prayer, to be given a sign.

"O my King and Lord, Ningirsu, tamer of the raging waters, begotten of Enlil, masterly and fearless; Lord, I would build for you a house, but have not yet received the sign. Hero God, oh let me know what is to be known; for I know not the

---

* The Imdugud bird is the lion-bird of Figure 16.

meaning of these things. Like the heart of the sea, you burst forth; like the world tree, you stand firm; you seethe like boiling water, and displode upon the enemy like storm. My King, you are as unfathomable as heaven.—But I? What know I?"

Said the god: "The day that Gudea, my shepherd true, sets hand to the building of my temple, Eninnu, there will be heard in the sky a wind of rain. And there will fall upon you abundance. The realm will swell with abundance. When the groundwork of my temple has been laid, abundance shall appear. The great fields shall produce bounteously. Water shall rise in ditches and canals: from the cracks of the earth water shall gush. There shall be oil in Sumer in abundance, to be poured; wool in abundance, to be weighed. The day that your pious hand is turned to the building of my temple, I will set foot upon the mountain, the place of the dwelling of the storm; from that dwelling of storm, the mountain, the pure place, I will send a wind, so that it may bring to your land the breath of life."

The King awoke; he had been sleeping. He shook himself: it was a dream. And when the temple was constructed, the god was carried to his shrine, and the marriage of Ningirsu with his goddess, Baba, was acclaimed. "For seven days," we read, "the handmaid and the mistress were equal; slave and master walked together; high and lowly sat side by side; and on evil tongues, bad words became good: orphans suffered no injustice from the rich, and righteousness shone from the sun." [38]

With the fall, c. 1950 B.C., of the last king of Dynasty III of Ur before an invasion from the cities of Elam, the end came of the unity of the old culture world of Sumer and Akkad; and, to quote once again Professor Moortgat:

A Mastery of "the four quarters" could no longer even be imagined. Everywhere the old city states again arose—for the most part governed, however, not by native, but by alien princes. The lesser number of these were of Elamite stock, a people strongly Semiticized, whose land had been a province of the empire of Sumer and Accad. But the larger number were desert nomads, members of a new Semitic wave, linguistically distinguishable from the earlier, Accadian, Eastern Semitic peoples, both by their dialect and by their names, their nearest kin being the Canaanites then moving into Syria and Palestine. . . . In Isin, Larsa, Babylon, Mari and later in Assur, these desert folk assumed the lead, gave battle to each other, com-

bined in coalitions, and waged war everywhere for top place—
until, after a century and a half, Elamites and Semites, each,
found their greatest warrior-statesmen: respectively, the Elamites Rimsin and the Semites Hammurabi. Then the greater of
the two, Hammurabi of Babylon, finally contrived to restore
for a time the unity and glory of the ancient world of Sumer
and Accad.[39]

Now it used to be the custom to place the reign of Hammurabi
somewhere between the years 2067 and 1905 B.C.,[40] and it was, in
fact, this dating that was then assigned also to Abraham on a supposed identification of King Amraphel of Shinar (Genesis 14:1)
with Hammurabi. Hammurabi's date now having been lowered by
new evidence to 1728–1686 B.C., however, Abraham's date has
been lowered too. And as Professor T. J. Meek remarks: "Although these identifications are now known to be false, the date
for Abraham may still be close to that of Hammurabi." [41]

Hammurabi's dynasty in Babylon survived until c. 1530 B.C.,
and then, like everything else in that fluent world, collapsed. But
the new waves continuing to pour in from all sides were now coming largely from the north, and of these there were three main
groups:

1. *The Hurrians:* A people of prodigious power and expansive
force, who had begun as early as c. 2200 B.C. to press down from
the Caucasus into northern Mesopotamia. By 1800 B.C., they had
reached the Persian Gulf, and thereafter they were moving westward into Syria and Palestine, where they displaced or infiltrated
with their blood many of the settled western Semites.

"It has long been noted by scholars," states Professor Meek,
"that there are certain details in the stories of the early Hebrew
patriarchs that do not fit into a purely Semitic background because
we have no Semitic parallels, but with our enlarged knowledge of
the Hurrians we now have exact Hurrian parallels." Esau's selling
of his birthright for a price, for example (Genesis 25:31–34), was
an unparalleled episode until the same sort of exchange was found
to have been practiced among Hurrians; and Rachel's theft of her
father's household goods and gods (Genesis 31:19), which had
long been a puzzle to scholars, became clear when it was found

that, according to Hurrian law, her possession of these ensured for her husband, Jacob, title to her father's property. "These and similar analogues between the early Hebrews and the Hurrians," states Professor Meek, "along with the occurrence of Hurrian names and references to the Hurrians in the Old Testament, indicate quite clearly that the two migrations went together. Hurrians and Habiru, or Hebrews, were found together in Mesopotamia, and it is likely that they would be found together in the west. . . ." [42]

Which opens a vast new prospect that no one has yet explored. For the Hurrians set up a short-lived but powerful kingdom— known as the kingdom of the Mitanni, c. 1500–c. 1250 B.C.— southwestward of Lake Van (in the area now called Kurdistan, at the juncture of Syria, Turkey, and Iraq), which included Abraham's station at Haran. Furthermore, in a treaty signed c. 1400 B.C. between these Mitanni and the neighboring Hittites—by whom they were presently to be conquered—the names appear of five Vedic gods: Indra, Mitra, Varuna, and the two Ashvins. The Hurrians, it now appears, were led, for some time at least, by an aristocratic upper class of chariot fighters of Indo-Aryan stock; and it may well have been these who introduced to the Near East the new war machine of the light two-wheeled battle car drawn by two steeds. For the war chariot was developed in the Aryan zone, c. 2000–1750 B.C., and appeared within the next three hundred years in almost every part of the ancient historic world, entering Egypt with the Asian Hyksos kings, c. 1670–1570 B.C., India with the Aryan tribes, c. 1500–1250 B.C., Greece at about the same time, and China, c. 1523, with the Shang. The prospect yet to be explored, therefore, is that of the possible—indeed inevitable—interplay, in the period ascribed to the Patriarchs, of Semitic and Aryan factors in the building of biblical myth. And some of the parallels with Chinese myth noted in *Oriental Mythology* [43] may also find their explanation here.

The other great intrusive groups of the period were the following:

2. *The Hittites:* Possibly related to the Hurrians, but surpassing them both in diplomacy and in war, these became the rulers, presently, of the better part of what is known today as Turkey. The

dates of their rise, at about the time of Hammurabi, their apogee, and then their abrupt collapse at about the time of Homer's Trojan War, were c. 1750–1150 B.C.

3. *The Kassites:* Descending from Elam (now Persia), whence China, from c. 2000 B.C., had been receiving a significant portion of its fundamental neolithic heritage, the Kassites occupied the riverine lands of Babylonia proper. And they appear to have made some kind of connection, before entering Mesopotamia, with the Indo-Aryan stems who were at that time entering India. The Kassites have left no written mythic texts, but we know from their personal names some of their gods; as, for example: Surias (Sanskrit, *Sūrya,* the Sun), Maruttas (Sanskrit, *Marut,* the Wind), and Burias (Greek, *Boreas,* the North Wind). Apparently, in some measure at least, they were of Aryan, perhaps Indo-Aryan, stock.

It was a world, in other words, of extreme complexity from which the book that has been the inspiration of the greater part of Occidental religious thought and practice took its rise. And it would be reasonable to believe that that complexity itself was one of the sources of its power and atmosphere of validity. However, although this power may convince and move our sentiments, the mind of the conscientious scholar striving to place his Patriarchs in the context of their time—even the time, let us say, of Hammurabi—is left still greatly in the lurch. For, as the eminent excavator of the city-mound of Jericho, Dr. Kathleen Kenyon, writes:

> It is certain that one cannot build up a chronology on the spans of years attributed to the Patriarchs, nor regard it as factual that Abraham was seventy-five years old when he left Harran and a hundred when Isaac was born, or that Isaac was sixty when Joseph was born and that Jacob was a hundred and thirty when he went into Egypt, for the evidence from the skeletons in the Jericho tombs shows that the expectation of life at this period was short. Many individuals seem to have died before they were thirty-five, and few seem to have reached the age of fifty.

But though an exact chronology is impossible, the setting of the period reflects that recorded in the Biblical story. The Patriarchs were semi-nomadic pastoralists, moving into the more fertile coastlands, and living in their tents among, but separate from, the Canaanites living in the towns of the type which archeology reveals. Pastoralists in their tents leave no evidence which archeology can recover, but we now know something of their surroundings.[44]

In the main, however, the episodes suggest mythology much more convincingly than chronicles of fact; as, for example, in the following curious tale, which already includes some of the motifs of the later Exodus under Moses:

Now there was a famine in the land. So Abram went down to Egypt to sojourn there, for the famine was severe in the land. When he was about to enter Egypt he said to Sarai his wife, "I know that you are a woman beautiful to behold; and when the Egyptians see you, they will say, 'This is his wife'; then they will kill me, but they will let you live. Say you are my sister, that it may go well with me because of you, and that I may be spared on your account." When Abram entered Egypt the Egyptians saw that the woman was very beautiful. And when the princes of Pharaoh saw her, they praised her to Pharaoh. And the woman was taken into Pharaoh's house. And for her sake he dealt well with Abram; and he had sheep, oxen, he-asses, menservants, she-asses, and camels.

But the Lord afflicted Pharaoh and his house with great plagues because of Sarai, Abram's wife. So Pharaoh called Abram, and said, "What is this you have done to me? Why did you not tell me that she was your wife? Why did you say, 'She is my sister,' so I took her for my wife? Now then, here is your wife, take her, and be gone." And Pharaoh gave men orders concerning him; and they sent him on the way, with his wife and all that he had. So Abram went up from Egypt, he and his wife, and all that he had, and Lot with him, unto the Negeb.[45]

This episode is from the Yahwist (J) Text; and to supplement it, we have the following from E, referring to a time, many years later, when Abram's name was called Abraham and his wife's Sarah; she now being over ninety years of age and he beyond a hundred.

Abraham journeyed toward the territory of the Negeb, and dwelt between Kadesh and Shur; and he journeyed in Gerar. And Abraham said of Sarah his wife, "She is my sister." And Abimelech king of Gerar sent and took Sarah. But Elohim came to Abimelech in a dream by night, and said to him, "Behold, you are a dead man, because of the woman you have taken; for she is a man's wife." Now Abimelech had not approached her; so he said, "Lord, wilt thou slay an innocent people? Did he not himself say to me, 'She is my sister'? And she herself said, 'He is my brother.' In the integrity of my heart and the innocence of my hands I have done this." Then Elohim said to him in the dream, "Yes, I know that you have done this in the integrity of your heart, and it was I who kept you from sinning against me; therefore I did not let you touch her. Now then restore the man's wife; for he is a prophet, and he will pray for you, and you shall live. But if you do not restore her, know that you shall surely die, you and all that are yours."

So, as the tale goes on to tell, Abimelech returned Sarah to Abraham, along with sheep and oxen, male and female slaves, and a thousand pieces of silver; after which Abraham prayed, and, as we read: "Elohim healed Abimelech, and also healed his wife and female slaves so that they bore children. For Yahweh had closed all the wombs of the house of Abimelech because of Sarah, Abraham's wife." [46]

Still another variant of the adventure is attributed to Abraham's son Isaac—once again in a Yahwist (J) passage—where it is declared that "Isaac went to Gerar, to Abimelech king of the Philistines." And when the men of the place asked about his wife, he said, "She is my sister," thinking, "lest the men of the place should kill me," etc. [47]

It is difficult to imagine how tales such as these could have been read even centuries ago as chronicles of fact, in "the full daylight of historical times"; but today the difficulty is even compounded, for we have found that the people called Philistines first arrived on the shores of Palestine from Crete only in the year 1196 B.C., [48] which, as we immediately perceive, carries the history of this remarkable family from Ur through a span of centuries that not even the lengths of life attributed to Abraham and his son suffice to explain. Furthermore, there is the additional inconvenience that Isaac, father of Jacob and grandfather of Joseph, is here described as flourishing in a period subsequent to Moses and the Exodus:

which difficulty is again compounded when it is recalled that Abraham, his father, when passing through Gerar, also played this turn on Abimelech.

Does it not, then, appear that we are dealing with the laws rather of myth, fairy tale, and legend than of any order of fact yet substantiated for either natural or human history? The past, as in every other folk tradition of the world, is here portrayed not with concern for what is known today as truth, but to give a semblance of supernatural support to a certain social order and its system of belief. That was then—as it is now and ever has been for those in whose mind the good of a society holds a higher place than truth—adequate justification for any fabrication that the mentality of the time might be persuaded to accept. All that is really exceptional about the present remarkable examples is that, whereas no modern thinker in his right mind would argue for the historicity of the fragments of myth brought together in the *Odyssey,* we have a modern literature of learning reaching from here to the moon and back, doing precisely that for those sewn together in these ancient tales of about the same date.

IV. The Age of Moses

Sigmund Freud delivered a shock to many of his admirers when he proposed in his last major work, *Moses and Monotheism,* that Moses was not a Jew but an Egyptian noble—specifically, of the household of the heretic pharaoh Ikhnaton, who reigned 1377–1358 B.C.—and that in the years directly following this pharaoh's death, which had entailed the collapse both of his court and of his cult of monotheism, Moses departed from Egypt with a company of Semitic settlers in the Delta, upon whom he strove to impress Ikhnaton's monotheistic belief. However, in the desert these people, oppressed by his disciplines, slew him, and his place of leadership was taken by the Midianite priest of an Arabian volcano god, Yahweh. Yet his memory and teaching (in Freud's words) "continued to work in the background, until it slowly gained more and more power over the mind of the people and at last succeeded in transforming the god Yahweh into the Mosaic God, and in waking to a new life the religion that Moses had instituted centuries before but which had subsequently been forsaken." [49]

Freud's theory has, of course, been attacked from every side, both with learning and without. However, according to his own by no means unlearned view, it furnishes the only plausible psychological explanation of the peculiarly compulsive character of biblical belief, which is in striking contrast to the relaxed, poetic, and even playful approaches to mythology of the Greeks of the same period. Biblical religion, according to Freud, has the character of a neurosis, where a screen of mythic figurations hides a repressed conviction of guilt, which, it is felt, must be atoned, and yet cannot be consciously faced. The screening myths are there to hide, not to reveal, a truth. Hence, they are insisted upon as factual—or, as people say today, "existential." The Jewish God is supposed to be, as the saying goes, a "living God," not a mere mythic god, like the others of the world; not a merely phantasmagoric symbol of something stemming, like a dream, from his worshipers' imagination. He was introduced from without by Moses and remains without, as a presumed fact.

Freud believed that his theory also accounted for the dual nature of Yahweh, who, on the one hand, exhibits the barbarous traits of the Midianite volcano god and of primitive serpent worship, but then comes forward with ever-increasing force in the teachings of the prophets as the universal God of righteousness of Moses and Ikhnaton. Also accounted for, Freud believed, were the inconsistencies of the Moses legend, where he appears at one time as an Egyptian noble and the next moment as an Arab shepherd boy who turns, in the end, into a desert shaman. "We cannot escape the impression," he wrote, "that this Moses of Kadesh and Midian, to whom tradition could even ascribe the erection of a brazen serpent as a healing god [Numbers 21:1–9], is quite a different person from the august Egyptian we have deduced, who disclosed to his people a religion in which all magic and sorcery were most strictly abhorred. Our Egyptian Moses differs perhaps no less from the Midian Moses than the universal god Aton differed from the demon Yahweh on his divine mountain." [50]

The great historian Eduard Meyer had also remarked this contrast. "Moses in Midian," he wrote in a passage aptly cited by Freud, "is no longer an Egyptian and Pharaoh's grandson, but a shepherd to whom Yahweh reveals himself. In the story of the ten plagues his former relationships are no longer mentioned, although they could have been used very effectively, and the order to kill the Israelite first-born is entirely forgotten." [51]

Now I am not going either to defend or to attack the views of Freud. They were not easy views for him to publish; for, as he wrote in the opening lines of his book, "to deny a people the man whom it praises as the greatest of its sons is not a deed to be undertaken lightheartedly—especially by one belonging to that people. No consideration, however, will move me to set aside truth in favor of supposed national interests." [52] Those are noble words, and I shall let them stand as the parting sign of one of the bravest creative spirits of our day—my own small intention being simply to offer a sketch of the setting of the problem of the Exodus, first in its screening, mythological aspect, and then in its screened, historical.

To begin with: the legend of Moses' birth is obviously modeled on the earlier birth story of Sargon of Agade (c. 2350 B.C.),* and is clearly not of Egypt, since in Egypt bitumen or pitch was not used before Ptolemaic times, when it was introduced from Palestine.[53]

> Now a man from the house of Levi [we read] went and took to wife a daughter of Levi. The woman conceived and bore a son; and when she saw that he was a goodly child, she hid him three months. And when she could hide him no longer she took for him a basket made of bulrushes and daubed it with bitumen and pitch; and she put the child in it and placed it among the reeds at the river's brink. And his sister stood at a distance, to know what would be done to him. . . .[54]

The episode is from the Elohim (E) document, which, as we know, was composed in the eighth century in Israel, not in Egypt; and the general mythic formula followed is that of the Myth of the

* Supra, p. 73.

Birth of the Hero discussed by Otto Rank in the work already named.* However, as Freud has pointed out, among the seventy-odd examples of the formula analyzed by Rank, this is the only one in which the exposed and adopted infant passes from a lowly to a noble house. The usual order is the other way.

Freud writes: "The first family, the one from which the babe is exposed to danger, is in all comparable cases the fictitious one; the second family, however, by which the hero is adopted and in which he grows up, is his real one. If we have the courage to accept this statement as a general truth to which the Moses legend also is subject, then we suddenly see our way clear: Moses is an Egyptian —probably of noble origin—whom the myth undertakes to transform into a Jew." [55]

The name Moses itself is Egyptian. It is the normal word for "child" and occurs among the names, for example, of the pharaohs of Dynasty XVIII. Years ago, Eduard Meyer suggested that in Moses' case the first part of the name—Ra-moses, Thut-moses, Ah-moses, or the like—may have been dropped, to obscure his Egyptian origin.[56] And in any case, the idea that an Egyptian princess could have thought the word to be Hebrew shows that story-tellers do not always think their problems through. As the pretty tale continues:

> Now the daughter of Pharaoh came down to bathe at the river, and her maidens walked beside the river; she saw the basket among the reeds and sent her maid to fetch it. When she opened it she saw the child; and lo, the babe was crying. She took pity on him and said, "This is one of the Hebrews' children." Then his sister said to Pharaoh's daughter, "Shall I go and call you a nurse from the Hebrew women to nurse the child for you?" And Pharaoh's daughter said to her, "Go." So the girl went and called the child's mother. And Pharaoh's daughter said to her, "Take this child away, and nurse him for me, and I will give you your wages." So the woman took the child and nursed him. And the child grew, and she brought him to Pharaoh's daughter, and he became her son; and she named him Moses [Hebrew Mosheh], for she said, "Because I drew him out [Hebrew mashah] of the water." [57]

* Supra, p. 73.

The legend bears comparison with the Greek story, of about the same period, told of Perseus, who was born of the princess Danaë. She was the daughter of Acrisius, king of Argos; but Acrisius, fearing the son prophesied, had imprisoned her in a dungeon, together with her nurse. Zeus, however, sent down a shower of gold, from which the virgin conceived. Mother and child together were then cast into the sea in a chest, which a fisherman drew ashore—and in the end, Perseus, by a curious slip, killed his grandfather, Acrisius, with a discus, symbol of the sun.[58]

We shall have more of Perseus later. For the present, the point is simply that there is precedent in legend for representing the Future Savior as a foster-grandson within the Tyrant Monarch's house. Whether Moses was actually such, we do not know. In fact, we do not really know whether the hero of such a legend should be thought of as an actual historical or as a merely symbolic figure associated with a certain body of teaching and belief. Either way, in the case of Moses, the Elohim (E) Text has provided this noble Egyptian background and legend of hero birth, while the Yahwist (J) tells the tale of our hero's marriage to one of the seven daughters of a Midianite priest of the desert.

"One day," this other story goes,

when Moses had grown up, he went out to his people and looked on their burdens; and he saw an Egyptian beating a Hebrew, one of his people. He looked this way and that, and seeing no one killed the Egyptian and hid him in the sand. When he went out the next day, behold, two Hebrews were struggling together; and he said to the man that did the wrong, "Why do you strike your fellow?" He answered, "Who made you a prince and a judge over us? Do you mean to kill me as you killed the Egyptian?" Then Moses was afraid, and thought, "Surely the thing is known." When Pharaoh heard of it, he sought to kill Moses. But Moses fled from Pharaoh and stayed in the land of Midian. And he sat down by a well.

Now the priest of Midian had seven daughters; and they came and drew water, and filled the troughs to water their father's flock. The shepherds came and drove them away; but Moses stood up and helped them, and watered their flock. When they came to their father Reuel, he said, "How is it that

you have come so soon today?" They said, "An Egyptian
delivered us out of the hand of the shepherds, and even drew
water for us and watered the flock." He said to his daughters,
"And where is he? Why have you left the man? Call him, that
he may eat bread." And Moses was content to dwell with the
man, and he gave Moses his daughter Zipporah. She bore a
son, and he called his name Gershom; for he said, "I have been
a sojourner [Hebrew *ger*] in a foreign land." [59]

The legendary analogues of this episode lead back to the matter
of the Patriarchs: the motifs suggest the marriage of Jacob. Like
Moses, fearing for his life, Jacob fled into the desert. He had not
murdered an Egyptian but had cheated Esau of his birthright, and
Esau, his brother, had said to himself, "I will kill my brother Jacob"
(Genesis 27:41). In the desert Jacob met his beloved Rachel at
a well and became her father's shepherd. He served seven years to
win her. (In the present case, we have seven daughters.) Cheated
by Laban, Jacob was given Leah instead of Rachel and to win the
latter had to work seven years more—after which he fled with his
two wives, two concubines and daughter, much wealth, and his
precious tribe of twelve sons.

Common to both tales are the lethal danger at home (associated with a relative: the brother Esau, the grandfather Pharaoh),
flight into the desert, the bride at the well (associated with the
number seven), and then servitude as shepherd to her father. In
both stories, furthermore, the desert flight leads to a direct meeting
with God and the reception of a great destiny: Jacob at Bethel,
where he lay with his head upon a stone and dreamed that there
was a ladder set up on the earth, the top of which reached to
heaven, the angels of God ascending and descending upon it, and
behold, Yahweh stood above it (Genesis 28:11–13); and comparably, Moses by a burning bush, where he heard the voice of the
same desert god.

As it comes to us, this episode presents an extremely complex
interlace of J and E Text elements, illustrating elegantly the manner
of cutting, splicing, and blending of the priestly fourth-century
editors. I reproduce J in roman type, E in italic, and retain the
numbers of the verses. The chapter is Exodus 3.

THE GOD IN THE BURNING BUSH

(1) *Now Moses was keeping the flock of his father-in-law, Jethro, the priest of Midian;* * *and he led his flock to the west side of the wilderness, and came to Horeb, the mountain of Elohim.* (2) And the angel of Yahweh appeared to him in a flame of fire out of the midst of a bush; and he looked, and lo, the bush was burning, yet it was not consumed. (3) And Moses said, "I will turn aside and see this great sight, why the bush is not burnt." (4) When Yahweh saw that he turned aside to see, *Elohim called to him out of the bush, "Moses, Moses!"* And he said, "Here am I." (5) Then he said, "Do not come near; put off your shoes from your feet, for the place on which you are standing is holy ground." (6) *And he said, "I am the God of your father, the God of Abraham, the God of Isaac, and the God of Jacob." And Moses hid his face, for he was afraid to look at Elohim.*

(7) Then Yahweh said, "I have seen the affliction of my people who are in Egypt, and have heard their cry because of their taskmasters; I know their sufferings, (8) and I have come down to deliver them out of the hand of the Egyptians, and to bring them up out of the land to a good and broad land, a land flowing with milk and honey, to the place of the Canaanites, the Hittites, and Amorites, the Perizzites, the Hivites, and the Jebusites. (9) *And now, behold, the cry of the people of Israel has come to me, and I have seen the oppression with which the Egyptians oppress them.* (10) *Come, I will send you to Pharaoh that you may bring forth my people, the sons of Israel, out of Egypt.*"

(11) *But Moses said to Elohim, "Who am I that I should go to Pharaoh, and bring the sons of Israel out of Egypt?"*

(12) *He said, "But I will be with you; and this shall be the sign for you, that I have sent you: when you have brought forth the people out of Egypt, you shall serve Elohim upon this mountain."*

(13) *Then Moses said to Elohim, "If I come to the people of Israel and say to them, 'The god of your fathers has sent me to you,' and they ask me, 'What is his name?' what shall I say to them?"*

(14) *Elohim said to Moses, "I Am Who I Am."* † *And he said, "Say this to the people of Israel, 'I Am has sent me to*

---

* Compare J text, supra, p. 129, where the name is Reuel.

† Or, "I Am What I Am," or "I Will Be What I Will Be."

you.' " (15) *Elohim also said to Moses, "Say this to the people of Israel,* 'Yahweh, the God of your fathers, the God of Abraham, the God of Isaac, and the God of Jacob, has sent me to you': this is my name forever, and thus I am to be remembered throughout all generations. (16) Go and gather the elders of Israel together and say to them, 'Yahweh, the God of your fathers, the God of Abraham, of Isaac, and of Jacob, has appeared to me, saying, "I have observed you and what has been done to you in Egypt; (17) and I promise that I will bring you up out of the affliction of Egypt, to the land of the Canaanites, the Hittites, the Amorites, the Perizzites, the Hivites, and the Jebusites, a land flowing with milk and honey." ' (18) And they will hearken to your voice; and you and the elders of Israel shall go to the king of Egypt and say to him, 'Yahweh, the God of the Hebrews, has met with us; and now, we pray you, let us go a three days' journey into the wilderness, that we may sacrifice to Yahweh, our God.' (19) *I know that the king of Egypt will not let you go unless compelled by a mighty hand.* (20) *So I will stretch out my hand and smite Egypt with all the wonders which I will do in it; after that he will let you go.* (21) *And I will give this people favor in the sight of the Egyptians; and when you go, you shall not go empty,* (22) *but each woman shall ask of her neighbor, and of her who sojourns in her house, jewelry of silver and of gold, and clothing, and you shall put them on your sons and on your daughters; thus you shall despoil the Egyptians."*

The question of the age and origin of the name and cult of Yahweh has been discussed by many, and the most lucid recent summary of the discussion is that of Professor T. J. Meek. He notes that in the text just quoted of Exodus 3:15, the god in the Midian desert gave his name as "Yahweh, the God of your fathers, the God of Abraham, of Isaac, and of Jacob," and then defined the meaning as "I am"; whereas in the priestly fourth-century text of a later passage, Exodus 6:3, the same god states that "I appeared to Abraham, to Isaac, and to Jacob as *El Shaddai,* but by my name Yahweh I did not make myself known to them."

The name [states Professor Meek] . . . was foreign to the Hebrews, and in their attempted explanation of it they connected it with the word *hāyāh,* "to be," just as the Greeks, who did not know the origin and exact meaning of "Zeus" connected the name with ζάω, "to live," whereas it is derived ultimately from Indo-European *dyu*, "to shine." The contention that Yahweh was of Arabian origin is clearly in accord with the Old Testament records, which connect him with the Negeb and with southern sanctuaries like Sinai-Horeb and Kadesh. . . . The most probable [origin of the name] in our opinion is . . . from the Arabic root *hwy*, "to blow." [60]

And so there we are: with an unsubstantial phantasmagoria of folklore motifs and a congeries of considerably differing gods: 1. a cruel, unnamed, fairy-tale pharaoh, persecuting a people whose presence in the Delta no one has explained (Tyrant-Ogre motif), 2. has a daughter, also unnamed, who finds a baby in a basket in the waters of the Nile and takes him to be reared, naming him Moses (Egyptian, "child"), which she believes to be a Hebrew word suggesting *mashah*, "to draw out" (modified Virgin Birth motif, with inverted Infant Exposure: from humble to noble household); 3. a Midianite priest of Kadesh, who is to become the hero's father-in-law (named Reuel in J Text, Jethro in E); 4. has seven daughters (magical 7: seven celestial spheres, colors of rainbow, etc.), 5. who are met at the well by a desert fugitive from Egypt who has just killed an Egyptian; 6. he marries one and becomes the shepherd of his father-in-law (parallel of the Jacob legend: flight to desert, bride at the well, service as shepherd of father-in-law, twice seven years); 7. the voice of Yahweh in the burning bush commits to this shepherd the cosmic task of rescuing his people from the clutches of the Tyrant Ogre; after which there follows 8. his magical contest, assisted by his suddenly present brother Aaron (Twin Hero theme), against the priests and magicians of Egypt (shaman contest), culminating in 9. the Plagues of Egypt (which, for some inhuman reason, Yahweh prolongs unconscionably by repeatedly "hardening Pharaoh's heart") and 10. the Exodus (Magic Flight motif, Passage through Water, Dissolution of Underworld Power at Threshold, Boon of Spoil from the Underworld, etc.: compare Abraham and Isaac despoiling Pharaoh and Abimelech by clever device).

Now the task of the priestly (P Text) editors of the fourth century

B.C., who put all this together, was to intertwine these two threads of legend into a single thread of argument, an argument, moreover, to which neither had been originally turned. As we read in the crucial P Text passages through which their new theme was introduced:

> These are the names of the sons of Israel who came to Egypt with Jacob, each with his household: Reuben, Simeon, Levi, and Judah, Issachar, Zebulun, and Benjamin, Dan and Naphtali, Gad and Asher. All the offspring of Jacob were seventy persons; Joseph was already in Egypt. . . . But the descendants of Israel were fruitful and increased greatly; they multiplied and grew exceedingly strong; so that the land was filled with them [Exodus 1:1–5 and 7]. . . . So the Egyptians made the people of Israel serve with rigor, and made their lives bitter with hard service, in mortar and brick, and in all kinds of work in the field; in all their work they made them serve with rigor [Exodus 1:13–14].

The great overall priestly argument by which the Pentateuch is unified was that all of the tribes of Israel were descended from a single parent, to whom a divine blessing had been given that was to be realized in their common history; namely, Abraham, the father of Isaac, who in turn begot Jacob, the father of those twelve sons who were supposed to have been the authors of the twelve tribes. The large narrative problem, therefore, was to bring the old myths and legends of the pastoral Patriarchs of the late Bronze Age into relation, first, to a supposed Egyptian interlude, and then to the epic lore of the Iron Age conquest and settlement of Canaan. Three obvious inconsistencies can be readily detected, however, which the masters of the priestly school either failed to recognize or ignored.

The first of these inconsistencies, which has not yet been quite rationalized either by theology or by science, derives from the fact that the Hebrew conquest of Canaan had already commenced long before the earliest plausible date yet assigned to the Exodus from Egypt; namely the date suggested by Freud, which, as we have seen, falls in the period just following the death of the heretic pharaoh Ikhnaton: specifically, the span of eight years, 1358–1350 B.C.,

that elapsed before the forceful restitution of the Amun orthodoxy under Haremhab.

"Moses' active nature," wrote Freud,

> conceived the plan of founding a new empire, of finding a new
> people, to whom he could give the religion that Egypt dis-
> dained. It was, as we perceive, a heroic attempt to struggle
> against his fate, to find compensation in two directions for
> the losses he had suffered through Ikhnaton's catastrophe.
> Perhaps he was at the time governor of that border province
> (Gosen) in which—perhaps already in "the Hyksos period"
> —certain Semitic tribes had settled. These he chose to be his
> new people. A historic decision!
>
> He established relations with them, placed himself at their
> head, and directed the Exodus "by strength of hand." In
> full contradistinction to the Biblical tradition we may sup-
> pose this Exodus to have passed off peacefully and without
> pursuit. The authority of Moses made it possible, and there
> was then no central power that could have prevented it.
>
> According to our construction the Exodus from Egypt
> would have taken place between 1358 and 1350 B.C.—that
> is to say, after the death of Ikhnaton and *before* the restitution
> of the authority of the state by Haremhab. The goal of the
> wandering could only be Canaan. After the supremacy of
> Egypt had collapsed, hordes of warlike Aramaeans had
> flooded the country, conquering and pillaging, and thus had
> shown where a capable people could seize new land. We know
> these warriors from the letters which were found in 1887 in
> the archives of the ruined city of Amarna. They are called the
> Habiru, and the name was passed on—no one knows how—
> to the Jewish invaders, Hebrews, who came later and could
> not have been referred to in the letters of Amarna.[61]

Freud, we see, solved the difficulty by assuming out of hand that
the Habiru were not Hebrews, whereas most scholars today think
they were.[62] Furthermore, to complicate things, there is the often
cited biblical statement that the persecuted Jews were forced to
build the cities of Pithom and Raamses (Exodus 1:11, from J
Text). These were constructed only in the period of Ramses II,
who reigned 1301–1234, which is one entire century later than
Ikhnaton. Hence, most of those modern scholars who think that

the Exodus can be dated situate it in this later time. Yet even here
there is disagreement. And the late dating even magnifies the problem of associating the Exodus with the beginnings of the Habiru
plundering and settlement of Canaan. As a way of letting the reader
choose a dating for himself, therefore, let me simply indicate in a
schedule of Dynasties XVIII and XIX some of the recently made
suggestions, together with Thomas Mann's interesting guess, in his
novel *Joseph in Egypt,* that the Patriarchs arrived precisely at the
time when Freud was causing their descendants to depart.

EXPULSION OF HYKSOS (EXODUS?): [63] C. 1570 B.C.

DYNASTY XVIII: 1570–1345

Ahmoses I	1570–1545
Amenhotep I	1545–1524
Thutmoses I and II	1524–c. 1502
Queen Hatshepsut	1501–1480
(The "Pharaoh's daughter" who saved Moses?) [64]	
Thutmoses III (contesting reign of Queen H.)	1502–1448
Exodus? (J. W. Jack's thesis) [64]	
Amenhotep II	1448–1422
Thutmoses IV	1422–1413
Amenhotep III	1413–1377
(Beginnings of Aton heresy)	
Amenhotep IV (Ikhnaton)	1377–1358
(Amarna period: Habiru incursions)	
Joseph enters Egypt? (Th. Mann's thesis) [65]	
Tutankhamon	1358–1349
(Period of slack: virtual interregnum)	
Exodus? (*Freud's thesis*) [66]	
(Amun cult restoration: 1350)	
Eye (Haremhab the virtual ruler)	1349–1345

DYNASTY XIX: 1345–1200

Haremhab	1345–1318
Ramses I	1318–1317
Seti I	1317–1301
Ramses II	1301–1234

(Building projects: cities of Pithom and Raamses)
Exodus? (Albright's thesis): c. 1280 [67]
   (Scharff's thesis): c. 1240–1230 [68]

Merneptah   1234–c. 1220
   Exodus? (Scharff's thesis): c. 1240–1230 [68]
("Israelite Stele" mentioning suppression of an "Israelite"
revolt in Palestine: first appearance of the term "Israelite")

Seti II   1220–1200
   *Exodus? (Meek's thesis): period of confusion following
   death of Seti II* [69] *

So much, then, for the first of the inconsistencies involved in the fourth-century priestly narrative deriving all the invading Hebrews of Canaan from the seed of Abraham by way of Egypt. A second difficulty derives from the fact that the Bedouin tribes in question were not of one family but many, having entered Canaan, furthermore, not in one fell swoop but in stages and from various directions. And a third very serious difficulty remains, that already mentioned, of finding a time when Joseph and his brothers could have entered Egypt, to remain.

Let us concede, in short, that no one has yet been able to explain when, how, or why any part of this imposing legend took place, let alone the continuity of its stages. Viewed, however, as a normal origin myth, instead of as a clue to history, the narrative reveals immediately both the form and the function of its message. The form is of a great cycle of descent into the underworld and return. What entered Egypt (Underworld: Land Below Waves) were the Patriarchs (Joseph into the well and on down to Egypt); what emerged were the People (Passage of the Red Sea).

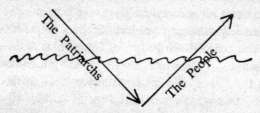

---

* Meek's dating of Seti's reign, however, is c. 1214–1194.

As in all such myths of descent and return, what is brought forth is a boon or elixir; in the present case: a) the knowledge of Yahweh, b) the nuclear force of the Chosen People, and c) the promise to that people of a destiny, with the gift of a Promised Land. However, in contrast to all other myths of this order, the hero here is not an individual—not even Moses—but the Jewish folk. It is highly significant that the later festival of the Passover which, as we have seen,* was first celebrated 621 B.C. in commemoration of the Exodus, occurs on the date of the annual resurrection of Adonis, which in the Christian cult became Easter. In both the pagan cult and the Christian, the resurrection is of a god, whereas in the Jewish it is of the Chosen People—who received the knowledge and support of their God while in the torment of the underworld of the King of Death. Thus a fundamental distinction emerges, which throughout the history of Judaism has remained its second point of high distinction among the religions of the world: namely, that whereas elsewhere the principle of divine life is symbolized as a divine individual (Dumuzi-Adonis-Attis-Dionysos-Christ), in Judaism it is the People of Israel whose mythic history thus serves the function that in other cults belongs to an incarnation or manifestation of God.

In the Hagadah of Passover, in the course of the family ceremonial, the following meditation is read aloud by the father of the household: "In every generation, one ought to regard himself as though he had personally come out of Egypt." Every Jew, that is to say, is of one substance with Israel—somewhat as every crumb of the transubstantiated wafer of the Roman Catholic Mass is the entire body and blood of the sacrificed and resurrected Christ, who descended into Hell and in three days rose from the dead. And the force of this Jewish principle of identification, not with God, who is transcendent, but with the People of God, which is the only entity in the universe through which his will for the future works, is even so strong that for a valid act of orthodox worship there must be present at least ten males above the age of thirteen (the *minyan*).

* Supra, pp. 96–97.

The individual has no relation to God save by way of this community, or consensus. God—the only God there is—is apart, and the body of his Chosen People is the one holy thing on earth. The individual apart from that is null.

Contrast to this emphatically social emphasis the Indian idea that the ultimate realization of truth is to be experienced alone, in yoga, in the forest; or the Chinese, that an accord is to be experienced with the Tao, the Way of nature and the universe, which is the Way of one's heart, as well. In the Book of Moses, on the contrary, the way of God, who is transcendent, is neither within nor in nature, but in the group—this group alone, with its laws, which are the only facts of real moment to be known.

The first two parts of the legendary cycle of the Chosen People may be said, then, to represent: I. The Entry of the Patriarchs into the Underworld of Death and Auguish, for Rebirth to a Higher Life, and II. The Rebirth, as a People, under Yahweh. Part III, The Desert Years, represents the phase of confirmation of the people in the ritual structure of the new life under Yahweh, to which they have been raised; and IV, The Conquest of the Promised Land, celebrates the entry of the Law of Yahweh, through the victory of his people, into world history.

The murder of Moses, deduced by Freud from the evidences both of Jewish psychology and of the numerous accounts of seriously violent revolts against Moses in the wilderness (for example, Numbers 16), would have supplied, according to his view, the nuclear event (latent content) of this entire mythic dream; and the myth (manifest content) he interprets, consequently, in the way rather of a screening than of a revealing structure. I do not wish to enter into any discussion of the relevancy of this theory specifically to this powerful and immensely influential legendary cycle of the Jewish people, but only to remark, with reference to the larger, general theory of our subject, that, indeed, two types of mythology must be recognized; namely, one (of which the biblical myths are the best-known examples) where all stress is placed on the historicity of the episodes, and the other (of which Indian mythology is an instance) where the episodes are *meant* to be read symbolically, as pointing through and beyond themselves. Of course, in Freud's view, the ultimate reference (latent content) of both types, finally, is an infantile desire to kill the father (Pharaoh: Moses) and enter the mother (Promised Land). However, my own impression is that even myths of the first type have something more to say than that; and that Freud in his Oedipus dogma has carried forward into science the biblical penchant for concretization. Exactly how much of the Patriarchal and Mosaic legend derives from factual occurrences of the second millennium B.C., and how much from creative priestly pens at work only in the first, remains—and will perhaps remain for all time—a question to which every answer must be symptomatic rather of the mind of him who answers than of the truth either of history or of God.

GODS AND HEROES OF THE
EUROPEAN WEST:
1500–500 B.C.

✦✦✦

I. The Dialogue of North and South

Fortunately it will not be necessary to argue that Greek, Celtic, or Germanic myths were mythological. The peoples themselves knew that they were myths, and the European scholars discussing them have not been overborne by the idea of something uniquely holy about their topic. Not many studies comparing these myths with the biblical have been made; but within the European field itself so much first-rate, sober scholarship has been deployed that in the present chapter we are at last, so to say, on home ground.

Friedrich Nietzsche was the first, I believe, to recognize the force in the Greek heritage of an interplay of two mythologies: the pre-Homeric Bronze Age heritage of the peasantry, in which release from the yoke of individuality was achieved through group rites inducing rapture; and the Olympian mythology of measure and humanistic self-knowledge that is epitomized for us in Classical art. The glory of the Greek tragic view, he perceived, lay in its recognition of the mutuality of these two orders of spirituality, neither of which alone offers more than a partial experience of human worth.

Nietzsche was but twenty-eight when *The Birth of Tragedy* appeared in 1872—the very year when his elder countryman Heinrich

Schliemann was unearthing Troy, to reveal within Homer's mythic world its core of historical fact. In his later years Nietzsche criticized his book as a work of youthful pessimism and aestheticism, composed within sound of the guns of the Franco-Prussian War, under a spell of Schopenhauer and Wagner. However, the justness of his insight has since been demonstrated by the findings of a century of archaeological research into fields of which not even the main outlines had appeared in his day.

As the record now stands, the earliest known population to enter Greece arrived c. 3500 B.C. There seem to have been no paleolithic or mesolithic settlements on the peninsula. The immigrants arrived from Asia Minor by sea, bearing a developed agrarian-pastoral culture of high neolithic style: fine ceramic wares, polished stone tools and weapons, knives of obsidian (from Melos?), which they continued to import, and the usual female figurines. They settled chiefly on the plains of Thessaly, Phocis, and Boeotia, building small, rectangular, flat-roofed homes of brick on stone foundations. A few moved north, to the banks of the river Haliacmon in southernmost Macedonia; others moved south into Attica, broached the Peloponnese, and settled here and there in Argolis, Arcadia, Laconia, and Messenia; but there was little or no expansion of these people west.

Then, however, as the ruins let us know, c. 2500 B.C. one of the northernmost of their towns, at Sérvia on the Haliacmon, was destroyed by fire; and there appear in the ruins, dramatically, the artifacts of a totally different, crude, pastoral people from the north.

"The intrusive culture," states Professor N. G. L. Hammond in his superb *History of Greece to 322 B.C.*, "is marked by a different style of pottery which is cruder in technique; its ornamentation includes incised parallel zigzag lines and the moulding of beaded and arcaded patterns."

> Two burials [he continues] have been discovered in the layer which succeeds the destruction by fire. In the first the body was buried in a pit, in a contracted attitude with one hand held up to the face; beside it lay vases and an obsidian blade. In the second, which lay over the first burial, there were

found beside the skeleton some fragments of a marble bracelet and lid, bone pins, and a clay phallus.

From Sérvia this intrusive culture, already influenced and enriched by contact with the Thessalian culture, spread eastwards into central Macedonia and Chalcidice and southwards into Thessaly. . . . The spread of the new culture is marked by incised pottery, spiral decoration, stone battle-axes, phallic emblems, and a new type of house. The phallic emblems, of which the first example occurs in the burial at Sérvia, indicate a worship of the masculine aspect of life, and are in marked contrast to the female statuettes of the Neolithic Thessalian culture. When the intruders settled at Dhimíni and Sésklo in Thessaly, they fortified their villages with a ringwall. Later they built houses with a porch, which was often supported on wooden pillars, and with an indoor hearth set towards one side. Such houses were probably the prototypes from which the typical Mycenaean house—the "Megaron"— developed centuries later.[1]

The subsequent stages of the dialogue of these two prehistoric cultures in Greece may be summarized for our purpose in the following schedule.

PHASE I: EARLY HELLADIC GREECE— TROY I TO V: c. 2500–1900 B.C.

Arrival and establishment of early Bronze Age forms: ready fusion with neolithic predecessors, impressive development of buildings.

Troy, controlling entrance to Dardanelles, grows from fishing village (Troy I) to large commercial port (Troy V).

In Greece, two regional pottery styles: 1. north of Isthmus, light figures on dark ground (trade with Troy and northwest Asia Minor), 2. south of Isthmus, dark figures on light ground (trade with Aegina and Cycladic Isles).

PHASE II: MIDDLE HELLADIC GREECE— TROY VI EARLY PHASE: c. 1900–1600 B.C.

Violent destructions in eastern Greece. Appearance of Megaron type of dwelling. Two new potteries: 1. matt-painted (developed from early Bronze Age styles), 2. gray "Minyan" ware (thrown on potter's wheel, imitating metal forms).

Fall of Troy V, founding of fortified Troy VI. In Troy, the horse appears (Hurrian-Kassite contribution from East?) *

New and powerful dynasty at Mycenae (Shaft Grave Dynasty I): skeletons in extended posture, some 5½ to 6 feet tall (far taller race than Minoan); elegant grave gear, excellent metalwork in gold, silver, and electrum (no resemblance to Minoan). Trade continues with Troy and Cycladic Isles. First direct contacts made with Crete.

From the remains of this stage it is evident that the Aryans, Nordics, or Indo-Europeans coming down from the north had already received a considerable cultural contribution from the "Painted Pottery" and other settled peoples of the Danube zone. They were not exactly paleolithic hunters, but developed pastoral nomads, comparable in culture—though not in temperament—to their contemporaries in the Near East, the Akkadians, who, under Sargon of Agade, had become the masters of the old Sumerian world. Having reached the southern shores of Greece and established contact with the elegant civilization of Crete, they were about to receive and submit to its cultural influence.

PHASE III: LATE HELLADIC I—TROY VI
EARLY MIDDLE PHASE: C. 1600–1500 B.C.

Period of the apogee of Crete (Late Minoan IA): dominance of Knossos throughout the Aegean.

Start of Minoization of Mycenae: new dynasty (Shaft Grave Dynasty II): skeletons in contracted posture, horse-drawn chariots, elegant inlaid daggers with graceful hunting and war scenes (Mycenaean motifs, craftsmen probably Minoan), boar's-tusk helmets (not Minoan), amber jewelry (Baltic amber unknown in Crete). In men's graves: breastplates and death masks of gold (mask showing visage with beard and mustache), swords, daggers, gold and silver cups, gold signet rings; stone, clay, and metal vessels. In

* Cf. Supra, pp. 120–22.

women's graves: gold frontlets, toilet boxes, jewelry, and disks. A Theban fresco shows the women in Minoan dress.

Great extension of Mycenaean influence throughout Argolis and into Boeotia: similar dynasties appear at Thebes, Goulas, and Orchomenus. Trade meanwhile increasing with Troy.

PHASE IV: LATE HELLADIC II — TROY VI
LATE MIDDLE PHASE: C. 1500-1400 B.C.

Rise of Mycenae over Crete (Late Minoan IB and II): new, very powerful Mycenaean dynasty (Tholos Tomb Dynasty I): large, circular, domed tombs carved directly into hillsides, covered with earth, faced with masonry, and closed by massive doors; approached by long, unroofed passages. Strong fusion of Mycenaean and Minoan art forms (Minoan dominant). Trade throughout Sea of Crete to detriment of Knossos.

c. 1450 B.C.: Cretan palaces destroyed (earthquake? attack?)
                Mycenaean-Cretan connections interrupted
                Mycenaean colony in Rhodes

c. 1425 B.C.: Mycenaean colony in Cos

High Bronze Age commerce now at apogee, circulating merchandise from Nubia (gold), Cornwall, Hungary, and Spain (tin), Sinai and Arabia (copper); Baltic amber; European hides, timber, wine, olive oil, and purple dye; Egyptian rope, papyrus, and linen.

Period of Egyptian Dynasty XVIII and Stonehenge III.

PHASE V: LATE HELLADIC III A —
TROY VI FINAL PHASE: C. 1400-1300 B.C.

Hittite hegemony in Asia Minor, associated with Troy: Hittite King Mursilis II (c. 1345-1315) mentions kings of Ahhiyava (Achaeans). Achaeans now fighting as allies of Hittites and as mercenaries in Egypt. (Period of Ikhnaton, 1377-1358: Habiru are harassing Syria and Palestine.)

c. 1400 B.C.: Mycenaean conquest of Crete.

c. 1350 B.C.: Palace of Mycenae greatly enlarged: cyclopean walls, "Lion Gate," etc.; vast tholos tombs ("Treasury of Atreus," dome 40 feet high). Cretan cities revive under Achaeans: invention of Linear B (Mycenaean) script. Troy also flourishing within massive fortifications.

c. 1325 B.C.: A new type of slashing sword appears in Aegean area (first used in Hungary), requiring new type of armor: small circular shield on arm (replacing great bull-hide shield hung from shoulder), peaked or horned helmet, deflecting downward slash.

c. 1300 B.C.: Troy VI destroyed by earthquake.

PHASE VI: HOMER'S TROY (TROY VII): c. 1300–c. 1184 B.C.

A mighty and wonderful city, exactly as in the Iliad, wealthy, and with flourishing trade. . . .

And so we arrive at the epic date of the deeds of Homer's heroes: the date, as well, of those of the Book of Judges. The two heroic ages were simultaneous. In both domains there had been a long period of interplay and adjustment between settled agricultural and intrusive pastoral-warrior peoples, after which, very suddenly, overwhelming onslaughts of fresh pastoral-warrior folk (in Palestine the Hebrews, in Greece the Dorians) precipitated a veritable *Götterdämmerung* and the end of the world age of the people of bronze. The exploits of Homer's "divine race of heroes" fall in the period c. 1250–1150, and following a lapse of about three centuries their epics took form, their dates coinciding approximately with the biblical; as follows:

c. 850 B.C.: Iliad—Yahwist (J) Text
c. 750 B.C.: Odyssey—Elohim (E) Text

It is all too neat for mere concidence; and, as Freud has remarked, there is the further problem of why in the case of Greece what appeared was poetry, and of the Jews, religion.

II. The Marriages of Zeus

It is instructive to contrast the history of the early Bronze Age cities of the Indus Valley with those of the Aegean. The dates of the two developments were about the same, c. 2500–1500 B.C., and the ultimate source of the two cultures also was the same, the nuclear Near East. But when the neolithic and Bronze Age arts and mythologies of village and city life spread to the Indus, they entered a zone of undeveloped paleolithic and mesolithic jungle villages: one of the major provinces of that tropical, timeless, equatorial "second kind of culture" that Leo Frobenius termed "the invisible counterplayer in the history of the culture of mankind." [2] And the influence of that environment on the subsequent history of Indian mythology and civilization was decisive.

The variously killed, cut-up, and rotting human corpses, buried portions of flesh, and other ritually handled remains of the grisly rites that are common to all tropical culture provinces are supposed, on the analogy of the slips of plants, to be generating fresh, continuing human social growth. "The people live," as Frobenius states, "in the spirit of the plant world; they identify themselves with it and it with themselves." [3] The leading mythological theme throughout the tropical, equatorial zone is of the killed and cut-up divine being out of whose body the food plants grow. And the primitive rites of the entire zone are counterparts of that myth.[4] But in the High Bronze Age mythologies, too, the leading theme was of death and resurrection, rendered in rites of human sacrifice, often on a lavish scale. Consequently, when these myths and rites reached primitive India, where they met and joined the tropical, a rich compound of high and low, sophisticated and unadorned, modes of ritual murder developed, of which the blood-soaked cult of the black goddess Kali and the burning of widows on their husbands' funeral pyres are the best-known illustrations.

The remoteness of India from the primary centers of Bronze Age civilization left the promising Indus cities of Mohenjo-daro and Harappa to expire, as it were, on the vine. No signs of local cultural evolution have appeared in the archaeology of their sites, but only of gradual devolution; [5] and the rest of the great subcontinent, meanwhile, remained at a level of development about comparable to that of Melanesia today—which is, perhaps, not too bad (it seems, indeed, to hold charm for anthropologists), but neither is it to be compared with the flourishing Mediterranean world trade of that time in copper, gold, silver, and bronze, uniting in one vast developing community Mesopotamia and Egypt, Nubia and Spain, Ireland, Hungary, Crete, and Arabia.

Moreover, when the Indo-Aryan chariot fighters, cattle-herders, and Vedic chanters with their pantheon of Aryan gods (Indra, Varuna, Mitra, Vayu, Agni, and the rest), shattered the Indus cities and passed on to the Gangetic plain, c. 1500–1000 B.C., they too were left on the vine; and their valor, as well as that of their gods, was presently absorbed into the timeless, all-absorbing and regenerating substance of the goddess-mother Kali, to the dreamy drone of "Peace! Peace! Peace! Peace to all living beings!" while the blood of beheaded victims poured in peace, continuously, as ambrosia, into her maw.

In the Aegean, on the other hand, the new orders of civilization came into a zone within call of descendants of the paleolithic Great Hunt on the broadly spreading animal plains of the north; who, furthermore, had been receiving and assimilating for centuries un-remitting influences from the chief creative centers of the nuclear Near East. The field was one of significantly heightened energy; and, as we have just seen, after the first of the Aryan or proto-Aryan waves struck south, c. 2500 B.C., there followed others, wave upon wave, until, in direct contrast to the Indian denouement, it was not the mythic order of the goddess that consumed the gods, but the other way around. And the order that was so consumed, furthermore, was not of Melanesian cannibal ogresses, but of those elegant, lovely Parisiennes whom we have learned to know from Crete.

We have already watched Olympian Zeus conquer the serpent son and consort of the goddess-mother Gaea. Let us now observe his behavior toward the numerous pretty young goddesses he met when he came, as it were, to gay Paree. Everyone has read of his mad turning of himself into bulls, serpents, swans, and showers of gold. Every Mediterranean nymph he saw set him crazy. And in consequence, when the Greeks became in time as civilized as the Cretans, the philanderings of their highest god proved embarrassing to theology—as they need not have done, however, since all of his goddesses were actually but aspects of the one, in a gown, so to speak, of changeable jade; while he in each of his epiphanies was as different from his last as was the goddess in the case from hers. The formula for such divine multiplicity in unity is given in the Christian doctrine of the Trinity: one divine substance, three (or more) divine personalities. Comparably, in the Old Testament the different "angels of Yahweh" that appeared, for example, to Jacob, to Moses, and to Gideon, both were and were not Yahweh. Gods throughout the world have a way of doing this sort of thing, which to a close student of their habits never is surprising; though one used only to the logic of Aristotle might suppose that something unusual had occurred and cry, "O Lord, thy ways are inscrutable to mankind!"

The particular problem faced by Zeus in that period was simply that wherever the Greeks came, in every valley, every isle, and every cove, there was a local manifestation of the goddess-mother of the world whom he, as the great god of the patriarchal order, had to master in a patriarchal way. And when all these conquests were brought together by the systematists of the Alexandrian age, they came to a vivid docket. One fortunate consequence of this supernatural scandal was that it ultimately relieved the Greeks of their elder theology altogether—an effect such as one could wish to have seen brought to pass in certain other provinces of archaic myth. However, in the palmy days of the god's marriages, they were of serious social worth, even though in the late narratives through which we hear of them they are presented with a certain levity.

For instance, a prime example both of the humor and of the logic and function of this mythology may be seen in the legend of the birth of Pallas Athene. The name already appears on a Linear B tablet of c. 1400 B.C. from the Cretan palace city of Knossos. "A-TA-NA PO-TI-NI-JA," we read: "To the Lady of Athana." [6] The word refers here to a place (as, for example, in the title "Our Lady of Chartres"), and is of pre-Hellenic speech. Professor Martin Nilsson believes the reference to be to a local goddess of the sort represented in the Cretan household and palace shrines (Figures

20 and 21). "The [Cretan] palace goddess," he writes, "was the personal protectress of the king, and such is the role assumed by Athene. . . . She is the guardian protectress of heroes." [7] However, as the world knows, in the Classical pantheon Athene is repre-

Figure 20. The Serpent Goddess

sented not as an ancient Cretan divinity but as a young and fresh Olympian, born, literally, from the brain of Zeus.

For Zeus, at the start of his long career of theological assault through marriage, had taken as first wife the goddess Metis, daughter of the primal cosmic-water couple Oceanus and Tethys—who were exact counterparts of the Mesopotamian Apsu and Tiamat. And, as the eldest child of the Mesopotamian primal pair had been their first-begotten son Mummu, the Word, the Logos, Lord of

Truth and Knowledge, so was Metis infinitely wise. She, in fact, knew more than all the gods. She knew, moreover, the art of changing shape, which she put to use whenever Zeus approached, until finally, by device, he made her his own and she conceived.

Figure 21. Aspects of the Serpent Goddess

But then Zeus learned that her second child, if born, would be the end of him; and so, inducing her to his couch (she pregnant still), he swallowed her at a gulp. And it was only some time later, while walking by a lake, that he began to feel an increasing headache. This grew until he howled; and, as some declare, Hephaestus, others say Prometheus, arrived with a double ax and gave his head a splitting blow: whereupon Athene, fully armed, sprang forth with a battle shout—and Zeus, thereafter, continued to claim that Metis, still sitting in his stomach, was giving him the benefit of her wisdom.[8]

We have here, certainly, a graphic instance of what Freud has termed "sublimation"; applied, however, to a large historical (not merely individual) situation. The case resembles that of Adam giving birth to Eve, except that in the present case the woman is born of the deity himself. Furthermore, as Eve in her pre-Hebraic incarnation was the consort of the serpent,* so in Crete the gifts presented to A-TA-NA PO-TI-NI-JA were addressed to a serpent goddess; and on the Gorgoneum, the magically potent aegis of the Classical Athene, worn upon her chest, the Medusa head is affixed, with its terrible hair of tangled hissing snakes.

We have already spoken of Medusa and of the powers of her blood to render both life and death.† We may now think of the legend of her slayer, Perseus, by whom her head was removed and presented to Athene. Professor Hammond assigns the historical King Perseus of Mycenae to a date c. 1290 B.C., as the founder of a dynasty;[9] and Robert Graves—whose two volumes on *The Greek Myths* are particularly noteworthy for their suggestive historical applications—proposes that the legend of Perseus beheading Medusa means, specifically, that "the Hellenes overran the goddess's chief shrines" and "stripped her priestesses of their Gorgon masks," the latter being apotropaic faces worn to frighten away the profane.[10] That is to say, there occurred in the early thirteenth century B.C. an actual historic rupture, a sort of sociological trauma, which has been registered in this myth, much as what Freud terms the latent content of a neurosis is registered in the manifest content of a dream: registered yet hidden, registered in the unconscious yet unknown or misconstrued by the conscious mind. And in every such screening myth—in every such mythology (that of the Bible being, as we have just seen, another of the kind)—there inheres an essential duplicity, the consequences of which cannot be disregarded or suppressed. Mother Nature, Mother Eve, Mother Mistress-of-

* Supra, pp. 9–31.
† Supra, p. 25.

the-World is there to be dealt with all the time, and the more sternly she is cut down, the more frightening will her Gorgoneum be. This may cause her matricidal son to achieve a lot of extremely spectacular escape work, and he may end by becoming master of the surface of the earth; but, oh, my! what a Sheol he will know—and yet not know—within, where his paradise should have been!

Well, anyhow: Medusa, in her lovelier, fresher, pre-Olympian centuries, had been one of the numerous granddaughters of Gaea, the goddess Earth, who, in the beginning, had brought forth of herself, without consort, Heaven (Uranus), the Hills (Urea), and the Sea (Pontus). Gaea had then conceived of her son Uranus the race of the Titans—which included Oceanus and Tethys, of whom Metis was born; also Cronus, Rheia, Themis, and, in a special manner, Aphrodite. Gaea, then conceiving of her son Pontus, gave birth to a second litter, amidst which Phorcys and Keto were numbered, who, in turn, became the parents of the Graeae, the Gorgons, and the serpent at the end of the world, who guards the golden apples of the Hesperides. Medusa's name means "mistress," "ruler," "queen." (We are on familiar ground, are we not?) And the god of the tides, Poseidon (whom we have also met before, as son and spouse of the Two Queens) * had begotten twins upon her, to whom, however, she was unable to give birth: Chrysaor, the hero "of the golden sword," and Pegasus, a winged horse.

Now, as we have seen,† there is still a certain mystery about the coming of the horse to the Aegean. The arrival seems to have taken place between c. 2100 and 1800 B.C., with Troy an outstanding center; but whether from the north, by way of Macedon,[11] or from the east, through Anatolia, introduced from the Indo-Aryan context by the Hurrians and Kassites, seems not to be known. What we do know, however, is that in the Vedic-Aryan horse sacrifice, which in India became the high rite of kings,[12] the structure and symbology were largely adapted from the earlier bull sacrifice. And it further appears that the ritual of the bull sacrifice was in the Aegean preceded by that of the pig, which belongs to an extremely

* Supra, pp. 47–48.
† Supra, p. 121.

primitive, widely disseminated order of mythic lore, strongly evident in the myths and rites of the goddesses Demeter and Persephone of Eleusis. In Greece, furthermore, the myths and rites of the pig sacrifice show precise analogies with those of Melanesia and the Pacific, which, in turn, rested on a base of lunar-serpent thought. I have discussed all this in *Primitive Mythology* [13] and need not repeat the argument beyond noticing the moon-serpent-pig-bull-horse continuity and sequence.

Medusa and the other Greek goddesses of the old Titan generation, who were certainly at home in Greece and the Aegean long before the Hellenes appeared, exhibit every possible sign of an original relationship to an extremely early neolithic—perhaps even mesolithic—lunar-serpent-pig context that is represented in the myths and rites on one hand of Melanesia and the Pacific, and, on the other, of Celtic Ireland. In fact, the usual form in which Medusa is shown—squatting, arms raised, tongue lolling over the chin, eyes wide—is a pose that is characteristic of the guardian of the other world in the pig cults of Melanesia. There she is a guardian demoness on the road to the yonder world, beyond whose ban the offering of a pig—offered in the way of a substitute for oneself —allows one to pass.[14] And Medusa is in exactly such a place in her cave beyond the edge of day, on the road to the golden apple tree. Compare, also, the sibyl Siduri of the Gilgamesh adventure.*

But, at the same time, Medusa was linked in Classical Greece to the very much later mythic context of the sacrificial horse. She and Poseidon together, in fact, were associated with a mythology of horses that can have become attached to them only *after* c. 2000 B.C. In the Mycenaean Linear B tablets of c. 1400–1200 offerings are recorded to a god I-QO (*hippo,* "horse"); and we know that Poseidon was called Hippios in Classical times.[15] Poseidon in the form of a horse mated with Medusa as a mare, whence she conceived the winged Pegasus and his human twin Chrysaor. There is, moreover, as Robert Graves points out, "an early representation of the goddess with a Gorgon's head and a mare's body." [16] Graves,

* Supra, pp. 90–91.

therefore, reads the Perseus myth to mean in full: "The Hellenes overran the goddess's chief shrines, stripped her priestesses of their Gorgon masks, and took possession of the sacred horses."

But now, just one more detail: Frazer, in *The Golden Bough*, has shown that there was a mythic association of the horse with Diana's grove at Nemi, where the ritual regicide was enacted even in late Roman times. The princely youth Hippolytus, dragged to his death by his own chariot horses when they were frightened by a bull of Poseidon that came up at them from the sea, is supposed to have been revived by Diana and to have reigned at Nemi as her king, the King of the Wood. "And we can hardly doubt," Frazer adds, "that the Saint Hippolytus of the Roman calendar, who was dragged by horses to death on the thirteenth of August, Diana's own day, is no other than the Greek hero of the same name, who, after dying twice over as a heathen sinner, has been happily resuscitated as a Christian saint." [17]

So that we must now add to our view of the mythic context of Poseidon, Medusa, and the hero deed of Perseus, the mythology of the death and resurrection of the lunar king, and with that the ritual regicide. In an early chapter of *Primitive Mythology* I presented the record from Ethiopia of a Greek-educated king named Ergamenes, who, in the period of the Alexandrian pharaoh Ptolemy II Philadelphus, 309–246 B.C., walked with a body of soldiers into the hitherto solemnly feared sanctuary of the Golden Temple, slew the priests who had been up to that time the readers of the oracle of the ritual regicide, discontinued the awesome old tradition, and reorganized things according to a new view of the destiny, function, and powers of a king. [18] By analogy, if Perseus was indeed the founder of a new dynasty at Mycenae, c. 1290 B.C., his violation of the neighboring goddess's grove must have marked the end of an ancient rite—possibly of regicide—there practiced. The myth of his miraculous birth from the golden shower of Zeus then would have been of great moment, as validating his act in terms of a divine patriarchal order of belief that was now to supplant the old, of the mother-goddess in whom death is life.

Perseus, we are told, was conceived of Zeus miraculously by the princess Danaë of Argolis, and sent floating with his mother in a water-worthy chest to sea. Drawn ashore on the isle of Seriphos by a fisherman, whose brother, Polydectes, was the local king, Danaë with her child became the king's slave—or, according to another version, his wife; or, according to still another, she remained with Dictys, the fisherman, his brother. But the king, like all monarchs in legends of this class, was a cruel ogre of a king, and to be rid of Perseus, so that he might enjoy his mother, he imposed upon the youth the very difficult—nay, impossible—task of procuring Medusa's head.

This terrible monster had two sisters, and all three were endowed with golden wings, hands of brass, heads and bodies wreathed with snakes, and countenances with boar's tusks, so dreadful to behold that anyone who saw them would be turned to stone. Perseus, on his way, passed through various mythic dangers, in the course of which adventures he received from the water nymphs a pair of winged sandals, a cap of invisibility, and a wallet in which to carry the captured head. With these he passed beyond the outermost sea, the outer rim of day, and, arriving in the realm of darkness into which stars and planets vanish for rebirth, he came first upon the curious triad of the Graeae. These were three old gray sisters, sharing a single tooth and eye, and when they were passing the eye, one to another, Perseus snatched and would not return it until they taught him the way to the Gorgons' cave—which they were supposed to be guarding. After which, as Aeschylus tells, "boarlike, he passed into the cave." [19]

The Gorgons within were asleep, and while Perseus's eyes were averted from the petrifying sight of Medusa, Athene, the patron goddess of heroes, gave guidance to his sword hand (or, as another telling has it, let him see his victim reflected in a shield). With a single stroke of his sickle-shaped blade, he took the trophy, stuffed it in his wallet, turned his back, and ran, while Pegasus and Chrysaor sprang from Medusa's severed neck. The two sisters pursued. But Perseus reached home, where he produced his appalling prize, holding it high for all to see; and the tyrant king with his entire company at dinner became stone—which is why the isle of Seriphos today is so full of rocks.[20]

III. The Night Sea Journey

The connotation of female personages in a patriarchal mythology is generally obscured by the device that Sigmund Freud termed, with reference to the manifest content of dream, "displacement of accent." A distracting secondary theme is introduced, around which the elements of a situation are regrouped; revelatory scenes, acts, or remarks are omitted, reinterpreted, or only remotely suggested; and "a sense of something far more deeply interfused" consequently permeates the whole, which, however, rather baffles than illuminates the mind.

In the patriarchal cosmogonies, for example, the normal imagery of divine motherhood is taken over by the father, and we find such motifs as, in India, the World Lotus growing from the reclining god Vishnu's navel—whereas, since the primary reference of the lotus in India has always been to the goddess Padma, "Lotus," whose body itself is the universe, the long stem from navel to lotus should properly connote an umbilical cord through which the flow of energy would be running from the goddess to the god, mother to child, not the other way. Or in the Classical image of Zeus bearing Athene from his brain, where we have already recognized an example of "sublimation," we now note that the "sublimation" has been rendered by means of an image of the type that Freud termed "transference upward": as the woman gives birth from the womb, so the father from his brain. Creation by the power of the Word is another instance of such a transfer to the male womb: the mouth the vagina, the word the birth. And one extremely important consequence of this bizarre, but highly honored, aberration upward, is the notion, common to all Occidental spirituality—and particularly stressed by our numerous bachelor and homosexual great teachers—that spirituality and sexuality are opposed.

"By the displacement of the accent and regrouping of the elements," Freud wrote in his elucidation of the censoring factor in dream, "the manifest content is made so unlike the latent thoughts that nobody would suspect the presence of the latter behind the former." [21] And so it has been throughout all patriarchal mythologies. The function of the female has been systematically devalued, not only in a symbolical cosmological sense, but also in a personal, psychological. Just as her role is cut down, or even out, in myths of the origin of the universe, so also in hero legends. It is, in fact, amazing to what extent the female figures of epic, drama, and romance have been reduced to the status of mere objects; or, when functioning as subjects, initiating action of their own, have been depicted either as incarnate demons or as mere allies of the masculine will. The idea of an effective dialogue seems never to occur, where the male, with himself or his world shattered by one of those blazing demonesses (tragedy, alas!), should receive from her (in the underworld, as it were) some revelation beyond the bounds of his former horizon of thought and feeling (illumination, completion, rebirth). Throughout the literature images appear that obviously, in some earlier, pre-patriarchal context, must have pointed to initiations received by the male from the female side; but their accent is always so displaced that they appear on first glance—though not, indeed, on second—to support the patriarchal notion of virtue, *arete,* which they actually, in some measure, refute.

Even modern Classical scholarship has been collaborating largely in this patriarchal displacement. In fact, it required a female Classical scholar, the late and wonderful Jane Ellen Harrison, to remark the triviality and vulgarity of the episode from which the whole constellation of the glories and tragedies of the Trojan War was supposed to have derived: the Judgment of Paris.

The myth in its present form [she wrote] is sufficiently patriarchal to please the taste of Olympian Zeus himself, trivial and even vulgar enough to make material for an ancient Satyr-play or a modern *opéra-bouffe.*

"Goddesses three to Ida came
   Immortal strife to settle there—
Which was the fairest of the three,
   And which the prize of beauty should wear."

The bone of contention is a golden apple thrown by Eris ["Strife"] at the marriage of Peleus and Thetis among the assembled gods. On it was written, "Let the fair one take it," or, according to some authorities, "The apple for the fair one." The three high goddesses betake them for judgment to the king's son, the shepherd Paris. The kernel of the myth is, according to this version, a καλλιστεῖον, a beauty contest.[22]

And the informing ethos of the myth, we might add, is that *arete,* or pride in excellence, which has been called the very soul of the Homeric hero—as it is the soul, also, of the Celtic and Germanic; or, indeed, everywhere, of the unbroken male.

But here it is represented as proper to the female soul as well— which is the rub. In this masculine dream world, the excellence of the female is supposed to reside in: a) her beauty of form (Aphrodite), b) her constancy and respect for the marriage bed (Hera), and c) her ability to inspire excellent males to excellent patriarchal deeds (Athene). Along with which, finally, of course, being a woman, the winner of the beauty contest cheats. Aphrodite promises Paris that if she is given the golden apple, she will procure for him the golden beauty Helen, who is already married to Menelaus. "A beauty contest," states Miss Harrison in undisguised disgust, "vulgar in itself and complicated by bribery still more vulgar." [23] Yet for generations this seems to have been accepted as the adequate mythic (i.e., unimportant) start of the world's most noble epic of "excellence" (ἀρετή), and all that followed in its train.

What followed were the *Nostoi,* "Returns," when the masters of excellence in the world of the outer deed returned to their neglected wives, who for ten years (or, in Odysseus's instance, twenty) had been supposed to be sitting faithfully, in the manner of Griselda, at home (redemption by love, patriarchal style). However, as we know, one of the returning heroes, at least, received a formidable shock.

There is a principle of complementarity operating in the psyche, in society, in history, and in the symbolism of myth, which Dr. Carl G. Jung has discussed throughout his writings and illustrated from every quarter of the globe. "No matter how much we make conscious," he once wrote, in discussion of the mechanics of this principle, "there will always be an indeterminate and indeterminable quantity of unconscious elements, which belong to the totality of the self." [24] But these unconscious elements do not simply rest in the psyche, inert. As unrealized potentialities, they are invested with a certain readiness for activation in compensatory counterplay to the conscious attitude; so that whenever in the sphere of conscious attention a relaxation of demand occurs and the individual is no longer required to bring all of his energies to bear upon his one intended goal—as, for example, the winning of the Trojan War— the released, disposable energies turn back, as it were, and flow to the waiting centers of potential experience and development. "It does not lie in our power," Jung declares, "to transfer 'disposable' energy at pleasure to a rationally chosen object." [25] On the contrary, the transfer is inevitably not only out of control, but also complementary to the conscious will; for, as Jung observes, quoting Heraclitus, who, as he says, was indeed a very wise man, "everything tends sooner or later to go over into its opposite."

The old Greek philosopher Heraclitus (c. 500 B.C.) called this process of psychological, historical, and cosmogonic overbalancing *enantiodromia,* "running the other way." And as an example of the process no better instance could be sought than that supplied by the two contrasting epics of Homer on which Heraclitus and his whole generation were raised: on one hand, the *Iliad,* with its world of *arete* and manly work and, on the other, the *Odyssey,* the long return, completely uncontrolled, of the wisest of the men of that heroic generation to the realm of those powers and knowledges which, in the interval, had been waiting unattended, undeveloped, even unknown, in that "other mind" which is woman: the mind that in the earlier Aegean day of those lovely beings of Crete had made its sensitive statement, but in the sheerly masculine Heroic Age had been submerged like an Atlantis.

Jane Harrison shows an illuminating series of scenes derived, not from the literary Homeric side of the Greek tradition of the Judgment of Paris, but from the elder, wordless heritage of ceramic art. And there we see, as for example in Figure 22, not a youth in the usual languid pose of an accomplished boulevardier, but a Paris in manifest alarm, whom the god Hermes—guide of souls to the underworld—has actually had to seize by the wrist to compel attendance to his task. "There is here," observes Miss Harrison, "clearly no question of voluptuous delight at the beauty of the goddesses." [26] And in fact, as one looks, there is not.

Figure 22. The Judgment of Paris

Conveniently for my present theme, the direction of Paris's flight in this picture is toward Troy, while the triad of the feminine principle, which he is obviously being required to face for some crisis in his own lot, not in theirs, stand on the side of the Greek homeland, where Agamemnon was to meet Clytemnestra, Menelaus his recaptured golden girl, and the great and wise Odysseus (who would be the only one up to the occasion) Penelope and her galaxy of suitors. I would suggest that we think of the short life full of deeds and fame, warcraft, *arete,* Zeus, and Apollo as off to the right, and on the left, besides the old goddesses of the time and tide of Mother Right, the mystic isles of Circe, Calypso, and Nausicaa, with Hermes in the role of the guide of souls to the underworld and to knowledges beyond death.

Heinrich Schliemann guessed correctly that there had actually been a Troy and Trojan War, and by following the lead of the epic found both Troy and the city of Mycenae. Likewise, Sir Arthur Evans unearthed Knossos and the palace of the labyrinth by following clues in the literature of Classical myth. "But," as Professor Martin Nilsson has remarked, "in one case the lead of mythology failed—when Dörpfeld searched for Odysseus' palace on Ithaca; and furthermore," he adds, "we now know why. For the *Odyssey* is not a semi-historical heroic saga, but a sheer novel, built on the well-known theme of the wife who remains true to her long departed husband thought to be dead." [27] Well, yes, in a way! So far, so good! But that particular way of reading this novel, my dear professor, is only from the displaced point of view of the patriarchal, secondary focus. There is a lot more depth to Penelope than that.

The patron god of the *Iliad* is Apollo, the god of the light world and of the excellence of heroes. Death, on the plane of vision of that work, is the end; there is nothing awesome, wondrous, or of power beyond the veil of death, but only twittering, helpless shades. And the tragic sense of that work lies precisely in its deep joy in life's beauty and excellence, the noble loveliness of fair women, the real worth of manly men, yet its recognition of the terminal fact, thereby, that the end of it all is ashes. In the *Odyssey*, on the other hand, the patron god of Odysseus's voyage is the trickster Hermes, guide of souls to the underworld, the patron, also, of rebirth and lord of the knowledges beyond death, which may be known to his initiates even in life. He is the god associated with the symbol of the caduceus, the two serpents intertwined; and he is the male traditionally associated with the triad of those goddesses of destiny —Aphrodite, Hera, and Athene—who, in the great legend, caused the Trojan War.

The war lasted ten years and Odysseus's voyage ten. But as the grand old master of Classical lore, Professor Gilbert Murray, pointed out some decades ago in his volume on *The Rise of the Greek Epic*, in the Classical period the effort to coordinate the lunar and solar calendars (the twelve lunar months of 354 days plus

a few hours, and the solar year of 364 days plus a few hours) culminated in the astronomer Meton's "Grand Cycle of Nineteen
Years," according to which (to quote Murray's statement): "On
the last day of the nineteenth year, which was also by Greek reckoning the first of the twentieth, the New Moon would coincide with
the New Sun of the Winter Solstice; this was called the 'Meeting
of Sun and Moon' (Σύνοδος Ἡλίον καὶ Σελήνης)—a thing which had
not happened for nineteen full years before and would not happen
again for another nineteen." [28]

Odysseus, Murray notes, returned to Ithaca "just at the rising of
that brightest star which heralds the light of the Daughter of Dawn"
(*Odyssey* v 93). He rejoined his wife "on the twentieth year"; i.e.,
he came as soon as the twentieth year came, as soon as the nineteenth was complete (ψ 102, 170; ρ 327, β 175). He came at the
new moon, on the day which the Athenians called "Old-and-
New," "when one month is waning and the next rising up" (τ 307,
ξ 162). But this new moon was also the day of the Apollo Feast,
or solstice festival of the sun (v 156, φ 258), and the time was
winter. Moreover, Odysseus had just 360 boars, of which one
died every day (ξ 20); likewise, the cattle of the sun are in seven
herds of fifty each, totaling 350. Odysseus goes under the world
in the West, visits the realm of the dead, and comes up in the
extreme East, "where the Daughter of Dawn has her dwellings and
her dancing-floors and the Sun is uprising" (μ 3) [29]—whereas
Penelope, as we all know, was sitting at home, weaving a web
and unweaving, like the moon.

The nineteenth- and early twentieth-century scholars always
liked to identify solar and lunar analogies in this way because they
confirmed a point that was becoming clear in their time, which was
that the imagery of our heritage of myth is in large part derived
from the cosmological symbology of the Age of Bronze. But we
now must add to this important insight the further realization that
a fundamental idea of *all* the pagan religious disciplines, both of
the Orient and of the Occident, during the period of which we are
writing (first millennium B.C.), was that the inward turning of
the mind (symbolized by the sunset) should culminate in a re-

alization of an identity *in esse* of the individual (microcosm) and the universe (macrocosm), which, when achieved, would bring together in one order of act and realization the principles of eternity and time, sun and moon, male and female, Hermes and Aphrodite (Hermaphroditus), and the two serpents of the caduceus.

The image of the "Meeting of Sun and Moon" is everywhere symbolic of this instant, and the only unsolved questions in relation to its universality are: a) how far back it goes, b) where it first arose, and c) whether from the start it was read both psychologically and cosmologically.

In the Indian Kundalini yoga of the first millennium A.D., the two spiritual channels on either side of the central channel of the spine, up which the serpent power is supposed to be carried through a control of the mind and breath, are called the lunar and solar channels; and their relationship to the center is pictured precisely as the two serpents to the central staff in our Figure 1—which is Hermes' staff. In Figure 2, we see the meeting of sun and moon again in significant relation to the serpent and the axial staff, tree, or spine. The symbolism was known to Europe, China and Japan, the Aztecs and the Navaho: it is unlikely that it was unknown to the Greeks.

And so—to say the very least—the union of Odysseus and Penelope at the start of the twentieth year is to be seen as of somewhat greater interest than the lot of the merely patient Griselda. And to say just a little more: since Penelope is the only woman in the book who is not of a magical category, it is clear (to me, at least) that Odysseus's meetings with Circe, Calypso, and Nausicaa represent psychological adventures in the mythic realm of the archetypes of the soul, where the male must *experience* the import of the female before he can meet her perfectly in life.

1. The first adventure of Odysseus, following his departure with *twelve ships* from the beaches of conquered Troy, was a pirate raid on Ismarus, a Thracian town. "I sacked their city and slew the people," he reported of this act. "And from out the city we took their wives and much substance and divided them amongst us." [30] The brutal deed was followed by *a tempest sent by Zeus,* by which

the sails of the ships were torn to shreds. They were blown, there-after, *out of control, for nine days,* and by that wind of God, carried beyond the bounds of the known world.

2. "On the tenth day," as Odysseus related, "we set foot on *the Land of the Lotus Eaters,* who eat a flowery food." But those of his men who ate of that fare had no more wish ever to return home (Lethe motif, forgetfulness: turn of the mind to the mythic, i.e., in-ward, realm); so that he dragged them weeping to their ships, bound them in the hulls, and rowed away.

3. Odysseus and his fleet were now in a mythic realm of diffi-cult trials and passages, of which the first was to be *the Land of the Cyclopes,* "neither nigh at hand, nor yet afar off," where the one-eyed giant Polyphemus, son of the god Poseidon (who, as we know, was the lord of tides and of the Two Queens, and the lord, furthermore, of Medusa), dwelt with his flocks in a cave.

"Yea, for he was a monstrous thing and fashioned marvelously, nor was he like to any man that lives by bread, but like a wooded peak of the towering hills, which stands out apart and alone from others."

Odysseus, choosing *twelve men,* the best of his company, left his ships at shore and sallied to the vast cave. It was found stocked abundantly with cheeses, flocks of lambs and kids penned apart, milk pails, bowls of whey; and when the company had entered and was sitting to wait, expecting hospitality, the owner came in, shepherding his flocks. He bore a grievous weight of dry wood, which he cast down with a din inside the cave, so that in fear all fled to hide. Lifting a huge doorstone, such as two and twenty good four-wheeled wains could not have raised from the ground, he set this against the mouth of the cave, sat down, milked his ewes and goats, and beneath each placed her young, after which he kindled a fire and spied his guests.

Two were eaten that night for dinner, two the next morning for breakfast, and two the following night. (*Six gone.*) But the com-panions meanwhile had prepared a prodigious stake with which to bore out the Cyclops' single eye; and when clever Odysseus, de-claring his own name to be *Noman,* approached and offered the giant a skin of wine, Polyphemus, having drunk his fill, "lay back," as we read, "with his great neck bent round, and sleep that conquers all men overcame him." Wine and the fragments of the men's flesh he had just eaten issued forth from his mouth, and he vomited, heavy with drink.

"Then," declared Odysseus,

I thrust in that stake under the deep ashes, until it should grow hot, and I spake to my companions comfortable words, lest any should hang back from me in fear. But when that bar of olive wood was just about to catch fire in the flame, green though it was, and began to glow terribly, even then I came nigh, and drew it from the coals, and my fellows gathered about me, and some god breathed great courage into us. For their part they seized the bar of olive wood, that was sharpened at the point, and thrust it into his eye, while I from my place aloft turned it about, as when a man bores a ship's beam with a drill while his fellows below spin it with a strap, which they hold at either end, and the auger runs round continually. Even so did we seize the fiery-pointed brand and whirled it round in his eye, and the blood flowed about the heated bar. And the breath of the flame singed his eyelids and brows all about, as the ball of the eye burnt away, and the roots thereof crackled in the flame. And as when a smith dips an ax or adze in chill water with a great hissing, when he would temper it—for hereby anon comes the strength of iron—even so did his eye hiss round the stake of olive. And he raised a great and terrible cry, that the rock rang around, and we fled away in fear, while he plucked forth from his eye the brand bedabbled in much blood. Then maddened with pain he cast it from him with his hands, and called with a loud voice on the Cyclopes, who dwelt about him in the caves along the windy heights. And they heard the cry and flocked together from every side, and gathering round the cave, called in to ask what ailed him. "What hath so distressed thee, Polyphemus, that thou criest thus aloud through the immortal night, and makest us sleepless? Surely no mortal driveth off thy flocks against thy will: surely none slayeth thyself by force or craft?"

And the strong Polyphemus spake to them again from out of the cave: "My friends, Noman is slaying me by guile, nor at all by force."

And they answered and spake winged words: "If then no man is violently handling thee in thy solitude, it can in no wise be that thou shouldst escape the sickness sent by mighty Zeus. Nay, pray thou to thy father, the lord Poseidon."

On this wise they spake and departed; and my heart within me laughed to see how my name and cunning counsel had beguiled them.

There remained, however, the problem of getting out of the blocked cave. The Cyclops, groaning, groping with his hands, lifted away the stone from the door, and himself then sat at the entry. And Odysseus cleverly lashed together three large rams of the flock, "well nurtured and thick of fleece, great and goodly, with wool as dark as violet." And he prepared in all six triads of this kind. The middle ram of each set was to carry a man clinging beneath, while the side pair were to give protection. And as for himself, he laid hold of a goodly young ram, far the best of all, and curled beneath his shaggy belly; and as soon as early dawn shone forth, the nineteen rams, together with the flock, issued from the cave, bearing seven men.

To note: the symbolic penetration of the eye ("bull's eye": analogous to the sun door to the yonder world); the symbolic name Noman (self-divestiture at the passage to the yonder world: because he did not assert his secular character, his personal name and fame, Odysseus passed the cosmic threshold guardian, to enter a sphere of transpersonal forces, over which ego has no control); identification with the ram (symbolically a solar animal: compare Egyptian Amun).

4. The ships sailed to *the Island of Aeolus,* god of the wind (*pneuma, spiritus,* spirit): a floating island where the god and his twelve children, six daughters and six sons, abode in halls of bronze. "And behold, he gave his daughters to his sons to wife; and they feast evermore by their dear father and their kind mother, and dainties innumerable lie ready to their hands."

"He gave me a wallet," said Odysseus, "made of the hide of an ox nine seasons old, and therein he bound the ways of all the noisy winds. . . . And he made it fast in the hold of the ship with a shining silver thong, that not the faintest breath might escape.

Then he sent forth the blast of the West Wind to blow for me, to bear our ships and ourselves upon our way."

For nine days and nights the ships sailed on the winds proceeding from the wallet, and on the tenth were in sight of home. But while Odysseus slept, his men, to see what wealth was in the wallet, opened it, and a violent blast bore the flotilla back to Aeolus, who, however, refused, this time, to receive them.

One can recognize in this and the following adventure symbolic representations of a common psychological experience: first, elation (Jung's term is "inflation"), then depression: the manic-depressive sequence common to sophomores and saints. Having achieved the first step—let us call it a threshold-crossing toward some sort of illumination—the company felt itself to be already at the goal; yet the enterprise had hardly begun. Phrased in terms of individual psychology: while Odysseus, the governing will, slept, his men, the ungoverned faculties, opened the wallet (the One Forbidden Thing). Phrased in sociological terms: the individual achievement was undone by the collective will. Or, putting the two sets of terms together: Odysseus had not yet released himself from identification with his group, group ideals, group judgments, etc.; but self-divestiture means group-divestiture as well. Hence, after enspirited social inflation, there followed:

5. *Deflation, humiliation, the Dark Night of the Soul:* "We sailed onward, stricken at heart. And the spirit of the men was spent beneath the grievous rowing by reason of our vain endeavor, for there was no more sign of a wafting wind." And the seventh day, laboring thus, they arrived at *the Land of the Laestrygons,* a rich place of many flocks, where a scouting party went ashore.

They saw a town ahead and, before the town, fell in with a damsel drawing water. She was the daughter of the king and introduced them to her home, where they met her mother, huge as a mountain peak and loathly in their sight. The mother called the king, and he, also a giant, clutching up one of the company, readied him for eating, while the rest of the startled party ran. The king raising a war hoot, Laestrygons without number flocked from every side and, making for the shore, shattered with rocks all the ships but one.

6. Thus humbled, reduced, and battered, our great voyager, Noman, now was ready for his first fundamental encounter with the female principle, not in terms of *arete,* beauty, constancy, patience, or inspiration, but in terms to be dictated by *Circe of the braided tresses,* a nymph begotten upon a daughter of Ocean by the sun who gives light to all men.

The ship put in to Circe's isle unknowing, and for two days and nights the men lay on the shore, consuming their hearts. But when the third day dawned, Odysseus, taking spear and sword, mounted a hill and spied smoke rising from the woodland beyond. Returning to his men, he slew a tall antlered stag, and they feasted, weeping for their lost companions. Then a party went off to reconnoiter, and in the forest glades they discovered the halls of Circe, built of polished stone.

> And all around the palace mountain-bred wolves and lions were roaming, whom she herself had bewitched with evil drugs that she gave them. Yet the beasts did not set on the men, but lo, they ramped about them and fawned on them, wagging their long tails. And as when dogs fawn about their lord when he comes from the feast, for he always brings them the fragments that soothe their mood, even so the strong-clawed wolves and the lions fawned around them; but they were affrighted when they saw the strange and terrible creatures. So they stood at the outer gate of the fair-tressed goddess, and within they heard Circe singing in a sweet voice, as she fared to and fro before the great web imperishable, such as is the handiwork of goddesses, fine of woof and full of grace and splendor. Then Polites, a leader of men, the dearest to me and the trustiest of all my company first spake to them:
>
> "Friends, forasmuch as there is one within that fares to and fro before a mighty web singing a sweet song, so that all the floor of the hall makes echo, a goddess she is or a woman; come quickly and cry aloud to her."
>
> He spake the word and they cried aloud and called to her. And straightway she came forth and opened the shining doors and bade them in, and all went with her in their heedlessness.

But Eurylochus tarried behind, for he guessed that there was some treason. So she led them in and set them upon chairs and high seats, and made them a mess of cheese and barley-meal and yellow honey with Pramnian wine, and mixed harmful drugs with the food to make them utterly forget their own country. Now when she had given them the cup and they had drunk it off, presently she smote them with a wand, and in the styes of the swine she penned them. So they had the head and voice, the bristles and the shape of swine, but their mind abode even as of old. Thus were they penned there weeping, and Circe flung them acorns and mast and fruit of the cornel tree to eat, whereon wallowing swine do always batten.

Terrified Eurylochus having carried the news to the ship, Odysseus took up his great blade of bronze, slung his bow about him, and made off: but, as he proceeded, then did *Hermes of the golden wand* meet him on the way, in the likeness of a young man with the first down on his lip, the time when youth is most gracious, clasped his hand, and lo, gave him *an herb of virtue,* Moly the gods call it, to protect him against her magic, warned him of her procedure, and said: "When it shall be that Circe smites thee with her long wand, even then draw thou thy sharp sword from thy thigh, and spring on her, as one eager to slay her. And she will shrink away and be instant with thee to lie with her. Thenceforth disdain not thou the bed of the goddess, that she may deliver thy company and kindly entertain thee. But command her to swear a mighty oath by the blessed gods, that she will plan nought else of mischief to thine own hurt, lest she make thee a dastard and unmanned, when she hath thee naked."

Hermes departed toward Olympus, up through the woodland isle, and Odysseus did as he was told. And when she had sworn and had done that oath, he at last went up into the beautiful bed of Circe, while her handmaids busied them in the halls, four maidens, born of the wells and of the woods and of the holy rivers that flow to the salt sea. The men who had been turned to swine were presently trotted in, and she went through their midst and anointed each one of them with another charm. "And so, from their limbs the bristles dropped away, wherewith the venom had erewhile clothed them that lady Circe gave them. And they became men again, younger than before they were, and goodlier far, and taller to behold."

This "sacred marriage" of a hero who had 360 boars at home to a goddess who turns men into swine and back again, goodlier and taller than before, leads us to recall that in the mythology and rites of Demeter and Persephone of Eleusis and of the festival of the Anthesteria the pig was the sacrificial beast, representing a theme of death and rebirth [31]—as it is, also, in the Melanesian rites to which we have already referred. Odysseus on Circe's isle, protected by the advice and power of Hermes, god of the caduceus, had passed to a context of initiations associated with the opposite side of the duplex Classical heritage from that represented by his earlier heroic sphere of life. In the *Odyssey,* as in the mythology of Melanesia, the goddess who in her terrible aspect is the cannibal ogress of the Underworld was in her benign aspect the guide and guardian to that realm and, as such, the giver of immortal life.

7. We learn next, therefore, that Circe has offered to guide Odysseus to *the Underworld*. "Son of Laertes, of the seed of Zeus, Odysseus of many devices," she said, "ye must perform another journey and reach the dwelling of Hades and of dread Persephone, to seek to the spirit of Theban Tiresias, the blind soothsayer, whose wits abide steadfast. To him Persephone hath given judgment, even in death, that he alone should have understanding; but the other souls sweep shadowlike around."

An extremely important point! Not all in the dwelling of Hades are mere shadows. Those who, like Tiresias, have seen and come into touch with the mystery of the two serpents and, in some sense at least, have been themselves both male and female, know the reality from both sides that each sex experiences shadowlike from its own side; and to that extent they have assimilated what is substantial of life and are, so, eternal.

There is a line of Sophocles, referring to the mysteries of Eleusis: "Thrice blessed are those among men, who, after beholding these rites, go down to Hades. Only for them is there life, all the rest will suffer an evil lot." [32]

This idea is basic to mature Classical thought and, in fact, is what distinguishes it from its echo in academic neo-Classicism. It is the expression of an organic synthesis of the two worlds of the Greek dual heritage and amounts, one might say, to an attainment of the second as well as first tree of the Garden—which to our sorry couple in the other school of virtue was denied.

Odysseus, following Circe's lead, now sailed his craft to the limits of the world, where he came to the land and city of the Cimmerians, shrouded in mist and cloud, a land of eternal night. There he poured his offerings for the dead into a trench dug in the earth (in contrast to the upward direction of Olympian offerings) and the ghosts flocked from every side with a wondrous cry. He talked with those he knew: his mother, Tiresias, Phaedra, Procris, Ariadne, and many more, Agamemnon and Achilles. And he saw there, moreover, the Cretan King Minos, son of Zeus, holding in his hand a scepter and from his throne sentencing the dead.

Presently, taken with fear, however, lest Persephone should send to him the head of Medusa, the voyager, departing, returned to Circe, his mystagogue, and received from her the ultimate instruction.

8. *The way and dangers of the way to the Island of the Sun:* The dangers of the way were as follows: a) the Sirens, and b) the Clashing Rocks, or, by an alternate route, b') Scylla and Charybdis. The first is symbolic of the allure of the beatitude of paradise, or, as the Indian mystics say, "the tasting of the juice": accepting paradisial bliss as the end (the soul enjoying its object), instead of pressing through to non-dual, transcendent illumination. The other two represent alike the ultimate threshold of unitive mystical experience, leading past the pairs-of-opposites: a passage in experience beyond the categories of logic (A is not B, thou art not that), beyond all forms of perception, to a conscious participation in the consciousness inherent in all things. Odysseus chose the route between the pair-of-opposites Scylla and Charybdis and passed through.

However, on the Island of the Sun, to which they came, his men, with human appetite, slew, cooked, and ate a number of the cattle of the sun while Odysseus slept; and when they next set sail, "of a sudden came the shrilling West Wind with the rushing of a great tempest, and the blast snapped the two forestays of the mast." The ship, foundering, sank with its entire company except Odysseus himself, who, clinging to a keel and mast, survived—alone at last.

And that was the climax of this spiritual voyage.

The analogy of this crisis to that of the first major threshold-crossing is manifest. And the contrast to the highest Indian ideal of illumination is apparent too. For had Odysseus been a sage of India, he would not now have found himself alone, floating at sea, on the way back to his wife Penelope, to put what he had learned into play in domestic life. He would have been united with the sun —Noman forever. And that, briefly, is the critical line between India and Greece, between the way of disengagement and of tragic engagement.

One can, in fact, compare the lesson of the two visits of Odysseus under the patronage of Circe, on the one hand to the Land of the Fathers and on the other to the Isle of the Sun, with "the two ways, of Smoke, and of Fire," taught in the Indian Upanishads of c. 700–600 B.C.[33] In India, as in Greece, the tradition of these two ways had belonged originally not to the Aryan but to the pre-Aryan component of the compound heritages. Furthermore, it was communicated to the Brahmanical gods of the Aryan patriarchy (according to a myth preserved in the Kena Upanishad) by a goddess: Uma Haimavati, who was a most charming manifestation of the awesome Kali.[34]

In both Greece and India a dialogue had been permitted to occur between the two contrary orders of patriarchal and matriarchal thought, such as in the biblical tradition was deliberately suppressed in favor exclusively of the male. However, although in both Greece and India this interplay had been fostered, the results in the two provinces were not the same. In India the power of the goddess-mother finally prevailed to such a degree that the principle of masculine ego initiative was suppressed, even to the point of dissolving the will to individual life;[35] whereas in Greece the masculine will and ego not only held their own, but prospered in a manner that at that time was unique in the world: not in the way of the compulsive "I want" of childhood (which is the manner and concept of ego normal to the Orient), but in the way of a self-responsible intelligence, released from both "I want" and "thou shalt," rationally regarding and responsibly judging the world of empirical facts, with the final aim not of serving gods but of developing and maturing man. For, as Karl Kerényi has well put it: "The Greek world is chiefly one of sunlight, though not the sun, but man, stands at its center." [36]

And so we come to the journey home, the return of Odysseus from the Underworld and the Island of the Sun.

9. *Calypso's Isle:* Miraculously, Odysseus on his bit of flotsam came coursing back between Scylla and Charybdis and for nine days more was borne upon the sea, to be cast, on the tenth, upon the beaches of the isle Ogygia, of Calypso of the braided tresses. And the lovely goddess, dwelling there in a cave amid soft meadows, flowers, vines, and birds, singing with a sweet voice while faring to and fro before her loom, weaving with a shuttle of gold, restored him. He dwelt with her eight years (an octave, an eon), assimilating the lessons learned of the first nymph, Circe of the braided tresses. And when the time came, at last, for his departure, Zeus sent the guiding god Hermes to bid her speed her initiate on his way; which she did, reluctantly. He built a raft, and when she had bathed him and clothed him in fair attire, she watched him push out to sea and fade away.

10. But Poseidon, angry still for the blinding of his son, the Cyclops (we are returning, level by level, station by station, through the waters of this deep, dark night-sea of the soul) sent a blast of storm to wreck the raft, and, tossed again into the brine, Odysseus swam for two days and nights.* He was presently flung ashore naked on *the Isle of the Phaeacians.* And there then followed the charming episode of the little princess, Nausicaa, with her company of maidens, coming to the beach, playing ball, the ball going into the water, the girls screaming, and the great man, prostrate in the

---

* Lucky for our athletic records that we do not take the myths of the Greeks as literally as we do the Bible!

bushes, waking to their cries. He appeared, holding a branch before him, and, after their moment of fright, the girls (the female principle again, but now in delightful childhood) gave him a cloth to wear and showed him the way to the palace.

That evening the great man from afar related to all, at dinner, the adventurers of his ten years; and the good and kind Phaeacians furnished both a ship and a fine crew to bear him home.

And they strewed for Odysseus a rug and a sheet of linen on the decks of the hollow ship in the hinder part thereof, that he might sleep sound. Then he too climbed aboard and laid him down in silence, while they sat upon the benches, every man in order, and unbound the hawser from the pierced stone. And so soon as they leant backwards and tossed the sea water with the oar blade, *a deep sleep fell upon his eyelids, a sound sleep, very sweet, and next akin to death.* . . .

11. "*. . . and the goodly Odysseus awoke where he slept on his native land.*"

Could it have been plainer said?

When, in the depths of the night, he had been approaching the palace of Circe, Hermes became Odysseus's guide, and when the time arrived to leave Calypso, again Hermes was the messenger: the guide of souls, lord of the caduceus and of the goddesses three. Whereas now that the long voyager had emerged from the night sea of mythic forms and again was on the plane of waking life, with its world of social realities (domestic realities now), his guide was to be *Athene*. She appeared to him on the beach in the guise of a young man, "most delicate, such as are the sons of kings. And she was wearing a well-wrought mantle that fell in two folds about her shoulders, and beneath her smooth feet she had sandals bound, and a javelin was in her hands. And Odysseus rejoiced when he saw her, came over against her, and uttering his voice, spake to her winged words. . . ."

Athene had already caused his son Telemachus to go forth from his mother's palace, which the visiting suitors suing for her hand, together with the maidservants, had been turning into a brothel and despoiling. She had come to the porch of the palace in the guise of a stranger; and the youth, who had been sitting with a heavy heart among the wooers, dreaming of his good father, saw the visitor and rose to greet her on the outer porch. After the dinner of that evening, she had advised him to go seek his father and had sent him on his way. She now, therefore, was to bring the two together.

And their meeting was to be in Odysseus's swineherd's hut.

So that, once again in this epic of departure, initiation, and return, we find that the archaic Eleusinian-Melanesian pig motif carries the great theme and frames the high moments of the merging of the two worlds of Eternity and Time, Death and Life, Father and Son.

The remaining episodes are as follows:

12. *Odysseus's arrival home:* Transformed by Athene into the semblance of a beggar (Noman, still), the returned master of the house was recognized only by his dog and his old, old nurse. The latter spied above his knee the old scar of a gash received from the tusk of a boar. (Compare Adonis and the boar, Attis and the boar, and, in Ireland, Diarmuid and the boar.) Hushing the nurse, Odysseus watched for some time the shameless behavior of the suitors and maidservants in his house; whereafter, and at last:

13. Penelope, offering to marry any one of those present who could draw the powerful bow of her spouse, set up a target of *twelve axes to be pierced.* None of the suitors could even string the bow. Several tried manfully. The recently come beggar then offered and was mocked. However, as we read:

He already was handling the bow, turning it every way about, and proving it on this side and on that, lest the worms might have eaten the horns when the lord of the bow was away. . . . And Odysseus of many counsels had lifted the great bow and viewed it on every side, and even as when a man that is skilled in the lyre and in minstralsy, easily stretches a cord about a new peg, after tying at either end the twisted sheep-gut, even so Odysseus straightway bent the great bow, all without effort, and took it in his right hand and proved the bowstring, which rang sweetly at the touch, in tone like a swallow. Then great grief came upon the wooers, and the color of their countenance was changed, and Zeus thundered loud showing forth his tokens. And the steadfast goodly Odysseus was glad thereat, in that the son of deep-counselling Cronus had sent him a sign. Then he caught up a swift arrow which lay by his table, bare, but the other shafts were stored within the hollow quiver, those whereof the Achaeans were soon to taste. He took and laid it on the bridge of the bow, and held the notch and drew the string, even from the settle whereon he sat, and with straight aim shot the shaft and missed not one of the axes, beginning from the first ax-handle, and the bronze-weighted shaft passed clean through and out at the last.

The solar hero having thus demonstrated his passage of the twelve signs and his lordship of the palace, he proceeded masterfully to the shooting down of the suitors. "And they writhed with their feet for a little space, but for no long while." After which, "Thy bed verily shall be ready," said the wisely wifely Penelope. "Come tell me of thine ordeal. For methinks the day will come when I must learn it, and timely knowledge is no hurt."

iv. The Polis

The leap from the dark age of Homer's barbaric warrior kings to the day of luminous Athens—which in the fifth century B.C. had become suddenly present, like a rapidly opening flower, as the most promising new thing in the world—is comparable to a passage without transition from boyhood dream (life mythologically compelled) to self-governed young manhood. The mind, having dared at last to slay the jangling old gold-plated dragon "Thou shalt!" had begun to give forth, with a sense of the novelty, its own lion roar. And as the blazing roar of the rising sun scatters the herds of stars, so the new life blew out the old, not for Greece alone, but (when it will one day have learned to open its eyes) for the world.

"Our form of government does not enter into rivalry with the institutions of others," declared Pericles (495?–429) in his celebrated funeral oration, extolling the life that the Athenians, in the Peloponnesian War, were at that time fighting to preserve.

We do not copy our neighbors, but are an example to them. It is true that we are called a democracy, for the administration is in the hands of the many and not of the few. But while the law secures equal justice to all alike in their private disputes, the claim of excellence is also recognized; and when a citizen is in any way distinguished, he is preferred to the public service, not as a matter of privilege, but as the reward of merit. Neither is poverty a bar, but a man may benefit his country whatever be the obscurity of his condition. There is no exclusiveness in our public life, and in our private intercourse we are not suspicious of one another, nor angry with our neighbor if he does what he likes. . . .

And we have not forgotten to provide for our weary spirits many relaxations from toil; we have regular games and sacrifices throughout the year; at home the style of our life is refined; and the delight that we daily feel in all these things helps to banish melancholy. Because of the greatness of our city the fruits of the whole earth flow in upon us; so that we enjoy the goods of other countries as freely as our own.

Then, again, our military training is in many respects superior to that of our adversaries. Our city is thrown open to the world, and we never expel a foreigner or prevent him from seeing or learning anything of which the secret if revealed to an enemy might profit him. We rely not upon management or trickery, but upon our own hearts and hands. And in the manner of education, whereas they from early youth are always undergoing laborious exercises which are to make them brave, we live at ease, and yet are equally ready to face the perils that they face. . . .

An Athenian citizen does not neglect the state because he takes care of his own household; and even those of us who are engaged in business have a very fair idea of politics. We alone regard a man who takes no interest in public affairs, not as a harmless, but as a useless character; and if few of us are originators, we are all sound judges of a policy. The great impediment to action is, in our opinion, not discussion, but the want of that knowledge which is gained by discussion preparatory to action. For we have a peculiar power of thinking before we act and of acting too, whereas other men are courageous from ignorance but hesitate upon reflection. And they are surely esteemed the bravest spirits who, having the clearest sense both of the pains and pleasures of life, do not on that account shrink from danger.

In doing good, again, we are unlike others; we make our friends by conferring, not by receiving favors. Now he who confers a favor is the firmer friend, because he would fain by kindness keep alive the memory of an obligation; but the recipient is colder in his feelings, because he knows that in requiring another's generosity he will not be winning gratitude but only paying a debt. We alone do good to our neighbors not upon calculation of interest, but in the confidence of freedom and in a frank and fearless spirit.[37]

The Greeks, after an ordeal of fire such as few could have survived, had beaten back decisively the numerically overwhelming hordes of Persia, not once alone, but four times, and were on the brink, now, of the most decisively productive century for the maturation of man's mind in the history of the world. And they were proud, as well they might be, of being men instead of slaves; of being the ones in the world to have learned, at last, how to live as men might live, not as the servants of a god, obedient to some conjured divine law, nor as the functionaries, trimmed to size, of some wheeling, ever-wheeling, cosmic order; but as rationally judging men, whose laws were voted on, not "heard"; whose arts were in celebration of humanity, not divinity (for even the gods now had become men); and consequently in whose sciences truth and not fancy was, at last, actually beginning to appear. A discovered cosmic order was not read as a design for the human order, but as its frame or limitation. Nor was society to be sanctified above the men within it. One can realize, after coming down through all these millenniums of religion, what a marvel of new thought the wonderful, earthly humanity of the Greek polis represented in the world. As Professor H. D. F. Kitto well says: "This certainly is what an ancient Greek would put first among his countryman's discoveries, that they had found out the best way to live." [38]

The impact of this turn upon the panorama of mythology is evident, first, in the extreme anthropomorphism of the Greek pantheon, and then in the vague yet always felt presence of the force of Moira, destiny, which limits even the gods. In contrast to the earlier Bronze Age view of a serene, mathematically ordered process defined by the rhythm of the planets, to the machinery of which all things are geared and as agents of which they serve, the Greek view suggests an indefinable circumscription, within the bounds of which both the gods and men work their individual wills, ever in danger of violating the undefined bounds and being struck down, yet with play enough—within limits—to achieve a comely realization of ends humanly conceived.

In contrast, also, to the biblical view (which becomes even more emphatic in Islam), where a freely willing personal god is antecedent to the order of the universe, himself unlimited by law, the Greek gods were themselves aspects of the universe—children of Chaos and the great Earth, just as men are. And even Chaos and the great Earth produced our world not through acts of creative will, but as seeds produce trees, out of the natural spontaneity of their substance. The secret of this spontaneity may be learned or sensed, in silence, in the mysteries and throughout life, but is not definable as the will, work, or divine plan of a personality.

It is true that in Homer's epics the great male Zeus stands above the action of the piece in a way that might seem at first to resemble the role of Yahweh. However, Zeus governs the field only in relation to man, being himself limited by the grain of destiny. Moreover, his power even within the field of his control is countered by other gods, indeed even by men who beguile other gods to their will. And in later writings, where a tendency appears to elevate Zeus beyond Moira, letting his personal will become destiny, the will then is not willful, but is known as natural law, and the personal accent of the god is so diminished that Zeus becomes merely a masculine name for what is otherwise known as Moira.

So that at no time in the history of properly Greek thought does the idea appear of a book of moral statutes revealed by a personal god from a sphere of being antecedent to and beyond the laws of nature. The type of scholarship characteristic of both the synagogue and the mosque, therefore, where the meticulous search for the last grain of meaning in scripture is honored above all science, never carried the Greeks away. In the great Levantine traditions such scholasticism is paramount and stands opposed to the science of the Greeks: for if the phenomenal world studied by science is but a function of the will of God, and God's will is subject to change, what good can there possibly be in the study of nature? The whole knowledge of the first world principle, namely the will of God, has been by the mercy of God made known to man in the book that he has furnished. Ergo: read, read, read, bury your nose in its blessed pages, and let pagans kiss their fingers at the moon.

The Greeks kissed their fingers at the moon—and men now will soon be riding on the moon, which has been found to be no deity after all. The rational study of the world as a field of facts to be observed began, as we all know, with the Greeks. For when they kissed their fingers at the moon, or at rosy-fingered dawn, they did not fall on their faces before it, but approached it, man to man, or man to goddess—and what they found was already what we have found: that all is indeed wonderful, yet submissive to examination.

Thales of Miletus, the first empirical philosopher on record and an old, old man when he died (c. 640–546 B.C.), is reputed to have believed that "water is the ἀρχή, the first principle or cause of all things," but also, that "all things are full of gods: the magnet is alive, for it has the power of moving iron."

Now it is a little difficult today to become excited about two statements of this kind, particularly since they seem to be saying little more than the myths had been saying for centuries, which is that all things are full of gods and emerged from the watery abyss. However, the novelty here is a new attitude: not faith or passive acceptance of a received doctrine, but active, reasoning inquiry. And the implications of this become clear when it is remarked that Thales' pupil Anaximander (c. 611–547 B.C.) did not repeat the ideas of his master, but said something entirely different; namely, that the ἀρχή is the ἄπειρον, "the infinite or boundless": neither water nor any other of the elements, but a substance different from all, which is infinite and from which arise all the heavens and the worlds within them.

In the infinite are the pairs-of-opposites: moist and dry, warm and cold, etc. Their alternation is what produces the world. "And back into that from which they have taken their rise things pass away once more, which," declares Anaximander, "is as it should be;

for thereby they make reparation and satisfaction for their injustice to each other in the course of time."

In the winter, cold commits injustice against heat; in the summer, heat against cold: but a principle of justice keeps the balance. The earth hangs free in space, supported by nothing, but held in place because equidistant from everything. Celestial spheres are wheels of fire; thunder and lightning, blasts of wind. Life emerged from the moist element as it was evaporated by fire, and man, in the beginning, was like a fish.

With Anaximander we have stepped far indeed from the earlier, personifying mode of myth. And with another pupil of Thales still another view is proposed: The ἀρχή is air, the breath, said Anaximenes (fl. c. 600). By virtue of rarefication and condensation it differs in different substances: dilated, air becomes fire; condensed, cloud, water, earth, and stone.

We must note that in India as well there was at this time a development of philosophical thought, best known to us in the Sankhya system and the classificatory science of the Jains; [39] and there too a rational inquiry was undertaken for the primal substance or element. It was identified variously as space or ether (ākāśa) from which the elements of air, fire, water, and earth are condensed in that order; as breath (prāṇa); as the duad of soul and non-soul (jīva—ajīva); as a numinous power (brahman); as the void (śunyatā). . . . Moreover, a classification of all beings, including gods, according to the number of their senses, a notion of the evolution and devolution of forms, and the correlation of all this with an interior, psychological science, promised greatly for an extremely refined development of objective research.

However, in India the principle of disinterest never gained the day over that of practical application, and particularly application to psychological and sociological ends. The brilliant cosmologies, developed by what must have been a great movement of creative thought (possibly c. 700–600 B.C.), had become, even in the Buddha's time (563–483 B.C.), mere icons: images for religious contemplation, used to move the mind *away from,* not toward, the world. Whatever spirit of inquiry may have brought them forth had already solidified into a static tradition of repetition by rote. And in the normal manner of religion, cosmologies were retained and taught to the uncritical young even when the known facts refuted them. R.I.P., therefore, to an Oriental science.

In the Greek world the trend of thought most closely suggesting that of India was in the line of the Dionysian-Orphic movement, which culminated in the sixth century B.C. in the militant puritanism of the Buddha's older contemporary, Pythagoras (c. 582–c. 500 B.C.). In the earlier Orphic system a negative attitude had been assumed toward the world. According to the great Orphic myth, man was represented as a compound of the ashes of Dionysus and the Titans.[40] The soul (Dionysus factor) was divine, but the body (Titan factor) held it in bondage. The watchword, therefore, was *soma sema,* "the body, a tomb." And a system both of thought and of practice, exactly paralleling that of Indian asceticism, was communicated by initiated masters to little circles of devotees. The soul, it was declared, returned repeatedly to life, bound to the wheel of rebirth (compare the Sanskrit *saṁsāra*). Through asceticism (Sanskrit, *tapas*), however, the body could be purged of its Titan dross (Sanskrit, *nirjarā,* "shedding") and the soul released (Sanskrit, *mokṣa,* "release"). Also, rituals fostering meditation on the godly factor were of help (Sanskrit, *bhakti,* "devotion"). And when, at last, in rapture (*samādhi*), the initiate cleaved to his own intrinsic being (*svasvarūpam*), he was divine (*Śivāhaṁ*, "I am Shiva").

> Where midnight Zagreus roves, I rove;
> I have endured his thunder-cry;
> Fulfilled his red and bleeding feasts;
> Held the Great Mother's mountain flame:
> I am Set Free and named by name
> A Bacchos of the Mailed Priests

> Robed in pure white I have borne me clean
> From man's vile birth and coffined clay,
> And exiled from my lips away
> Touch of all meat where Life hath been.[41]

The disciplines included vegetarianism, as the last two lines inform us; and if we are to read literally the earlier verse, "I have . . . fulfilled his red and bleeding feasts," there must have been a ritual "eating of raw flesh" (*omophagia*) in the Orphic as well as in the Dionysian cult. It appears also that a sacred marriage of some kind was either enacted or simulated. We hear, first, of the veiling of the neophyte as a bride; then of the bearing into his presence of a liknon, a shovel-shaped basket made of wicker, containing a phallus and filled with fruits (compare above, Figure 7), and finally a snake of gold was let down into the bosom and taken from below: the god, as father of himself, reborn of the devotee.

I cannot find any *fundamental* difference between any of this and the Indian Jain-Sankhya-Vedantic line of the teaching of release, unless it be that in Greece the doctrine never gained the field, but remained secondary and at odds with the generally positive spirit of the culture. There have been those who sought to show that the movement stemmed from India, but the likelihood is not great. More likely is a common source in the archaic Bronze Age order, which in its last phases underwent the negative transformation that I have termed *The Great Reversal*,[42] when a literature of lament arose from Egypt to Mesopotamia, following centuries of invasion, murder, and rapine. The center of religious focus then turned for many from this world to the next, and disciplines that in earlier times had been directed to an achievement of perfection here became translated into disciplines of escape.

The name Orpheus itself belongs to the oldest level of Greek names: those ending in -eus (for example, Atreus). Such are pre-Homeric. Early representations show him singing, drawing animals to him by the power of his song; also as a festival singer, whose listeners—significantly—are men. Dr. Karl Kerényi plausibly suggests that the basic idea is of an initiator whose power transforms even the wildest creatures, animals and men who live in the wilderness. Such a figure would have been associated with the initiation of young men—in the wilds of nature, excluding women. There something significant was disclosed to them in music and song that delivered them from their blood-spilling savagery and gave a deep sense to the ceremonies of transit from immaturity to adulthood. And the announcer of this mystery played the lyre, but was not a mere singer.

Later on, in the period of Greek urban life, detached from the earlier ground of the tribal-bound secret men's rites, the so-called Ορφεοπελεταί, "initiating priests of Orpheus," revised their spiritual arts to the new spiritual needs. And their modes of presentation now were divided into a lower, largely ritualistic category, and a higher, purely spiritual, philosophical one, where the initiators were, indeed, philosophers: first the Pythagoreans, but then others also: Empedocles and onward to our dear and well-known Platonic banqueteers.[43]

In the teaching of Pythagoras the philosophic quest for the ἀρχή, the first cause and principle of all things, was carried to a consideration of the problem of the magic of the Orphic lyre itself, by which the hearts of men are quelled, purified, and restored to their part in God. His conclusion was that the ἀρχή is number, which is audible in music, and by a principle of resonance touches—and adjusts thereby—the tuning of the soul. This idea is fundamental to the arts of both India and the Far East and may go back to the age of the Pyramids. However, as far as we know, it was Pythagoras who first rendered it systematically, as a principle by which art, psychology, philosophy, ritual, mathematics, and even athletics were to be recognized as aspects of a single science of harmony. Moreover, his approach was entirely Greek. Measuring lengths of string of the same tension, stopped so as to sound differing notes, he discovered the ratios, 2:1 for the octave, 3:2, for the fifth, and 4:3, for the third. And then, as Aristotle states, the Pythagoreans supposed the elements of numbers to be the elements of all things, and the whole heaven to be a musical scale and number.[44] So that, finally, knowledge, not rapture, became the way to realization; and to the ancient ways of myth and ritual art there was joined harmoniously the dawning enterprise of Greek science, for the new life.

THE AGE OF THE GREAT CLASSICS

THE PERSIAN PERIOD:

5 3 9 – 3 3 1   B . C .

++

I. Ethical Dualism

It was in November 1754 that a young Frenchman, Abraham Hyacinthe Anquetil-Duperron (1731–1805), enlisted as a private in the French army to sail for India, where he hoped to find—and where he did find—what remained in the world of the works of the fabled Persian prophet Zoroaster. In 1771 his publication of the Zend Avesta appeared; and the progress that Oriental scholarship has since made toward an understanding of the relationship of those texts to the doctrines of both Christianity and Islam has been—though extremely slow—secure and convincing.

The Persian prophet's words have come down preserved like gems in the setting of a later liturgical work known as the Yasna, "Book of the Offering," which is a priestly compilation of prayers, confessions, invocations, and the like, arranged according to the rituals in which they were employed. The chapters are in three divisions: Chapters 1–27, priestly invocations; Chapters 28–34, 43–51, and 53, the Gathas of the Prophet (sermons, songs, and revelations, in a dialect considerably earlier than that of the remainder of the work); and Chapters 35–42, 52, and 54–72, again priestly invocations, revealing a more highly systematized theology than that of the basic Gathas themselves.

Professor L. H. Mills, in the introduction of his translation of the Yasna, suggests for the Gathas a period roughly between c. 1500 and 900 B.C.[1] Professor Eduard Meyer dates the prophet c. 1000 B.C.[2] And Professor Hans Heinrich Schaeder, observing that the social order represented in the Gathas sets the prophet in a world of "petty regional princes, who are obviously not subject to a common overlord," assigns to him a date preceding the rise of the Median Empire in the seventh century B.C.[3] But, on the other hand, there is an influential school that would equate a certain King Vishtaspa named in the Gathas [4] with King Darius's father, Hystaspes, and so place the prophet as late as c. 550 B.C.[5] The problem is extremely complicated, with arguments and arguers on every side. However, the evidence for the antiquity of the language, social order, and religious atmosphere cannot be lightly—or even ponderously—brushed aside. There it stands. And, as the masterful Professor Meyer, in learned amazement, remarks: "That scholars still should exist who believe it possible, or even discussable, that King Vishtaspa [of the Gathas] should be identified with Darius's father Hystaspes, is one of those incomprehensible anomalies that have been particularly prominent and bothersome in this field, and which only prove how remote from many of our leading philologists all understanding must be of history and historical thinking." [6]

Meyer has termed Zoroaster "the first personality to have worked creatively and formatively upon the course of religious history." [7] The pharaoh Ikhnaton was, of course, earlier, but "his solar monotheism did not endure"; [8] whereas, throughout the entire history of Occidental ethical religiosity—in contrast to the metaphysical religiosity of the Orient—the great themes first sounded in the Gathic dialogues of the God of Truth, Ahura Mazda, with his prophet, Zoroaster, can be heard echoed and re-echoed, in Greek, Latin, Hebrew and Aramaean, Arabic, and every tongue of the West.

The first novelty of this radically new teaching lay in its treatment in purely ethical terms of the ultimate nature and destiny of both mankind and the world. In the Orient of India no attempt was ever made to bring into play in the religious field any principle of fundamental world reform or renovation. The cosmic order of eons, ever cycling in a mighty round of ineluctably returning ages —from eternity, through eternity—would never, by any act of man, be changed from its majestic way. The sun, the moon, the stars in their courses, the various animal species, and the orders of the castes of the orthodox Indian social system would remain forever established in their modes; and truth, virtue, rapture, and true being lay in doing, as before, whatever had been traditionally done—without protest, without ego, without judgment—precisely as taught. The individual had, therefore, but two courses: one, to accept the entire system and strive to play his part as an actor in the play, competently, without hope or fear; and the other, to resign, disengage himself, and let the play of fools run on. The ultimate Being of beings (or, in Buddhist terms, the Void of the phantasmagoria of appearance) lay beyond the reach of ethical judgment—indeed, beyond all pairs-of-opposites: good and evil, true and false, being and non-being, life and death. So that the wise (as those were termed who had at last arrived, through many lives, at the point of recognizing the futility of hope), "scorched," as we read, "with the fire of an endless round of birth, death, and the rest—like one whose head is on fire rushing to a lake—" [9] either retired to the forest, there to plunge beyond the non-being of being, or else remained in the fire, to be burned willingly to nought through an unremitting giving of themselves, without hope, but with compassion, to futility.

The orientation of such an order of thought was metaphysical; not ethical or rational, but trans-ethical, trans-rational. And in the Far East, as well as in India, whether in the mythic fields of Shinto, Taoism, and Confucianism, or in the Mahayana, the world was not to be reformed, but only known, revered, and its laws obeyed. Personal and social disorder stemmed from departure from those cosmic laws, and reform could be achieved only by a return to the unchanging root.

In Zoroaster's new mythic view, on the other hand, the world, as it was, was corrupt—not by nature but by accident—and to be reformed by human action. Wisdom, virtue, and truth lay, therefore, in engagement, not in disengagement. And the crucial line of decision between ultimate being and non-being was ethical. For the primal character of creation had been light, wisdom, and truth, into which, however, darkness, deception, and the lie had entered, which it was now man's duty to eradicate through his own virtue in thought, word, and deed.

Specifically, according to this teaching, two contrary powers made and maintain the world in which men live: first, Ahura Mazda, the Lord of Life, Wisdom, and Light, Creator of the Righteous Order; but then, too, his antagonist, Angra Mainyu, the Demon of the Lie, who, when the world had been made, corrupted every particle of its being. These two powers are coeval; for they have existed from all eternity. However, not both are eternal, for the Demon of the Lie is to be undone at the end of time, when truth alone will prevail. Thus we note, beside the primary novelty of the ethical posture of the Zoroastrian system, a second novelty in its progressive view of cosmic history. This is not the old, ever-revolving cycle of the archaic Bronze Age mythologies, but a sequence, once and for all, of creation, fall, and progressive redemption, to culminate in a final, decisive, irrefragable victory of the One Eternal God of Righteousness and Truth.

"Yea," we read, in the words of the prophet,

> of the world's two primary powers, I will proclaim; of whom the more bountiful thus addressed the hurtful: "We are at one neither in our thoughts nor in our commands, understandings nor beliefs, deeds, consciences, nor souls."
> I will declare, thus, the world's first teaching, which the all-wise Ahura Mazda has proclaimed to me. And those of you who will not fulfill and obey this holy word, as I now conceive and proclaim it, the issue of life will be in woe.[10]

A third teaching is of certain powers proceeding from the Creator, which awaken their counterparts in man. Foremost of these are the archangels Good Mind and Righteous Order, to whom Perfect Sovereignty and Divine Piety bring support, accompanied by Excellence and Immortality. Opposed to these are the powers of the Lie, known as Evil Mind and False Appearance, Cowardice, Hypocrisy, Misery, and Extinction. These were later systematized as opposed hierarchies of beneficent Amesha Spentas and malignant Daevas—whence the Christian orders of angels and devils were derived. However, in the Gathas there is no sign yet of any such systematized angelology; the various powers are named and called upon almost without distinction, to activate the spirit of the devotee. Furthermore, they are both "god" and "of God"; and they are matched in the "Better Mind" of each man.

> O Great Creator, Living Lord! Inspired by Thy Kindly Mind, I approach You Powers, and beseech of Thee * to grant me as a bountiful gift—furthering the worlds both of body and of mind—those attainments derived of Divine Righteousness, by means of which that personified Righteousness within us may conduct those who receive it to Glorious Beatitude.[11]

Of high importance throughout is the idea of individual free will and decision. One is not to follow rote and command, like a herding beast, but to act as a man with a mind. We read the celebrated verse:

> Hear ye then with your ears; see the bright flames with the eyes of the Better Mind. It is for a decision as to religions, man and man, each individually for himself. Before the great effort of the cause, awake ye to our teaching.[12]

Each having chosen his cause, he must cleave to it, not in thought alone, but in word and deed as well. "He who would bend his mind till it attains to the better and more holy," wrote the prophet, "must pursue the Good Religion closely in word and act. His will and wish must be consistent with his chosen creed and fealty." [13] And when the course of life is run, the soul at the Chinvat Bridge, the Bridge of Judgment, learns the nature of its earned reward.

There is a memorable representation of this bridge in a late Zoroastrian work known as "The Vision of Arda Viraf," composed at some undetermined date during the late Sassanian period of post-Alexandrian, Zoroastrian restoration (226–641 A.D.). The document gives an account of an ardent visionary's Dantean visit in trance, while yet alive, to the other world.

* Plural You and singular Thou and Thee interchange throughout.

Taking the first footstep with the Good Thought, the second footstep with the Good Word, and the third footstep with the Good Deed, I came [wrote the visionary at the beginning of his account] to the Chinvat Bridge, the very wide and strong, created by Ahura Mazda. And when I came up there, I saw a soul of the departed, which in the first three nights remained seated upon its body, uttering these words of the Gatha: "Well is he who has caused his own benefit to become the benefit of another."

And in those three nights there came to that soul as much benefit, comfort, and enjoyment as it had beheld in the world, which was in proportion to the comfort, happiness, and joy it had caused. Whereupon, when the third dawn arrived, that pious soul departed into the sweet scent of trees, the scent that had graced his nose among the living, and that wind of fragrance came to him from the south, the quarter of God.

And there stood before him his own Religion and Deeds, in the form of a damsel, a beautiful appearance, matured in virtue, with prominent breasts; that is to say, her breasts swelled downward, which is charming to heart and soul. And her form was as brilliant as the sight of it delightful and the observation of it desirable. The soul at the bridge asked the damsel, "Who art thou? What person art thou? Never in the world of the living did I see any damsel of more elegant form and more beautiful body than thine." To which she answered, "O Youth of good thoughts, good words, good deeds, and good religion, I am your own actions. It is because of your own good will and acts that I am as great and good, sweet scented, triumphant and undistressed as what you see. For in the world you intoned the Gathas, consecrated the good water, tended the fire, and proffered honor to the pious who came to you from far and from near. Though buxom in the beginning, I was made more so by yourself; though virtuous, more virtuous, though seated on a resplendent throne, I am enthroned more resplendently through you; and though exalted, I am made more exalted through you— through your good thoughts, good words, and good deeds." [14]

When he had observed this beautiful meeting of the soul with its Fravashi (its unearthly alter-ego, poetically called its "Spirit of the Road") the visiting Arda Viraf was taken by the hand by two angels, Divine Obedience and the Flaming Fire of Thought; the bridge widened; and he went across, to where other angels, also, gave protection. Moreover, numerous Spirits of the Road of the Just, who were there waiting for their living counterparts, bowed to him in greeting. And there was an angel, Justice, who bore in his hand a yellow golden balance, wherewith to weigh the pious and the wicked. His two guardians said to Arda Viraf, "Come, let us show you heaven and hell: the place of the true and the place of the false: the reality of God and the archangels, the non-reality of Angra Mainyu and his demons: the resurrection of the dead, and the future body."

The two guardians, Divine Obedience and the Flaming Fire of Thought, led the visionary first to a place where he saw the souls of people who remained ever in the same position. "Who are these?" he asked. "And why do they so remain?" To which his two guardians answered: "They call this place the Ever Stationary. The souls here will remain till the resurrection of the future body. They are the souls of those in whom good works and sin were equal. Their punishment is cold or heat from the revolution of the atmosphere; and they have no other pain."

The visionary and his guides advanced a first step, to the Star Tract, the place where good thoughts receive their reward. The radiance of the souls there ever increased, like the glittering of stars; and their throne and seat, beneath the radiance, were splendorous, full of glory. "What place," asked the voyager, "is this? What people, these?" And he was told: "These are the souls of those who, in the world, offered no prayers, intoned no Gathas, failed to contract next-of-kin marriages, and exercised no sovereignty, rulership, or chieftainship, but through other good works became pious."

The Zoroastrian Dante passed a second step, to the Moon Tract, where good works find their reward. "These are the souls," he was told, "who, in the world, offered no prayers, intoned no Gathas, failed to contract next-of-kin marriages, but through other works came hither; and their brightness matches the moon."

His third step was to the Sun Tract, where good deeds find their reward; and there was there the radiance called the Highest of the Highest, where he saw the pious on thrones and carpets made of gold. They were as bright as the brightness of the sun. "These are the souls," he was told, "who, in the world, exercised good sovereignty, rulership, and chieftainship."

He passed on, a fourth step, to the place of radiance called All Glorious, where there came to meet him souls of the departed who asked blessing, offering praise, and said, "How is it, O pious one, that you come to us? You have come from that perishable, evil world to this imperishable, untroubled world. Taste, therefore, immortality; for here you see bliss eternal."

From a throne of gold the archangel Good Mind arose. He took the visitor's hand, and with the words, "Good thought, good word, good deed," brought him into the midst of God, the archangels, and the blessed, besides the Spirits of the Road of Zoroaster and his sons, as well as other leaders and upholders of religion, brilliant and excellent beyond any he had ever seen.

"Behold! Ahura Mazda!" said the archangel Good Mind; and Arda Viraf offered worship. But when Ahura Mazda spoke, he was amazed; for though he saw a light and heard a voice and understood, "This is Ahura Mazda," he saw no body. "Arda Viraf, salutation!" said the voice. "And welcome! You have come from that perishable world to this pure place of illumination." Ahura Mazda addressed the two guides. "Take Arda Viraf. Show him the place of reward of the pious and the punishment of the wicked."

He was taken, therefore, to the place of the liberal, who walk adorned, and of those who had intoned the Gathas. They were in gold-embroidered and silver-embroidered raiment. He saw the souls of those who had married their next of kin; those of the good rulers and monarchs; the great and truthful speakers; women of excellent thoughts, words, and deeds, submissive to control, who had considered their husbands lords, had honored water, fire, earth, trees, cattle, sheep, and all other good creations of God, performing the rituals of religion, practicing without doubt. These were in clothing of gold and silver, set with gems. There were the souls, also, of those who had known the scriptures by heart, who had solemnized the rites; warriors and kings whose excellent arms were of gold, set with gems, beautifully embossed. He saw the souls of those who had killed many noxious creatures in the world; agriculturalists in thick, majestic clothing, offering praise before the spirits of water and earth, trees and cattle; artisans who, in the world, had well served their rulers and chieftains; shepherds who had preserved their flocks from the wolf, thief, and tyrant; householders and justices, heads of village families, teachers and inquirers, interceders and peace seekers, and those pre-eminent for piety: all seated upon thrones, great, splendid, and embellished, in a glorious light of space, much perfumed with sweet basil, full of glory and every joy, without satiation.

Then I came [wrote the voyager in his account of his great vision] to a great and gloomy stream, dreadful as hell, on which there were many souls and Spirits of the Road; and some of these were not able to cross, some crossed only with difficulty, others, however, with ease. And I inquired: "What stream is this? And who are these people so distressed?" Divine Obedience and the Flaming Fire of Thought said to me, "This stream is the river of tears that men shed in lamentation for their dead. They shed those tears unlawfully, which swell into this stream. Those unable to cross are those for whom there was much weeping; those who cross more easily are those for whom less was made. Speak, when you return to the world, and say, 'When in the world, do not make unlawful lamentation; for of it may come much harm and difficulty to your departed.'"

And Arda Viraf then returned to the Chinvat Bridge.

But now [he tells] I saw a soul of one of the wicked, to whom, in those three nights of sitting above his corpse, there was shown so much distress as never had been seen by him in the world. And I asked, "Whose soul is this?" A cold, stinking wind came to meet him from the quarter of the demons, the north, and he saw coming therein his own Religion and Deeds in the form of a profligate woman, naked, decayed, gaping, bandy-legged, lean-hipped and infinitely blotchy, so that blotch was joined to blotch; and indeed, she was the most hideous, noxious, filthy creature, and stinking.

The wicked soul spoke thus: "Who art thou, than whom I have never seen creation of the God of Truth and Demon of the Lie uglier, filthier, and more stinking?"

"I," she said, "am your own bad actions, O youth of evil thoughts, words, deeds, and religion. It is because of your will and actions that I am hideous and vile, iniquitous, diseased, rotten, foul-smelling, miserable and distressed, as you see. For when you saw anyone performing rites, in the praise, prayer, and service of God, preserving and protecting water, fire, cattle, trees, and the other good creations, you, on the other hand, did the will of the Lie and his demons, with improper acts. And when you saw one who provided hospitable reception, with deserved gifts and charity, for the good and worthy who came from far and near, you, on the contrary, were avaricious and shut up your door. So that though I have been unholy, I have been made by you more unholy; though I have been frightful, I have been made by you more frightful; though I have been tremulous, I have been made by you more tremulous; and though I am settled in the northern region of the demons, I have been settled by you farther north: as a consequence of those evil thoughts, words, and deeds that you have practiced."

Then that wicked soul advanced the first step, to the tract of Evil Thoughts; second, to the tract of Evil Words; and third, to the tract of Evil Deeds. But the angels took my hand and I went along, through all, unhurt, beholding cold, heat, drought and stench, to such a degree as I had never seen or heard of in the world.

I saw the greedy jaws of hell: the most frightful pit, descending, in a very narrow, fearful crevice and in darkness so murky that I was forced to feel my way, amid such a stench that all whose nose inhaled that air, struggled, staggered, and fell, and in such confinement that existence seemed impossible. Each one thought, "I am alone"; and when a mere three days had elapsed supposed that the end of the nine thousand years of time had come, when time would cease and the resurrection of the body occur. "The nine thousand years are run," he would think, "yet, I am not released." In that place even the lesser noxious creatures are as high as mountains, and these so tear, seize, and worry the souls of the wicked as would be unworthy of a dog. But I passed easily thereby in the guidance of Obedience and Thought.

I saw the soul of a man through whose fundament a snake went in, like a beam, and came forth out of the mouth; and many other snakes ever seized his limbs. "What sin," I inquired, "was committed by this body whose soul suffers so severe a punishment?" "This," I was told, "is the soul of a man who, in the world, committed sodomy."

A woman's soul I saw, to whom they gave to drink one cupful after another of the impurity and filth of men, I asked, "What sin was committed by the body whose soul thus suffers?" "Having failed to abstain," they replied, "this wicked woman approached water and fire during menstruation." I saw, also, the soul of a man, the skin of whose head was being flayed . . . who, in the world, had slain a pious man. I saw the soul of a man into whose mouth they poured continually the menstrual discharge of women, while he cooked and ate his own child. . . . "While in the world," I was told, "that wicked man had intercourse with a menstruating woman."

The sights of this terrible pit of pain continued. A woman hung by her breasts, who, in the world, had been adulterous, gnawed from below by noxious beasts; there were men and women, variously gnawed, who, in the world had walked without shoes, gone without proper clothing, or had urinated standing; one whose tongue was out upon his jaw, being consumed by noxious creatures, who, in the world, had been a slanderer; then a miser, stretched upon a rack, upon whose whole body a thousand brutal demons trampled, smiting him with violence; women digging into hills with their breasts, who had denied milk to their infants; others gashing their breasts with iron combs, who had been untrue to their husbands; one who continually licked a hot stove with her tongue, who, in the world, had been abusive to her lord; many who hung by one leg, through all the apertures of whose bodies frogs, scorpions, snakes, ants, flies, worms, and other noxious creatures went and came, who, in life, had been untrue; and then a man who stood up in the form of a serpent, as a column, but with human head, who had committed apostasy. . . .

There is unpleasant food for thought in the consideration that both in this vision of Arda Viraf and in Dante's Divine Comedy the agonies of hell are far more vividly described, with infinitely more imagination, than the bliss of paradise, where all that we ever see are various amplitudes of light, and mild companies, sitting, standing, or strolling, very beautifully clothed. The really horrible chronicle of torment continues for pages; and when the whole course of the vile and stinking pit has been viewed: "Then," writes the visionary, "then I saw that Evil Spirit, the deadly world destroyer, whose religion is wickedness, ever ridiculing and mocking those in hell, to whom he called, 'Why did you ever do my work and, thinking not of your Creator, practice only my will?' "

> After which [as he then relates] my two angelic guides, Divine Obedience and the Flaming Fire of Thought, brought me out of that dark and terrible, awful place to Eternal Light and the place of assembly of Ahura Mazda and his angels. And when I wished to offer homage, Ahura Mazda said to me graciously, "A perfect servant you have been, O pious Arda Viraf. You have come as a messenger from my worshipers on earth. Go back to them now, and as you have seen and understood, so speak truly to the world. Say to my worshipers, Arda Viraf, 'There is but one way of piety, the way of the prime religion; the other ways are no ways. Take the one way that is piety and turn not from it in prosperity, or in adversity, or in any wise; but practice good thoughts, good words, and good deeds. And be aware, also, of this: that cattle are dust, the horse is dust, silver and gold are dust, and the body of man is dust. He alone mingles not with dust who, in the world, gives praise to piety and performs duties and good works.' You are perfect, Arda Viraf, go and prosper: for every purity and purification that you perform and keep, being mindful of God, I know, I know them all."

"And when I had heard these words," the marvelous work concludes, "I made a profound bow to the Creator, Ahura Mazda; after which those two great angels, Divine Obedience and the Flaming Fire of Thought, conveyed me bravely and successfully to this carpeted place where I now write.

"May the glory of the good religion of the Mazdayasnians triumph!

"Completed in health, pleasure, and joy." [15]

II. The Cosmic Fall and Renovation

The Persian myth of Creation, Fall, and World Renovation, which has influenced fundamentally not only the Messianic ideas of Judaism and Christianity, but also their parody in the Marxian proletariat apocalypse of the closing chapter of the first volume of *Das Kapital,* is itself preserved only in a late Pahlavi (Middle Persian) work, the Bundahish, "The Book of Creation," which, like "The Book of Arda Viraf," was a production of the late Sassanian restoration, 226–641 A.D. It was not completed in its present form until c. 881 A.D.[16] Consequently it includes much that is both of later date and of a more popular order of belief than the prophecies from which its main theme of the resolution of the cosmic conflict of good and evil has been derived. However, as the old master of Persian scholarship, James Darmesteter, has observed of the Zoroastrian tradition: "There has been no other great belief in the world that ever left such poor and meager monuments of its past splendor." [17] The ravages, first of Alexander the Great (331 B.C.), and then, after painful reconstruction, of the zealots of Islam (641 A.D.), have left for later centuries pitifully little, even of ruins, of the once great structure of imperial Persian religion.

According, then, to the Bundahish:

The two Creators through whose dialectic everything in this world has been wrought, so that it shows in every part a nature that is both good and evil, in conflict with itself and characterized by disorder, were existent from all eternity: but they are not both to remain for all eternity. In the end, which is inevitable, the dark and evil power, Angra Mainyu, with all his brood, is to be destroyed forever in a crisis of world renovation to which all history tends— and to the realization of which every individual is categorically summoned.

> For thus [in the words of the prophet Zoroaster himself] are the two primeval spirits who, as a pair, yet each independent in his action, have been known from of old. They are a Better and a Worse, as to thought, to word, to deed. And between these two let the wisely choosing choose aright. So, choose, then, not as evil doers! And may we thus be such as those who bring about the great renovation and make this world progressive, till its perfection shall have been achieved.[18]

Ahura Mazda, through omniscience (we read in the Bundahish), knew a priori, from all eternity, that Angra Mainyu existed; but the latter, because of his backward, a posteriori, knowledge, was not aware of the existence of the light. Creation commenced when Ahura Mazda produced spiritually certain spiritual beings who remained for three thousand years in a perfectly spiritual state: motionless, without thought, and with intangible bodies. At the close of that time, the power of darkness, rising, perceived the glory and, because of the malice of his nature desirous only of destruction, he rushed to annihilate the light. Its power he found greater than his own, however, and, returning chagrined to his abyss, he created fiends there, who, in concert, rose against the light.

Then the Lord of Light and Truth, through omniscience knowing what the end would be, went to meet the monster of the Lie, proposing peace. The latter thought: "Ahura Mazda, being powerless, offers peace." But Ahura Mazda said: "You are neither omniscient nor omnipotent; hence, can neither undo me nor cause my creatures to defect. However, let us appoint a period of nine thousand years of intermingling conflict." For he knew that for three thousand years all would be according to his own will; for three there would be an intermingling of the two wills; and in the last three thousand years, following the birth of Zoroaster, the will of the other would be broken. Together with the first three thousand of the stationary state, these nine would compose in all twelve thousand years. And Angra Mainyu, not knowing, because of his backward knowledge, was content with this arrangement. He returned to his abyss, and the play commenced.

Ahura Mazda, as a first step, produced Good Mind and Sky; the other, Evil Mind and the Lie. Good Mind yielded the Light of the World, the Good Religion, Righteous Order, Perfect Sovereignty, Divine Piety, Excellence, and Immortality. Whereafter, as second step, the lord Mazda produced the army of the constellations with four captains in the quarters, the moon, the sun, and then water, earth, plants, animals, and man.

Angra Mainyu, meanwhile, had returned to sleep. But at the end of those three thousand years a female fiend, Jahi (Menstruation), appeared, and she shouted at him: "Arise, O father of us all! For I shall now cause in the world that contention from which the misery and injury of Ahura Mazda and his Archangels are to proceed. I shall empoison the righteous man, the laboring ox, the water, plants, fire, and all creation." Whereupon Angra Mainyu, starting up, kissed her on the forehead, and the pollution called menstruation appeared on the demoness. "What is your wish," he asked, "that I may give it to you?" "A man is my wish," she answered; "give it to me." The form of Angra Mainyu, which had been of a loglike lizard, thereupon changed to that of a young man of fifteen years; and this brought to him Jahi's zeal.

Angra Mainyu, then raging with malice, sprang up like a snake at the constellations, against which he flung the moving planets, so that the fixed order of the sky was destroyed. His second venture was against water, upon which drought descended. Next, into the earth he poured the serpent, scorpion, frog, and lizard, so that not so much as the point of a needle remained free of noxious things. The earth shook and mountain ranges rose. Angra Mainyu pierced it, entering to its center, which passage now is the road to hell. And fourth, he desiccated the plants. But the Angel of Vegetation, pounding these small, mixed them with water that the Angel of Rain poured down. Then over the whole world plants sprang up like hairs on the heads of men. And from the germs of all these plants the Tree of All Seeds arose in the middle of the world ocean, which is of a single root, without branches, without bark, juicy and sweet. And the griffon bird rests upon it, which, when he flies forth from it, scatters seed into the water, which then is rained back to earth with the rain.

Moreover, in the vicinity of this first tree a second, the Gao-kerena, White Haoma (Sanskrit, *Soma*) Tree arose, which counteracts old age, revives the dead, and bestows immortality. At its root Angra Mainyu formed a lizard for its injury; but to keep away that lizard ten kar-fish were created, which at all times circle round its root in such a way that the head of one is turned continually toward the lizard. And between those two trees there rose a mountain with 9,999,000 myriads of caves, to which is given the function of protecting the waters; so that water streams from its caves in channels to all lands.

And as to the nature of plants: before the coming of Angra Mainyu none had thorn or bark upon it, but, like the Tree of All Seeds, they were sweet and smooth.

Now the fifth of Angra Mainyu's sallies was against the Sole-Created Ox, the primal beast, which, on the bank of the river Daiti, in Eran Vej, the central land of the seven lands of earth, was grazing in the form of a cow, white and brilliant as the moon, when the enemy came rushing like a fly. Avarice, want, pain, hunger, disease, lust, and lethargy were diffused into the beast; and when that Sole-Created Ox passed away, it fell to the right. Its soul came out, stood before it, and cried to Ahura Mazda, as loudly as ten thousand men when all cry out at once. "In whom, then, has the guardianship of creatures been confided, since ruin has broken upon the earth? Where is the man of whom you once declared: 'I will produce him, that he may teach the doctrine of Care'?"

The Lord of Light replied: "You are ill, O Soul of the Ox, of the illness caused by Angra Mainyu. If the time had come to have produced that man upon the earth, Angra Mainyu would have had no effect."

The Soul of the Ox proceeded to the Star Tract and cried in the same manner; to the Moon Tract; to the Sun Tract. But there the Spirit of the Road of the Prophet Zoroaster was shown to her, and she was appeased. She said: "I will nourish the creatures of the earth." She had renewed her consent to an earthly creation in the world.

Meanwhile, when the body of the Sole-Created Ox had fallen to the right, its seed, delivered to the moon, had become purified in moonlight. From that purified seed a male and a female animal then arose, after which pairs appeared on earth of two hundred and eighty-two species: birds in the air, quadrupeds on land, fish in the waters. And where the marrow of the Ox came out, fifty-five kinds of grain grew and twelve kinds of healing plant. From its horns grew peas, from its nose the leek, from its blood the vine of which wine is made; from its lungs the rue-like herbs, and from the midst of its heart thyme.

The sixth attack of Angra Mainyu, then, was against the first-created man, Gayomart, who, in his spiritual form, had been living with the Sole-Created Ox in Eran Vej, the central land of the seven lands of the earth. Ahura Mazda, the Lord of Light, had previously brought forth a sweat on Gayomart, for the length of time required for the recitation of one stanza of a prayer. He formed of that sweat the youthful body of a man of fifteen years, tall and radiant; and this body of Gayomart had issued from that sweat, with eyes that looked out for the Great One. It saw, however, the world as dark as night, and the earth as though not a needle's point were free of vermin. The great sphere of heaven was in revolution; the sun and moon were in motion; the planets were in battle with the stars.

Angra Mainyu let forth upon Gayomart the Demon of Death; but his appointed time had not come: his life was to endure for thirty years. Avarice, want, pain, hunger, disease, lust, and lethargy then were diffused into Gayomart. And when he passed away, he fell to the left and gave forth seed. That of the Ox had been purified by the moon; that of Gayomart was purified by the sun. Moreover, when he passed away there rose eight kinds of precious metal from his members: gold, silver, iron, brass, tin, lead, quicksilver, and adamant.

The gold remained in the earth forty years, preserved by the Angel of Perfect Meditation, when there grew from it, in the form of a plant of one stem with fifteen leaves—each leaf a year—the first human couple, wrapped in each other's arms and their bodies so close together that it could not be seen which was the male, which the female, or whether, as yet, they had separate living souls. From the form of a plant, they became two human beings, Mashya and Mashyoi; the breath entered them, which is the soul, and Ahura Mazda said: "You are Man, the ancestry of the world, created perfect in devotion. Perform the duties of the law, think good thoughts, speak good words, do good deeds, and do not worship demons."

The first thought of each was, to please the other. The first deed was, to go and thoroughly wash. Their first words were, that Ahura Mazda had created water and earth, plants, animals, stars, the moon and sun, and all prosperity. But then the enemy, Antagonism, rushed into their minds, and they declared that Angra Mainyu had created all.

They had gone thirty days without food, garbed with a raiment of leaves, when they came upon a goat and milked the milk from the udder with their mouths. Mashya said: "Before drinking that milk I was happy. But now that my vile body has drunk, my delight is more delightful." The second part of that evil speech enhanced the power of the demons, who thereupon reduced the taste of food, so that of one hundred parts, only one remained.

After thirty more days they chanced upon a sheep, fat and white-jawed, which they slaughtered. Angels taught them to produce fire from wood and they made a roast of the meat. They dropped three handfuls in the fire, saying, "This is Fire's share," and tossed one piece to the sky, saying, "This share is of the angels." A vulture carried some away from before them, and a dog consumed the first bite. They donned now a clothing of skins, dug a pit in the earth from which they procured iron, and when they had beaten this out with stones to a cutting edge, they chopped wood with it and built a wooden shelter from the sun.

Angra Mainyu caused the couple to quarrel, however, tearing at each other's hair and cheeks. Demons shouted, "You are men! Worship the demon, so that your demon of malice may be quelled." Mashya killed a cow and poured the milk toward the northern quarter, and the demons gained so much power thereby that for the next fifty years the couple had no desire for intercourse. Then, however, the source of desire rose first in Mashya, next Mashyoi: for he said to her: "When I see your sex my desires rise." She said: "When I see your great desire rise, I too am agitated." So it became their mutual wish, and they reflected: "This, even for those fifty years, was our duty."

There were born to them a male and female, and, owing to their tenderness for offspring, the mother devoured one, the father the other. Ahura Mazda therefore took such tenderness away, so that the child should be cherished alive. And there were born to them, then, seven sets of twins, each a brother and sister-wife. . . .[19]

Like the second chapter of Genesis, this Zoroastrian myth betrays its derivation from the planting complex discussed in *Primitive Mythology*.[20] However, in the mythologies of primitives there is no such moral criticism of life and the world as in these Levantine doctrines of the Fall; nor any theme, consequently, of Restoration.

Both the Bible and the Bundahish represent the Fall as the answer to the moral enigma of evil in the world; yet their two views of the mythic incident differ absolutely, as do their views, also, of the Restoration. For in the Persian myth evil is regarded from a cosmic point of view, as antecedent to the Fall of man, which indeed was but its culminating episode; whereas in the Bible the Fall proceeds *from* man, whose acts of disobedience entail calamity in the natural world as well as to himself. As the late Professor Joseph Klausner of Hebrew University, Jerusalem, states in his important work on *The Messianic Idea in Israel:*

> Natural evil (catastrophe) was in the eyes of the prophets the result of human evil. God, the creator of nature, cannot be the source of evil: if this were not so, two forces, good and evil, would be used by Him in mixed confusion and His character would not be complete, harmonious, essentially great. The deeds of man are, therefore, the source of evil both in society and in nature.[21]

And again (the italics are Professor Klausner's):

> The wise men of Israel, contrary to those of Greece, saw natural evil (disaster) not as an independent entity, but as the result of human evil (wrongdoing). Since the prophets believed in a one and only God, not in many gods which embody the powers of nature, good and evil, they were *forced* to conclude that both good and evil proceed from the one and only God. And if good and evil proceed from the *one* Supreme Being, whose nature must be absolutely perfect and harmonious (otherwise he would not be *one* and only, and therefore there would be a place for belief in dualism), then the Supreme Being of necessity creates evil *because* of evil persons and *for* evil persons. Thus, if the evil of evil persons, that is, human evil, should come to an end, *all evil* would cease, even natural evil in general.[22]

How evil can have had its source in God and yet not in God but in evil persons, I shall not attempt to argue; but the contrast of this tangle of thought with the Zoroastrian system warrants a moment of consideration. For in the Persian myth the cause indicated for the corruption of creation is not a personage, but a principle, the Lie, which is, philosophically, a counterpart of the Indian principle of *māyā,* the world-creating power of illusion; whereas the sin of Adam and Eve was disobedience, which is a matter rather of pedagogical than of ontological, or even properly ethical, interest— particularly since the ethics of the command itself may be open to question. A great deal of the stress of Old Testament thought rests on obedience to a multitude of apparently arbitrary orders of this kind (food taboos, sabbath laws, aniconic worship, circumcision, endogamy, and the rest). In Zoroastrianism, too, a great deal of stress is placed on such concerns: next-of-kin marriage, disposal of clipped hair and fingernails, dry wood for the fire, menstrual impurity, etc. But when the serious, deeper aspects of the two traditions are compared—beyond the sphere of their elevation of tribal custom into cosmic law—it is seen that they offer two contrasting orders of possible development.

The biblical view, placing the Fall within the frame of human history as an offense against its god, cuts out the wider reach of a challenge to the character of that god, denigrates the character of man, and fosters, furthermore, an increasingly untenable insistence on the historicity of its myth; while the other, cosmic view of the problem is actually symbolized philosophy, and, as later centuries would show, was to become one of the leading inspirations of every major spiritual threat to the hegemony of biblical literalism in the West.

The Messianic idea in Israel, as Professor Klausner well shows, was in essence not cosmological, but political. Its central concern was the elevation of Israel to leadership in the world. "In the belief in the Messiah of the people of Israel," Klausner writes (and again the italics following are his), *"the political part goes arm in arm with the ethical part, and the nationalistic with the universalistic."* [23] In the period before the fall of Jerusalem (586 B.C.), the stress of prophetic teaching had been on the requirement to adhere to the statutes of the Lord; that is to say, to live as Jews, not as gentiles. The Messiah exalted by the First Isaiah (c. 740–700 B.C.) had been specifically the young king of Judah of that time, King Hezekiah (r. 727–698 B.C.); and Professor Klausner, to this point, cites the following Talmudic saying: "The Holy One, blessed be He, wished to appoint Hezekiah as the Messiah and Sennacherib as Gog and Magog" (Sanhedrin 94*a*); also the saying of the Amora R. Hillel: "There shall be no Messiah for Israel, because they have already enjoyed him in the days of Hezekiah" (ib., 98*b* and 99*a*).[24] The term "the Day of the Lord" in that period had no reference to the world end or the end of time, with the resurrection of the dead, and all the rest. Those ideas had not yet entered the biblical stream of belief from their Zoroastrian source.

But in that source the idea of the redemption was cosmological, not political, and to occur at the end of the world span of twelve thousand years, foreknown by Ahura Mazda, when he would appear and judge the living and the dead. The ultimate aim of the prophet Zoroaster, therefore, had been, seriously and entirely, to bring about through his teaching the transfiguration of the earth, following which the world would be again as it was in the beginning, uncovered of darkness, sorrow, and death. "And it will thenceforth," as we read in a late Avestan text, "never age and never die, never decay and never rot, ever living and ever increasing, being master of its own wish: when the dead will rise, life and immortality come, and the world be restored to its wish." [25]

As an actual character on the plane of earth in the first millennium B.C., Zoroaster may not be accurately represented in the meager notices of his life that have come down to us. But on the plane of symbol, as representing the Zoroastrian perfect man, he appears in these in clearest light, in what is obviously not the chronicle but the myth of his career—like the lives of the Buddha and Christ; that is to say, as a revelation or symbolization of the truth in which he lived, whose glory cleaved to him, and which he taught. For, as we read:

> He thought according to the Law, spoke according to the Law, and did according to the Law; so that he was the holiest

in holiness in all the living world, the best ruling in exercising rule, the brightest in brightness, and most glorious in glory, the most victorious in victory. And at his sight the demons rushed away.[26]

His birth and teaching in the world marked the opening of the final three thousand of the world span of twelve thousand years— at the end of which term his spiritual son Saoshyant, "the Coming Savior," the World Messiah, would appear, to culminate the victory of Truth over the Lie and establish forever the restoration of the pristine creation of God.

As the legend tells, the birthplace of Zoroaster, like that of the first man Gayomart and the Sole-Created Ox, was beside the river Daiti, in the central land of the seven lands of the earth, Eran Vej. He laughed when he was born. As we read: "In his birth, in his growth, the waters and trees rejoiced. In his birth, in his growth, the waters and trees increased. In his birth, in his growth, the waters and trees exclaimed with joy." [27]

The demons, however, were of a different disposition. Angra Mainyu rushed from the regions of the north, crying to his horde, "Annihilate him!" But the holy babe chanted aloud the prayer known as the Ashi Vanguhi, and the demons were dispersed. "The will of the Lord is the Law of Holiness," he prayed. "The riches of Good Mind are his who labors in this world for Ahura Mazda, wielding the power—according to His Law—bestowed of Him, to relieve the poor." [28]

It is recounted that the prophet's wives were three. But that in these we are to recognize rather mythology than history is shown by the further notice that, "He went to his first and privileged wife, named Hvov, three times, and each time, the seed entered the ground." That is to say, she was the goddess Earth herself. "And the angel who had received the seed of the first-created man Gayo-mart received the strength and brilliance of this seed as well." [29] For there were to be born of that seed three sons, at the time of the cosmic Renovation: Ukhshyat-ereta, Ukhshyat-nemangh, and, finally, the Messiah Saoshyant.[30]

For a maid, Eredad-ereta, bathing in Lake Kansava, was to

conceive by that seed at the end of the world span of twelve thousand years, and bring forth the savior Saoshyant; his two forerunners having been born in the same manner, by two other virgins, Srutad-fedhri and Vanghu-fedhri.[31]

But concerning the nature of the Renovation to come, it is revealed that:

Whereas Mashya and Mashyoi, who had grown as a plant from the earth, fed first upon water, then upon plants, then milk, then meat, and when their time of death arrived, desisted first from meat, then milk, then bread, till, when about to die, they fed upon water; so, likewise, in the millennium of the final years, the strength of appetite will diminish. One taste of consecrated food will be more than enough for three days and nights. People then will desist from flesh food and eat vegetables and milk. Next they will abstain from milk, and after that, from vegetable food and feed on water. And for ten years before the coming of Saoshyant, they will remain without food altogether, and not die.[32]

According to the Bundahish, the resurrection of the dead is to follow the coming of Saoshyant. First the bones of Gayomart will be roused, next Mashya and Mashyoi, and then the remainder of mankind. When all have resumed their bodies, each will know his father, mother, brother, wife, and the others of his kind.

Then [we read] there will be the assembly where all mankind will stand, and each will see his own good deeds and evil deeds. And there in that assembly, a wicked man will stand out as conspicuously as a white sheep among black. Moreover, in that assembly, the wicked man will complain to the righteous one who was his friend in the world, saying, "Why did you not acquaint me, while in the world, with the good deeds that you yourself were practising?" And if the righteous man had not informed him, then in that assembly he would suffer shame.

Next they set the righteous apart from the wicked, and the righteous then is for heaven, but the wicked they cast back to hell. Three days and nights they inflict bodily punishment in hell, and then the wicked beholds for three days and nights the happiness of heaven. It is said that on the day when the righteous man is parted from the wicked, the people's tears run down their legs. And when they set apart a father from his spouse, brother from brother, friend from friend, they suffer, each for his own deeds, and they weep, the righteous for the wicked and the wicked for themselves. For there may be a father who is righteous and a son wicked, one brother who is righteous and one wicked. . . .

And when a great meteor then falls the distress of the earth will become as of a sheep fallen upon by a wolf. Fire and the angel of Fire will melt the metal in the hells and mountains, which then will flow upon the earth as a river. All men then pass into that metal and become pure: when one is righteous it seems to him like walking in warm milk, but when wicked, then it seems to him that he is walking in molten metal.

And in the end, with the greatest affection, all come together, father and son, brother and friend, and they ask each other thus: "Where have you been these many years and what was the judgment on your soul? Were you righteous, or were you wicked?" The first soul the body sees, it inquires with these words. All men become then of one voice in praise lifted loud to Ahura Mazda and his angels. Saoshyant with his assistants slaughter ceremonially an ox, from whose fat and the white Haoma a drink of immortality is prepared, which is given to all men, who become thereby immortal for ever.

And this, too, it says: whoever had been full grown when on earth, they give the age of forty years; whoever less, they give an age of fifteen; and they give to every one his wife and show him his children with his wife; and so they behave now as in the world, but there is no begetting of children any more. And this, too: that whoever performed no worship in the world and bestowed no clothes as a righteous gift is naked there; but he performs worship and the angels then provide him with the use of clothes.

And then, in the end, Ahura Mazda seizes Angra Mainyu, and each archangel his opposite. The fallen meteor incinerates the serpent in the melted metal and the stench and pollution of hell are burned in that metal too, until hell becomes quite pure. Ahura Mazda brings the land of hell back for the enlargement of the world, the renovation of the universe occurs, and all is immortal for ever.

And this too it says: that the earth becomes an iceless, slopeless plain. Even the mountain whose summit is the support of the Chinvat Bridge, they draw down, so that it disappears.[33]

III. The King of Kings

The mighty Assyrian monarch Tiglath Pilesar III (r. 745–727 B.C.) was the inventor of a new method of breaking the will of conquered populations. It was a device continued through this dynasty by Shalmaneser V (726–722), Sargon II (721–705), Sennacherib (704–681), Asarhaddon (680–669), and Ashurbanipal (668–626)—from the shattered cuneiform library of the last of whom most of our knowledge of the old Semitic world has been derived. One of the favored earlier customs of such conquerors had been simply to massacre all living things within a city—as we are told, for example, of Joshua's warriors in Jericho: "They utterly destroyed all in the city, both men and women, young and old, oxen, sheep, and asses, with the edge of the sword," [34] and so again at Ai,[35] Gibeon, Makkedah, Libnah, Gezer, Eglon, Hebron, Debir, and the whole land of the Negeb, "in order," as it is written, "that they should be utterly destroyed, and should receive no mercy but be exterminated, as Yahweh commanded Moses." [36] Or, on the other hand, the victor might reduce whole cities to servitude and tribute, as Manasseh reduced Megiddo, and Zebulun reduced Kitron.[37] But the former custom had the disadvantage of depriving the victor of subjects, and the latter, of leaving populations intact, ready for revolt.

Tiglath Pilesar's genial idea, therefore, was to sever the primary lifelines of attachment to the soil by transferring conquered populations to lands distant from their own. Babylonia was conquered in 745, and a large part of its people was removed: inscriptions name no less than thirty-five separate populations of that country thus broken and transferred.[38] In the year 739 Armenia was crushed, and about that time thirty thousand miserable persons from the province of Hamath were herded by the king to the province Tushan of the upper Tigris. A like number were taken from Syrian Calneh, and in their place Aramaeans were transferred from Elam.[39] The prophet Amos, crying in Israel, held up as warnings to the people these neighboring national catastrophes. "Woe to those who are at ease in Zion," he cried, "and to those who feel secure on the mountain of Samaria. . . . Pass over to Calneh, and see; and thence go to Hamath the great; then go down to Gath of the Philistines." [40] Populations were being tossed from east to west, west to east, north to south, and south to north, until not a vestige of the earlier, ground-rooted sense of a national continuity remained.

The world historic role of the Kings of Assyria can be described, therefore, as the erasure of the past and creation of a thoroughly mixed, internationalized, interracialized Near Eastern population that has remained essentially thus ever since. For themselves, meanwhile, however, they were accumulating an extremely dangerous karma. In the year 616 B.C. an alliance of King Nabopolassar of a revived Babylon with the Aryan King Kyaxares of the Medes, who were coming down now from the northeast, rose against the Assyrian, whose capital, Nineveh, was taken in 612; and the outraged populations of the empire then did their work with such effect that, as Eduard Meyer describes the result: "It was a catastrophe of the mightiest kind. Not only did an empire go to pieces that but a moment before had controlled all of Hither Asia, but practically the entire people who for centuries had been the scourge and horror of the nations was annihilated. . . . No people has ever been more completely wiped out than the Assyrians." [41]

For seventy-five years thereafter the mastery of the Near East was shared by the Medes, controlling the north, and the Babylonian Chaldean kings in the south. Of the latter the most notable was Nebuchadnezzar II (r. 604–562 B.C.), whom the prophet Jeremiah characterized as the servant of Yahweh, chastising the people of Judah for their sins of disobedience. [42] The northern kingdom, Israel, had succumbed, in 721, to an alliance of Judah and Assyria, and Judah itself then fell, in 586, to Nebuchadnezzar, "Yahweh's servant." Both populations were removed. However, during the middle of the sixth century a new type of master appeared in the Near Eastern political theater, with a new idea of the state. In four masterful strokes, the Persian Cyrus the Great first overthrew King Astyges of the Medes in the year 550, and instead of putting his eyes out, flaying him alive, or otherwise mishandling him in the manner of all kings before, assigned to him a residence in his capital; next, when threatened with an alliance of Nabonidus of Babylon, Amasis of Egypt, the powerful Croesus of Lydia, and the Greek city state of Sparta, he advanced directly against the chief antagonist, Croesus, and by the end of the year 546 was the ruler of Anatolia—whereupon he bestowed on his defeated enemy the government of the city of Barene, near Ecbatana; third, in the year 539, on his march south to Babylon, he was met by an open invitation, from the priesthood of the god Marduk of the chief temple of that city, to enter and take possession, which he did; and fourth, having become master of all of Hither Asia, he paid worship in the city of Babylon to Marduk, the god of that city, removed from the temple the captured images of the deities of numerous leading cities of the Near East, which he returned to their proper sites, and, finally, gave order that the people of Judah should be returned to their place and the temple of Jerusalem rebuilt. "The nobility of his character shines forth to us equally," Professor Meyer writes, "from the writings of the Persians whom he led to world mastery, the Jews whom he freed, and the Greeks whom he overthrew." [43]

"Cyrus the king," we read in Ezra,

> brought out the vessels of the house of Yahweh which Nebu- chadnezzar had carried away from Jerusalem and placed in the house of his gods. Cyrus the king of Persia brought these out in charge of Mithredath the treasurer, who counted them out to Sheshbazzar the prince of Judah. And this was the number of them: a thousand basins of gold, a thousand basins of silver, twenty-nine censers, thirty bowls of gold, two thousand four hundred and ten bowls of silver, and a thousand other vessels; all the vessels of gold and of silver were five thousand four hundred and sixty-nine. All these did Sheshbazzar bring up, when the exiles were brought up from Babylonia to Jerusa- lem.[44]

The Second Isaiah, writing c. 539 B.C., in the period of the return from exile, termed the noble king Cyrus of Persia "the anointed of Yahweh," whom Yahweh himself had grasped by his right hand, "to subdue nations before him and ungird the loins of kings, to open doors before him that gates may not be closed"; [45] and whereas Cyrus himself had supposed Ahura Mazda to have been his guide, the Hebrew prophet knew, on the contrary, that the voice of the god he had heard had been of Yahweh, saying:

> I will go before you and level the mountains, I will break in pieces the doors of bronze and cut asunder the bars of iron, I will give you the treasures of darkness and the hoards in secret places, that you may know that it is I, Yahweh, the God of Israel, who call you by your name.
>
> For the sake of my servant Jacob, and Israel my chosen, I call you by your name, I surname you, though you do not know me.
>
> I am Yahweh, and there is no other, besides me there is no God; I gird you though you do not know me, that men may know, from the rising of the sun and from the west, that there is none besides me; I am the Lord, and there is no other.

On top of which, in direct argument against the dualism of Zoroastrian doctrine, Yahweh is supposed to have said to Cyrus: "I form light and create darkness, I make weal and create woe, I am Yahweh, who do all these things." [46]

The prophet then goes on to disparage all the other local gods whom the King of Kings, anointed of the Lord, had been at pains to restore to their temples; and he exults then, with eloquent song, in the miracle of restoration which the Lord had brought about through an alien king.

But the priests of the god Marduk of Babylon also were exuberant in praise; for the last Chaldean king, Nabonidus, had been a devotee of the moon-god Sin of Harran, whose cult he had favored and restored, to the embarrassment of the clergy of Marduk.[47] Cyrus, in his noble way, had assigned a residence to Nabonidus in Carmania, while in the city of Marduk the temple scribes, in their religious way, gave praise to the redeeming king. Their eulogy is preserved on a cylinder of clay—the Cylinder of Cyrus—which after seven or eight mutilated lines at the start, complaining of the heresy of Nabonidus, yields the following interesting text:

. . . the daily offerings were neglected . . . the service of Marduk, King of the Gods. . . . The people were crushed to earth by an unrelenting yoke. . . .

And the Lord of Gods, giving heed to their cries, was moved mightily to wrath. . . . He turned to them in mercy. He passed the nations in review, searching, to find a righteous prince, after His heart, to take him by his hand.

Cyrus, King of Anshan, whose name He uttered, He summoned to universal lordship. The land of Gutium, the whole realm of the Kings of the Medes, He bowed beneath his feet. The black-haired people, who were delivered into his hands, the king received in righteousness and justice; and Marduk, the great Lord, protector of mankind, looked with joy upon his good deeds and righteous heart.

Marduk commanded him to march to Babylon, His city; advanced him on the road to Babylon, while He walked, as friend and fellow, at his side. And his troops, mighty in extent, innumerable as river waters, were at his side with weapons. Without battle, without slaughter, He caused him to enter Babylon, His city. Babylon He protected from affliction. Nabonidus the King, by whom Marduk had not been revered, Marduk delivered into Cyrus' power. And the people of Babylon, altogether, all of Sumer and Akkad, the mighty and the governors, bowed before him, kissed his feet, rejoiced in his lordship, and their faces shone. The lord who, in his majesty, had restored the dead to life, redeeming all from extinction and wrong, they blessed with joy, in celebration of his name.

The text then attributes the following to the new King of Kings:

I am Cyrus, King of the Universe, the great king, the mighty king, king of Babylon, king of Sumer and Akkad, king of the four quarters of the world . . . whose dynasty Bel [Marduk] and Nabu [the messenger of Bel] love, and for whose kingdom they rejoice in their hearts. When I made my gracious entry into Babylon and, amid rejoicing and delight established myself in the seat of lordship, the palace of the kings, Marduk, the great Lord, turned the noble heart of the Babylonians toward me, and I gave daily thought to His worship. My widely spread out troops moved peacefully throughout Babylon. In all Sumer and Akkad I permitted no enemy to rise. I respected gladly the interior of the city and all its holy sites. I released the inhabitants from their dishonoring yoke. I restored their fallen dwellings and had the ruins cleared.

And Marduk, the mighty lord, rejoicing in my pious deeds, showed Himself gracious both to me, Cyrus the King, who revered him, and to my beloved son Cambyses, and to all my troops, while we, in turn, gave praise sincerely and in joy to His exalted godhead. All the kings dwelling in palaces of all quarters of the world, from the Upper to the Lower Sea, and all the kings of the West, who dwell in tents, brought their heavy gifts and in Babylon kissed my feet. And I returned to their places the gods who dwelt in the cities of Assur and Susa, Agade, Eshnua, Zamban, Me-Turnu, Deri, the land of Gutium, and the cities of the Tigris, settled from of old. And I had built for them eternal dwellings. I restored the communities to their people, whose habitations I rebuilt. On the command of Marduk, the mighty lord, I allowed the gods to find, unmolested, a dwelling in their sanctuaries for the pleasure of their hearts: the gods of Sumer and Akkad, whom Nabonidus —to the anger of the gods—had caused to be brought to Babylon.

May all the gods whom I have thus brought into their cities pray daily before Bel and Nabu for long life for me and say to Marduk my lord: "May Cyrus, the king, who worships you, and Cambyses, his son, be blessed. . . ." [48]

It is not known how many of the priesthoods of the other folk- and city-gods were as eager as those of Jerusalem and Babylon to claim the credit of the general victory, overreading the course of history in terms of their own system of supernatural causality; but we do know that at least one considerable party of Cyrus's own Zoroastrian religion was incensed by this entire development— much as the Yahwist party of the Jews had been by the whoring of their kings after alien gods. For when, in the year 529 B.C., Cyrus fell in battle in a war being waged against the raiding tribes of the northeast Iranian border, a dangerous cloak-and-dagger intrigue of the Persian priesthood—the Magians—threatened for a moment to undo everything he had accomplished and to break up the Persian state from within, as the blood baths of the Yahwists had undone the Hebrew state.

Cyrus's son, Cambyses, following the pattern of his father, had in the year 525 conquered Egypt and so completed the work of uniting in a single mighty intercultural, interracial empire the entire domain of antiquity, from the Aegean to the Indus, and from the Caspian Sea to the Nubian Sudan.* And as Cyrus had in Babylon, so Cambyses in Egypt paid reverence to the local gods, bowed before them, and assumed the mantle of their blessing. Cambyses became pharaoh. And he remained in Egypt three years. But he had had a younger brother, Smerdis by name, whom his father had made governor of Bactria, Chorasmia, Parthia, and Carmania; and to protect himself against possible intrigue from that quarter, Cambyses had had his brother murdered before departing for the Nile.

The murder had been held secret. But a Magian priest named Gaumata, who resembled the murdered brother, stepped into his role and incited dissident elements to revolt. There is considerable evidence that the revolt was, in part at least, religious; for numerous temples were demolished by the priestly usurper. And in the summer of the year 522 this false Smerdis claimed the Persian throne. Cambyses, rushing from Egypt, fell in battle in March 522, confessing before his death, however, the murder of his brother. Yet no one dared to rise against the pretender until a young, fairly distant cousin of the Achaemenid house, Darius by name, took destiny into his thought, and in October 522 slew the usurper and the whole number of his court. By the end of February 521 the insurrection had been suppressed, and the young King of Kings, Darius I, was the ruler of the world.[49]

At Behistun there is a famous rock inscription in three languages, Old Persian, Elamite, and Babylonian, announcing this victory and describing it in detail, with the recognition, many times repeated, of the guidance—neither of Yahweh nor of Marduk, but of the Persian god.

---

* It was exactly in this period that the old Nubian capital, Napata, was taken and the seat of rule transferred to Meroë, which is supposed to have been named after Cambyses' sister. We have thus returned in a great circle to the point of time suggested as the background of the Sudanese tale of Napata-Meroë recounted in *Primitive Mythology*, pp. 151–64.

I am Darius, the great king, King of Kings, king of Persia, king of the Lands, son of Hystaspes, grandson of Arsames, the Achaemenid. . . .

King Darius speaks: Eight of my family have been kings, I am the ninth. Nine of us, in two lines, have been kings. . . . By the will of Ahura Mazda, I am king. Ahura Mazda conveyed to me the Lordship. . . . In these lands, the man who was circumspect, I have treated well; him who was inimical, I have sternly punished. By the will of Ahura Mazda, these lands have obeyed my laws. What I have commanded, they have done.

King Darius speaks: And this, by the will of Ahura Mazda is what I did, on becoming king:

One by name Cambyses, Cyrus' son, of our dynasty, here was king. That Cambyses had a brother, Smerdis, of the same mother and the same father as Cambyses. Cambyses murdered that Smerdis. And when Cambyses murdered Smerdis, it was not known to the people that Smerdis had been slain. Thereafter, Cambyses went to Egypt. When Cambyses had gone to Egypt, the people became his enemy and the Lie became great in the land, as well in Persia as in Media and the other lands.

King Darius speaks: There was a man, a certain Magian, Gaumata by name, who rose in rebellion from Pishijau-uada, from the mountain called Arakadrish. It was the 14th of Addaru [March 11, 522 B.C.] when he rebelled. He lied to the people, as follows: "I am Smerdis, Cyrus' son, Cambyses' brother." Whereupon the whole people deserted Cambyses and went over to that other, as well the Persians as the Medes and the other lands. He seized the mastery. It was the 9th of Garmapada [April 2, 522] when he seized the mastery. Then Cambyses died by his hand.

King Darius speaks: This mastery, which Gaumata the Magian seized from Cambyses, had belonged to our family from of old. Then Gaumata took from Cambyses, Persia as well as Media and the other lands, appropriated them, made them his own, and became king.

King Darius speaks: There was no one—neither Persian, nor Mede, nor any one of our line—who recovered the mastery from that Gaumata the Magian. The people greatly feared him: he would have killed many who had formerly known Smerdis: he would have killed many of the people, [thinking:] "so that the people should not know that I am not Smerdis,

Cyrus' son." No one dared speak a word with reference to Gaumata the Magian till I came.

Then I prayed to Ahura Mazda: Ahura Mazda brought me aid. On the 10th day of Bagajadish [September 29, 522], I slew with a few men that Gaumata the Magian and those who had been his foremost followers. There is a fortress called Sikajau-uatish in a region called Nisaja in Media: there I slew him, tore from him the mastery. By the will of Ahura Mazda I became king. Ahura Mazda conferred upon me the lordship.

King Darius speaks: The mastery that had been taken from our line I recovered and established in its place, as before. I built again the temples that Gaumata had destroyed. I returned to the people the pasturelands, the cattle herds, and the dwellings and buildings that Gaumata the Magian had taken from them. I placed the people in their places, as before, in Persia, Media, and the other lands. I gave back what had been taken, as before. I took pains in accord with the will of Ahura Mazda, until it was just as though Gaumata the Magian never had carried off our house.

King Darius speaks: And I did as follows. . . .[50]

The text goes on at considerable length, recounting for all centuries to come the wonders of the reign of one of the greatest creative rulers in the history of the world, Darius I, the master of the whole Near East from 521 to 486 B.C. He was a contemporary of the Buddha (563–483 B.C.) and Confucius (551–478 B.C.), and can properly be named in the same breath as representing with them the image of supreme spiritual authority by which each mythological province thereafter was to be hallmarked: respectively, the Levantine Despot under God, the Indian Yogi, and the Chinese Sage. In his own words Darius had been king by the will of Ahura Mazda. His reign, therefore, had been the vehicle of that will and, as such, the sole measure of moral right; and every enemy of such a king is an agent of the enemy of God—Angra Mainyu, the Demon of the Lie.

IV. The Remnant

Oswald Spengler seems to have been the first to point out that, from the time of the Persians onward, the cultural development of the Near East has taken place in terms not of nations but of churches, not of post-neolithic, earth-rooted, primary communities, but of freely floating sects without geographical bounds. The terrible plowing, pulverizing, and tossing about of peoples that the whole culture province had suffered during the centuries had wiped out the earlier continuities. The first world age of the birth and primary flowering of civilization in the Near East was ended, and in the making was a new birth—of unprecedented kind.

The empire of Darius extended from the Greek Ionian isles to the Indus Valley, and from the Caspian Sea to the upper cataracts of the Nile; and during two millenniums to come there would germinate and flower in this united field a new and brilliant civilization of contending, mutually disparaging sects, related closely in spirit, yet in doctrines set wide apart. And as it would be impossible to know anything of Europe without recognizing, on the one hand, that France, Germany, and England are in spirit different, yet, as components of the European order, of one spirit, so to understand the force and interplay of the differing yet related burgeoning sects of the Near East, from the period of Cyrus the Great to Mohammed and the Crusades, we shall have to consider, on one hand, the affinities, and, on the other, the differences, first, of the Persian, Jewish, and Chaldean myths of the earliest phase of this development, next of the Primitive Christian, Byzantine, and Gnostic, of the age of the flowering of the culture, and finally, of the rise and total victory of Islam.

Spengler, with his eye for the symbolically significant, saw the architectural interior created by the dome (Hadrian's Tomb in Rome, Sancta Sophia in Constantinople, and the mosques throughout Islam) as exemplifying the new Levantine sense of space and, therein, the wonder-world of creation. The dome of the sky, as seen from a desert or plain, supplies the model for the bounded, yet soaring, cavern-like interior created by the architectural dome. And in the myths of the new Levant—as in the Zoroastrian myth of the world span of twelve thousand years—time as well as space had symmetrically measured bounds, a beginning, middle, and end, within which everything, every happening, had both its time and its meaning or reason.

There is, in fact, a certain fairy-tale quality of wonder about everything in this bounded cavern world of the mythologies of the Levant, as though one pervading spirit dwelt within all. We are everywhere caught in the measured spell of one space, one span of time, one all-pervading spirit—and the idea of one true teaching. Each such teaching, furthermore, in a magical, fairy-tale way, has been revealed, once and for all, to be the permanent treasure of a certain group; and so, there is one authorized group as well.

Such a group, as I have already said, is not a geographical nation but a church, a sect, the company in possession of a magical treasure; and the functioning of its treasure is conditioned by certain fairy-tale laws, which are the statutes of the group. Membership, therefore, is not a matter of either time or place, but of the knowledge and execution of the statutes, which are at once secular and religious; revealed, not invented by man; and categorical, not subject to review. When obeyed, they produce boons beyond anything the world has ever known—fairy-tale boons; however, when violated, even accidentally, they produce a magical catastrophe against which the force and will of the individual—or even of the now unfortunate group of which he is an organ—are as nought. Hence, finally, the weal and woe, virtue and value of all and each lie not in creative individual thought and effort but in participation in the customs of the group; so that as far as the principle of free will is concerned, which is generally argued for in this culture, its effect is only to make the individual responsible for his decision either to obey or to disobey. It is not his province to decide what is good and what bad.

As Spengler defines the character of the moral order of this new Levantine, or, as he terms it, Magian world-feeling:

The Magian man is but *part of a pneumatic "We"* which, descending from above, is one and the same in all members. As body and soul he belongs to himself alone, but something else, something alien and higher, dwells in him, making him with all his glimpses and convictions just a member of a consensus, which, as the emanation of God, excludes error, but excludes also all possibility of the self-asserting Ego. Truth is for him something other than for us [i.e., for us of specifically European mentality]. All our epistemological methods, resting upon the *individual* judgment, are for him madness and infatuation, and its scientific results a work of the Evil One, who has confused and deceived the spirit as to its true dispositions and purposes. Herein lies the ultimate, for us unapproachable, secret of Magian thought in its cavern-world—the impossibility of a thinking, believing, and knowing Ego is the presupposition in all the fundamentals of all these religions.[51]

The first Isaiah (c. 740–700 B.C.) had supposed the young King Hezekiah to be the Messiah. Two centuries later a second Isaiah (c. 545–518 B.C.) all but applied the concept to Cyrus. The first had foreseen that after Yahweh's day of wrath a "remnant," purged as it were by fire, would remain to renew and bear the promise. As he wrote in a famous prophecy:

> In that day the remnant of Israel and the survivors of the house of Jacob will no more lean upon him that smote them, but will lean upon Yahweh, the Holy One of Israel in truth. A remnant will return, the remnant of Jacob, to the mighty God. For though your people Israel be as the sand of the sea, only a remnant of them will return. Destruction is decreed, overflowing with righteousness. For the Lord, Yahweh of Hosts, will make a full end, as decreed, in the midst of all the earth. [52]

To the second Isaiah, and to the priest Ezra, who followed him by a century, the decree of Cyrus the Great, renewing Jerusalem and the temple, had seemed a fulfillment of that prophecy. Its words, according to Ezra, were these:

> Yahweh, the God of heaven, has given me all the kingdoms of the earth, and he has charged me to build him a house at Jerusalem, which is in Judah. Whoever is among you of all his people, may his God be with him, and let him go up to Jerusalem, which is in Judah, and rebuild the house of Yahweh, the God of Israel—he is the god who is in Jerusalem; and let each survivor, in whatever place he sojourns, be assisted by the men of his place with silver and gold, with goods and with beasts, besides freewill offerings for the house which is in Jerusalem.[53]

The response was not immediately encouraging. The number of those who returned to the shattered city is given as "forty-two thousand three hundred and sixty, besides menservants and maidservants, of whom there were seven thousand three hundred and thirty-seven; and they had two hundred male and female singers." [54] It is supposed that this group arrived in 537 or 536 B.C. The rebuilding of the temple was begun in the reign of Darius, 520. Its dedication took place 516. After that, however, we have little news until the reign of Artaxerxes I (465–424 B.C.), when Nehemiah, who declares himself to have been "cupbearer to the king," [55] was sent, on his own request, to Jerusalem, to be its governor, and he found the city still largely in ruins.[56] He began the rebuilding of its walls. But the great day that is marked as the day of the proper founding of modern Judaism arrived only in the reign of Artaxerxes II (404–358 B.C.), when, in the year 397 B.C., Ezra the Scribe, with a large company of the faithful and authority from the king, came from Babylon to Jerusalem and was scandalized by what he found.

> The officials [he wrote] approached me and said, "The people of Israel and the priests and the Levites, have not separated themselves from the peoples of the lands with their abominations, from the Canaanites, the Hittites, the Perizzites, the Jebusites, the Ammonites, the Moabites, the Egyptians, and the Amorites. For they have taken some of their daughters to be wives for themselves and for their sons; so that the holy race has mixed itself with the peoples of the lands. And in this faithlessness the hand of the officials and chief men has been foremost." And when I heard this, I rent my garments and my mantle, and pulled hair from my head and beard, and sat appalled.[57]

Ezra prayed and apologized for his people to God and cast himself down before the house of God, and a very great assembly of the people gathered, men, women, and children, who joined him in his pain and wept. After which, as we read,

> a proclamation was made throughout Judah and Jerusalem to all the returned exiles that they should assemble at Jerusalem

and that if any one did not come within three days, by order of the officials and the elders all his property should be forfeited, and he himself banned from the congregation of the exiles.

Then all the men of Judah and Benjamin assembled at Jerusalem within the three days; it was the ninth month, on the twentieth day of the month. And all the people sat in the open square before the house of God, trembling because of this matter and because of the heavy rain. And Ezra the priest stood up and said to them, "You have trespassed and married foreign women, and so increased the guilt of Israel. Now then make confession to the Lord the God of your fathers, and do his will; separate yourselves from the peoples of the land and from the foreign wives."

Then all the assembly answered with a loud voice, "It is so; we must do as you have said. But the people are many, and it is a time of heavy rain; we cannot stand in the open. Nor is this a work for one day or for two; for we have greatly transgressed in this matter. Let our officials stand for the whole assembly; let all in our cities who have taken foreign wives come at appointed times, and with them the elders and judges of every city, till the fierce wrath of our God over this matter be averted from us." Only Jonathan the son of Asahel and Jahzeiah the son of Tikvah opposed this, and Meshullam and Shabbethai the Levite supported them.

Then the returned exiles did so. Ezra the priest selected men, heads of fathers' houses, according to their fathers' houses, each of them designated by name. On the first day of the tenth month they sat down to examine the matter; and by the first day of the first month they had come to the end of all the men who had married foreign women. . . . And they put them away with their children.[58]

Thus, for a while at least, peace had again been made with their god by the remnant of the people of his trust.

v. The God of Love

The King of Kings of Persia illuminated with the radiance of his justice, on one hand the Greek Ionian city states of westernmost Asia Minor, as Satrapy I of his unprecedented domain, and, on the other, the most ancient centers of Indian civilization, in the Punjab, as Satrapy XX. Moreover, the image of his grandiose lordship, as symbolized in the glory of his throne and palace in Persepolis, and the methods of despotism that in his hands became the nerves and sinews of the most powerful social organization the world had up to then seen, were in his time so prodigiously impressive that, though they endured for hardly two centuries, they have remained, through all centuries since, the ultimate figure and symbol of kingly majesty and rule. In India, in the court and theòry of government of Chandragupta Maurya (c. 322–293 B.C.), whose art of despotism is epitomized in Kautilya's Arthashastra, "Textbook of the Art of Gaining Ends," and in China, in the reign of Shih Huang Ti (221–206 B.C.), whose counterpart of Kautilya's work is the Shang Tzu, "Book of the Lord Shang," the model of the Persian King of Kings was copied and made definitive for all Oriental ideals of political method and achievement to this day. Furthermore, in the Old Testament prophetic visions of the majesty of God, the imprint of the King of Kings of Persia can be recognized as finally the source. We read of his reign and the methods of his reign in the work of his Greek subject Herodotus. His radiance was of Ahura Mazda; but the instrument of his majesty was the whip.

In the luminous little Greek peninsula beyond the benevolence of that divine Levantine government, however, in the polis eulogized by Pericles in his celebrated oration, a quite different notion was developing of majesty and rule, and of the deity whose presence was the best support of law as well as of life. For it was inevitable that where individual excellence was to such an extent revered as in Greece, the force and principle of Love—Eros—should have been recognized not merely as a god but as the informing god of all things. For no one achieves excellence in his life task without love for it, in himself without love for himself, or in his family without love for his home. Love brings everything to flower, each in terms of its own potential, and so is the true pedagogue of the open, free society. "For," as Agathon declared in his banquet speech, immortalized in Plato's account of the grandest drinking party in the history of the world, "all serve him of their own free will, and where there is love as well as obedience, there, as the laws which are the lords of the city say, is justice." [59]

Professor Warner Fite of Princeton years ago pricked the bubble of a late Victorian version of Plato's ideal of love by pointing out to a generation ignorant of Greek that Professor Jowett's translation (which was the one that all were then reading in school) renders *orthos paiderastein,* "the right kind of pederasty," as "true love." [60] So that all then knew—as most had already guessed— that boy-love, pederasty or sodomy, which in most of the published moral codes of the world counts as a heinous offense against nature, was for Plato's model company the one true way to spirituality and the sublimation of mere nature into fine discourse, poetry, science, excellence, and the perfect city state.

In such primitive rites of initiation as those of the natives of Australia, pederasty plays a role in the translation of boys away from Mother to the secret knowledges of manhood: but they are then led by way of further rites back to the village and to marriage.[61] Also, in the pedagogical sphere and atmosphere of the Orphic wilderness singers above described,* the participation of youths, for a time, in a purely masculine society was, in the way of a preparatory school, preparatory for life. But in the high circle of the lions of Athens, during a great period of late fifth- and early fourth-century Greece, 450–350 B.C., the pedagogical atmosphere became, as it were, embalmed. Everything that we read of it has a wonderful adolescent atmosphere of opalescent, timeless skies— untouched by the vulgar seriousness of a heterosexual commitment to mere life. The art, too, of the lovely standing nude, for all its grace and charm, is finally neuter—like the voice of a singing boy— as appears immediately when the eye turns for comparison to the art of Gupta, Chalukya, and Rashtrakuta India. To quote an observation of Heinrich Zimmer:

> Greek sculpture developed to its acme of perfection through a portrayal of the handsome athletic bodies of the attractive boys and youths who won prizes for wrestling and racing at the

* Supra, p. 185.

national religious contests at Olympia and elsewhere; Hindu, on the other hand, in its great period, rested on those intimate experiences of the living organism and mysteries of the life-process that derive from the inward awareness gained through yogic experiences—and simultaneously had a definitely hetero-sexual flavor, distilled and refined to a subtle enchanting fragrance. Greek art was derived from experiences of the eye; Hindu from those of the circulation of the blood.[62]

There is a telling line of the Roman satirist and poet Juvenal (60–140 A.D.), where he speaks with disapproval of what went on in one of the secret women's cults:

> *nil ibi per ludum simulabitur, omnia fient*
> *ad verum. . . .*

"Nothing will there be imitated as in play, everything will be done in earnest. . . ." [63]

As in adolescence it is fortunate for a youth if he can live and think and play for some time in a world exclusively of males, where the mind, unassaulted by the female system of seriousness, can develop in its own playful way toward science and aesthetics, philosophy and athletics, the world, in short, of the Logos, where even Eros appears with an exhalation of inorganic scent; so also for the West and the world it was a moment of great good fortune that bestowed upon us—for a certain time—the boys' singing school of the Greeks: of which the great banquet scene of the young and old lions at the home of the poet Agathon was the apogee.

The reader recalls the magical moment. Socrates arose to tell of love—as he had learned of it from the wise woman Diotima, of whom we know nothing more than what he tells.

"I want to talk about some lessons I was given, once upon a time, by a Mantinean woman called Diotima," he said: "a woman who was deeply versed in this and many other fields of knowledge. It was she who brought about a ten years' postponement of the great plague of Athens on the occasion of a certain sacrifice, and it was she who taught me the philosophy of Love." [64]

Like Zeus with Metis in his belly, so was Socrates with Diotima.*

* Supra, pp. 150–52.

In his celebration of love we may recognize the percolation upward of an earlier, pre-Hellenic wisdom, from the world of the serpent queens of Crete, of Circe also, and Calypso. But in the male womb of his brow the lore has been transmuted to accord with the inorganic atmosphere of the perfume of the banquet. We can only guess what it might have been from Diotima herself. As it comes to us from Socrates, thus alone do we know it. And so:

Well then, she began [declared the old satyr to his company], the candidate for this initiation cannot, if his efforts are to be rewarded, begin too early to devote himself to the beauties of the body. First of all, if his preceptor instructs him as he should, he will fall in love with the beauty of one individual body, so that his passion may give life to noble discourse. Next he must consider how nearly related the beauty of any one body is to the beauty of any other, when he will see that if he is to devote himself to loveliness of form it will be absurd to deny that the beauty of each and every body is the same. Having reached this point, he must set himself to be the lover of every lovely body, and bring his passion for the one in due proportion by deeming it of little or of no importance.

Next he must grasp that the beauties of the body are as nothing to the beauties of the soul, so that wherever he meets with spiritual loveliness, even in the husk of an unlovely body, he will find it beautiful enough to fall in love with and to cherish —and beautiful enough to quicken in his heart a longing for such discourse as tends toward the building of a noble nature. And from this he will be led to contemplate the beauty of laws and institutions. And when he discovers how nearly every kind of beauty is akin to every other he will conclude that the beauty of the body is not, after all, of so great moment.

And next, his attention should be diverted from institutions to the sciences, so that he may know the beauty of every kind of knowledge. And thus, by scanning beauty's wide horizon, he will be saved from a slavish and illiberal devotion to the individual loveliness of a single boy, a single man, or a single institution. And, turning his eyes toward the open sea of beauty, he will find in such contemplation the seed of the most fruitful discourse and the loftiest thought, and reap a golden harvest of philosophy, until, confirmed and strengthened, he will come upon one single form of knowledge, the knowledge of the beauty I am to speak of.

And here, Diotima said to me, you must follow me as closely as you can.

Whoever has been initiated so far in the mysteries of Love and has viewed all these aspects of the beautiful in due succession, is at last drawing near the final revelation. And now, Socrates [she said], there bursts upon him that wondrous vision which is the very soul of the beauty he has toiled so long for. It is an everlasting loveliness which neither comes nor goes, which neither flowers nor fades, for such beauty is the same on every hand, the same then as now, here as there, this way as that way, the same to every worshiper as it is to every other.

Nor will his vision of the beautiful take the form of a face, or of hands, or of anything that is of the flesh. It will be neither words, nor knowledge, nor a something that exists in something else, such as a living creature, or the earth, or the heavens, or anything that is—but subsisting of itself and by itself in an eternal oneness, while every lovely thing partakes of it in such sort that, however much the parts may wax and wane, it will be neither more nor less, but still the same inviolable whole.

And so, when his prescribed devotion to boyish beauties has carried our candidate so far that the universal beauty dawns upon his inward sight, he is almost within reach of the final revelation. And this is the way, the only way, he must approach, or be led toward, the sanctuary of Love. Starting from individual beauties, the quest for the universal beauty must find him ever mounting the heavenly ladder, stepping from rung to rung—that is, from one to two, and from two to *every* lovely body, from bodily beauty to the beauty of institutions, from institutions to learning, and from learning in general to the special lore that pertains to nothing but the beautiful itself —until at last he comes to know what beauty is.

And if, my dear Socrates, Diotima went on, man's life is ever worth the living, it is when he has attained this vision of the very soul of beauty. And once you have seen it, you will never be seduced again by the charm of gold, of dress, of comely boys, or lads just ripening to manhood; you will care nothing for the beauties that used to take your breath away and kindle such a longing in you, and many others like you, Socrates, to be always at the side of the beloved and feasting your eyes upon him, so that you would be content, if it were possible, to deny yourself the grosser necessities of meat and drink, so long as you were with him.

But if it were given to man to gaze on beauty's very self—unsullied, unalloyed, and freed from the mortal taint that haunts the frailer loveliness of flesh and blood—if, I say, it were given to man to see the heavenly beauty face to face, would you call *his,* she asked me, an unenviable life, whose eyes had been opened to the vision, and who had gazed upon it in true contemplation until it had become his own forever?

And remember, she said, that it is when he looks upon beauty's visible presentment, and only then, that a man will be quickened with the true, and not the seeming, virtue—for it is virtue's self that quickens him, not virtue's semblance. And when he has brought forth and reared this perfect virtue, he shall be called the friend of God, and if ever it is given to man to put on immortality, it shall be given to him.[65]

We have ascended now to such an Elysian height as to have transcended words. However, libraries are filled with the words that have been devoted to this immortal discourse of the wise Diotima. And, of all that might be remarked concerning her exposition of the Way of Beauty and Love, I shall take notice only of two outstanding points, which apply to the metamorphosis of mythology in the fifth century B.C. And these are, namely:

1. *The accent on the body:* Spengler has made what seems to me to be an extremely important point in his designation of the body (*soma*), the beautiful, standing nude, as the signature and high symbol of the Classical—or, as he terms it, Apollonian—order of experience. In contrast, on one hand, to the Magian sense of the World Cavern, with its one space, one span of time, one all-inhabiting spirit, and, on the other hand, to the later, north European, Gothic—or, as Spengler terms it, Faustian—sense and yearning for infinitude, the Greek mind was focused almost exclusively on what is present to the senses. And this concentration was expressed as well in the stone body of the Classical temple as in the art of the sculptured nude. It was the inspiration, furthermore, of Euclidean mathematics (a mathematic of static bodies) and of the

politics of the polis (the area of land visible from its acropolis). Or, in Spengler's own words:

> The Classical statue in its splendid bodiliness—all structure and expressive surfaces and no incorporeal *arrière-pensée* whatsoever—contains without remainder all that Actuality is for the Classical eye. The material, the optically definite, the comprehensible, the immediately present—this list exhausts the characteristics of this kind of extension. The Classical universe, the *Cosmos* or well-ordered aggregate of all near and completely viewable things, is concluded by the corporeal vault of heaven. More there is not. The need that is in us to think of "space" as being behind as well as before this shell was wholly absent from the Classical world-feeling. The Stoics went so far as to treat even properties and relations of things as "bodies." For Chrysippus, the Divine Pneuma is a "body," for Democritus seeing consists in our being penetrated by material particles of the things seen. The State is a body which is made up of all the bodies of its citizens, the law knows only corporeal persons and material things. And the feeling finds it last and noblest expression in the stone body of the Classical temple. The windowless interior is carefully concealed by the array of columns; but outside there is not one truly straight line to be found. Every flight of steps has a slight sweep outward, every step relatively to the next. The pediment, the roof-ridge, the sides are all curved. Every column has a slight swell and none stands truly vertical, or truly equidistant from the others. But swell and inclination and distance vary from the corners to the centers of the sides in a carefully toned-off ratio, and so the whole corpus is given a something that swings mysterious about a center. The curvatures are so fine that to a certain extent they are invisible to the eye and only to be "sensed." But it is just by these means that direction in depth is eliminated. While the Gothic style *soars,* the Ionic *hovers.* The interior of the cathedral pulls up with primeval force, but the temple is laid down in majestic rest.[66]

The Greek concept and experience of Eros, then, is locked firmly to the body and, as the wise woman Diotima tells, all penetration beyond, to "beauty's very self," not only must begin with bodily specificity but also must remain in the end with "beauty's visible presentment." The leap is not taken by the Greek spirit to any such sphere of dis- or pre-embodiment as becomes typical of certain strains of post-Classical Neoplatonic thought. And yet there *is* a penetration—which brings us to our second point.

2. *The idea of beauty everywhere:* Thales, we have seen, believed that "water" was the ultimate ground (ἀρχή) of all perceptible things; Anaximander, the "unlimited"; Anaximenes, "air"; the Pythagoreans, "number": and we have now entered a world of thought, a century or so later, where love—of and as beauty—has become the ἀρχή, or prime substance of all things. As every sophomore in philosophy knows, Plato and his school identified this principle, in a very interesting way, with the earlier principle of number, harmony, and the music of the spheres, which, as we have also seen, had already been linked to the mystery of the magic of the music of the Orphic lyre and song that quelled even the heart of Hades and the animals of the wild. Moreover and finally, it has been shown that the figure of Dionysus looms behind the Orphic, who is ultimately that same mighty lord of death and resurrection whom we have recognized in Osiris, Tammuz, and the beautifully bearded golden bull of the graceful harp of the royal tombs of Ur. So that there is now breaking into the scene a really tremendous torrent of earlier mythic themes, figures, and motifs, bearing fragments, variously assorted, of the whole deep, dark, and turbid well of the serpent lord and his bride: the symbolism of the lunar bull, the dead and resurrected godly king, those fascinating harps of the moon king of the royal tombs of Ur, and the great names of Osiris, Tammuz, Attis, Adonis, Dionysus, and the rest.

In Hesiod's *Theogony* (c. 750 B.C.) the god of love, Eros, had been one of four separate deities named as original. One was Chaos; another, Gaea, Mother Earth; Tartarus, the dark pit of Hades beneath the earth, was given as third; while the fourth was Eros—"who is love, handsomest among all immortals, who breaks the limbs' strength: who, in all gods, in all human beings, overpowers the intelligence in the breast and all their shrewd planning." [67]

Hesiod tells no more of this god. Eros does not appear at all in Homer. He derives from the old pre-Hellenic Aegean stratum of mythological thought. He is linked definitely and firmly to Aphrodite as her child, and in the later, allegorical mythologies appears (as Cupid, child of Venus) with his bow and poisoned arrow, piercing brutal as well as gentle hearts, to their death or to their healing in delight. The allegory is apt and appealing, denoting in a literary way the impact of love upon the individual. But, as our whole survey of the prehistory of the Aegean has shown, the goddess Aphrodite and her son are exactly the great cosmic mother and her son, the ever-dying, ever-living god. The variety of myths of Eros's parentage point, without exception, to such a background. He is the issue of Chaos. He is hatched from the egg of Night. He is the son, now of Gaea and Uranus, now of Artemis and Hermes, now again of Iris and Zephyrus: all transformations of the same mythological background, pointing, without exception, to the timeless catalogue of themes with which we are now familiar: of that willing victim in whose death is our life, whose flesh is our meat and blood our drink; the victim present in the young embracing couple of the primitive ritual of the love-death, who at the moment of ecstasy are killed, to be sacramentally roasted and consumed; [68] the victim present in Attis or Adonis slain by a boar, Osiris slain by Seth, Dionysus torn apart, roasted, and consumed by the Titans. In the charming later allegories of Eros (Cupid) and his victim, *the god is in the role of the dark enemy*—the rushing boar, the dark brother Seth, the Titan band—and *the lover is the incarnate dying god*. But, as we know, in this mythology, based as it is on the mystery that in old Egypt was known as "the Secret of the Two Partners," [69] the slayer and his victim, though on the stage apparently in conflict, are behind the scenes of one mind—as they are, too, it is well known, in the life-consuming, life-redeeming, -creating, and -justifying dark mystery of love.

In the old myths of the primitive and archaic worlds to which we have devoted so many pages, the accents in the rites and retellings of this theme were laid generally upon the godly, or mythic aspect of the mystery. The sentiments and disaster of the human victim were systematically and sublimely disregarded. The Indian rituals of suttee and of human sacrifice before Kali not only were thoughtless of the individual but, in fact, were disciplines intended to inspire and consummate a spirituality of egoless devotion to the archetypes, mythologically based, of the social order.[70] But in Greece, with its Apollonian appreciation for and delight in the individual form, its beauty and its particular excellence, the accent of the same old basic mythic themes dramatically moved from the side of the ever-repeated archetype to that of the unique individuality of each particular victim: and not only to his particular individuality, but also to the entire order of values that may be termed properly personal, as opposed to the impersonal of the group, or of the species, or of the sheerly natural order. It is this dramatic, epochal, and—as far as our documentation tells—unprecedented shift of loyalty from the impersonal to the personal that I want to characterize here as the Greek—the European— miracle. It is comparable to an evolutionary psychological mutation. Elsewhere the particularities of the individual, novelties of his thought, and qualities of individual desire and delight were sternly wiped away in the name of the absolute norms of the group; but in Greece the particular excellencies of each were at least theoretically—though not always actually (as, for example, if the individual chanced to be a woman or a slave)—legally and pedagogically respected. Also, the human mind and its reasoning were honored. The norm for human conduct became not the nursery norm of obedience ("being good," doing as taught and told), but a rational individual development ("the good life") under laws that were not supposed to be from God, but were recognized to be the products of purely human judgment. And, indeed, as far as godhead was concerned, even Zeus could think, reason, learn, and improve morally through time.

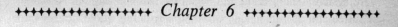

Chapter 6

HELLENISM:

331 B.C.–324 A.D.

I. The Marriage of East and West

It has been argued that Greek mythology declined from the status of religion to literature because of the highly critical Greek mind, which was already turned against it in the sixth and fifth centuries B.C. Often implied in this argument is the idea that polytheism is an inferior form of religion, vulnerable to criticism, whereas monotheism is not: consequently, when the Greek mind got to work on it, polytheism was liquidated and the way was cleared for the revealed Christian Truth of the One God in Three Persons, with his pantheon of angels, counter-pantheon of devils, communion of saints, forgiveness of sins, and resurrection of the body, as well as the multiple presence (in every consecrated drop of wine and wafer of the Mass) of the dead and resurrected Son of God—true God and true Man—who was born miraculously of the Virgin Mother Mary. Actually, however, the Olympians never were confused by the Greeks with the ultimate Being of being. Like men, the gods had been born of the Great Mother. Though stronger and of longer life than men, they were their brothers. Moreover, they were but temporary governors of the universe, which they had wrested from an earlier generation of divine children of the goddess, and they would lose it—as Prometheus knew—to a later. Properly, they were the archetypes of the ideals of the Greek city state, and with its passing they passed too.

But in the Hellenistic period, when the brilliant pupil of Aristotle, Alexander the Great, having smashed across the whole Levant into India, had brought together in one world Greece, India, Persia, Egypt, and even the Jews outside of Jerusalem, Greek religion advanced to a new phase: on one hand, of grandiose universalism, and on the other, of personal, inward immediacy. In fact, the beautiful gods, far from dying, sent the inspiration of their breath across all Asia, to waken new religious and aesthetic forms in Maurya India, Han China, and ultimately Japan; while in the West they wakened Rome and in the South brought a new significance to the old, old cults of the goddess Isis and her spouse.

An appreciation of the point of view of the Hellenistic Greeks toward religion can be obtained from the Alexandrian mythographer Maximus of Tyre (fl. second century A.D.):

> God Himself, the father and fashioner of all that is, older than the Sun or the Sky, greater than time and eternity and all the flow of being, is unnameable by any lawgiver, unutterable by any voice, not to be seen by any eye. But we, being unable to apprehend His essence, use the help of sounds and names and pictures, of beaten gold and ivory and silver, of plants and rivers, mountain-peaks and torrents, yearning for the knowledge of Him, and in our weakness naming all that is beautiful in this world after His nature—just as happens to earthly lovers. To them the most beautiful sight will be the actual lineaments of the beloved, but for remembrance' sake they will be happy in the sight of a lyre, a little spear, a chair, perhaps, or a running-ground, or anything in the world that wakens the memory of the beloved. Why should I further examine and pass judgment upon Images? Let men know what is divine ($\tau o \ \theta \epsilon \hat{\iota} o \nu \ \gamma \acute{\epsilon} \nu o s$), let them know: that is all. If a Greek is stirred to the remembrance of God by the art of Phidias, an Egyptian by paying worship to animals, another man by a river, another by fire—I have no anger for their divergences; only let them know, let them love, let them recall.[1]

In the vast international, intercultural empire of the Persians, though a fine tolerance was practiced toward the gods of conquered peoples, no attempt was ever made, either by the King of Kings or by any priest of the Magian clergy, to further a general system of syncretic universalization. Persian religious tolerance was political and prudent, not an expression of belief. Nor when it suited political ends did the Persians for a minute hesitate to desecrate alien shrines. Alexander, invading Persia in the years 336–330 B.C., gave strict orders that no sacred object whatsoever should be injured; but when the Persians, nearly two centuries before, had sought to overpower Greece, they had destroyed temples, burned the images of gods, and desecrated shrines, with the same sort of righteous zeal as had moved Elijah and Elias, Josiah and Hezekiah—for, after all, they too were Levantine "monotheists," for whom there was no true god but their own.[2] The Greeks were both incensed and horrified by such impiety; and Aeschylus, in his patriotic tragedy *The Persians,* attributed to these godless acts of sacrilege and hubris the obviously miraculous defeat of the mighty Persian fleet in its incredible disaster at Salamis. "Those godless," he wrote; "those of pride infatuate who made Greece their prey, nor held it shame to rob her gods and give her shrines to flame":

> Altars lie wrecked and images of God
> O'erthrown, disbased, and down in rubbish trod.
> For which dire sin, dire suffering now is theirs,
> And direr yet shall be. . . .[3]

Darius I, having made himself master of the world, sent a fleet to subdue Athens in the summer of the year 490 B.C. His army landed on the shore at Marathon—and every schoolboy knows the rest. Aeschylus fought, and his brother died, in the battle: 6400 Persians and 192 Athenians lay dead upon the field; and Darius commenced immediately to prepare a second, larger, much larger, fleet and army for a second try. He died, however; and his son, Xerxes the Great (r. 486–465 B.C.), one decade after Marathon, sent against Athens the largest military force the world had ever seen assembled—about half a million men, drawn from every quarter of his empire, and a fleet of some 3000 ships, with himself in personal command. However, at Thermopylae, Leonidas with 300 Spartans, absolutely brave, held the pass for three full days. They died, enveloped by an army driven on with whips; and about them lay 4000 Persian dead. Whereafter, in the harbor of Salamis

—September 23, 480 B.C.—the flower of the Persian fleet, 1200 vessels strong, outmaneuvered and outfought by a Greek fleet of 380, went to ruin before the appalled eyes of the King of the Four Quarters—and the Orient, we may say, had found its bound.[4]

Alexander was Europe's answer. And within two generations of his death at the age of thirty-three, he was celebrated in the Orient as a god.

He was at least the creator of a new world. And of the numerous things that might be said of that world, four stand as of particular pertinence to our study of the history of myth.

First, as already remarked, we note not merely respect for the gods of all religions, but an almost scientific effort to recognize analogies; so that specific deities of the various lands began to be identified and worshiped as equivalent to each other: Isis and Demeter, Horus and Apollo, Thot and Hermes, Amun and Zeus. The Greeks in Bactria and in India identified Krishna with Heracles, Shiva with Dionysus, and in the West the later Romans saw, not only in the Greek gods but also in the Celtic and Germanic, respectable counterparts of their own. Before the Alexandrian period there had been many regional syncretic movements, as, for instance, that of the great Egyptian priestly syntheses of Re and Amun, Ptah and Osiris, and the masterful joining of Re, Osiris, Seth, Horus, and Thot in a single grandiose mythology. Likewise in India and in China regional syncretisms had abounded, and there was generally, as in Greece, a decent regard for other people's gods. However, nowhere before the period of Alexander the Great does the idea seem to have emerged—or, at least, to have been put into operation—of a transcultural syncretism, systematically cultivated. We may see in this an extension of the Greek regard for the individual beyond the bounds of Greece itself, as well as an application of the idea of an empire not of tyranny but of free men to the sphere of thought. For in this period the Periclean ideal of the polis expanded to the Alexandrian ideal of cosmopolis: the *oecumene,* or inhabited world as a whole, as the common possession of civilized mankind.

The second point to be observed for this period is the role of philosophy and science in the higher reading and development of myth. In sixth- and fifth-century Greece, the philosophers had recognized a relationship of the Dionysian-Orphic complex to philosophical thought, and in the cults of the Orient they now discovered analogous possibilities. In Babylonian astronomy and mathematics —from the archaic period of which practically all the high mythologies of both East and West had originated [5]—they found new inspiration for a deepening of their own cosmological vision; and from the new developments of both these sciences in Alexandrian times entirely fresh ideas concerning the structure of the universe were derived, which remained basic to Occidental mythic thought (as, for example, in Dante's *Divina Commedia*) until the century of Copernicus, when the sun displaced the earth at the center of the macrocosmic order.

Point three to be observed, then, is the breakthrough of the Greek inquiring intellect with Alexander into India, where a totally unforeseen species of philosophic inquiry had been developed in the various yogic schools of the Jain, Buddhist, and Brahmanic centers. A far deeper understanding of the practical psychological—as opposed to cosmological—relevancy of mythology was represented in those disciplines than anything the West was to achieve until the century of Nietzsche, Freud, and Jung. However, in the meantime a formidable influence of only half-comprehended psychosomatic mystic lore was to come pouring out of India into the hermitages and monasteries, schools and universities of the comparatively callow West—from which a number of colorful gnostic, theosophical, and hermetic cults and movements were derived.

And then, finally, as a fourth point to be remarked in the rich context of the Hellenistic world, we must note that, after about two centuries of European influence upon Asia, the tide began to turn, until presently a powerful surge of reaction developed, which culminated with the victories of Christianity over the gods and philosophies of Classical antiquity and the subsequent collapse—for a spell of seven centuries—of the civilization of the European West.

II. Syncretistic and Ethnic Monotheism

Polytheism we may define as the recognition and worship of a plurality of gods; monalatry as the worship of a single god—one's own—while recognizing others.* Monotheism is the belief that there is finally but one substantial god; and of monotheism two types are to be distinguished: 1. the inclusive, cosmopolitan, open, syncretic type, and 2. the ethnic, closed, and exclusive. Ethnic monotheism is the belief that the only god is the god worshiped by one's own group, all others being false. Syncretic monotheism, recognizing that all concepts of deity are limited, infers an ultimately inconceivable god above all, to whom all refer; as in the "Universal Prayer" of Alexander Pope (put forth in 1738), of which the following three stanzas—in their mincing minuet—suffice to make the point:

> Father of All! in ev'ry Age,
>   In ev'ry Clime ador'd,
> By Saint, by Savage, and by Sage,
>   Jehovah, Jove, or Lord!
>
> . . . .
>
> Let not this weak, unknowing hand
>   Presume thy bolts to throw,
> And deal damnation round the land,
>   On each I judged thy Foe.
>
> . . . .
>
> To thee, whose Temple is all Space,
>   Whose Altar Earth, Sea, Skies,
> One Chorus let all Being raise,
>   All Nature's Incense rise! [6]

The outstanding instance of ethnic monotheism is, of course, the post-exilic monotheism of the Bible, which then passed to Chris-

---

* In recent theological writings the term henotheism has been incorrectly used in this sense. Henotheism was a term invented by Max Müller with reference specifically to Vedic theology, where one god after another is celebrated as supreme. In later Hinduism, likewise, a worshiper may celebrate as supreme first Shiva, then Vishnu, and then again the Goddess; in the spirit of the Vedic saying "Truth is one, the sages call it by many names" (*Rg Veda* X. 164.46).

tianity and Islam; while the most richly developed systems of syncretic monotheism have been those of the Hellenized Near East, Rome, Gupta and post-Gupta India, and (in the broadest sense) the humanistic learning of Europe since the Renaissance. Epicureanism, Buddhism, and the higher reaches of Hinduism are exceptional in as much as their final terms are not personified, or in any way anthropomorphized, as "God." However, in the higher reaches of syncretic monotheism and even, occasionally, of ethnic, where the godhood may be recognized as absolutely unknown (*deus absconditus:* "god concealed"), a point of contact is afforded for a valid juncture of theology with these trans- or non-theological orders of belief.

In Classical Greece an early prelude to the Hellenistic and Roman, Renaissance and eighteenth-century types of monotheism is to be recognized in the often-cited statement of Xenophanes of Colophon (fl. 536 B.C.), the reputed founder of the Eleatic school from which Plato derived certain mythologically colored strains of his philosophy.

> There is one God, greatest among gods and men, neither in shape nor in thought like unto mortals. . . . He is all sight, all mind, all ear. . . . He abides ever in the same place motionless, and it befits him not to wander hither and thither. . . . Yet men imagine gods to be born, and to have raiment, voice, and body, like themselves. . . . Even so the gods of the Ethiopians are swarthy and flat-nosed, the gods of the Thracians, fair-haired and blue-eyed. . . . Even so Homer and Hesiod attributed to the gods all that is shame and a reproach among men—theft, adultery, deceit, and other lawless acts. . . . Even so oxen, lions, and horses, if they had hands wherewith to carve images, would fashion gods after their own shapes and make them bodies like to their own.[7]

And again, we have the words of Antisthenes (born c. 444 B.C.): "God is not like anything; hence one cannot understand him by means of an image."[8]

Xenophanes was a contemporary of the Buddha (563–483 B.C.), and, according to Aristotle, "the first to believe in the unity of all things."[9] According to Simplicius, on the authority of Theophrastus, Xenophanes conceived the One, the Unity of all Things that was God, as neither limited nor limitless, neither in motion nor at rest [10]—which is a view close enough to the Indian of brahman or the Void to allow for comparison. Antisthenes was the founder of the Cynic (*kynikos*, "doglike") school, and his most celebrated disciple, Diogenes (412?–323 B.C.), suggests comparison with a certain type of Hindu ascetic. Dwelling (significantly) in a large discarded earthen pot outside the temple of the Great Mother, to illustrate the "doggishness" of his back-to-nature philosophy he would shamelessly relieve himself whenever nature moved. Alexander the Great is supposed to have visited him, as the next most celebrated man in the world, and when the young monarch asked if there were any boon the beggar desired, the Cynic replied, "You are between me and the sun, please move aside." Thus, with considerably more thoroughness than his later counterpart, Jean Jacques Rousseau, Diogenes went all the way in his return to what he took to be man's state in nature. The conscientious "doggishness" of the later Zen masters of China and Japan was another statement of the same rejection of both the amenities and the ideals of civilization; as, likewise, the Chinese Taoist notion—just about contemporary with Diogenes—of returning to the state of "the uncarved block," the sage sitting with blank mind.[11] And we should perhaps also recognize something of the same in Christ's rejection of the world: "If you would be perfect, go, sell what you possess and give to the poor, and you will have treasure in heaven; and come, follow me." [12]

"If I were not Alexander, I would be Diogenes," the political master of the known world is reported to have said; and the Cynic: "If I were not Diogenes, I would be Alexander." However, the main line of Greek religiosity never accepted the Cynic notion of man without civilization as properly *man*. For the Greek, indeed for the European mind, the faculty of reason is to such a degree particular to man that to erase it is not to return to nature but to escape from it—from *man's* nature. And if the excellence, *arete*, of any species must be recognized as rising from a life lived according to its nature, then for man it must be according to reason—neither to ecstatically communicated, so-called "divine revelations," nor to animalistic or vegetal erasures of the human faculties. Moreover, the faculty of reason develops not in sheer solitude, but in society; for as the Emperor Marcus Aurelius (whom Matthew Arnold has termed "perhaps the most beautiful figure in history"),[13] wrote in his memoirs of admonition to himself:

> If our intellectual part is common, the reason also, in respect of which we are rational beings, is common: if this is so, common also is the reason which commands us what to do, and what not to do; if this is so, there is a common law also; if this is so, we are fellow-citizens; if this is so, we are members of some political community; if this is so, the world is in a manner a state. For of what other common political community will anyone say that the whole human race are members? And from thence, from this common political community comes also our very intellectual faculty and reasoning faculty and our capacity for law; or whence do they come? For as my earthly part is a portion given to me from certain earth, and that which is watery from another element, and that which is hot and fiery from some peculiar source (for nothing comes out of that which is nothing; as nothing returns to non-existence), so also the intellectual part comes from some source.[14]

And he writes again: "The prime principle then in man's constitution is the social." [15] "Men exist for the sake of one another." [16]

Furthermore, since there are joy and beauty, as well as excellence, in a life lived according to its nature, therefore excellence —i.e., "virtue," properly understood—must be and *is* its own reward. Or, as we read further, in the words of the philosopher king:

> One man, when he has done a service to another, is ready to set it down to his account as a favor conferred. Another is not ready to do this, but still in his own mind he thinks of the man as his debtor, and he knows what he has done. A third in a manner does not even know what he has done, but he is like a vine which has produced grapes, and seeks for nothing more after it has once produced its proper fruit. As a horse when he has run, a dog when he has caught the game, a bee when it has made its honey, so a man when he has done a good act, does not call out for others to come and see, but he goes on to

another act, as a vine goes on to produce again the grapes in season. Must a man, then, be one of these, who in a manner acts thus without observing it? Yes.[17]

Somewhat the same idea might at first seem to have been implied in the words of Jesus: "Do not let your left hand know what your right hand is doing"; however, the full text of the Christian admonition changes the point of view:

> Beware of practicing your piety before men in order to be seen by them; for then you will have no reward from your Father who is in heaven. Thus, when you give alms, sound no trumpet before you, as the hypocrites do in the synagogues and in the streets, that they may be praised by men. Truly, I say to you, they have their reward. But when you give alms, do not let your left hand know what your right hand is doing, so that your alms may be in secret; and your Father who sees in secret will reward you.[18]

As Matthew Arnold temperately remarks: "The motives of reward and punishment have come, from the mis-conception of language of this kind, to be strangely overpressed by many Christian moralists, to the deterioration and disfigurement of Christianity." [19] And, for contrast, he cites the above quoted passage of the Stoic Caesar.

The view and estimate of virtue that is running through all this is the same, essentially, as that of the Homeric *arete*. However, a new inwardness, maturity, or adulthood, has appeared. For the comparatively youthful ideal of the buoyant, wonderfully physical earlier centuries, when all had been going well for the battle-ready Greeks, had long since been undermined by the sickening devolution of the late fifth and early fourth centuries B.C. The victories over Persia of the generation of Aeschylus had been followed by a sequence of interior disasters: the Peloponnesian Wars, 431 and 413–404 B.C.; Corinthian War, 395–387; Theban War, 371–362; and finally, 335 B.C., the frightful destruction of Thebes by Alexander the Great and the transfer of Greek hegemony to the young and ruthless master from the north.

Professor Gilbert Murray has termed the centuries between the flowering of classical Athens and the growth of the radically different garden of the early Christian era the period of the Failure of Nerve.[20] It was an age comparable to that of India in the Buddha's time and of China in the period of Confucius; for in each of these the earlier social structure was in process of dissolution, the centers of higher civilization were crumbling before the sheer power of comparative barbarians, and the central task of philosophy had become, on one hand socio-political, how to restore a dissolving civilization to health, and on the other, moral and psychological, how an individual in the shattering world might retain and develop his own humanity. The Buddha's sermon is well known:

> All life is suffering;
> The cause of suffering is ignorant craving;
> The suppression of suffering [*nirvāṇa*] can be achieved;
> The Way is the Noble Eightfold Path:
>   Right Views, Aspiration, Speech, and Conduct;
>   Right Vocation, Effort, Mindfulness, and Rapture.

The laws of the universe were of no interest in themselves to the Buddhist seeker of the way out. There was no moral law derived from God; for there was no God, and the gods or principles by which the world was held in form were themselves the nets, traps, and obstacles that the yogi must elude. The Buddha's Eightfold Path was a path entered upon voluntarily, against the order of the universe. And when the victor had thoroughly killed all fear and desire in himself, there supervened, paradoxically, a rapture both of transcendence and of compassion for all self-bounded beings.

Confucius's sagely teaching, in contrast to this yogic way of individual disengagement, was of social reconstruction through individual integrity; and the noble humanity of this line of thought has suggested to many a comparison with the Greek. However, a difference lies in the conservatism of the Chinese in contrast to the inventive, rational experimentations of the Greek schools, in every field. Both in Confucianism and in Taoism, the Chinese ideal was to place the individual in accord with the order both of his own nature and of the world; and in the Stoic tradition of the West the leading idea was—apparently—the same. Likewise in both East and West, the cosmic order itself was conceived in terms of the old

Sumero-Babylonian idea of an eternal round of eons, ever returning, with man, the microcosm, an organ of the whole. As the Taoist
teachers of quietism renounced society to place themselves in
harmony with nature, so, likewise, the Greek Cynics; and as the
Confucians sought to bring the principles of life-in-accord-with-
nature (in accord with the Tao) into play in the social nexus, so
too the Greek Stoics and, more effectively, the Roman. However,
in their approaches to the study of nature as well as in their views
of the individual and the state, the Classical and Chinese thinkers
were as far as possible apart.

In the first place, whereas the Chinese view of the universe remained archaic, Greek science during the Hellenistic age was in a
phase of unexampled transformation. While the Oriental sages were
brooding philosophically on the alternating influences of the male
(*yang*) and female (*yin*) forces in the cosmic harmony of heaven,
earth, and man, the Greeks, building forward from Sumero-Babylonian beginnings, were already arguing the problem of a helio-
centric astronomy against a geocentric. Aristarchus of Samos (c.
310–230 B.C.) proposed the view that the earth and all the planets
revolved around the sun in circles, while the sun itself and the stars
were stationary. He could not *prove* his point, however, and so,
when Hipparchus of Nicea (c. 146–126 B.C.) appeared to have
solved the problem better with a geocentric hypothesis, employing
epicycles and eccentric circles to explain the planetary orbits, his
system prevailed until Copernicus (1473–1543 A.D.) set the matter
straight.[21] Eratosthenes of Cyrene (275–200 B.C.), meanwhile, had
measured to within two hundred miles the circumference of the
earth, concluded that one might sail from Spain westward to India,
and suggested that the Atlantic might be divided longitudinally by
a land mass (America).[22] While in medicine Herophilus of
Chalcedon (third century B.C.) discovered the relationship of the
brain and spinal column to the nerves, and Erasistratus of Iulis
(also third century B.C.) recognized the difference between the
motor and sensory nerves.[23] In the Greek and Roman Stoic system
the nature to which man was called to accord, therefore, was not
that of the older mythic world views, even though in the notion of

nature as one great organism and of the ever-recurrent cycles of world emergence and dissolution highly significant old Sumerian themes were retained.

Another point of difference, though in many ways the Greek and Chinese sages might seem to have been thinking in much the same terms,[24] is that whereas Chinese education remained an elegant affair of the elite—owing in part to the recondite nature of the Chinese script—Hellenistic education was general. And correlatively, whereas Chinese government was in theory as well as in practice an expression of archaic mythic notions of a divine appointment of the emperor, who ruled by the mandate of heaven as an organ of the cosmos, the Greek idea and experience of government was of human beings—whether despots or elected—administering conventional human laws, not laws superhumanly ordained.

It was in the writings of the great personalities of the Hellenistic and Roman Stoic school that the most enduring and influential statements of the moral, political, and cosmological implications of Hellenistic syncretic monotheism appeared; and notably in the works of its Greco-Phoenician founder, Zeno (336?–264 B.C.), the Roman author Seneca (4 B.C.–65 A.D.), the crippled Phrygian-Roman slave Epictetus (c. 60?–120 A.D.), and the emperor, Marcus Aurelius Antoninus (121–180 A.D.). Epictetus and Aurelius are of particular interest, since they represent most emphatically the two extremes of social destiny; so that we may know that each speaks out of life. The slave, on one hand, asks:

> How can it be that one who has nothing, neither raiment, nor house, nor home, nor bodily tendance, nor servant, nor city, should yet live tranquil and contented? Behold God has sent you a man to show you in act and deed that it may be so. Behold me! I have neither city nor house, possessions nor servants: the ground is my couch; I have no wife, no children, no shelter—nothing but earth and sky, and one poor cloak. Yet, what do I lack? Am I not untouched by sorrow, by fear? Am I not free? [25]

And from the other pole, the emperor:

> How small a part of the boundless and unfathomable time is assigned to every man? for it is very soon swallowed up in the

eternal. And how small a part of the whole substance? and how small a part of the universal soul? and on what a small clod of the whole earth you creep? Reflecting on all this consider nothing to be great, except to act as your nature leads you, and to endure what the common nature brings.[26]

Zeno of Citium in Cyprus, a shy and silent foreigner, in part at least of Phoenician background, first became known to Athens about 300 B.C., as a philosopher talking to those who would listen, in a public colonnade, the Painted Porch. His school became known, therefore, as the Stoa, the Porch. And because the virtue of his life matched that of his teaching, the nobility of his character as well as lore drew to him a following of excellent young men. When he died, the city of Athens gave him the funeral of a hero.[27]

His two leading disciples, Cleanthes of Assos in the Troad (fl. c. 260 B.C.) and Chrysippus of Soli in Cilicia (d. 206 B.C.), developed the doctrine, the former with a Platonic accent and the latter assimilating the deities, heroes, and mantic cults of the folk; while Posidonius of Alamea in Syria (135?–50? B.C.), who settled in the great Hellenistic seafaring station of Rhodes, produced with immense learning an encyclopedic synthesis of the religious and scientific thinking of his age that was both the culminating Stoic theoretical work and one of the wonders of the ancient world. According to Posidonius, physics and theology are two aspects of one knowledge, since God is immanent throughout nature as well as infinitely transcendent. Science, therefore, deals with the material body of which God is the living spirit.

For all these thinkers, God, the informing spirit of the world, is rational and absolutely good. Nothing, therefore, can occur that is not—in the frame of the totality—absolutely good. The doctrine, essentially, is that satirized by Voltaire in *Candide,* of the best of all possible worlds. But in strong terms it was reaffirmed by Nietzsche in his rhapsodic *Thus Spake Zarathustra,* where the word "good" is read not as "comfortable" but as "excellent," and a call is issued to each to love his fate: *amor fati.* Oswald Spengler also represents this view in his motto, adopted from Seneca: *Ducunt fata volentem, nolentem trahunt:* "The fates guide him who will, him who won't they drag." It is a view derived rather from courage and joy than from rational demonstration: from a life zeal and affirmation, beyond any kind of pleasure-pain calculation. It leaves the Buddhist sentiment of compassion (*karuṇā*) far behind; for compassion contemplates suffering. And Job's problem also is left behind; for that too rests upon the recognition of suffering. In Seneca's words: "Not what you bear but how you bear it is what counts." [28] And again: "Within the world there can be no exile, for nothing within the world is alien to man." [29]

"Great is God," declared the lame slave Epictetus:

> This is the rod of Hermes: *touch what you will with it,* they say, *and it becomes gold.* Nay, but bring what you will and I will transmute it into Good. Bring sickness, bring death, bring poverty and reproach, bring trial for life—all these things through the rod of Hermes shall be turned to profit.[30]

> *Great is God,* for that He has given us such instruments to till the ground withal:
> *Great is God,* for that He has given us hands, and the power of swallowing and digesting; of unconsciously growing and breathing while we sleep!

> Thus should we ever have sung: yea and this, the grandest and divinest hymn of all:—

> *Great is God,* for that he has given us a mind to apprehend these things, and duly to use them! [31]

> You yourself are a fragment torn from God: you have a portion of Him within yourself.[32]

The ideal of indifference to pain and pleasure, gain and loss, in the performance of one's life task, which is of the essence of this Stoic order, suggests the Indian ideal of Karma Yoga described in the Bhagavad Gita. "The calm spirit, indifferent to pain and pleasure, whom neither can disturb: he alone is fit for immortality." [33] "Therefore, without attachment, do what has to be done: that is the way the highest state is achieved." [34] However, the Indian life task is imposed upon each by his caste statutes, whereas the Greco-Roman task is that recognized and imposed on each by his own reason: for God here is Intelligence, Knowledge, and Right Reason.[35] Furthermore, the condition of *nirvāṇa,* disengagement in trance rapture, which is the ultimate goal of Indian yoga, is entirely different from the Greek ideal of *ataraxia,* the *rational* mind undisturbed by pleasure and pain. Yet, between the two views there is much to be compared, and particularly their grounding in what Christian scholars like to call "pantheism," which is fundamental both to the Orient—whether India or the Far East—and to the Classical world: against which the biblical view, whether in Jewish, Christian, or Islamic thought, stands in unrelenting, even belligerent, argument.

Within a world that is itself divine, where God is immanent throughout, in the impulse of the flight of birds, the lightning, the falling rain, the fire of the sun, there is an epiphany of divinity in all sight, all thought, and all deeds, which—for those who recognize it—is a beginning and end in itself. There is for all, and within all, a universal revelation. Whereas within a world that is not itself divine, but whose Creator is apart, the godhead is made known only by *special* revelation—as on Sinai, or in Christ, or in the words of the Koran; and righteousness then consists in placing oneself in accord, not with nature but with Sinai, with the lesson of Christ or with the Koran; and one lives not simply to play the part well that is in itself the end, like the grapevine producing grapes, but, as Christ has said, "so that the Father may reward." The goal is not here and now, but somewhere else.

As the conservative Jewish scholar Jacob Hoschander has pointed out, the first unmistakably monotheistic, as distinguished from monalatrous, utterances of the Bible are to be found in Second Isaiah, about 539 B.C., in the period of Cyrus the Great.[36] Yet the God so universalized was still specifically the God of the house of Jacob, who was supposed to have brought Cyrus to victory so that his people should be restored.[37] And in the subsequent utterances of Ezra, in the P Text authors by whom the Pentateuch was put together, and in Jewish writings into Roman times there was no break from this fundamental line. In fact, as Professor Klausner has demonstrated, even Philo Judaeus (c. 20 B.C.–54 A.D.), the most Hellenized of the Jewish semi-Platonist philosophers, could not bring himself to think of God as immanent. "The Logos of Philo," Klausner writes,

> is different in a fundamental respect from that of Heraclitus and the Stoics. While for them the universal intelligence or "inspirited matter" (matter into which an animating breath has been blown) and deity are the same thing, and thus they reach pantheism as well as a certain materialism (even "inspirited matter" is matter)—by contrast Philo the Jew sees that for him deity is a separate entity (included in the world). . . . There is nothing in common except the name between the "Logos" of Philo and "Word" of the Gospel of John (which depends on Philo) on the one hand, and the "Logos" of Heraclitus the Stoic and of Epictetus on the other hand. The Philonic "Logos" is an almost completely original creation, the fruit of Jewish thought and teaching based on the Scriptures (Midrash).[38]

"In the world as it is," as Klausner has said, "there are good and evil; so how could God, who is absolutely good and perfect, form a world which contains evil, the essence of imperfection?" [39]

To which the lame Phrygian slave, from the other side, has already answered:

> When we are invited to a banquet, we take what is set before us; and were one to call upon his host to set fish upon the table or sweet things, he would be deemed absurd. Yet in a word, we ask the gods for what they do not give; and that, although they have given us so many things! [40]

Epictetus's magic, to make all things gold, was that of Hermes' staff.

III. Mystery Cult and Apocalypse

In Japanese the term *jiriki,* "one's own strength," refers to such self-reliant disciplines as Stoicism or, in the Orient, Zen Buddhism, while *tariki,* "outside strength, another's strength," refers to ways that rely on the idea of a savior: in Japan, Amida Buddhism. Through invoking the name of the infinitely radiant Solar Buddha of the Land of Bliss, one is reborn, at death, in his paradise, there to attain nirvana.[41] During the Hellenistic age Western counterparts of this popular Buddhism were the numerous mystery cults that flourished with increasing influence until, in the late Roman period, first Mithraism, then Christianity, gained imperial support and, thereby, the field.

For not all of us are philosophers. Many require an atmosphere of incense, music, vestments and processions, gongs, bells, dramatic mimes and cries, to be carried beyond themselves. And for such the various styles of religion exist—where, for the most part, however, truth is so enveloped in symbol as to be imperceptible to anyone who is not already a philosopher. Degrees of initiation have been developed, through which the mind is meant to be carried beyond the fields of the symbols to increasingly exalted realization—passing, as it were, through veil beyond veil. But the ultimate realizations differ, according, on one hand, to those cults in which divinity is seen as at once immanent and transcendent, and, on the other, to the orthodox Zoroastrian, Jewish, Christian, and Mohammedan liturgies, where the ontological distinction is retained between God and Man, Creator and Creature.

In cults of the former type the two strengths, "outside" and "within," are finally to be recognized as identical. The savior worshiped as without, though indeed without, is at the same time one's self. "All things are Buddha things." Whereas in the great Near Eastern orthodoxies no such identity can be imagined or even credited as conceivable. The aim is not to come to a realization of one's self, here and now, as of one mystery with the Being of beings, but to know, love, and serve in this world a God who is apart (mythic dissociation)[42] though close at hand (omnipresence), and to be happy with him when time shall have ceased and eternity been attained. The referent (the "God") of cults of the first type is never a personage somewhere else, to be known, loved, served, and some day beheld (which, in fact, is the notion to be dispelled), but a state of realization to be attained by way of the initiatory, knowledge-releasing imagery of the "God," as through a sign. The function of such signs is to effect a psychological change of immediate value in itself, while that of the orthodox mythology is to fix the mind and will upon a state of soul to come.

As an example of the first or pagan-Oriental type, we may take the once powerful cult, derived from Iran, of the Mysteries of Mithra, which came to flower in the Near East during the Hellenistic age as a kind of Zoroastrian heresy, and in the Roman period was the most formidable rival of Christianity both in Asia and in Europe, reaching as far north as to the south of Scotland. In it were offered seven degrees of initiation. In the first, the neophyte was known as "Raven" (*corax*), and in the rites the celebrants wore masks representing animals of the zodiac: for astronomy was undergoing a new development in this period through an application of Greek thought to the data of the centuries of Sumero-Chaldean observation. In all religions of the age, the zodiac had come to represent the bounding, ever-revolving sphere of time-space-causality, within which the unbounded Spirit operates—unmoved yet moving in all. The orbits of the seven visible spheres—Moon, Mercury, Venus, Sun, Mars, Jupiter, and Saturn—were conceived as so many envelopes around the earth, through which the soul had descended when coming to be born. The individual had derived from each a specific temporal-spatial quality, which on the one hand contributed to his character, but on the other was a limitation. Hence, the seven stages of initiation were to facilitate passages of the spirit, one by one, beyond the seven limitations, culminating in a realization of the unqualified state.

The Raven, the black bird of death with whom the mystic was identified in the first initiation, carried him symbolically beyond the lunar sphere, which was the sign—here as everywhere—of the waxing and waning of the life-round of birth and death: the nutritive, vital energies of the vegetal aspect of existence. Identified with the Raven, the mystic imagination left the physical body to the work of change and dissolution, flying, as it were, through the lunar gate, to the second sphere: that of Mercury (Greek Hermes; Egyptian Thot; Germanic Woden, Othin), the sphere of occult powers and of magic, and of the wisdom of rebirth.

In a second rite the candidate, known now as "Hidden Master" (*cryphius*), passed from Mercury to Venus's sphere of mystically toned delusions of desire, where, again, certain disciplines of initiation were experienced. Assuming the character of "Soldier" (*miles*), he passed next to the circle of the sun, the realm of intellectual arrogance and power, to be presented with a crown upon a sword, which he thrust back with his hand, so that it fell, declaring that Mithra alone should be his crown. He became here a "Lion" (*leo*) and participated in a sacramental meal of bread and water mixed with wine, as a rite of supreme graduation, whence he passed through the solar gate to the fifth zone, Mars—of daring and audacity—where he donned the Phrygian cap and loose Iranian garb of the Savior Mithra himself, assuming the title of "Persian" (*perses*).

Two further transformations remained. First, quenching in his heart the rashness of audacity, he passed to Jupiter, to be known as "Runner of the Sun" (*heliodromus*); and finally, from Jupiter mounting to Saturn, he was sanctified as "Father" (*pater*). The trials along the way had served to cultivate the Stoic virtue of indifference to pleasure and pain, while symbolic apparitions had impressed upon the mind certain essential attitudes. The rites were celebrated, normally, in a grotto symbolic of the world cave, in which the old mythological theme of the unity of the macrocosm (the universe), mesocosm (the liturgy), and microcosm (the soul) was illustrated. And in contemplation of the doctrine of the immanence of God, the mystic was led by degrees to an experience, in his final stage, of the transcendent reality of his own being.

The god who was to be the inspiration, and to become in time the incarnate form of the initiate, was the old Aryan deity Mithra—Vedic Mitra—the first known occurrence of whose name was in the treaty, previously mentioned, c. 1400 B.C., between the Hittites and Mitanni.* There this god appeared as one of five Vedic Aryan deities summoned to witness and approve the pact, namely: Mitra, Varuna, the monster-slayer Indra, and the twin horsemen, the Ashvins or Nasatya. Both his antiquity and his northern Aryan

* Supra, p. 121.

derivation can therefore be presumed, even though he is not mentioned in the Gathas of Zoroaster. In the Yashts of the later Avesta (about sixth century B.C.) the name recurs in its Persian form, as the greatest of an order of angels known as the Yazatas, as "adored ones." Called "the lord of wide pastures," he is there praised by the Creator himself and said to have "a thousand ears, ten thousand eyes," like the Vedic monster-killer Indra. "I created him," Ahura

Figure 23. Mithra Tauroctonus

Mazda is supposed to have declared to his prophet Zoroaster, "to be as worthy of sacrifice and as worthy of prayer as myself." [43]

Mithra seems not to have attained to the status of a paramount symbol, however, until the Hellenistic period, when he appeared in two related but contrasting manifestations. Figure 23 shows an example from the second century A.D. of an image of which literally hundreds of counterparts have been found throughout Europe. The model seems to have been created by a sculptor of the school of Pergamon toward the close of the third century B.C., possibly with the features of Alexander as inspiration.[44] In loose Iranian garb, and wearing the characteristic Phrygian cap adopted many centuries later (and not at all by accident) by the prophets of the light of reason of the French Revolution, the flashing hero-savior is performing his supreme symbolic act as Tauroctonus, Slayer of the Primeval Bull—which was the role assigned in the orthodox Zoroastrian system to the wicked Angra Mainyu, the Antagonist.*

It will be recalled that in the normal Zoroastrian view all evil in the world is attributed to the Demon of the Lie, who, in the end, is to be undone, when the savior Saoshyant appears, and there is a reference of all acts of virtue forward toward the realization of that Messianic day. A historically oriented, progressive, apocalyptic theme underlies the whole tradition. Whereas here, in this Hellenistic representation of the Persian god and savior Mithra, there is expressed a new—or perhaps resurgent, primitive—interpretation of the immemorial mythic symbol of the sacrifice.

Let me refer the reader once again to the brutal rites, described in *Primitive Mythology,* of the murdered, cut-up, and buried divine being from whose body all food plants grow.[45] According to the primitive view represented in those rites, the world is to be not improved but affirmed, even in what to the rationalizing moralist appears to be its most horrible, ungodlike sinfulness: for precisely in that resides its creative force, since out of death, decay, violence, and pain comes life. As in the words of William Blake: "The roaring of lions, the howling of wolves, the raging of the stormy sea, and the destructive sword, are portions of eternity, too great for the eye of man." [46] The virtue of heroism must lie, therefore—according to a view of this kind—not in the will to reform, but in the courage to affirm, the nature of the universe. And in the mystery cults of the Greco-Persian Hellenistic age it was this mystical, world-loving—not the orthodox world-improving—type of optimistic affirmation that prevailed.

Professor Franz Cumont, to whose researches we owe most of what we know of Mithraism, has observed that in the finer examples of the image of Mithra Tauroctonus the features of the god bear an expression of dolor and compassion as he drives the knife, and so takes upon himself the guilt—if such it must be termed—

* Compare supra, p. 204.

of life, which lives upon death.[47] In the corresponding Christian image of the Sacrifice of the Cross, though the savior there is declared to have taken on his shoulders the sins of mankind, a certain terrible guilt remains attached to the Jews by whom he was condemned, to Judas who betrayed him, and to Pontius Pilate, by whom he was crucified. For the god-man is there the victim, the sacrificial lamb, whereas here, the god-man is the sacrificial priest. Compare the Cretan sacrifice of Figure 18. He is himself performing the brutal deed by which the world is ever, and ever again, renewed. He is the lion-bird, the solar bird, of Figure 16; and though the bull is suffering in our view, he is in fact the same as the cosmic bull of the archaic smile.

We note in Figure 23 that where the knife runs into the bull the blood comes forth as grain—conforming to the old myth already recalled, as well as to the Zoroastrian theme of grain from the marrow of the Ox.* A serpent glides beneath, representing, as the serpent always does, the principle of life bound to the cycle of renewal, sloughing death. The dog, who is in Iranian myth the friend and counterpart of man and in the episode of the first couple ate the first bite of meat,† here eats the grain (the blood), as the archetype of life nourished by the sacrifice, while the scorpion gripping the bull's testicles typifies the victory of death as well—since death as well as life is an aspect of the one process of existence.

There is also an astronomical reference to be recognized in the symbols of the bull and scorpion; for in the centuries during which the foundations of all astrological iconography were laid (c. 4300–2150 B.C.), the zodiacal sign of Taurus, the Bull, stood at the vernal equinox, and Scorpio, the Scorpion, at the autumnal. Leo, the Lion, was then the sign of the midsummer sun, when its decline toward winter began, and Aquarius, the Water Carrier, was in the house of the winter solstice, where the sun god, *Sol invictus,* was annually reborn, on December 25.

In the grottoes of the Hellenistic Mithra cult all these festivals of the solar round were celebrated in masked rites, to which the rites

* Supra, p. 204.
† Supra, p. 206.

of initiation were attached. And we are informed from numerous sources of an actual bull sacrifice, the *taurobolium,* which was performed above a pit in which the initiate lay, so that he was baptized in a cascade of hot bull's gore.[48] Two attendants, one before and one behind the sacrifice, held flaming torches, one turned up, the other down, to represent respectively the rise of light to the upper and descent to the nether world: sunrise, sunset, the vernal and autumnal equinox, birth, death, and the circulation of the energy of light from the central act of the sacrifice. Or these two so-called Dadophors might carry the heads of a bull and a scorpion, as Taurus and Scorpio. They have been compared to the two thieves crucified with Christ, one of whom was to ascend to heaven and the other descend to hell; likewise, to the medieval Christian motif of the wise and foolish virgins, the former holding lamps burning upward, and the latter, lamps out, turned down.[49] However, in the usual Christian reading a moral turn is given to such signs, so that their mystic sense disappears; for, with this retained, hell itself would be redeemed, whereas the whole point of the Christian dualism is that sin is absolutely evil, hell eternal, and its souls forever damned.

Amidst the little that we know of the mythic biography of the Persian savior Mithra, a number of parallels appear both to Christian and to Zoroastrian themes. However, just as in the case of the Dadophors, whereas they are on one level analogous, and in fact derive from the same source, they represent a completely different reading of the nature of the universe and of man: a mystical affirmative, as against a moral corrective, and a reassertion of the elder, primitive, and generally pagan designation of the sacrifice.

Mithra, like Gayomart, of whom he is in a certain sense the antithetic counterpart, was born beside a sacred stream beneath a sacred tree. In works of art he is shown emerging as a naked child from the "Generative Rock" (*petra genetrix*), wearing his Phrygian cap, bearing a torch, and armed with a knife. His birth is said to have been brought about *solo aestu libidinis,* "by the sole heat of libido (creative heat)," [50] and, as Dr. Carl G. Jung has pointed out in one of his numerous discussions of this subject, here all the elemental mother symbols of mythology are united, earth (the rock), wood (the tree), and water (the stream).⁵¹ The earth has given birth—a virgin birth—to the archetypal Man. And so that we may know the birth to be symbolic (not prehistoric, as the claim would be for, say, an Adam or a Gayomart) nearby are shepherds witnessing the birth, coming with their flocks to pay the savior worship, as in Christmas nativity scenes. Christ, the Second Adam, was the renewer of the image of man. In the Persian savior Mithra the two Adams are united; for there was no sin, no Fall, involved in his enactment of the deeds of temporal life. With his knife the child culled the fruit of the tree and fashioned clothing of its leaves: once again like Adam—but without sin. And there is another scene, which shows him shooting arrows at a rock, from which water pours to refresh a kneeling suppliant. We do not possess the myth, but the episode has been compared to that of Moses producing water from the rock in the desert with his rod (Exodus 17:6). However, Moses sinned, for he struck twice, and consequently, was denied entry into the Promised Land—as Adam sinned and was denied paradise. But the savior Mithra both ate the fruit of the mother tree and drew the water of life from his mother rock—without sin.

The primal bull was grazing on a mountainside when the young athletic god, seizing it by its horns, mounted, and the animal, wildly galloping, presently unseated him, but, clinging to its horns, he was dragged until the great beast collapsed. He then seized it by its hind hoofs, which he hoisted to his shoulders, and the so-called *transitus,* or difficult task of hauling the live bull, head down, along the way of many obstacles to his cave, began. This painful ordeal both of hero and of bull became symbolic both of human suffering in general and of the specific trials of the initiate on his way to illumination—corresponding (though with hardly comparable force) to the *Via Crucis* of the later Christian cult. When he had reached his cave, a raven sent by the sun brought the savior word that the moment of sacrifice had arrived, and, seizing his victim by the nostrils, he plunged the knife into its flank. (We note the raven of the first initiation here associated with the sacrifice of the bull, the lunar beast: and see again Figure 16.) Wheat sprang from the bull's spinal cord and from its blood the vine—whence the bread and wine of the sacramental meal. Its seed, gathered and purified by the moon—as in the orthodox Zoroastrian myth *—produced the useful animals by which man is served. And, as we have ob-

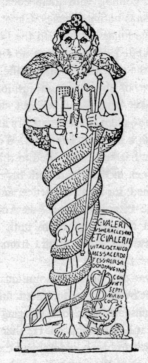

Figure 24. Zervan Akarana

served already in the pictured scene, the animals of the goddess-mother of death and rebirth arrived to perform their several tasks: the scorpion, dog, and serpent.[52]

But this myth and ritual of the initiate "washed in the blood of the bull" was only introductory to a deeper, larger mystery symbolized in the second major apparition of the cult: Zervan Akarana, "Boundless Time." The image of this mystery shown in Figure 24

* Supra, p. 204.

was found in the ruins of the Mithra temple of the Roman port of Ostia, where it was dedicated in 190 A.D. by a certain C. Valerius and his sons. A nude male body wears the head of a lion. Four wings issue from his back, bearing the symbols of the seasons of the year. In each hand is a key, and in the left a scepter of authority as well. A serpent winding in six turns up the body rests its head (turn 7) above the brow. And the symbol on the man's chest is of the fiery thunderbolt, which nothing can resist.[53]

But this symbol of the fiery bolt, in exactly the same form, is the normal attribute of a certain aspect of Buddhahood, known as the Buddha Vajradhara, "Bearing the Bolt," who stands for that Supreme Illumination of which the Buddhas who appear in time and space are but the visible manifestations. Such a bolt may appear in the Buddha's hand or engraved upon his chest, where it signifies (to quote the words of Heinrich Zimmer), "the weapon or substance of adamantean truth and reality, compared with which all other substances are fragile." [54] The Sanskrit term *vajra* means both "thunderbolt" and "diamond." As the diamond cannot be cut by other stones, so do all things fall before the bolt; they belong to the merely phenomenal sphere and can offer no resistance. And in that branch of Buddhism known as the Vajrayana, "Thunderbolt Way" (Shingon in Japan), which is an extremely bold and colorful, magico-mystical form of Tantric Buddhist discipline,[55] the Buddhist mystic, through meditation, postures, and the pronunciation of spells, may substantialize the *vajra* power immanent within himself, which then can be applied either to sorcery or to the attainment of ultimate Illumination.[56]

In *Oriental Mythology* I have shown that a distinct Iranian influence can be discerned in the popular Chinese and Japanese sects of the Solar Buddha Amitabha-Amitayus (*amitābha,* "immeasurably radiant"; *amitāyus,* "forever enduring"; known as Amida in Japan), whose veneration first appeared in northwestern India c. 100 A.D. and spread thence to the Far East.[57] The cult is of the "outside strength" (*tariki*) type, and is characterized by the oft-repeated aspiration, *Namu Amida Butsu,* "Glory to Amida Buddha," through which the mind and heart are readied for the saving grace of this infinitely compassionate savior. But now it must be noted that in exactly the same centuries the influence of Hellenized Iran was spreading even more strongly toward the West, where the Roman armies stationed throughout Europe were celebrating Mithraic rites. Sanctuaries abound throughout the Danube and Rhine valleys, Italy and the south of France, with extensions into Spain. Many of the Levantine slaves brought into Roman Europe were initiates, as were also a number of the late emperors, from Commodus (r. 180–192 A.D.) to Julian (r. 361–363). The imperial cult of *Sol invictus,* instituted by Aurelian (r. 270–275 A.D.), was syncretized with that of Mithra. And since syncretism was no less congenial to the native religions of Europe than to those of the Orient, there developed throughout the post-Alexandrian world—from Scotland to North Africa and eastward into India, with extensions even to the Far East—a single, rich, and colorful religious empire with an infinite wealth of forms, joining and harmonizing on many levels all the pantheons of the nations: Celtic, Germanic, Roman, Greek, and Oriental.

Do we not hear, indeed, the echo of *Namu Amida Butsu* in the aspiration inscribed on the Mithraic shrines of second- and third-century Europe: *Nama, nama Sebazio?* [58] The deity here invoked is clearly the Greek Sabazios, who, as Jane Harrison has shown, was a doublet of Dionysus—symbolized by that golden serpent which, in the Orphic rites of initiation, was let glide "through the bosom" in symbolic suggestion of the unity of god and devotee.* And do we not recognize our very lion-man in the popular Hindu figure of Vishnu as the Man-Lion, Narasimha?

Returning to Figure 24, we note in the lower left-hand corner the tongs and hammer of the god Vulcan, of fire and metalcraft: the fire by which the metal is brought from its ore and by which the craftsman creates forms. At the lower right is the cock, announcer of the new sun. Before him lies the pine cone symbolic of the seeds of life produced by the ever self-renewing cosmic tree. And finally, the serpent winding up the body of the lion-man is duplicated in the caduceus, which corresponds not only in form, but also certainly in

* Supra, p. 184.

sense, to that of the cup of King Gudea of Lagash (Figure 1). The single serpent of the main figure has become in the caduceus two —as Adam became Adam and Eve. And these wind up the axial pole (*axis mundi*), the spinal line of the lion-man himself, who is the Alpha and Omega of all the productions of time.

In other words, the syncretic mythic lore of this cosmopolitan period was in no sense a mere hotchpotch raked together from every corner of the earth. The symbolism throughout was as consistent as could be, and in accord, furthermore, with a common heritage shared by all from of old. For, as all these religions of the agriculturally based high cultures had been developed, actually, from a few (astonishingly few) insights of the neolithic, Bronze, and Iron ages, locally adapted to landscapes and to manners of somewhat (though not absolutely) differing requirement, so in this age of intercultural exchanges they could be readily brought together again by anyone properly trained in his own tradition. The parallels, in fact, are not difficult to recognize, even today—at least for those scholars who are not so committed to the usual Judeo-Christian notion of transcendence that they cannot spell out the alphabet of immanence even after working at it all their lives.

In the Vedic Aryan tradition, to which the Aryan Persian is akin, the god Mitra (Persian Mithra) always appears in association with Varuna—so intimately, indeed, that these two are generally named in a single dual noun, *Mitrāvaruṇau*. In the hymns, Varuna is described as the lord of the cosmic rhythm (*ṛta*) of the cycling starry sky; [59] while his other half, the god Mitra, brings forth the light of dawn, which at night was covered by Varuna. In the late Vedic ritual literature it is prescribed that Mitra must receive a white and Varuna a dark victim at the sacrificial post. And in the Shatapatha Brahmana the compound person of Mitra-Varuna is analyzed as "the Counsel and the Power." "These," it is said, "are his two selves. Mitra is the Counsel, Varuna the Power; Mitra the Priesthood, Varuna Royal Rule; Mitra the Knower, Varuna the Executive." [60] Comparing Figure 24, we see that Zervan Akarana is also a dual god: a naked lion-man enveloped by a snake of seven folds. The lion is symbolic of solar light, which is eternal; the serpent, of the rhythmic, circling round of the lunar tides of time, which never cease. Thus the figure is precisely what its name tells: Zervan Akarana, "Boundless Time," in which eternity and time are one, yet two. But if anyone should suppose that he would ever meet this figure anywhere beyond the bounds of time (which is boundless), he would have missed the point of his initiation, and would have to be sent back, I should think, to his Raven suit.

The serpent is of seven folds: these are the folds of temporality. They were identified in the Hellenistic world with the seven celestial spheres after which our days of the week are named, as Sun-day, Moon-day, Mars (Germanic Tīwes) day, Mercury (Germanic Woden's) day, Jupiter (Germanic Thor's) day, Venus (Germanic Frigg) day, and Saturn-day. We have already seen that the progress of the mystic way cut through these seven veiling folds to the adamantean truth. And that truth now has been shown to us in the symbol of the lion-man.

Midway along the path of initiation, as we have seen, the *taurobolium* was enacted, as a repetition of the savior Mithra's slaying of the bull. Analogously, in the Indian Vedic mythology, Indra, the warrior king and savior of the gods, slew the all-enveloping Vritra, who, though a serpent, is described also as a bull. He is the negative aspect of the power of Varuna; and Indra, his slayer, is on many counts the analogue of the Persian Mithra Tauroctonus. Both are said to have a thousand eyes. Both are active foreground aspects of the light or solar force at play in time. Both renew the world by their deed. And in rites performed for the benefit of eligible individuals, the priestly re-enactment of their sacrifice endows the beneficiary with the knowledge of eternal life. As we read, for instance, in the Vedic Taittiriya Samhita: "By means of Mitra the priest sacrifices Varuna for him [the beneficiary] . . . sets him free from Varuna's noose, so that even if his life be almost gone he verily lives." [61] Thus the symbols of the Persian lion-man and slayer of the bull correspond, in a way that is quite precise, to those of the Vedic Mitra-Varuna and slayer of dragon-bull.

Moreover, as the two torchbearers, the Dadophors, attended the deed of the Persian Mithra Tauroctonus, so in the Indian Vedic context we have a matched pair who also represent the principle of syzygy—the unity of apparent opposites—namely, the Nasatya, twin horsemen, or Ashvins. These are identified, amongst other associations, with sky and earth (i.e., up and down), eternity and time, priest and king, as the two halves of one spiritual person.[62] So let me call attention once again, to the names of the five Vedic dieties who were invoked to witness that treaty, c. 1400 B.C., of the Hittite and Mitanni kings. They were, exactly, Mitra, Varuna, Indra, and the Nasatya, the twin horsemen; precisely those five most perfectly matched by Zervan Akarana (= *Mitrāvaruṇau*), Mithra Tauroctonus, and the Dadophori of the Mithraic cult—which seems to have originated, by the way, in just that part of the Near East where the Hittites and Mitanni had flourished eleven hundred years before.[63]

There is a lot more to be told; but we have already followed the subject about as far as is appropriate for a work of the present scope. And I would hope to have made it perfectly clear, at least, that if certain scholars of this subject have found it difficult to recognize anything but a hotchpotch of puerilities in the syncretistic mystery cults of the Hellenistic period, the fault lies not altogether in Antiquity. The function of these cults was to bring about, by one means or another, a psychological transformation in the candidate for knowledge, as a result of which his mind should come to rest in the realization that divinity inheres in, as well as transcends, every particle of the universe and all its beings; the realization that duality is secondary; and the realization that man's goal cannot be to make duality disappear at the end of time, as in the ethical, dualistic teaching of the prophet Zoroaster, since time, being boundless, never ends. Boundless Time, Zervan Akarana, holds everything in its tongs; shapes all things with its hammer; yet yields through its hard initiations knowledge of the adamantean reality, which is here and now, beyond the obscuring veil of duality, the true eternity of us all.

This teaching is the same, essentially, as that of the yogic schools of India; and a particularly striking analogy is the Kundalini Yoga of the Gupta and post-Gupta periods. For there the aim was to bring the "Serpent Power," the spiritual force of the yogi, from its lowest seat at the base of the spine, up an interior path to the crown of the head, completing seven stages, at each of which the psychological limitations of the lower planes of commitment are surpassed.[64] As in India, so in these Hellenistic mysteries, the accomplished initiate both realized his own divinity and was honored as a god: for what better sign of godhood could there be than a human being in whom his own godhood had been realized? or what better guide to one's own perfection? Nor was the impact of the pagan mystery cults of this age felt only by such confused minds as, dear reader, you and I might be warranted to pity or despise. No less a one than Marcus Tullius Cicero (106–43 B.C.) wrote in his *De Legibus* of the Greek mysteries of Eleusis:

> Among the many excellent and divine institutions that your Athens has developed and contributed to human life, there is none, in my opinion, better than these mysteries, by which we have been brought forth from our rustic and savage mode of existence, cultivated, and refined to a state of civilization: and as the rites are called "initiations," so, in truth, we have learned from them the first principles of life and have gained the understanding, not only to live happily, but also to die with better hope.[65]

The rites of Demeter and Persephone of Eleusis, Isis of Alexandria, Mithra of the Persians, and the Great Mother, Cybele, of Asia Minor, mutually influenced and enriched each other in the course of these centuries—all in terms of a common ability to sense and experience the miracle of life itself as divine, and wonderfully so. In contrast to which we find that in the orthodox Zoroastrian church, as well as in Judaism and, later, Christianity and Islam—where the ultimate view was not of boundless time but of a time when time began, as well as of a time when time would end: moreover, where it was supposed that the world and its inhabitants might be judged as, for the most part, evil, yet susceptible of some sort of ontological correction: and finally, where (particularly in Judaism, Christianity, and Islam) no immanent divinity was recognized in the material world, but God, though omnipresent and (in the phrase of the Korān) "closer to man than his neck vein," was absolutely other and apart—the ultimate goal was not, and could not be, the realization of eternal life in this world. Consequently, whereas in pagan mysteries the symbolism of world annihilation always applied, finally, to a psychological, spiritual crisis in the initiate, whereby the shadowplay of phenomenality was annihilated as by a thunderbolt and the adamantean Being of beings realized immediately and forever, in the orthodox, ethically scaled Levantine religions, the same symbolism of world annihilation was applied, rather, historically, as referring to a day to come of terminal doom.

In the earlier Jewish writings of the Day of the Messiah, the underlying notion had been simply of the restoration of the Jewish state under a king of the line of David, and the willing recognition, then, by all nations, of the truly Chosen People of God. However, in the Hellenistic period, notably from c. 200 B.C. to c. 100 A.D., there burst upon certain Jewish minds the highly thrilling idea that their own national Messiah would be, in fact, the cosmic Messiah at the end of time (like Saoshyant)—upon whose appearance there would follow gloriously, amid thunderous phenomena, the resurrection of the dead, liquidation of time, and all the rest. Moreover, that day was at hand. An abundant, imaginative Apocalyptic literature burst into bloom, first among Jews, but then also among Christians: the Book of Enoch, Testaments of the Twelve Patriarchs, Apocalypse of Baruch, Assumption of Moses, et cetera; and, above all, in the Christian series, the words attributed to Christ himself, touching the end of days and his own return in glory. It is well worth repeating these here in full; for, in direct contrast to the initiatory symbolism of the mystery cult just studied, they bring out very clearly the typical point of view of an Apocalypse—besides revealing fully the cosmology of bounded time of the early Christian church and (apparently) of Christ himself. For, as we read:

> And as he sat on the Mount of Olives opposite the temple, Peter and James and John and Andrew asked him privately, "Tell us, when will this be, and what will be the sign when these things are all to be accomplished?" And Jesus began to

say to them, "Take heed that no one leads you astray. Many will come in my name, saying, 'I am he!' and they will lead many astray. And when you hear of wars and rumors of wars, do not be alarmed; this must take place, but the end is not yet. For nation will rise against nation, and kingdom against kingdom; there will be earthquakes in various places, there will be famines; this is but the beginning of the sufferings.

"But take heed to yourselves; for they will deliver you up to councils; and you will be beaten in synagogues; and you will stand before governors and kings for my sake, to bear testimony before them. And the gospel must first be preached to all nations. And when they bring you to trial and deliver you up, do not be anxious beforehand what you are to say; but say whatever is given you in that hour, for it is not you who speak, but the Holy Spirit. And brother will deliver up brother to death, and the father his child, and children will rise against parents and have them put to death; and you will be hated by all for my name's sake. But he who endures to the end will be saved.

"But when you see the desolating sacrilege set up where it ought not to be (let the reader understand),* then let those who are in Judea flee to the mountains; let him who is on the housetop not go down, nor enter his house, to take anything away; and let him who is in the field not turn back to take his mantle. And alas for those who are with child and for those who give suck in those days! Pray that it may not happen in winter. For in those days there will be such tribulation as has not been from the beginning of the creation which God created until now, and never will be. And if the Lord had not shortened the days, no human being would be saved; but for the sake of the elect, whom he chose, he shortened the days. And then if any one says to you, 'Look, here is the Christ!' or 'Look, there he is!' do not believe it. False Christs and false prophets will arise and show signs and wonders, to lead astray, if possible, the elect. But take heed; I have told you all things beforehand.

"But in those days, after the tribulation, the sun will be darkened, and the moon will not give its light, and the stars will be falling from heaven, and the powers in the heavens will

---

* This parenthetical aside is taken as evidence by modern scholars that the words here accredited to Jesus were not actually his.

be shaken. And then they will see the Son of man coming in clouds with great power and glory. And then he will send out the angels, and gather his elect from the four winds, from the ends of the earth to the ends of heaven.

"From the fig tree learn its lesson: as soon as its branch becomes tender and puts forth its leaves, you know that summer is near. So also, when you see these things taking place, you know that he is near, at the very gates. Truly, I say to you, this generation will not pass away before all these things take place. Heaven and earth will pass away, but my words will not pass away.

"But of that day or that hour no one knows, not even the angels in heaven, nor the Son, but only the Father. Take heed, watch; for you do not know when the time will come. It is like a man going on a journey, when he leaves home and puts his servants in charge, each with his work, and commands the doorkeeper to be on the watch. Watch therefore—for you do not know when the master of the house will come, in the evening, or at midnight, or at cockcrow, or in the morning— lest he come suddenly and find you asleep. And what I say to you I say to all: Watch." [66]

IV. The Watchers of the Dead Sea

If the Battle of Marathon may be said to mark the crucial point of resistance of the European spirit to Asia, the counterpole of Levantine tolerance of the paganism of Europe may be seen registered in the reaction of the true "remnant" to the installation of a Greek altar—the "Abomination of Desolation"—on the Jewish altar in the temple court of Jerusalem. The year was 167 B.C., and the perpetrator of the indignity was the Seleucid emperor of Syria, Antiochus IV Epiphanes (r. 175–164 B.C.).

"In those days," we read in the First Book of the Maccabees,

Mattathias the son of John, the son of Simeon, arose; a priest of the sons of Joarib, from Jerusalem, and dwelt in Modin. And he had five sons. . . . And when he saw the blasphemies that were committed in Judah and Jerusalem, he said, "Woe is me! Wherefore was I born to see this misery of my people and of the holy city, and to dwell there when it was delivered into the hand of the enemy, and the sanctuary into the hands of strangers? All her ornaments are taken away; of a free woman she is become a bondslave. And, behold, our sanctuary, even our beauty and our glory, is laid waste, and the gentiles have profaned it. To what end therefore shall we live any longer?" Then Mattathias and his sons rent their clothes, and put on sackcloth, and mourned very sore.

In the meanwhile the king's officers, such as compelled the people to revolt, came into the city Modin, to make them sacrifice. And when many of Israel came unto them, Mattathias also and his sons came together. Then answered the king's officers, and said to Mattathias on this wise. "Thou art a ruler, and an honorable and great man in this city, and strengthened with sons and brethren. Now therefore come thou first, and fulfill the king's commandment, as all the heathen have done, yea, and the men of Judah also, and such as remain at Jerusalem. So shalt thou and thy house be in the number of the king's friends, and thou and thy children shall be honored with silver, gold, and many rewards."

And Mattathias answered and spake with a loud voice: "Though all the nations that are under the king's dominion obey him and fall away every one from the religion of their fathers, and give consent to his commandments, yet will I and my sons and my brethren walk in the covenant of our fathers. God forbid that we should forsake the Law and the Ordinances. We will not hearken to the king's words, to go from our religion, either on the right hand, or on the left."

Now when he had left speaking these words, there came one of the Jews in the sight of all to sacrifice on the altar which was at Modin, according to the king's commandment. Which thing when Mattathias saw, he was inflamed with zeal and his loins trembled, neither could he forbear to show his anger according to judgment. Wherefore he ran, and slew him upon the altar. Also the king's commissioner, who compelled men to sacrifice, he killed at that time, and the altar he pulled down.

And Mattathias cried throughout the city with a loud voice, saying: "Whosoever is zealous of the Law and maintaineth the Covenant, let him follow me." So he and his sons fled into the mountains, and left all that ever they had in the city. Then many that sought after justice and judgment went down into the wilderness, to dwell there: both they and their children, their wives and their cattle, because afflictions increased sore upon them.[67]

And so, we are told, the uprising began that led to the founding of the Jewish state of the Maccabean (also called Hasmonean) priest-kings.

Meanwhile, however, not all the People were of one mind; nor were all, by any means, in Palestine. There were communities in Egypt, Babylon, Syria and Anatolia, in the Greek isles, and in Rome. Moreover, the privilege of judging themselves by their own laws had become in many places a formally granted right. And in many of these widely scattered synagogue communities the services were conducted not in Hebrew but in Greek. In fact, it was for these—and in particular the large Jewish community of Egyptian Alexandria—that the task was undertaken, in the third to first centuries B.C., of translating the Old Testament into Greek: which produced the version called the Septuagint, from the Latin word for "seventy"—since, according to the legend, there were seventy-two translators (six from each of the twelve tribes) and their renditions of the holy text were miraculously identical.*

But with the Greek language and customs came, of course, Greek thought. Some of the communities tolerated mixed marriages; some of their members, joining gymnasiums, exercised naked, like Greeks, and, when dressed, preferred Greek clothes. Some even neglected circumcision. Furthermore, there were proselytes from other faiths who were not required to be circumcised, but only kept the sabbath, worshiped Yahweh, and obeyed the food ordinances. There were even Jews who participated in Hellenistic cults. In Mesopotamia, as Professor W. W. Tarn points out, Jewish women had for centuries joined their neighbors in the annual wailing for Tammuz; and now, in Asia Minor, Yahweh himself had received a Greek name, *Theos Hypsistos,* God the Highest—a name later used even by Philo. "Sabazios, too," as Tarn remarks, "was equated with the god of the Jews, from a fancied identity of Lord Sabazios with Lord Sabaoth"; and indeed, in the year 139, a number of Jews were expelled from Rome ostensibly for introducing the cult of Zeus Sabazios.

* For the force of the number 72 in relation to Sumero-biblical astrology, see *The Masks of God: Oriental Mythology,* pp. 117–21 and 129.

Zeus—Sabazios—Sabaoth—Yahweh—Hypsistos: "These cults," suggests Professor Tarn, "may conceivably have been sufficiently important to make Antiochus IV think that there would be no insuperable difficulty in introducing even in Judaea, the worship of Zeus." [68]

Only a few brief years before the issuing of his offensive order, two contenders for the high priesthood of the temple of Jerusalem had approached him separately and successively for support, Jason of the Oniad family, and Menelaus of the Tobiads. Both were Hellenizers. First Jason won, then Menelaus; and there burst upon the community open civil war—with Syria, Egypt, Arabia, and a criss-cross of all sorts of family and sectarian factions contributing, besides Rome, which now was rising in the West as a growing threat to Antiochus—and Persia, moreover, in the resurgent East.

An idea of the lengths to which those who in the Book of the Maccabees are termed "the wicked men who went out of Israel" (I Maccabees 1:11) actually went in their adoption of Greek ways may be gained from a glance at Figures 25 and 26—which are by no means even exceptional for the period. As Professor Erwin R. Goodenough has shown (in whose monumental twelve-volume work on *Jewish Symbols in the Greco-Roman Period* these amulets are discussed), already in early Palestinian graves many seals appear bearing Jewish names along with figures of the gods of Egypt, Syria, and Babylon; while in the Second Book of Maccabees there is a passage (II Maccabees 12:32–45) where it is told that when the bodies of several Jews who had died fighting for Yahweh were

Figure 25. Iaw

prepared for burial, there was discovered on each "an amulet of the idols of Jamnia." [69]

The representations in our figures are of a type known to scholarship as "the Anguipede," or Snake-footed God. On amulets he is usually labeled *Iaw*. Noteworthy is the cock's head. In some examples this becomes a lion's head, and we seem to be on the way back to the Mithraic Zervan Akarana. Both cock and lion are solar symbols. Other figures show a phallic emphasis, which is appropriate enough in a god whose initiatory rite is circumcision: however, the further association in one of our examples with an eagle wound round by a serpent is rather special. The odd little horned figure at the right of this composition, Goodenough identifies with the old Egyptian god Anubis, bearing a sistrum in his left hand and "a peculiar pronged instrument" in his right.[70]

The Jewish Anguipede is represented normally as a war god, bearing on his right arm a shield and in his left hand the whip of Helios. On his head in one case we see the figure of Ares, the Greek god of war. Still another example shows him as Helios, the sun, standing on a lion, which, in turn, is trampling down a crocodile. The second, smaller human figure in this case is the god Harpocrates—a late Egyptian form of the child Horus—with his left hand to his mouth and a cornucopia on his right arm. In the Hellenistic-Roman age the hand to lips of this child was read as an admonishment to silence; and we learn the sense of this from the following Mithra text.

"When the gods look directly at you and bear down upon you, straightway put your finger to your mouth and say, 'Silence,

Figure 26. Iaw

Silence, Silence, Symbol of the living indestructible God. Protect me, Silence: *nechtheir thanmelou.*" After which one is to give a long whistle, a cluck, and pronounce other magical words.[71]

In the age of the Maccabees the leaders in Jerusalem of the Hellenizing party were the Sadducees, among whom were priestly families claiming descent from the priestly patriarch Zadoc (Zadoc > Sadducee), and these were opposed chiefly by the Pharisees, or "Separatists," who believed themselves to be of a stricter orthodoxy—though, in fact, they had combined the old Hebrew heritage of a Day of Yahweh to come with the idea of the world end of Zoroastrian eschatology. The Jewish historian Joseph ben Matthias, or, as he preferred to write his name, Flavius Josephus (c. 37–95 A.D.), wrote of these two sects in his *De Bello Judaico.*

"The Pharisees," in his words, "are those who are esteemed most skillful in the exact explication of their laws and are regarded as the first sect. They ascribe all to fate and to God, and yet allow that to act as is right, or the contrary, is principally in the power of men: although fate does cooperate in every action. They say that all souls are incorruptible, but that the souls of good men only are removed into other bodies, whereas the souls of bad men are subject to eternal punishment." [72]

In other words, though strict enough in their practice of the ceremonial laws, they had added to their beliefs the idea of the immortality of the soul, the resurrection of the body, and a future retribution. Besides, they also believed in a Messiah to come in the last days of the world, as well as in a pantheon of angels.

"But the Sadducees," states Josephus, "are those that compose the second order, and take away fate entirely, and suppose that God is not concerned in our doing or not doing what is evil. And they say that to act what is good or what is evil is at man's own choice, and each man attaches himself to the one or the other as he will. They also take away the belief of the immortal duration of the soul and the punishments and rewards in Hades." [73]

Actually, the Sadducees, for all their Hellenizing, were those who in matters of doctrine held to the old law exclusively, rejecting every one of the popular traditions that had been absorbed from the Persians by their challengers. Moreover, in politics they were closer than the Pharisees to the reigning spirit of the Maccabees, who, after all, were still vassals of the Hellenistic Seleucids, though free now to worship as they pleased. The Sadducees were, in short, the aristocratic party: intelligent, conservative, sophisticated snobs. "Whereas," states Josephus, "the Pharisees are friendly to one another, and are for the exercise of concord and regard for the public, the Sadducees, even toward each other, show a more disagreeable spirit, and in their relations with men of their own kind are as harsh as though they were gentiles." [74]

Now it is simply a fact, signally illustrated in the history of the Levant and particularly in Judaism and Islam, that when religion is identified with community (or, as we have expressed the idea, with a consensus),* and this community, in turn, is not identified with an actual land-based socio-political organism, but with a transcendental principle embodied in the laws of a church or sect, its effects on the local secular body politic, within which it thrives but with which it does not identify itself, are inevitably and predictably destructive. The Old Testament Book of Kings describes in detail the terrible effects of such intransigence in the history of the monarchy of David, and we are now to watch it once again come into play—with cumulative fury—in the calamitous disintegration from within of the state so bravely fought for by the Maccabees.

For when the bold Mattathias and his sons—we are told—had made good their cause against the Greek altars, they and their friends went round about, "and what children soever they found within the coast of Israel uncircumcised, those they circumcised valiantly. They pursued also after the proud men and the work prospered in their hand. So they recovered the law out of the hand of the gentiles and out of the hand of kings, and neither suffered the sinner to triumph." [75]

Mattathias was followed by his eldest son, Judas Maccabeus, who, "in his acts was like a lion, and like a lion's whelp roaring for his prey, for he pursued the wicked and sought them out, and burnt up those that vexed his people." Indeed, he succeeded even in slay-

* Supra, pp. 138–39.

ing Antiochus's agent, Apollonius, who, as we read, "gathered the gentiles together, and a great host out of Samaria, to fight against Israel. Which thing when Judas perceived, he went forth to meet him, and so he smote him, and slew him: many also fell down slain, but the rest fled. Wherefore Judas took their spoils, and Apollonius' sword also, and therewith he fought all his life long." [76] Judas made league with the rising power of Rome. But he was slain in battle when he went against a Syrian army that had been treacherously summoned against him by the Hellenizing high priest of Jerusalem, Alcimus.

Judas was succeeded by his younger brother Jonathan (r. 160–143); however, as the tale now turns: "the wicked began to put forth their heads in all the coasts of Israel and there rose up all such as wrought iniquity." [77] Alcimus, the Hellenizing high priest, now was in actual command of the city and, in keeping with his program to integrate Jewish and contemporary life, he relaxed the observance of the Mosaic code and even removed the walls of the inner court of the temple. Intrigues, on one side with Rome, while on the other simultaneously with Syria, miracles of supernatural intervention, famines and executions followed throughout Israel in bewildering succession. Jonathan took refuge in a desert city, which he fortified, and in 152 B.C., some years after Alcimus had died, Jonathan, with Syrian help, returned victoriously to Jerusalem, restored the wall, and resanctified the city.[78]

There was now, however, no consecrated high priest. Besides, the late tenant of the office, Alcimus, had been of the upstart Tobiad, not authentic Oniad, family; and to compound the impropriety of the situation, Jonathan the Maccabee now contrived to have himself installed in that sacred office at the Feast of Tabernacles of the year of his victory. He died nine years later, and the office passed to his brother Simon, who was confirmed by "the priests and people and the heads of the nation and the elders of the country," as well as by the Seleucid emperor of Syria; and this outrage was commemorated by a bronze plaque in which it was stated that Simon should be "their governor and high priest forever, until a prophet should arise, and that, furthermore, he should be obeyed by all and that all documents in the country should be written in his name, and that he be clothed in purple and wear gold." [79]

Simon reigned but eight years (142–134); for while he was on a tour of inspection, in Jericho, his son-in-law, at a great banquet given ostensibly in his honor, got him drunk and had him slain. His wife and two of his sons were imprisoned—later cruelly murdered [80]—but his third son, John Hyrcanus, managing to escape, assumed immediately the high priesthood and reigned thereafter for thirty-one fairly prosperous years (135–104), waging war on every hand with considerable success. However, as Josephus states, "these successes made him envied, and occasioned a sedition in the land; and many there were who got together and would not be at rest till they broke out into open war—in which war they were beaten." [81]

Now those who had thus risen and been beaten were the Pharisees, whom, in the first years of his reign, John Hyrcanus had favored but subsequently betrayed. He had invited a number of their leaders to a feast and, when the dinner was over, asked for approval of the godliness of his rule. Whereupon, one old Pharisee present, whose name was Eleazar, let him hear that if he truly wished to be righteous he should lay aside the priesthood, to which his family properly had no claim. After that, Hyrcanus not only turned his favor to the Sadducees but formally forbade the observance of Pharisaic rites. And it was apparently in the course of this reign, c. 110 B.C., that the recently discovered Dead Sea Scroll retreat was built, far eastward in the desert, about ten miles from the Jordan site where John the Baptist later was to baptize.

For in the city of Jerusalem the battle of the two contending sects continuously increased, and to such a point that many thought the prophesied war at the end of days, the apocalyptic moment, had arrived. John Hyrcanus died in 104 B.C., bequeathing the government to his wife and the high priesthood to his son Aristobulus. The son, however, threw his mother into prison, where he let her die of starvation, [82] and, as Josephus states, "changed the government into a kingdom, and was the first to put a diadem on his head." [83] This added sacrilege to sacrilege; for if the family had no right to the high priesthood of Zadoc, it had no more to the kingship of David; and besides, the act of assuming to himself both anointments amounted practically to an assumption of the ultimate apocalyptic Messiahhood.

Aristobulus was not to live long to enjoy his blasphemous act. For he caused his brother Antigonus to be slain by an assassin, and when he himself then coughed up blood and it was being carried away by a servant, by chance the servant stumbled and the blood spilled on the very spot stained by his brother's blood. Asking the meaning of the shocked cry without, he was told, and immediately expired, having reigned but one miserable year (104–103).[84]

Aristobulus's widow, Alexandra, let his surviving brothers out of the jail in which he had kept them and married the eldest, who seemed to her to be the most moderate and responsible in temper, Alexander Jannaeus (r. 103–76 B.C.)—who, however, embarked straightway on a series of wars, to the north, south, east, and west, suppressing meanwhile with his foreign troops all Jewish insurrections. The Pharisees were heating up. "He slew," according to Josephus, "not fewer than fifty thousand Jews in the interval of six years. Yet he had no reason to rejoice in these victories, since he was only consuming his own kingdom; till at length he left off fighting and endeavored to come to a composition with them by talking with his subjects. But this mutability and irregularity of his conduct made them hate him the more. And when he asked them why they so hated him and how he might appease them, they said, by dying." [85]

In the course of all this the Pharisees invited the Syrian Seleucid, Demetrius, to assist them, and he came, of course. He came against Jerusalem with an army of both Jews and Syrians, which defeated Alexander Jannaeus's force; but after the victory six thousand of his Jews deserted to Jannaeus, and the Syrian king withdrew.[86] Whereafter the king and high priest of Jerusalem took revenge upon the Pharisees. "His rage," states Josephus, "became so extravagant that his barbarity proceeded to impiety, and when he had ordered eight hundred crucified in the middle of the city, he had the throats of their wives and children cut before their eyes. And he watched these executions while he was drinking, lying down with his concubines. Upon which so deep a terror seized on the people, that eight thousand of his opposers fled away the very next night, out of all Judea, whose flight was only terminated by Alexander's death." [87]

And with that death, 76 B.C., the Pharisees came to power, and the internecine tide only ran the other way. New purges, fratricides, betrayals, liquidations, and miracles kept the kingdom in uproar until, after a decade of such madness, the Roman legion of Pompey was invited by one of two brothers who were then contending for the crown to assist him in his holy cause; and it was in this way that the city of God, Jerusalem, passed in the year 63 B.C. into the sphere of Rome.

The recently unearthed desert retreat of the Dead Sea Scroll community, near the preaching place of John the Baptist, belongs precisely to this time; and it surely is no wonder (since all believing Jews supposed in that period that the history of their own people was the destiny of creation) that the idea should have gained currency that the end of the world was at hand; indeed, that the final war and upheaval of "the birth-throes of the Messiah," terrible Armageddon, was already in full course. Mythology had become history, and prophets were recognizing on every side radiant miracles both of promise and of doom. The Sadducees and Pharisees, along with the mighty Maccabees (who were now being called Hasmoneans, after a supposed ancestor of Mattathias) had turned their own Promised Land into a veritable hell on wheels—while a fourth and very different sect withdrew in deep solemnity to the desert and the Dead Sea, with intent there to prepare themselves for the day of days, at hand.

These were the sect called the Essenes, who supposed themselves to be members of the final generation of the world, and they were in training for that ultimate moment of the Lord when the Messiah would appear. The war was to terminate in victory, as a result largely of their own participation on the side of the principle of light, and the earth then would be renewed. As they had read in the words of the prophet Habakkuk: "The earth will be filled with the knowledge of the glory of the Lord, as the waters cover the sea" (Habakkuk 2:14). The dating of the Dead Sea Scrolls now is fixed between c. 200 B.C. and the time of the First Jewish Revolt against Rome, 66–70 A.D. They are the oldest Hebrew manuscripts now known. And their contents are of two kinds:

1. Fragments of Bible text from the period of the Septuagint; * hence, older by as much as three centuries than the orthodox Masoretic version of the Old Testament, and by more than a thousand years than the earliest formerly known Hebrew manuscript of the Bible (Codex Babylonicus Petropolitanus, 916 A.D.); and

2. Writings original to the Essene sect, of which the chief examples are the following:

A) THE SCROLL OF THE WAR OF THE SONS OF LIGHT WITH THE SONS OF DARKNESS

This is a nearly perfect scroll of leather, more than nine feet long, six inches wide, wrapped in a covering of parchment.[88] In it is projected, in detail, a forty-year war plan, by which the Essenes were to conquer the world for God in three military campaigns. The first two campaigns were to be against Mesopotamia, Syria, Egypt, and the other immediate neighbors, which together would last six years, after which there was to follow a sabbatical year of rest. Then the last campaign was to be undertaken against the more distant peoples of the world, and would require twenty-nine years, with four interpolated sabbaticals (which the enemy too apparently were to honor). The title of this scroll suggests the Zoroastrian influence, which is apparent throughout, mingled with echoes of the early Hebrew prophets, here interpreted, however, as referring to an age of which those earlier jeremiads had no idea. And although everything was foreknown, even to the length of each campaign, mankind (or, at least, those elect of mankind who were the members of this sect) would have to participate with all vigor in the action.

* Supra, p. 273.

Some idea of the spirit of this war plan may be gained from the following instruction:

On the trumpets of the assembly of the congregation they shall write "The Called of God"; on the assembly of the commanders they shall write "The Princes of God"; on the trumpets of the connections they shall write "The Order of God"; on the trumpets of the men of renown they shall write "The Chiefs of the Fathers of the Congregation." When they are gathered together to the house of meeting they shall write "The Testimonies of God for the Holy Council." On the trumpets of the camps they shall write "The Peace of God in His Holy Camps"; on their trumpets of breaking camp they shall write "The Powers of God for Scattering the Enemy and Putting to Flight Those Who Hate Righteousness and Turning Back Kindness against Those Who Hate God." On the trumpets of the ranks of battle they shall write "The Ranks of the Banners of God for the Vengeance of His Anger against All the Sons of Darkness." On the trumpets of assembly of the champions, when the war gates are opened to go forth to the array of the enemy, they shall write "Memorial of Vengeance in the Assembly of God"; on the trumpets of the slain they shall write "The Mighty Hand of God in Battle to Cast Down all the Faithless Slain"; on the trumpets of ambush they shall write "The Mysteries of God for the Destruction of Wickedness"; on the trumpets of pursuit they shall write "God's Smiting All the Sons of Darkness—His Anger Will Not Turn Back until They Are Destroyed." . . .

When they go to the battle they shall write on their standards "The Truth of God," "The Righteousness of God," "The Glory of God," "The Justice of God," and after these the whole order of the explanation of their names. When they draw near to the battle they shall write on their standards "The Right Hand of God," "The Assembly of God," "The Panic of God," "The Slain of God," and after these the whole explanation of their names. When they return from the battle they shall write on their standards "The Extolling of God," "The Greatness of God," "The Praises of God," "The Glory of God," with the whole explanation of their names.[89]

B) THE MANUAL OF DISCIPLINE

A manuscript of leather in two rolls, nine and one-half inches wide and perhaps originally, when sewn together, some six or seven feet long.[90] The matter of the text is of two sorts: one, a manifesto of the Doctrine of Two Spirits; the other, a statement of the regulations by which the sect was organized and prepared for its historic work.

God created man to have dominion over the world, and made for him two spirits, that he might walk by them until the appointed time of his visitation; they are the spirits of Truth and of Error. In the abode of light are the origins of Truth, and from the source of darkness are the origins of error. In the hand of the Prince of Lights is dominion over all the sons of righteousness; in the ways of light they walk. And in the hand of the Angel of Darkness is all dominion over the sons of error; and in the ways of darkness they walk. . . . But the God of Israel and his angel of truth have helped all the sons of light. For he created the spirits of light and darkness, and upon them he founded every work and upon their ways every service. One of the spirits God loves for all the ages of eternity, and with all its deeds he is pleased forever; as for the other, he abhors its company, and all its ways he hates forever. . . .

But God in the mysteries of his understanding and in his glorious wisdom has ordained a period for the ruin of error, and in the appointed time of punishment he will destroy it forever. And then shall come out forever the truth of the world, for it has wallowed in the ways of wickedness in the dominion of error until the appointed time of judgment which has been decreed. And then God will refine in his truth all the deeds of man, and will purify for himself the frame of man, consuming every spirit of error hidden in his flesh, and cleansing him with a holy spirit from all wicked deeds. And he will sprinkle upon him a spirit of truth, like water for impurity, from all abominations of falsehood and wallowing in a spirit of impurity, to make the upright perceive the knowledge of the Most High and the wisdom of the Sons of Heaven, to instruct those whose conduct is blameless. For God has chosen them for an eternal covenant, and theirs is all the glory of man; and there shall be no error, to the shame of all works of deceit. . . .

For in equal measure God has established the two spirits until the period which has been decreed and the making new; and he knows the performance of their works for all the periods of eternity. And he causes the sons of men to inherit them, that they may know good and evil, making the lots fall for every man according to his spirit in the world until the time of visitation.[91]

"And this," we next read, "is the order for the men of the community who have offered themselves to turn from all evil and to lay hold of all that he commanded according to his will, to become a community in law and in wealth. . . ."

Most notable in the strictly ordered manner of communal, puritanical, pseudo-military barracks life that the Essenes thought to be necessary for the accomplishment of their end are the vows of chastity, poverty, and obedience, the years and stages of noviatiate, the semi-sacred communal meals, and the emphasis on a kind of ritual bathing. Almost certainly the mother house of the sect was the large building complex recently unearthed in the Wady Qumran, at the northwest corner of the Dead Sea. In its neighborhood there is an extensive cemetery containing mostly males; and it was round about, in various hidings—caves and rock crannies of the desert—that the precious texts were hurriedly stowed for safekeeping at the time of the Jewish Revolt. The dates of occupancy of the site are now reckoned as from c. 110 B.C. to 67/70 A.D., with a lapse of vacancy during the period of the reign of Herod, 31–4 B.C., for which no explanation has been found.

It is believed that around the mother house there was a camp and that there were also in the cities of the land cells or meeting groups of Essenes. Josephus noted the resemblance of the Essene to the Orphic movement of the Greeks, both in mythology and in custom; and connections now may be suggested as well with the Buddhist-Hindu ideal of monastery life. For we have sufficient evidence of the entry of Indian influence into the Hellenistic-Levantine sphere at this time. A recently found rock-wall inscription of the Buddhist king Ashoka (r. 268–232 B.C.), near Kandahar, South

Afghanistan, bears a text in both Greek and Aramaic.[92] And another Ashokan text declares that the Buddhist king sent missionaries to Antiochus II of Syria, Ptolemy II of Egypt, Magas of Cyrene, Antigonas Gonatas of Macedonia, and Alexander II of Epirus [93]—all influential monarchs in major centers of the Hellenistic world.

The archaeological dating of the ruins, the paleographic dating of the scrolls, our knowledge of the history of the Maccabees, and the passage of Josephus on the Essenes perfectly combine to place us in the general socio-historic field from which the Qumran sect emerged; and as a further contribution to our knowledge of their thought, there is, in addition:

c) THE HABAKKUK COMMENTARY

This is a badly damaged fragment, only five feet long and about five and a half inches wide, decayed along the edges, with a loss, apparently, of about two inches.[94] Here appear passages from the Old Testament Book of Habakkuk, sixth century B.C., reread as referring to the Maccabean age, the rationalization being that the prophet was referring to the wars of the "last days," which, indeed, were these.

> *For, lo, I am rousing the Chaldeans, that bitter and hasty nation* (Habakkuk 1:6). This means [states the Commentary] the Kittim [the Romans], who are swift and men of valor in battle, overthrowing rulers and subduing them in the domination of the Kittim. They take possession of many lands and do not believe in the statutes of God. . . . Over smooth ground they go, smiting and plundering the cities of the earth.[95]

At the opening of this text two characters are named, who, in the first flush of excitement following the publication of the document, seemed to some to suggest that the whole mythology of the life, crucifixion, resurrection, and second coming of Jesus the Messiah had been anticipated in the founder of the Essene community of Qumran. As we read:

> *So the law is slacked* (Habakkuk 1:4). This means that they [the leaders of the Jews] rejected the law of God. *And*

justice never goes forth, for the wicked man encompasses the righteous man. This means that the wicked man is the Wicked Priest, and the righteous man is the Teacher of Righteousness.[96]

It is now practically certain that the person referred to as the Wicked Priest was one or another of the reigning high priests of Jerusalem. A number of scholars hold that he was Jonathan Maccabeus (r. 160–142 B.C.), who, as we have just seen, was the first of his line to assume the sacred office.[97] Others give the role to Simon (r. 142–134 B.C.), who was confirmed formally in the role by a decree inscribed in bronze.[98] A third suggestion has been John Hyrcanus (r. 134–104 B.C.), who assumed the anointment not only of high priest, but also of king—in which case the bold challenger Eleazar may have been the Teacher of Righteousness, and a retreat to the desert of the Pharisees (or perhaps of an extreme wing of the Pharisaic party) may then have been the occasion for the founding of the center at Qumran, c. 110 B.C., which is within the span of years of this reign.[99]

In the language of the Scrolls, the Wicked Priest is termed the Preacher of the Lie, the Man of the Lie, the One who Preached with Lies, the Man of Falsehood, and the Man of Scoffing, all of which epithets suggest the Zoroastrian concept of the Lie as the Lord of Darkness, and Truth as the quality of Light.

Another text of the Dead Sea complex, a mere fragment of a commentary on the Old Testament Book of Nahum, speaks of "the Lion of Wrath . . . who hangs men alive," who is to be identified, in all likelihood, as Alexander Jannaeus (r. 104–78 B.C.), who, as we have seen, crucified eight hundred Jews of Jerusalem in one night, and slew their wives before their eyes, while himself enjoyed his concubines.[100] And, as Josephus tells, many Jews thereafter fled for refuge to the desert. "It was a night," writes the Reverend Duncan Howlett, "such as the world has seldom seen. Need we look further for the Wicked Priest of the Dead Sea Scrolls!"[101]

For the Wicked Priest we thus find at least four qualified candidates, whereas for the Teacher of Righteousness, whom the Wicked

Priest is declared to have persecuted, the only name that has been suggested—and this without great conviction—is the brave old Pharisee Eleazar. Were the Essenes, then, a splinter group from the Pharisees? The question is open. Was the Teacher of Righteousness the founder of the sect? Was he crucified by the Wicked Priest? Did he rise again from the dead? And will he come again in the character of Messiah? Let me quote Professor Millar Burrows to these points.

"The teacher may have been crucified. . . . He may have been stoned or put to death in some other way. On the other hand, he may have died a natural death. . . . Neither the Habakkuk Commentary nor any other Qumran text published thus far says or clearly implies that the teacher was put to death." Furthermore: "There is certainly no evidence that he was believed to have risen already." And finally, according to Burrows, it is "quite uncertain" as to whether the Teacher himself was identified with the prophet or Messiah at the end of days.[102] We know from another text of the movement, the so-called Damascus Document (discovered in 1895, and formerly thought to be a Pharisaic text), that there were expected still to come "a teacher of righteousness, an interpreter of the law, a prophet, and two Messiahs," but, as Professor Burrows concludes, "What connection, if any, the teacher of righteousness who had already come was thought to have had with any of these coming persons is quite uncertain." [103]

What is certain, on the other hand, is that we have found in the Dead Sea Scrolls the *Sitz in Leben* (to use Professor F. M. Cross's term) [104] of the Jewish apocalyptic movement of the late Hellenistic age, and that it was from the general neighborhood of this movement that the Christian mission sprang. To quote Professor Cross: "Like the primitive Church, the Essene community was distinguished from the Pharisaic associations and other movements within Judaism precisely in its consciousness 'of being already the called and chosen Congregation of the end of days.' " [105] However, a distinction is to be remarked. For, whereas the Essene, in his view of "the end of days" in which he lived, looked forward to the Messiah, for the early Christian the Messiah had already come. He stood, so to say, on later ground.[106] The leading theme of the Dead Sea community was that Yahweh, as of yore, had brought the armies of the gentiles down upon his people as a punishment for their sins; and in this sense the Essenes stood directly on the line of the old prophets. However, whereas Amos, Hosea, Jeremiah, and the rest had conceived of the Hebrew calamity in historical terms, the ideology now was shot through with Zoroastrian eschatological thought. According to the earlier view, the people were being punished, but a remnant would survive to restore the world power of the messianic House of David. The idea now, on the contrary, was that the day at hand was to mark the end of historic time itself, the end of the cosmic struggle of the two Spirits of Light and Darkness; moreover, that in the tumult of that day of God, which now was in full career, the remnant passing on into the perfect age to come would not be the members of any other Jewish sect but this, sternly training for its high destiny in its monastery of the desert by the Dead Sea.

Much the same was the early Christian view. But, as a number of scholars have observed, the Old Testament legalism and exclusivism, which still are to be recognized in every passage of the Dead Sea Scrolls, had been left behind by the Christians, standing as they were, on the "later ground." The cosmic crisis of the War of the Sons of Light and the Sons of Darkness had been passed, and the old ethic of Judgment therefore could yield to Love. We read in the Dead Sea Manual of Discipline that the candidate for admission to the order of the Community of God was "to seek God; . . . to love all that he has chosen and to hate all that he has rejected; . . . to love all the Sons of Light, each according to his lot in the counsel of God, and to hate all the Sons of Darkness, each according to his guilt in vengeance of God." [107] Whereas in the messianic sphere itself the words to be heard were, rather:

> You have heard that it was said, "You shall love your neighbor and hate your enemy." But I say to you, Love your enemies and pray for those who persecute you, so that you may be sons of your Father who is in heaven; for he makes his sun rise on the evil and on the good, and sends rain on the just

and on the unjust. For if you love those who love you, what reward have you? Do not even the tax collectors do the same? And if you salute only your brethren, what more are you doing than others? Do not even the Gentiles do the same? You, therefore, must be perfect, as your heavenly Father is perfect.[108]

Which is to say, in Zoroastrian terms, you must go beyond Good and Evil, the intertwining serpents, to the posture of the lion-man. Compare the previously discussed mystery of Tiresias, and, in biblical terms, the state of man before the Fall.

So far, then, it would seem that the origins of Christian mythology might be interpreted as a development out of Old Testament thought, under Persian influence, with nothing as yet particularly Greek—unless the emphasis on love and (possibly) a conception of Mankind instead of specifically Jewish Man. However, in relation to the term Messiah something more has to be told; and for this we turn our eyes to Rome.

GREAT ROME:
c. 500 B.C. – c. 500 A.D.

✦✦✦

I. The Celtic Province

Caesar's Gallic wars, commencing in 58 B.C., opening Europe to the empire of Rome as Pompey's wars had opened the Levant, broke the power of the Celts, who for centuries had been harassing the cities of the south. Spain they had entered and occupied in the fifth century B.C., as far as to Cadiz, and their seven-month siege of Rome itself in the year 390 B.C. had been but one of numerous inroads into Italy. Eastward, in 280 B.C., Thessaly was overrun, Greece invaded, Delphi sacked, and the following year the uplands of Asia Minor, which are known to this day as Galatia, became a center out of which war parties ranged even into Syria, until 232 B.C., when King Attalos I of Pergamon subdued the Galatians. The famous Hellenistic victory statue of the "Dying Gaul" depicts one of their handsome fair-haired warriors, wearing a typical Celtic torque or collar of gold.

The earliest matrix of the Celtic culture complex was the Alpine and South German area; and the centuries of its development were those of the early Iron Age in Europe, in two phases: 1. The Hallstatt Culture, c. 900–400 B.C., and 2. the La Tène, c. 550–15 B.C. The first was characterized at the outset by a gradual introduction of iron tools among bronze, fashioned by a class of itinerant smiths, who in later mythic lore appear as dangerous wizards— for instance, in the German legend of Weyland the Smith. The

Arthurian theme of the sword drawn from the stone suggests the sense of magic inspired by their art of producing iron from its ore. Professor Mircea Eliade, in a fascinating study of the rites and myths of the Iron Age, has shown that a leading idea of this mythology was of the stone as a mother rock and the iron, the iron weapon, as her child, brought forth by the obstetric art of the forge.[1] Compare the savior Mithra born from a rock with a sword in his hand.*

"Smiths and shamans are from the same nest," declares a Yakut proverb cited by Eliade.[2] The allegedly indestructible body of the shaman who can walk on fire is analogous to the quality of a metal brought forth through the operation of fire. And the power of the smith at his fiery forge to produce such immortal "thunderbolt" matter from the crude rock of the earth is a miracle analogous to that of spiritual (viz. Mithraic or Buddhist) initiation, whereby the individual learns to identify himself with his own immortal part. In certain Buddhist temples of Japan there is to be seen the image of a strenuously meditating sage, Fudo, "Immovable" (Sanskrit, *Acalanātha*, "Lord Immovable"), seated, grim-faced, amidst a roaring blaze, holding a sword upright in his right hand with adamantine stability, like Mithra rising from the rock. And in the biblical idea of the remnant, which appeared first in Isaiah 10:21–22 (c. 740–700 B.C.), we have an application of the idea to the concept of the hero not as a clarified individual but as a purged people, a tried and true consensus, bearing the purpose of Yahweh through all time.

We may surmise, then, that the iron implements found among the earliest Hallstatt remains (c. 900 B.C.) must represent an entry into Europe of the ritual lore of drawing swords from stones, both in the smithy of the soul and in the fires of the forge. Hallstatt itself, the type site, is in Austria, about thirty miles southeast of Salzburg. Pigs, sheep, cattle, dogs, and the horse were the beasts domesticated. Log cabins and corduroy log roads testify to the crude physical circumstances; and the ornamentation of ceramic and metallic wares, weapons, horse and chariot harness, brooches, et

* Supra, p. 260.

cetera, was inelegant as well: lifeless, crudely symmetrical, geo-
metrical, and stiff. The European peasant smock and a kind of
pointed skullcap seem to have been the normal dress. And the
usual funeral rite was cremation, though burial also was practiced. The earliest locus of the culture was Bohemia and South
Germany, but it spread, in its final century, as far as to Spain and
Brittany, Scandinavia and the British Isles, to furnish a base upon
which the subsequent Celtic flowering of the La Tène period then
appeared, c. 550–15 B.C.

The type site of La Tène, the brilliant second Iron Age of
Central and Western Europe, is in Switzerland, some five miles
from the town of Neuchâtel. Found here were a ten-spoked chariot
wheel, three feet in diameter, bound with an iron tire; two yokes,
each for a pair of horses; parts of a pack saddle, and numerous
smaller equestrian trappings; oval shields, parts of a long bow, 270
spearheads, and 166 swords—several of the latter being in bronze
sheaths, gracefully decorated in the typical high Celtic curvilinear
style.

It was during this period that Rome was besieged by the Celts
and Asia Minor was entered. The tide spread eastward into southern Russia, but the main trend was to the west, where it over-
flowed the earlier Hallstatt sites. In the late fifth century B.C.
the Rhineland and Elbe areas were occupied, and in the early
fourth the Channel was crossed, bearing the tribes known as
Brythons to what now is England, and the Goidels to Ireland—
who then, by invasion, entered Scotland, Cornwall, and Wales.
Gaul and Spain also were occupied by tribal groups of the La
Tène complex, and until Caesar, in the year 52 B.C., defeated
Vercingetorix and the Helvetic confederacy, a vigorous common
civilization flourished throughout the European north and west,
bearing influences from Etruria, Greece, and the centers of the
Near East, but, in the main, of a barbaric brilliance all its own.

"Throughout Gaul," wrote Julius Caesar in the sixth book of his
Gallic War,

> there are two classes of persons of definite account and dignity.
> As for the common folk, they are treated almost as slaves,

venturing nothing of themselves, never taken into counsel. The greater part of them, oppressed as they are by debt, by the heavy weight of tribute, or by the wrongs of the more powerful, commit themselves in slavery to the nobles, who have, in fact, the same rights over them as masters over slaves. Of the two classes above mentioned one consists of Druids, the other of Knights. The former are concerned with divine worship, the due performance of sacrifices, public and private, and the interpretation of ritual questions: a great number of young men gather about them for the sake of instruction and hold them in great honor. In fact, it is they who decide in most all disputes, public and private; and if any crime has been committed, or murder done, or there is any dispute about succession or boundaries, they also decide it, determining rewards and penalties: if any person or people does not abide by their decision, they ban such from sacrifice, which is their heaviest penalty. Those that are so banned are reckoned as impious and criminal; all men move out of their path and shun their approach and conversation, for fear they may get some harm from their contact, and no justice is done if they seek it, no distinction falls to their share.

Of all these Druids one is chief, who has the highest authority among them. At his death, either any other that is preeminent in position succeeds, or, if there be several of equal standing, they strive for the primacy by the vote of the Druids, or sometimes even with armed force. These Druids, at a certain time of the year, meet within the borders of the Carnutes,* whose territory is reckoned as the center of all Gaul, and sit in conclave in a consecrated spot. Thither assemble from every side all that have disputes, and they obey the decisions and judgments of the Druids. It is believed that their rule of life was discovered in Britain and transferred thence to Gaul; and today those who would study the subject more accurately journey, as a rule, to Britain to learn it.

The Druids usually hold aloof from war, and do not pay war taxes with the rest; they are excused from military service and exempt from all liabilities. Tempted by these great rewards, many young men assemble of their own motion to receive their training; many are sent by parents and relatives. Report says that in the schools of the Druids they learn by heart

* The French name *Chartres* is from the Latin *Carnutes*. The tribe inhabited the area now covered approximately by Eure et Loire and Loiret.

a great number of verses, and therefore some persons remain twenty years under training. And they do not think it proper to commit these utterances to writing, although in almost all other matters, in their private and public accounts, they make use of Greek letters. I believe that they have adopted the practice for two reasons—that they do not wish the rule to become common property, nor those who learn the rule to rely on writing and so neglect the cultivation of the memory; and, in fact, it does usually happen that the assistance of writing tends to relax the diligence of the action of the memory. The cardinal doctrine which they seek to teach is that souls do not die, but after death pass from one to another; and this belief, as fear of death is thereby cast aside, they hold to be the greatest incentive to valor. Besides this, they have many discussions concerning the stars and their movement, the size of the universe and of the earth, the order of nature, the strength and powers of the immortal gods, and hand down their lore to the young men.

The other class are the Knights. These, when there is occasion, upon the incidence of a war—and before Caesar's coming this would happen well-nigh every year, in the sense that they would either be making attacks themselves or repelling such—are all engaged therein; and according to the importance of each of them in birth and resources, so is the number of liegemen and dependents that he has about him. This is the one form of influence and power known to them.

The whole nation of the Gauls is greatly devoted to ritual observances, and for that reason those who are smitten with the more grievous maladies and who are engaged in the perils of battle either sacrifice human victims or vow to do so, employing the Druids as ministers for such sacrifices. They believe, in effect, that, unless for a man's life a man's life be paid, the majesty of the immortal gods may not be appeased; and in public, as in private, life they observe an ordinance of sacrifices of the same kind. Others use figures of immense size, whose limbs, woven out of twigs, they fill with living men and set on fire, and the men perish in a sheet of flame. They believe that the execution of those who have been caught in the act of theft or robbery or some crime is the more pleasing to the immortals; but when the supply of such fails they resort to the execution even of the innocent.

Among the gods, they most worship Mercury.* There are numerous images of him; they declare him the inventor of all arts, the guide for every road and journey, and they deem him to have the greatest influence for all money-making and traffic. After him they set Apollo, Mars, Jupiter, and Minerva. Of these deities they have almost the same idea as all other nations: Apollo drives away diseases, Minerva supplies the first principles of arts and crafts, Jupiter holds the empire of heaven, Mars controls wars. To Mars, when they have determined on a decisive battle, they dedicate as a rule whatever spoil they may take. After a victory they sacrifice such living things as they have taken, and all the other effects they gather into one place. In many states heaps of such objects are to be seen piled up in hallowed spots, and it has not often happened that a man, in defiance of religious scruple, has dared to conceal such spoils in his house or to remove them from their place, and the most grievous punishment, with torture, is ordained for such an offense.

The Gauls affirm that they are all descended from a common father, Dis, and say that this is the tradition of the Druids. For that reason they determine all periods of time by the number, not of days, but of nights [because Dis is the lord of the underworld], and in their observance of birthdays and the beginnings of months and years day follows night. In the other ordinances of life the main difference between them and the rest of mankind is that they do not allow their own sons to approach them openly until they have grown to an age when they can bear the burden of military service, and they count it a disgrace for a son who is still in his boyhood to take his place publicly in the presence of his father.[3]

There being no Celtic literature from the Hallstatt, La Tène, or even Roman periods, we have to rely, first, on the accounts of Caesar, Strabo, Pliny, Diodorus Siculus, and a few others; [4] next, on certain monuments in stone from the Roman period; and finally—but best—an abundance of clues from the late Celtic literatures of Ireland, Scotland, and Wales, to which the fairy lore of modern Ireland and the basically Celtic wonderland of Arthurian romance are to be added.

* Caesar's naming of these Celtic gods only in terms of their Roman counterparts leaves us a little in the dark. However, their likely Celtic names and characters can be suggested, as will appear.

There is, for instance, a curious poetic charm supposed to have been recited by the chief poet, Amairgen, of the invading Goidelic Celts, when their ships scraped to beach on the Irish shore:

> I am the wind that blows o'er the sea;
> I am the wave of the deep;
> I am the bull of seven battles;
> I am the eagle on the rock;
> I am a tear of the sun;
> I am the fairest of plants;
> I am a boar for courage;
> I am a salmon in the water;
> I am a lake in the plain;
> I am the word of knowledge;
> I am the head of the battle-dealing spear;
> I am the god who fashions fire [= thought] in the head.
>
> Who spreads light in the assembly on the mountain? *
> Who foretells the ages of the moon? †
> Who tells of the place where the sun rests? ‡

Much has been written around this poem and certain others of its kind, suggesting affinities of Druidic thought with Hinduism, Pythagoreanism, and the later philosophy of the Irish Neoplatonist Scotus Erigena (d.c. 875 A.D.). The text of the charm is from the Irish "Book of Invasions" (*Lebor Gabala*), which, though preserved only in manuscripts of late medieval date, is a compendium of ancient matters put together no later than the eighth century A.D., and may contain material from as early, indeed, as the first arrivals in Ireland of the Goidels.[5] Caesar's observation that the Celts were not afraid to die because they believed that they would live again has seemed to some to support the claim of this poem to antiquity, although others hold it to be a late composition of the high period of the courts of Tara and Cashel, the fourth and early fifth centuries A.D.[6]

In either case, what the poem renders in the way of a world philosophy is a form rather of pan-wizardism than of developed

* Gloss: "Who clears up each question but I?"
† Gloss: "Who but I tell you the ages of the moon?"
‡ Gloss: "Unless it be the poet?"

mystical theology.[7] As one authority has put it, the comparison to be made is with "the bragging utterances of savage medicine-men"; [8] and another: "what is claimed for the poet is not so much the memory of past existences as the capacity to assume all shapes at will; this it is which puts him on a level with and enables him to overcome his superhuman adversaries." [9] Such ideas are basic to shamanistic practice.[10] However, they can be readily developed into something higher, as in India, where the shaman became the yogi and the realization was attained of one's self as the cosmic Self and therewith the essence of all things. Compare, for instance, with Amairgen's chant the stanza already cited of the Shvetashvatara Upanishad:

> You are the dark-blue bird and the green parrot with red eyes.
> You have the lightning as your child. You are the seasons and
>   the seas.
> Having no beginning, you abide with all-pervadingness,
> Wherefrom all beings are born.*

It is not possible to separate categorically the shaman from the mystic. Furthermore, from primitive shamanism to the highest orders of archaic and Oriental thought, where the microcosm and macrocosm unite and are transcended, there is not so great a step as from these to the way of thought of the man for whom God is without and apart. In fact, throughout the history of European myth, the tendency of the later mystic modes to unite with, and to find support in, the modes of both Celtic and Germanic myth has been decisive for the development of much that in our literature is of the highest spiritual strain.

The Irish mythological cycles tell of a number of waves of invaders entering Ireland from the Continent, of which the last was that of the people of the poet Amairgen, the so-called Sons of Mil, or Milesians. However, the diligent Christian monks to whose pens we owe the preservation of these texts were at pains to link their characters with the no less mythic figures of the Bible, and so what has come down to us, finally, is a kind of camelopard

* Supra, p. 108.

combined of two lineages of nonsense, which no amount of scholarship has yet been able to relate firmly to any portion of the actual history of mankind.

For example, the first arrivals in Ireland were Banba and two other daughters of Cain, who came by sea with a company of fifty women and three men, but then died there of the plague. Next, three fishermen arrived, who "with hardihood took possession of the island of Banba of Fair Women." However, having returned home to fetch their wives, they perished in the Deluge.[11] The granddaughter of Noah, Cessair to wit, arrived with her father, her husband, and a third gentleman, Ladru, "the first dead man of Erin," again with fifty damsels; but their ship was wrecked, and all but Finntain, her spouse, who survived for centuries, perished in the Deluge.[12]

Banba, the reader must know, is the name of a goddess after whom Ireland itself is affectionately named; and the meaning of the word is "pig"; so that we are again on familiar ground: the island of a northern Circe. An Irish folktale recounted in *Primitive Mythology* tells of the daughter of the king of the Land of Youth, who appeared on earth as a maid with the head of a pig—which, however, could be kissed away.[13] Classical authors have written of islands in the Celtic fastnesses inhabited by priestesses. Strabo describes one near the mouth of the Loire, devoted to orgiastic cults, where no man was allowed to set foot, and another, near Britain, where the sacrifices resembled those to Demeter and Persephone at Samothrace.[14] The Roman geographer Mela (fl. c. 43 A.D.) tells of nine virgins on the tiny Isle of Sein, off Pont du Raz on the western coast of Brittany, who were possessed of marvelous powers and might be approached by those sailing especially to consult them.[15] Pigs figured prominently in the myths and rites of Demeter and Persephone, who themselves might appear as pigs.[16] The pig is linked, furthermore, to cults of the dead. Hence, in discussion of the Celtic isles of women, scholars have remarked that important pre-Celtic cemeteries have been excavated on the small Channel islands Alderney and Herm, as well as on Er Lanic in the Morbihan Gulf. "The graves," states one authority, "take us back to pre-

Celtic peoples and, therefore, encourage the belief that the island-cults represented a deeply rooted faith of the indigenous folk and were not necessarily of Celtic origin. Indeed, if we accept the stories of these communities of women, we can scarcely avoid admitting at the same time that they probably existed in addition to, and not as part of, the druidic religious system, and thus must have continued the observances of a pre-druidic faith." [17]

Following the antediluvian series of Banba, the company of fishermen, and the granddaughter of Noah, there came to the Emerald Isle a grotesque race called Fomorians, some of whom were footless; some had only one side, and all were descendants of the biblical Ham. They were giants, yet were defeated by the next arrivals, the race of Partholan from Spain, who were "no wiser one than the other." All but one of these died of a plague, however—and it was that one, Tuan mac Caraill by name, who, surviving into Christian times, communicated the whole history of ancient Ireland to Saint Finnen.[18]

Next to arrive were the people of Nemed, further descendants of Noah, who, like the Partholanians, came by way of Spain. They were subdued by the Fomorians, who had recovered from defeat and were governing the land from a tower of glass on Tory Island, off the northwest coast of Donegal. The Nemedians thereafter had to pay every year, on Halloween, two-thirds of the year's harvest and of children born.

Now came the Firbolgs. A number of scholars have thought that these might represent the actual pre-Celtic population of Ireland and that the Fomorians were their gods. Among the latter were a god of war named Net, his dangerous grandson, Balor of the Evil Eye, and a god of knowledge, Elatha. The Firbolgs came from Greece, by way of Spain, like the builders of the megaliths, and were supposed to have been governed by a queen, Taltiu by name. According to the chronicles, they overcame the Fomorians but were themselves defeated by the race next to arrive, the shining Tuatha De Danann, the People (Tuatha) of the goddess Dana—who, in turn, were overcome by the last of this legendary series: the race of the poet Amairgen, the Milesians, who are thought by some to have been the Celts. Whereupon the conquered Tuatha withdrew from view into fairy hills, invisible as glass, where they dwell throughout Ireland to this day.

A few of the outstanding traits of the colorful mythology of the Tuatha De Danann may be noted here. The first is the prominence of a constellation of goddesses who in many ways are counterparts of both the great and lesser goddesses of Greece. Dana (genitive, Danann), who gives her name to the entire group, is called the mother of the gods and is the counterpart of Gaea. She is the Earth Mother, bestower of fruitfulness and abundance, and may have been one of the deities to whom human sacrifices were presented. Two hills in Kerry are called "the Paps of Anu," Anu being a variant of her name associated with the verbal root *an,* "to nourish."

Brigit or Brig (Irish *brig,* "power"; Welsh *bri,* "renown"), the patroness of poetry and knowledge, represents another aspect of the goddess and was the Celtic Minerva named by Caesar. The popular cult of Saint Brigit, which carried her worship into Christian times, was represented in Kildare by a sacred fire that was not to be approached by any male and was watched daily by nineteen vestal nuns in turn and on the twentieth day by the saint herself. Brigit, furthermore, was the giver of civilization. As Professor John A. MacCulloch remarks: "She must have originated in the period when the Celts worshiped goddesses rather than gods, and when knowledge—leechcraft, agriculture, inspiration—were women's rather than men's." [19]

The great father figure of this pantheon was the underworld god equated by Caesar with Dis, Pluto, or Hades. His Gallic name was Cernunnos, perhaps meaning "horned," from *cerna,* "horn," [20] and in the Irish epics he is called the Dagda, from *dago devos,* "the Good God." In the Gallic monuments he is represented with horns or antlers and wearing a Celtic torque (as in the altar from Reims reproduced in *Oriental Mythology,* Figure 20), or with three heads, heavily bearded (as in a statue found at Condat, France); and he may carry on his arm a sack of abundance from which a river of grain proceeds.

On the monuments he is a figure of imposing mien. In the Irish epics, on the other hand, he is a kind of clown—and here we touch upon one of the most profound traits of all of the North European mythologies, whether Celtic or Germanic: for even the greatest of their gods and goddesses appear in manifestations that to sober eyes suggest no relation whatsoever to religion.

The Dagda was the father both of Banba and of Brigit and possessed, moreover, a caldron from which "no company ever went unthankful," whose contents both restored the dead and produced poetic inspiration. Such a caldron suggests, however, derivation from a goddess; and the assignment to a god of the fatherhood of earlier goddesses also betrays the appropriation by a patriarchal deity of matriarchal themes—in the manner of the victories of Zeus, Apollo, and Perseus over the Bronze Age goddesses and priestesses of the Aegean.

We shall not be surprised to learn, therefore, that on a certain day the Dagda met and lay with the great war goddess Morrigan: the same who in later romance was to become the fateful sister of King Arthur, Fata Morgana, Morgan la Fée. He spied her when she was washing in a river, with one foot at Echumech in the north and the other at Loscuinn in the south. But he, that very day, had been challenged by the Fomorians to drink a certain broth. They had filled the prodigious caldron of their own king, Balor of the Evil Eye, with four times twenty gallons of milk, four times twenty of meal and fat, and had put in goats, sheep, and pigs besides: all of which they had boiled together and then poured into a vast hole in the ground. But the Dagda, a mighty god, took a ladle large enough for a man and woman to lie in the bowl of it, and he went on putting the full of the ladle into his mouth until the entire hole was empty; after which he put his hand down and scraped up all that remained amidst the earth and gravel.

Sleep then overcame the Dagda, and the Fomorians all were laughing; for his belly was the size of the caldron of a great house. But he presently got up, and, heavy as he was, made his way away. And indeed his dress was in no way sightly either; for he wore a cape to the hollow of his elbows and a brown coat, long before but short behind; the brogues on his feet were of horsehide, hair without; and he held in his hand a wheeled fork it would take eight men to carry, so that the track he left behind him was deep enough for the boundary ditch of a province. And it was while he was on the way home in this state that he chanced upon the Morrigan, the old Battle Crow, prodigious at her bath.[21]

But as already the pillow colloquy of Queen Meave and her Celtic spouse Ailill has let us know, the pre-Celtic goddesses, though subjugated in Ireland, were by no means out of power. The grotesque epic of the war of the Brown Bull of Cooley, precipitated by the brazen action of Meave, when she sent for the bull and offered herself in part payment, is filled with a sense of the force of female powers over the destinies even of war—considerably in contrast to the spirit of the Greek epic, where, though Aphrodite and Helen were the true and deeper fates, the gods and heroes for the most part usurped the scene.

Cuchullin, for example, the Irish Achilles of this curious Irish Iliad, awoke one night to a terrible cry sounding in the north, so suddenly that he fell out of his bed and hit the ground like a sack. He rushed out of the east wing of his house without weapons, gaining the open air; and Emer, his wife, pursued with his armor and his garments. Across the great plain he ran, following the sound, and presently, hearing the rattle of a chariot from the loamy district of Culgaire, he saw before him a car harnessed with a chestnut horse.

The animal had but one leg, and the pole of the chariot passed through its body, so that the peg in front met the halter passing over its forehead, and within the car there sat a woman, eyebrows red, and with a crimson mantle around her. The mantle fell behind, between the wheels, so that it swept along the ground. And a big man walked beside. He too wore a crimson coat, and he carried on his back a forked staff, while he drove before him a cow.

"That cow," said Cuchullin to the man, "is not pleased to be driven on by you." To which the woman said: "She does not belong to you; nor to any of your associates or friends." Cuchullin turned to her. "The cows of Ulster in general belong to me," he said. She retorted: "You would give a decision, then, about the cow? You are taking too much on yourself, O Cuchullin!" He asked: "Why is it the woman who accosts me, and not the man?" She said: "It was not the man to whom you addressed yourself." He answered: "Oh yes it was. But it was you who answered in his stead." "He is Uar-gaeth-sceo Luachair-sceo," said the woman.

"Well, to be sure," Cuchullin said, "the length of the name is astonishing. Speak to me then yourself; for the fellow does not talk. What is your own name?"

"The woman to whom you are speaking," said the man, "is called Faebor beg-beoil cuimdiuir folt scenb-gairit sceo uath."

Said Cuchullin: "You are making a fool of me." And he made a leap into the chariot, put his two feet on her shoulders and his spear on the parting of her hair. She warned: "Do not play your sharp weapons upon me." "Then tell me your true name," he said. "Go further off me then. I am a female satirist," she answered. "And he is Daire son of Fiachna of Cuailgne. Moreover, I carry off this cow as reward for a poem that I made." "Let us hear your poem," said Cuchullin. "Only move further off," she told him. "Your shaking over my head is not going to influence me at all."

Cuchullin stepped away, until he stood between the two wheels, and she sang to him a song of insult. Whereat he prepared to leap again upon her; but horse, woman, chariot, man, and cow, all had disappeared. Then he perceived that she had transformed herself into a black bird, close by, on a branch.

"A dangerous enchanted woman you are!" said Cuchullin.

She answered: "Henceforth this place shall be called, the Enchanted Place." And so it was, indeed.

Cuchullin said: "If I had only known it was you, we should not have parted thus."

"Whatever you would have done," she said, "it would have brought you ill luck."

"You cannot harm me," said Cuchullin.

"Certainly I can," said she. And it was then that the old Battle Crow let him know what she held in store. "Indeed," she said, "I am guarding now your deathbed, and shall be guarding it henceforth. This cow I have brought out from the Fairy Hill of Cruachan, so that she might breed by the bull of Daire son of Fiachna, which is named the Brown of Cuailgne.

So long as her calf is not yet a year old, so long shall your life be. And it is this that is to be the cause of the Cattle Raid of Cuailgne."

The two exchanged a lively series of threats, touching the battle ahead, in which he was to die, when, as she said, he would be in combat with a man as strong, victorious, dexterous, terrible, untiring, noble, great, and brave as himself, when she would become an eel and throw a noose around his feet in the ford, so that heavy odds would be against him.

"I swear," said Cuchullin, "by the gods by whom Ultonians swear, that I will bruise you against a green stone of the ford."

"I will become a gray wolf for you," she said, "and take the flesh from your right hand as far as to your left arm."

"I will encounter you with my spear," he said, "until your left or right eye is forced out."

"I will become a white red-eared cow," she said, "and I will go into the pond beside the ford in which you are in combat, with a hundred white red-eared cows behind me. And I and all behind me will rush into the ford, and the Fair Play of Men that day shall be brought to a test, and your head shall be cut off from you."

"Your right or your left leg," he said, "I will break with a cast of my sling, and you shall never have any help from me, if you leave me not."

Thereupon the Morrigan departed into the Fairy Hill of Cruachan in Connacht, and Cuchullin returned to his bed.[22]

The goddess Morrigan, as an apparition of fate from the Fairy Forts of the Tuatha De Danann, is known as Badb, the crow or crane of battle, and, like the other goddesses of the Celtic, Germanic, Greek, and Roman worlds, she appears commonly in triplicate. Figures 27 and 28 are from two sides of a Celtic altar found in Paris at the site of Notre Dame, now preserved in the Cluny Museum. In the first is a figure in woodman's clothes cutting down a tree, with his name, *Esus,* above. On the other is a bull beneath an extension of the tree that seems actually to be growing from his body, and with three cranes standing on his back. Above, we read the words, *Tarvos Trigaranos,* "The Bull with the Three Cranes."

The great Celtic scholar of a generation past, H. D'Arbois de

Jubainville, associated the bull of this Gaulish altar with the Brown Bull of the Irish epic, Esus with Cuchullin, the cranes with the goddess Morrigan, and the episode depicted with the passage we have just reviewed.[23] Professor MacCulloch suggests that the Brown Bull's calf, whose life was to be the measure of the hero's life, was the animal counterpart of Cuchullin; and since the Gallic Esus seems to have been a god of vegetation, to whom human sacrifices were hung on trees, the myth may have been associated with a bull sacrifice for the furtherance of vegetation.[24] Analogies

Figure 27. Esus

with the Mithra mythology are indicated: the bull slain with vegetation springing from his flesh, and the sacrifice as an act performed by the human counterpart of the bull (see above, Figure 23). In the Gallo-Roman period, to which these altar panels belong, such cross-cultural analogies could not possibly have been missed. And so we now must recognize that, in the wildly grotesque hero deeds of this epic of the north, the goddess of the Fairy Hill, who appears variously as earth-mother, culture-giver, muse, and a goddess of fate and war, in human or in animal form, is ultimately analogous with the great goddesses of the nuclear Near East; while the Celtic warrior heroes, with Cuchullin as supreme example, carry in their mythic deeds motifs that have come down from the old Bronze Age serpent-son and consort of the Great Mother, Dumuzi-Tammuz.

Figure 28. The Bull with Three Cranes

II. Etruria

On the fair plain of Tuscany westward of the Apennines, situated between the Celts of the north and the rising power of Rome, were the twelve autonomous cities of the old Etruscan Confederation, symbolically centered around the sacred lake Bolsena. The origins of their culture date from the Villanova period, c. 1100–700 B.C., which overlaps the northern Hallstatt * and represents in the south about the same level of development. A great number of curious funerary urns, buried close together in great fields, suggest not only an abiding concern for the dead, but also a certain idea of the purging and transforming power of fire in relation to the future state of the soul. Dr. Otto-Wilhelm von Vacano has interpreted the symbolism of these urns.

"When the bones," he writes, "were gathered up from the funeral pyre as it ceased to glow, the remains of the ashes were all put into the cavity of the urn, to ensure that even the smallest piece of bone should be included." Many of the urns were of human form and were even set upon ceramic thrones; others were in the forms of huts.

> Underlying all this [von Vacano goes on to explain] is a belief that the dead will be transformed in the grave into beings of new and enhanced power, the idea that they are for the time being helpless as newborn babes, and must therefore in this interim period depend on the care of the survivors, while they are, as it were, germinating in the womb of the earth in order to sprout into a new life. . . .
>
> Conceptions of this kind swept in waves over Europe at this time, and were also influential in Asia. Possibly their birthplace was the Caucasus or Persia. . . . In the sphere of influence of these early iron cultures the urn is a sort of hermetic vessel, in which a mysterious process of transformation and creation takes place. . . .

"One notable special feature in all this," he then points out in a statement that corroborates very nicely our own observations in relation to the Celtic Iron Age,

> is the belief in the purifying and transforming power of fire. Such conceptions have found expression in countless tales and legends of smiths, in the stories of the "little man who

---

* Supra, p. 291.

was burned till he became young," the reviving cauldron boiling over the fire, the Medea-Pelias myth. On the other hand it is in the initiation rites of the shamans that we hear of a certain dream process whereby the novice is torn apart and cut to pieces by the spirit of one of his ancestors and his bones cleaned of all blood and flesh. Only his skeleton is preserved and is then clothed in new flesh and blood and thus transformed into a creature that is lord over time and space.[25]

The high period of the confederation of the cities of Tuscany extended from c. 700 B.C. to the year 88 B.C., which they themselves regarded as their last. Repeatedly harried from the north by the barbaric La Tène Celts, and gradually undone from the south by the growing power and realistic politics of Rome, they remained in their time an enclave of provincial, colonial conservatism, preserving the sense of style and holiness of an age in full decline. Professor von Vacano has pointed out that the number twelve of the cities of their confederation was a holy, symbolic sum, determined by religious, not practical, considerations. "Like constellations round the Pole Star these hallowed places grouped themselves around the grove of the god Voltumna, the site of which has not yet been located but which lay in the territory of Bolsena, called Volsinii by the Romans and Velzna by the Etruscans themselves." [26]

The god of this grove, Voltumna, was androgynous—beyond the pairs of opposites. Annually, at a festival celebrated in the grove amid the usual Classical festival events of athletic and artistic competition, the Year Nail was driven into the wall of the temple of the goddess Nortia (Fortuna), symbolizing the inevitability of fate.[27] Figure 29 is from the back of an Etruscan mirror, dating c. 320 B.C. The winged goddess in the center with a hammer in her right hand is holding the Year Nail in her left. Her name, inscribed above, is Athrpa, related to the Greek Atropos. And we note the boar's head associated with the hand holding the nail, as well as the posture of the hammer, precisely at the genitals of the young man at the goddess's right. He is Adonis (Etruscan Atune), who was gored, slain, and emasculated by the boar. The female at his side is Aphrodite, his beloved. And the opposite lovely couple, the writing tells, are Atalanta and Meleager, whose destiny, too, was sealed by a boar.

The old story goes that at the birth of Meleager the Fates appeared to his mother, and the first of them, Clotho, prophesied that he would be a man of noble spirit, the second, Lachesis, that he would be a hero, and the last, Atropos, that he would live as

Figure 29. The Driving of the Year Nail

long as the log burning then on the hearth was not consumed. The mother, Althaia, springing from her bed, caught the brand from the fire and hid it in a chest. Meleager grew and became devoted to the hunt. But the goddess Artemis of the Wild Things, who had been offended when his father, King Oineus of Calydon, had failed to honor her with an offering at a great sacrificial feast, released a boar so mighty that no one could destroy it. In the words of the Roman poet Ovid, re-rendered by our own poet Horace Gregory:

> Both blood and fire wheeled in his great eyes;
> His neck was iron; his bristles rose like spears,
> And when he grunted, milk-white foaming spittle
> Boiled from his throat and steamed across his shoulders. . . .
> Only an elephant from India
> Could match the tusks he wore, and streams of lightning
> Poured from wide lips, and when he smiled or sighed
> All vines and grasses burnt beneath his breath.[28]

The troubled King Oineus invited all the heroes of the lands of Greece to compete in the killing of this boar, and all the great names arrived: Castor and Pollux, Idas and Lynceus, Theseus, Admetus, Jason, Peleus, and many more. But of interest beyond all was the beautiful maid Atalanta, whose skill in many arts had already been exhibited when she had slain a pair of centaurs who had tried one day to ravish her, and when, at the funeral games of a certain prince, she had thrown in wrestling Peleus, the father of Achilles.

Many were killed by the boar in the course of that celebrated hunt. The first spear to graze the beast was Atalanta's; Meleager's felled him. But the youth had already been more gravely struck by the beauty of the fair huntress (who engaged in all these manly sports stripped naked like a male) than the boar had been by her lance; and when the beast was killed, he bestowed on her its hide.

This act was gravely resented by his uncles, the brothers of his mother, who wished the prize to be kept within the matriarchal family, and a brawl ensued of almost Irish magnitude, in the course of which the uncles tore the prize from the girl, whereupon Meleager slew them. And his mother, in a rage at the murder of her kin (but also, perhaps, rankled by the brazenness of the hoyden who had brought this all about), took the charred brand from its hiding and threw it into the fireplace, and her son died while still carving up the boar.[29]

Once again the pig emerges focally in the symbolism of death, destiny, the underworld, and immortality! Of the personages represented on the mirror, Adonis, slain by a boar, was a god; Meleager, a prince. Both gods and men, that is to say, are governed by the power of the goddess, symbolized by the boar.

It is amazing, but now undeniable, that the vocabulary of symbol is to such an extent constant through the world that it must be recognized to represent a single pictorial script, through which realizations of a *tremendum* experienced through life are given statement. Apparent also is the fact that not only in higher cultures, but also among many of the priests and visionaries of the folk cultures, these symbols—or, as we so often say, "gods"—are not thought to be powers in themselves but are signs through which the powers of life and its revelations are recognized and released: powers of the soul as well as of the living world. Furthermore, as in the case of this Etruscan composition, the signs may be arranged to make fresh poetic statements concerning the great themes of ultimate concern; and from such a pictorial poem new waves of realization ripple out through the whole range of the world heritage of myth. So that a polymorphic, cross-cultural discourse can be recognized to have been in progress from perhaps the dawn of human culture, opening realizations of the import inherent both in the symbols themselves and in the mysteries of life and thought to which they bring the mind to accord.

The *Disciplina Etrusca* continued to a late date the spirit of the old Bronze Age cosmology of the ever-revolving, irreversible cycles; and the image of space also was of the orthodox traditions: four quarters and the points between, each presided over by a deity, with a ninth, supreme Tinia, the lord of heaven, whom the Romans equated with Jupiter. The kings of the separate cities, who were Tinia incarnate, each wore a cloak symbolizing heaven, embroidered with stars. Each colored his face red, bore a scepter topped by an eagle, and rode in a chariot drawn by white steeds. At each quarter of the moon the king displayed himself ceremonially to his people, offering sacrifices to learn the will of destiny; and on the field of battle he rode before his men. As among the Celts, the king may have been sacrificed at the expiration of a term of eight or twelve years. The magnitude of the tumuli of these kings and the luxury of the furnishings bear witness to a royal death cult, while the custom of the grove at Nemi, analyzed by Frazer in *The Golden Bough,* makes it almost certain that this cult retained to a late date the old rite of the regicide.

With the fall of the city of Veii to Rome in the year 396 B.C., the fate of Etruria was sealed. But though the military might and secular laws of the growing empire prevailed and the people of Etruria, in 88 B.C., were granted Roman citizenship, authority in priestly affairs nevertheless remained with the old Etruscan masters. As late as 408 A.D. Etruscan conjurers offered their advice and aid to the Romans, who were then being threatened by Alaric and his Goths, and there is even a report that Pope Innocent I, who was then bishop of the city, allowed them to give a public demonstration of their skill in the conjuring of lightning.[30]

"This," wrote the Roman Stoic Seneca, "is what distinguishes us from the Tuscans, masters in the observation of lightning. We think that lightning arises because clouds bump against each other; they on the other hand hold the belief that the clouds bump only in order that lightning may be caused. For as they connect everything with God they have the notion that lightning is not significant on account of its appearance as such, but only appears at all because it has to give divine signs." [31]

And so we pass, at last, from the ancient to the modern world.

III. The Augustan Age

Plutarch relates of Romulus and Remus that they were twins of a young virgin of the royal line of Aeneas, who had been forced by her father Amulius, the brother of King Numitor of Alba, to become a Vestal Virgin. Shortly following her assumption of the vow, she was found to be with child, and would have been buried alive had not her cousin, daughter of the king, pleaded for her life. Confined, she brought forth two boys of more than human size and beauty, whom her father, alarmed, turned over to a servant to be cast away. But the man put them in a small trough, which he carried to the river and left upon the bank; and the river, rising, bore the little boat downstream to a smooth place where a large

wild fig tree grew. A she-wolf came and nursed them; a wood-
pecker brought them food: which two creatures, being esteemed
holy to Mars, gave credit—as Plutarch states—to the mother's
claim that Mars, the god, had been their father; whereas some
declared the father to have been her own father, Amulius, who had
come to her disguised in armor as the god.

Following a period of being cared for by animals, the twins were
discovered by Amulius's swineherd, who brought them up in secret;
though, as others tell, with the knowledge and assistance of the
king: for it is said they went to school and were instructed well in
letters. They were called Romulus and Remus from the word *ruma,*
"dug"—of the wolf. And in their growing they proved brave. To
their comrades and inferiors they were dear, but the king's overseers
they despised; and they engaged themselves in study, as well as in
running, hunting, repelling thieves, and delivering the oppressed.

A quarrel arose between two cowherds, one of the king, the other
of his brother, in the course of which Remus fell into the hands,
first of the brother, then of the king. Romulus attacked the city,
released his twin, slew the tyrant king and brother; and the twins,
then bidding their mother farewell, departed to build a city of their
own in the place where they had spent their infancy. A quarrel
arose as to where this city should stand, which they agreed to settle
by divination. But when Remus saw six vultures and Romulus
claimed twelve, they came to blows and Remus was slain.

Plutarch reports that when Romulus set about founding Rome
he sent for men of Tuscany to direct the ceremonies according to
the *Disciplina Etrusca.*

> First [Plutarch declares] they dug a circular trench around
> what is now the comitium, or Court of Assembly, and into this
> they solemnly threw the first fruits of all things sanctioned
> either by custom as good or by nature as necessary. Then,
> every man bearing a small portion of the earth of his native
> land, they all threw these in together. They call this trench, as
> they do the heavens, *Mundus;* and taking this as center, they
> described the city in a circle around it. Whereupon the
> founder, having fitted to a plow a brazen plowshare, and
> having yoked to it a bull and a cow, he himself drove a deep

line of furrow, circumscribing the bounds, while the task of those that followed him was to see that whatever earth was thrown up should be turned inward, toward the city, and that no clod should lie outside. With this line they laid the course of the wall . . . and where they proposed to have a gate, they lifted the plow out of the ground and left a space; for which reason they regard the whole wall as holy, except where the gates are: for had they deemed these also sacred, they could not, without offense to religion, have given free entrance and exit to those necessities of life that are of themselves unclean.[32]

Romulus stocked his city with women through his famous raid and rape of the Sabines, who became thereby first relatives, then citizens, of Rome. Other wars enlarged the realm. And presently he died, or rather disappeared—in a manner of interest to all who might like to think about the mythological air of the Roman Empire in the century of the birth and death, resurrection and disappearance of Christ.

For the life span of Plutarch, our biographer (c. 46–c. 120 A.D.), includes the years both of the mission of Saint Paul (d. c. 67 A.D.) and of the writing of the Gospels (c. 75–c. 120 A.D.); while the contrast of the Roman's "modern" attitude toward miracles with the "religious" of the saints of the Levant is of relevance both to our present theme and to any general understanding of the scientific/religious schizophrenia of the modern Occidental "church." Let me quote my author, word for word.

Plutarch has just told of the Roman conquest of Etruria and the fall of its chief city, Veii.

When Romulus [he continues] of his own accord then parted among his soldiers the lands that had been acquired by war and restored to the city of Veii the hostages he had taken, without asking the Roman senate either to consent or to approve, it seemed that he had put upon his senate a great affront. Consequently, on his sudden and strange disappearance a short time later, the senate fell under suspicion and calumny. Romulus disappeared on the Nones of July, as they call the month that was then Quintilis, leaving nothing of certainty to be related of his death except the time, as just mentioned;

for on that day many ceremonies are still performed in representation of what happened.

Nor is this uncertainty to be thought strange, seeing that the manner of the death of Scipio Africanus, who died at his own home after supper, has been found capable neither of proof nor of disproof: for some say he died a natural death, being of sickly habit; others, that he poisoned himself; others again, that his enemies, breaking in upon him in the night, stifled him. Yet Scipio's dead body lay open to be seen of all, and any one, from his own observation, might form his suspicions and conjectures, whereas Romulus, when he vanished, left neither the least part of his body, nor any remnant of his clothes to be seen.

So that some fancied, the senators, having fallen upon him in the temple of Vulcan, cut his body into pieces, and took each a part away in his bosom; others think his disappearance was neither in the temple of Vulcan, nor with the senators only by, but that it came to pass that, as he was haranguing the people without the city, near a place called the Goat's Marsh, on a sudden strange and unaccountable disorders and alterations took place in the air; the face of the sun was darkened, and the day turned into night, and that, too, no quiet, peaceable night, but with terrible thunderings, and boisterous winds from all quarters; during which the common people dispersed and fled, but the senators kept close together. The tempest being over and the light breaking out, when the people gathered again, they missed and inquired for their king; the senators suffered them not to search, or busy themselves about the matter, but commanded them to honor and worship Romulus as one taken up to the gods, and about to be to them, in the place of a good prince, now a propitious god. The multitude, hearing this, went away believing and rejoicing in hopes of good things from him; but there were some, who, canvassing the matter in a hostile temper, accused and aspersed the patricians, as men that persuaded the people to believe ridiculous tales, when they themselves were the murderers of the king.

Things being in this disorder, one, they say, of the patricians, of noble family and approved good character, and a faithful and familiar friend of Romulus himself, having come with him from Alba, Julius Proculus by name, presented himself in the forum; and, taking a most sacred oath, protested before them all, that, as he was traveling on the road, he had seen Romulus coming to meet him, looking taller and comelier than ever, dressed in shining and flaming armor; and he, being affrighted at the apparition, said, "Why, O King, or for what purpose have you abandoned us to unjust and wicked surmises, and the whole city to bereavement and endless sorrow?" and that he made answer, "It pleased the gods, O Proculus, that we, who came from them, should remain so long a time amongst men as we did; and having built a city to be the greatest in the world for empire and glory, should again return to heaven. But farewell; and tell the Romans, that, by the exercise of temperance and fortitude, they shall attain the height of human power; we will be to you the propitious god Quirinus." This seemed credible to the Romans, upon the honesty and oath of the relater, and indeed, too, there mingled with it a certain divine passion, some preternatural influence similar to possession by a divinity; nobody contradicted it, but, laying aside all jealousies and detractions, they prayed to Quirinus and saluted him as a god.[33]

Who, on reading this passage, can have failed to recall that other meeting on the road, recounted in the twenty-fourth chapter of Luke?

That very day two of them were going to a village named Emmaus, about seven miles from Jerusalem, and talking with each other about all these things that had happened. While they were talking and discussing together, Jesus himself drew near and went with them. But their eyes were kept from recognizing him. And he said to them, "What is this conversation which you are holding with each other as you walk?" And they stood still, looking sad. Then one of them, named Cleopas, answered him, "Are you the only visitor to Jerusalem who does not know the things that have happened there in these days?" And he said to them, "What things?" And they said to him, "Concerning Jesus of Nazareth, who was a prophet mighty in deed and word before God and all the people, and how our chief priests and rulers delivered him up to be condemned to death, and crucified him. But we had hoped that he was the one to redeem Israel. Yes, and besides all this, it is now the third day since this happened. Moreover, some women of our company amazed us. They were at the tomb early in the morning and did not find his body; and they came back saying that they had even seen a vision of angels, who said that he was alive. Some of those who were with us went to the tomb, and found it just as the women had said; but him they did not see." And he said to them, "O foolish men, and slow to believe all that the prophets have spoken! Was it not necessary that Christ should suffer these things and enter into his glory?" And beginning with Moses and all the prophets, he interpreted to them in all the scriptures the things concerning himself.

So they drew near to the village to which they were going. He appeared to be going further, but they constrained him, saying, "Stay with us, for it is toward evening and the day is now far spent." So he went in to stay with them. When he was at table with them, he took the bread and blessed and broke it, and gave it to them. And their eyes were opened, and they recognized him; and he vanished out of their sight.[34]

Let us now return to the other.

"This," wrote the sober Roman, commenting on the apparition of Romulus,

resembles certain Greek fables of Aristeas the Proconnesian, and Cleomedes the Astypalaean; for they say Aristeas died in a fuller's workshop, and his friends, coming to look for him, found his body vanished; and that some presently after, coming from abroad, said they met him traveling toward Croton. And that Cleomedes, being an extraordinarily strong and gigantic man, but also wild and mad, committed many desperate freaks; and at last, in a school-house, striking a pillar that sustained the roof with his fist, broke it in the middle, so that the house fell and destroyed the children in it; and being pursued, he fled into a great chest, and, shutting the lid to, held it so fast, that many men, with their united strength, could not force it open; afterwards, breaking the chest to pieces, they found no man in it alive or dead; in astonishment at which, they sent to consult the oracle at Delphi; to whom the prophetess made this answer:

"Of all the heroes, Cleomedes is last."

They say, too, the body of Alcmena, as they were carrying her to her grave, vanished, and a stone was found lying on the bier. And many such improbabilities do your fabulous writers relate, deifying creatures naturally mortal; for though altogether to disown a divine nature in human virtue were impious and base, so again, to mix heaven with earth is ridiculous. Let us believe with Pindar, that

> All human bodies yield to Death's decree,
> The soul survives to all eternity.

For that alone is derived from the gods, thence comes, and thither returns; not with the body, but when most disengaged and separated from it, and when most entirely pure and clean and free from flesh: for the most perfect soul, says Heraclitus, is a dry light, which flies out of the body as lightning breaks from a cloud; but that which is clogged and surfeited with body is like gross and humid incense, slow to kindle and ascend. We must not, therefore, contrary to nature, send the bodies, too, of good men to heaven; but we must really believe that, according to their divine nature and law, their virtue and their souls are translated out of men into heroes, out of heroes into demi-gods, after passing, as in the rite of initiation, through a final cleansing and sanctification, and so freeing themselves from all that pertains to mortality and sense, are thus, not by human decree, but really and according to right reason, elevated into gods and admitted thus to the greatest and most blessed perfection. . . .

It was in the fifty-fourth year of his age and the thirty-eighth of his reign that Romulus, they tell us, left the world.[35]

The Romans employed two words to designate divine presences or powers, namely *deus,* which we generally translate "god," and *numen,* for which we have no proper term. The root NV-, from which the latter is derived, means (curiously enough) "nod," whence the connotation "command or will," and then, "divine will or power, divine sway." [36] Anthropologists have found for this Roman term a number of primitive counterparts; for instance, Melanesian *mana,* Dakotan *wakon,* Iroquoian *orenda,* and Algonquian *manitu,* all of which refer to an *immanent* magical force infecting certain phenomena. The "nod," therefore, would have been experienced as coming not from without, but from within the object contemplated. Thus, whereas the Latin word *deus,* from the root DIV-, "shine," is related to the Sanskrit *deva,* "god," and suggests a being with defined personality, *numen* suggests, rather, the impulse of a will or force of no personal definition. We may recall here the Japanese sense of divine presences—*kami*—discussed in *Oriental Mythology,* under Shinto.[37] For, as in Japan, so in early Rome: the living universe was regarded, both in its great and in its lesser aspects, with a sense of wonder before its sheer existence. There is a pertinent passage in one of Seneca's letters:

> When you find yourself within a grove of exceptionally tall, old trees, whose interlocking boughs mysteriously shut out the view of the sky, the great height of the forest and the secrecy of the place together with a sense of awe before the dense impenetrable shades will awaken in you the belief in a god. And when a grotto has been hewn into the hollowed rock of a mountain, not by human hands but by the powers of nature, and to great depth, it pervades your soul with an awesome sense of the religious. We honor the sources of great rivers. Altars are raised where the sudden freshet of a stream breaks from below ground. Hot springs of steaming water inspire veneration. And many a pond has been sanctified because of its hidden situation or immeasurable depth.[38]

Most important of the Roman *numina* were those of the home, where the leading celebrant was the *pater familias.* The family cult was concerned, first, with the mystery of its own continuity in time, as represented in rituals honoring the ancestors (*manes*) and in festivals of the general dead (*parentes*). The *numina* of the household also were revered: those of the larder (*penates*) and of household effects (*lares*). The guardian of the hearth, Vesta, was personified as a goddess, and that of the door, Janus, as a god. There was the idea also of a *numen* of the procreating power of each male, his *genius,* and of the conceiving and bearing power of the female, her *juno. Genius* and *juno* came into being and expired with the individual. They stood beside him in life as protecting spirits and could be represented as serpents. Under Greek influence the power of the *juno* later became developed into the goddess Juno, as the guardian of childbirth and motherhood, who was identified then with the Greek Hera. A series of *numina* of the various phases of the agricultural process also were celebrated: Sterculinius, the power effective in the fertilizing of the fields; Vervactor, the first plowing of the soil; Redarator, the second;

Imporcitor, the third; Sator, the sowing of the field . . . and so on, to Messia, the reaping; Convector, the harvest home; Noduterensis, the threshing floor; Conditor, the storing of the grain in the barn; Tutilina, its resting there; and Promitor, its removal to the kitchen.[39]

Other *numina,* of more constant presence, acquired more substantial character, as Jupiter, lord of the brilliant heavens and of storm, later identified with Zeus; Mars, the war god, equated with Ares; Neptune, the god of waters, identified with Poseidon; Faunus, the patron of animal life; Silvanus, god of the woods. Comparably, of the female forces, Ceres became identified with Demeter; Tellus Mater, with Gaea; Venus, originally a market goddess, with the Cyprian Aphrodite; and Fortuna with Moira. We hear too of Flora, goddess of flowers; Pomona, goddess of fruits; Carmenta, a goddess of springs and of birth; Mater Matuta, first a goddess of dawn, then of birth.[40]

In the larger sphere of the cult of the state the counterpart of the *pater familias* was the king, originally a god-king. His palace was the chief sanctuary; his queen was his goddess spouse. We have remarked that in the home the *numen* of the hearth was the goddess Vesta. In the larger family of the state, the same holy principle was honored throughout the history of pagan Rome in a circular temple, where a pure flame was attended by six highly revered women. The flame was extinguished at the end of each year and relighted in the primitive way, with firesticks. The dress of the Vestal Virgins resembled the gown of a Roman bride; and on assuming her vow, the dedicated nun was solemnly clasped by the Pontifex Maximus, the chief priest of the city, who said to her: *Te, Amata, capio!* "My Beloved, I take possession of thee!" The two were symbolically man and wife. And if the Vestal broke her vow of chastity, she was buried alive.

The correspondence of this Vestal Fire context, in every single detail, with the rites of the regicide and relighting of the holy fire described in *Primitive Mythology* [41] could hardly be more exact. The mythology of such rites was of the neolithic and Bronze ages. Hence, although no written matter has come down to us from the earliest centuries of the city, it is evident that the same great mythology of the cycling eons, years, and days that shaped every one of the other civilizations of the world, shaped also that of Rome—both spatially, in the city plan itself, as described in the legend of Romulus's foundation ceremony, and calendrically, in the disciplines of its life.

At an early date, the latter part of the sixth century B.C., an Etruscan royal house, the Tarquins of Tarquinia (now Corneto), governed Rome. They were expelled about 509 B.C., and it was then that the epochal process of the Hellenization of the Roman religion began, which brought its local, archaic customs into accord with the new humanism of the rapidly growing chief centers of civilization. In the decades of Etruscan rule temples had been constructed and cult images fashioned of stucco; but for stone, Rome had to wait for the coming of Greek artisans in the second century B.C., at which time the Sibylline Books also arrived from Cumae in the south: an ancient holy site, some twelve miles west of Naples, founded by the Greeks as early as the eighth century B.C., and celebrated particularly for its oracular cave, where the Sibyl prophesied of whom Virgil wrote in Eclogue IV. The old woman incumbent visited the city with a bundle of nine prophetic books, of which three were purchased and buried for safekeeping in the temple of Jove, where at intervals they were consulted until they perished in the fire of 82 B.C.

As Plutarch tells, their prophecies were of "many mirthless things . . . many revolutions and transportations of Greek cities, many appearances of barbarian armies and deaths of leading men." [42] They seem also to have divided the history of the world into ages to which various metals and deities were assigned.[43] And, as we may judge from Virgil's celebrated words, the Sibylline round, declining to its end, was to be followed—as everywhere in such mythic cycles—by a golden age of rebeginning.

> Now is come [he wrote] the last age of the Cumaean prophecy: the great cycle of periods is born anew. Now returns the Maid, returns the reign of Saturn: now from high heaven descends a new generation. And O holy goddess of childbirth

Lucina, do thou be gracious at that boy's birth in whom the
Iron Race shall begin to cease and the Golden to arise all over
the world. . . .[44]

This poem, with its wonderful Boy, was taken in the Christian
Middle Ages to have been a prophecy of Christ, and Virgil was
honored, therefore, as a kind of pagan prophet. His thought of the
coming Golden Age somewhat resembles the eschatology of the
Jewish Apocalyptic writers, and his dates, 70–19 B.C., fall perfectly
within the period of the Essenes of Qumran. However, in the gentle
Roman poem there is no tumult of any War of the Last Days. The
image is of a *return* of the Golden Age in the natural course of an
ever-revolving cycle, not the epochal passage in a "day of the
Messiah" to an everlasting terminal state of the universe. And the
Boy in question, finally, was not a Messiah of any kind, but a
normal human child, born to a distinguished family of the poet's
acquaintance at a time that Virgil regarded, properly, as the dawn
of a universal age of peace (for those willing to enjoy it) under
the empire of Rome. Nor is the sense of Virgil's imagery to be
taken literally and concretely, but poetically, as a Classical figure
of speech.

About the year 100 B.C. the Roman Pontifex Maximus, Q. Mucius
Scaevola, in the spirit of a Stoic sage, proposed a theory of a threefold order of gods: the gods of poets, of philosophers, and of statesmen; of which the first two were unfit for the popular mind and only
the second true. However, a fourth and far more potent order of
gods than any of those of which he had taken thought was already
becoming known to Rome in his day: those, namely, of the Near
East, whose appeal was, in the Greek sense, neither poetic nor
philosophic, and whose force, furthermore, would ultimately effect
not the preservation but the undoing of the moral order of Rome
and its civilization.

The first occasion for the introduction of these highly charged
alien powers had occurred in the year 204 B.C., when the Carthaginian army of Hannibal was still a threat within Italy. Repeated
storms and hail had produced the impression that the gods themselves, for some reason, were at odds with the people of Rome,

and the Sibylline Books were consulted. Their reply was that the enemy would be expelled only when the cult of the Great Goddess of the Phrygian city of Pessinus was introduced into Rome. This Magna Mater was Cybele, the mother-bride of the ever-dying, ever-resurrected savior Attis; and these two were simply the local forms of the pair that we have come to know so well: Inanna and Dumuzi, Ishtar and Tammuz. In the high Etruscan age, as Figure 29 shows, the cognate myth of Aphrodite and her dead and restored lover Adonis had been introduced into Italy. Now, on the advice of the Sibylline Books, Cybele Magna Mater, under the aspect of a large black stone, was imported and set up in a temple on the Palatine. We have already commented on the influence of the Mithra cult within the empire. A third religion of this order, derived from Alexandria, was that of the now Hellenized Isis, and her spouse, now called Serapis (from the name Osiris-Apis). All these formerly local cults had in the Hellenistic age been syncretized with the related Greek traditions of the Dionysian, Orphic, and Pythagorean movements—to which a modicum of late Chaldean-Hellenistic astrology had been added, to form a compound of macro-microcosmic lore that was to remain dominant in the Occident, one way or another, until the science of the Renaissance undid the old cosmology of a geocentric universe and opened marvels beyond anything dreamed of by the sages of the ancient mystic ways.

Outstanding figures in this development were the Greek Stoic Posidonius, already mentioned (c. 135–50 B.C.),* his eloquent pupil Cicero (106–43 B.C.), Cicero's friend, Publius Nigidius Figulus (c. 98–45 B.C.), and then Virgil (70–19 B.C.), Ovid (40 B.C.–17 A.D.), Apollonius of Tyana (fl. first century A.D.), Plutarch (c. 46–120 A.D.), Ptolemy (fl. second century A.D.), and Plotinus (c. 205–270 A.D.). In the works of all these there is sounded a certain modern note; for the sciences of their time, like those of our own, were disclosing facts of the natural order that could not be absorbed by the old cosmologies, so that the problem of the day was to retain the substantial spiritual insights of the past even while pressing on to new horizons.

* Supra, p. 250.

Perhaps the most lucid single instance of the manner in which the ancient lore was being translated into terms congenial to the new is to be seen in Cicero's "Dream of Scipio Africanus the Younger," with which he concluded the argument of his *Republic*. The youth whom he selected to be the subject of this work had lived c. 185–129 B.C. and was supposed to have seen his grandfather in vision, Scipio Africanus the Elder (237–183 B.C.), who many years before had invaded Africa and defeated Hannibal. The Elder is represented as revealing to his grandson, besides something of the future before him, a new spiritual view both of the universe and of man's place within it.

"I fell into a deeper sleep than usual," the youth is supposed to have reported; "and I thought that Africanus stood before me, taking the shape that was familiar to me from his bust rather than from his person."

The psychological inflection is already interesting. The vision is subjectively disposed. We are not asked to believe in it as an actual case of revenance from the dead. The atmosphere is of poetic, not religious myth.

Africanus said: "How long will your thoughts be fixed upon the lowly earth? Do you not see what lofty regions you have entered?" And he pointed to the marvels of a universe of nine celestial spheres. "The outermost, heaven, contains all the rest," he said, "and is itself the supreme God, holding and embracing within itself all the other spheres. In it are fixed the eternal revolving courses of the stars, and beneath it are seven other spheres, which revolve in the opposite direction to that of heaven." Africanus named these in order: Saturn, Jupiter, Mars, and the Sun, Venus, Mercury, and the Moon. "Below the moon," he said, "there is nothing but what is mortal and doomed to decay, except the souls given to men by the bounty of the gods, whereas above the moon all is eternal. And the ninth or central sphere, which is the earth, is immovable, lowest of all, and toward it all ponderable bodies are drawn by their own natural tendency downward."

The cosmology is that of Hellenistic science, which was later systematized by Ptolemy and carried on to Dante. It is derived ultimately from the astrology of the ziggurat, but the earth has become a sphere poised in the midst of a sort of Chinese box of concentric spheres; not the flat disk of yore, surrounded by a cosmic sea.

Said the dreamer: "What is this loud and agreeable sound that fills my ears?" And the vision answered:

That is produced by the onward rush and motion of the spheres themselves; the intervals between them, though unequal, being exactly arranged in a fixed proportion, by an agreeable blending of high and low tones various harmonies are produced. For such mighty motions cannot be carried on so swiftly in silence; and Nature has provided that one extreme shall produce low tones while the other gives forth high. Therefore this uppermost sphere of heaven, which bears the stars, as it revolves more rapidly, produces a high, shrill tone, whereas the lowest revolving sphere, that of the moon, gives forth the lowest tone. For the earthly sphere, the ninth, remains ever motionless and stationary in its position in the center of the universe; but the other eight spheres, two of which move with the same velocity, produce seven different sounds—a number that is the key of almost everything.

Learned men, by imitating this harmony on stringed instruments and in song, have gained for themselves a return to this region, as others have obtained the same reward by devoting their brilliant intellects to divine pursuits during their earthly lives. Men's ears, ever filled with this sound, have become deaf to it; for you have no duller sense than that of hearing. . . . But this mighty music, produced by the revolution of the whole universe at the highest speed, cannot be perceived by human ears, any more than you can look straight at the sun, your sense of sight being overpowered by its radiance.

The number theory of Pythagoras, in relation to the principle of harmony in the universe, in the arts, and in the soul, is here set forth in terms of the new image of the universe and a modern, secularized mode of life. The archaic order of the hieratic state with its castes, sacrifices, and all, and of the arts as serving largely to illuminate such a state, is of the past. The arts and those other "divine pursuits" of "brilliant intellects" here touched upon are conceived in Hellenized, humanistic terms. Yet nothing has been lost of the essence of the doctrine.

The apparition continued, referring now to the sphere of the earth, its poles, and its torrid and temperate zones.

> You will notice [he remarked] that the earth is surrounded and encircled by certain zones, of which the two that are most widely separated, and are supported by the opposite poles of heaven, are held in icy bonds, while the central and broadest zone is scorched by the heat of the sun. Two zones are habitable. Of these, the southern (the footsteps of whose inhabitants are opposite to yours) has no connection with your zone. Examine this northern zone which you inhabit, and you will see what a small portion of it belongs to the Romans. For that whole territory which you hold, being narrow from north to south, and broader from east to west, is really only a small island surrounded by that sea which you on the earth call the Atlantic, the Great Sea, or the Ocean. Now you see how small it is in spite of its proud name!

In surprising contrast to all mythological arguments up to this time, the native land with its local value system and circle of horizon is here diminished, not augmented, in importance. The view is of a reasonable human intellect, aware of the magnitude of the world, and greeting, not resisting, the opening vistas to which the new science, politics, and possibilities of life were inviting it. Statecraft and politics now were to be of a secular, not pseudo-religious stamp; yet, as the following portions of the discourse show, neither statecraft nor the spirit of man was to suffer one whit thereby.

> The spirit is the true self [said Africanus], not that bodily form which can be pointed to by the finger. Know, therefore, that you are a god, if a god be that which lives, feels, remembers, and foresees, and which rules, governs, and moves the body over which it is set, just as the supreme God above us rules this universe. And just as the eternal God moves the universe, which is partly mortal, so an immortal spirit moves the frail body. . . .
> For that which is always in motion is eternal; but that

which communicates motion to something else, but is itself moved by another force, necessarily ceases to live when this motion ends. Therefore, only that which moves itself never ceases its motion, because it never abandons itself; nay, it is the source and first cause of motion in all other things that are moved. But this first cause has itself no beginning, for everything originates from the first cause, while it can never originate from anything else: for that would not be a first cause which owed its origin to anything else. And since it never had a beginning, it will never have an end. . . .

Therefore, now that it is clear that what moves of itself is eternal, who can deny that this is the nature of spirits? For whatever is moved by an eternal impulse is spiritless; but whatever possesses a spirit is moved by an inner impulse of its own; for that is the peculiar nature and property of a spirit. And as a spirit is the only force that moves of itself, it surely has no beginning and is immortal. Use it, therefore, in the best pursuits!

We are brought thus to the question of the best pursuits for man, and the answer again is of a man of reason.

"The best pursuits," said the old soldier statesman, "are those undertaken in defense of your native land. A spirit occupied and trained in such activities will have a swifter flight to this, its proper home and permanent abode. And this flight will be still more rapid if, while still confined in the body, it looks abroad, and, by contemplating what lies outside itself, detaches itself as much as it may from the body."

The typically Roman accent here, placed on the spiritual value of a dedication to the state, is one that the figure of this elder savior of his native city was well fitted to represent. And it stands in sturdy contrast to the Oriental, world-denying tone of many of the incoming cults, where a dissociation of the temporal and eternal orders was taken to imply that for spiritual realization a total renunciation of the one and dedication to the other was necessary. In the Orphic-Pythagorean movement such a notion was expressed in the *soma-sema* ("the body, a tomb") aphorism. Cicero, the good Stoic, now directly confronts that theme.

"I asked Africanus," he lets the young visionary say, "whether he and my father and the others whom we think of as dead were really alive. And he answered: 'Surely all those are alive who have escaped, as from a prison, from the bondage of the body; but that life of yours, which men so call, is really death.' "

The youth in despair then cried to his father, Paulus: "O best and most blameless of fathers, since that is life, as I learn from Africanus, why should I remain longer on earth?"

And his father, appearing to him, answered:

Not so: for unless that God whose temple is everything that you see has freed you from the prison of the body, you cannot gain entrance to these heavens. For man was given life that he might inhabit that sphere called Earth, which you see in the center of this temple; and he has been given a soul out of those eternal fires that you call stars and planets, which, being round and globular bodies animated by divine intelligences, circle about in their fixed orbits with marvelous speed. Wherefore you, Publius, and all good men, must leave that soul in the custody of the body, and must not abandon human life except at the behest of him by whom it was given you, lest you appear to have shirked the duty imposed upon man by God. . . .

Love justice and duty, which are indeed strictly due to parents and kinsmen, but most of all to the fatherland. Such a life is the road to the skies, to that gathering of those who have completed their earthly lives and been relieved of the body, and who live in yonder place which you now see and which you on earth call the Milky Way.[45]

Thus, while recognizing the Orphic *soma-sema* thesis, Cicero, as a truly Roman spirit, gave all moral stress to the destiny of the human spirit in time.

All those who have preserved, aided, or enlarged their fatherland [he wrote] have a special place prepared for them in the heavens, where they may enjoy an eternal life of happiness. For nothing of all that is done on earth is more pleasing to that supreme God who rules the whole universe than the assemblies and gatherings of men associated in justice, which are called states. Their rulers and preservers come from that place, and to that place they return.[46]

The doctrine hardly differs from that of the Indian *karma yoga* taught by the kingly sages Ajatashatru and Jaibali in the earliest Upanishads.[47] And like the Indian masters both of themselves and of their states, Cicero, in his noble vision, teaches detachment as well as duty. "The spirits of those who are given over to sensual pleasures and have become, as it were, their slaves," he declares, "and who violate the laws of gods and men at the instigation of those desires, which are subservient to pleasure, after leaving their bodies fly about close to the earth, and do not return to this heavenly place except after many ages of torture." [48]

It would be difficult to invent a closer analogue to the doctrine of reincarnation of the Orient—and yet the whole tone of the Roman is as different from the Indian as is the Roman concept of man's duties from the Indian. For the Roman citizen's "divine pursuits" were not determined by caste but by the judgments of his own faculties; nor was their ultimate reference release from the world but intelligent service to human ends while within it. Virgil, in the sixth book of the *Aeneid,* presented another version of this same mythology, and in doing so became eligible to conduct Dante through a later revelation of this landscape of the soul. Yet between Virgil and Dante too there was a difference, in as much as for the Roman the intelligence in the center of the earth was not Satanic but divine.

Christian writers, even of the most liberal sort, have never been able to appreciate the piety of the pagan Romans: for instance, that veneration of the emperor which the patron of Virgil, Augustus, caused to be instituted as a policy of state. Cicero's two declarations, that the way to heaven is through service to one's fatherland, and that each is to know himself to be a god, set the mood for the later worship of the emperor, which Virgil supported in a prominent passage of his *Aeneid,*[49] and Ovid too in his *Metamorphoses.*[50] For, after all, where every fish and fly carries divinity within, why should not the master of the state be revered as *primus inter pares?* No comparison is to be made of such an attitude of respect with the Christian deification of Augustus's contemporary, Jesus. For in the Christian view the world and its creatures are not suffused with divinity. The deification of Jesus marks a radical designation, far beyond anything possible where all things are in essence *numina*. And from the Roman point of view the Christian refusal to concede a pinch of incense to an image of the emperor was an act not only of rebellion but also of atheism, vis-à-vis that divinity of the universe which every myth and philosophic view in the known history of mankind (save only that of the up to then completely unknown Bible) had taught as the ultimate Truth of truths.

Augustus, reigning from 27 B.C. to the year 14 A.D., while retaining as far as possible the semblance of the state as a republic, refreshed in imperial grandeur the old religious foundations of the city. His own palace became the focal sanctuary of the state, as in ancient times the palace of the god-king had been. A new temple of the Vestal Virgins was built in association with the palace, and the public honors bestowed on the Vestals were increased. To Apollo, his patron deity, to whom he credited the victory at Actium over Antony and Cleopatra, a temple was raised on the Palatine, and in a prominent part of the new forum a temple was built to Mars Ultor, "The Avenger," divine ancestor of the Julian house, to whom the avenging of Caesar's murder was attributed. The latter then became the sanctuary for all family rites of the dynasty, as well as for the installation of provincial magistrates, conclusion of senatorial decisions on peace and war, preservation of triumphant battle insignia, and ceremonial driving of the Year Nail.

In the year 17 B.C. a stupendous jubilee, the Festival of the Saeculum, was celebrated, to render in impressive form the idea of the World Renewed announced by Virgil in his Fourth Eclogue. Heralds to all quarters announced the required participation of all, slaves alone being excluded. Mourning rites were suspended, court proceedings deferred. From May 26 to 28, fumigants were distributed for the purification of homes. From May 29 to 31, the authorities received from the citizens contributions of grain for distribution to the performers and audiences of the festival games. And on the night preceding the day of June 1, the great three-day celebration began.

Let me tell of these days in the words of the late Professor L. A. Deubner of the University of Freiburg, whose article on Roman Religion in Professor Chantepie de la Saussaye's standard *Lehrbuch der Religionsgeschichte* first opened my own eyes, nearly forty years ago, to the common background in archaic myth of Virgil's Boy of the Golden Age and the Christian Apocalyptic Messiah.

The opening night, Augustus offered nine sheep and nine goats to the Fates, after which theatrical pieces were performed and one hundred and ten matrons set up religious banquets to Juno and Diana. The day of June 1st, Augustus, and after him his son-in-law Agrippa, offered each an ox to Jupiter, after which, in a wooden theater on the Field of Mars, Latin plays were produced. The next night, Augustus sacrificed nine cows of each of three varieties to the goddess of birth, Ilithyia, and the day of June 2nd Agrippa offered a cow to the Capitoline Juno Regina. Following his prayer for himself and Augustus, Agrippa pronounced another for the hundred and ten matrons, and the plays that day were the same as the day before.

The final night, Augustus offered a pregnant sow to Mother Earth, and the matrons again prepared banquets. During the next, the final day, Augustus and Agrippa offered to Apollo and Diana nine cows of each of the varieties that had been sacrificed the second night. Through all these nights and days the prayers pronounced at the offerings had begged protection for the state and its people in war and peace; victory, health, and blessings for the people and the legions, the person and family of the sacrificing emperor, and the college of the Sibylline priesthood. Terminating the ceremonies of June 3rd, a chorus of 27 boys and 27 girls, all of whose parents were alive, sang the festival song composed by Horace, first on the Palatine, where Apollo and Diana were revered, and then on the Capitoline. . . . The concluding hours of the day were filled with stage plays, chariot races, and the performances of jugglers. After all of which there were added, finally, a couple of days of various types of performance, during which the excitement of the festival settled down.

When this Augustan Festival of the Saeculum is compared with earlier feasts of the kind [Professor Deubner comments], the idea involved comes unmistakably to light. The earlier had been exclusively night festivals, addressed to the dark deities of the underworld, Pluto and Persephone. Their function had been to rectify evils, wash away sin, appease the powers of darkness, placate the jaws of death, and set bounds between what had been and what was to be. The new festival, on the other hand, joined the night festival to one of day. Thus it proclaimed the triumphant message to all who would hear: From Night to Light. And even in the nightly celebrations the deities called upon were not Pluto and Persephone, but the life-giving powers resident in the darkness of the earth. These were to pour forth from their domain those blessings for the world of light that Rome so fervently required. The Festival of Death of the Old Saeculum had transformed itself into the Resurrection Festival of the New; and the Emperor of the joyous populace appeared in the role of the Savior of the Dawning Era, bathed in the glory of Apollo's light.[51]

One cannot fail to recognize in this idea the prelude to the transfer of the Day of God in the Christian tradition from Saturday, the "Day of Saturn" (the god and planet of cold darkness and obstruction), to the New Testament "Day of the Sun," Sunday: *Sol invictus,* the sign of light, victory over darkness, and rebirth.

Augustus, after his death, was elevated to the circle of the gods of the Roman state, in which role the murdered Julius Caesar had preceded him, to whom a temple had already been erected in the Forum. Augustus, during his lifetime, had not permitted his person to be directly worshiped in Rome—offerings had been addressed only to his *genius;* however, in the provinces he had been worshiped as the vehicle of the spirit of the Roman state, and to refuse him reverence in this character had been a political crime punishable by death. After his passing, a special priesthood was founded for the services of his cult—as in future years special priesthoods were to appear for each of the deified emperors, until, as Professor Deubner remarks, "a complete devaluation of the idea of apotheosis supervened." [52]

Commodus (r. 180–192 A.D.) was the first to allow himself to be worshiped in Rome as a god while living; Aurelian (r. 270–275) allowed himself to be addressed as "Lord and God" (*dominus et deus*); and Diocletian (r. 284–305) went all the way, ordering that he should be known as Jovius, "of Jove," and his viceroy Maximian as Herculius, "of Hercules." And in those declining days of the empire, when the holy remains of an emperor were placed on a vast pyre of many stages and cremated, it was contrived that at just the right time there should appear flying from the summit of this flaming Cosmic Tower an eagle, bird of the sun, as the soul of the deceased, released from its earthly coil, now winging home.

IV. The Risen Christ

The recurrent mythological event of the death and resurrection of a god, which had been for millenniums the central mystery of all of the great religions of the nuclear Near East, became in Christian thought an event in time, which had occurred but once, and marked the moment of the transfiguration of history. Through Adam's Fall by the Tree in the Garden, death had come into the world. Through God's covenant with the Children of Israel a people had been prepared to receive and to clothe in flesh the Living God. Through Mary that divine being had entered the world, not as myth, not as symbol, but in flesh and blood, historically. And on the cross he had offered to the eye and heart a silent sign—which has been variously read from the points of view of the various sects, yet has been for all, however read, of prodigious affective as well as symbolic force.

We do not really know whether, historically, Jesus the Nazarene knew that he was going to die on the cross. It could be argued, I suppose, that in his character as True Man he cannot have known, though as True God he must have known from all eternity. The paradoxology of life, which is both tragic and beyond tragedy, is implicit in his silent sign. But whether known, or in what manner known, to the inspired and inspiring young proclaimer of the Day of God who was crucified under Pontius Pilate (the Roman procurator of Judea from 26 to 36 A.D.), it is a fact that within two decades of his death, his Cross had become for his followers the countervailing symbol of the Tree of the Fall in the Garden.

The earliest Christian documents to come down to us are Paul's letters, 51 to 64 A.D., written to his converts in the busy Hellenistic market towns to which he had introduced the new faith, and in these the fundamental mythic image of the Fall by the Tree and Redemption by the Cross was already firmly defined. "For as by a man came death," wrote Paul, "by a man has come also the resurrection of the dead. For as in Adam all die, so also in Christ shall all be made alive." [53] And in his epistle to the Philippians, written c. 61–64 A.D., there is a remarkable quotation from an early Christian hymn, the earliest of which we have knowledge, where already Jesus Crucified is hailed as the Messiah, "who," as we read,

> though he was in the form of God, did not count equality with God a thing to be grasped, but emptied himself, taking the form of a servant, being born in the likeness of men. And being found in human form he humbled himself and became obedient unto death, even death on the cross. Therefore God has highly exalted him and bestowed on him the name which is above every name, that at the name of Jesus every knee should bow, in heaven and on earth and under the earth, and every tongue confess that Jesus Christ is Lord, to the glory of God the Father.[54]

This, however, is a very different concept of the Messiah from that of the orthodox Jewish expectation, where there is no idea of the Messiah as God. As Professor Joseph Klausner formulates the expectation, it was—and is—(the italics are Professor Klausner's) of

> a truly pre-eminent man, to the extent that the *Jewish* imagination could picture him: he was supreme in strength and heroism; he was also supreme in moral qualities. A great personality, which is incomparably higher and stronger than ordinary people, a personality to which all very willingly make themselves subject and which can overcome all things, but for these very reasons feeling a very strong sense of obligation—this is the pre-eminent man of Judaism. Of a pre-eminent man like this it is possible to say, "Thou hast made him a little lower than God." For from a pre-eminent man like this to God is but a step. But this step Judaism did *not* take. It formed within the limits of a humanity which is continually raising itself up, the ideal of flesh and blood, "the idea of the ultimate limit of man" (in the language of Kant), this

great personality, only by means of which and by the help of which can redemption and salvation come to humanity— the King-Messiah.[55]

In contrast, the Christian legend, from an early date (how early, however, is a matter of debate) took to itself a motif already well known both in Greek mythology—as in the myths of Leda and the Swan, Danaë and the Shower of Gold—and in the Zoroastrian myth of Saoshyant; namely

THE VIRGIN BIRTH

According to Luke:

In the sixth month the angel Gabriel was sent from God to a city of Galilee named Nazareth, to a virgin betrothed to a man whose name was Joseph, of the house of David; and the virgin's name was Mary. And he came to her and said, "Hail, O favored one, the Lord is with you! Blessed are you among women!" But she was greatly troubled at the saying, and considered in her mind what sort of greeting this might be. And the angel said to her, "Do not be afraid, Mary, for you have found favor with God. And behold, you will conceive in your womb and bear a son, and you shall call his name Jesus. He will be great, and will be called the Son of the Most High; and the Lord God will give to him the throne of his father David, and he will reign over the house of Jacob for ever; and of his kingdom there will be no end." And Mary said to the angel, "How can this be, since I have no husband?" And the angel said to her, "The Holy Spirit will come upon you, and the power of the Most High will overshadow you; therefore the child to be born will be called holy, the Son of God" . . . And Mary said, "Behold I am the handmaid of the Lord; let it be to me according to your word." And the Angel departed from her.[56]

On the level simply of legend, without regard to the possibility of an actual miracle, the Virgin Birth must be interpreted as a mythic motif from the Persian or Greek, not Hebrew, side of the Christian heritage; and in the two recorded versions of the Nativity scene, more motifs appear from this gentilic side.

THE BABE IN THE MANGER

Again according to Luke:

In those days a decree went out from Caesar Augustus that all the world should be enrolled. This was the first enrollment, when Quirinius was governor of Syria. And all went to be enrolled, each to his own city. And Joseph went up from Galilee, from the city of Nazareth, to Judea, to the city of David, which is called Bethlehem, because he was of the house and lineage of David, to be enrolled with Mary, his betrothed, who was with child. And while they were there, the time came for her to be delivered. And she gave birth to her first-born son and wrapped him in swaddling cloths, and laid him in a manger, because there was no place for them in the inn.

And in that region there were shepherds out in the field, keeping watch over their flock by night. And an angel of the Lord appeared to them, and the glory of the Lord shone around them, and they were filled with fear. And the angel said to them, "Be not afraid; for behold, I bring you good news of a great joy which will come to all the people; for to you is born this day in the city of David a Savior, who is Christ the Lord. And this will be a sign for you: you will find a babe wrapped in swaddling cloths and lying in a manger." And suddenly there was with the angel a multitude of the heavenly host praising God and saying, "Glory to God in the highest, and on earth peace among men of good will!"

When the angels went away from them into heaven, the shepherds said to one another, "Let us go over to Bethlehem and see this thing that has happened, which the Lord has made known to us." And they went with haste, and found Mary and Joseph, and the babe lying in a manger. And when they saw it they made known the saying which had been told them concerning this child; and all who heard it wondered at what the shepherds told them. But Mary kept all these things, pondering them in her heart. And the shepherds returned, glorifying and praising God for all they had heard and seen, as it had been told them.[57]

This scene echoes in the detail of the shepherds a motif familiar from the legend of Mithra's birth from the mother rock. The angelic host, also, is suggestive rather of a Zoroastrian background, particularly since the glory of the Lord shines around it. Such a radiance—Avestan, *Xvarnah,* "Light of Glory" [58]—is the light of Ahura Mazda's pristine creation symbolized by the halo, which appears first in Persian art and then passes eastward into the Buddhist and westward to the Christian sphere. A totally different version of the Nativity is given in the Gospel according to Matthew —as far as possible from the idyllic atmosphere of Luke's peaceful pastoral scene.

THE VISIT OF THE MAGI

Now when Jesus was born in Bethlehem of Judea in the days of Herod the king, behold, wise men from the East came to Jerusalem, saying, "Where is he who has been born king of the Jews? For we have seen his star in the East, and have come to worship him." When Herod the king heard this, he was troubled, and all Jerusalem with him; and assembling all the chief priests and scribes of the people, he inquired of them where the Christ was to be born. They told him, "In Bethlehem of Judea; for so it is written by the prophet: 'And you, O Bethlehem, in the land of Judah, are by no means the least among the rulers of Judah; for from you shall come a ruler who will govern my people Israel' [Micah 5:2]." Then Herod summoned the wise men secretly and ascertained from them what time the star appeared; and he sent them to Bethlehem, saying, "Go and search diligently for the child, and when you have found him bring me word, that I too may come and worship him." When they had heard the king they went their way; and lo, the star which they had seen in the East went before them, till it came to rest over the place where the child was. When they saw the star they rejoiced exceedingly with great joy; and going into the house they saw the child with Mary his mother, and they fell down and worshiped him. Then, opening their treasures, they offered him gifts, gold and frankincense and myrrh. And being warned in a dream not to return to Herod, they departed to their own country by another way. [59]

The Feast of the Visit of the Magi is now celebrated January 6, which was the date of the festival in Egyptian Alexandria of the birth of the new Aion (a syncretistic personification of Osiris) from

Kore, "the Maiden," who was there identified with Isis, of whom the bright star Sirius (Sothis) rising on the horizon had been for millenniums the watched-for sign. The rising of the star announced the rising of the flood waters of the Nile, through which the world-renewing grace of the dead and resurrected lord Osiris was to be poured over the land. Writing of the Festival of Kore in her temple in Alexandria, Saint Epiphanius (c. 315–402 A.D.) states that "on the eve of that day it was the custom to spend the night in singing and attending to the images of the gods. At dawn a descent was made to a crypt, and a wooden image was brought up, which had the sign of a cross and a star of gold marked on hands, knees, and head. This was carried round in procession, and then taken back to the crypt; and it was said that this was done because 'the Maiden' had given birth to 'the Aion.' " [60]

The present custom of celebrating the Nativity on December 25 seems not to have been instituted until the year 353 or 354, in Rome, under Pope Liberius, possibly to absorb the festival of the birth of Mithra that day, from the mother rock. For December 25 marked in those centuries the winter solstice: so that Christ, now, like Mithra and the Emperor of Rome, could be recognized as the risen sun.[61] Thus we have two myths and two dates of the Nativity scene, December 25 and January 6, with associations pointing on one hand to the Persian and on the other to the old Egyptian sphere.

THE FLIGHT INTO EGYPT AND SLAUGHTER OF THE INNOCENTS

The Matthew version continues:

Now when they had departed, behold, an angel of the Lord appeared to Joseph in a dream and said, "Rise, take the child and his mother, and flee to Egypt, and remain there till I tell you; for Herod is about to search for the child, to destroy him." And he rose and took the child and his mother by night, and departed to Egypt, and remained there until the death of Herod. This was to fulfill what the Lord had spoken by the prophet, "Out of Egypt have I called my son" [Hosea 11:1].

Then Herod, when he saw that he had been tricked by the wise men, was in a furious rage, and he sent and killed all the male children in Bethlehem and in all that region who were two years old and under, according to the time which he had ascertained from the wise men. Then was fulfilled what was spoken by the prophet Jeremiah: "A voice was heard in Ramah, wailing and loud lamentation, Rachel weeping for her children; she refused to be consoled, because they were no more" [Jeremiah 31:150].

But when Herod died, behold, an angel of the Lord appeared in a dream to Joseph in Egypt, saying, "Rise, take the child and his mother, and go to the land of Israel, for those who sought the child's life are dead." And he rose and took the child and his mother, and went to the land of Israel. But when he heard that Archelaus reigned over Judea in place of his father Herod, he was afraid to go there, and being warned in a dream he withdrew to the district of Galilee. And he went and dwelt in a city called Nazareth, that what was spoken by the prophets might be fulfilled, "He shall be called a Nazarene." [62]

It is of interest to compare with this account of the malice of the tyrant-king a Jewish legend of the birth of Abraham, drawn from a late Midrash:

Abraham's birth had been read in the stars by Nimrod; for this impious king was a cunning astrologer, and it was manifest to him that a man would be born in his day who would rise up against him and triumphantly give the lie to his religion. In his terror of the fate foretold him in the stars, he sent for his princes and governors, and asked them to advise him in the matter. They answered, and said: "Our unanimous advice is that thou shouldst build a great house, station a guard at the entrance thereof, and make known in the whole of thy realm that all pregnant women shall repair thither together with their midwives, who are to remain with them when they are delivered. When the days of a woman to be delivered are fulfilled, and the child is born, it shall be the duty of the midwife to kill it, if it be a boy. But if the child be a girl, it shall be kept alive, and the mother shall receive gifts and costly garments, and a herald shall proclaim, 'Thus is done unto the woman who bears a daughter!'

The king was pleased with this counsel, and he had a

proclamation published throughout his whole kingdom, summoning all the architects to build a great house for him, sixty ells high and eighty wide. After it was completed, he issued a second proclamation, summoning all pregnant women thither, and there they were to remain until their confinement. Officers were appointed to take the women to the house, and guards were stationed in it and about it, to prevent the women from escaping thence. He furthermore sent midwives to the house, and commanded them to slay the men children at their mothers' breasts. But if a woman bore a girl, she was to be arrayed in byssus, silk, and embroidered garments, and led forth from the house of detention among great honors. No less than seventy thousand children were slaughtered thus. Then the angels appeared before God, and spoke, "Seest Thou not what he doth, yon sinner and blasphemer, Nimrod son of Canaan, who slays so many innocent babes that have done no harm?" God answered and said: "Ye holy angels, I know it and I see it, for I neither slumber nor sleep. I behold and I know the secret things and the things that are revealed, and ye shall be witness to what I will do unto this sinner and blasphemer, for I will turn My hand against him to chastise him."

It was about this time that Terah espoused the mother of Abraham, and she was with child. When her body grew large at the end of three months of pregnancy, and her countenance became pale, Terah said to her, "What ails thee, my wife, that thy countenance is so pale and thy body so swollen?" She answered and said, "Every year I suffer with this malady." But Terah would not be put off thus. He insisted: "Show me thy body. It seems to me thou art big with child. If that be so, it behooves us not to violate the command of our god Nimrod." When he passed his hand over her body, there happened a miracle. The child rose until it lay beneath her breasts, and Terah could feel nothing with his hands. He said to his wife, "Thou didst speak truly," and naught became visible until the day of her delivery.

When her time approached, she left the city in great terror and wandered toward the desert, walking along the edge of a valley, until she happened across a cave. She entered this refuge, and on the next day she was seized with throes and gave birth to a son. The whole cave was filled with the light of the child's countenance as with the splendor of the sun, and the mother rejoiced exceedingly. The babe she bore was our father Abraham.

His mother lamented, and said to her son: "Alas that I bore thee at a time when Nimrod is king. For thy sake seventy thousand men children were slaughtered, and I am seized with terror on account of thee, that he hear of thy existence, and slay thee. Better thou shouldst perish here in this cave than my eye should behold thee dead at my breast." She took the garment in which she was clothed, and wrapped it about the boy. Then she abandoned him in the cave, saying, "May the Lord be with thee, may He not fail thee nor forsake thee."

Thus Abraham was deserted in the cave, without a nurse, and he began to wail. God sent Gabriel down to give him milk to drink, and the angel made it to flow from the little finger of the baby's right hand, and he sucked at it until he was ten days old. Then he arose and walked about, and he left the cave. . . .[63]

In India a like tale is told of the beloved savior Krishna, whose terrible uncle, Kansa, was, in that case, the tyrant-king. The savior's mother, Devaki, was of royal lineage, the tyrant's niece, and at the time when she was married the wicked monarch heard a voice, mysteriously, which let him know that her eighth child would be his slayer. He therefore confined both her and her husband, the saintly nobleman Vasudeva, in a closely guarded prison, where he murdered their first six infants as they came.

For in those days a number of demons, having seduced the women of the earth by various wiles, had contrived to become born throughout the world as tyrants, of whom Kansa was the greatest. And the weight of their tyranny was such that the goddess Earth, unable to bear the burden of their warring hosts, took the form of a cow and, piteously weeping, went before the gods to beg for aid, on the summit of the cosmic mountain. These then, together with the cow, proceeded to the shore of the Cosmic Ocean, upon the surface of which the Lord of the Universe, reposing on the endless snake Ananta, slept forever, dreaming the dream that is the universe. And at the shore of the Cosmic Sea, the leader of the assembled gods, Brahma the Creator, bowed and prayed to the great form seen far out on the deep. "O Thou, great Vishnu, both possessed of form and without form, simultaneously one and multiform; hearing without ears, seeing without eyes, knowing all yet known of none: thou art the common center, protector of all things, in whom all rest. There is nothing but thyself, O Lord, nor will anything else ever be. Glory to thee, largest of the great, smallest of the least, pervader of all. Behold this goddess Earth, who comes to thee now terribly oppressed!"

The prayer being ended, there was heard a voice, deep, vast, yet gentle and auspicious, like the roll of distant thunder, bidding all to be at peace, while the radiant slumbering form, of the hue of a blue lotus, reposing on the milk-white serpent coils of the multiheaded Ananta, plucked from itself two hairs, a milk-white and a blue-black, which it then released into the air.

The white hair, white as Ananta, was born as the seventh child of Devaki, the savior Balarama, and the black hair as the eighth, black Krishna. But now the good lady's spouse, Vasudeva, had seven wives, of whom one had been sent across the river Jumna, to a district known as Cow Land; and when the child Balarama was conceived, he was by a miracle transferred to the womb across the river, and a report went to the tyrant king that Devaki had miscarried. The eighth child, however, was allowed to mature where it was, and while she carried him, the mother was invested with such light that no one could gaze upon her. And the gods, invisible to mortals, praised her continually from the time that Vishnu, as the incarnation Krishna, entered into her person.

The four quarters were alight with joy on the day of the birth. All the virtuous, that day, experienced new delight; violent winds were hushed; and the rivers glided tranquilly. The seas, murmuring, made a music to which the nymphs of heaven danced. And at midnight the clouds, emitting a low, pleasing sound, poured a rain of flowers to greet the birth.

But when Vasudeva beheld the babe, who was of a luminous, dark blue complexion with four arms and on his breast a curl of white hair, "Thou art born!" said the father, terrified. "But, O sovereign God of Gods, bearer of the conch, discus, and mace, in mercy withhold this thy celestial form!" And Devaki, the mother, also prayed. And the god, by his maya, took the form of an ordinary new-born babe.

Vasudeva then picked him up and hurried forth into a night of rain; for the guards, charmed by the power of Vishnu, were asleep. The many-headed cosmic serpent closely followed, spreading his broad milk-white hoods above the heads of the father and child. And when Vasudeva, wading the river, crossed to the farther shore the waters became calm, so that he passed easily to Cow Land. There again he found the world asleep. And a good woman there, Yashoda by name, with whom his second wife was staying, had just given birth to a girl. Vasudeva exchanged his son for that child, placing him at the sleeping mother's side; so that when she woke she found, to her delight, that she had been delivered of a boy. And bearing off the other, he crossed the river again, to his own wife's side, unobserved, and the gates of the city, as well as of the prison, closed of themselves.

Whereupon the cry of the newborn babe awoke the guards and, starting up, they alarmed the tyrant, who rushed immediately to the chamber, tore the infant from the mother's breast and flung her against a rock. The intended victim rose into the air, however, and expanded into the figure of a huge goddess with eight arms, each wielding a formidable weapon: a bow, a trident, arrows and a shield, a sword, a conch, a discus, and a mace. And laughing terrifically, this vision cried at him: "O Kansa, of what avail is it to you now to have hurled me to the ground? The one who is to kill you is already born." For she was the goddess Mahamaya, "The Great Illusion." She was the world-supporting dream-power of Vishnu himself; and when he had entered the womb of Devaki, she had entered that of Yashoda, precisely for this stroke. Clad in glorious raiment and with many gorgeous garlands, ornaments, and jewels, hymned by the spirits of air and earth, she filled the heavens —and dissolved into the sky.[64]

If miracles are required, India wins, every time. The text that I have abridged here is from the Bhagavata Purana, a popular work of the tenth century A.D.—from which I drew, in *Oriental Mythology*, one of the versions there compared to the moonlight dance of

Krishna and the Gopis.[65] But the worship of Krishna is mentioned much earlier, by the Greek envoy Megasthenes at the court of Chandragupta Maurya (300 B.C.), who compares the Indian hero-god to Heracles. The earliest documents of his deeds are the epic Mahabharata (c. 400 B.C.–400 A.D.) and its appendix, the Harivamsa (sixth century A.D.). Thus the period of the growth of the Krishna legend about parallels that of the post-exilic Hebrew development, with Persia, the Greeks, and finally Rome contributing to the intercultural traffic.

There can be no doubt that the mythologies bear close relationships to each other, with, however, important contrasts of implication as well as of style. The Levantine legends gave stress to a sociological argument, celebrating their own cults to the defamation of whatever others happened to be known, whereas the Indian developed an essentially psychological symbology, where the tyrant-demon signified not an alien religion, but the orientation of a mind locked to ego and the fear of death, while the savior was a manifestation of that spirit, beyond life and death, which is the inherent reality of us all. The passage to the yonder shore, to Cow Land (compare the shepherds and their flocks), denotes a transfer of accent from the orientation of ego, the world of the tyrant-king, to that of the reality manifest throughout nature, the world of the great goddess Earth, personified from early neolithic times in the aspect of a cow.* The myths are very much the same; but it would not be appropriate to elucidate one according to the meaning of another. They are a hair's breadth, and yet universes, apart.

Moreover, they are all considerably later than the Greek legend of the birth of Zeus recounted in Hesiod's Theogony, c. 750 B.C.

> Rheia [we there read] submissive in love to Kronos [her brother-spouse], bore glorious children—Histia and Demeter, Hera of the golden sandals, and strong Hades, who under ground lives in his palace and has a heart without pity; the deep-thunderous Earthshaker, and Zeus of the counsel, who is the father of gods and of mortals, and underneath whose thunder the whole earth shudders. But as each of these chil-

---

* Compare Egyptian Hathor, Sumerian Ninhursag, etc. *The Masks of God: Oriental Mythology*, pp. 36–112, and supra, p. 59.

dren came from the womb of its mother to her knees, great Kronos swallowed it down, with the intention that no other of the proud children of the line of Ouranos should ever hold the king's position among the immortals. For he had heard, from Gaia and from starry Ouranos, that it had been ordained for him, for all his great strength, to be beaten by his son, and through the designs of great Zeus. Therefore he kept watch, and did not sleep, but waited for his children and swallowed them, and Rheia's sorrow was beyond forgetting.

But when she was about to bear Zeus, the father of mortals and gods, then Rheia went and entreated her own dear parents, and these were Gaia and starry Ouranos, to think of some plan by which, when she gave birth to her dear son, the thing might not be known, and the fury of revenge be on devious-devising Kronos the great, for his father, and his own children whom he had swallowed. They listened gladly to their beloved daughter, and consented, and explained to her all that had been appointed to happen concerning Kronos, who was King, and his son, of the powerful spirit, and sent her to Lyktos, in the fertile countryside of Crete at that time when she was to bring forth the youngest of her children, great Zeus; and the earth, gigantic Gaia, took him inside her in wide Crete, there to keep him alive and raise him. There Earth arrived through the running black night, carrying him, and came first to Lyktos, and holding him in her arms, hid him in a cave, deep in under the secret places of earth, in Mount Aigaion which is covered with forest. She wrapped a great stone in baby-clothes, and this she presented to the high lord Kronos, son of Ouranos who once ruled the immortals, and he took it then in his hands and crammed it down into his belly, hard wretch, nor saw in his own mind how there had been left him instead of the stone a son, invincible and unshakable for the days to come, who soon by force and his hands defeating him must drive him from his title, and then be lord over the immortals.

And presently after this the shining limbs and the power of the lord, Zeus, grew great, and with the years circling on great Kronos, the devious-devising fooled by the resourceful promptings of Gaia, once again brought up his progeny. First he vomited up the stone, which last he had swallowed, and this Zeus took and planted in place, on earth of the wide ways, at holy Pytho, in the hollow ravines under Parnassos, to be a portent and a wonder to mortal men thereafter. Then he set free from their dismal bonds the brothers of his father, the sons of Ouranos, whom his father in his wild temper had enchained, and they remembered, and knew gratitude for the good he had done them, and they gave him the thunder, and the smoky bolt, and the flash of the lightning, which Gaia the gigantic had hidden till then. With these to support him, he is lord over immortals and mortals.[66]

The myth goes back to the millennium of Crete and, beyond that, to the neolithic earth-goddess and her son. We recall from later Greece the birth of Perseus, and from the legend of Zoroaster the complaint of the soul of the cow. We recall, in fact, a multitude innumerable of such tales and episodes, and in view of them all have to conclude, in sum, that a rich environment of mythic lore was diffused with the neolithic arts of agriculture and settled village life across the whole face of the earth, from which elements have been drawn everywhere for the fashioning of hero myths, whether in Mexico of Quetzalcoatl, in Egypt of Osiris, in India of Krishna and the Buddha, in the Near East of Abraham or of Christ. Zoroaster, the Buddha, and Christ seem to have been historical characters. Some of the others may not have been. But whether fictional or historical, the names and figures of the great and little heroes of the world act irresistibly as magnets to those floating filaments of myth that are everywhere in the air. Professor Charles Guignebert of the Sorbonne, treating of the history of the Gospels, states that in the course of development of the Christian legend, "Jesus the Nazarene disappeared and gave place to the glorified Christ."[67] It could not have been otherwise. In the Buddhist sphere, the biography of Gautama was turned into a supernatural life through a constellation of many of the same motifs. Through such a process history is lost; but history also is made. For the function of such myth-building is to interpret the sense, not to chronicle the facts, of a life, and to offer the artwork of the legend, then, as an activating symbol for the inspiration and shaping of lives, and even civilizations, to come.

Let us regard a few more significant episodes from this legend of the Man who was God.

THE BAPTISM IN THE JORDAN

Much has been made throughout the centuries of the fact that in the Gospel according to Mark there is no account either of the Virgin Birth or of the infancy of the Savior. The text begins with his baptism, and the descent, then, of the Spirit as a dove. It is as brief and simple a statement as could be:

> In those days Jesus came from Nazareth of Galilee and was baptized by John in the Jordan. And when he came out of the water, immediately he saw the heavens opened and the Spirit descending upon him like a dove; and a voice came from heaven, "Thou art my beloved Son; with thee I am well pleased." [68]

The baptism is the first event of the biography to appear in all three synoptic gospels, and the version according to Mark being the earliest of the series, c. 75 A.D., it supplied the matter from which the other two were derived. Nevertheless, in one authoritative text of the Gospel according to Luke the voice from heaven declares, not "Thou art my beloved Son," but "This day have I begotten thee." [69]

Now the controversy over the dignity of Mary hinges on the question as to whether Jesus was the very son of God from conception or became endowed with his divine mission only at the moment of his baptism by John. Apparently the historicity of John the Baptist cannot be denied. The almost contemporary Jewish historian Josephus (c. 37–95 A.D.) states that "he was a good man and commanded the Jews to exercise virtue through justice toward one another and piety toward God, and by so doing to arrive at immersion; for immersion would be acceptable to God only if practiced not to expiate sins but for purification of the body after the soul had first been thoroughly purified by righteousness." And further: "Because many affected by his words flocked to him, Herod * feared that John's great influence over the people might lead to revolt (for the people seemed likely to do whatever he

---

* I.e., Herod Antipas, who ruled over Galilee and Peraea from 4 B.C. to 39 A.D.

counseled). He therefore thought it best to slay him in order to prevent any mischief he might engender, and to avoid possible future troubles by not sparing a man who might make him repent of his leniency when too late. Accordingly, because of Herod's suspicious nature, John was imprisoned in the fortress Machaerus, and there put to death." [70]

The Gospel according to Mark tells of the beheading of John the Baptist in its famous tale of Salome's dance.[71] And of John's teaching and baptizing the same gospel relates, further, that he

> appeared in the wilderness, preaching a baptism of repentance for the forgiveness of sins. And there went out to him all the country of Judea, and all the people of Jerusalem; and they were baptized by him in the river Jordan, confessing their sins.
> Now John [the text continues] was clothed with camel's hair, and had a leather girdle around his waist, and ate locusts and wild honey. And he preached, saying, "After me comes he who is mightier than I, the thong of whose sandals I am not worthy to stoop down and untie. I have baptized you with water; but he will baptize you with the Holy Spirit." [72]

The site of John's activity, as already remarked,* was within ten miles of the Essene community of Qumran, where a white-clothed army of the Lord was waiting, watching, and preparing for exactly such a one as he foretold. The air of the desert in those days, in fact, was filled with the expectation of a Messiah and the Messianic Age. John, however, was no Essene, as we know both from his garb and from his diet. He was in the line, rather, of Elijah, who is described in the Book of Kings as a man who wore "a garment of haircloth, with a girdle of leather about his loins." [73] And the rite of baptism that he preached, whatever its meaning at that time may have been, was an ancient rite coming down from the old Sumerian temple city Eridu, of the water god Ea, "God of the House of Water," whose symbol is the tenth sign of the zodiac, Capricorn (a composite beast with the foreparts of a goat and body of a fish), which is the sign into which the sun enters at the winter solstice for rebirth. In the Hellenistic period, Ea was called *Oannes*, which is in Greek *Ioannes*, Latin *Johannes*, Hebrew *Yoḥanan*,

* Supra, p. 281.

English *John*. Several scholars have suggested, therefore, that there was never either John or Jesus, but only a water-god and a sun-god. The chronicle of Josephus seems to guarantee John, however;[74] and I shall leave it to the reader to imagine how he came both by the god's name and by his rite.

The episode of the baptism, then, whether taken as a mythological motif or as a biographical event, stands for the irrevocable passage of a threshold. The counterpart in the Buddha legend is the long series of visits to hermitages and ascetics, terminating with the five fasting mendicants on the bank of the river Nairanjana, after his stay with whom the Future Buddha bathed in the waters of the stream and departed alone to the Tree of Illumination.[75] Analogously, John the Baptist and his company represent the ultimate horizon of saintly realization antecedent to the victory of the Savior: the last outpost, beyond which his lonesome, individual adventure now was to proceed. And as the future Buddha, having tested all the sages of his time, bathed in the river Nairanjana and departed to his tree alone, so likewise Jesus, half a millennium later, leaving behind the wisdom of the Law and teaching of the Pharisees, came to the ultimate teacher of his time—and passed beyond.

In the Gospel according to Mark, as we have said, this event is the first recounted of the Savior: there is no notice in that text of the Virgin Birth. But there is no mention of it either in Paul or in John—or even in Matthew and Luke beyond the two passages above noted, which may be late interpolations. Moreover, in Matthew and Luke two quite different genealogies appear, both of which, however, trace the line of the house of David down to Jesus by way of Joseph.[76] It is reasonably certain that in the earliest, strictly Jewish stage of the development of this legend, the completely un-Jewish idea of the begetting of a hero by a god can have played no role, and that the episode of the initiatory baptism in Jordan must have marked the opening of the Messianic career.

THE TEMPTATION IN THE DESERT

After the words, "Thou art my beloved Son," the Mark gospel goes on: "The Spirit immediately drove him out into the wilderness. And he was in the wilderness forty days, tempted by Satan; and he was with the wild beasts; and the angels ministered to him." [77]

Matthew and Luke amplify this narrative. The following is from Luke:

And Jesus, full of the Holy Spirit, returned from the Jordan, and was led by the Spirit for forty days in the wilderness, tempted by the devil. And he ate nothing in those days; and when they were ended, he was hungry. The devil said to him, "If you are the Son of God, command this stone to become bread." And Jesus answered him, "It is written, 'Man shall not live by bread alone' [Deuteronomy 8:3]." *

And the devil took him up and showed him all the kingdoms of the world in a moment of time, and said to him, "To you I will give all this authority and their glory; for it has been delivered to me, and I give it to whom I will. If you, then, will worship me, it shall all be yours." And Jesus answered him, "It is written, 'You shall worship the Lord your God, and him only shall you serve' [Deuteronomy 6:13]."

And he took him to Jerusalem, and set him on the pinnacle of the temple, and said to him, "If you are the Son of God, throw yourself down from here; for it is written, 'He will give his angels charge of you, to guard you,' and 'On their hands they will bear you up, lest you strike your foot against a stone' [Psalm 91:11–12]." And Jesus answered him, "It is said, 'You shall not tempt the Lord your God' [Deuteronomy 6:16]." † And when the devil had ended every temptation, he departed from him until an opportune time.‡

It is to be remarked that the Puritan Milton's epic poem *Paradise Regained* is devoted to this episode of the conquest of the devil in the desert of the mind; whereas a Gothic author, on the other hand, or a Catholic today, would have expected that a work bear-

* Matthew's account is about the same, but adds: ". . . but by every word that proceeds from the mouth of God."

† Matthew reverses the order of temptations two and three.

‡ Luke 4:1–13. Matthew ends: "Then the devil left him, and behold, angels came and ministered to him" (Matthew 4:1–11).

ing such a title should deal with the world-redeeming sacrifice of
the Cross.

To be remarked also is the resemblance—though with contrast—
of this temptation of the World Savior by a devil into whose hands
the glory and authority of the kingdoms of the world had been delivered, to that of the Buddha—the earlier World Savior—by the
lord of the world illusion whose name is "Desire and Death."
Having considered all the teachings of the sages and practices of
ascetics, and having bathed in the stream Nairanjana, the Future
Buddha came forth and sat upon the bank. A herdsman's daughter,
moved and guided by the gods, brought him a rich bowl of milk,
on which he restored his emaciated body; whereafter, he proceeded
alone to the Tree of Enlightenment, beneath which he placed himself—and there appeared to him then the creator of the world illusion.

I have given the tale in *Oriental Mythology* [78] and need not repeat it here, beyond suggesting its relationship to the desert scene
of Christ. The first temptation of the Buddha was of desire (*kāma*),
the second, of fear, the fear of death (*māra*), which two correspond
to the two mainsprings of delusion recognized in modern psychi-
atric schools: desire and aggression, eros and thanatos.[79] They are
the chief motivations of life, and by transcending them the Buddha
rose to a sphere of knowledge that the world delusion occludes—
after attaining which, he taught for some fifty years.

In the Christian scene, the first temptation was economic: First
eat, seek the spirit later— which is the philosophy of Nietzsche's
"flies of the market place": security, the marketing orientation,
economic determinism; while the second temptation (according
to Luke, third according to Matthew) was political: Rule the
world (in the name, of course, of God, as always in the Levant)
—which was the plane of concern of the Old Testament Messianic
hope. For, to quote once again Professor Klausner (with his usual
italics):

The definition of belief in the Messiah is: *The prophetic hope
for the end of this age, in which a strong redeemer, by his
power and his spirit, will bring complete redemption, political*

*and spiritual, to the people of Israel, and along with this, earthly
bliss and moral perfection to the entire human race. . . .
In the belief in the Messiah of the people of Israel, the
political part goes arm in arm with the ethical part, and
the nationalistic with the universalistic.* It is Christianity which
has attempted to remove the political and nationalistic part
which is there, and leave only the ethical and spiritual part.[80]

In the Christian temptation scene we have, exactly, the counterpart in symbolic terms of this authoritative verbal definition of the
change from Old to New Testament thought. And so it appears that
even in the earliest Christian reading of the Messianic Age, the
political-economic orientation had been rejected and a plane of
universalism attained that was neither national nor racial. Whether
Christ himself was responsible for this, no one can surely say; but
in any case, it is fundamental to the Gospels and is, in fact, the
basis for the classification of Christianity, like Buddhism, as a
World (not Ethnic, Tribal, Racial, or National) Religion.

However, the danger of what Dr. Jung has termed "inflation" is
the next temptation, the elevation of the mystic mind when it believes it has surpassed the earth.* Transported by Satan to the
pinnacle of the temple, the Son of God who has just overcome the
two material claims of what Schopenhauer termed the "vegetal" and
"animal" orders of existence now is to suppose himself to be an
angel, without taint of earth, without weight. But Christ, True Man
as well as True God, is (to use another Jungian term) a "uniting"
or "transcendent" symbol, showing the way between antitheses, in
this case earth and sky. And so the next we learn is that, instead of
passing away in ecstasy, this Son of Man, as well as of God, has
returned to his community, to teach.

THE WORLD TEACHER

Again according to Mark:

Now after John [the Baptist] was arrested, Jesus came into
Galilee, preaching the gospel of God, and saying "The time
is fulfilled, and the kingdom of God is at hand; repent, and
believe in the gospel." And passing along by the Sea of

* Compare the Aeolus episode of the Odyssey discussed supra, p. 168.

Galilee, he saw Simon and Andrew the brother of Simon casting a net in the sea; for they were fishermen. And Jesus said to them, "Follow me and I will make you become fishers of men." And immediately they left their nets and followed him. And going on a little farther, he saw James the son of Zebedee and John his brother, who were in their boat mending their nets. And immediately he called them; and they left their father Zebedee in the boat with the hired servants, and followed him. And they went into Capernaum; and immediately on the sabbath he entered the synagogue and taught. And they were astonished at his teaching, for he taught them as one who had authority, and not as the scribes.

And immediately there was in their synagogue a man with an unclean spirit; and he cried out, "What have you to do with us, Jesus of Nazareth? Have you come to destroy us? I know who you are, the Holy One of God." But Jesus rebuked him, saying, "Be silent, and come out of him!" And the unclean spirit, convulsing him and crying with a loud voice, came out of him. And they were all amazed, so that they questioned among themselves, saying, "What is this? A new teaching! With authority he commands even the unclean spirits and they obey him!" And at once his fame spread everywhere throughout all the surrounding region of Galilee.[81]

Viewed from a distance, the wandering sage of Galilee with his cluster of disciples, teaching, performing miracles, and challenging the established readers of the law, resembles many others, both before and since: the Buddha, the numerous World Teachers of the Jains, Elijah and Elisha, Pythagoras, Parmenides, Apollonius of Tyana. And the miracles, in particular, suggest the archetypal figure of the Oriental wonder-worker. Indeed, a number of such characters are named in the New Testament itself: Simon Magus of Samaria (Acts 8:9–24), Bar-Jesus and Elymas the Magician (Acts 13:6–12); at Ephesus, seven sons of the Jewish high priest Sceva (Acts 19:13–20), and at Caesarea, Agabus the Prophet (Acts 21:10–11). The Church has made a great deal of Christ's miracles: however, one can only wonder why such occult signs should ever have been supposed by men of intelligence to constitute the proof, or even desirability, of an elevated religion; for, as Professor Guignebert has observed:

All the religions that have so desired have had their miracles, the *same* miracles, and, on the other hand, all have shown themselves equally incapable of producing certain other miracles. The unprejudiced scholar is not surprised at this, because he knows that the same causes everywhere produce the same effects. But what is strange is that the believer is not surprised at it either. He merely insists that . . . *his* miracles are the only genuine ones; others are mere empty appearances, fabrications, frauds, uncomprehended facts, or witchcraft.[82]

Viewed more closely, on the other hand, in the context of his heritage, the gospel of the Nazarene represents two profound innovations. The first had to be reinterpreted when its promise failed of fulfillment, yet supports to this day the basic mythological expectation of the faithful; while the second has given the Christian world its ethical and spiritual, as distinct from clerical and sacramental, ground.

For already in the first recorded cry of the Good News, the conviction was announced that the kingdom of God was at hand; and throughout the first century of the Church this proclamation was interpreted literally, in apocalyptic, historical terms: as, for instance, in Paul's epistle to the Romans. "You know what hour it is, how it is full time now for you to wake from sleep. For salvation is nearer to us now than when we first believed; the night is far gone, the day is at hand." [83] The Day of the Messiah foreseen by the Essenes had arrived.

Yet the Messiah himself, in contrast to the waiting and watching Essenes, in contrast also to the Baptist, was neither a moralist nor an ascetic in the usual sense of these terms. He deliberately, on occasion, broke the statutes of the Mosaic Law, declaring, "The sabbath was made for man, not man for the sabbath; so the Son of Man is lord even of the sabbath"; [84] and again: "No one puts new wine into old wineskins; if he does, the wine will burst the skins, and the wine is lost; but new wine is for fresh skins." [85] And when it was complained that he sat and ate with sinners, he replied: "I came not to call the righteous, but sinners." [86] Moreover, in what represents the most vivid line of contrast of the Christian to the Essene view of purity of heart, whereas the white-clothed brotherhood of Qumran had taught love for those of their own brotherhood of light but hatred for all sons of darkness, we have the words of Jesus: "Love your enemies." [87] And when asked by one of the scribes, "Which commandment is the first of all?" he replied: "The first is, 'Hear, O Israel: The Lord our God, the Lord is one; and you shall love the Lord your God with all your heart, and with all your soul, and with all your mind, and with all your strength' [Deuteronomy 6:4]. The second is this, 'You shall love your neighbor as yourself' [Leviticus 19:18]. There is no other commandment greater than these." [88]

THE POWER OF THE KEYS

"Now," as we read in the gospel according to Matthew,

> when Jesus came into the district of Caesarea Philippi, he asked his disciples, "Who do men say that the Son of Man is?" And they said, "Some say John the Baptist, others say Elijah, and others Jeremiah or one of the prophets." He said to them, "But who do you say that I am?" Simon Peter replied, "You are the Christ, the Son of the living God." And Jesus answered him, "Blessed are you, Simon Bar-Jona! For flesh and blood has not revealed this to you, but my Father who is in heaven. And I tell you, you are Peter, and on this rock I will build my church, and the powers of death shall not prevail against it. I will give you the keys of the kingdom of heaven, and whatever you bind on earth shall be bound in heaven, and whatever you loose on earth shall be loosed in heaven." Then he strictly charged the disciples to tell no one that he was the Christ.
>
> From that time Jesus began to show his disciples that he must go to Jerusalem and suffer many things from the elders and chief priests and scribes, and be killed, and on the third day be raised. And Peter took him and began to rebuke him, saying, "God forbid, Lord! This shall never happen to you." But he turned and said to Peter, "Get behind me, Satan! You are a hindrance to me; for you are not on the side of God, but of men." [89]

In the life and legend of the Buddha there is a comparably ambivalent relation between the World Teacher and his beloved body servant Ananda, who, like Peter, never got spiritual things quite right, yet was made the head of the church. We note that in later Christian legend Peter is not placed within the heavenly sanctuary but as porter stands at the gate; and it might be supposed accordingly, that the flock in his keep, the good folk of the church of which he is the bedrock, also must be just outside. Certainly in the Buddhist fold, where the ministrations of the clergy represent simply a preparatory herding of the good sheep *toward* an experience that each in the silence of his heart must ultimately come to on his own, such is the meaning of the tenderly represented, cumbersome humanity of Ananda; and one cannot but suspect that in the writings of the Evangelists, too, there may have been some such implication in their representation of Peter as a good—indeed, a very good—loyal, honorable, and doting devotee of his master, just a little short of the insight that would have brought him through the gate to realization.

THE LAST DAY

And when it was evening [the first day of Unleavened Bread, when they sacrificed the passover lamb] Jesus came with the twelve; and as they were at table eating, Jesus said: "Truly I say to you, one of you will betray me, one who is eating with me." They began to be sorrowful, and to say to him one after another, "Is it I?" He said to them, "It is one of the twelve, one who is dipping bread in the same dish with me. For the Son of man goes as it is written of him, but woe to that man by whom the Son of man is betrayed! It would have been better for that man if he had not been born." And as they were eating, he took bread, and blessed, and broke it, and gave it to them, and said, "Take; this is my body." And he took a cup, and when he had given thanks he gave it to them, and they all drank of it. And he said to them, "This is my blood of the covenant, which is poured out for many. Truly, I say to you, I shall not drink again of the fruit of the vine until that day when I drink it new in the kingdom of God."

And when they had sung a hymn, they went out to the Mount of Olives. And Jesus said to them, "You will all fall away; for it is written, 'I will strike the shepherd, and the sheep will be scattered' [Zechariah 13:7]. But after I am raised up, I will go before you to Galilee." Peter said to him, "Even though they all fall away, I will not." And Jesus said to him, "Truly, I say to you, this very night, before the cock crows twice, you will deny me three times." But he said vehemently, "If I must die with you, I will not deny you." And they all said the same.

And they went to a place which was called Gethsemane; and he said to his disciples, "Sit here, while I pray." And he took with him Peter and James and John, and began to be greatly distressed and troubled. And he said to them, "My soul is very sorrowful, even to death; remain here, and watch." And going a little farther, he fell on the ground and prayed that, if it were possible, the hour might pass from him. And he said, "Abba, Father, all things are possible to thee; remove this cup from me; yet not what I will, but what thou wilt." And he came and found them sleeping, and he said to Peter, "Simon, are you asleep? Could you not watch one hour? Watch and pray that you may not enter into temptation; the spirit indeed is willing, but the flesh is weak." And again he went away and prayed, saying the same words. And again he came and found them sleeping, for their eyes were very heavy; and they did not know what to answer him. And he came a third time, and said to them, "Are you still sleeping and taking your rest? It is enough; the hour has come; the Son of man is betrayed into the hands of sinners. Rise, let us be going; see, my betrayer is at hand."

And immediately, while he was still speaking, Judas came, one of the twelve, and with him a crowd with swords and clubs, from the chief priests and the scribes and the elders. Now the betrayer had given them a sign, saying, "The one I shall kiss is the man; seize him and lead him away safely." And when he came, he went up to him at once, and said, "Master!" And he kissed him. And they laid hands on him and seized him. But one of those who stood by drew his sword, and struck the slave of the high priest and cut off his ear. And Jesus said to them, "Have you come out as against a robber, with swords and clubs to capture me? Day after day I was with you in the temple teaching, and you did not seize me. But let the scriptures be fulfilled." And they all forsook him, and fled.

And a young man followed him, with nothing but a linen

cloth about his body; and they seized him, but he left the linen cloth and ran away naked.

And they led Jesus to the high priest; and all the chief priests and the elders and the scribes were assembled. And Peter had followed him at a distance, right into the courtyard of the high priest; and he was sitting with the guards, and warming himself at the fire. Now the chief priests and the whole council sought testimony against Jesus to put him to death; but they found none. For many bore false witness against him, and their witness did not agree. And some stood up and bore false witness against him, saying, "We heard him say, 'I will destroy this temple that is made with hands, and in three days I will build another, not made with hands.' " Yet not even so did their testimony agree. And the high priest stood up in the midst, and asked Jesus, "Have you no answer to make? What is it that these men testify against you?" But he was silent and made no answer. Again the high priest asked him, "Are you the Christ, the Son of the Blessed?" And Jesus said, "I am; and you will see the Son of man sitting at the right hand of Power, and coming with the clouds of heaven." And the high priest tore his mantle, and said, "Why do we still need witnesses? You have heard his blasphemy. What is your decision?" And they all condemned him as deserving death. And some began to spit on him, and to cover his face, and to strike him, saying to him, "Prophesy!" And the guards received him with blows.

And as Peter was below in the courtyard, one of the maids of the high priest came; and seeing Peter warming himself, she looked at him and said, "You also were with the Nazarene, Jesus." But he denied it, saying, "I neither know nor understand what you mean." And he went out into the gateway and the cock crowed. And the maid saw him, and began again to say to the bystanders, "This man is one of them." But again he denied it. And after a little while again the bystanders said to Peter, "Certainly you are one of them; for you are a Galilean." But he began to invoke a curse on himself and to swear, "I do not know this man of whom you speak." And immediately the cock crowed a second time. And Peter remembered how Jesus had said to him, "Before the cock crows twice, you will deny me three times." And he broke down and wept.

And as soon as it was morning the chief priests, with the

elders and scribes, and the whole council held a consultation; and they bound Jesus and led him away and delivered him to Pilate. And Pilate asked him, "Are you the King of the Jews?" And he answered him, "You have said so." And the chief priests accused him of many things. And Pilate again asked him, "Have you no answer to make? See how many charges they bring against you." But Jesus made no further answer, so that Pilate wondered. Now at the feast he used to release for them any one prisoner whom they asked. And among the rebels in prison, who had committed murder in the insurrection, there was a man called Barabbas. And the crowd came up and began to ask Pilate to do as he was wont to do for them. And he answered them, "Do you want me to release for you the King of the Jews?" For he perceived that it was out of envy that the chief priests had delivered him up. But the chief priests stirred up the crowd to have him release for them Barabbas instead. And Pilate again said to them, "Then what shall I do with the man whom you call the King of the Jews?" And they cried out again, "Crucify him." And Pilate said to them, "Why, what evil has he done?" But they shouted all the more, "Crucify him." So Pilate, wishing to satisfy the crowd, released for them Barabbas; and having scourged Jesus, he delivered him to be crucified.

And the soldiers led him away inside the palace (that is, the praetorium); and they called together the whole battalion. And they clothed him in a purple cloak, and plaiting a crown of thorns they put it on him. And they began to salute him, "Hail, King of the Jews!" And they struck his head with a reed, and spat upon him. And when they had mocked him, they stripped him of the purple cloak, and put his own clothes on him. And they led him out to crucify him. And they compelled a passer-by, Simon of Cyrene, who was coming in from the country, the father of Alexander and Rufus, to carry his cross. And they brought him to the place called Golgotha (which means the place of the skull). And they offered him wine mingled with myrrh; but he did not take it. And they crucified him, and divided his garments among them, casting lots for them, to decide what each should take. And it was the third hour, when they crucified him. And the inscription of the charge against him read, "The King of the Jews." And with him they crucified two robbers, one on his right and one on his left. And those who passed by derided him, wagging their heads, and saying, "Aha! You who would destroy the temple and build it in three days, save yourself, and come down from the cross!" So also the chief priests mocked him to one another and the scribes, saying, "He saved others; he cannot save himself. Let the Christ, the King of Israel, come down now from the cross, that we may see and believe." Those who were crucified with him also reviled him.

And when the sixth hour had come, there was darkness over the whole earth until the ninth hour. And at the ninth hour Jesus cried with a loud voice, "Eloi, Eloi, lama sabachthani?" which means, "My God, my God, why hast thou forsaken me?" And some of the bystanders hearing it said, "Behold, he is calling Elijah." And one ran and filled a sponge full of vinegar, put it on a reed and gave it to him to drink, saying, "Wait, let us see whether Elijah will come to take him down." And Jesus uttered a loud cry and breathed his last.

And the curtain of the temple was torn in two, from top to bottom. And when the centurion, who stood facing him, saw that he thus breathed his last, he said, "Truly this man was a son of God!"

There were also women looking on from afar, among whom were Mary Magdalene, and Mary the mother of James the younger and of Joses and Salome, who, when he was in Galilee, followed him, and ministered to him; and also many other women who came up with him to Jerusalem. And when evening had come, since it was the day of Preparation, that is, the day before the sabbath, Joseph of Arimathea, a respected member of the council, who was also himself looking for the kingdom of God, took courage and went to Pilate, and asked for the body of Jesus. And Pilate wondered if he were already dead; and summoning the centurion, he asked him whether he was already dead. And when he learned from the centurion that he was dead, he granted the body to Joseph. And he bought a linen shroud, and taking him down, wrapped him in the linen shroud, and laid him in a tomb which had been hewn out of the rock; and he rolled a stone against the door of the tomb. Mary Magdalene and Mary the mother of Joses saw where he was laid.

And when the sabbath was past, Mary Magdalene, and Mary the mother of James, and Salome, bought spices, so that they might go and anoint him. And very early on the first day of the week they went to the tomb when the sun had risen. And they were saying to one another, "Who will roll away the stone for us from the door of the tomb?" And looking up, they saw that the stone was rolled back; for it was very large. And entering the tomb, they saw a young man sitting on the right side, dressed in a white robe; and they were amazed. And he said to them, "Do not be amazed; you seek Jesus of Nazareth, who was crucified. He has risen, he is not here; see the place where they laid him. But go, tell his disciples and Peter that he is going before you to Galilee; there you will see him, as he told you." And they went out and fled from the tomb; for trembling and astonishment had come upon them; and they said nothing to any one, for they were afraid.[90]

v. The Illusory Christ

It is clear that, whether accurate or not as to biographical detail, the moving legend of the Crucified and Risen Christ was fit to bring a new warmth, immediacy, and humanity, to the old motifs of the beloved Tammuz, Adonis, and Osiris cycles. Indeed, it was those early myths, filling the atmosphere of the whole eastern Mediterranean, that had furnished the ambient of readiness within which the Christian legend so rapidly grew and spread. But the pagan mythologies and their cults were, at that time, themselves in a phase of burgeoning transformation. The Hellenistic concept of "humanity" as a totality, transcending all racial, national, tribal, and sectarian forms, was operating everywhere to effect a cross-fertilization of cults. And a massive shift in social emphasis from rural to cosmopolitan populations had, centuries before, converted the old, beloved field divinities into intimately personal, psychologically effective spiritual guides, appearing in elite as well as in popular rites of initiation. Moreover, a general association of mystical and philosophical thought with the symbols of religion made it possible, everywhere, to pass from one mode of communication to the other, from new verbal definitions to new iconographic combinations, and vice versa. Certain influences from India, dating from the Buddhist missions of Ashoka (268–232 B.C.),* also were at work. The multiplication of cults was, consequently, great,

---

* Supra, pp. 285–86, and *The Masks of God: Oriental Mythology*, p. 294

as was also the multiplication of myths. And in such an atmosphere it was inevitable that the savior image of the Christians should be in danger not only of contamination from the pagans, but also of absorption, one way or another, into related pagan cults.

Already in one of the later letters of Paul, sent from Rome, c. 61–64 A.D., to his newly founded community in Colossae in Asia Minor, there is mention of a growing Gnostic heresy among the membership of that young congregation. "See to it," he warned his distant flock,

> that no one makes a prey of you by philosophy and empty deceit, according to human tradition, according to the elemental spirits of the universe, and not according to Christ. . . . He disarmed the principalities and powers and made a public example of them, triumphing over them in him. . . . Let no one disqualify you, insisting on self-abasement and worship of angels, taking his stand on visions, puffed up without reason by his sensuous mind, and not holding fast to the Head from whom the whole body, nourished and knit together through its joints and ligaments, grows with a growth that is from God. . . . Put to death therefore what is earthly in you: immorality, impurity, passion, evil desire, and covetousness, which is idolatry. On account of these the wrath of God is coming. In these you once walked, when you lived in them. But now put them all away.[91]

Until recently it was not known what the actual teachings had been of those Gnostic Christian sects that in the first centuries flourished throughout the Roman Empire; for with the victory of the Orthodox Church in the fourth and fifth centuries A.D., the banned writings, teachings, and teachers disappeared. Our reports of them came only from their enemies, the Church Fathers; notably, Justin Martyr and Irenaeus (second century), Clement of Alexandria (late second and early third centuries), Hippolytus (d.c. 230 A.D.), and Epiphanius (c. 315–402 A.D.). Hence, it was an event no less important than that of the finding of the Dead Sea Scrolls when a large jar was unearthed near Nag-Hamadi in Upper Egypt in 1945, containing forty-eight Coptic Gnostic works, totaling over seven hundred pages. Most of these are now in the

Coptic museum, Cairo. One arrived in 1952 at the Jung Institute in Zurich. Editions and translations are in progress, much remains to appear, and scholars of the next decade will possess a far greater knowledge of Gnosticism than is possible today. However, certain leading principles and themes of the movement have already been ascertained.

In 1896, when the Berlin Museum acquired a papyrus codex of about the date of these Hamadi texts, three important Gnostic works came to light: "The Sophia of Jesus Christ," "The Apocryphon of John," and "The Gospel of Mary." A 1785 acquisition of the British Museum, now known as Pistis Sophia, of which translations began to appear in the middle 1850s, also has provided information. And, finally, an often-cited work of mixed Gnostic and orthodox strains, known as the "Acts of John," ascribed to the supposed author of the Fourth Gospel, was read aloud, in part, at the Council of Nicaea, 325 A.D., and formally condemned. When we review these in the light of what we now have come to know, both from the great Nag-Hamadi trove and from our understanding, recently gained, of the Docetic doctrines of Mahayana Buddhism (the growth and flowering of which exactly coincided with the high period of the Gnostic movement), the implications of their imagery can be judged with enlarged appreciation.

For example, in the Acts of John we find the following astonishing rendition of the scene of Christ's summoning of his apostles at the Sea of Galilee. The Messiah has just come from his desert fast of forty days and his victory there over Satan. John and James are in their boat, fishing. Christ appears on the shore. And John is supposed to be telling, now, of the occasion:

> For when he had chosen Peter and Andrew, who were brothers, he came to me and James my brother, saying: "I have need of you, come unto me." And my brother, hearing that, said to me: "John, what does that child want who is on the shore there and called to us?" And I said: "What child?" And he said again, "The one beckoning to us." And I answered: "Because of the long watch we have kept at sea, you are not seeing right, my brother James. But do you not

see the man who is standing there, comely, fair, and of cheerful countenance?" But he answered: "Him, brother, I do not see. But let us go, and we shall see what he wants."

And so, when we had brought our boat to land, we saw him, also, helping us to settle it; and when we left, thinking to follow him, he appeared to me to be rather bald, but with a beard thick and flowing, but to James he seemed a youth whose beard had newly come. We were therefore, both of us, perplexed as to what we had seen should mean. And as we followed him, continuing, we both were, little by little, even more perplexed as we considered the matter. For in my case there appeared this still more wonderful thing: I would try to watch him secretly, and I never at any time saw his eyes blinking, but only open. And often he would appear to me to be a little man, uncomely, but then again as one reaching up to heaven. Moreover, there was in him another marvel: when we sat to eat he would clasp me to his breast, and sometimes the breast felt to me to be smooth and tender, but sometimes hard, like stone. . . .[92]

Another glory, also, would I tell to you, my brethren: namely, that sometimes when I would take hold of him, I would meet with a material and solid body, but again, at other times, when I touched him, the substance was immaterial and as if it existed not at all. And if at any time he were invited by some Pharisee and accepted the invitation, we accompanied him; and there was set before each of us a loaf by those who entertained; and with us, he too received one. But his own he would bless and apportion among us. And of that little, every one was filled, and our own loaves were saved whole, so that those who had invited him were amazed. And often when I walked with him, I desired to see the print of his foot, whether it appeared on the earth; for I saw him, as it were, sustaining himself above the earth: and I never saw it.

And these things I tell you, my brethren, for the encouragement of your faith in him; for we must, at present, keep silence concerning his mighty and wonderful works, in as much as they are unspeakable and, it may be, cannot at all either be uttered or be heard.[93]

The term "docetism" (from the Greek *dokein*, "to appear") denotes such a view of the Savior, which holds that Christ's body, as seen by men, was a mere appearance, the reality being celestial

or divine; and its appearance furthermore, a function of the mentality of the seer, not of the reality of the seen: a mere mask, that
might change but not be removed. We must remark, moreover,
that in India, in just these first centuries A.D., the Mahayana was
developing, where the appearance of the Buddha was interpreted
exactly this way. The Buddha of the Mahayana is not a mere man
who achieved Illumination, but the manifestation of Illumination
itself, which appeared in the form of a teacher, expressly to illuminate those entangled in the coils of their own masking delusions,
delusions derived from the universal thirst for life and fear of death.
In the Mahayana Buddhist view, the entire world, as seen, was
equally delusory, its substance, in fact, being the Buddha.

> Stars, darkness, a lamp, a phantom, dew, a bubble;
> A dream, a flash of lightning, and a cloud:
> Thus should we look upon the world.[94]

Or, in Shakespeare's wonderful language:

> . . . . We are such stuff
> As dreams are made on, and our little life
> Is rounded with a sleep.[95]

But with this we are in the realm again, properly of myth, not
pseudo-history. For here God does not become Man; but man, the
world itself, is known as divine, a field of inexhaustible spiritual
depth. And the problem of creation is the problem of the origin of
delusion, which, as in Buddhism, is treated psychologically. The
problem of redemption, therefore, is, according to this view, psychological too.

In a late Greek-Egyptian body of pagan Gnostic teaching known
as the Corpus Hermeticum, put forth as a revelation of the syncretic
god Hermes-Thot, the guide of souls, there is a perfectly glorious
passage, to this point, as follows:

> If then you do not make yourself equal to God, you cannot
> apprehend God; for like is known by like. Leap clear of all
> that is corporeal, and make yourself grow to a like expanse
> with that greatness which is beyond all measure; rise above
> all time, and become eternal; then you will apprehend God.
> Think that for you too nothing is impossible; deem that you

too are immortal, and that you are able to grasp all things in your thought, to know every craft and every science; find your home in the haunts of every living creature; make yourself higher than all heights, and lower than all depths; bring together in yourself all opposites of quality, heat and cold, dryness and fluidity; think that you are everywhere at once, on land, at sea, in heaven; think that you are not yet begotten, that you are in the womb, that you are young, that you are old, that you have died, that you are in the world beyond the grave; grasp in your thought all this at once, all times and places, all substances and qualities and magnitudes together; then you can apprehend God. But if you shut up your soul in your body, and abase yourself, and say "I know nothing, I can do nothing; I am afraid of earth and sea, I cannot mount to heaven; I know not what I was, nor what I shall be"; then, what have you to do with God? Your thought can grasp nothing beautiful and good, if you cleave to the body, and are evil.

For it is the height of evil not to know God; but to be capable of knowing God, and to wish and hope to know him, is the road which leads straight to the Good; and it is an easy road to travel. Everywhere God will come to meet you, everywhere he will appear to you, at places and times at which you look not for it, in your waking hours and in your sleep, when you are journeying by water and by land, in the nighttime and in the daytime, when you are speaking and when you are silent; for there is nothing which is not God. And do you say "God is invisible"? Speak not so. Who is more manifest than God? For this very purpose has he made all things. Nothing is invisible, not even an incorporeal thing; mind is seen in its liking, and God in his working.

So far, thrice-greatest one, I have shown you the truth. Think out all else in like manner for yourself, and you will not be misled.[96]

In one of the recently discovered Gnostic codices of the jar of Nag-Hamadi we find the following, attributed to Jesus:

I am the Light that is above them all,
I am the All.
The All came forth from Me and the All attained to Me.
Cleave a piece of wood, I am there:
Lift up the stone, you will find me there.[97]

It has been determined that the words attributed to Jesus in the Gospels of the New Testament were derived from a common stock of "sayings" (*logia*), preserved and passed about, at first orally, among the communities of the faithful, which then became fixed in various ways in various writings. The editors of the Gospels according to Mark, Matthew, and Luke (in that order, between c. 75 and 90 A.D.), drew from these in the fashioning of their separate, mutually contradictory accounts. Matthew and Luke drew independently from Mark, but also from another text, now lost, known to scholarship as "Q" (from the German *Quelle,* "Source"), which is believed to have been a collection merely of "Sayings." Mark also may have drawn from "Q"; but Matthew and Luke certainly did. And each set the "Sayings" in his own way, like pearls in settings of his own invention.

But now, suddenly, from Nag-Hamadi there has come a collection of such sheer "Sayings" in which a Gnostic turn has been given to words long known to us in quite another sense from the orthodox Gospels. For example:

> Let him who seeks, not cease seeking until he finds, and when he finds, he will be troubled, and when he has been troubled, he will marvel and he will reign over the All.

> His disciples said to him, "When will the Kingdom come?" And Jesus said: "It will not come by expectation; they will not say, 'See here,' or 'See there.' But the Kingdom of the Father is spread upon the earth and men do not see it."

> If those who lead you say to you: "See, the Kingdom is in heaven," then the birds of the heaven will precede you. If they say to you: "It is in the sea," then the fish will precede you. But the Kingdom is within you and is without you. If you will know yourselves, then you will be known and you will know that you are the sons of the Living Father. But if you do not know yourselves, then you are in poverty and you are poverty.[98]

Luke apparently drew from a saying related to the last of these when he attributed to Jesus, in a discourse to the Pharisees, the following, much argued, words:

"The Kingdom of God is not coming with signs to be observed; nor will they say, 'Lo, here it is!' or 'There!' for behold, the kingdom of God is in the midst of you"—ἐντὸς ὑμῶν ἐστιν—or, as others have read the Greek phrase, "is within you." [99]

The trouble with the latter reading, when applied to a canonical, not Gnostic, Christian passage, however, is that it implies a theology of immanence, which is exactly what the Church, following the footsteps of the prophets, has been condemning as heresy and purging with fire and sword these many centuries. In the words of Charles Guignebert, written long before the finding of the Nag-Hamadi jar:

> Linguistic arguments seem to justify the translation of ἐντὸς as *within:* but probability is definitely against it. Jesus could hardly tell the Pharisees, without appearing absurd, that the Kingdom of God was within them, in their hearts. And ignoring the Pharisees, none of his disciples, who were all authentic Jews, could have understood such a strange utterance, which is unsupported by any teaching in the Gospels. If this *logion* is the focal point of the whole teaching of Jesus concerning the Kingdom, its isolation is incredible. These objections raise, and to all appearances dispose of, the problem of its authenticity.
>
> Nor is this all. If we read the verse in its context with ἐντὸς as *within,* a contradiction results. Luke makes this utterance a kind of introduction to a teaching on the coming of the Kingdom (17:22 ff.).* But the coming of the Son of Man is there referred to as destined to be sudden: 17:24, "For as the lightning that lighteneth shines from one end of heaven to the other, so shall also the Son of Man be in his day." In the view of all his disciples the only object of his coming was the inauguration of the Kingdom. He could therefore hardly say in the same breath, that the Kingdom was in the hearts of his hearers, and that he would come to establish it suddenly, in a day when he was not expected.
>
> The obvious conclusion then is that ἐντὸς ὑμῶν means *in the midst of you,* which seems equally to imply the actual presence of the Kingdom. But then there arises the question

---

* The substance of this also occurs in Matthew 24; Luke joins it up with the apocalyptic discourse of Mark 13 [supra pp. 269–71]. Q doubtless provides the basis for this. [*Guignebert's note.*]

whether the verb ἐστὶν is the real present tense or a prophetic present, that is to say, the future. This would change everything, even if ἐντὸς be taken to mean *within*. The probable meaning of the whole passage is: "When the Kingdom comes no one will have any difficulty in recognizing it, or will need to ask where it is. It will suddenly be in your midst, or in your hearts: that is, those who have suitably prepared themselves in accordance with the teaching of Jesus himself will enter into it."

. . . Jesus taught, in conformity with current Jewish belief, that the Kingdom would come as a gift of God. But he perhaps believed, or at least his disciples after him believed, that, his own mission being to announce the imminent approach of this manifestation, his teaching, or from another angle, the belief in his vocation, was the outer chamber through which men had to pass to reach the Kingdom. . . . The Kingdom is primarily and essentially the material transformation of this present evil world.[100]

It is a fine, but important, point; for on it hangs the whole contrast between the way of the Church of Peter and Paul and the ways, numerous as the varieties of inward experience, of the Gnostics.

The "Gospel According to Thomas," which is the text from which I have been quoting, contains 114 *logia*. Its Coptic manuscript is of c. 500 A.D., but the Greek text of which it was the translation belonged to c. 140 A.D., which is well within the period of the shaping of the Gospels, all four of which continued to be touched and retouched until the canon finally was fixed in Rome, toward the opening, only, of the fourth century A.D.

The high flowering time of the Gnostic movement was the middle of the second century, notably that period of the Antonines— Antoninus Pius (r. 138–161) and Marcus Aurelius (r. 161–180) —which Edward Gibbon marked as the apogee of the glory of the Roman Empire: the world system, as he wrote, that at that time "comprehended the fairest part of the earth and the most civilized portion of mankind," and when the various modes of worship that prevailed in the known world "were all considered by the people, as equally true; by the philosopher, as equally false; and by the magistrate, as equally useful," so that "toleration produced not only mutual indulgence, but even religious accord. Rome gradually became the common temple of her subjects; and the freedom of the city was bestowed on all the gods of mankind." [101]

Let me conclude this glimpse of the mysteries of the anathematized Gnostic heritage with a second passage from the Acts of John: the passage that was read and condemned at the Council of Nicaea. It is the most illuminating statement remaining to us of the Docetic —or, as one could as properly say, Mahayana—view of the silent sign of the crucifix. For, as it is written:

Now before he was taken by the lawless Jews, who had their law from the lawless serpent,* he gathered all of us together and said: "Before I give myself up to them, let us praise the Father in a hymn of praise, and so go forth to meet what is to come." Then he bade us make a circle, holding each other's hands, and he was in the middle. And he said: "Answer me with Amen." After which he began to sing a hymn of praise:

"Glory be to thee, Father!"

And we all, going around in a ring, answered, "Amen."

"Glory be to thee, Word!
Glory be to thee, Grace!"—"Amen."

"Glory be to thee, Divine Spirit!
Glory be to thee, Holy One!
Glory be to thee, Transfiguration!"—"Amen."

"We praise thee, Father!
We give thanks to thee, O Light,
Wherein there is no darkness!"—"Amen."

"And wherefore we give thanks, that will I tell:
"I will be saved, and I will save!"—"Amen."

* Cf. the serpent Nehushtan of II Kings 18:4, which was worshiped in Solomon's temple. See also, Figures 25, 26, and 30. According to the Gnostic view, if the world is evil, its creator was evil: its creator was exactly Satan, who appeared to Christ in the desert and is the Yahweh of the Old Testament. The Buddhist counterpart is the tempter of the Buddha, Kama-Mara, who is represented in the Upanishads as the Self, out of whose Desire and Fear the world came into being. See *The Masks of God: Oriental Mythology*, pp. 9–10, 13–22.

"I will be freed, and I will free!"—"Amen."
"I will be wounded, and I will wound!"—"Amen."
"I will be begotten, and I will beget!"—"Amen."

"I will be consumed, and I will consume!"—"Amen."
"I will hear, and I will be heard!"—"Amen."
"I will be known, who am all spirit!"—"Amen."
"I will be washed, and I will wash!"—"Amen."

"Grace paces the round.
I will blow the pipe.
Dance the round, all!"—"Amen."

"I will mourn: mourn all!"—"Amen."

"The Pantheon of Eight [the Ogdoad] sings praise with us!"
      —"Amen."
"The Number Twelve paces the round aloft!"—"Amen."
"To each and all it is given to share in the dance!"—"Amen."
"He who joins not in the dance mistakes the event!"—
      "Amen."

"I will flee and I will stay."—"Amen."
"I will adorn and I will be adorned."—"Amen."
"I will be understood and I will understand."—"Amen."

"A mansion I have not, and mansions I have."—"Amen."
"A torch am I to you who perceive me."—"Amen."
"A mirror am I to you who discern me."—"Amen."
"A door am I to you who knock at me."—"Amen."
"A way am I to you who pass."

   "So as you respond to my dancing, behold yourself in me,
the speaker. And when you see what I do, keep silent concerning my mysteries. You that dance, ponder what I do, for
yours is this passion of humanity that I am about to suffer.
For you could not at all have understood your suffering, had
I not been sent to you as the Word of the Father. When you
saw my suffering, you saw me as the sufferer; and seeing it, you
stood not fast, but were all shaken. In your drive toward
wisdom, you have me for a bed: rest upon me. You will know
who I am when I depart. What now I am seen to be, that I
am not. You shall see when you arrive.—Had you known how
to suffer, you would have been able not to suffer. See through
suffering, and you will have non-suffering. What you know
not, I myself will teach you. I am your God, not the betrayer's

God. I will bring the souls of the saints into harmony with myself. In me know the Word of Wisdom.—Say with me again:

> "Glory to thee, Father!
> "Glory to thee, Word!
> "Glory to thee, Holy Spirit!"

"And if you would understand what I am, know this: all that I have said I have uttered playfully, and I was by no means ashamed thereby. I danced; but as for you, consider the whole, and having considered it, say:

> "Glory be to thee, Father!—Amen!" [102]

The narrator, John, is now about to proceed to a view of the crucifixion itself from the standpoint of this Docetic understanding of the mystery. The Father receiving praise in these ejaculations cannot be identified either with the God of the Old Testament or with the Father of the New. The best analogy is with Ahura Mazda of the Persian myth. Yahweh or Elohim is then approximately the counterpart of Angra Mainyu, the creator of the world of the Lie, in which we live and from which the savior is to set us free. Moreover, this savior, like Zoroaster, descends from the sphere of Light; but, unlike Zoroaster, partakes only apparently of the nature of the world.

> And thus, my beloved, having danced with us, the Lord went forth. And like men gone astray or dazed with sleep, we fled this way and that. And I, then, when I saw him suffering, did not abide his suffering, but fled to the Mount of Olives, weeping for what had come to pass. And when he was hung upon that thorn of a cross, darkness fell at the sixth hour on the whole earth.
>
> And lo, my Lord was standing in the middle of the cave, and illumined it, and spoke: "John, for the multitude below in Jerusalem I am being crucified and pierced with lances and staves; vinegar and gall are given me to drink. But to you I speak, and to what I speak, give ear. Secretly, I caused you to ascend this mountain, so that you should learn what a disciple must learn from his master, and man from God."
>
> With these words he showed me an implanted cross of light and about the cross a great multitude that had not one uniform

shape. And in that cross of light there was one form and one appearance. And upon the cross I saw the Lord himself, and he had no shape, but only a voice: and a voice not such as was familiar to us, but one sweet and kind and truly of God, saying to me: "John, it is needful that there be one who hears these things from me, for I have need of one that will hear. This cross of light is sometimes called the Word by me for your sakes, sometimes Mind, sometimes Jesus, sometimes Christ, sometimes Door, sometimes Way, sometimes Bread, sometimes Seed, sometimes Resurrection, sometimes Son, sometimes Father, sometimes Spirit, sometimes Life, sometimes Truth, sometimes Faith, sometimes Grace. So it is for men. But what it is in truth, as conceived in itself, as spoken between us, it is the marking off of all things, and the firm uplifting of things fixed out of things unstable, and the harmony of wisdom—of the wisdom that is harmony.

"But there are forces of the right and forces of the left, potencies, angelic powers and demons, efficacies, threats, upsurges of wrath, devils, Satan, and the lower root from which the nature of Becoming issued. And so it is this cross which spiritually bound the All together, and which marked off the realm of change and the lower realm, and which caused all things to rise up.

"It is not that cross, the wooden cross that you will see when you go down from here; nor am I whom you now cannot see but whose voice alone you hear he that is on the cross. I was thought to be what I am not, not being what I was to those many others: what they will say of me is wretched and unworthy of me. Those who neither see nor name the place of stillness will much less see the Lord.

"The multitude not of one aspect that throngs around the cross is the lower nature. And if those whom you see by the cross have as yet no single form, then all the parts of him who descended have not been gathered together. But when the nature of mankind has been taken up and a generation of men moved by my voice comes close to me, you, who hear me now, shall be united therewith, and what now is shall no longer be. But you will then stand above those, as I now do. For until you call yourself mine own, I shall not be what I am. When you hear me, however, you will be a hearer like myself. For this you are through me.

"Therefore have no concern for the many and despise the

profane. Know that I am wholly with the Father and the Father wholly with me. Nothing of what they will relate of me have I suffered. Even the passion that I revealed to you and the others in the round dance, I would that it were called a mystery. For what you are, that you see, and I have shown it to you: but what I am, I alone know, and no man else. Suffer me then to keep what is mine, but what is yours, behold through me; and see me in mine essence, not as I have said I was, but as you, being akin to me, know me.

> "You heard that I suffered, but I suffered not.
> An unsuffering one was I, yet suffered.
> One pierced was I, yet I was not abused.
> One hanged I was, and yet not hanged.
> Blood flowed from me, yet did not flow.

"In brief, what they say of me, that have I not suffered; but what they do not say, that have I suffered. What it is, that I intimate in a riddle; for I know you will understand. Know me, then, as the praise of the Word, the transfixing of the Word, the blood of the Word, the wound of the Word, the hanging up of the Word, the suffering of the Word, the nailing of the Word, the death of the Word. And thus in my discourse have I distinguished the man from myself.

"First, therefore, know the Word, the inwardness, the meaning. Then you will know the Lord, and thirdly, the man and what he has suffered."

When he had spoken thus to me and still more, which I know not how to say as he would have me, he was caught up and none of the multitude saw him. And when I went down, I laughed at them all, for he had told me what they have said concerning him; holding fast this one thing in myself: that the Lord carried out everything symbolically, for the conversion and salvation of men.[103]

VI. The Mission of Paul

During the first centuries of the Christian era, three main views of the mission of Jesus were in play. The earliest was that of the Jewish Christians of Palestine, of whom we read in the first chapter of the Acts of the Apostles, that when they had come together and the risen Christ appeared to them, they asked, "Lord, will you at this time restore the kingdom to Israel?"[104] For these there can have been no mythology of the Virgin Birth. Their teacher was the Messiah, the Anointed of the Lord, as prophesied for Israel from of old, and the new thing was simply that the Day of Yahweh now had come, actually and historically: the day when Israel should be glorified and justified before the world. This we may call the primary apocalyptic view. Isaiah had prophesied of that day: "Thy dead shall live, their bodies shall rise." [105] Christ had risen: that was the clarion call (Isaiah 27:13). The day had dawned of which Yahweh had declared through his prophet: "For behold, I create new heavens and a new earth; and the former things shall not be remembered or come into mind. . . . I will rejoice in Jerusalem." [106]

The second view was that of the Gnostics. This, we have seen, was in its theology older than Christianity and alien to the Jews, and during the first century was linked only loosely to the Christian movement. However, in the course of the second century, when the grandiose promise of the early Christian apocalyptic vision failed to come to pass, so that the expectation had somehow to be spiritualized, the seeds of Christian Gnosticism took root and gained in force. Moreover, a still more dangerous threat to the authority of the Pauline Church arose in the vigorous heresiarch Marcion (fl. c. 150 A.D.), of whom Justin Martyr wrote that "by the help of devils he has caused many of every nation to speak blasphemies, and to deny that God is the maker of the universe and to assert that some other being greater than He has done greater works." [107]

For Marcion stressed the contrast between the Old and New Testament views of God and proposed a Christian canon completely independent of the Old, based largely on Paul and Luke. His own doctrine was that the God of the Old Testament had indeed been the creator of the world we know as evil. He had created man from matter and imposed on him a strict law that none could keep, and so the whole race had fallen under his curse. He was not the highest God, however, though he thought himself to be so. Above him was another power, of which he had no conception, who, in love and pity for the world in torment, sent his son, Christ, as a redeemer. Clothed in a visionary body, in the likeness of a man of thirty years, the Son made his appearance in the fifteenth year of the Emperor Tiberius (r. 14–37 A.D.), preaching in the synagogue in Capernaum. The Jews mistook him for their national Messiah, and even his apostles failed to understand. Moreover, the Old Testament deity himself had no idea of the dignity of this teacher, but in fear caused him to be crucified, and by that act accomplished his own doom. Christ, according to Marcion, appeared after his crucifixion to Paul, who, alone of all, understood the gospel and, opposing the Jewish Christians, founded properly Christian churches among the gentiles—which, however, were now being corrupted by Judaizing tendencies, against which Marcion had been appointed by the true God to preach.

In contrast to the Gnostic way, Marcion placed his emphasis not on knowledge, but on faith, which had, of course, the more popular appeal, and his doctrine, consequently, was a real threat to the early Church. It was, in fact, so real a threat that the Fathers were stirred to shape their own version of a New Testament largely to refute the earlier canon of the Marcionites; and for one entire century—150–250 A.D.—it actually appeared that the independent Testament of the heresiarch might gain the field.

The book that won, however, was that according to which the New Law was interpreted as a fulfillment of the Old, but on a plane rather of spiritual than of socio-political ideals: even though it continued to be hoped that in the end the doomsday prophesied would come to pass—largely in Zoroastrian terms, with Christ in the role of Saoshyant at the right hand of the Father, to judge the living and the dead—which then would be the literal end of the world. For some reason, Christian writers like to interpret this belief and hope as a positive, world-affirmative doctrine, and place it in contrast to the Gnostic, which they term negative. Also, they commonly tell of the great "danger" of Gnosticism, since it fostered —and would foster still—a diversity and multiplication of cults; whereas, with the victory of the one true Church in the fourth century A.D., there prevailed a "universal" religion, which (to quote one distinguished authority) "did not view itself as a coterie of the spiritually elite," [108] and (to quote another) "stood for an entirely new concept of religion," which "could not develop, according to the law of its own nature, unless it broke loose from the insidious forces which would have anchored it to a bygone world." [109]

Actually, in Gnosticism, as in Buddhism to this day, there was diversity because (as the Church was to find out in due time) individuals have differing spiritual capacities and requirements, so that, as already told in that sensible episode in the Acts of John, of Jesus on the shore,* no one can safely pretend to have grasped Truth once and for all: least of all a committee (whether of cardinals or of presbyters) legislating in the name of the great majority of a popular, so-called universal religion, for whom metaphysical speculation, experience, and symbolization must remain on a fairly elementary level. There is an old Roman proverb: *Senatus bestia est; senatores, boni viri;* which neither time nor tithe has rendered out of date.

Moreover, the paramount concern of a popular religion cannot be, and never has been, "Truth," but the maintenance of a certain type of society, the inculcation in the young and refreshment in the old of an approved "system of sentiments" upon which the local institutions and government depend. And, as the documentation of our subject shows, the history of society itself has been marked over the millenniums by a gradual—ever so gradual—enlargement of group horizons: from the tribe or the village to the race or the nation, and beyond that, finally, with Buddhism and Hellenism, to the all-embracing concept of humanity—which is, however, not a governable but a spiritual unit of individuals. And in such a unit there have to be many mansions, as there were in Gnosticism. Nor is it proper to denigrate such separated orders (each minding its own business) by calling them coteries. They are rather schools for those of like disposition, for mutual instruction: more like, for example, Alcoholics Anonymous than, say, the Women's Christian Temperance Union, which latter would teach us all to abstain from spirits too strong for some to imbibe.

We have to recall of Paul that he commenced his career as a

* Supra, pp. 364–65.

persecutor of the early Jewish Christians in the name of his Pharisaic heritage. He was present, as we learn from the New Testament Acts of the Apostles, at the stoning to death of Saint Stephen. "The witnesses," it is written, "laid down their garments at the feet of a young man named Saul. . . . And Saul was consenting to his death. And on that day a great persecution arose against the church in Jerusalem. . . . Saul laid waste the church, and entering house after house, he dragged off men and women and committed them to prison." [110]

It could be said that in turning from Pharisee to Christian, Paul simply transferred his temperament to the other side of the line and that the Christian Church that he founded thus inherited and carried into Europe the stamp of his Levantine regard for the monolithic consensus. The first principle of his doctrine was that in Christ the Law had been abrogated. Indeed, like Marcion, he held that the Law had been a curse upon man; for, as he wrote: "Christ redeemed us from the curse of the law . . . that we might receive the promise of the spirit through faith." [111] And again: "The law was our custodian until Christ came, that we might be justified by faith. But now that faith has come, we are no longer under a custodian. . . . There is neither Jew nor Greek, there is neither slave nor free, there is neither male nor female; for you are all one in Christ Jesus." [112] Those are burning, wonderful words. But in the very next letter we read that a new enforcement was in operation, of which Paul could cite the book:

> I appeal to you, brethren, by the name of our Lord Jesus Christ, that all of you agree that there be no dissensions among you, but that you be united in the same mind and the same judgment. . . . I wrote to you in my letter not to associate with immoral men. . . . not to associate with anyone who bears the name of brother if he is guilty of immorality or greed, or is an idolater, reviler, drunkard, or robber—not even to eat with such a one. . . . Drive out the wicked person from among you. . . . [113]

> To each is given the manifestation of the Spirit for the common good. . . . For just as the body is one and has many members, and all the members of the body, though many, are

one body, so it is with Christ. For by one Spirit we were all baptized into one body—Jews or Greeks, slaves or free—and all were made to drink of one Spirit. . . . Now you are the body of Christ and individually members of it. And God has appointed in the church first apostles, second prophets, third teachers, then workers of miracles, then healers, helpers, administrators, speakers in various kinds of tongues. . . .[114]

I want you to understand that the head of every man is Christ, the head of a woman is her husband, and the head of Christ is God. Any man who prays or prophesies with his head covered dishonors his head, but any woman who prays or prophesies with her head unveiled dishonors her head—it is the same as if her head were shaven. For if a woman will not veil herself, then she should cut off her hair; but if it is disgraceful for a woman to be shorn or shaven, let her wear a veil. For a man ought not to cover his head, since he is the image and glory of God; but woman is the glory of man. (For man was not made from woman, but woman from man. Neither was man created for woman, but woman for man.) That is why a woman ought to have a veil on her head, because of the angels.[115]

"Be imitators of me," wrote Paul to his sheep, "as I am of Christ." [116] Which is to say: let no one conceive or follow his own image of Christ, as in the Acts of John, but only that of Paul and his community. And so it was that in the name of this community, as its own image of Christ gradually matured, the history of the West for the next two thousand years was to be carved and trimmed.

The first epochal event in the history of this new consensus had been the stoning of Stephen. "On that day," as we read in the Acts of the Apostles, "a great persecution arose against the church in Jerusalem; and they were all scattered throughout the region of Judea and Samaria, except the apostles." [117]

The frightened scattering led to a dissemination of the doctrine beyond Jerusalem and Galilee, which then Paul continued, even preaching outside the Jewish fold to the gentiles—specifically, of those racially and culturally mixed trading towns where Jew and Greek (to use Paul's recurrent phrase) were thrown together. In the purely Greek city of Athens he had almost no success, and in purely Jewish Jerusalem he escaped barely with his life.

"At Athens," we are told, "his spirit was provoked within him as he saw that the city was full of idols." The idols, of course, were those luminous works of art of the Acropolis which stand, to this hour, among the crowning glories of the human spirit. And to those who had gathered about him in the middle of the Areopagus (for, as we read: "all the Athenians and the foreigners who lived there spent their time in nothing except telling or hearing something new"), he declaimed: "Men of Athens, I perceive that in every way you are very religious. For as I passed along, and observed the objects of your worship, I found also an altar with this inscription, 'To an unknown god.' What therefore you worship as unknown, this I proclaim to you."

Which, from the pagan point of view, was, of course, an elementary mistake; for the Ineffable is not named or by anyone proclaimed, but is manifest in all things, and to claim knowledge of it uniquely is to have missed the point entirely. Besides, the altar in question had not been erected to the Ineffable, but to whatever significant god or gods unknown might have been omitted from the local cult. And in this character the god proclaimed by Paul might easily have been welcomed; however, the preacher was not proclaiming his god in that character.

"The God who made the world and everything in it," Paul announced to the city in which Xenophanes, Socrates, Plato, Aristotle, and Zeno had taught,

> does not live in shrines made by man, nor is he served by human hands, as though he needed anything, since he himself gives to all men life and breath and everything. And he made from one every nation of men to live on all the face of the earth, having determined allotted periods and the boundaries of their habitation, that they should seek God, in the hope that they might feel after him and find him. Yet he is not far from each one of us, for "In him we live and move and have our being": as even some of your poets have said, "For we are indeed his offspring."

Being then God's offspring [Paul continued], we ought not

to think that the Deity is like gold, or silver, or stone, a representation by the art and imagination of man. The times of ignorance God overlooked, but now he commands all men everywhere to repent, because he has fixed a day on which he will judge the world in righteousness by a man whom he has appointed, and of this he has given assurance to all men by raising him from the dead.

Some mocked, we are told, but others said, "We will hear you again about this." A few joined Paul and believed. But his harvest was disappointing. So he shook the dust of Athens from his feet and went to the trading city of Corinth,[118] where he lived and taught among both Greeks and Jews for eighteen months.

In Jerusalem, to which holy city Paul presently returned, he fared even worse than he had fared in Athens—almost as badly, indeed, as Stephen had fared before his own eyes, many years before. For there, as it is chronicled,

All the city was aroused, and the people ran together; they seized Paul and dragged him out of the temple, and at once the gates were shut. And as they were trying to kill him, word came to the [Roman] tribune of the cohort that all Jerusalem was in confusion. He at once took soldiers and centurions, and ran down to them; and when they saw the tribune and the soldiers, they stopped beating Paul. Then the tribune came up and arrested him, and ordered him to be bound with two chains. He inquired who he was and what he had done. Some in the crowd shouted one thing, some another; and as he could not learn the facts because of the uproar, he ordered him to be brought into the barracks. And when he came to the steps, he was actually carried by the soldiers because of the violence of the crowd; for the mob of the people followed, crying, "Away with him!" [119]

Paul, indeed, was between two worlds. But time was on his side. For both the religion of the polis and the religion of the tribal god had been left behind by the interplay of peoples throughout the empire of great Rome. And Rome itself, furthermore, would presently pass high noon.

vii. The Fall of Rome

In the year 167 A.D., the sixth in the reign of Marcus Aurelius, Germanic hordes from the north broke through the Roman wall between the upper Rhine and Danube, swarming into northern Italy; and since they could not be repulsed, they were allowed to settle as farmers on assigned lands within the frontier. Marcus Aurelius died in the year 180; his dissolute son Commodus succeeded; and revolts erupted in Germany, Gaul, Britain, Northwest Africa, and Judaea. A conspiracy in Rome itself was suppressed in 183, but nine years later the emperor was slain. His successor, Pertinax, was overthrown the following year by a mutiny of the guard, and the great catastrophe of the empire began.

The army in Rome elevated M. Didius Julianus to the throne; but the army in Syria supported C. Pescennius Niger; that in Britain, D. Clodius Albinus; and that on the Danube border, L. Septimius Severus, who ultimately won, after some four years of furious internecine war. Severus reigned sternly amidst wars until 211 A.D., to be followed by his son Caracalla, who in the year 213 repulsed a German invasion into Gaul, the following year subdued Armenia, and the next a revolt in Egypt. In 216 he turned against Parthia but was assassinated by his own guard—and so it went, from one amazement to the next. The Goths along the northern shore of the Black Sea took to piracy and, passing to the Mediterranean, raided everywhere as they went. Other German tribes pressed into Italy; still others into Gaul and Spain; a few crossed to Africa: and Roman cities, villages, and farms throughout the realm were going up in flame.

The Germans were an Aryan folk dwelling northeastward of the Celts, beyond the Elbe, from the Baltic to the Black Sea. Fairhaired, blue-eyed, and of towering stature, they were—like the Celts—courageous warriors; and the Roman legions, no longer what they had been in Caesar's time, were finding them more than a match. However, these semi-nomadic fighting herdsmen, threatening with ever increasing force the northern defenses, represented only one of three great pressures to which the civilization of Rome was at that time being subjected, to its doom. The second lay beyond the Tigris, in the ill-protected East, in the form of the new Persian dynasty of the Sassanids, by whom the Parthians had been overthrown 226 A.D. And whereas the northern, German danger was mainly physical, representing in a sense a barbarization and rejuvenation of the European spirit itself, the new Persian threat was rather a danger to that very spirit.

Diocletian (r. 284–305 A.D.) moved his Roman court to Asia Minor to meet the new military power, which he matched with considerably more success than the powers to the north; but he was no match at all for the seduction of the Oriental mythology of his foe. The Sassanids were Zoroastrians. The Bundahish and other sacred texts were edited, interpreted, and amplified in their period; and a state church came to flower under a powerful Magian clergy. The openness of the West to Persian religious ideas can be judged from the rapid spread of Mithraism throughout the Roman Empire from the reign of Vespasian (69–79 A.D.); but in Persia itself the Zoroastrian revival, far from generating any sense of intercultural coexistence, was in true Levantine style antipathetic to the gentile world, particularly the West, or more specifically, Hellenism and syncretism, which the preceding Parthian dynasty had favored.

Diocletian, having set up his Asian court in Nicomedia, in Asia Minor, assumed the garb and pose of an Asian despot: the symbolic heavenly robe, embroidered with the pearls and precious stones of the bounding constellations of the universe. And, as the sun shines in the midst of all, as the golden door to eternity, so the kingly head with its diadem rose gloriously above the robe. The footstool of the world was at his feet, before which all had to bow. And as a further result of the force of the archaic Asian ideal, the Roman Empire itself was transformed into an Oriental machine state. Taxation had greatly increased in the century since Aurelius, and it now had become the custom to assign responsibility for the levy of each district to the wealthy men of the region: what they could not extract from the people they had to render from their own wealth; and so the middle class had collapsed. The peasant class had long since been devastated by the wars. Everywhere indigence, beggary, robbery, and violence were increasing; and Diocletian, to correct the trend, produced laws forbidding men to quit or change their occupation. Guild and union membership was made obligatory and could not be changed; so that a veritable caste system resulted, and with all working for the state. Wages and prices were determined by the state. The emperor's ears and eyes, his spies, were everywhere observing, to make sure that all the rules were being obeyed. Professor James Breasted many years ago summarized the situation, in a paragraph that has lingered in my mind ever since my student years, as the prophecy of a time to come in our own fair land of the free:

> Staggering under his crushing burden of taxes, in a State which was practically bankrupt, the citizen of every class had now become a mere cog in the vast machinery of the government. He had no other function than to toil for the State, which exacted so much of the fruit of his labor that he was fortunate if it proved barely possible for him to survive on what was left. As a mere toiler for the State, he was finally where the peasant on the Nile had been for thousands of years. The emperor had become a Pharaoh, and the Roman Empire a colossal Egypt of ancient days. The century of revolution which ended in the despotic reorganization by Diocletian completely destroyed the creative ability of ancient men in art and literature, as it likewise crushed all progress in business and affairs. In so far as the ancient world was one of progress in civilization, its history was ended with the accession of Diocletian.[120]

The Germans on one hand, the Orient on the other, had brought into being this Rome, into which Christianity now was to enter as a third transforming force. Diocletian dealt harshly with the Christians, recognizing them as enemies of the state, but Galerius, his successor (r. 304–311), issued an edict of toleration on the good old pagan principle that every god is entitled to the worship of its own people; and in the course of the complicated interludes of murder, palace intrigue, open wars, and massacre that bridged the years between Galerius's death and Constantine's accession (i.e. 311–324 A.D.), the issue of the Christian cause hung precariously in the balance, until—as the famous legend goes, on the word of

Constantine himself to his biographer Eusebius—in the course of his preparation for the crucial battle with Maxentius, his chief rival for the crown, who was inimical to the Christians, the still pagan Constantine beheld in the sky a shining cross bearing the words *Hoc vince,* and his army saw it too. In a dream the following night, Christ appeared and bade him adopt that sign for his standard, which he did and, victory won, his loyalty thereafter was to the cross.[121]

The place of Constantine the Great in relation to the history of Christianity can be compared to that of Ashoka in the Buddhist cause. Each arose three centuries after the lifetime of his savior, and each converted what had been a religion indifferent to politics and even to the current social order into the secular religion of an empire. The comparable dates are these:

Jesus Christ	Gautama Buddha
c. 3 B.C.–30 A.D.	563–483 B.C.
Constantine the Great	Ashoka the Great
r. 324–337 A.D.	r. 268–232 B.C.

Whereas, however, Ashoka preached and practiced non-violence and religious tolerance,[122] Constantine set to work, as soon as he had won his throne, to extirpate two heresies. The first was that of the Donatists of North Africa. These maintained that the efficacy of a sacrament depends on the spiritual state of the priest: anyone betraying the faith, they declared, is in possession not of the faith, but of guilt (*qui fidem a perfido sumserit, non fidem percipit sed reatum*). The orthodox answer to this heresy was that the sacraments are sacred in themselves, not by virtue of men (*sacramenta per se esse sancta, non per homines*). And the danger of the controversy was that, if the Donatists were right, the entire ceremonial edifice of the Church would be dependent on the moral character of the clergy and no one could ever be sure that a given rite had been supernaturally effective; whereas, if the Donatists were wrong, a sacrament might be effectively administered even by a heretic or heathen.

The second controversy faced by Constantine was even more essential. It was that of the followers of Arius, who maintained that Christ was neither True God nor True Man. God, they averred, is absolutely unknowable and alone. Christ, though pre-existent to his incarnation, is a created being and therefore not truly God, though worshipful as the creator of all other creatures. In his incarnation as Jesus, the Son had assumed a human body but not a human soul. Hence, he was neither True God nor True Man.[123]

Perhaps in contrasting the attitudes of Ashoka and Constantine toward differences in belief, one should take into account the fact that the Indian had already gained his empire when the terrible spectacle of the carnage and calamity wrought by his armies struck him to the soul with an arrow of remorse, and he was converted to the Buddhist ethic of non-injury and compassion; whereas Constantine saw a vision of future victory and was converted thereby to something that has since been called Christianity—though it is difficult to construe its relationship to the lesson of Christ's temptation in the desert.* The next observation would have to be, however, that whereas the Buddhist empire of Ashoka collapsed only half a century after his death, the Christian empire of Constantine endured until the fall of Constantinople to the Turks, eleven hundred and twenty-nine years after his gaining of his throne. And the crucial remark for the general theory of our subject, then, would perhaps have to be that in East and West the contrary destinies of the two great secular religions of salvation were established by the contrary characters of their first great kingly converts, not by the prophets to whose names they are referred.

For Ashoka's recognition of suffering had been of the order (though not the intensity) of that of the Buddha himself when he stated, as the First of his Four Noble Truths, "All life is sorrowful." Hence, in the royal edicts the essence of the teaching was honestly retained, and non-violence and compassion were sincerely fostered. But in the Occident, the religion of Christ became with Constantine the handmaid (or, better, fairy godmother) of politics, and authority for the dominance of a certain social order was alleged to have been derived from one who was supposed to have said: "My kingship is not of this world; if my kingship were of this

* Supra, pp. 351–53.

world, my servants would fight." [124] Hence, to the world-dividing question, "Are you interested in society or in Truth?" the Occidental monarch, answering honestly, would have had to have said, "In the former," whereas the Indian could have said, "In Truth."

And yet, ironically, whereas in the West the religion of the Savior has suffered throughout its history the degradation of an identification with politics, our Western political practices have been mollified to a significant degree through its influence, whereas, in contrast, Oriental political thought has remained governed to this day by the elementary political law of nature; which is, simply and forever, the Law of the Fishes (Sanskrit, *matsya nyāya*): The big ones eat the little ones, and the little ones have to be smart.

Constantine the Great was born in Dacia (now Rumania) c. 274 A.D. His mother, Helena, was a woman of low degree from Bithynia (in Northwest Asia Minor) and the concubine of Constantius, who put her aside, however, in the year 293, to marry the stepdaughter of Maximian, Theodora. Constantius then became Caesar of Rome and the young Constantine was removed to the Asian court of the Emperor Diocletian—with whom he marched to Egypt, where he met Eusebius, the future bishop of Caesarea and, later, his biographer. The young prince took as concubine a young woman named Minervina and begot on her his son Crispus— though he had been betrothed as early as 293 to the infant daughter of Maximian, Fausta. Affairs turning against him at court, he escaped to Gaul, where, when his father died quelling a rebellion in Britain, he assumed and presently won command of the empire of the West. We read of his wars in Gaul, from 306 to 312, that "even heathen feeling was shocked when he gave barbarian kings to the beasts, along with their followers by thousands at a time." [125] And we know, too, that almost immediately after summoning and presiding over the Council of Nicaea, where the will and nature of God were proclaimed and defined for all mankind, he slew—for some unknown reason—both his son Crispus and his wife Fausta. Some kind of Phaedra tragedy has been suggested. But whatever the occasion may have been, it is clear that Constantine was a man of sterner stuff than Ashoka.

Having gained for himself the whole empire by 324 A.D., Constantine the Great set about welding it into one spiritual block, and to this end summoned, in 325 A.D., the Council of Nicaea. Over three hundred bishops attended, from every province of the realm, and after a sermon from the emperor on the necessity for unity, these set to work, first to fix a date for Easter and then to anathematize the Arians. The creed finally accepted (composed by the young deacon Athanasius of Alexandria) ran as follows:

> We believe in one God, the Father all-Sovereign, maker of all things, both visible and invisible:
> And in one Lord Jesus Christ, the Son of God, begotten of the Father, an only-begotten;
> that is, from the essence (οὐσία) of the Father,
> God from God, Light from Light, true God from true God —begotten, not made—being of one essence (ὁμοούσιον) with the Father;
> by whom all things were made, both things in heaven and things on earth;
> who for us men and for our salvation came down and was made flesh, was made man, suffered, and rose again the third day, ascended into heaven, cometh to judge the quick and the dead:
> And in the Holy Spirit.
> But those who say that "there was once when he was not," and "before he was begotten he was not," and "he was made of things that were not," or maintain that the Son of God is of a different essence (ἐξ ἑτέρος οὐσίας ἢ ὑποστάσεως), or created or subject to moral change or alteration—these doth the Catholic and Apostolic Church anathematize.[126]

In the reign of Constantine Christianity was accorded equal status with the pagan religions of the empire, but half a century later, in the reign of Theodosius the Great (r. 379–395), it was declared to be the only religion allowed; and with that the period was inaugurated by imperial decree that has since been known as the Dark Ages. Edward Gibbon tells of its onset; and I can think of no more appropriate way to ring down the curtain on the Age of the Great Classics than with a passage of his classic prose.

"In Syria," he states, after reviewing scenes in various other of the Roman provinces,

the divine and excellent Marcellus, as he is styled by Theodoret, a bishop animated with apostolic fervor, resolved to level with the ground the stately temples within the diocese of Apamea. His attack was resisted by the skill and solidity with which the temples of Jupiter had been constructed. The building was seated on an eminence: on each of the four sides the lofty roof was supported by fifteen massy columns, sixteen feet in circumference; and the large stones of which they were composed were firmly cemented with lead and iron. The force of the strongest and sharpest tools had been tried without effect. It was found necessary to undermine the foundations of the columns, which fell down as soon as the temporary wooden props had been consumed with fire; and the difficulties of the enterprise are described under the allegory of a black daemon, who retarded, though he could not defeat, the operations of the Christian engineers. Elated with victory, Marcellus took the field in person against the powers of darkness; a numerous troop of soldiers and gladiators marched under the episcopal banner, and he successively attacked the villages and country temples of the diocese of Apamea. Whenever any resistance or danger was apprehended, the champion of the faith, whose lameness would not allow him either to fight or fly, placed himself at a convenient distance, beyond the reach of darts. But this prudence was the occasion of his death; he was surprised and slain by a body of exasperated rustics; and the synod of the province pronounced, without hesitation, that the holy Marcellus had sacrificed his life in the cause of God. In support of this cause, the monks, who rushed with tumultuous fury from the desert, distinguished themselves by their zeal and diligence. They deserved the enmity of the Pagans; and some of them might deserve the reproaches of avarice and intemperance, which they indulged at the expense of the people, who foolishly admired their tattered garments, loud psalmody, and artificial paleness. A small number of temples was protected by the fears, the venality, the taste, or the prudence of the civil and ecclesiastical governors. The temple of the Celestial Venus at Carthage, whose sacred precincts formed a circumference of two miles, was judiciously converted into a Christian church; and a similar consecration has preserved inviolate the majestic dome of the Pantheon at Rome. But in almost every province of the Roman world, an army of fanatics, without authority and without discipline, invaded the peaceful inhabitants; and the ruin of the fairest structures of antiquity still displays the ravages of *those* barbarians who alone had time and inclination to execute such laborious destruction. . . .

The temples of the Roman empire were deserted or destroyed; but the ingenious superstition of the Pagans still attempted to elude the laws of Theodosius, by which all sacrifices had been severely prohibited. The inhabitants of the country, whose conduct was less exposed to the eye of malicious curiosity, disguised their *religious* under the appearance of *convivial* meetings. On the days of solemn festivals they assembled in great numbers under the spreading shade of some consecrated trees; sheep and oxen were slaughtered and roasted; and this rural entertainment was sanctified by the use of incense and by the hymns which were sung in honour of the gods. But it was alleged that, as no part of the animal was made a burnt-offering, as no altar was provided to receive the blood, and as the previous oblation of salt cakes and the concluding ceremony of oblations were carefully omitted, these festal meetings did not involve the guests in guilt or penalty of an illegal sacrifice. Whatever might be the truth of the facts or the merit of the distinction, these vain pretences were swept away by the last edict of Theodosius, which inflicted a deadly wound on the superstition of the Pagans. This prohibitory law is expressed in the most absolute and comprehensive terms. "It is our will and pleasure," says the emperor, "that none of our subjects, whether magistrates or private citizens, however exalted or however humble may be their rank and condition, shall presume in any city or in any place to worship an inanimate idol by the sacrifice of a guiltless victim." The act of sacrificing and the practice of divination by the entrails of the victim are declared (without any regard to the object of the inquiry) a crime of high treason against the state, which can be expiated only by the death of the guilty. The rites of Pagan superstition which might seem less bloody and atrocious are abolished as highly injurious to the truth and honour of religion; luminaries, garlands, frankincense, and libations of wine are specially enumerated and condemned; and the harmless claims of the domestic genius, of the household gods, are included in this rigorous proscription. The use of any of these profane and illegal ceremonies subjects the offender to the forfeiture of the house or estate where they have been performed; and if he has artfully chosen the property of another for the scene of his impiety, he is compelled to discharge, without delay, a heavy fine of twenty-five pounds of gold, or more than one thousand pounds sterling. A fine not less considerable is imposed on the connivance of the secret enemies of religion who shall neglect the duty of their respective stations, either to reveal or to punish the guilt of idolatry. Such was the persecuting spirit of the laws of Theodosius, which were repeatedly enforced by his sons and grandsons, with the loud and unanimous applause of the Christian world. . . .

The ruin of the Pagan religion is described by the sophists as a dreadful and amazing prodigy, which covered the earth with darkness and restored the ancient dominion of chaos and night. They relate in solemn and pathetic strains that the temples were converted into sepulchres, and that the holy places, which had been adorned by the statues of the gods, were basely polluted by the relics of Christian martyrs. "The monks" (a race of filthy animals, to whom Eunapius is tempted to refuse the name of men) "are the authors of the new worship, which, in the place of those deities who are conceived by the understanding, has substituted the meanest and most contemptible slaves. The heads, salted and pickled, of those infamous malefactors, who for the multitude of their crimes have suffered a just and ignominious death; their bodies, still marked by the impression of the lash and the scars of those tortures which were inflicted by the sentence of the magistrate; such" (continues Eunapius) "are the gods which the earth produces in our days; such are the martyrs, the supreme arbitrators of our prayers and petitions to the Deity, whose tombs are now consecrated as the objects of the veneration of the people."

. . . The satisfactory experience [Gibbon concludes] that the relics of saints were more valuable than gold or precious stones stimulated the clergy to multiply the treasures of the church. Without much regard for truth or probability, they invented names for skeletons, and actions for names. The fame of the apostles, and of the holy men who had imitated their virtues, was darkened by religious fiction. To the invincible band of genuine and primitive martyrs they added myriads of imaginary heroes, who had never existed, except in the fancy of crafty or credulous legendaries; and there is reason to suspect that Tours might not be the only diocese in which the bones of a malefactor were adored instead of those of a saint.[127]

Theodosius the Great died in 395 A.D., and exactly fifteen years later the Visigoths, under Alaric, ravaged Rome. Saint Augustine (354–430 A.D.) wrote his great work *The City of God* to answer the argument that though the city had flourished for a millennium under its own gods, when it turned to Christ it perished. The City of Man, of sin, of damnation, had fallen, the good bishop conceded, but in its stead the City of God, the Church, the Living Body of Christ, would endure to all eternity. "And in that blessed city," he wrote, as one who could be depended upon to know,

> there shall be this great blessing, that no inferior shall envy any superior, as now the archangels are not envied by the angels, because no one will wish to be what he has not received, though bound in strictest concord with him who has received; as in the body the finger does not seek to be the eye, though both members are harmoniously included in the complete structure of the body. And thus, along with his gift, greater or less, each shall receive this further gift of contentment to desire no more than he has.[128]

All very well! But meanwhile throughout Europe there ranged, without impediment, the barbarians not of Europe alone, but of Asia as well. For Attila the Hun, with his horde of battle-riders, entering Europe from the Russian steppes, set up a capital of barbaric splendor in the neighborhood of present Budapest and harried half the continent until his death in 453. The Vandals poured through Spain to Africa, followed by the Visigoths, who in Spain set up a Visigothic kingdom. Britain, abandoned by the Romans, was invaded and settled by Germanic Jutes, Angles, and Saxons, while the Franks settled in Gaul, to which they gave their name as France. Rome itself came in charge largely of Christianized Germanic officers, who made and unmade a terminal series of pitiful puppet emperors until September 476, when the tall and fair Odoacer took the government to himself and there would be no emperor more in the West for the next 324 years—until another German, Charlemagne, should set the solar crown upon his own head, Christmas Day, 800 A.D., in Saint Peter's Church in Rome, having received that radiant symbol of Ahura Mazda from the hands of Pope Leo III.

THE AGE OF THE GREAT BELIEFS

The Dialogue of Europe and the Levant

During the reigns of Trajan (98–117 A.D.) and his successor Hadrian (117–138) the forms of the dome and arch had begun to appear in the architecture of Rome, and therewith—as Spengler recognized—the world-feeling of the rising Levant was announced. In his words: "The Pantheon . . . is *the earliest of all mosques*." [1] And at the same time the eyes of the portrait busts of emperors began to have their pupils bored, whereas in earlier Classical sculpture eyes had been as though blind: there had been no gazing forth of an interior spirit into space.[2] For, just as the Greek temple had stressed the exterior with its columns, there being but a simple cella within, affording no sense of interior space but only of outside physicality, so (again to use Spengler's words) for Classical man "the Temple of the Body, too, had no 'interior.' " [3]

The mosque, in contrast, was all interior: an architectural like-ness of the world-cavern, which appears to the Levantine mind to be the proper symbol of the spiritual form of the universe. "An ingeniously confusing interpenetration of spherical and polygonal forms," as Spengler writes of it, "a load so placed upon a stone drum that it seems to hover weightless on high, yet closing the in-terior without outlet; all structural lines concealed; vague light ad-mitted, through a small opening in the heart of the dome but only the more inexorably to emphasize the walling-in—such are the characteristics that we see in the masterpieces of this art, St. Vitale in Ravenna, Hagia Sophia in Constantinople, and the Dome of the Rock (the Mosque of Omar) in Jerusalem." [4]

An awesome, all-pervading sense of bounded space and time, as a kind of Aladdin cave within which light and darkness, good and evil, grace and willfulness, spirit and soul, interplay to create, instead of history, a mighty fairy tale of divinely and diabolically motivated agents, fills all the mythologies of the Levant—whether of Judaism, Zoroastrianism, Mithraism, Manichaeism, Eastern Christianity, Neoplatonism, Gnosticism, the late Classical Mysteries, or Islam. And the cognate view of the individual in this world is not of an individual at all, but of an organ or part of the great organism—as in Paul or Augustine's view of the Living Body of Christ. In each being, as throughout the world cavern, there play the two contrary, all-pervading principles of Spirit and Soul—Hebrew *ruach* and *nephesh,* Persian *ahu* and *urvan,* Mandaean *manuhmed* and *gyan,* Greek *pneuma* and *psyche.*

"*Ruach,*" as Spengler observes, "means originally 'wind' and *nephesh* is always in one way or another related to the bodily and earthly, to the below, the evil, the darkness. Its effort is the 'upward.' The *ruach* belongs to the divine, to the above, to the light. Its effects in man when it descends are the heroism of a Samson, the holy wrath of an Elijah, the enlightenment of the judge (the Solomon passing judgment), and all kinds of divination and ecstasy. It is poured out." [5]

The manifestation of a newly developing culture through the forms of an alien heritage—such as is represented by the appearance of the dome in late Roman architecture and the pupils in the eyes of Roman portraits—Spengler has denominated by the term "pseudomorphosis." The word, derived from the vocabulary of mineralogy, properly refers to the deceptive outer shape, the "false formation," of a crystal that has solidified within a rock crevice, or other mold, incongruous to its inner structure. As Spengler defines the category:

> By the term "historical pseudomorphosis" I propose to designate those cases in which an older alien culture lies so massively over the land that a young culture, born in this land, cannot get its breath and fails not only to achieve pure and specific expression forms, but even to develop fully its own self consciousness. All that wells up from the depths of the young soul is cast in the old molds, young feelings stiffen in senile works, and instead of rearing itself up in its own creative

power, it can only hate the distant power with a hate that grows to be monstrous.[6]

In the case of the Levantine culture, as he shows, this condition prevailed, one way or another, from start to finish. Its earliest stage of germination lay entirely within the ambit of the ancient Babylonian civilization; the next, from c. 529 B.C., was marked by the dictatorship of a small Persian clan, primitive as the Ostrogoths, whose domination of two hundred years, till the victory of Alexander, was founded on the infinite weariness of the worn-out Babylonian populations. "But from 300 B.C. onward," Spengler states "there begins and spreads a great awakening in the young Aramaic-speaking peoples between Sinai and the Zagros range." Yet precisely at this juncture came the Macedonians, who laid down a thin sheet of Classical civilization as far as to India and Turkestan. With the victories of Pompey in Syria and then of Augustus at Actium (30 B.C.), the heavy toga of Rome fell over the land. And for centuries thereafter, until the veritable explosion of Islam into sudden form, Levantine thought and feeling had to express itself— except in the released realm of the Persian Sassanian kings—under forms that our scholars have consistently misinterpreted as representing an interval largely of transition from the Classical to the Gothic stages of our own European civilization.

"The Magian Culture," as Spengler seems to have been the only historian to observe,

> geographically and historically, is the midmost of the group of higher Cultures—the only one which, in point both of space and of time, was in touch with practically all others. The structure of its history as a whole in our world-picture depends, therefore, entirely on our recognizing the true inner form which the outer molds distorted. Unhappily, that is just what we do not yet know, thanks to theological and philological prepossessions, and even more to the modern tendency of over-specialization which has unreasonably subdivided Western research into a number of separate branches—each distinguished from the others not merely by its materials and its methods, but by its very way of thinking—and so prevented

the big problems from being even seen. In this instance the consequences of specialization have been graver perhaps than in any other. The historians proper stayed within the domain of Classical philology and made the Classical language frontier their eastern horizon; hence they entirely failed to perceive the deep unity of development on both sides of their frontier, which spiritually had no existence. The result is a perspective of "Ancient," "Medieval," and "Modern" history, ordered and defined by the use of the Greek and Latin languages. For the experts of the old languages, with their "texts," Axum, Saba, and even the realm of the Sassanids were unattackable, and the consequence is that in "history" these scarcely exist at all. The literature-researcher (he also a philologist) confuses the spirit of the language with the spirit of the work. Products of the Aramaean region, if they happen to be written in Greek or even merely preserved in Greek, he embodies in his "Late Greek literature" and proceeds to classify as a special period of that literature. The cognate texts in other languages are outside his department and have been brought into other groups of literature in the same artificial way. And yet here was the strongest of all proofs that the history of a literature never coincides with the history of a language. Here, in reality, was a self-contained ensemble of Magian national literature, single in spirit, but written in several languages—the Classical amongst others. For a nation of Magian type has no mother tongue. There are Talmudic, Manichaean, Nestorian, Jewish, or even Neopythagorean national literatures, but *not* Hellenistic or Hebrew.

Theological research, in its turn, broke up its domain into subdivisions according to the different West-European confessions, and so the "philological" frontier between West and East came into force, and still is in force, for Christian theology also. The Persian world fell to the student of Iranian philology, and as the Avesta texts were disseminated, though not composed, in an Aryan dialect, their immense problem came to be regarded as a minor branch of the Indologist's work and so disappeared absolutely from the field of vision of Christian theology. And lastly the history of Talmudic Judaism, since Hebrew philology became bound up in one specialism with Old Testament research, not only never obtained separate treatment, but has been *completely forgotten* by all the major histories of religions with which I am acquainted, although these find room for every Indian sect (since folklore, too, ranks as a specialism) and every primitive Negro religion to boot. Such is the preparation of scholarship for the greatest task that historical research has to face today.[7]

In the remaining pages of the present volume we shall regard only in broad lines—hardly touching even the most important of the numerous special traditions—the interplay of the two great spiritual worlds of the Levantine and European souls, through a colorful maze of mutual and self misunderstanding; and herewith two contrary pseudomorphoses will appear. Of the first, Spengler has just informed us; namely, the germination of Levantine forms beneath an overlay of Hellenistic-Roman formulae. And the second might be termed the Levantine revenge; namely, the massive diffusion of Pauline Christianity over the whole culture field of Europe, after which the native Celtic and Germanic sense of being, and manner of experience, were compelled to find both expression and support in alien terms, antipodal, or even antipathetic, to every native sentiment and impulse. The breakthrough of the released Levantine spirit in a late yet powerful statement will be seen in the vivid, definitive victory of Islam from the seventh century on. And the comparable breakthrough of the released European mind will appear in the double victory of individual conscience with the Reformation and of unencumbered science, joined to a revived humanism, with the Renaissance. We shall attempt an aerial survey, so to say, first of the Levantine province and then of the European to c. 1350 A.D., when the cracks in the old pseudomorphy began to split apart. And our aim will be to bring out through a few significant forms the main lines both of each native order and of the distorting force of each overlay on the proper growth.

++++++++++++++++++ *Chapter 8* ++++++++++++++++++

THE CROSS AND THE
CRESCENT

+++

I. The Magi

Next to nothing is known of the Parthian phase of the religion of Iran. Under the Greek Seleucidae (312–64 B.C.) Alexander's ideal of a marriage of East and West seemed generally to be prospering. However, the whole of the rising new Levant could not be held under one scepter. In c. 212 B.C. a Macedonian governor in Bactria, Euthydemus, had been able to establish an independent state.[1] Palestine, some four years later, revolted with the Maccabees. Then Rome began lopping off western provinces. And it was in those years that in Parthia (East Iran) the native dynasty arose that is known as the Parthian or Arsacid. Founded by an obscure tribal chief, Arsaces, c. 250 B.C., it was made firm by two brothers, Phraates I (r. c. 175–170) and Mithradates I (r. c. 170–138); and though continuously at war on every side—to the north and east against the Scythians, Bactrians, and Kushanas, and westward, first against the Seleucidae, then, for two centuries, against Rome—the rugged dynasty increased its hold and endured until 226 A.D., when it was displaced from within by another Persian house, the Sassanian, which remained until the conquest by Islam in 641.

In the Denkart, a late Sassanian work of the sixth century, it is recorded that in the first century A.D.

Valakhsh the Arsacid [Vologaeses I, r. 51–77 A.D.] commanded that a memorandum should be sent to all provinces, with instructions to preserve in whatever state they appeared as much of the Avesta and Zend as came to light and was genuine; also, any teachings derived from it: which, though scattered, owing to the chaos and confusion that Alexander had carried in his wake and the pillage and looting of the Macedonians in the kingdom of Iran, might have survived either in writing or in authoritative oral communication.[2]

In the main, throughout the Parthian period a strong Hellenizing trend had prevailed. However, in this notice the beginning is registered of a Magian Zoroastrian revival, which in the period of Sassanian rule was strengthened and enforced. The founder of the new dynasty, Ardashir I (r. 226–241 A.D.), set about immediately to review the religious heritage of his empire, with the idea of establishing an orthodoxy through which its heterogeneous population should be amalgamated; and he selected to direct this task a member of the Zoroastrian clergy, Tansar, whose accomplishment is registered in the Denkart.

> His Majesty the King of Kings Ardashir son of Papak, following Tansar as religious authority, commanded all those scattered teachings [formerly gathered by Valakhsh] to be brought to the court. Tansar set about his task, selected one version, excluded others from the canon, and issued this decree: "The interpretation of all the teachings from the Religion of the Worshipers of Mazda is our responsibility; for now there is no lack of certain knowledge concerning them."[3]

Just as the Christian canon was taking shape, so too was an orthodox Zoroastrian. However, a challenge to this reconstruction of the Zoroastrian heritage under the Magian priest Tansar appeared in the teachings of the greatest sage and preacher of the age, the Babylonian prophet Mani (216?–276? A.D.), whose grandiose Manichaean synthesis of Zoroastrian with Buddhist and Christian-Gnostic ideas seemed for a time to promise to the King of Kings an even broader amalgamation of beliefs than a canon simply of Zoroastrian lore. Hence, the second monarch of the dynasty, Shapur I (r. 241–272), a man of widely ranging view, was impressed. As we read of him, continuing our text:

The King of Kings Shapur son of Ardashir further collected those writings of the Religion that were dispersed throughout India, the Byzantine Empire,* and other lands, and which treated of medicine, astronomy, movement, time, space, substance, creation, becoming, passing away, qualitative change, logic, and other arts and sciences. These he added to the Avesta and commanded that a fair copy of all of them be deposited in the Royal Treasury: and he examined the possibility of basing every form of academic discipline on the Religion of the Worshipers of Mazda.[4]

Mani, who began his mission in 242 A.D., was granted an interview with Shapur and given liberty to preach wherever he wished. Apparently the King of Kings himself dallied for a time in Manichaean doctrine. However, this liberal-minded monarch passed away in 272 A.D., and the prophet, in his thirtieth year of teaching, was turned over to the orthodox clergy by the second following king, Bahram I (r. 273–276): whereupon, in the capital, in true Levantine style, he was executed for teaching heresy—according to his legend, crucified, like Christ.

Following the death of Shapur, the Magian reaction to his broadly humanistic, Hellenistic point of view was enforced by his own high priest Karter—the inquisitor by whom Mani was condemned. "Under him," states Professor R. C. Zaehner in his recent work, *The Dawn and Twilight of Zoroastrianism,*

Zoroastrianism appears for the first time as a fanatical and persecuting religion. The list of the sects persecuted, however, shows how justified the early Sassanian kings were in seeking a unifying force that would weld their Empire together; for not only do we find Jews, Christians, Manichees, and Mandaeans mentioned, but also Buddhists and Brahmans; all these Karter claims to have chastised. . . . "Heretics and apostates," Karter tells us, "who were within the Magian community, were spared for the religion of the worshipers of Mazda and the rites of the gods but not for the spread of propaganda: I chastised and upbraided them and improved them."

Uniformity of belief [Professor Zaehner comments] was,

* The Byzantine Empire had not yet been established. The term in the text is anachronistic.

then, certainly enforced, and the probability is that this unity was along strictly dualist and Mazdaean lines. Karter's policy must then be seen as a reaction, under a series of weak kings, against the personal religious policy of Shapur.[5]

Let me suggest that we formulate the sociological principle, formerly illustrated by the Maccabean and now by this Magian reaction to the force of Hellenism, in organic-chemical terms of "tolerance": the constitutional capacity of a system to endure a food or drug that to a certain degree or for a certain time can be assimilated even profitably, but beyond that becomes intolerable and is spontaneously expelled.

Without arguing the point as to whether a state can survive without compelling its subjects to accept as Absolute Truth whatever system of belief the dominant elite may have decided to put forth as divine revelation, we shall observe only that in the history of the Levant this pseudo-religious form of sociology can be studied in variety and, so to say, in purest style. And where once allowed to prevail, it only grows in force and terror as the violated, coerced factors become increasingly intractable through the operation of a second natural law, namely, that gods suppressed become demons; which is to say, that psychological and sociological factors neither assimilated nor recognized by the consciously controlled system become autonomous and must ultimately break the approved system apart.

From the next statement of the Denkart we learn that during the reign of King Shapur II (310–379)—who was an exact contemporary of Constantine, Saint Augustine, and Theodosius the Great—the Persian reaction to what the orthodox mind calls heresy was in full career. And the great man of piety now was Aturpat, to whom, as Professor Zaehner states, "the Pahlavi books look back as to the very embodiment of orthodoxy. Aturpat submitted himself to the ordeal by molten metal and emerged from it victorious 'during his controversy with all manner of sectarians and heretics.' "[6] According to the Denkart:

The King of Kings, Shapur, son of Ohrmazd [Shapur II], summoned men from all lands to examine and study all doctrines, so that all cause for dispute might be removed. After Aturpat had been vindicated by the consistency of his argument against all the other representatives of the different sects, doctrines, and schools, he issued a declaration to the following effect: "Now that we have seen the Religion upon earth, we shall leave no one to his false religion and we shall be exceeding zealous." And so did he do.[7]

However—and who should be surprised?—the danger to the empire of heresy, right and left, still was rampant two full centuries later, in the period of Chosroes I (r. 531–579), a contemporary of his Christian counterpart Justinian (r. 527–563), whose problems and solutions were approximately the same. We shall let his own text stand as our final exhibit from the Denkart, which was a work composed in his reign.

His present Majesty, the King of Kings, Khusraw, son of Kavat [Chosroes I], after he had put down irreligion and heresy with the greatest vindictiveness according to the revelation of the Religion in the matter of all heresy, greatly strengthened the system of the four castes and encouraged precise argumentation, and in a diet of the provinces he issued the following declaration:

"The truth of the Religion of the Worshipers of Mazda has been recognized. Intelligent men can with confidence establish it in the world by discussion. But effective and progressive propaganda should be based not so much on discussion as on pure thoughts, words, and deeds, the inspiration of the Good Spirit, and the worship of God paid in absolute conformity to the Word. What the chief Magi of Ohrmazd [= Ahura Mazda] have proclaimed, do we proclaim; for among us they have been shown to possess spiritual insight. And we have asked and continue to ask of them the fullest exposition of doctrine both in the matter of spiritual insight and in its practical application on earth, and for this we give thanks to God.

"Fortunately for the good government of the country, the realm of Iran has gone forward relying on the doctrine of the Religion of the Worshipers of Mazda, that is, the synthesis of the accumulated knowledge of those who have gone before us throughout the whole of this central clime. We have no dispute with those who have other convictions, for we ourselves possess so much both in the Avestan language through pure oral tradition and in written records, in books and memoranda, and in the vulgar idiom by way of exegesis—in short, the whole original wisdom of the Religion of the Worshipers of Mazda. Whereas we have recognized that, in so far as all dubious doctrines foreign to the Religion of the Worshipers of Mazda reach this place from all over the world, further examination and study prove that to absorb and publish knowledge foreign to the Religion of the Worshipers of Mazda does not contribute to the welfare and prosperity of our subjects as much as one religious leader, who has examined much and pondered much in his recital of the liturgy; with high intent and in concert with the perspicacious, most noble, most honorable, most good Magian men, we do hereby decree that the Avesta and Zend be studied zealously and ever afresh, so that what is acquired therefrom may worthily increase and fertilize the knowledge of our subjects.

"Those who tell our subjects either that it is not possible to acquire, or that it is possible to acquire in its entirety, knowledge of the Creator, the mystery of spiritual beings, and the nature of the Creator's creation, are to be deemed men of insufficient intellect and freethinkers. Those who say that it is possible to understand reality through the revelation of the Religion and by analogy, are to be deemed researchers after truth. Those who expound this doctrine clearly are to be deemed wise and versed in the Religion. And since the root of all knowledge is the doctrine of the Religion, both in its spiritual power and through its manifestation here on earth, a man who speaks in this cause speaks wisely, even if he derives the doctrine from no Avestan revelation. So he should be esteemed as speaking in accordance with the Religion, the function of which is to give instruction to the sons of men." [8]

II. Byzantium

"While Classical man stood before his gods as one body before another," Spengler writes,

the Magian deity is the indefinite, enigmatic Power on high that pours out its Wrath or its Grace, descends itself into the dark or raises the soul into the light as it sees fit. The idea of individual wills is simply meaningless, for "will" and "thought" in man are not prime, but already effects of the deity upon him. Out of this unshakable root-feeling, which is merely re-expressed, never essentially altered, by any conversions, illumination or subtilizing in the world, there emerges of necessity the idea of the Divine Mediator, of one who transforms this state from a torment into a bliss. All Magian religions are by this idea bound together, and separated from those of all other Cultures.[9]

In the Zoroastrian sector of the Magian world the key question of mythology on which the various contending sects went apart was that of the relationship of Angra Mainyu to Ahura Mazda, the relationship of the power of darkness to the source and being of light; in other words, the origin and the ultimate nature of evil. For the Christian fold, on the other hand, the chief knot of discord was the problem of the Incarnation, the nature of the Mediator who entered the realm of time, matter, and sin, to save mankind. In the councils of the Church that followed Nicaea in rapid series, this was the issue on which all either held or went apart. We need not review the controversy in all of its exquisite convolutions. However, the force of sheerly political considerations in the determination of what was represented as a theological dispute, "not of this world," warrants a few pages of thought. For it is in the history of these councils that the growth of Christian doctrine as a function of the usual Levantine requirement for a monolithic consensus of opinion (which then is to be taken for unarguable truth) comes best to view.

To the argument there were four leading parties: 1. the great Egyptian theological school of Alexandria (of which the young deacon Athanasius, of the Council of Nicaea and the Athanasian Creed, had been a product),* where Christ's *divinity* was stressed: in the present development of controversy this school was to be represented principally by two powerful bishops, Cyril and Dioscurus, of whom the first would be canonized and the second anathematized for holding essentially the same view; 2. the Cappadocian-Syrian school of Antioch, where Christ's *humanity* was stressed: represented chiefly by the great heresiarch Nestorius, who

* Supra, p. 389.

would be condemned by Saint Cyril and destroyed; 3. the emperor on his throne in Constantinople, the New or Second Rome, whose high concern would be to keep the empire from disintegrating in argument; and 4. the pope on his throne in Rome itself, striving to assert the primacy of his see, on the claim of its establishment by Peter: as Peter had been made head of the apostles, so the pope should now be of all bishops. However, the vast majority of the bishops were Levantines, and Rome was no longer the seat of imperial rule.

PHASE ONE (C. 370-431)

The first capital phase of the great conflict was opened when the vigorously anti-Arian Bishop Apollinarius of Laodicea (a city just south of Antioch) proposed, about 370 A.D., to answer a certain troublesome argument, which was that, if all men are sinners and Christ was not a sinner, then Christ cannot have been truly man. The good Bishop Apollinarius's reply was that in Christ the place of the human soul was taken by the Logos, the Word made Flesh, but since the human spirit was created in the image of the Logos (Genesis 1:28), Christ was not the less, but the more, human for the difference. The Logos and man were not alien beings, but joined in their inmost nature, and, in a sense, each was incomplete without the other.[10]

It was an adroit reply. However, instead of quelling, it only exacerbated argument; and it placed Apollinarius himself, moreover, almost on the side of those Gnostics who argued for the illusionary appearance of the Savior.* He was condemned at the Second Ecumenical Council, at Constantinople in 381, and died nine years later. But his argument revived in the year 428, when Nestorius became the bishop of Constantinople. Trained at Antioch, where the doctrine of the reality of Christ's human nature was argued, the new bishop of the Second Rome proposed that Mary had not been the mother of God (θεοτόκος), but only the mother

* Supra, pp. 364-66.

of Christ's human nature. "I cannot speak of God as being two or three months old," he is reported to have said; and again: "Well, anyhow, don't make the Virgin a goddess!"

At which point the great bishop Cyril of Alexandria broke into the controversy with a volley of letters to the court of Constantinople—to the Emperor Theodosius II (r. 408–450), whom he addressed as "the image of God on earth," and to his sisters, "the most pious princesses," notably the eldest, Pulcheria, who had superintended Theodosius's education as a child, ruled as regent during his minority, chosen for him a consort who would not challenge her own authority, and vowed both herself and her sisters to perpetual virginity—with a view not only to a lofty place in heaven but also to unchallenged authority in the palace of the empire. The ladies spent their innocence placing flowers before altars, spinning, and exchanging counsels with the clergy and eunuchs of high station.

Cyril of Alexandria, writing to these and their brother, justified the term θεοτόκος with quotations from numerous authorities, and in letters to Nestorius charged him with having failed to understand the Nicene Creed. Letters passed also between Cyril and the pope in Rome, who at that time was Celestine I (422–432): whereupon there was called in Rome a synod at which Nestorius was condemned, and at another synod, in Alexandria, again he was condemned. But he issued counter-anathemas from his own high see of Constantinople: and at this point the emperor stepped in.

Theodosius II summoned a council in the year 431 at Ephesus, which happened to be the city in Asia Minor that, for millenniums before the Christian era, had been the chief temple site of the great Asian goddess Artemis, mother of the world and of the ever-dying resurrected god. We can reasonably assume that her lingering influence, no less than that of the virginal matriarchs of the palace, worked upon the counsels of the bishops there assembled. For it was there that the Virgin Mother was declared to be θεοτόκος, the Mother of God—five days before the delegates from Antioch arrived. Nestorius had refused to attend. He was condemned and deprived of his see. Together with the Antioch group, however, he held a council of his own, condemning Cyril, but in the end was forced to acquiesce. And in exile, in the desert of Egypt, he finally was slain, by the hand, apparently, of a great and well-known desert monk, Senuti.[11]

Yet his doctrine had a life course of its own. It split off eastward, away from the church of Rome and Constantinople, to flourish through Persia and as far as to Madras and to Peking. Marco Polo (1254–1323) found Nestorian churches along the caravan routes, where the Mahayana Buddhist monks also had their sanctuaries. And if anyone desires to enter a field of study as yet hardly explored, he will find a rich, though difficult, gain in those Asian marts of exchange, where the iconographic currencies of Buddhist and Brahmanical, Taoist and Confucian, Manichaean, Nestorian, and Zoroastrian stamp were all accepted and passed along as tender.

PHASE TWO (448–553)

The second capital phase of the argument over the nature of the Incarnation opened in the year 448. Bishop Cyril had died four years before—to be canonized—and the incumbent of his Alexandrian see was Dioscurus. The controversy resumed when a certain aged abbot named Eutyches, who from his cloister near Constantinople had been volubly opposed to Nestorius, was accused of disseminating errors of the opposite kind. Brought before a council in the capital, he stated his rather clumsy belief that Christ had been of *two natures* (God and Man) before their union in the Incarnation but of *one nature* thereafter; whereupon he was condemned and degraded. He appealed, however, to the emperor, to Pope Leo the Great (440–461), and to the monks of Constantinople. Theodosius called a second council to revise the findings of the first, and Dioscurus of Alexandria was invited to preside. Pope Leo was the one who now began writing, however, to the emperor, to Pulcheria, and to numerous other high personages, stating: 1. that Eutyches was in error, 2. that if there was to be a council at all, the place for it was Rome, and 3. that it was he, as successor of Peter, who was to compose the authoritative statement, or Tome, of the points of controversy to be discussed. The council was summoned in 449—by the emperor: not at Rome, but at Ephesus; and not Leo, but Dioscuorus, the bishop of Alexandria, presided. Leo dispatched three delegates, a bishop, a priest, and a deacon; but his Tome was not even read. Those who had condemned Eutyches were themselves condemned, and by the signatures of 115 bishops the old abbot was declared orthodox and reinstated. The sole protest—*Contradicitur*—was pronounced by Hilarius, the pope's delegated deacon, who escaped for his life and carried the news of the catastrophe to Rome, where Leo bestowed on the council the name by which it still is known, the Robber Council.

When Theodosius II fell from his horse into the river Lycus, broke his back, and died, in July 450, Pulcheria was proclaimed Empress, "and the Romans, for the first time," writes Gibbon, "submitted to a female reign." [12] She married a prudent senator, Marcian, who respected her virginity and, as emperor, supported with her Pope Leo's demand for another council—which he summoned, however, not in Rome, as expected, but in Chalcedon, near Constantinople. The pope's Tome prevailed this time, and Dioscurus, anathematized, was banished from his see: but with the disconcerting result that, before the decade had elapsed, the Alexandrian church had in large part split away from Constantinople and was seating bishops of its own in defiance of imperial appointments.

Thus arose the independent Coptic Monophysite (One Nature) branch of the rapidly separating Living Body of Christ. Of tremendous influence in its shaping were the multitudes of hermits who, since the period of Saint Anthony (251–356??), had infested the various Egyptian deserts, practicing the most bizarre austerities. Some, for instance, the so-called Stylites and Dendrites, like certain yogis of India,[13] condemned themselves to perpetual immobility, the former sitting atop columns left among the ruins of old temples, the latter perched on the branches of trees. Others, known as Browsers, fed like animals on grass. More chained themselves to rocks. Some bore on their shoulders heavy yokes. Yet multitudes were available for mob scenes, shouting slogans such as "One Nature! One Nature!" when Alexandrian theologians required conspicuous support.

In a zone of its own, after the schism of Chalcedon, the Coptic Monophysite Church developed outside the pale of European concern, linked to a little-studied civilization that arose in the lands around the Arabian Sea: Abyssinia and Somaliland, Hadramaut, Bombay and Malabar. Who, for example, has written of the life and times of the forty-odd monolithic churches of Ethiopian Lalibela, and of their relationship to the cave-temples of Ajanta? [14] And what of the legendary serpent king of nearby Axum, from whose slayer the present Nahas or Negus (compare Sanskrit *nāgas,* "serpent, serpent king"), Haile Selassie of Ethiopia, is descended? [15] Or who has searched the background of the legends of Issa (Jesus) and of the kings of Persia and Rome that Leo Frobenius traced through the Sudan as far west as to the Niger? [16] It is all, as far as the modern science of mythology, as well as the Catholic Church, is concerned, a lost world.

But the virtual loss of Africa was not the only calamity of the Council of Chalcedon; for a split began to appear, as well, between Byzantium and Rome. The see of Peter had previously played almost no role in the church councils, all of which had been summoned by emperors, held in Levantine cities, and attended by literally hundreds of bishops of the Orient with scarcely half a dozen from the West. The pope's high claim to the dignity of Peter had been simply disregarded. Whereas now Leo the Great, a man of stature and character, standing amid the ruins of his city, who, as shepherd of his flock, was in the year 451 to outface the Hun Attila at the gate of Rome and by outfacing him—somehow, with some power unexplained—actually cause him to retreat: this Leo was not the man to leave the papal claim unasserted. And the Orient, aware of his stature, replied at Chalcedon with the following challenge, known as Canon XXVII. Commencing with a reaffirmation of the findings of the council of Theodosius, the bishops proceeded to their point:

> Following in all things [they declared] the decisions of the holy Fathers and acknowledging the canon, which has just

been read, of the One Hundred and Fifty Bishops beloved-of-
God (who assembled in the Imperial city of Constantinople,
which is New Rome, in the time of the Emperor Theodosius
of happy memory), we also do enact and decree the same
things concerning the privileges of the most holy Church of
Constantinople, which is New Rome. For the Fathers rightly
granted privileges to the throne of Old Rome, because it was
the imperial city. And the One Hundred and Fifty most religious Bishops, actuated by the same consideration, gave
equal privileges to the most holy throne of New Rome, justly
judging that the city which is honored with the Sovereignty and
the Senate, and enjoys equal privileges with the old imperial
Rome, should in ecclesiastical matters also be magnified as she
is, and rank next after her; so that [and here comes the catch]
in the Pontic, the Asian, and the Thracian Dioceses, the metropolitans only, and such bishops also of the Dioceses aforesaid
as are among the barbarians, should be ordained by the aforesaid most holy throne of the most holy church of Constantinople; every metropolitan of the aforesaid Dioceses, together
with the bishops of his province, ordaining his own provincial
bishops, as has been declared by the divine canons; but that,
as has been above said, the metropolitans of the aforesaid
Dioceses should be ordained by the archbishop of Constantinople, after the proper elections have been held according to
custom and have been reported to him.[17]

The Byzantine ideal of the Kingdom of God on Earth, like the
Old Testament ideal of Israel, was political, material, and con-
crete. As Moses to Aaron, so the emperor to the priesthood, in a
state that was itself conceived as the sole vehicle of God's law in the
history of the world. "The pivotal point of the [Byzantine] structure," as Professor Adda B. Bozeman writes in her masterful survey
of the interplay of *Politics and Culture in International History,*
"was the concept of the centralized state, and this concept was
realized by many separate but interlocking institutions of government. Each of these institutions had its own frame of reference because it was designed to serve a particular aspect of the state. But
all, including those concerned with ecclesiastical affairs, proceeded
from the premise that the ultimate success of all government is
dependent upon the proper management of human susceptibilities

rather than upon the faithful obeisance to preconceived theories and images. [18]

Furthermore: "Since the state was generally regarded as the paramount expression of society it was taken for granted that all human activities and values were to be brought into a direct relationship to it. This meant that knowledge was not to be pursued for its own sake alone but also as a service to the state. It meant, in fact, that learning had an official political value, just as faith did." [19] And not only faith, we must add, but the mythology of faith, the awe of faith, and the will to serve.

Robert Eisler, in his encyclopedic study of the symbolism of the kingly robes and thrones of Europe and the world, quotes the following description of the royal presence in Byzantium from the writings of a contemporary visitor:

> By the imperial throne there stood a brazen, gilded tree, whose branches were filled with brazen, gilded birds of various kind, each of which, according to its kind, emitted the notes of a species of bird. And the emperor's throne was itself so contrived that it might appear, now low, now higher, and now mightily exalted. It was guarded, as it were, by lions of prodigious size, whether of bronze or of wood I do not know, but covered all with gold, and these, with lashing tails, open jaws, and moving tongues, emitted roars. I was led before the emperor. But as, at my entry, the lions roared and birds sang, each according to its kind, I was shaken neither with fear nor with awe. When I had thrice prostrated myself in obeisance to the emperor, I raised my head, and the one whom I had seen seated at a moderate height from the floor I now beheld, clothed in different garments seated high up, near the ceiling; and how this had come to pass I could not imagine, if not, perhaps, by some such machine as those by which the boom is hoisted of a wine press.[20]

Dr. Eisler observes that "since Chosroes I is supposed to have had a wonder throne of this kind—with moving stars beneath its canopy—we shall hardly go astray if we assume that the Roman emperor took over this venerable but finally very childish contraption, only in order not to fall behind his Persian rival." The symbolism involved goes back to early Sumerian times, and in the

Middle Ages it passed from Byzantium both to Western Europe and to Russia, largely as a result, we may assume, of its effect upon the emissaries from those barbarous regions to the great court. As Professor Norman H. Baynes suggests in a passage cited to this point by Adda Bozeman:

> Picture for a moment the arrival of a barbarian chieftain from steppe or desert in this Byzantine Court. He has been royally entertained, under the vigilant care of imperial officials he has seen the wonders of the capital, and today he is to have audience with the Emperor. Through a dazzling maze of marble corridors, through chambers rich with mosaic and cloth of gold, through long lines of palace guards in white uniforms, amidst patricians, bishops, generals and senators, to the music of organs and church choirs he passes, supported by eunuchs, until at last oppressed with interminable splendor he falls prostrate in the presence of the silent, motionless, hieratic figure of the Lord of New Rome, the heir of Constantine, seated on the throne of the Caesars: before he can rise, Emperor and throne have been caught aloft, and with vestments changed since last he gazed the sovereign looks down upon him, surely as God regarding mortal men. Who is he, as he hears the roar of the golden lions that surround the throne or the song of the birds on the trees, who is he that he should decline the Emperor's behests? He stays not to think of the mechanism which causes the lions to roar or the birds to sing: he can scarce answer the questions of the logothete speaking for his imperial master: his allegiance is won: he will fight for the Roman Christ and his Empire.[21]

With this ridiculous scene in mind, we discover an unsuspected dimension in Saint Cyril's flattery of such a royal clown as "the image of God on earth."

God in heaven, however, is without a wife. The emperor had an empress. And while the mighty monarch Justinian, who assumed this playful throne in the year 527 A.D., was engaged in the delicate task of sealing mythologically, and thereby politically, the inherited breach with Rome, his immensely powerful, adored spouse, Theodora, began offending Rome by favoring openly her personal friends and intimates, the Monophysites.

"Theodora the Great," let us call her, was anything but a replica of Pulcheria. The daughter of one of the bear-keepers of the Constantinople hippodrome, she had already, through a lurid stage career, achieved something like world renown, when the bachelor prince Justinian, at about the age of thirty-seven, fell hopelessly in love with her beauty, intelligence, and wit. Many historians have suggested that she was a greater political talent than her husband, and that her recognition of the spiritual affinities of Byzantium with the Levant—while he was striving to heal an organic separation of two incompatible culture worlds—would have made the Second Rome a far stronger and more durable stronghold of Christendom than it became as a result of Justinian's misguided course. In any case, the cosmic cloak-and-dagger novel that developed as a consequence of her Levantine talent for political theology was wonderful. Gibbon gives it all in his chapters. The only aspect of essential relevancy here, however, was its effect upon the credo of Pope Vigilius (537–555).

Justinian had assumed his throne at the age of forty-five, in the year 527, and was to reign for thirty-eight years, seven months, and thirteen days. Setting to work immediately to exterminate all remaining pagans, he closed the University of Athens in the second year of his reign, effected multitudes of conversions by imperial decree, and was restrained from a severe persecution of the Monophysites of Egypt only by the soft but fateful hand of his beautiful wife.

In the year 543, under advice from this audacious empress, Justinian issued an edict condemning as heretical the writings of three deceased theologians of the School of Antioch, which it was supposed would serve both to heal the breach with the Monophysites and to force Rome to accord; for the new pope, Vigilius, had been elevated to his station largely through Theodora's influence and was expected to comply with her will. He delayed so long in fulfilling his given word to her to support her husband's edict that Justinian had him kidnaped and brought to Constantinople, where he issued his *Judicatum,* Easter Eve, 548, under force. However, the clergy of the West reacted with such an uproar that Justinian, for the time being, allowed his victim to retract his statement.

Theodora, that year, died of cancer at about the age of forty, and the case rested, with the pope still captive, until at last, in the year 557, Justinian, to force the issue, called the Fifth Ecumenical Council, which Vigilius refused to attend. He produced, instead, his own unsatisfactory document known as the *Constitutum ad Imperatorem,* in which he condemned only sixty passages of but one of the Antioch theologians and not the author himself, on the ground that it was not customary to condemn the dead. Nor would he condemn even the works of the other two, on the ground that they had both been declared free of heresy at the Council of Chalcedon. Justinian's council, on the other hand, thereupon condemned not only the works and authors in question but also the captive pope; and, thoroughly undone, the poor man finally joined his name to theirs and, permitted to return to his see, died in Syracuse on the way.[22]

PHASE THREE (630–680)

The last chapter of this tale of Shehrzad opened eight long decades later, in the reign of the Emperor Heraclius (r. 610–641), when the patriarch of Constantinople, Sergius, offered a formula that he believed would finally resolve the entire mytho-political broil; namely, of a single "energy" in Christ behind his two "natures" and operating through each. Heraclius, the emperor, thought the idea promising, and when the Monophysites of Alexandria accepted it, in the year 633, an optimistic letter was sent to the pope —now Pope Honorius (625–638)—who accepted it as well, suggesting, however, the term "will" instead of "energy." Thus everything seemed solved, with Byzantium, Rome, and Alexandria finally in accord, when, alas, a new county was heard from. The patriarch Sophronius of Jerusalem took it upon himself to issue a vigorous synodical letter, declaring the single-"energy" theory to be tantamount to Monophysitism, and all went again into motion: Church, Empire, and all.

In 638 the emperor, through his patriarch Sergius, proclaimed the orthodoxy of the doctrine of a single "will," prohibiting the use of the term "one energy" as well as the doctrine of "two wills."

In both East and West a hurricane of protests arose, and the following emperor, Constans II (r. 641–668), simply forbade discussion of the matter. However, a bold new pope, Martin (649–654), defiantly summoned a council in Rome and condemned both the "one will" doctrine of his predecessor and the prohibition of discussion by the emperor; for which diligence he was kidnaped, conveyed to Constantinople, exposed to public gaze, stripped all but naked, and, with a chain around his neck and a sword held in front of him, dragged over rough stones to a common prison to be beheaded. Reprieved, he was banished to the Crimea, where, as a result of the maltreatment, he expired.[23]

The ultimate word then had to wait for the Sixth Ecumenical Council, of the year 680, when the doctrine of "two natures" was confirmed, and the entire cast of characters of the earlier "one will" compromise, along with all the great Monophysites, were condemned.[24]

However, a new and much less complex theology had already been cried forth from Araby: *Lā ilāha illa 'llāh;* and one can readily understand that by now this simple cry, "There is no god but God," would have had considerable appeal. The shout took away the entire Near East within two blazing decades and, flying the breadth of North Africa, overran Spain in 711. By 732 it was on the point of engulfing France, when there eventuated another of those moments—as of Marathon and the Maccabees—when the limit of an East-West-East-West-East pendulation was attained. For, as every such moment has shown, there is a point beyond which the character of an invaded major culture province cannot be contravened. And this arrived, this time, in Europe, at the Battle of Poitiers, when the Frankish king Charles the Hammer smote the criers of Islam back to the Pyrenees.

III. The Prophet of Islam

In the name of God, most gracious, most merciful,
Praise be to God, the cherisher and sustainer of the worlds:
most gracious and most merciful, Master of the Day of Judgment.

Thee do we worship and Thine aid do we seek. Show us the way that is straight, the way of those on whom Thou hast bestowed Thy grace, whose portion is not wrath, and who go not astray.[25]

We are reading the Holy Koran. The text continues with a version of the biblical creation myth and Fall.

Behold, the Lord said to the angels: "I will create a vice-regent on earth." They said: "Will you place therein one who will make mischief and shed blood, while we are celebrating your praises and glorifying your name?" He said: "I know what you do not know."

He taught Adam the names of all things, then placed these before the angels; and he said: "Tell me the names of these, if you are knowing." But they answered: "Glory be to Yourself! We have no knowledge but what you have taught us. Truly it is you who are both in knowledge and in wisdom perfect." He said: "O Adam! Announce to them the names." And when he had done so, God said: "Did I not declare to you that I know the secrets of the heavens and of earth, and know what you yourselves reveal and what you conceal?"

And behold, We said to the angels: "Bow down to Adam!" They bowed. Not so, however, Iblis, who refused. He was haughty. He was of those who reject the faith. We said: "O Adam, dwell—both you and your wife—in the Garden. Eat of the bounty therein as you will, but approach not to this tree, lest you approach darkness and transgression." Satan then made them slip from it and caused their banishment from the place in which they were.*

We said: "Get you down! There shall be enmity between

* *Iblis*, "the Calumniator," with the root idea of rebellion; *Satan*, "the Hater," with the root idea of perversity or enmity. These are two names of the Power of Evil, the Koranic counterpart of Zoroastrian Angra Mainyu.

We read in a later verse of the Koran that Iblis was a jinni: "He was one of the jinn, and he broke the command of his Lord" (15:50). The present text implies, however, that Iblis was an angel. Jinn are the old desert demons of the pre-Mohammedan Arabs, taken over by Islam, whereas angels derive from the biblical-Zoroastrian side of the inheritance. "God," we read in the Koran, "created man, like pottery, from sounding clay, and he created jinn from fire free from smoke" (55:14–15). The jinn are of two kinds: those who have accepted, and those who have rejected, Islam. The Power of Evil, Iblis, can be interpreted, therefore, either as a fallen angel or as an unconverted jinni. There will be more to tell of Iblis.

you. On earth shall be your dwelling place and your provision, for a certain time." Adam learned from his Lord the words of prayer and his Lord turned to him; for he is oft-returning and most merciful. We said: "Get you down from here, all together. And if—as is certain—guidance comes to you from me, whosoever shall follow my guidance, on him shall be no fear, nor shall he grieve. But those who reject the Faith and regard our signs as false: these shall be companions of the fire, and in it they shall abide." [26]

It is obvious that in every syllable Islam is a continuation of the Zoroastrian-Jewish-Christian heritage, restored (as it is claimed) to its proper sense and carried (as it is further claimed) to its ultimate formulation. The whole legend of the patriarchs and the Exodus, golden calf, water from the rock, revelation on Mount Sinai, etc., is rehearsed with its lessons time and time again throughout the Koran, as are, also, certain portions of the Christian myth.

The basic Koranic origin legend is of a descent of both the Arabs and the Jews from the seed of Abraham, of whom it is told already in the Bible that he had two wives, Sarah and Hagar, of whom Hagar, an Egyptian slave woman, was the first to conceive: and she bore Ishmael to Abraham, who then was eighty-six years old. But when Abraham was ninety-nine years old, Sarah, his first wife, conceived and bore Isaac.

And the child grew [we read in the Book of Genesis] and was weaned; and Abraham made a great feast on the day that Isaac was weaned. But Sarah saw the son of Hagar the Egyptian, whom she had born to Abraham, playing with her son Isaac. So she said to Abraham, "Cast out this slave woman with her son; for the son of this slave woman shall not be heir with my son Isaac." And the thing was very displeasing to Abraham on account of his son. But God said to Abraham, "Be not displeased because of the lad and because of your slave woman; whatever Sarah says to you, do as she tells you, for through Isaac shall your descendants be named. And I will make a nation of the son of the slave woman also, because he is your offspring." So Abraham rose early in the morning, and took bread and a skin of water and gave it to Hagar, putting it on her shoulder, along with the child, and sent her away.

And she departed, and wandered in the wilderness of Beer-sheba.[27]

According to the Koranic version of this ancient family history, Abraham and Ishmael built the Kaaba of the Great Mosque of Mecca some years before this separation took place. "And remember," it is there stated,

> Abraham and Ishmael raised the foundations of the House with this prayer: "O Lord! Accept from us this service; for Thou art the All-hearing, the All-knowing. O Lord! Make of us Moslems, bowing to Thy Will, and of our progeny a Moslem people, bowing to Thy Will. Show us our places for the celebration of due rites. And turn to us; for Thou art the oft-returning, most Merciful." [28]

Furthermore, not only Abraham and his sons, but also Jacob and his sons were Moslems. "Were you witness," the text continues, "when Death appeared before Jacob? Behold, he said to his sons: 'What will you worship after me?' They said: 'Your God we shall worship, and the God of your fathers, of Abraham, Ishmael, and Isaac: the One true God: to Him we bow in Islam.' " [29]

The uninstructed reader will perhaps ask: "How then am I to believe this bit of news, which I never heard before?" And the answer will be such as every Jew or Christian surely will recognize; namely that the Book (here, however, the Koran) is revealed of God.

"Or do you say," we read, "that Abraham, Ishmael, Isaac, Jacob and the Tribes were Jews or Christians? Say: Do you know better than God? Ah, who is more unjust than those who conceal the testimony they have received from God? But God is not unmindful of what they do!" [30]

"The People of the Book," as the Jews are termed in the Koran, are declared to have closed their eyes to the confirmation of their own heritage when they rejected the message of Islam; and the Christians, with their trinitarian doctrines, added gods unto God, misreading the words of their own prophet Jesus, which are to be understood directly in the line of Abraham, Moses, Solomon, and Mohammed.

"O Children of Israel!" God now calls to the Jews. "Call to mind the special favor that I bestowed on you, and fulfill your Covenant with me as I fulfill mine with you. Fear none but me. And believe what I now reveal, confirming the revelation that is with you: and be not the first to reject faith therein. Neither sell my signs for a small price. Fear me, and me alone!" [31]

> We gave Moses the Book and followed him with a succession of messengers. We gave to Jesus, son of Mary, clear signs of his mission and strengthened him with the holy spirit. Is it, then, that whenever a messenger comes to you with what you yourselves do not desire, you puff yourselves up with pride? Some you called impostors; others you kill!—They say: "Our hearts are the wrappings that preserve God's Word: we need no more." Nay, God has cursed them for their blasphemy: little is it they believe.[32]

It is not exactly known how the Koran was received from heaven and written down. In fact, the greater part of Mohammed's life is a matter of conjecture. The basic biography, by a certain Mohammed ibn Ishaq, was written for the Caliph Mansur (r. 754–775) more than a century after the Prophet's death; and this work itself is known only as preserved in two still later writings, the Compendium of Ibn Hisham (d. 840 A.D.) and the Chronicle of Tabiri (d. 932 A.D.). In brief, the biography, as reconstructed, falls naturally into four main periods.[33]

1. CHILDHOOD, YOUTH, MARRIAGE, AND FIRST CALL: C. 570–610 A.D.

Born at Mecca to a family of the powerful Kuraish tribe, the child was bereaved of its father shortly after birth and of its mother but a few years later. Reared by relatives of little means but with numerous children, the youth, when about twenty-four, entered the service of a wealthy woman named Khadija, older than himself, twice married and with several children, who sent him to Syria on a commercial mission, from which he returned to become her husband. She bore him two sons, both of whom died in infancy, and several daughters.

In his fortieth year Mohammed began receiving revelations, of which the first is said to have been that of Sura 96: "Proclaim! In the name of thy Lord and Cherisher, who created, created man from a clot of blood: Proclaim! For thy Lord is most bountiful, who has taught man the use of the pen—taught man what he knew not before!" [34]

The accepted Moslem legend tells that this revelation came to Mohammed in a cave in the side of Mount Hira, three miles north of Mecca, to which he used to retire for peaceful contemplation—often alone, but sometimes with Khadija. As we read in one retelling, he was there pondering the mystery of man of corruptible flesh when a dazzling vision of beauty and light overpowered his soul and senses, and he heard the word, "Proclaim!" He was confused and terrified; but the cry rang clear, three times, until the first overpowering confusion yielded to a collected realization of his mission. Its author was God; its subject, man, God's creature; and its instrument, the pen, the sanctified Book, which men were to read, study, recite, and treasure in their souls.

His soul was filled with divine ecstasy; but when this passed he returned to the world of time and circumstance, which now seemed dark tenfold. His limbs were seized with a violent trembling and he turned straightway to the one who shared his life, Khadija, who understood, rejoiced, gave comfort to his shaken nerves, and knew it had been no mere illusion. She consulted her cousin, Waraka ibn Naufal, who was a worshiper of God in the faith of Christ; and when he heard, he rejoiced as well, and Khadija returned to her husband.

"O Chosen One," she said, "may you be blessed! Do we not see your inner life, true and pure? Do not all see your outer life: kind and gentle, loyal to kin, hospitable to strangers? No thought of ill or malice ever has stained your mind; no word that was not true and did not quiet the passions of narrower men has ever passed your lips. Ever ready in the service of God, you are he of whom I bear witness: There is no god but God, and you are his Chosen Apostle." [35]

2. THE FIRST CIRCLE OF FRIENDS:
c. 610–613 A.D.

For three years Mohammed and Khadija engaged in private propaganda, first in the family and among friends, then among neighbors. Mecca, their city, was a prosperous trading station in a barren valley, some fifty miles inland from the Red Sea. In its center stood a perfectly rectangular stone hut, known as the Kaaba, the "Cube," containing an image of the patron god, Hubal, as well as some other sacred objects, besides the black stone, possibly of meteoric origin, that is today the central object of the entire Islamic world. This stone is now said to have been given by Gabriel to Abraham; and its hut, to have been the house that Abraham constructed with the aid of Ishmael. And in fact, even before Mohammed's time the whole region around Mecca was regarded as a place of sanctity. An annual festival took place there, to which crowds streamed from all quarters; and many of those who came paid visits to the Kaaba.

One of the literary problems of the Koran is the source of the biblical lore that abounds in it, derived largely from the Christian side, and of a distinctly Nestorian cast; for tradition holds that the Prophet was unable to read. However, certainly from childhood he must have been made aware of many types of religion: principally, of course, the tribal and regional cults of the Arabs, but also Christianity, Judaism, and perhaps Zoroastrianism as well. Some two hundred miles to the north, in Medina, was a large community of Jews. Directly across the Red Sea, in Ethiopia, was a Coptic Christian kingdom. His wife's cousin, Waraka, was a Christian, probably of Monophysite persuasion. And the great trading routes from north to south, down the Red Sea and across to India, had for centuries been bearing philosophers, missionaries, and other men of learning, as well as merchants, back and forth.

One need only suppose a boyhood and youth of alert interest in the oral lore and religious life round about: a little pitcher with big ears; and then a youth of high intelligence, ardent religious sensibilities, and an extraordinary capacity for extended periods of

auditory trance: a youth of great physical strength and persuasive
presence, furthermore, as the later episodes of his biography prove.
And as a rock loosed from a snowy peak, gathering snow in descent,
may grow into an avalanche, so the enterprise of Mohammed and
Khadija. Among their first converts were Mohammed's young
cousin, Ali, who would later become his son-in-law; an older, sturdy
friend (though a member of another clan), the wealthy Abu Bakr;
and a faithful servant of Khadija's house, Zaid.

As the legend tells:

> Khadija believed, above all women exalted in faith. Ali the
> well beloved, then a child of but ten, yet lion-hearted, plighted
> faith and became from that instant the right hand of Islam.
> Then Abu Bakr, sincere and true-hearted, a man of wealth
> and influence, who used both without stint for the cause,
> joined as sober counselor and inseparable friend. And Zaid,
> the freedman of Mohammed, counted freedom as naught com-
> pared with the service of God. These were the first fruits of
> the mission: a woman, a child, a man of wealth, and a freed-
> man, banded in equality in Islam.[36]

3. THE GATHERING COMMUNITY IN MECCA: C. 613–622 A.D.

> O thou, folded in garments! Stand to prayer by night, but
> not all night—half, or a little less, or a little more: and in
> slow, measured, rhythmic tones, say forth the Koran. For soon
> We shall send down to thee a weighty message.[37]

These imposing lines of Sura 73 are supposed to represent the
second recorded revelation given to Mohammed, which is believed
to have come only some time after the first—perhaps two years,
perhaps six months—and again, as it is supposed, in the cave.

The term "folded in garments" (*muzzamil*), which is one of the
titles of the Prophet, is to be understood in several senses. Literally,
it refers to the physical state of the Prophet in his arduous moments
of trance-ecstasy, when, according to tradition, he would lie or sit,
wrapped in a blanket, uttering divine verses while copiously per-
spiring. A second meaning, however, is referred to every Moslem at
prayer. Like the Prophet of pure heart, each is to be "properly

dressed for prayer: folded in a mantle, as one renouncing the vanities of this world." And finally, on the mystic plane, by the mantle we may understand the outward wrappings of phenomenality, which are essential to existence, but are presently to be outgrown, whereupon one's inner nature is to proclaim itself with all boldness.[38] In the next Sura this image is continued:

> O thou, wrapped in a mantle! Arise, and deliver thy warning! Do thou magnify thy Lord. Keep thy garments free from stain and shun abominations! Nor expect, when giving, any increase to thyself, but, for the Lord's cause, be patient and be constant! That will be—that Day—a Day of Distress, far from easy for those without faith.[39]

The old apocalyptic sense of the coming Day of Judgment filled the message of the Prophet with the urgency of immediate event. We do not know what other prophetic movements may have been stirring in the Arab world of the time. Ecstatics of one type or another surely abounded, then, as now. And there were, besides, prophets of a type known as Hanifs, who represented, in various ways, the influence of a general monotheistic trend deriving from the Zoroastrian, Jewish, and Christian centers round about. Khadija's relative, Waraka ibn Naufal, may have been one of these. Another was the Meccan Zaid ibn 'Amr, who appears to have died during Mohammed's boyhood.[40] In any case, there were in Mecca people enough in Mohammed's time prepared to respond to the call of a prophetic voice to constitute, within a few years, a typical Magian consensus, ready to make the world over in its own image.

The first large group to whom Mohammed's message was addressed was the membership of his own large and influential tribe. The Kuraish were custodians of the Kaaba and a leading folk of the region. He called upon them to eliminate all pagan images from their sanctuary and to recognize their deity as the One God of Islam. An early Sura, dating from this period so adjures them:

> In gratitude for the covenants of divine protection and security enjoyed by the Kuraish—their covenants covering journeys by winter and by summer—let them adore the Lord of this House [the Kaaba], who provides them with food against hunger and security against fear.[41]

The fervor of the Prophet's increasing group provoked, in time, reactions among those of the city for whom the old deities of their tribe and the prospects of trade were life concerns enough. And these presently became so strong that Islam could be thought of by its membership as a persecuted sect—with all the advantages to group solidarity and zeal that stem from such a circumstance. Mohammed, to protect his company, shipped them across the Red Sea to Axum, in Christian Abyssinia, where the king welcomed them with such sympathy that the population of Mecca began to have cause to fear that the nightmare of an earlier series of Abyssinian raids and devastations might be repeated. The Prophet himself, remaining in Mecca, was abused, reviled, and in deep trouble. And it was at about this time that he was joined—providentially— by a new and wonderful convert, the young and brilliant Omar ('Umar ibn al-Khaṭṭab), a youth who, up to that time, had been publicly opposed to the new faith, but was now—as a kind of Paul —to become its most effective leader.

However, a great and deep sorrow fell upon the already troubled Prophet when his beloved wife, Khadija, passed away: "the great, the noble lady," as she had been termed in appropriate praise,

> who had befriended him when he had been without resource, trusted him when his worth had been little known, encouraged and understood him in his spiritual struggles, and believed in him with trembling steps when he took up the Call. She withstood obloquy, persecution, insults, threats, and torment, till she was gathered to the saints in his fifty-first year: a perfect woman, she was the mother of those who believe.[42]

Then came, marvelously, the miracle: the sounding, as it were, of the muezzin cry of planetary destiny, announcing the dawn of a new world age. For a summons came to Mohammed from the city of Medina, two hundred miles to the north, where strife between the two leading Arab tribes, the Aus and the Khazraj, had brought things to such a pass that a body of leading citizens begged Mohammed to come and exert his influence to restore peace. It was feared that the considerable Jewish community there, constituted largely of converted Arabs, might gain the ascendancy if the Arab feud went on. Mohammed, sensibly, sent his whole community ahead, and then, late in the epochal year of 622 A.D., made his own secret escape, together with Abu Bakr, from Mecca to Medina, hiding for some days, on the way, in his cave.

> For [as we read in the Koran] God did indeed help him, when the Unbelievers drove him out. He had no more than one companion. These two were in the Cave, and he said to his companion: "Have no fear, for God is with us." God sent down his peace upon him, and strengthened him with forces that were invisible, and humbled to the depths the word of the Unbelievers. But the word of God is exalted to the heights. God is exalted in might and most wise.[43]

4. MOHAMMED IN MEDINA: 622–632 A.D.

The "Emigration" or Hegira (Arabic, *hijrah,* "flight") of the Prophet to Medina marks the opening of the year from which all Mohammedan dates are reckoned; for it represents the passage of the Law of Islam from the status of theory to practice and to manifestation in the field of history. At Medina, as Professor H. A. R. Gibb has pointed out, Mohammed sat astride Mecca's vital trade route to the north, and for seven years made brilliant use of this advantage to break the resistance of the oligarchy of his city.[44] First, operating as a mere brigand, he captured caravans and enriched the new community under God with booty taken from its neighbors. Next, as a brilliant generalissimo, he met and defeated (often with angelic aid) * larger forces than his own, sent against him by the desperate merchants of his native place. And finally, having won to his side a number of the Bedouin tribes, he returned to Mecca unopposed, in the year 630, and with a grand symbolic sweep established the new order by destroying every idol in the city. One of the local goddesses, Na'ila, is said to have appeared at this time in the form of a black woman, and to have fled away

---

* As Constantine and his army had seen the "Shining Cross" before the crucial defeat of Maximian (supra, pp. 385–86), so Mohammed and his army, during the crucial battle at Badr, saw the angels giving them aid. The turbans of all except Gabriel were white, whereas his, according to eye witnesses, was yellow. (A. A. Bevan, "Mahomet and Islam" in *The Cambridge Medieval History,* Vol. II, p. 318, note 1, citing Ibn Hisham).

shrieking.[45] But the black stone of the Kaaba remained—which was originally white, we are told; for it is one of the stones of Paradise, turned black by the kisses of sinful lips.[46]

However, at the summit of victory, the Prophet, two years later, passed away—to his eternal home, as we may suppose, where the golden Koran of his vision shines forever. And thereon is written of God:

> Not merely in idle sport did We create the heavens, earth, and all between, but for just ends. However, most do not understand. Verily, the Day of Sorting Out is the day appointed for them all, the day when no protector shall avail his client and no help shall any receive except such as receive God's Mercy: for He is exalted in might, the Most Merciful.
>
> Verily, the Tree of Hell, Zakkum it is called, will afford the food of the sinful. Like molten brass it will boil in their insides, like the boiling of scalding water. And a voice shall cry out, "Seize him! Drag him into the midst of the Blazing Fire, pour over his head the penalty of Boiling Water! Taste this! Mighty and full of honor you were! And, indeed, it was this you doubted!"
>
> But as to the righteous, they shall be in a place of security, among gardens, among springs. Dressed in finest silk and in rich brocade, they will greet each other. So it shall be! And We will join to them Companions with beautiful, big, lustrous eyes. There can they call for every kind of fruit in security and peace. Nor shall they there taste death, except the first death. And We shall preserve them from the Blazing Fire. As a boon from your Lord, that will be the supreme achievement!
>
> Moreover, We have made the Koran easy: in your own tongue, that all may heed. So watch and wait: for they are waiting too.[47]

iv. The Garment of the Law

The mask of God named Allah is a product of the same desert from which the mask Yahweh had come centuries before. In fact, the word *Yahweh,* as Professor Meek has shown,* is not of Hebrew but of Arabic source. Hence we are forced, to some extent, to agree with Mohammed's startling claim that people of his own

---

* Supra, pp. 132–33.

Semitic stock were the first worshipers of the God proclaimed in the Bible.

As a god of Semitic desert folk, Allah reveals, like Yahweh, the features of a typical Semitic tribal deity, the first and most important of which is that of not being immanent in nature but transcendent. Such gods are not to be known through any scrutiny of the natural order, whether external (as through science) or internal (through meditation); for nature, whether without or within, does not contain them. And the second trait is a function of the first. It is, namely, that for each Semitic tribe the chief god is the protector and lawgiver of the local group, and that alone. He is made known, not in the sun, the moon, the cosmic order, but in the local laws and customs—which differ, of course, from group to group. Hence, whereas among the Aryans, for whom the chief gods were those of nature, there was always and everywhere a tendency to recognize one's own divinities in alien cults, a tendency toward syncretism, the tendency of Semites in the worship of their tribal gods has always been toward exclusivism, separatism, and intolerance.

On the primitive level there is no requirement, or even possibility, that a local tribal god should be regarded as lord of the entire world. Each group has simply its own lawgiver and patron; the rest of the world—if there is such a thing—can take care of itself, under its own gods; for each people is supposed to have a divine lawgiver and patron of its own. We call such thought *monalatry.** And accordingly, during the first long and terrible phase of the Israelite occupation of Canaan, Yahweh was conceived simply as a tribal god more powerful than the rest.

The next epochal phase of the biblical development occurred when the god so regarded became identified with the god-creator of the universe. No nation of all those on earth but Israel could then claim to know and worship, or to be the concern of, this one true God of all.

> Thus says the Lord: "Learn not the way of the nations, nor be dismayed at the signs of the heavens because the nations are dismayed at them, for the customs of the peoples are false."

* Cf. supra, p. 242.

. . . There is none like thee, O Yahweh; thou art great, and thy name is great in might. Who would not fear thee, O King of the nations? For this is thy due; for among all the wise ones of the nations and in all their kingdoms there is none like thee. They are both stupid and foolish; the instruction of idols is but wood! . . . But Yahweh is the true God.[48]

Ironically, the concept of this god of cosmic stature did not occur to the desert Habiru until they had entered the higher culture sphere of the settled civilizations, where writing had been known for millenniums and mathematical records kept of the movements not only of the general heavens but even of the planets amid them. The cosmic order as understood by the priests of those High Bronze Age civilizations had been of a marvelously mathematical regularity, ever revolving, ever rising into being and declining into chaos, according to fixed laws of which the priestly watchers of the stars were the first to know. And the ultimate ground of this rhythm of being had not been represented as a willful personality: such a god, for example, as Yahweh. On the contrary: personality, will, mercy, and wrath had in these systems been only secondary to an absolutely impersonal, ever-grinding order, of which the gods—all gods —were the mere agents.

In dramatic, unresolvable contrast to this view, the peoples of the Semitic desert complex held to their own tribal patrons when they entered the higher culture field; and, although accepting, roughly, the idea of a cosmic order, instead of submitting their own god to it they made him its originator and support—though in no sense its immanent being. For he was still, as ever, an entity apart: personal, anthropomorphic. And he was to be known, furthermore, even as in the tribal desert days, only through the social laws of his still solely favored group. Not the laws of nature, open to all eyes and minds with the wit to observe and to think, but uniquely the laws of this particular social molecule in the vast and teeming history of humanity, were to be known as rendering the one sole lesson of God. Hence the warning of Jeremiah not "to be dismayed at the signs of the heavens because the nations are dismayed at them, for the customs of the people are false," and of Mohammed: "We see the turning of thy face for guidance to the heavens: now shall We turn thee to a *qibla* * that shall please thee. Turn then thy face toward the sacred Mosque. Wherever you are, turn your face in that direction." [49] "If anyone desires a religion other than Islam, never will it be accepted of him; and in the Hereafter he will be in the ranks of those who have lost." [50]

Certain differences obtain, however, between the biblical and Koranic concepts of the group favored of God and the character of God's law, the first and most obvious of these being that whereas the Old Testament community was tribal, the Koran was addressed to mankind. Islam, like Buddhism and Christianity, was in concept a world religion, whereas Judaism, like Hinduism, remained in concept as well as in fact an ethnic form. For in Mohammed's day the Alexandrian vision of humanity had reached even the peoples of the desert. "Aliens," the Hebrew Isaiah had declared, "shall stand and feed your flocks, foreigners shall be your plowmen and vinedressers; but you shall be called the priests of Yahweh, men shall speak of you as the ministers of our God; you shall eat the wealth of nations, and in their riches you shall glory." [51] In clear contrast, there is no tribe or race triumphant in the Koran, but absolute equality in Islam. "Verily," says the Book, "in this there is a message for any that has a heart and understanding, or gives ear and earnestly witnesses the truth." [52] The desert concept of the one authentic social order under its god had become magnified to match the new knowledge of a larger world.

And yet, a certain difficulty followed. For the laws of God, as conceived under the earlier desert revelation of Yahweh, had been the mores of an actual society in being, whereas the laws of God as conceived in Islam were to be derived from a series of utterances emitted in a state of trance by a single individual in the course of but twenty-three years; and to enlarge these to a viable system for a living world community was to be a feat of unmatched temerity —which, *mirabile dictu,* was achieved.

* *Qibla:* the direction of address of prayer. For Islam the *qibla* is the Kaaba of the Great Mosque of Mecca, which is not a "natural" but a socio-historical symbol, referring specifically to the history and legend of Islam itself.

In the invention of this Moslem legal order three controls were recognized, of which the first was, of course, the Koran itself. Where there were clearly stated commands and prohibitions in the Koran, these precluded argument and were to be unquestionably obeyed. There were contingencies not so covered, however, and for these the Moslem jurists had to establish other "roots." Their second support, therefore, was a marginal body of tradition called the "statements" or *hadīth*. These were anecdotes about the Prophet, supposed to have been related by one or another of his immediate companions. A vast body of such "statements" came into being during the first two or three centuries of Islam, and the most trustworthy were collected in canonical editions—notably those of al-Bukhari (d. 870) and Moslem (d. 875)—which then, as Professor H. A. R. Gibb has shown, "rapidly acquired almost canonical authority." [53]

Yet, in practice, points of law still arose that were not covered by any clear statement either in Koran or in Hadith, and to deal with these, decisions were determined by "analogy" (*qiyās*), which is to say (to quote again Professor Gibb), "the application to a new problem of the principles underlying an existing decision on some other point which could be regarded as on all fours with the new problem."

Professor Gibb continues:

> On this apparently narrow and literalist basis the theologians and lawyers of the second and third centuries worked out not only the law, but also the rituals and the doctrines, which were to be the special property of the Islamic community, in distinction from other religions and social organizations. Yet the narrowness is more apparent in theory than in practice, for . . . a great deal became naturalized in Islam from outside sources through the medium of traditions claiming to emanate from the Prophet and in other ways.
>
> But because the principles on which this logical structure was built up were immutable, so also the system itself, once formulated, was held to be immutable, and indeed to be as divinely inspired as the sources from which it was drawn. From that day to this, the *Sharī'a* or *Shar'*, as it is called, the

"Highway" of divine command and guidance, has remained in essentials unchanged.[54]

Spengler, comparing this approach to law with the Classical, states that

Whereas the Classical law was made by burghers on the basis of practical experience, the Arabian came from God, who manifested it through the intellect of chosen and enlightened men. . . . The authoritativeness of Classical laws rests upon their success, that of the Arabian on the majesty of the name that they bear. But it matters very considerably indeed in a man's feelings whether he regards law as an expression of some fellow man's will or as an element of the divine dispensation. In the one case he either sees for himself that the law is right or else yields to force, but in the other he devoutly acknowledges (*Islām*). The Oriental does not ask to see either the practical object of the law that is applied to him or the logical grounds of its judgments. The relation of the cadi to the people, therefore, has nothing in common with that of the praetor to the citizens. The latter bases his decisions upon an insight trained and tested in high positions, the former upon a spirit that is effective and immanent in him and speaks through his mouth. But it follows from this that their respective relations to written law—the praetor to his edict, the cadi to the jurist's texts—must be entirely different. It is a quintessence of concentrated experience that the praetor makes his own, but the texts are a sort of oracle that the cadi esoterically questions. It does not matter in the least to the cadi what a passage originally meant or why it was framed. He consults the words—*even the letters*—and he does so not at all for their everyday meanings, but for the *magic* relations in which they must stand toward the case before him. We know this relation of the "spirit" to the "letter" from the Gnosis, from the early Christian, Jewish, and Persian apocalyptic and mystical literature, from the Neopythagorean philosophy, from the Kabbalah; and there is not the slightest doubt that the Latin codices were used in exactly the same way in the minor judicial practice of the Aramaean world. The conviction that the letters contain secret meanings, penetrated with the Spirit of God, finds imaginative expression in the fact that all religions of the Arabian world formed scripts of their own. in which the holy books had to be written and which maintained themselves with astounding tenacity as badges of the respective "Nations" even after changes of language.[55]

Both Gibb and Spengler, as well as everyone else who has ever written seriously of Islam, point out, furthermore, that the body of tradition (*sharī'a,* the "highway") that has been wrought through the interaction of the precepts of the Koran (*kitāb,* the "book"), the sayings of tradition (*hadīth*), and extensions by analogy (*qiyās*), is supposed to be an exact expression of the infallibilty of the group (*ijmā',* "consensus") in all matters touching faith and morals. "It is one of the boasts of Islam," writes Professor Gibb,

> that it does not countenance the existence of a clergy, who might claim to intervene between God and man. True as this is, however, Islam, as it became organized into a system, did in fact produce a clerical class, which acquired precisely the same kind of social and religious authority and prestige as the clergy in the Christian communities. This was the class of the *Ulamā,* the "learned" or the "doctors," corresponding to the "scribes" in Judaism. Given the sanctity of Koran and Tradition and the necessity of a class of persons professionally occupied with their interpretation, the emergence of the Ulama was a natural and inevitable development, though the influence of the older religious communities may have assisted the rapid establishment of their social and religious authority.
>
> As their authority became more firmly held and more generally conceded by the public opinion of the community the class of Ulama claimed (and were generally recognized) to represent the community in all matters relating to faith and law, more particularly against the authority of the State. At an early date—probably some time in the second century [of Islam]—the principle was secured that the "consensus of the community" (which in practice meant that of the Ulama) had binding force. *Ijmā'* was thus brought into the armory of the theologians and jurists to fill up all the remaining gaps in their system. As the Tradition was the integration of the Koran, so the consensus of scholars became the integration of the Tradition.
>
> Indeed, on a strict logical analysis, it is obvious that *ijmā'* underlies the whole imposing structure and alone gives it final validity. For it is *ijmā'* in the first place which guarantees

the authenticity of the text of the Koran and of the Traditions. It is *ijmā'* which determines how the words of their texts are to be pronounced and what they mean and in what direction they are to be applied. But *ijmā'* goes much farther; it is erected into a theory of infallibility, a third channel of revelation. The spiritual prerogatives of the Prophet—the Muslim writers speak of them as the "light of Prophecy"—were inherited not by his successors in the temporal government of the community, the Caliphs, but by the community as a whole. . . .

When, therefore, a consensus of opinions had been attained by the scholars of the second and third centuries on any given point, the promulgation of new ideas on the exposition of the relevant texts of the Koran and Hadith was as good as forbidden. Their decisions were irrevocable. The right of individual interpretation (*ijtihād*) was in theory (and very largely in practice also) confined to the points on which no general agreement had yet been reached. As these were narrowed down from generation to generation, the scholars of later centuries were limited to commenting and explaining the treatises in which those decisions were recorded. The great majority of Muslim doctors held that the "gate of *Ijtihād*" was shut once and for all and that no scholar, however eminent, could henceforth qualify as a *mujtahid,* an authoritative interpreter of the law; although some few later theologians did from time to time claim for themselves the right of *ijtihād*.[56]

Professor Gibb points out that there is a certain analogy between this settlement of doctrine by "consensus" in Islam and the councils of the Christian Church, in spite of the divergences of outer form, and that in certain respects the results, also, were very similar. "It was, for example," as he states, "only after the general recognition of *ijmā'* as a source of law and doctrine that a definite legal test of 'heresy' was possible and applied." [57] Spengler, too, points out these analogies and, in line with his view of the historic form of the Magian-Levantine spiritual community, interprets them in general contrast to the properly European sense of the value of the individual.

We seek to find truth [he states] each for himself, by personal pondering, but the Arabian savant feels for and ascertains the general conviction of his associates, which cannot err because the mind of God and the mind of the community are the same. If *consensus* is found, truth is established. *Ijmā'* is the key of all Early Christian, Jewish and Persian Councils, but it is the key, too, of the famous Law of Citations of Valentinian III (426), which . . . limits the number of great jurists whose texts were allowed to be cited to five, and thus set up a canon —in the same sense as the Old and New Testaments, both of which also were summations of texts which might be cited as canonical.[58]

In a very interesting way one is reminded also of the councils, purges, manifestoes, and pretensions of the so-called people's governments of the Iron Curtain culture province, where the precepts of the Prophet Marx, reinterpreted by an elite of Ulamas, are put forth as the *ijmā* of a purely mythical entity, the People. Remarkable too is the power of the symbols even of such a clown-parody of the City of God to work upon the nerves of free individuals outside of the geographical control of that consensus, but in whom the Magian system of sentiments still lives. Like the virtue of the Sacraments of the Roman Catholic Church, which are unaffected by the realities of the world, the fall of Christian empires, the personal lives of the clergy, or the total refutation through science of the mythology on which they rest, so, too, the garment of Islam —and now likewise of the People—is of a transcendental order untouched by the realities of time, or by the sins of those upon whose shoulders it descends. As we are warned by the recent prophecy of a London-tailored Indian Moslem poet and philosopher, Sir Mohammed Iqbal (d. 1938), which has been aptly cited in Adda Bozeman's work:

Believe me, Europe today is the greatest hindrance in the way of man's ethical achievement. The Muslim, on the other hand, is in possession of these ultimate ideas on the basis of a revelation, which, speaking from the inmost depths of life, internalizes its own apparent externality. With him the spiritual basis of life is a matter of conviction for which even the least enlightened man among us can easily lay down his life; and in view of the basic idea of Islam that there can be no further revelation binding on man, we ought to be spiritually one of the most emancipated peoples on earth. . . . Let the Muslim today appreciate his position, reconstruct his social life in the light of ultimate principles, and evolve, out of the hitherto partially revealed purposes of Islam, that spiritual democracy which is the ultimate aim of Islam.[59]

One more remark concerning the contrast of the Jewish, Byzantine, Moslem, and Communist conceptions of the ungainsayable consensus: The first three of these four Magian churches obviously are distinguished from the last in as much as their ultimate appeal is to God, whereas the last takes particular pride in its Robert Ingersoll type of hard-skulled late-nineteenth-century atheism: its sacred object, the Worker, is a mythic being supposed to be incarnate in every factory of the world. But this transfer of the mystique of authority from heaven to a supposed social entity on earth simply adjusts to a modern, secular mode of symbolization the shared concept of an authentic law, known only to those of the faithful in whom orthodox knowledge resides, which is to break into full manifestation when the day of days arrives. Meanwhile, the so-called laws of the nations are but delusions, afflicting all in whose hearts the light has not yet dawned.

"But say, then," as we read in the Koran,

> what is the matter with them that they turn away from admonition? As if they were affrighted asses, fleeing from a lion! . . . For those Rejecters we have prepared chains, yokes and a blazing fire. But as to the Righteous: . . . Reclining in the Garden on raised thrones, they will see there neither the sun's excessive heat nor the moon's excessive cold; and the shades of the Garden will come low over them, and the bunches of fruit there will hang low in humility. And amongst them will be passed around vessels of silver and goblets of crystal, crystal-clear, made of silver: they will determine the measure thereof according to their wishes.[60]

The contrast between the Jewish and the other three ideals of the Law, on the other hand, is that between a law derived, in some measure at least, organically from life, the actual experiences of an actual community, and laws spun out of an established text, to be impressed upon, or rendered through, an ideal community to come.

The Jewish is an organic, pliant growth, the others, in contrast, being of a cerebrated, relatively brittle, and—for those standing outside of the system—unconvincing artificiality, or even incredible absurdity, to which their claims to universal application give a threatening turn of terror that far surpasses the merely fairy-tale threat of the Jewish-Apocalyptic Day of the Lord.

v. The Garment of the Mystic Way

God is not subject to the Law, but above it, not to be known or judged in its terms. Consequently, for those in whom a desire to know as well as to serve God burns, there must be a way beyond the Law, as God himself is beyond it, and as the Prophet, Mohammed, gazed beyond.

The term Sunna (*sunnah*) denotes the general, orthodox, conservative body of Islam, for whom the Garment of the Law, as announced and administered by and for the community, the consensus (*ijmā'*), suffices. Two other powerful movements have challenged, however, the absolute authority of this conservative Sunna. They are, first, the Shi'a, also called Shi'ites (Arabic *shī'i*, "a partisan" [of Ali]), whose politically formulated esotericism bears an aggressive anarchistic stamp, and second, the Sufis (Arabic *sūfi*, "man of wool," i.e., wearing a woolen robe, an ascetic), in whose raptures all the normal themes and experiences of both ascetic and antinomian mysticism have come to roost, ironically, in Islam. We have all read Omar Khayyam (d. 1123? A.D.):

> In Paradise, they tell us, Houris dwell,
> And fountains run with wine and oxymal:
>   If these be lawful in the world to come,
> Surely 'tis right to love them here as well. . . .
>
> Heed not the Sunna, nor the law divine:
> If to the poor his portion you assign
>   And never injure one, nor yet abuse,
> I guarantee you heaven, and now some wine! . . .
>
> In taverns better far commune with Thee,
> Than pray in mosques, and fail Thy face to see! [61]

More sternly and threateningly, a like attack was launched by Jalalu'ddin Rumi (1207–1273), the founder of a mystic Whirling Dervish order:

Many are they that do works of devotion and set their hearts on being approved and rewarded for the same. But 'tis in truth a lurking sin: what the pietist thinks pure is really foul.—As in the case of the deaf man who thought he had done a kindness, which, however, had had an opposite effect.

The deaf man sat down well pleased, saying, "I have paid my respects to my sick friend, I have performed what was due to my neighbor"; but he had only kindled a fire of resentment against himself in the invalid's heart and burned himself. Beware, then, of the fire that you have kindled: in truth you have increased in sin. . . .

For the deaf man had said to himself, "Being hard of hearing, how shall I understand the words of the sick neighbor I am going to visit?—Well, when I see his lips moving, I shall, by analogy from myself, form a conjecture as to his meaning. When I ask, 'How are you, O my suffering friend?' he will of course reply, 'I am fine,' or 'I am pretty well.' I shall then say, 'Thanks be to God! What have you had to drink?' He will reply, 'Some sherbet,' or 'A decoction of kidney beans.' Then I shall say, 'May you enjoy health! Who is the doctor attending you?' He will answer, 'So-and-so.' And I shall remark, 'He is one who brings great good fortune; since he has come, all will go well with you. I have myself experienced the benefit of his treatment: wherever he goes, the desired end is attained."

The deaf man, having made ready these reasoned answers, went to visit his sick friend. "How are you?" he asked. "I am at the point of death," the other said. "Thanks be to God!" said the deaf man—at which the patient became resentful and indignant, murmuring to himself, "What cause for thanksgiving is this? He has been my enemy." The deaf man had made a reasonable conjecture, but, as now appears, it proved false. Next he asked what his friend had drunk. "Poison," he said. "May it do you good and bring you health," said the visitor; and the invalid's wrath increased. Then he inquired, "What doctor is attending you?" He answered, "The Angel of Death! Get you gone!" Said the deaf man, "His arrival is a blessing. Rejoice!"

Thus, by analogical reasoning, a ten years' friendship was annulled; and so, likewise, O Master, you must particularly eschew conclusions by analogy, drawn by the lower senses, in regard to Revelation—which is illimitable. Know that if your sensuous ear is tuned to the understanding of the letter of the Revelation, the ear that receives the occult meaning is deaf.[62]

The Shi'a sect goes back for its origin to the period just after the passing of the Prophet, when the question of succession to the headship of Islam was settled by a series of murders.

For the first Companion to be hailed as caliph—largely through the influence of Omar—was the grand old Abu Bakr, who died, however, two years later (634 A.D.), after appointing Omar to succeed. Exception was strongly taken to this exchange by the partisans (shī'i) of Mohammed's cousin Ali, who had married the Prophet's daughter Fatima and fathered Mohammed's two beloved grandsons, Hasan and Husain. Affairs at that time, however, were going exceedingly well for Omar and the cause. A threatening fermentation among the Arab tribes of the peninsula had been quelled by Islamic generals in a brilliant series of battles, after which bold marches against both Persia and the Second Rome brought Syria, Palestine, Iraq, and, presently, all Iran under Moslem rule. The Byzantine army of Heraclius * was shattered in the Yarmuk valley in 636 A.D. Damascus, Baalbek, Emesa, Aleppo, and Antioch were then invested easily; and though the more strongly Hellenized cities of Jerusalem and Caesarea held out longer, they fell, respectively, in 638 and 640. In 637 a Persian army had been routed on the Euphrates, and in 641 Mosul fell. Byzantine Egypt collapsed in 643. And at the height of his glory the Caliph Omar was murdered in 644 by a Persian slave.

This set the whole problem of the caliphate in full play; for instead of designating a successor, Omar had appointed a committee to elect one, composed of Ali, Othman, and four others. Othman was selected. But he survived little more than a decade, to be slain while at prayer, June 17, 655, under circumstances that have led many to suppose connivance from the partisans of Ali.

Othman had been a member of the powerful Umayyad clan,

* Supra, p. 418.

which was an old Meccan family that for years had opposed the Prophet but after his victory had joined his camp and migrated to Medina. One of its distinguished members, Mu'awiya ibn Abu Sufyan, who had been appointed by Omar to be governor of Syria, now engaged in a complicated military and diplomatic battle (actually a family vendetta) for the caliphate against Ali and his sons. Ali claimed the office from his capital, Kufa, in Iraq. However, the Umayyad outmaneuvered him both in war and in devices and in July 660 proclaimed himself caliph in Jerusalem. Ali then was slain by a dagger, January 24, 661, after which his elder son, Hasan, conceded victory in return for a monetary allowance. Hasan died in 669 (said, perhaps falsely, to have been poisoned), and Husain, his brother, was slain in battle, October 10, 680, when he sought to unseat the second Umayyid caliph, Yazid—which date then became the Good Friday, so to say, of the Shi'a. "Revenge for Husain" is the watchword and cry that can still be heard wailed, long and loud, amidst din of ritual keen, throughout those provinces of Islam where the Shi'a lament his martyrdom to this day. The youth is honored almost above the Prophet himself, and his tomb, the Mashhad Husayn, at Kebala in Iraq, where he died, is for the Shi'a the most holy place on earth.

Briefly, the Shi'a position is that the reigning caliphs both of the Umayyad and of the subsequent Abbasid dynasties were usurpers and that, consequently, historic Islam is a falsification: the caliph is a pretender, the Sunna deluded, and the *ijmā'* a false guide. Islam in the proper sense of the Koran resides in the knowledge, lost to the popular community, that passed from the Prophet to Ali and has come down only in the line of the true Imams.

The word *imām* means spiritual leader and is applied generally to leaders of the services of the mosque, and, more specifically, according to Sunna usage, to the founders of the four orthodox theological schools; but by the Shi'a it is applied only to the disinherited, true leaders of the line of Ali and the Prophet. Their known number is but twelve; for somewhere between the years 873 and 880 A.D. the Imam then alive, Mohammed al-Mahdi, disappeared. He is known as the Hidden Imam, is still in this world, and his second coming, as "The Guided One" (*mahdī*), to restore Islam, is awaited by the faithful. A variant view is that the seventh Imam was the one who disappeared; still another names the fifth. Numerous pretenders to the character have emerged, here and there, at various times, to precipitate political upheavals, "the Mad Mullah of Somaliland," for instance, and "the Mahdi of the Sudan," put down by British troops. Many Shi'a sects exist, in all of which esotericism and politics are explosively combined *—the cardinal tenet of all being that both spiritual authority and temporal power properly reside not in the consensus (*ijmā'*) of the Sunna, but in the person of the Hidden Imam, to whom absolute submission is demanded, and in whom alone God is made known. Indeed, in the most extreme of these sects, Ali and his descendant Imams are regarded as incarnations. By all they are held to have been sinless and infallible. And about them there has accumulated an esoteric mythology, shot through with Christian, Gnostic, Manichaean, and Neoplatonic thought, that is excellently illustrated in a myth of World Creation described by the late French master of this lore, Louis Massignon, drawn from a work by one of the early Shi'a leaders in Kufa, named Moghira (d. 736 A.D.).

"In a mythological guise that is only apparently naïve," states Professor Massignon in discussion of this text,

> Moghira presents a Gnostic doctrine that is already in a highly developed stage. God has a form of light and the appearance of a man whose limbs are composed of the letters of the alphabet; and this Light Man has a heart that is the Well of Truth. When he wished to create, he uttered his own supreme name, which flew forth and settled on his head as a crown.

* One may name the *Zaidiyah*, who follow Zaid, the grandson of Husain, as their Imam; the *Isma'ilians*, who are extreme in their attitude of renunciation, secrecy, and service to the Imam; the *Carmatians*, a violent activist variety of Isma'ilian; the *Fatimids*, another such, who established an Egyptian dynasty that ruled from 909 to 1171; the *Assassins*, still another terrorist variety of Isma'ilian, whose Grand Master, known as the Shaikh of the Mountains, terrorized half the Near East until crushed by the Tatars under Hulagu in the year 1256: the Aga Khan is the most recent descendent of the Master. And in the Black Moslem movement now stirring in the United States one may recognize Shi'a inspiration.

Then he wrote on the palms of his hands the deeds of men and was indignant at the sins they were to commit. His indignation broke forth as sweat and formed two oceans, one of salt, the other of sweet water; one dark, the other light. He beheld his own shadow in these, and tore out the shadow's eyes, from which he made the sun and moon—that is to say, Mohammed and Ali. Whereupon he destroyed what remained of his shadow and created everyone else from the two oceans: Believers from the light, Unbelievers from the dark. These he created as shadows; for all of this took place before the creation of the physical world.—God proposed to men that they should recognize Ali as their ruler; but two there were who refused. These were the first Antagonists: Abu Bakr and Omar —unreal shadows of his two eyes on the dark sea.[63]

Generally in Islam the spiritual character of women is rated very low. According to at least one Shi'a text, they were created from the sediment of the sins of demons, to serve as temptations to sinners. They are not admitted to initiations, and are of value only as vehicles for the entry into the world of spirits condemned temporarily to take on flesh in punishment for their sins; they themselves being, however, without soul.[64] And yet, in the mythology of these sects the person of Fatima, Ali's bride, daughter of Mohammed and mother of Hasan and Husain, has been transformed into a being— a divine being—antecedent even to the being of her own father. In a recently found Persian Shi'a text of Gnostic affinities called the Omm-al-Kitab, we find the following astonishing visionary narration:

When God concluded with men a covenant at the time of his creation of the material world, they prayed him to show them Paradise. He showed them, thereupon, a being ornamented with a million varicolored shimmering lights, who sat upon a throne, head crowned, rings in the ears, and a drawn sword at the girdle. The radiating rays illuminated the whole garden; and when the men then asked who this was, they were told it was the form of Fatima as she appears in Paradise: the crown was Mohammed; the earrings, Hasan and Husain; the sword was Ali; and her throne, the Seat of Dominion, was the resting place of God, the Most High.[65]

Fatima is revered by the whole Mohammedan world; for she was the only daughter of the Prophet who bore sons to continue his heritage. She was his favorite and died only a few months after himself. But in certain Shi'a sects her veneration goes to such lengths that she is even termed the "Mother of her Father," "Source of the Sun," and given a masculine name, *Fātir,* signifying "Creator," the numerical value of the letters of which—290—is the same as that of Maryam, Mary, the mother of Jesus. For, as daughter, wife, and mother, she personifies the center of the genealogical mystery; and at least one Shi'a poet has compared her to the Burning Bush of Moses; to the Aqsa Mosque in Jerusalem, where the Prophet is supposed to have experienced his Heaven Journey; and to the Night of Power,[66] when the Angel of Destiny, Gabriel, descending to earth, brought forgiveness to mankind.[67]

The Shi'a, finally, are dualists, and in their abjuration of the state of the world they approach the Gnostic-Docetic point of view.* Persecuted frightfully by the various governments of Islam, they were faced early in their history with the enigma of an evil world in which every loyal lover of God is cruelly destroyed; and from this profound mystery, as Professor Massignon points out, two questions emerged:

1. Does the martyrdom of love entail any actual physical suffering, or is the suffering only apparent? and 2. What happens after death to the willing victim who permits himself, for love, to be condemned in the name of God?

The Koran states of the crucifixion of Jesus that another, and not he, was hung upon the cross. "They killed him not, nor crucified him, but so it was made to appear to them." [68] The Christian Gnostics held the same view, as we have already seen.† Likewise, according to the Shi'a, martyrs in the cause of Ali suffer only in appearance. Their true bodies are lifted to heaven, while in the hands of their executioners mere substitutes remain. The popular Passion Play of Husain, representing his betrayal and murder at the battle of Kerbala in the year 680, is enacted every year on the

---

* Supra, pp. 365–66.
† Supra, pp. 373–75.

tenth day of the month of Moharram. The muezzin cries that morning from the summit of the minaret: "Oh Shi'a, this day is a day of sorrow: the body of Husain lies in the desert, naked." But those of extreme Gnostic persuasion give praise that day with joy, since the martyred one could not possibly have suffered, but in his true body returned, that day, to heaven, while an unknown suffered death for him on the field.[69]

Among the mystic Sufis, on the other hand, suffering is viewed as a reality, a blessed reality: the means itself to salvation. As in the words of the greatest of all Sufi martyrs and masters, al-Hallaj (858–922 A.D.):

> The moth plays about the lamp till dawn, then returns to its companions, to recount to them in sweetest terms the tale of what occurred. Then again it flies to play about the trusted power of the flame, in the wish to attain complete bliss. . . . Not the light suffices, nor the warmth. It plunges into the light now entire. And its companions, meanwhile, await its return, for it to reveal to them its experience.
>
> It did not trust the mere accounts of others, but now burns, goes up in smoke, remains without body in the flame, without name, without a sign. And with that—in what condition or to what end should it return to its companions, when it now is in full possession?
>
> For since it is itself now He Who Has Seen and Knows, it has ceased listening to mere accounts. It is now one with what it saw: to what end should it still see?
>
> Oh do not lock yourself away from me any longer! If you really believe, then you are able to say: "That am I!" [70]

The roots of the Sufi movement do not rest in the Koran, where Mohammed comes out clearly against the monastic way of life, but in the Christian Monophysite and Nestorian monk communities of the desert and, beyond those, their Buddhist, Hindu, and Jain models farther east. For Islam, like Judaism, is oriented principally to the furtherance of a sanctified secular consensus, wherein marriage and begetting, by way of a circumcised—i.e. ritually dedicated—organ, is the first communal duty. "Marry!" it is said in the Koran; "O those among you who are single!" [71] However, in the second century of Islam, ascetics explicitly "in imitation of Jesus" were already donning undyed garments of wool (*sūf*) as a mark of personal penitence,* and at that time the first traces also appeared both of hermit retreats and of meetings for the rapturous recitation of the Koran, with constant repetition (*dhikr*) of the name of God and with spiritual song (*samā*), leading to ecstasis.

The earliest phase of this movement, according to Professor Gibb, was inspired not by the love but by the fear of God, and specifically his Wrath to Come, "the same fear that had inspired Muhammad." [72] But in the eighth century A.D. a celebrated woman saint, Rabi'a al-Adawiya (d. 801), brought forward the idea of divine love as both the motive and the end of the mystic way. In her zeal for God all other interests ("gods") were extinguished. She declared that she knew neither fear of hell nor desire for paradise, but only such an absorbing love for God that neither love nor hate for any other being—not the Prophet himself—remained in her heart.[73] Like Epictetus, she is said to have been a slave. Her parentage is unknown. But in her poetry we hear the song eternal again of the mystics of all time, whether of India, Spain, Japan, or Persia:

> Two ways I love Thee: selfishly,
> And next, as worthy is of Thee.
>
> 'Tis selfish love, that I do naught
> Save think on Thee with every thought.
> 'Tis purest love, when Thou dost raise
> The veil to my adoring gaze.
>
> Not mine the praise, in that or this;
> Thine is the praise in both, I wis.[74]

It is a law of our subject, proven time and time again, that where the orthodoxies of the world go apart, the mystic way unites. The orthodoxies are concerned primarily with the maintenance of a certain social order, within the pale of which the individual is to

---

* Gibb in his *Mohammedanism,* p. 132, cites the protest of Ibn Sirin (d. 729), who declared, "I prefer to follow the example of the Prophet, who dressed in cotton."

function; in the interest of which a certain "system of sentiments" must be instilled into every member; and in defense of which all deviants are to be, one way or another, either reformed, deformed, or liquidated. The mystic way, on the other hand, plunges within, to those nerve centers that are in all members of the human race alike, and are at once the well springs and ultimate receptacles of life and all experiences of life.

I have discussed this matter in *Primitive Mythology,* and need not return to it here.[75] What is of special interest in the present context is the fact that even in such a straitjacket as the Garment of the Law of Islam men and women can awaken to a generally valid *human* experience—if they keep their counsel prudently to themselves. There are some words of Emerson, quoted on the motto page of the last published work of E. E. Cummings, that are worth repeating here. "Society everywhere is in conspiracy against the manhood of every one of its members. . . . The base doctrine of the majority of voices usurps the place of the doctrine of the soul." [76] In Islam particularly, but also, in general, throughout the Levantine world of the consensus, the force of this terrible dichotomy is great. In India and the Far East the mystic way is accorded a recognized and even honored place in relation to the common social order; but in the orthodox Levant, where the notion prevails that the Way of God is exclusively that of the local, sanctified legal statutes (whether ethnic, as in Judaism, or, as in the Moslem world, algebraically developed from a given set of axioms) the individual is cut down to such an approximation of zero that an alien can only wonder whether the ministrations of a Sigmund Freud must not have been wanted in the whole province centuries ago.

The female mystic Rabi'a al-Adawiya of Basra seems to have been the first to employ in her writings the imagery of wine, as "divine love," and the cup, as "the filled soul or heart," which became subsequently a typical trope of the mystics of Islam. The Persian Abu Yazid (Bayazid) of Bistan (d. 874 A.D.) carried the image to an absolutely Indian conclusion when he sang: "I am the Wine-drinker, the Wine, and the Cupbearer!" "God speaks

with my tongue and I have vanished." "I came forth from Bayazid-
ness, like a snake from its skin. Then I looked. And I saw that
lover, beloved, and love are one; for in the world of unity all can
be one." "Glory to me!"

Compare the Indian Ashtavakra Samhita, of approximately the
same date: "Wonderful am I! Adoration to myself! . . . I am that
stainless Self in which, through ignorance, knowledge, knower, and
the knowable appear!" [77]

Such excitement was permissible, even normal, in India; in Islam,
however, dangerous. And so it came to pass that when the next
great mystic in this line, al-Hallaj, uttered what, anywhere else,
would have been recognized as a mystic truism, "I am God. . . .
I am the Real," he was crucified. The model of the mystic life for
Hallaj was Jesus, not Mohammed; and his concept of the way (as
we have learned from his fable of the moth) was, through suffering,
surrender. When he saw the cross prepared for him, and the nails
—absolutely after the model of his *Imitatio Jesu*—he turned to
those present and prayed, concluding with these words:

> And these Thy servants who are gathered to slay me, in
> zeal for Thy religion and in desire to win Thy favor, forgive
> them, O Lord, and have mercy upon them; for verily, if Thou
> hadst revealed to them what Thou hast revealed to me, they
> would not have done what they have done; and if Thou hadst
> hidden from me what Thou hast hidden from them, I should
> not have suffered this tribulation. Glory unto Thee in what-
> soever Thou doest, and glory unto Thee in whatsoever Thou
> willest! [78]

The critical social problem of the mystic everywhere is to abide
in God, either as a manifestation of God or as God's devotee, and
at the same time to abide in phenomenality, as a material, social
phenomenon. For the dualist this remains difficult: God and World,
for him, are apart. For the non-dualist, however, the difficulty exists
only at a preliminary stage of the mystic way, antecedent to realization, since for him, finally, all is found to be in some manner God
—as in the words of the Gnostic Thomas Gospel, previously cited,
attributed to Jesus: "I am the All, the All came forth from Me and

the All attained to Me. Cleave the wood and I am there; lift up the stone, you will find me there." *

In the writings of Bayazid two stages of the mystic way are distinguished: first, the "passing away of the self" (fanā), and second, the "unitive life in God" (baqā).[79] The first suggests a verse of the Koran: "All that is on earth will perish"; and the second, the next verse of the same Sura: "But forever abides the Face of the Lord, full of Majesty, Bounty, and Honor." [80] Among the Sufis every nuance of the mystic attitude and experience is represented—with, however, as in India, stress going chiefly to the world-dissolving disciplines of fanā, rapture. The candidate for ecstasy submits in full surrender to a Master (Sanskrit guru; Arabic shaikh or pīr), and passes by that door to the larger full surrender in God, or, beyond even that, the Void. But now, the orthodox Koranic aspiration, "There is no god but God," can, by a change of emphasis, be read to mean, esoterically; "All is God. Every stick or stone, person or power, that has ever been revered as a god, is indeed God; for God is all." And by other such dexterous readings, numerous Koranic passages have been turned to a mystic, non-dual sense; for example: "We are closer to man than his neck vein," [81] or, "Wheresoever you turn, there is God's Presence: the All-Pervading, All-Knowing." [82]

After the crucifixion of Hallaj—to which the mystic gave himself as the moth, rapturously, to the flame (and we may ask whether in the crucifixion of Jesus there may not have been a like moment) —a new strain of caution entered the Sufi movement, which is typified in the spiritual formula of the one who (as they say) "makes the Law his outer garment and the mystic Way his inner garment." Here the observation of the Law itself is accepted as the crucifixion through which fanā, the "passing away of the self," is to be realized. In the works of the great culminating theologian of Islam, al-Ghazali (1058–1111)—who was an exact contemporary of Omar Khayyam—Sufism, by this formula, became acceptable as orthodox, and the high period of the primary saints of Islam came to an end, giving place to that of the mystic poets: Omar

* Supra, p. 367.

Khayyam, 1050?-1123?, Nizami, 1140-1203, Sadi, 1184-1291 (sic!), Rumi, 1207-1273, Hafiz, 1325-1389, and Jami, 1414-1492.

The suffering of love, then, is itself, for the Sufis, the redemptive moment, in contrast to the Shi'a view of the suffering of the martyr as unreal. And an equally characteristic answer is proposed to the second question asked above, namely, as to what happens after death to the willing sacrifice who permits himself, for love, to be condemned in the name of God. Might such a one, for example, be condemned, according to the law of God, to eternal damnation for love?

The case of Satan is examined as an instance of the possibility, with a result that will cause the reader, I dare say, a certain catch of surprise. For, as we have read at the opening of the Koran, he was condemned for refusing to bow down with the other angels to Adam—which, of course, was correct, since none but God is to be worshiped. Satan has to be regarded, then, as the type of the true Mohammedan. Loving and worshiping God alone, he could not bring himself to bow before man, even though commanded, inconsistently, by his God, who, before, had commanded him to worship none but God. God—as in the Book of Job—is above justice, above consistency, above all law and order whatsoever. The lesson of the Book of Job, carried through properly, as it began, would have ended with this Sufi thought of the exile of Satan, the perfect devotee, in the pains everlasting of hell. And as the great Hallaj, in his consideration of this profound theme, proposed as a further depth of the mystery: Satan in the pit of hell maintained intact his love; for indeed, that precisely was what held him there, removed from his beloved object—the pain of that loss of God, itself, being the greatest torment of all. And if we ask by what he is there sustained, in loss and pain, through all time: it is the rapture of his heart in the memory of the sound of God's beloved voice, when it pronounced his judgment: Depart!

Nor was Satan (or Job, for that matter) unjustly condemned after all. For he had himself already abandoned his beloved for the idea that he had formed of his beloved, which idea was an idol in the highest sense. That is to say: Satan's (Job's, Mohammed's, Abraham's) rigid monotheism was but another form of godlessness, and the worship of Adam by the angels was—correct.[83] For once again, as we read in the Koran: "God shall lead the wicked into error." [84]

VI. The Broken Spell

When the Umayyads were overthrown in 750 A.D. by the Abbasids, the capital of the now vast Islamic empire was moved to Baghdad, Arab domination of the culture gave place to an increasing Persian influence, and the puritanism of the desert yielded to the arts of a brilliant Levantine civilization. Baghdad, the capital, was pre-eminently a metropolis of pleasure, and the extent, as well as wealth, of the empire at the peak of its expansion in the period of Harun al-Rashid (r. 786–809) was enormous.

In Africa: Egypt, Fez, Tripoli, Tunis, Algiers, and Morocco were secure. In Europe: Spain had been taken, as well as nearly half of France, along with Corsica, Sardinia, Sicily, and Malta. In Asia, beyond Arabia, Palestine, Syria, and parts of Anatolia, the realm extended through Armenia and Iraq, Persia, Turkestan, Baluchistan, Afghanistan, and Sind, to the bounds of the flourishing Buddhist world of India and the Far East. And this, moreover, was the golden age of Asia. The arts and literatures, philosophies, divine sanctuaries of pilgrimage, and palaces of kings that have illuminated the fantasies of mankind through centuries since were then present actualities—where now are deserts and debris.

Caravans across the Mongolian wastes interlaced the empires of T'ang China, Rashtrakuta India, and the caliphate. Merchants sailed the seas in Arab, Chinese, and Pallava sailing craft of now forgotten make, boldly venturing to unknown isles that live in fable as bizarre domains of fairy: the wondrous Seven Isles of Wac Wac, beyond the Land of the Jinn, where a tree grows that bears fruit like human heads, which, when the sun sets or rises, cry: "Wac! Wac! Glory be to the Creating King!" [85] or those lands described in wonder tales of the shipwrecked merchant Sindbad: near India, for example, where a king's young mares used to be tethered at the seashore, to be covered, each new moon, by magical stallions rising from the sea, whose colts, when sold, brought treasuries of gold; or again, that land where the marvelous bird Roc fed its young on elephants, where valleys were paved with scattered diamonds, and from the trees liquid camphor poured.

We have ourselves explored, even mapped, all those distant lands today, but their magic, somehow, has vanished. For the marvel of the Asian golden age was that everywhere reality, fierce and difficult though it was for all (as the records of history show), was translated, not only in fable but also in belief and experience, into wonder—which, of course, as our own physicists now show, is exactly what reality is. The chief lost art of antiquity might be said, therefore, to have been the art of living in realization of the sheer wonder of the world: passing readily back and forth between the plane of experience of its hard crust and the omnipresent depth of inexhaustible wonder within. The Persian poets wrote of this mystery in their figure of the cup and its wine; as in Omar Khayyam:

> Man is a cup, his soul the wine therein,
> Flesh is a pipe, spirit the voice within;
>   O Khayyam, have you fathomed what man is?
> A magic lantern with a light therein.[86]

"The world of Magian mankind is filled with a fairy-tale feeling," as Spengler has well observed. "Devils and evil spirits threaten man; angels and fairies protect him. There are amulets and talismans, mysterious lands, cities, buildings, and beings, secret letters, Solomon's Seal, and Philosopher's Stone. And over all this is poured the quivering cavern-light that the spectral darkness ever threatens to swallow up." [87]

In the great golden period of Islam, T'ang China, and the glory that was India, an infinitely beautiful and promising flowering of the arts, and, with the arts, of aristocratic sensibility and civilization, threw its spell across the world, from Cordova to Kyoto—and beyond, as it now appears, even to Yucatan and Peru. The Levantine sense of the magical body of the infallible consensus met and joined harmoniously with the Indian of Dharma and the Chinese of the Tao; for in all these there prevailed the idea of a superimposed order to which the individual had simply and humbly to bow, in submission and, where possible, in rapturous realization. For neither in the Far East nor in India was there any teaching in which the doctrine of free will played a fundamental part, while in all those "churches" of the Levant where the doctrine of free will did indeed play a part, its only virtue lay in submission to the consensus—which is to say, to whatever "Law of God" (or, as we now say, *mores*) constituted the local, socially maintained "system of sentiments." "Disobedience," the exercise of individual judgment and freedom of decision, was exactly Satan's crime. The moral and spiritual adulthood of the Greek and Roman Classical masters had vanished from the earth with the Fall of Rome; and Europe, a regressed outland, lay apart from the broad field of higher civilization, in the condition of what today would be called an "undeveloped area." Charlemagne, contemporary with Islam's Harun al-Rashid, was a kind of high Congo-chieftain of the great northwestern forest, to whom the great caliph sent an elephant as a present, as today we are sending helicopters and yachts and in the nineteenth century sent beads. No one viewing the earth in that glorious day of the burgeoning Great Beliefs would have supposed that the seeds of thought and spirit of the millennium next to come were germinating in neither Baghdad, Ch'ang-an, nor Benares, but in the little palace school of *Carles li reis, nostre emperere magnes,* and his not yet Gothic basilica at Aix-la-Chapelle.

Something, however, occurred:

In the year 1258 A.D. Baghdad was put to the sword by the Mongol Hulagu and his golden horde, whose brothers, Mangu and Kublai Khan, were at the same time doing the same fell work upon China. India had already been disintegrated by the steamroller of Islam (commencing with Mahmud al-Ghazni, 1001 A.D.), and a century later would be entered and again treated to the sword by the Central Asian hordes of Tamerlane (1398). The radiant dream of divinity in civilization dissolved; and the mighty Orient, thenceforth, from Peking to Casablanca, became a culture field rather of second than of primary growth.

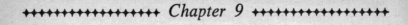
EUROPE RESURGENT

1. The Isle of Saints

When Ireland then had first and vaguely heard Christ's name the disposition of Christian devotion had its first origin in Kieran; his parents and every other one marveling at the extent to which all his deeds were virtuous. Before she conceived Kieran in her womb his mother had a dream: as it were a star fell into her mouth; which dream she related to the magicians and to the knowledgeable ones of the time, and they said to her: "Thou wilt bear a son whose fame and whose virtues shall to the world's latter end be great." Afterward that holy son Kieran was born; and where he was brought forth and nursed was on the island which is called Clare. Verily God chose him in his mother's womb. He was mild in his nature, and of converse sweet; his qualities were attended with prosperity, his counsel was instruction, and so with all else that appertained to a saintly man.

One day that he was in Clare there it was that, he being at the time but a young child, he made a beginning, of his miracles; for in the air right over him a kite came soaring and, swooping down before his face, lifted a little bird that sat upon her nest. Compassion for the little bird took Kieran, and he deemed it an ill thing to see it in such plight; thereupon the kite turned back and in front of Kieran deposited the bird half dead, sore hurt; but Kieran bade it rise and be whole. The bird arose, and by God's favor went whole upon its nest again.

A score and ten years now before ever he was baptised Kieran spent in Ireland in sanctity and in perfection both of body and of soul, the Irish being in that time all non-Christians. But the Holy Spirit being come to dwell in His servant,

456

in Kieran, he for that length lived in devotion and in perfect ways; then he heard a report that the Christian piety was in Rome and, leaving Ireland, went thither, where he was instructed in the Catholic faith. For twenty years he was there: reading the Holy Scripture, collecting his books and learning the rule of the Church; so that when the Roman people saw our Kieran's wisdom and cunning, his devotion and his faith, he was ordained into the Church. Afterwards he reached Ireland again; but upon the way from Italy Patrick had met him, and when they (God's people) saw each other they made much rejoicing and had great gladness.

Now at that time Patrick was not a bishop, but was made one later on. Pope Celestinus [422–432] * it was that made a bishop of him and then sent him to preach to the Irish; for albeit before Patrick there were saints in Ireland, yet for him God reserved her magistracy and primacy until he came; nor till his advent did their kings or their lords believe by any other's means.

Said Patrick to Kieran: "Precede me into Ireland; and in the meeting of her northern with her southern part, in her central point, thou shalt find a well. At such well (the name of which is Uaran) build thou a monastery; there shall thine honor abide for ever and thy resurrection be."

Kieran answered and said: "Impart to me the spot where the well is."

Patrick said to him: "The Lord will be with thee: go thou but straight before thee; take to thee first my little bell, which until thou reach the well that we have mentioned shall be speechless; but when thou attainest to it the little bell will with a clear melodious voice speak out: so shalt thou know the well, and at the end of nine years and a score I will follow thee to that place."

They blessed and kissed each other, and Kieran went his way to Ireland; but Patrick tarried in Italy. Kieran's bell was without uttering until he came to the place where was the well of which Patrick spoke: Uaran namely; for when Kieran was come into Ireland God guided him to that well, which when he had reached, straightway the little bell spoke with a bright clear voice: *barcán Ciaráin* 'tis called, and for a token is now in Kieran's parish and in his see. . . .

And touching that well of which we have spoken: the

* Cf. supra, p. 410.

very spot in which it is is in the mearing betwixt two parts
of Ireland, Munster being the southernmost part and Ulster
the northern; howbeit in Munster actually the country is which
men call Ely. In that place Kieran began to dwell as a hermit
(for at that time it was all encircled with vast woods) and
for a commencement went about to build a little cell of flimsy
workmanship (there it was that later he founded a monastery
and metropolis which all in general now call *Saighir Chi-
aráin*).

When first Kieran came hither he sat him down under a
tree's shade; but from the other side of the trunk rose a wild
boar of great fury which, when he saw Kieran, fled and then
turned again as a tame servitor to him, he being by God rendered gentle. Which boar was the first monk that Kieran had
there; and moreover went to the wood to pull wattles and
thatch with his teeth by way of helping on the cell (human
being there was none at that time with Kieran, for it was alone
and away from his disciples that he came on that eremite-
ship). And out of every quarter in which they were of the
wilderness irrational animals came to Kieran: a fox, namely,
a brock, a wolf, and a doe; which were tame to him, and
as monks humbled themselves to his teaching and did all that
he enjoined them.

But of a day that the fox (which was gross of appetite,
crafty, and full of malice) came to Kieran's brogues he e'en
stole them and, shunning the community, made for his own
cave of old and there lusted to have devoured the brogues.
Which thing being shown to Kieran he sent another monk
of the monks of his familia (the brock to wit) to fetch the fox
and to bring him to the same spot where all were. To the
fox's earth the brock went accordingly, and caught him in the
very act to eat the brogues themselves (their lugs and thongs
he had consumed already). The brock was instant on him
that he should come with him to the monastery; at eventide
they reached Kieran, and the brogues with them. Kieran
said to the fox: "Brother, wherefore hast thou done this
thievery which was not becoming for a monk to perpetrate?
seeing thou needest not to have committed any such; for we
have in common water that is void of all offence, meat too we
have of the same. But and if thy nature constrained thee to
deem it for thy benefit that thou shouldst eat flesh, out of the
very bark that is on these trees round about thee God would

have made such for thee." Of Kieran then the fox besought remission of his sins and that he would lay on him a penance; so it was done, nor till he had leave of Kieran did the fox eat meat; and from that time forth he was righteous as were all the rest.* [1]

The coming of Patrick to Ireland is traditionally set at 432 A.D.; but the date is suspect, and particularly so since when multiplied by 60 (the old Sumerian sexagesimal *soss*) it yields the number 25,920, which is precisely the sum of years of a so-called "Great" or "Platonic year," i.e., the sum of years required for the precession of equinoxes to complete one cycle of the zodiac. I have discussed this interesting figure in *Oriental Mythology*,[3] where it appeared that in the Germanic deity Odin's warrior hall there were 540 doors through each of which 800 warriors fared to the "war with the Wolf" at the end of the cosmic eon. $540 \times 800 = 432,000$, which is the sum of years ascribed, also, in India to the cosmic eon. The earliest appearance of this number in such an association, however, was in the writings of the Babylonian priest Berossos, c. 280 B.C., where it was declared that between the legendary date of the "descent of kingship" to the cities of Sumer and the date of the mythical deluge, ten kings reigned for 432,000 years. I have remarked that in Genesis, between the creation of Adam and the time of Noah's deluge, there were ten Patriarchs and a span of 1656 years. But in 1656 years there are *86,400 seven-day (i.e., Hellenistic-Hebrew) weeks,* while if the Babylonian years be reckoned as days, 432,000 days constitute *86,400 five-day (i.e. Sumero-Babylonian) weeks.* And, finally, $86,400 \div 2 = 43,200$: all of which points to a long-standing relationship of the number 432 to the idea of the renewal of the eon; and such a renewal,

---

* From Egerton MS 112 in the British Museum, written 1780–82 by Maurice O'Conor of Cork, probably from a copy (now in the Royal Irish Academy) made by his tutor: John Murphy of Raheenagh near Blarney. "The text," states Standish O'Grady, "is a specimen of good modern (say 17th century) Irish, formally and as to vocabulary correct; it is however too close a translation from the Latin (Codex Kilkenniensis, printed by the Irish Franciscan John Colgan, priest, in his Acta Sanctorum Hiberniae: Louvain, 1645) to be 'streng irisch' in style." Kieran's chronology is altogether obscure.[2]

from the pagan to the Christian eon is exactly what the date of Patrick's arrival in Ireland represents.

Patrick's actual life span seems to have been c. 389–461 A.D.,* and we note that Pope Celestine I, by whom he is supposed to have been appointed, did in fact die in the year 432. Thus the period of Patrick's life was that of, on the one hand, the end of Classical paganism at the hands of Theodosius I (r. 379–395) and, on the other hand, the breakthrough of the German tribes and the fall to them of much of Europe. Ireland, however, was not invaded at this time, so that there a distant colony of Christ remained intact, cut off from Rome, while England and the Continent fell prey to contending Germanic tribes.

Now Patrick's life was, of course, ornamented with miracles. "Just born," we read in an Old Irish version of his biography,

he was brought to be baptized to the blind flat-faced boy named Gornias; but Gornias had no water wherewith to perform the baptism. So with the infant's hand he made the sign of the cross over the earth, and a wellspring of water broke forth therefrom. Gornias put the water on his own face and it healed him at once, and he understood the letters of the alphabet though he had never seen them before. So that here, at one time, God wrought a threefold miracle for Patrick, the wellspring of water out of the earth, his eyesight to the blind youth, and skill in reading aloud the order of baptism without knowing the letters beforehand. Thereafter Patrick was baptized.[4]

When Patrick fared as primate to Ireland, twenty-four men were of his number, and he found a light sailing craft in readiness before him on the strand of the sea of Britain.

But when he had come into the boat, a leper asked him for a place and there was no empty place therein. So he put out before him to swim in the sea the portable stone altar whereon he used to make offering every day. *Sed tamen,* God wrought

---

* According to legend, however, Patrick died in the year 492 or 493 at the age (like Moses) of 120 years. Cf. Whitley Stokes, *The Tripartite Life of Patrick with Other Documents Relating to That Saint* (London: Eyre and Spottiswoode, 1887), Vol. I, p. cxxvi.

a great miracle here, to wit, the stone went not to the bottom, nor did it stay behind them; but it swam round about the boat with the leper on it until it arrived in Ireland.

Then Patrick saw a dense ring of demons around Ireland, to wit, a six days journey from it on every side.[5]

Now the fierce heathen High King of Ireland in those days was Laeghaire (Leary) son of Niall (r. 428–463), and it came to pass that when Patrick had been for some time there, preaching, he brought his ship, one Easter Eve, into the estuary of the Boyne. There was just then a feast in progress at the royal residence in Tara, during the period of which no fire was permitted to be lighted. Nevertheless, Patrick left his vessel and went along the land to Slane, where he pitched his tent and kindled a Paschal fire that lighted up the whole of Mag Breg; and the folk at Tara saw that fire from afar.

The king said: "That is a breach of the ban of our law; go find out who has done that." And his wizards said: "We too have remarked the fire. Furthermore, we know that unless it be quenched on the night on which it has been made, it will not be quenched till doomsday; and he who kindled it, moreover, unless he be forbidden, will have the kingdom of Ireland forever."

The king, hearing that, was mightily disturbed; and he said: "That must not be. We shall go and kill him." His chariots and horses were yoked, and he and his men, at the end of the night, proceeded toward the fire.

Said his wizards: "Go not thou to him, lest it be a token to him of honor; but let him come to thee, and let none rise up before him: and we shall argue in thy presence." Thus, therefore, it was done. And when Patrick saw the chariots and horses being unyoked, he chanted: "Some in chariots, some in horses trust, but we in the name of the Lord our mighty God."

They were all sitting before him with the rims of their shields against their chins, and none rose up, save only one, in whom there was a nature from God; namely Erc, later Bishop Erc, who is venerated at Slane. Patrick bestowed a blessing upon him, and he believed in God, confessed the Catholic Faith, and was baptized. Patrick said to him: "Thy city on earth will be high, will be noble."

Patrick and Laeghaire then asked tidings, each of the other; and one of the wizards, Lochru to wit, went angrily and noisily, with contention and questions against Patrick, and went astray into blaspheming the Trinity. Patrick thereupon looked upon him wrathfully and called with a great voice unto God, and he cried: "Lord, who canst do all things, and on whose power dependeth all that exists, and who hast sent us hither to preach Thy name to the heathen: let this ungodly man, who blasphemeth Thy name, be lifted up, and be destroyed in the presence of all."

Swifter than speech, at Patrick's word, demons uplifted the wizard in the air, and they let him down against the ground; his head struck a stone on which his brains were scattered and dust and ashes were made of him before all. And the heathen hosts that were biding there were adread.

King Laeghaire thereupon was greatly enraged at Patrick and desired at once to kill him. He said to those about him: "Slay the cleric!" And when Patrick perceived the onfall of heathen upon him, he exclaimed again with a great voice: "Let God arise, and let his enemies be dispersed: let these that hate him flee before him. As smoke vanishes, so let them. And as wax melts at a fire, so let the ungodly before God!" Immediately darkness came over the sun, a great earthquake and trembling of arms took place: it seemed the sky dropped on the earth; horses fled in fright and the wind whirled the chariots through the fields. And all in the assembly turned against each other, so that each was after slaying the other, and there were left along with the king but four persons only in that place, to wit, himself, his queen, and two of his wizard priests.

And the queen, namely, Angas, daughter of Tassach, son of Liathan, came in terror to Patrick. She said to him: "O just and mighty man, do not destroy the king. He shall come to thee and do thy will and kneel and believe in God." So Laeghaire went and knelt to Patrick, and pledged to him a false peace; some little time after which, he said to him: "Come, O cleric, follow me to Tara,

that I may recognize thee in the presence of the men of Ireland."
And he had set an ambush on every path.

Yet Patrick and his company of eight, along with his gillie (his
boy servant) Benén, went together past all these ambushes in the
form of eight deer and, behind them, one fawn with a white bird on
its shoulder: that is, Benén with Patrick's writing tablets on his
back.[6]

The most famous deed of the conversion was Patrick's con-
frontation on the hillock at Mag Slecht of the large stone image
known as Cenn or Cromm Cruach, the "Head" or "Crooked One
of the Mound," which was surrounded by twelve smaller idols, all
of stone. It has been said that at Halloween (Samhain) the Irish
offered a third of their children to this god—who was probably
an aspect of that Dagda of the Tuatha De Danann, whose caldron
never lacked food, whose trees were always laden with fruit, and
whose swine (one living, one always ready for the cooking) were
the inexhaustible banquet of the ever-living ones of his sidhe.*
The legend of Patrick tells that he went by water to Mag Slecht,
where there was that chief idol of Ireland covered with gold and
silver, and the other twelve around it covered with brass. And when
he saw that thing from the water and drew nigh to it, he raised up
his hand to put his staff upon it and, though his staff was not long
enough, nevertheless it smote its side. The mark of the staff still
remains on its left side, yet the staff did not move out of Patrick's
hand. And the earth swallowed up the other twelve as far as to
their heads, where they still stand in token of the miracle. He
cursed the demon and expelled him into hell; then founded a
church in that stead, namely Domnach Maige Slecht, where he left
Mabran, who was his relative and a prophet. And there, too, is
Patrick's well, wherein many were baptized.[7]

However, the most important aspect of the Christianization of
Ireland for our study is not the conflict but the ultimate accord that
was reached between the older mysteries of the fairy forts and the
new of the Roman Catholic Church. The magic of King Laeghaire's

* For the Dagda, cf. supra, pp. 301–303.

wizards was surpassed by that of Patrick's mighty God, and the island, even in the lifetime of the saint, was turned to Christ, with all the necessary machinery of cloisters, churches, relics, and the voice of bells. However, a culture historian today surely has a right to ask the meaning of such a mass conversion as takes place when a pagan king submits to baptism and all his people follow. And the question is compounded when the doctrines of the new religion are still in the process of being hammered out in conventions held two thousand miles away.

We have already had occasion to remark the heresy of the Donatists, combated, first by the monarch Constantine (r. 324–337), and then by Saint Patrick's North African contemporary, Saint Augustine (354–430).* The argument turned on the question as to whether a sacrament depends for its validity on the spiritual state of the human being who administers it, and the orthodox reply was that it did not: the Church (in the words of Augustine's predecessor, Optatus of Mileum) is an institution "whose sanctity is derived from the sacraments, and not estimated from the pride of persons. . . . The sacraments are holy in themselves and not through men." [8] So much for the doctrine! What, however, of the Celtic natives who received it? Surely it is permissible (indeed, in a work such as this, necessary) to ask: How, exactly, was this Levantine institution with its supporting myth received and understood by the recently pagan, hyperborean population, to whose well-being in the yonder world its magic now was to be applied?

One important clue to the temper of the north may be seen in the heresy of two Irishmen, contemporaries of Patrick, Pelagius and his chief disciple Caelestius. In their essentially Stoic doctrine of free will and the innate goodness of nature, which is not corrupted but only modified by sin, they opposed diametrically their great antagonist Augustine, for whom (as for the Church), nature, though created good, was so corrupted by the sin of Adam that virtue is impossible without grace: grace proceeds only from the sacraments by virtue of Jesus Christ: without grace, man's free will can will only vice, and therewith hell: and, consequently, man

---

* Supra, pp. 386 and 393.

(fallen man) cannot redeem himself but is rendered virtuous only by that incorruptible Levantine dispensary which Augustine had already manfully defended against the Donatists. Man's sins, that is to say, could not corrupt the Church, nor man's merely human virtues restore man. Against what Pelagius decried as the Manichaeism of his North African adversary, the Irish heretics proclaimed the following six doctrines, for which they were formally condemned:

1. That Adam would have died even if he had not sinned;

2. That the sin of Adam injured himself alone, not the human race;

3. That newborn children are in the same condition in which Adam was before the Fall; corollary: that infants, though unbaptized, have eternal life;

4. That the whole human race does not die because of Adam's death or sin, nor will it rise again because of Christ's resurrection;

5. That the Old Testament Law, as well as the New Testament Gospel, gives entrance to heaven; and

6. That even before the coming of Christ there were men who were entirely without sin.

According to this heresy, it follows from the goodness and righteousness of God that everything created by him is good. Human nature is indestructibly good and can be modified only accidentally. Sin, which consists in actively willing to do what righteousness forbids, is such a modification: it is always a momentary self-determination of the will and can never pass into nature so as to give rise to an evil nature. But if this cannot happen, so much the less can evil be inherited. Moreover, the will, which is thus uncorrupted, is always of itself capable of willing good. And Christ works by his example, the sacraments functioning not as power but as teaching. All of which adds up, in sum, to a variant of the Oriental and Stoic doctrine of self-reliance (Japanese, *jiriki:* "own strength"),* or in Pelagian phrase: *homo libero arbitrio emancipatus a deo:* man, created free, is with his whole sphere independent

* *The Masks of God: Oriental Mythology,* pp. 304, 492–93, and supra, p. 253.

of God and of the Church, the Living Body of Christ—though Christ, Church, and sacraments mightily teach and help.[9]

A second clue to the temper of the north may be seen in the Irish Neoplatonic philosopher—"the most learned and perhaps also the wisest man of his age," Professor Adolph Harnack has termed him [10]—Johannes Scotus Erigena (c. 815–c. 877 A.D.), who, when he was about thirty-two years of age, was invited by Charles the Bald to France to conduct the Carolingean court school. His basic work, *De divisione naturae* (c. 865–870), views nature as a manifestation of God, in four aspects, which are not forms of God but forms of our thought. These are, namely: I. The Uncreated Creating, II. The Created Creating, III. The Created Uncreating, and IV. The Uncreated Uncreating. The first is God conceived as the source of all things. The second is nature in the aspect of those immutable divine acts of will, primordial ideas or archetypes, that are the Forms of forms. The next is nature in the aspect of individual things, or forms, in time and space. And the fourth is God conceived as the final end of all things. No student of Schopenhauer will have the least difficulty here. It is impossible to know God as he is. *The same predicate may rightly be both affirmed and denied of God: however, the affirmation (e.g., God is Good) is only metaphorical, whereas the denial is literal (God is not Good), since God is beyond all predicates, categories, and oppositions.* Moreover, God does not know what he is, since he is not a what: this "divine ignorance" surpasses all knowledge, and true theology, therefore, must be negative. Nor does God know evil; if he knew it, evil would exist, whereas evil is an effect merely of our own misknowledge (the Created Uncreating). All apparent differences in time and space, of quality and quantity, of birth and death, male and female, etc., are effects of this misknowledge. All that God creates, on the other hand, is immortal; and the incorruptible body, which is our God-created Form, is hidden, as it were, in the secret recesses of our nature, and will reappear when this mortality is put away from our mind. Sin is the misdirected will and is punished by the finding that its misjudgments are vain. Hell is but the inner state

* Compare supra, p. 3.

of a sinning will. And the Paradise and Fall of Genesis, consequently, are allegorical of states of mind, not to be understood as episodes in the prehistoric past. Correction of the mind is facilitated by philosophy (reason) and religion (authority), but the criterion of the latter is the former, not vice versa. It follows that the Living Body of Christ is not the Church but the world; for God is in all things, and all things, therefore, both are and are not.

Needless to say, Erigena's Neoplatonic philosophy was condemned by Rome; and there is, furthermore, a possibly true story (not unlikely of a great teacher) of his students' having stabbed him to death with their pens.[11]

As a final clue to the manner of thought of the minds of the north, let me call attention to the curious illuminations of the Irish Book of Kells, which are of the period of Scotus Erigena * and of which I reproduce in Figure 30 † the so-called Tunc-page, bearing the words of the Gospel according to Matthew: "Then there were crucified with him two thieves" (*Tunc cru/cifixerant/*XPI *cum eo du/os la/trones*).[12]

We recognize the cosmic self-consuming, self-renewing serpent, whose lion-head recalls the old Sumerian lion-bird, while the T of the word *Tunc* is a lion with serpentine attributes, either swallowing or emitting (or both) a tangled pair-of-opposites. The serpent, as we have learned, is generally symbolic of both the self-consuming and self-renewing powers of life; that is to say, the lunar mystery of time, while the lion is the solar power, the sun door to eternity. The circumscribing serpent, therefore, is the demiurgic, world-creating and -maintaining principle, or, in the Gnostic-Christian view, the God of the Old Testament, while the lion of the T is the road of escape from this vale of tears: the "way and the light," that is to say the Redeemer.

The Greek letters XPI, inserted in the text after *crucifixerant,* are the signa of Christ (Greek χριστός). The same three letters

---

* Following Sir Edward Sullivan, *The Book of Kells* (London: The Studio, Limited, 4th edition, 1933), p. vii: "the latter end of the ninth century."

† The figure has been very kindly drawn for me by Mr. John Mackey, from Sullivan, op. cit., plate XI.

Figure 30. "Then There Were Crucified with Him Two Thieves"

furnish the base of the whole design, as appears when the page is
turned clockwise, to lie on its right side. In this position, the great
initial unites with the central bar to form P: the middle letter of
the sign, symbolizing the Savior between the two thieves, which
latter now are represented by the X and I, and are thus one with
—indeed parts of—XPI, or Christ. Compare the Dadophors of the
Mithra sacrifice, discussed above.*

* Supra, p. 260.

Moreover, on the *fifteenth* day of each lunar month, the setting full moon (lunar bull: sacrifice) confronts the blaze of the rising sun (Mithra Tauroctonus), which strikes it directly across the plane of the earth, and the moon thereafter wanes. We note in the border formed by the serpent's body three groups of five men, which is to say, fifteen. Easter is now celebrated the first Sunday after the full moon on or following the vernal equinox; and, according to the reckoning of the Synoptic Gospels, the crucifixion took place on the fifteenth day of the Jewish month of Nisan (March–April: first month of the Jewish year). It looks as though a reference to this lunar theme of death and resurrection were intended here. Furthermore, it may be relevant to remark that the letter T is one of the forms and symbols of the cross, the cross being a traditional sign, moreover, of the earth, or principle of space, while the word *Tunc,* of which T is the initial, meaning "then," is a word of time: space-time being the field of phenomenality, the field, that is to say, of the mystery of the Incarnation and Crucifixion. Finally, the flame is the normal Christian symbol of the Paraclete, the Holy Spirit, as well as of that state of Gnostic Illumination (Sanskrit, *bodhi;* Greek, *gnosis*) by which the World Illusion is destroyed. And so, as a considered guess, it might be suggested that in the circumscribing serpent the powers symbolized are the Father and Holy Spirit (possibly associated with Erigena's Uncreated Creating and Uncreated Uncreating), while in the lion we have the Son in the field of space and time—which interpretation may (or may not) be supported by the fact that in the Irish *Lebar Brecc,* where Patrick's biography is recorded, Christ, the Son, is represented not as second but as *third* person of the Trinity.[13]

In any case, the symbols of this important page are certainly not mere scrimshaw but a commentary on the text, suggesting, moreover, an association of the Christian with earlier symbolic forms. And the background of their statement, equally certainly, was a form of Christianity not yet in accord with the Augustinian orthodoxy of the Byzantine Church councils. Sir Edward Sullivan, from whose beautiful publication of twenty-four color plates of The Book of Kells our figure has been drawn, has remarked that in the orthodox Latin Vulgate translation of the Gospel according to Matthew the passage here illuminated does not read *Tunc crucifixerant,* but *Tunc crucifixi sunt;* which is another sign, among many, of a differing line of communication.[14]

The main point that I would bring out through all this, however, is simply that in the remote, recently pagan Irish province there was not such a radical rejection by the monks either of the virtues of natural man or of the symbols of pagan iconography as was to be characteristic of the later missionizing of the German tribes. In the words of Professor T. G. E. Powell in his recent study of *The Celts:*

> Whereas in the early Teutonic kingdoms of Post-Roman Europe, the Church found but the most rudimentary machinery for rule and law, in Ireland the missionaries were confronted by a highly organized body of learned men with specialists in customary law, no less than in sacred arts, heroic literature, and genealogy. Paganism alone was supplanted, and the traditional oral schools continued to flourish, but now side by side with the monasteries. By the seventh century, if not earlier, there existed aristocratic Irish monks who had also been fully educated in the traditional native learning. This led to the first writing-down of the vernacular literature, which thus became the oldest in Europe next after Greek and Latin. . . . The continuity of native Irish traditional learning, and literature, from Medieval times backwards into prehistory is a matter of great significance, and one that has been little appreciated.[15]

The old druidic training of the filid, or bards, by which they learned not only the entire native mythological literature by heart but also the laws according to which mythological analogies were to be recognized and symbolic forms interpreted, was applied in the early Christian period both to a reading of the symbolism of the Christian faith and to the recognition of analogies between this and the native pagan myths and legends. The dates of the birth and death of Cuchullin's uncle, King Conachar, for example, were made to coincide with those of Christ's nativity and crucifixion. Moreover, he was declared to have died as a result of learning, through the clairvoyance of a druid, of the crucifixion of Christ. And the soul of Cuchullin, after his death at the hand of Lugaid (when he had strapped himself to a pillar-stone so that he might die standing, not seated or lying down), was seen by thrice fifty queens who had loved him, floating in his spirit chariot, chanting a song of the Coming of Christ and the Day of Doom. He returned, furthermore, from his pagan Irish otherworld to converse cordially with Saint Patrick, as did, also, numerous other grand old heroes. And according to all accounts (all penned, it must be born in mind, by clerics), Patrick blessed the old pagans, delighted by their tales, all of which his scribe recorded in the work known to us as The Colloquy with the Ancients.

For instance, there was the giant Caeilte, who appeared with a company of his kind and their huge wolfdogs just when Patrick, lauding the Creator, was blessing an ancient fort in which Finn MacCumhaill (Finn McCool) once had dwelt. The clerics saw the big men draw near and fear overcame them; for those were not people of the same time or epoch of these clergy. Then Patrick, apostle to the Gael, rose and took his spergillum, to sprinkle holy water on the old heroes, floating over whom there were a thousand legions of demons. Into the hills and skalps, into the outer borders of the region and country, the demons thereupon departed in all directions; after which the great men sat down.

"Good now," Patrick said to Caeilte; "what name hast thou?"

"I am Caeilte," said he, "son of Crundchu son of Ronan."

The clergy marveled greatly as they gazed; for the largest man of them reached but to the waist, or else to the shoulder, of any given one of the old pagans, and they sitting.

Patrick said: "Caeilte, I am fain to beg of thee a boon." Who replied: "If I have but that much strength or power, it shall be had: at all events, enunciate the same." "To have in our vicinity here a well of pure water," Patrick said, "from which we might baptize the people of Bregia, of Meath, and of Usnach." Said the giant: "Noble and righteous one, that I have for thee." And they, crossing the fort's circumference, came out. In his hand the big man took the saint's, and in a little while they saw a loch-well right in front of them, sparkling and translucid. . . .

Patrick said: "Was not he a good lord with whom ye were; Finn MacCumhaill that is to say?" Upon which Caeilte uttered the following tribute of praise:

"Were but the brown leaf which the wood sheds from it gold,
Were but the white billow silver:
Finn would have given it all away."

"Who or what was it that maintained you so in your life?" Patrick asked; and the other answered: "Truth, which was in our hearts, strength in our arms, and fulfillment in our tongues."

Many days they passed together, and on one of those days Patrick baptized them all, whereupon Caeilte reached across to the rim of his shield, from which he tore off a ridgy mass of gold in which there were three times fifty ounces, saying: "That was Finn the Chief's last gift to me and now, Patrick, take it for my soul's sake, and for my commander's soul."

And the extent to which that mass of gold reached on Patrick was from his middle finger's tip to his shoulder's highest point, while in width and in thickness it measured, as they say, a man's cubit. And this gold was then bestowed upon the mission's canonical hand bells, on psalters, and on missals.

But finally, after many days of strolling conversation, when the time came for the big men to be off and on their way, Caeilte addressed the saint. "Holy Patrick, my soul," said he; "I hold that tomorrow it is time for me to go."

"And wherefore goest thou?" Patrick asked.

"To seek out the hills and bluffs and fells of every place in which my comrades and my foster-fellows and the Fian-chief were along with me," he answered; "for I am wearied with being in one place."

They abode that night; the next day all arose; Caeilte laid his head on Patrick's bosom, and the saint said to him: "By me to thee, and whatsoever be the place—whether indoors or abroad—in which God shall lay hand on thee, Heaven is assigned."

Then the Christian King of Connaught, who had joined them, went his way to exercise royal rule; Patrick also went his way, to sow faith and piety, to banish devils and wizards out of Ireland, to raise up saints and righteous, to erect crosses, station stones and altars, also to overthrow idols and goblin images, and the whole art of sorcery. And touching Caeilte now: on he went northward, to the wide plain of the plains of Boyle, across the waterfall of Nera's son, northward yet into the Curlieu mountains, in Keshcorann, and out upon the Corann's level lands. . . .[16]

II. The Weird of the Gods

The Roman, P. Cornelius Tacitus (c. 55–c. 120 A.D.), in his *Germania,* has given the earliest known account of the life and religion of the German tribes beyond the Danube and the Rhine, who in his day were already threatening Rome and in the next three hundred years were to become its ruin.

In their ancient songs [states Tacitus], their only form of recorded history, the Germans celebrate the earth-born god Tuisto. They assign to him a son, Mannus, the author of their race, and to Mannus three sons, their founders, after whom the people nearest Ocean are named Ingaevones, those of the center Herminones, the remainder Istaevones. The remote past invites guesswork, and so some authorities record more sons of the god and more national names, such as Marsi, Gambrivii, Suebi and Vandilici; and the names are indeed genuine and ancient. As for the name of Germany, it is quite a modern coinage, they say. The first people to cross the Rhine and oust the Gauls are now called Tungri, but were then called Germans. It was the name of this tribe, not that of a nation, that gradually came into general use. And so, in the first place, they were all called Germans after the conquerors because of the terror these inspired, and finally adopted and applied the new name to themselves.

Hercules, among others, is said to have visited them, and they chant his praises before those of other heroes on their way into battle. . . .[17] They also carry into the fray figures taken from their sacred groves. . . .[18]

Above all gods they worship Mercury, and count it no sin to win his favor on certain days by human sacrifices. They appease Hercules and Mars with the beasts normally allowed. Some of the Suebi sacrifice to Isis also. I cannot determine the origin and meaning of this foreign cult, but her emblem, made in the form of a light war-vessel, proved that her worship came in from abroad. They do not, however, deem it consistent with the divine majesty to imprison their gods within walls or represent them with anything like human features. Their holy places are the woods and groves, and they call by the name of god that hidden presence which is seen only by the eye of reverence. . . .[19]

The oldest and noblest of the Suebi, so it is said, are the Semnones, and the justice of this claim is confirmed by a religious rite. At a set time all the peoples of this blood gather, in their embassies, in a wood hallowed by the auguries of their ancestors and the awe of ages. The sacrifice in public of a human victim marks the grisly opening of their savage ritual. In another way, too, reverence is paid to the grove. No one may enter it unless he is bound with a cord. By this he acknowledges his own inferiority and the power of the deity. Should he chance to fall, he must not get up on his feet again. He must roll out over the ground. All this complex of super-stition reflects the belief that in that grove the nation had its birth, and that there dwells the god who rules over all, while the rest of the world is subject to his sway. Weight is lent to this belief by the prosperity of the Semnones. They dwell in a hundred country districts and, in virtue of their magnitude, count themselves chief of all the Suebi.

The Langobardi, by contrast, are distinguished by the few-ness of their numbers. Ringed round as they are by many mighty peoples, they find safety, not in obsequiousness but in battle and its perils. After them come the Reudigni, Aviones, Anglii, Varini, Eudoses, Suarini and Nuitones behind their ramparts of rivers and woods. There is nothing par-ticularly noteworthy about these people in detail, but they are distinguished by a common worship of Nerthus, or Mother Earth. They believe that she interests herself in human affairs and rides through their peoples. In an island of Ocean stands a sacred grove, and in the grove stands a car draped with a cloth which none but the priest may touch. The priest can feel the presence of the goddess in this holy of holies, and attends her, in deepest reverence, as her car is drawn by kine. Then follow days of rejoicing and merry-making in every place that she honors with her advent and stay. No one goes to war, no one takes up arms; every object of iron is locked away; then, and then only, are peace and quiet known and prized, until the goddess is again restored to her temple by the priest, when she has had her fill of the society of men. After that, the car, the cloth and, believe it if you will, the goddess herself are washed clean in a secluded lake. This service is performed by slaves who are immediately afterwards drowned in the lake. Thus mystery begets terror and a pious reluctance to ask what that sight can be which is allowed only to dying eyes. . . .[20]

In the territory of the Naharvali one is shown a grove, hallowed from ancient times. The presiding priest dresses like a woman; the gods, translated into Latin, are Castor and Pollux. That expresses the character of the gods, but their name is Alci. There are no images, there is no trace of foreign cult, but they are certainly worshiped as young men and as brothers. . . .[21]

Turning to the right shore of the Suebian sea, we find it washing the territories of the Aestii, who have the religion and general customs of the Suebi, but a language approximating to the British. They worship the Mother of the Gods. They wear, as emblem of this cult, the masks of boars, which stand them in stead of armor or human protection and ensure the safety of the worshiper even among his enemies. They seldom use weapons of iron, but cudgels often. They cultivate grain and other crops with a patience quite unusual among lazy Germans. Nor do they omit to ransack the sea; they are the only people to collect the amber—*glaesum* is their own word for it—in the shallows or even on the beach. Like true barbarians, they have never asked or discovered how it is produced. For a long time, indeed, it lay unheeded like any other jetsam, until Roman luxury made its reputation. They have no use for it themselves. They gather it crude, pass it on unworked and are astounded at the price it fetches.[22]

The Germans believe that there resides in women an element of holiness and prophecy, and so they do not scorn to ask their advice or lightly disregard their replies. In the reign of our deified Vespasian we saw Veleda long honored by many Germans as a divinity, whilst even earlier they showed a similar reverence for Aurinia and others, a reverence untouched by flattery or any pretence of turning women into goddesses. . . .[23]

There is no pomp about their funerals. The one rule observed is that the bodies of famous men are burned with special kinds of wood. When they have heaped up the fire they do not throw robes or spices on the top; but only a man's arms, and sometimes his horse, too, are cast into the flames. The tomb is a raised mound of turf. They disdain to show honor by laboriously rearing high monuments of stone; they would only lie heavy on the dead. Weeping and wailing are soon abandoned—sorrow and mourning not so soon. A woman may decently express her grief in public; a man should nurse his in his heart.[24]

Notable is the prominence given here to female divinities and their association with the soil, with planting, with the pig, with human sacrifice, and with such a festival car procession as may be witnessed to this day in any part of the world in which the cult of the goddess still prevails. The Aestii, whose language resembled the Celtic tongue of the Britain of that time, cultivated grain, held the boar sacred, and worshiped the mother of the gods. With this syndrome we are already familiar. The Anglii (Angles, the future English) worshiped the goddess Nerthus, Mother Earth, whose image was honored in a car procession and bathed—after which those who had bathed the image were drowned in a lake on her sacred isle. One thinks of the legend of the Greek hunter Actaeon, who, chancing upon Artemis bathing in her forest pool, was transformed by her into a stag, to be slain by his own hounds; and one thinks, too, of the impudent young adept in the temple of the goddess in Egyptian Sais, who, when he made bold to lift the veil of her image was struck so with amaze that his tongue was thereafter ever dumb. For it was she who had declared: "There is none who has lifted my veil" (οὐδεὶς ἐμὸν πέπλον ἀνεῖλε); that is to say: none who has lived to reveal the secret of my divine motherhood of the world.[25]

The priest of the Naharvali, furthermore, garbed as a woman, supervising the sacred grove where twins resembling Castor and Pollux were revered, suggests the eunuch priests of the great Syrian goddess Cybele. And finally, the goddess whom Tacitus identified with Isis—honored like her as a goddess of the sea and of ships— may or may not have been the late import he supposed. For the evidence given by these Germanic forms, of an ancient continuity from as far back as the earliest neolithic infiltration of Europe, is strong enough to support almost any theory of dating that one might wish to propose. In fact, these various goddesses of the German tribes of the first century A.D. are exactly what one should have expected to find in a zone of numerous strains of neolithic diffusion. The tribal genealogies from the god Tuisto, born of the goddess Earth, resembling as they do the Earth-born genealogies of Hesiod, lend to this picture additional support. And so it appears that we may safely assert that whether in the early Greek and Celtic, or in the later Roman and Germanic zones, the European neolithic heritage produced largely homologous mythic forms, derived from and representing the old order of the great Age of the Goddess: and it was upon this basic stratum that the later layerings of high culture myth were superimposed.

The question remains then as to what these later layerings may have been; and germane to this question is Tacitus's naming of Hercules, Mercury, and Mars as the Latin counterparts of three important German deities to whom, in his time, sacrifices were addressed. These have been identified unquestionably as Thor, Wodan, and Tiu—after whom, as we have seen, our Thursday, Wednesday, and Tuesday have been named. In the brilliant literature of the Icelandic Eddas and Middle High German Nibelungenlied, from which Wagner drew his mighty Ring, they are among the most prominent male divinities. And just as in the period of Tacitus's account, so also in the Eddic period, one long millennium later, the figure of Wodan-Mercury was the god paramount, above all.

The figure of Thor, however, shows signs of being the eldest of the pantheon, even going back, possibly, to the paleolithic age, when his celebrated hammer would have been properly a characteristic weapon. He is never equipped with a sword or lance, or mounted on a steed, like Wodan, but walks against his foes. And as a clever giant-killer, he has counterparts in the monster-killers of practically every primitive hunting mythology on record.[26] Heracles, among the Greeks, belonged to this primitive hero-type as well. But in the outrageously grotesque humor of the victories of Thor—which in many ways bear comparison with the legendry of the Dagda of the Celts *—there is more of the primary mythic flavor of the old shaman-deeds of the heroes of the peoples of the Great Hunt than there is to be found among even the most bizarre of the epic hero tales of the Greeks.

For instance, when he was at one time full of wrath against the entire race of the giants, having just been tricked into playing the fool in their city, Jotunheim, he set forth to wreak revenge upon the most notable of their race, namely the Midgard Worm, the Cosmic Serpent, whose dwelling was the world-surrounding ocean. Thor assumed the unimpressive form of a mere lad and, walking so, came, one evening, at the edge of the world, to the dwelling of the giant named Hymir, of whom he asked shelter for the night. The following dawn, Hymir, the giant, got up quickly and dressed, with the idea of rowing out alone to sea, to fish; but Thor, perceiving, got up as quickly and dressed to go along. Hymir rebuffed him, saying that he would be of no help, being puny and a mere lad, and that he would freeze sitting out so far and long as the giant always sat; and the lad Thor became so angry at this insult that he withheld the fling of his hammer, Mjollnir, only because he intended a far greater feat at sea. Thor replied merely that he could row as far and sit as long as he pleased, and that it was not certain who would be the first out there to want home. He asked what bait they would be using and Hymir bade him fetch his own bait, whereat the lad turned and, setting out in his wrath to where he saw the giant's herd of oxen, grabbing the largest bull, who was named "He Who Bellows to Heaven," he tore off the animal's head. Then he came lunging with this to the sea, where Hymir had already shoved out the boat.

The visitor boarded, sat on the bottom, took up two oars, and rowed; and to Hymir it seemed they made speed. The giant himself was rowing in the bow, and they made such speed that soon he could declare they had reached his fishing grounds for halibut. The guest said, however, that he wished to go on, so they pulled another stretch, until Hymir called out that they had come so far it would

* Supra, pp. 301–303.

be dangerous to fare farther, because of the Worm. The lad, however, said again that he would go on, which he did; and the giant now was afraid.

Thor laid up the oars and made ready a strong line, nor was the hook that he had brought with him small, thin, or inadequate. He fixed the ox-head to this hook and flung it out to sea. To the bottom it descended, and the Midgard Worm, perceiving it, was fooled. The serpent struck at the ox head: the hook caught in his upper jaw: and when he felt that, he jerked back with such force that Thor's two fists smacked on the gunwale. Angered, the god put forth then every bit of his strength, planting his feet so hard upon the bottom of the boat that when he pulled they went right through, and he was standing with them on the floor of the sea as he drew his catch up the side.

And it may be said that no more fearful sight was ever seen in the world than that which appeared when Thor's eyes flashed upon the serpent, and the serpent, glaring up from below, let blow at him its venom. Then Hymir, the giant, grew pale, became yellow, and was afraid: when he saw the Midgard Worm itself there, and how the sea was rushing in and out through his boat. Thor reached for his hammer and raised it for the blow; but Hymir, snatching up his fish-knife, cut the line at the gunwale and the serpent sank into the sea. Thor flung his hammer at it and, some say, lopped off its head against the bottom. Others believe, however, that the Midgard Worm still lives and lies in the abyss of the all-embracing ocean. But the god, incensed, doubled his fist and drove it against Hymir's ear, who went overboard, head first. And Thor then waded back to land.[27]

Thor is called, in Scandinavia, The Defender of the World, and amulet miniatures of his hammer have for centuries been worn to afford protection. At Stockholm, the museum holds one of amber from a late paleolithic date; and from the early metal ages fifty or more tiny T-shaped hammers of silver and gold have been collected. In fact, even to the present—or, at least, to the first years of the present century—Manx fishermen have been accustomed to wear the T-shaped bone from the tongue of a sheep to protect them from the sea; and in German slaughterhouses workers have been seen with the same bone suspended from their necks.[28]

An unforeseen, somewhat startling overtone is added by this observation to the T-motif that has already been discussed in connection with the Celtic Christian Tunc-page (which is of a date when the Celtic and Viking spheres of influence were in many ways interlaced); and, of course, then vice versa: the apparently merely grotesque fishing episode acquires a new range of possible significance when the T of the Celtic page is identified with Thor's hammer as well as with Christ's cross. We might, in fact, even ask whether in Manx and German folklore the T-shaped bone of the sheep—the sacrificial lamb—may not have been consciously identified with the world-redeeming cross of the man-god Christ, as well as with the world-defending hammer of the native, far more ancient, even possibly paleolithic, man-god Thor.

In Tacitus's day, as we have seen, Thor was identified with Hercules; but in later Germano-Roman times, the analogy was rather with Jove. Jove's Day in the Latin world (*giovedi* in Italian; *jeudi* in French) became Thor's Day (Thursday) among the Germans. Thor's hammer, accordingly, was identified with the fiery bolt of Zeus—and with this analogy a vast range of new associations opens into the sphere of Hellenistic syncretistic thought.

Let us consider, first, the association of Jove and his planet Jupiter with the principle of justice and law. Scandinavian assemblies generally were opened on Thursday—Thor's Day. The gavel of order is still Thor's hammer. And at the Icelandic *Things* (court assemblies) the god invoked in testimony of oaths, as "the Almighty God," was Thor.[29]

The bolt of Jove, moreover, is cognate both in meaning and in origin with the *vajra,* "diamond," "lightningbolt," of the Mahayana Buddhist and Tantric Hindu iconographies. For, as already remarked,* the lightningbolt is the irresistible power of truth by which illusions, lies, are annihilated; and again, more deeply read, the power of eternity through which phenomenality is annihilate.

* Supra, p. 263.

Like a flash of initiatory knowledge, lightning comes of itself and is followed by the roar and tumult of awakening life and rain—the rain of grace. And the idea of the diamond, too, has point in this connection; for as the lightning shatters all things, so does the diamond cut all stones, while the hard, pure brilliance of the diamond typifies the adamantean quality both of truth and of the true spirit.

The two ideas of lightning and diamond, then, which are combined in the Indian *vajra,* may be readily applied to the hammer of Thor. We have already noted a relationship between this sign and the great Mithraic lion-serpent man, Zervan Akarana (Figure 24). It is the weapon of Shiva and of the Solar Buddha Vairochana, the fiery bolt of Jove, and now, the mighty hammer of Thor. It is also the Cretan double ax of the Bull Sacrifice, and the knife in the hero Mithra's hand with which he slew the World Ox.

Let us look once again at Thor's fishhook—at its bait—and turn to Figure 23, where the World Serpent comes to the Mithraic sacrifice. Let us look once again, as well, at the Tunc-page of The Book of Kells and recall that, in the Christian view, Christ, the sacrifice who appeased the Father's wrath, was by analogy the bait by which the Serpent Father was subdued. As the priest at Mass consumes the consecrated host, so did the Father consume the Willing Victim, his ever-dying, ever-living Son, who was finally, of course, his very Self.

How much of all this was rendered in the mythologies of the Germans of Tacitus's day no one can know. There can be no doubt, however, of the period of the Eddas, Sagas, and Nibelungenlied. Nor is it even difficult to identify the paths and ways by which the great Hellenistic, syncretistic style of mythic communication penetrated beyond Roman reach, into the ramparts of the German rivers and woods.

First of all, we have the evidence of the runic script, which appeared among the northern tribes directly after Tacitus's time. It is now thought to have been developed from the Greek alphabet in the Hellenized Gothic provinces north and northwestward of the Black Sea. Thence it passed—possibly by the old trade route up the Danube and down the Elbe—to southwestern Denmark, where it appeared about 250 A.D. and whence the knowledge of it was soon carried to Norway, to Sweden, and to England. The basic runic stave was of 24 (3 × 8) letters, to each of which a magical —as well as a mystical—value was attributed. In England the number of letters was increased to 33; in Scandinavia, reduced to 16. Monuments and free objects throughout the field of the German Völkerwanderung bear inscriptions in these various runic scripts, some telling of malice, others of love. For instance, on a late seventh-century stone standing in Sweden: "This is the secret meaning of the runes: I hid here power-runes, undisturbed by evil witchcraft. In exile shall he die by means of magic art who destroys this monument." And on a sixth-century metal brooch from Germany: "Boso wrote the runes—to thee, Dallina, he gave the clasp." [30]

The invention and diffusion of the runes mark a strain of influence running independently into the barbarous German north, from those same Hellenistic centers out of which, during the same centuries, the mysteries of Mithra were passing to the Roman armies on the Danube and the Rhine. We do not know what "wisdom" was carried with the runes at that early date, but that in later times their mystic wisdom was of a generally Neoplatonic, Gnostic-Buddhist order is hardly to be doubted. Othin's (Wodan's) famous lines in the Icelandic Poetic Edda, telling of his gaining of the knowledge of the runes through self-annihilation, make this relationship perfectly clear:

> I ween that I hung on the windy tree,
> Hung there for nights full nine;
> With the spear I was wounded, and offered I was
> To Othin, myself to myself.
> On the tree that none may ever know
> What root beneath it runs.
>
> None made me happy with loaf or horn,
> And there below I looked;
> I took up the runes, shrieking I took them,
> And forthwith back I fell.

> Then began I to thrive and wisdom to get,
>   I grew and well I was;
> Each word led me on to another word,
>   Each deed to another deed.[31]

No one knows who wrote these lines. They occur in the precious manuscript known as *Codex Regius,* in the Royal Library in Copenhagen, which appears to have been written c. 1300 A.D., and of which the contents (judging from the form of the language) must have been composed between c. 900 and 1050 A.D.[32] That is to say, the period of composition was that of the great Viking expeditions out of Scandinavia against the coasts and lands of France and the British Isles—on to Iceland, to Greenland, to Nova Scotia, and to Massachusetts; the age, as well, of the Viking kings and princes of Novgorod and Kiev, from whose appellation, Rhos or Rus (from the Old Norse, *rodr,* "rowing road"?),[33] the name of Russia is derived: years when to the prayers of the European Christian litanies the aspiration was added "From the fury of the Norsemen, deliver us!"

Much had come to pass since the period of Tacitus's primitive account. In the first place, the impact of the Hunnish raids from Asia had set the entire German constellation in movement, so that tribes had been tossed from east to west, north to south, and back and forth from all sides. Secondly, a continuing stream of influence had come pouring into this caldron, first from Byzantium in the southeast, commencing strongly in the sixth century, and then, suddenly, from Islam in Sicily and in Spain. The Irish, meanwhile, largely from St. Columba's island monastery of Iona (founded 563 A.D.)—whose missionaries, shaved from ear to ear across the front of the head and with long flowing locks behind, bearing in their hands long staves and with leathern water-bottles hanging from their backs together with food-wallets, writing-tablets, and relic-cases [34]—were diligently bearing the message of Christ back to the lands from which they themselves had received it, penetrating as far south as to Lake Constance and Milan. By the time the Viking period opened, c. 750 A.D., the Germans of the earlier phase of movement were already settled members of an established, crude but Christian, European culture province, marked off, on the one hand, from the Moors of the southwest and, on the other, from the now tottering Byzantine Christian Empire of the southeast: not in any sense a mere continuation or after-civilization of the earlier, worn-out Roman order, but the new and rapidly forming promise of a Gothic order, soon to be. And the Vikings of the marginal north were not the primitive tribesmen of Tacitus's account seven centuries before, but developed, powerful barbarians, building and sailing great sea-craft, elegantly decorated, that were sent to sea in fleets of up to six hundred vessels, many of them twenty-five yards in length and of a register of some thirty tons.

"The number of ships grows," wrote a chronicler of about 800 A.D.

> The endless stream of Vikings never ceases to increase. Everywhere the Christians are victims of massacres, burnings, plunderings: the Vikings conquer all in their path, and no one resists them: they seize Bordeaux, Perigueux, Limoges, Angoulême and Toulouse. Angers, Tours and Orléans are annihilated and an innumerable fleet sails up the Seine and the evil grows in the whole region. Rouen is laid waste, plundered and burnt: Paris, Beauvais and Meaux taken, Melun's strong fortress levelled to the ground, Chartres occupied, Evreux and Bayeux plundered, and every town besieged. Scarcely a town, scarcely a monastery is spared: all the people fly, and few are those who dare to say, "Stay and fight, for our land, children, homes!" In their trance, preoccupied with rivalry, they ransom for tribute what they ought to defend with the sword, and allow the kingdom of the Christians to perish.[35]

And from the other side of the fiery scourge we have the following boyhood poem of the great Viking skald and warrior-magician, Egil Skallagrimsson (fl. c. 930 A.D.):

> This did say my mother:
> that for me should be bought
> a ship and shapely oars,
> to share the life of Vikings—
> to stand up in the stem and
> steer the goodly galley,

> hold her to the harbor
> and hew down those who meet us.[36]

If the god Thor retains in his character something of the crude dawn memories of his people—the paleolithic hammer and the bold works of the primitive giant-killer—in the character of Wodan (Othin, Odin), primitive traits have all but disappeared, giving place to a steely-bright symbolic figure, highly fashioned and of great surface brilliance, but also of astounding depth. Wodan is the all-father of a securely structured, vastly conceived cosmology, inspired, like all of the great orders that we have studied, by the system of the priestly minds of ancient Sumer: developed, however, under influences from Zoroastrian, Hellenistic, and possibly, also, Christian thought; with the force of a type of warrior-mysticism that has already been represented to us in the military mysteries of Mithra and with a particular sense of destiny that is epitomized in the awesome old Anglo-Saxon word *wyrd*—from which our own word "weird," as meaning "fate," derives: the weird of the Weird Sisters of Macbeth.

We have already remarked that in Wodan's heavenly warrior hall 432,000 warriors reside,[37] who, at the end of the cosmic eon, are to rush forth to the "war with the Wolf," the battle of mutual slaughter of the gods and giants. On the dawn of that day the watchman of the giants, Eggther, would strike his harp, and above him the cock would crow, namely Fjalar, red and fair. To the gods would crow the cock Gollinkambi; and below the earth another cock would crow, rust-red, in the bowels of the goddess Hel. And then, as we read in the fate-laden verses, the hellhound Garm before its cave would howl, the fetters would burst and the wolf run free: "Much do I know," states the prophetess of these lines, "and more can see of the weird of the gods":

> Brothers shall fight and fell each other,
> And sisters' sons shall kinship stain;
> Hard is it on earth, with mighty whoredom;
> Ax-time, sword-time, shields are sundered,
> Wind-time, wolf-time, ere the world falls;
> Nor ever shall men each other spare.

> Yggdrasil shakes, and shiver on high
> The ancient limbs, and the giant is loose.

> How fare the gods? how fare the elves?
> All Jotunheim groans, the gods are at council;
> Loud roar the dwarfs by the doors of stone,
> The masters of the rocks: Would you know yet more? [38]

Another apocalypse thus appears before us.

From eastward come the giants faring in their ship Naglfar, formed of fingernail parings, steered by the giant Hrym with his shield held high. Alongside swims the Midgard Worm, and a giant eagle screams above. From the north there sails another ship, filled with the people of Hel, the shape-shifter Loki in control. And from the south appears a third ship, having Surt, the ruler of the fire-world at its helm, with a scourge of branches. Othin comes to engage the Wolf. The god Freyr seeks out Surt. Othin falls and his son Vithar avenges him, thrusting his sword to the Wolf's heart. Thor confronts the Worm again. The bright snake gapes to heaven above and Thor in anger slays him, but turning walks nine paces and falls dead.[39]

> The sun turns black, earth sinks in the sea,
> The hot stars down from heaven are whirled;
> Fierce flows the steam and the life-feeding flame,
> Till fire leaps high about heaven itself.

But then, behold!

> Now do I see the earth anew
> Rise all green from the waves again;
> The cataracts fall, and the eagle flies,
> And fish he catches beneath the cliffs.

> Then fields unsowed bear ripened fruit,
> All ills grow better, and Baldr comes back;
> Baldr and Hoth dwell in Hropt's battle-hall,
> And the mighty gods: Would you know yet more? [40]

There is no need to argue. The entire system of images of the cosmic tree of life and runic wisdom, the four cosmic directions with their companies of powers, the great eon of 432,000 years terminating in a cosmic battle, dissolution and renewal, accords perfectly with the pattern with which we are by now familiar. In this case, a point of great interest is the powerful sense of an impersonal cosmic process that infects the entire myth, while, at the same time, there is an insistence on the interplay of opposites that has suggested to some scholars a Persian, Zoroastrian source. The giant ship Naglfar, made of fingernail parings, suggests Persia also, where it was regarded as a fault to fail to make proper disposition of such parings. However, in the Eddic mythology the opposites in play are not conceived of in ethical terms; nor is it expected that in the future round the conflict of opposites will have ceased.

The old Germanic concept of the world beginning and rebeginning was of an essentially physical, not moral, conflict or interaction. As Snorri Sturluson tells in his Prose Edda:

In the beginning, there was but a Yawning Gap. In the north, then, the frigid Mist-World appeared, in the midst of which there was a well, from which the world rivers flowed. In the south appeared the world of heat, glowing, burning, and impassable to such as have not their holdings there. And those frigid streams from the north, pressing toward the south, sent up a yeasty venom that hardened to ice, which halted, and the mist congealed to rime. And when the breath of southern heat met the rime, it melted, dripped, and life was quickened from the yeast drops in the form of a great sleeping giant Ymir.

A sweat came over Ymir and there grew under his left hand a male and female, one of his feet begat a son with the other, and thus the Rime Giants appeared. Moreover, there condensed from the rime a cow, her name Audumla, four streams of milk flowing from her udder; and she nourished Ymir. She licked the ice-blocks, which were salty, and the first day she licked, hair appeared on the blocks; the next day, a man's head; and the next, the whole man was there. His name was Buri, fair of feature, great and mighty.

Buri begat Borr, who married the daughter of a giant and had three sons: Othin, Vili, and Ve, who slew the giant Ymir and fashioned of his body the earth: of his blood the sea and waters, land of his flesh, crags of his bones, gravel and stones from his teeth and broken bones; heaven they made of his skull, set over the earth, and under each corner they set a dwarf; fire and sparks from the south they scattered, some to wander in the sky, others to stand fixed, and so were made the sun, moon, and stars. And the earth was circular, with the deep sea round about. They assigned the outer edge of the earth to the giants; for the inward part they made a great citadel round about the world: and they called this Midgard. Of Ymir's brain they made the clouds. And they fashioned man and woman of two trees,* to which they gave spirit and life, wit and feeling, and then form, speech, hearing, and sight, clothing and names. Moreover, in the middle of the world they fashioned a city for themselves, of which there are many tidings and tales. Othin sat there on high, his wife was Frigg; and their race is the race known as Aesir. All-father he is called, because he is the father of all the gods and of men, and of all that was fulfilled of him and of his might.[41]

The gods give judgment every day at the foot of the Ash Yggdrasil, the greatest of all trees and best; its limbs spread over all the world, and it stands upon three roots: one is among the Aesir, one among the Rime Giants where formerly was the Yawning Void, and a third stands over the Mist World, beneath which last is the great worm Nidhoggr who gnaws the root from below.† Under the root among the Rime Giants lies Mimir's well of wisdom, of which Mimir is the watcher; and he is full of ancient lore, since he ever drinks of the well. But the root among the Aesir is in heaven, where there is the very holy well known as Urdr, whereby the gods hold tribunal. Atop the Ash sits an eagle and between his eyes sits a hawk, at the root is the gnawing worm, and a squirrel, Ratatoskr, runs up and down the trunk of the Ash, bearing envious words between Worm and Eagle. Four harts, moreover, run among the limbs and bite the leaves. . . .

As we have seen, All-father Othin hung upon that tree and, like Christ upon the cross, was pierced by a lance: the lance, his own; and he, a sacrifice to himself (his self to his Self) to win the wisdom of the runes. The analogy to be made, however, is rather to the Buddha at the Bodhi-tree than to Christ upon the cross, for

---

* Cf. supra, p. 205.
† Cf. supra, pp. 51–52.

the aim and achievement here was illumination, not the atonement of an offended god and the procurement thereby of grace to redeem a nature bound in sin. But on the other hand, in contrast to the Buddha, the character of this Man of the Tree is entirely *with* the world, and, specifically, in heroic-poetic disposition. Every day, in his great warrior hall, the champions at dawn arise, put on armor, go into the court, and fight and fell each other. That is their sport. And at evening they return to be served by Valkyries an inexhaustible mead, to sit later with them in love. And of the mead of poesy, as well, this god is the possessor and dispenser. For it was in the arts of war, in the arts of skaldic verse, and in the wisdom of the runes, that the power and glory of the Viking fleets consisted.

Poetry itself was Othin's ale, and in poetry of his sort resided the power of life. But of himself there are so many forms and names that, as a bewildered royal candidate for his wisdom once complained: "It must indeed be a goodly wit that knows all the lore and the examples of what chances have brought about each of these names." To which the god himself, in the disguise of a mystic teacher, made reply: "It is truly a vast sum of knowledge to rake into rows. But it is briefest to say, that most of his names have been given him by reason of this chance: there being so many branches of tongues in the world, all people believed that it was needful for them to turn his name into their own tongue, by which they might the better invoke him and entreat him on their own behalf. But some occasions for those names arose, also, in his wanderings; and that matter is recorded in tales. Nor canst thou ever be called a wise man if thou canst not tell of those great events." [42]

Perhaps of all Othin's wonders the most remarkable, however, is the fact that the last of his poets, to whom we owe the passage of his knowledge to ourselves, were professing Christians. Both Saemund the Wise (1056–1133), to whom the compilation of the Poetic Edda is credited, and Snorri Sturluson (1179–1241), the great warrior chieftain, skaldic poet, and author of the Prose Edda, prefigure something of the spirit of those poets of the Renaissance

for whom the gods of the Greeks supplied the mystic language of
an order of revelation antecedent to that of the Church. The Eddic
system was—for those who knew how to read—eloquent of the
same Stoic and Neoplatonic themes out of which the noblest minds
of Europe had for centuries gathered strength; and for those of a
Pelagian conviction of heart, for whom nature could never be convincingly traduced, the old gods were not unfitting associates of the
angels. They were, in fact, the northern counterparts of the very
gods of those Hellenistic mysteries of the noughting of the self,
out of whose iconographies the ritual lore and setting of the gospel
of Christianity itself had been derived. Thus in the Eddas, no less
than in the Celtic hero tales, we have, as it were, the serpent-lions
of The Book of Kells without the Gospel text: the setting (one of
faith might say) without the jewel of price. However, to those who
had learned the reading of the runes—for which Othin gave himself in gage—nature itself revealed the omnipresent jewel.

III. ROMA

The following authoritative formulation of the Christian myth
was set forth by the mighty Pope Innocent III (1198–1215) at
the Fourth Lateran Council, November 1215. Its purpose was to fix
for all time the ultimate Procrustean bed to which all thinking men
were thenceforth to be trimmed. And they were being trimmed to
it indeed in the time of this shining statesman of the Church, from
whose elegant pen no less than 4800 masterfully composed personal letters have survived. Historians name him "the greatest of
the popes." In the annals of religion the Fourth Lateran Council,
which he summoned and over which he presided, marked the con-
summation of the most awesome victory over heresy by an orthodox consensus that the world had yet beheld, and therewith
the apogee of papal power in its implementation of a gospel that
has been venerated for two thousand years as the purest statement
known to mankind of the principle of love.

"We firmly believe and simply confess," wrote this great inheritor of Peter's keys,

that there is only one true God, eternal, without measure and unchangeable; incomprehensible, omnipotent, and ineffable, the Father, and the Son, and the Holy Spirit: three persons indeed, but one simple essence, substance, or nature altogether; the Father of none, the Son of the Father alone, and the Holy Spirit of both alike, without beginning, always and without end; the Father begetting, the Son being born, and the Holy Spirit proceeding; consubstantial, and co-equal, and co-omnipotent, and co-eternal; one principle of all things; the creator of all things visible and invisible, spiritual and corporal; who by His omnipotent virtue at once from the beginning of time established out of nothing both forms of creation, spiritual and corporal, that is the angelic and the mundane, and afterwards the human creature, composed as it were of spirit and body in common. For the devil and other demons were created by God; but they became evil of their own doing. But man sinned by the suggestion of the devil.

This Holy Trinity, undivided as regards common essence, and distinct in respect of proper qualities of person, at first, according to the perfectly ordered plan of the ages, gave the teaching of salvation to the human race by means of Moses and the holy prophets and others His servants.

And at length the only-begotten Son of God, Jesus Christ, incarnate of the whole Trinity in common, being conceived of Mary ever Virgin by the cooperation of the Holy Spirit, made very man, compounded of a reasonable soul and human flesh, one person in two natures, showed the way of life in all its clearness. He, while as regards His divinity He is immortal and incapable of suffering, nevertheless, as regards His humanity, was made capable of suffering and mortal. He also, having suffered for the salvation of the human race upon the wood of the cross and died, descended to hell, rose again from the dead, and ascended into heaven; but descended in spirit and rose again in flesh, and ascended to come in both alike at the end of the world, to judge the quick and the dead, and to render to every man according to his works, both to the reprobate and to the elect, who all shall rise again with their own bodies which they now wear, that they may receive according to their works, whether they be good or bad, these perpetual punishment with the devil, and those everlasting glory with Christ.

There is moreover one universal Church of the faithful,

outside which no man at all is saved, in which the same Jesus Christ is both the priest and the sacrifice, whose body and blood are truly contained in the sacrament of the altar under the species of bread and wine, the bread being transubstantiated into the body and the wine into the blood by the divine power, in order that, to accomplish the mystery of unity, we ourselves may receive of His that which He received of ours. And this thing, the sacrament to wit, no one can make but a priest, who has been duly ordained, according to the keys of the Church, which Jesus Christ Himself granted to the apostles and their successors.

But the sacrament of baptism, which is consecrated in water at the invocation of God and of the undivided Trinity, that is of the Father, and of the Son and Holy Spirit, being duly conferred in the form of the Church by any person, whether upon children or adults, is profitable to salvation. And if anyone, after receiving baptism, has fallen into sin, he can always be restored by true penitence.

Not only virgins and the continent, but also married persons, deserve, by right faith and good works pleasing God, to come to eternal blessedness.[43]

Implicit in this stately doctrine, as in all pronouncements of the Church, was the belief, which had been argued by Augustine against the heresy of Pelagius, that through Adam's fall human nature had been so corrupted that the will, though free, is able to will only what is sinful until blessed (through no merit of man's own but by God's free act alone) with divine grace; and implicit, also, is the no less basic notion, argued by Augustine against the Donatists, that the authenticity of the Church as the only valid dispensary on earth of the grace by which man is saved is not contingent on the character of its clergy. Ironically, although in the period of Augustine such a guaranteed monopoly in the invisible commodity called grace (for which no proof could be furnished or demanded either of delivery or of failure) may have been advantageous to the unchallengeable growth and spread of the dispensing institution among those in whom a demand for the commodity had been instilled, nevertheless, in the period of Innocent III the dark and dangerous side of the guarantee of power to an unimpeachable clergy had become to such an extent evident that the council itself had been summoned to confront it. Heresies of both Gnostic and Donatist type, protesting the abuse by the orthodox clergy of their powers, were frighteningly increasing both in number and in force. In the words of Henry Charles Lea in his classic *History of the Inquisition:* "The affection of the populations was no longer attracted by the graces and loveliness of Christianity; submission was purchased by the promise of salvation, to be acquired by faith and obedience, or was extorted by the threat of perdition or by the sharper terrors of earthly persecution." [44] And the clergy themselves, meanwhile, were illustrating virtues on the side rather of the goats at the left than of the sheep at the right hand of the Judgment Seat of the Second Coming of the Lord. Two examples will suffice, from the period of Innocent himself; the first, Gérard de Rougemont, Archbishop of Besançon, and the second, the Bishop of Toul, Maheu de Lorraine.

In the year 1198 de Rougemont's chapter accused him of perjury, simony, and incest, but when he was summoned to Rome the accusers did not dare to prosecute their charges. They did not, however, withdraw them, and the great master of the Law of God, Innocent III, charitably quoting Christ in the case of the woman taken in adultery ("Let him who is without sin among you be the first to throw a stone at her"),[45] sent the prelate back home to purge himself and be absolved. And de Rougemont returned home indeed: to live in incest with his cousin, the Abbess of Remiremont, and in less exceptionable intimacy with his other concubines, one of whom was a nun, a second the daughter of a priest; whereas, meanwhile, no church in his province could be consecrated without a payment to himself, monks and nuns who could bribe him were allowed to quit their convents to marry, and his regular clergy were reduced by his exactions to live like peasants, by their own hands. In the year 1211 there was initiated a second attempt to remove him, which, however, simply dragged on until, at last, about the time of the Lateran Council itself, his people rose and drove him out. He retired to the Abbey of Bellevaux, where he died peacefully in the year 1225.[46]

The Bishop of Toul, Maheu de Lorraine, who was a devotee of the chase, had as favorite concubine his own daughter by a nun of Epinal. He was consecrated in 1200. Two years later his chapter, reduced to poverty, applied to Innocent for his removal, and it was only after a most intricate series of commissions and appeals, interspersed with acts of violence, that he was in 1210 deposed. Seven years later he caused his successor, Renaud de Senlis, to be murdered, after which, his own uncle, Thiebault, Duke of Lorraine, chancing to meet him, slew him on the spot.[47]

From the troubadour Peire Cardenal (c. 1205–1305?) who had himself, for a time, been a student of theology, comes the following verse:

> 'Tis true the monks and friars make ample show
> Of rules austere which they all undergo,
>   But this the vainest is of all pretences,
> In sooth, they live full twice as well, we know,
> As e'er they did at home, despite their vow,
>   And all their mock parade of abstinences,
> No jollier life than theirs can be, indeed;
> And specially the begging friars exceed,
>   Whose frock grants license as abroad they wander.
> These motives 'tis which to the Orders lead
> So many worthless men, in sorest need
>   Of pelf, which·on their vices they may squander,
>   And then the frock protects them in their plunder.[48]

The great Minnesinger Walther von der Vogelweide (fl. 1198–1228) wrote as well:

> Thy ministers rob here and murder there,
> And o'er thy sheep a wolf has shepherd's care.[49]

While from Saint Bernard of Clairvaux (1090–1153) comes the question: "Whom can you show me among the prelates who does not seek rather to empty the pockets of his flock than to subdue their vices?"[50] and from Saint Hildegarde of Bingen (1098–1179): "The prelates are ravishers of the churches; their avarice consumes all that it can acquire. With their oppressions they make us paupers and contaminate us and themselves."[51]

It is hardly to be wondered, then, why in the course of the twelfth century there should have developed throughout Europe a deep trend, not merely of anti-clericalism but of radical heresy, of which the Cathari or Albigenses of the fairest cities and lands of the south of France were the most threatening examples. We need not rehearse the whole length of the well-known, terrible history of the papal extirpation of this sect. The main point to our present purpose is that Albigensianism seems to have been a resurgent variant of the Manichean religion, which had recently entered Europe by way of Bulgaria, Bosnia, Hungary, and then Italy, to flourish largely in the southern France of the troubadours.

Like the Christianity of Augustine, Manichaeism viewed nature as corrupt; however, not because of Adam's fall, but because created by an evil god. And redemption was to be attained not through sacraments functioning, as by magic, of themselves, but through virtue. It has been the fashion of Christian critics to ridicule the Manichaean notion that the virtue of their clergy was the actual and sole agency by which the principle of spirit and light, caught in the meshes of material darkness, was to be released and returned to its proper state. Bizarre as the myth may have seemed to those who were not initiate to its sense (though it is, of course, no more bizarre than the Christian myth itself, or any other myth, in fact, that is read as literal prose), it had what, for that time, was the astonishing result of producing a type of clergyman who could be honored as a model of the virtues that he preached. And the result was a vast and, for the Church, dangerous popularity, against which the most vigorous measures were invoked.

There were, apparently, numerous Albigensian sects, but the outstanding characteristic of all was the extreme austerity of their supreme living saints, who were known as the "purified" or "perfected": *Cathari*. As in Buddhism, so here, the basic idea was of reincarnation and release: the progress through many lives of the soul trapped in ignorance and delusion to an ultimate state of release through illumination. Like the living Buddhas, so the Cathari served both as initiators and as models for those "believers" who were not yet spiritually ready for the great renunciations of the ultimate leap to release. The believers, *auditores,* might marry and eat meat: the perfected, *boni homines,* were ascetic vegetarians. Since the writings of the Albigensian Cathari have been destroyed, and our knowledge of their practice comes mainly from their enemies, little can be said of the finer points. We seem to know, however, that the *boni homines* were themselves venerated by the *auditores;* that the all-important Catharan rite was a mystery of spiritual initiation known as the Consolamentum; that a form of ritual suicide through absolute fast, known as the Endura, might occasionally be practiced by the saints (as by the Jains of India); [52] and that when offered, under Christian persecution, the alternative of recantation or the stake, both the mere believers and the perfected chose inevitably the latter.

Indeed, in the words of Henry Charles Lea, "If the blood of the martyrs were really the seed of the Church, Manichaeism would now be the dominant religion of Europe." [53] As early as 1017, which is the earliest recorded date of a public burning of heretics, thirteen Albigensians out of a group of fifteen apprehended in Orléans remained steadfast and were taken to the stake. At Toulouse in 1022 another such execution is recorded; in 1051 there was another in Goslar, in Saxony.[54] At Cologne, a century later, 1163, those who were burned produced a profound impression by the cheerful ease with which they accepted incineration. Arnold, their leader, when already blazing, placed a liberated arm on the heads of those burning at his side and calmly said, "Be ye constant in your faith; for this day ye shall be with Lawrence!" The leader, Gerhard, of another group burned in Oxford at that time, sang, as he walked with his flock to the fire, "Blessed are ye when men shall revile you." And in southern France, during the utterly detestable Albigensian Crusade of 1209–1229, after the capture of the Castle of Minerve, one hundred and eighty went together to the stake, and the monkish chronicler of the festival remarked, "no doubt these martyrs of the devil passed, all, from temporal to eternal flames." [55]

The problem for the Church in southern France lay in the indifference of the aristocracy to anathemas, excommunications, bulls, embassies, legates, or anything else emanating from Rome to frustrate the rising heresy. And the climax came in the year 1167, when the Cathari actually held a council of their own at St. Felix de Caraman near Toulouse. Their highest dignitary, Bishop Nicetas, came from Constantinople to preside; bishops were elected for the vacant sees of Toulouse, Val d'Aran, Carcassonne, Albi, and France north of the Loire; commissioners were named to settle a boundary dispute between the sees of Toulouse and Carcassonne; and "in short," as Lea remarks, "the business was that of an established and independent Church, which looked upon itself as destined to supersede the Church of Rome." [56]

Rome, however, replied. Pope Alexander III (1159–1181) summoned a Lateran Council that in the year 1179 took the unprecedented step of proclaiming within Christendom itself a crusade. Two years' indulgence (that is to say, a shortening of the soul's term in purgatory by two years) was promised to all who should take up arms, and those who might die in the cause were assured of eternal salvation. An army thus was raised, to serve without visible pay, and in the year 1181 this spiritual force fell upon the territories of the Viscount of Béziers and took, after siege, the fortified city of Lavaur (between Albi and Toulouse) where the Viscountess Adelaide and several other leading Cathari had sought refuge. The fortified city, according to account, was taken only by miracle, and throughout France consecrated wafers dropping blood announced to believers the victory of their Christian arms.[57] The crusading force, having gained heaven for itself, disbanded, and nothing more was done about the continuing heresy until Pope Innocent III, in the year 1209, launched an army of great magnitude, from the city of Lyons, for the kill.

These were centuries, throughout Europe, of all kinds of hysterical group seizures. Through the preaching of the First Crusade (1096–1099), first by the pope, Urban II, and then by a type of wandering fanatic of whom Peter the Hermit was the most famous (whose very donkey became an object of religious veneration), the peasants were uprooted from the land and sent by thousands on waves of ardor to meet disaster, one way or another, either on the roads or in the Holy Land itself. The celebrated pied piping of the Children's Crusade of the year 1212 was but another such group seizure; and like phenomena of lesser magnitude were both various and common everywhere: as, for example, in the curious dance epidemics that came to a climax in the fourteenth century, in the years of the Black Death.[58] Swarms of flagellants, naked to the waist, heads enveloped in cloths, bearing standards, lighted candles, and streaming scourges, beating themselves to the sound of spiritual songs, also might be encountered on the roads.[59] It was an age when the admonition of Christ—when you pray, go into your room and there shut the door [60]—was little regarded. The call of Innocent for an army, therefore, had met with a rather highly charged emotional response. Recruits both of noble and of menial blood were drawn from every quarter of Europe, as far away as Bremen, as nearby as Burgundy and Nevers; and in Germany towns and villages became filled with spiritually inflamed women, who, unable to expend their religious ardor by joining the pope's army of the cross, had stripped and were to be seen silently running, naked, singly and in groups, about the streets and along the roads.

Pope Innocent, two years before the massing of his horde, had excommunicated Count Raymond of Toulouse, who had been one of the leading protectors of the rights of his Albigensian relatives and friends to worship as they would; and shortly following this excommunication, which had released all the count's subjects from their loyalty, oaths, and obligations to him, it came to pass that a papal legate, almost immediately after an argument with the count, was slain by a knight's lance. Raymond seemed to have been the author of the deed—though in fact he may not have been—and to clear his character and soul he offered, in confusion, to yield in penance to the pope's conditions. These, as he then found, were that he should place in the hands of the Church his seven most important strongholds, after which, if he could prove himself free of guilt, he would be absolved.

Raymond, to his sorrow, failed to bear in mind, in this contingency, the recognized Christian principle that covenants contracted with heretics could—or even should—be disregarded. He allowed himself, therefore, to be brought, stripped to the waist, before the papal legates at the portal of the Church of St. Gilles, where he swore upon the relics of St. Gilles to obey the Church in all matters whereof he was accused. The legate placed a stole around his neck in the way of a halter and, while he was being scourged on naked back and shoulders, led him through a curious crowd that had gathered to witness the degradation of their lord to the high altar, where he was absolved—on condition that he should extirpate heresy from his realm, dismiss all Jews from office, restore all despoiled Church property, abolish all arbitrary tolls, and join himself to the crusade. Then, when the cities that he gave had been occupied, he was excommunicated once again—which had been actually Innocent's plan—and the great advance of the mighty army of the Christian Cross commenced, into the richest lands of France.

There were some twenty thousand cavaliers and two hundred thousand foot. All moneys of the empire were under contribution, under pain of excommunication, and the salary of eternal reward was lavishly available to all. The walls of the fair city of Béziers were the first to fall, and the massacre that followed was up to that day without parallel in European history: the papal legates report a slaughter of nearly twenty thousand—seven thousand in the Church of Mary Magdalene alone, to which they had fled for asylum; and when the empowered legate in charge was asked whether Catholics should be spared, fearing that some of the heretics then might escape by feigning orthodoxy, he replied, with the true spirit of a man of God in his heart, "Kill them all, for God knows his own!" The city caught fire and the sun that evening set upon a smoking scene perfectly fit to illustrate the Catharan view that the pope and his Church were not of the seed of divine love, AMOR, but the reverse (as the word, read backward, seemed to show), the very fashioners of hell on earth, which, according to their teaching, is the only hell there is. The fall of Carcassonne followed: the city, in fear, submitted, and its population were allowed to leave, bearing with them nothing but their sins, the men in their breeches, the women in their shifts, and the army, paid with a promise of the

Kingdom of Christ, moved in. By summer's end the mighty pope could write, in his elegant Latin style, of his fervent joy at the wonderful wresting of five hundred cities and castles from the servants of the wiles and wickedness of the devil.[61]

Count Raymond's Toulouse was the next city on the list. . . . But the interested reader can pursue the rest of this sordid history alone. It continued for another twenty years, leaving southern France a ruin and the Church of Rome no more secure in its seat of tyranny than before. For, in contrast to the great histories of China, India, and the Levant, where, as we have seen, the governing elites could pretend without serious challenge to have been supernaturally endowed, in Europe this high mythic posture never gained for long the field. Neither in Greece and Rome, nor in the later Celto-Germanic West, has the normal Oriental view that certain parties, whether kings or priests, have a divine right and power to assert not only what men must do but also what men must think, ever inspired the best native minds. During the early Middle Ages, when the primary Christian mission was in progress, the clergy may have imagined that in time they would imprint their myth on the land forever and thereby rule as the bureaucracy of a kind of European caliphate or papal pharaonic court. But already at the apogee of their power, in the reign of Innocent III, the entire project was in conspicuous decay and could develop only toward collapse. Men had begun to think, and the European sense of the individual in his own right simply disintegrated the pretext of an absolute, Levantine consensus.

The symptom of the Catharan heresy was but one of a mounting number, which no amount of threats, burnings, lashings, or anathemas could abolish or even abate. For example:

Joachim of Floris (c. 1145–1202), founder of the abbey of San Giovanni in Fiore, on Monte Nero, which on January 21, 1204, received the approval of Innocent III, died in the good graces of his church. In his interesting *Expositio in Apocalypsin,* however, he had defined a view of history that in a council held at Arles in 1260 was condemned, together with all his works, and together, moreover, with all those ecstatic monastic movements that had followed in his wake. Briefly, his idea was that the history of mankind was to be divided in three periods: 1. The Age of the Father (the Old Testament); 2. the Age of the Son (the New Testament and Church); and 3. the Age of the Holy Spirit, when the hierarchy of Rome would be dissolved and the whole world become, as it were, a monastery of souls in direct communion with God.

Joachim's anti-papal polemic appealed to a great many zealots of his day, including numerous Franciscans, who believed they saw in Francis of Assisi (1182–1226) the initiator of Age Three, when the papal structure would disappear. A number of curious movements developed, also, around certain figures who were thought to be incarnations of the Holy Ghost; notably a pious lady, Guglielma, who arrived in Milan about 1260 and died 1281, and an interesting, very simple youth, Segarelli by name, who appeared in Parma in the garb of an apostle, also in the fateful year 1260— which had been foretold by Joachim of Floris as the year of the Age of the Holy Ghost. Segarelli became the center of an at first relatively harmless anti-clerical sect, which rapidly gained extensive influence and, in reaction to persecution, became fanatically violent, yielding many members to the stake. Segarelli himself was burned in the year of the great papal Jubilee 1300, and the leaders of the largest company of his followers—the brave Dolcino, his adjutant Longino Cattaneo, and Margherita di Trank—after one of the most amazing episodes of desperate guerrilla warfare in the history of Europe, were captured seven years later and executed: the woman, of noble family and recognized beauty, was roasted slowly before Dolcino's eyes, and he himself was then driven about the city of Vercelli in a cart, being gradually torn to bits with a battery of red-hot pincers, while his colleague, Cattaneo, was suffering the same piecemeal dismemberment for the edification of the Christian town of Biella.[62]

Dante Alighieri (1265–1321) placed the monk Joachim in paradise,[63] but appears to have appointed Dolcino to hell [64]— while proposing, as we know, his own mythic answer to the worldly arrogance of the popes, having himself, in the year 1302, been sentenced by the papal party to be burned. Dante's proposition was

that the empire of Rome had been established by divine appointment no less than the kingdom of Jerusalem; and that the emperor,
inheriting from Rome, represented the secular order, as the pope,
inheriting from Jerusalem, represented the spiritual, whose kingdom, as Christ had said, was not of this world. "Not force but
reason, and moreover divine reason, was the beginning of the
Roman empire," Dante wrote in the Fourth Treatise of the *Convivio;* [65] and he showed in what a marvelous way the histories of
the two orders, of Rome and of Jerusalem, had coincided through
the ages: the coming to Italy of Aeneas had coincided with the
birth of David; the perfection of Rome under Augustus had coincided with the birth of Christ. Further, the whole growth of Rome
had been fostered by a sequence of divinely inspired citizens and
protected by divine miracles. Dante reviewed the series and ex-
claims at the conclusion, "Verily, I am of firm opinion that the
stones that are fixed in her walls are worthy of reverence, and the
soil where she sits more worthy than man can preach or prove." [66]

The capital point of this exposition was that in the Christian
world the powers of state and church are equally of divine origin,
and, by implication, authority, having each its appointed sphere;
and that, whereas the heritage of the religious derived from the
Covenant of Moses and teaching of the prophets, that of the secular
sphere was of Roman law. We cannot in this volume review the
mounting series of disasters through which the effort of the Church
to usurp the functions of the state broke down. The first came in
Dante's own time, when Pope Boniface VIII (1294–1303), whom
he assigned in his *Divine Comedy* to the eighth circle of hell, set
forth in a celebrated bull known as *Unam Sanctam* the boldest
claim to world rule that any monarch in the world had ever made.
"We declare," this pope had written, "we declare, say, define, and
pronounce that it is a necessity of salvation for every human
creature to be subject to the Roman pontiff." [67] And in a second
statement, delivered to the king of the Romans, he had added that
as God had made both sun and moon, so had He also made the
metaphorical sun of ecclesiastical power and metaphorical moon
of the secular power: "And as the moon has no light save that

which it received from the sun, so too no earthly power has anything save that which it received from the ecclesiastical power." [68] What a surprise it must have been, therefore, to that metaphorical sun, Boniface himself, when in June 1303 the king of France, Philip IV the Fair (r. 1285–1314), accusing him of heresy, sent an armed band to arrest him. The old prelate died of the shock; and the following pope was a Frenchman, dwelling not in Rome but in Avignon.

By 1377 there were two popes, one in Avignon, one in Rome, each excommunicating the other, until 1409, when a council of cardinals at Pisa elected still another, so that of popes there then were three. The great council at Constance, 1414–1418, attended by some 6500 persons—of whom at least 1600 were of noble blood and 700 public women (the latter, according to report, supplemented by innumerable succubi) *—only advanced the rampant process of decomposition of the Church through its entrapment and burning of the popular John Huss (c. 1373–1415), which, as one authority has remarked, was "the most momentous act of the century." [69]

Having come to the council of his own free will under a guarantee of safe conduct to present his argument for reform, the gentle Bohemian priest was entrapped, chained feet and hands to the wall of a noisome cell, implacably ordered to confess that he had taught doctrines which he had never taught, and, when he refused thus to perjure himself, was, on July 6, 1415, at the most gorgeous *auto da fe* on record, stripped ceremoniously of his priestly vestments before a distinguished multitude at the cathedral of Constance, shorn of his tonsure with a scissors, and after his fingers had been scraped (to remove the skin, which at the time of his ordination had been anointed with priestly oil), he was given a tall conical paper hat painted with devils, on which were inscribed the words, "This is the heresiarch," and turned over to the secular agents of the Church's infallible will, to be burned. "Christ Jesus, Son of the living God, have mercy upon me!" his voice was heard

* Succubi are devils in female form that appear to men in sleep and seduce them.

to exclaim twice, while a wind blew the flames and smoke about his upright form. The ashes and all the earth round about were then thrown into the Rhine, to prevent their veneration as relics.[70] Exactly one century later, however, the sun of Luther rose from those ashes, and the Roman Catholic Church was, thereafter, but one of a constellation of contending Christianities in the European West.

IV. AMOR

In the broadest view of the history of world mythology, the chief creative development in the period of the waning Middle Ages and approaching Reformation was the rise of the principle of individual conscience over ecclesiastical authority. This marked the beginning of the end of the reign of the priestly mind, first, over European thought and then, as today we see, in all the world. And therewith a new world age dawned, which is already as great in its advance beyond the high cultures of the past—spiritually and morally, as well as materially—as were these beyond the simple tribal orders of paleolithic man.

Through our survey of the mythologies of the Primitive, Oriental, and Occidental worlds we have found that during the almost endless first period of our species, when hunting and vegetable-collection were the sole means of sustenance, social groups were comparatively small and there was little or no specialization of individuals. The roles of the sexes were, indeed, distinct, and there was a recognized difference, also, between those endowed with the gift of shamanistic vision and the rest of the community. However, in the main, as remarked in *Primitive Mythology,* in the period of the early hunting tribes, "every individual was technically a master of the whole cultural inheritance, and the communities were therefore constituted of practically equivalent individuals." [71]

A new and grandiose epoch dawned with the invention of the arts of food-cultivation, agriculture and animal husbandry, in the nuclear Near East, between c. 7500 and 5500 B.C. As a consequence, communities arose of considerable size, within which variously specialized types of man and knowledge were developed.

And the most important of these for our study was the class of professional, full-time priest, devoted, among other concerns, to the observation of the movements of the starry heavens. In the earlier, primitive cultures, the orientation had been toward the animal and plant kingdoms of the immediate neighborhood. The myths and rites of the roving tribesmen of the Great Hunt, for whom the animals, large and small, of the rolling plains were the chief manifestations of the powers and mysteries of nature, were based largely on the idea that between mankind and the beasts a covenant existed. The food animals gave their bodies willingly to be slain, provided certain rites were enacted to insure their rebirth and return. Animals also appeared in vision, to become the guardians, initiators, and vehicles of the shamans, bestowing upon them knowledge, power, and spiritual insight. And the people, in their rites, dressed as and imitated beasts.

In regions, on the other hand, where the plant world predominated both as food source and as exemplar of the mysteries of life, the dominant myths were inspired by a recognition of analogies between the processes of vegetal and human existence—birth and growth out of death and decay, indifference toward the individual —and the rites, accordingly, were characterized by a concentration, often lavishly, on forms of human sacrifice, through which the powers of life (thought to be derived from death) were supposed to be enhanced.

It appears, furthermore, that in the nuclear Near East, where the earliest agricultural villages of the neolithic stage of civilization arose, a vegetal mythology prevailed that was closely allied to that of the primitive planting zones. We have discussed the evidence in *Primitive Mythology* and need not repeat the demonstration.

And we have discussed there also the epochal appearance toward the dawn of the Age of Bronze of an entirely new priestly mythology, oriented principally neither to the animal nor to the plant world as manifestations of the laws and mystery of being, but to the cycling, mathematically calculable order of the stars, the sun and moon, with Mercury, Venus, Mars, Jupiter, and Saturn.

As in heaven, so on earth. To the priestly knowers of that cosmic order an absolute, divinely directed moral authority was attributed; and from the time of the rise of the earliest great temples of the ancient Near East (c. 4000 B.C) to the period to which our reading now has brought us, every known high civilization—except, for a time, the Greco-Roman—took its spiritual instruction from these priestly watchers of the sky, who were supposed to have derived from the cosmic order a knowledge of the order proper as well to men on earth.

Both in *Oriental Mythology* and in this volume, we have followed the growth and spread across the world of the majestic mythologies derived from these celestial observations, to which all the orders of human experience, thought, yearning, and realization were required to be subordinate. And we have seen, too, how, in their diffusion, they encountered and absorbed—or, on the other hand, were absorbed by—the mythologies of the more primitive folk among whom they came.

Entering India, the high mythology of the ritual regicide was introduced to a realm in which the brutal sacrificial rites of the tropical planter complex were already flourishing, and the two lines were united to compose one of the most richly developed traditions of ritual murder in the history of our subject. Entering Europe, on the other hand, the same high culture complex came into the classic lands of the northern, paleolithic Great Hunt, the lands of the great caves and cave art of the Dordogne and Pyrenees. And we have seen that in this area there prevailed in the paleolithic period no such plant-inspired emphasis on ritual cannibalism as among the villages of the tropics. Nor did the characteristic myths center on a deity ritually killed so that the village, tribe, or universe should prosper.

Among tribesmen depending on the hunting skills of individuals for their existence, the individual is fostered: even the concept of immortality is individual, not collective. Spiritual leadership, furthermore, is exercised primarily by shamans, who are individuals endowed with spiritual power through personal spiritual experience, not socially installed priests, made members of an organiza-

tion through appointment and anointment.[72] We have seen that in
the early interplay of these northern hunter and warrior forms with
those of the entering neolithic and Bronze Age cultural orders,
there developed not a fusion but a process of interaction, of mounting amplitude and force. And so it was again, in the millennium
of the Christian mission, which arrived, like the other higher culture
forms, from the nuclear Near East.

Like them, the Christian order both carried and was supported
by a mythology of priestly authority, derived—it was alleged—
from a supernatural source. The priests were not required, or
even expected, to have had spiritual experiences of their own; indeed, those who had had such were in danger of the stake. They
were installed by anointment and appointment, and their personal
power derived not from the dignity of their persons, but from the
institution they served, and this, in turn, was valued, not for its
contribution to the earthly dignity of man, but for its supposed
derivation from on high. We have seen that after a moment of high
victory in the reign of Innocent III, the authority of this priestly
organization was challenged and substantially overthrown. And as
our next volume is to record, it was immediately thereafter that a
new mythology—quite new—neither of animal nor of plant divinities, nor of the cosmic order and its God, but of man, gradually
came (and is still coming) to the fore, which is, in fact, the only
creative breath now operating for the future of a mankind centered
in its own terrestrial truth, blessedness, and will.

Let me note before passing on, however, that even in the
twelfth- and early thirteenth-century flowering of Arthurian Romance the beginnings may be recognized of this new mythology of
man who in his native virtue is competent both to experience and
to render blessedness, even in the mixed field of this our life on
earth. Take the mystery of the Grail: For what reason, pray, should
a Christian knight ride forth questing for the Grail when at hand, in
every chapel, were the blessed body and blood of Christ literally
present in the sacrament of the altar for the redemption and
beatitude of his soul?

The answer, obviously, is that the Grail Quest was an individual adventure in experience. The backgrounds of the legend lay in pagan, specifically Celtic, myth. Its heroes were the old champions, Cuchullin and the rest, returned in knightly armor as Gawain, Perceval, or Galahad, to engage, as ever, in marvelous adventure. There had been added, furthermore, through the influence of Islam, related symbols, loaded with the mystic lore of Asia; elements, also, from Byzantium and from even farther East. By various schools of modern scholarship the Grail has been identified with the Dagda's caldron of plenty, the begging bowl of the Buddha in which four bowls, from the four quarters, were united, the Kaaba of the Great Mosque of Mecca, and the ultimate talismanic symbol of some sort of Gnostic-Manichaean rite of spiritual initiation, practiced possibly by the Knights Templar.[73] All such alien, primitive, or related Oriental forms, however, were in the European romances reinterpreted and applied to the local, immediate spiritual situation. Specifically, the legend refers to the restoration of a land laid waste through a Dolorous Stroke dealt to its king by an unworthy hand, which took possession of a sacred lance that in the later versions of the legend is identified with the lance that pierced Christ's side.[74] And we do not have to ask or guess what the reference of such a legend may have been, or why the allegory in its time touched so many hearts: the condition of the Church, above described, explains this well enough.

The Grail Hero—particularly in the person of Perceval or Parzival, the "Great Fool"—is the forthright, simple, uncorrupted, noble son of nature, without guile, strong in the purity of the yearning of his heart. In the words of the poet Wolfram von Eschenbach (c. 1165–c. 1220), describing his Grail Hero's childhood in the forest: "Of sorrow he knew nothing, unless it was the birdsong above him; for the sweetness of it pierced his heart and made his little bosom swell: His nature and his yearning so compelled him." [75] His widowed, noble mother, in their forest retreat had told him of God and Satan, "distinguished for him dark and light." [76] However, in his own deeds light and dark were mixed. He was not an angel or a saint, but a living, questing man of deeds, gifted with the paired virtues of courage and compassion, to which was added loyalty. And it was through his steadfastness in these—not supernatural grace—that he won, at last, to the Grail.

Or what shall we say of the other great theme of Arthur's Table Round: the passionate loves in adultery of Tristan and Iseult and of Lancelot and Queen Guinevere? It is again a mystic theme of individual experience in depth, opposed to the sacramental claim—this time, of marriage. For in the Middle Ages marriage, sanctified by the Church, was a socio-political arrangement, bearing no relationship to the mystery and wonder of love. In the words of Professor Johan Huizinga in his eloquent little book, *The Waning of the Middle Ages,* "From the side of religion maledictions were poured upon love in all its aspects." [77] From the side of the court, on the other hand, and of the poetry of experience (again to quote a phrase of Huizinga), love "became the field where all moral and cultural perfection flowered." [78] Love was a divine visitation, quelling mere animal lust, whereas feudal marriage was a physical affair. The lover, whose heart was rendered gentle by the discipline of his lady, was initiate to a sphere of exalted realizations that no one who had experienced such could possibly identify (as the Church identified them) with sin. One has but to read the poems of Dante's *Vita Nuova* to realize to what spheres of mystic transport the courtly way of love might lead.

There is considerable evidence that a number of the troubadours were associated with the Albigensian heresy. Numerous links are known, furthermore, to the mystic poetry of the Sufis of Islam. Analogies appear, as well, to the Shakti cults of India and above all to the poetry of Jayadeva's Gita Govinda, the date of which, c. 1175, is about that of the Tristan of Chrétien of Troyes.[79] We also recognize—here as in the Grail context—strains from the Celtic mythic sphere. The proven prototypes of Mark, Tristan, and Iseult were the Irish legendary favorites, Finn MacCumhaill, his lieutenant Diarmuid, and his abducted bride-to-be, Grianne.

There is, in short, between the pagan past and high Middle Ages of Europe an impressive continuity of spirit and development, over which, for a time, the overlay of an Oriental type of spiritual despotism was heavily spread, only to be disintegrated, assimilated, and absorbed. In courtly and poetic circles the ideal of individual experience prevailed over that of the infallible authority of men whose character was supposed to be disregarded. And in the Church as well, the principle of such fallibility was called into doubt, questioned and rejected. John Wycliffe (d. 1384) wrote in England that all the hierarchy, from the pope down, were accursed by reason of their greed, simony, cruelty, lust for power, and evil lives: the popes of the period were Antichrist and not to be obeyed, their decretals were as naught and their excommunications to be disregarded. And unless they give satisfaction, he wrote, "thai schul be depper dampned than Judas Scarioth." "Certes," he wrote again, "as holy prestis of lyvynge and cunnynge of holy writte han keyes of heven and bene vicaris of Jesus Christ, so viciouse prestis, un-konnynge of holy writte, ful of pride and covetise, han keyes of helle and bene vicaris of Sathanas." [80]

Wycliffe, practically, was a Donatist, as were also Huss and his followers. No one in mortal sin, Huss wrote, could be a temporal lord, a prelate, or a bishop. And in Germany, where the Reformation finally would come to its full statement, Meister Eckhart (c. 1260–c. 1327), who was almost precisely a contemporary of Dante, led the way to a new Christian mystic life within:

> Where [he preached to his congregation] is he who is born King of the Jews? Now concerning this birth, mark where it befalls. I say again, as I have often said before, that this birth befalls in the soul exactly as it does in eternity, neither more nor less, for it is the same birth: this birth befalls in the ground and essence of the soul.[81]

> God is in all things as being, as activity, as power. But he is procreative in the soul alone; for though every creature is a vestige of God, the soul is the natural image of God. . . . Such perfection as enters the soul, whether it be divine light, grace, or bliss, must needs enter the soul in this birth and no other wise. Do but foster this birth in thee and thou wilt experience all good and all comfort, all happiness, all being, and all truth. What comes to thee therein brings the true being and stability; and whatsoever thou mayest seek or grasp without it perishes, take it how thou wilt.[82]

Kill thy activities and still thy faculties if thou wouldst realize this birth in thee. To find the newborn King in thee, all else thou mightest find must be passed by and left behind thee. May we outstrip and leave behind such things as are not pleasing to the newborn King. So help us thou who didst become a child of man that we might become the children of God. Amen.[83]

We are on the edge of India here; as we are, too, when gazing at the charming little Madonna in the Cluny Museum of Paris shown in Figures 31 and 32. Eckhart's sermon on the birth of Jesus Christ in the soul might be taken as a reading of the import of this image; which is an image comparable, also, to the Shi'a Fatima described above,* as well as to the Bronze Age goddess-mother of the universe and of its Living God—in whom the macro- and microcosmic orders are to be known as one.

From Eckhart, another word:

A maid is given to a man, hoping to bear his child. And God did make the soul, intending her to bear in her his only begotten Son. The occurrence of this birth in Mary spiritual was to God more pleasing than his being born of her in flesh. And this same birth today in the God-loving soul delights God more than his creation of the heavens and the earth.[84]

Still another word; and one more:

I am as certain as I live that nothing is so close to me as God. God is nearer to me than I am to my own self; my life depends upon God's being near me, present in me. So is he also in a stone, a log of wood, only they do not know it.[85]

I say: had Mary not borne God in spiritual fashion first, he never had been born of her in flesh. The woman said to Christ, "Blessed is the womb that bore thee." To which Christ replied, "Blessed not alone the womb that bore me: blessed they that bear the word of God and keep it." It is more worth to God his being brought forth spiritually in the individual virgin or good soul than that he was born of Mary bodily.

But this involves the notion of *our* being the only Son whom

* Supra, pp. 445–46.

Figure 31. Madonna and Child

the Father has eternally begotten. When the Father begat all creatures, he was begetting me; I flowed out with all creatures while remaining within in the Father. It is like what I am now saying: it springs up within me, then I pause in the idea, and thirdly I speak it out, when all of you receive it: but really it is in me all the while. Just so am I abiding in the Father.[86]

Moses saw God face to face, so the scriptures say. This theologists deny. They argue in this way: Where two faces show, God is not seen, for God is one not two. Who sees God sees nothing but one. . . . The soul is one with God—not united.[87]

And finally:

If you would know and recognize the really sane and genuine seers of God, whom nothing can deceive or misinform, they can be detected by four and twenty signs. The first sign is told us by the chief exponent of knowledge and wisdom and transcendental understanding, who is himself the

Figure 32. The Mother of the Living God

truth, or Lord Jesus Christ. He says, "Thereby ye shall know
that ye are my disciples, if ye love one another and keep my
commandment. What is my commandment? That ye love one
another as I have loved you," as though to say, ye may be my
disciples in knowledge and in wisdom and high understanding,
but without true love it shall avail you little if anything at all.
Balaam was so clever he understood what God for many hundred years had been trying to reveal. This was but little help
to him because he lacked true love. And Lucifer, the angel,
who is in hell, had perfectly pure intellect and to this day
knows much. He has the more hell pain, and all because he
failed to cleave with love and faith to what he knew.—The
second sign is selflessness: they empty themselves out of
themselves, giving free furlough to things.—The third sign:
they have wholly abandoned themselves to God: God works in
them undisturbed.—The fourth sign: wherever they still find
themselves they leave themselves; sure method of advance-
ment.—The fifth sign: they are free from all self-seeking:
this gives them a clear conscience.—The sixth sign: they wait
unceasingly upon God's will and do it to their utmost.—The

seventh sign: they bend their will to God's will, till their will coincides with God's.—The eighth sign: so closely do they fit and bind themselves to God and God to them in the power of love, that God does nothing without them and they do nothing without God.—The ninth sign: They naught themselves and make use of God in all their works and in all places and all things.—The tenth sign: they take no single thing from any creature, neither good nor bad, but all from God alone, albeit God effect it through his creature.—The eleventh sign: they are not snared by any pleasure or physical enjoyment or by any creature.—The twelfth sign: they are not forced or driven by insubordination.—The thirteenth sign: they are not misled by any spurious light nor by the look of any creature; they go by the intrinsic merit.—The fourteenth sign: armed and arrayed with all the virtues, they emerge victorious from every fight with vice.—The fifteenth sign: they see and know the naked truth and praise God without ceasing for his gnosis.—The sixteenth sign: perfect and just, they hold themselves in poor esteem.—The seventeenth sign: they are chary of words and prodigal of works.—The eighteenth sign: they preach to the world by right practice.—The nineteenth sign: they are always seeking God's glory and nothing at all besides.—The twentieth sign: if any man fight them, they will let him prevail before accepting help of any sort but God's.—The twenty-first sign: they desire neither comfort nor possessions, of the least of which they deem themselves all undeserving.—The twenty-second sign: they look upon themselves as the most unworthy of all mankind on earth; their humbleness is therefore never-failing.—The twenty-third sign: they take the life and teaching of our Lord Jesus Christ for the perfect exemplar of their lives and in the light of this are always examining themselves with the sole intention of removing all unlikeness to their high ideal.—The twenty-fourth sign: to outward appearance they do little, who are working all the time at the virtuous life, hence the disesteem of many people, which, however, they prefer to vulgar approbation.

These are the signs of the true ground wherein lives the image of the perfect truth and he who does not find them in himself may account his knowledge vain, and so may other people.[88]

Eckhart, of course, was excommunicated: by the bull of Pope John XXII, March 27, 1329; after which his writings passed, as it were, into the underground, to become what have been called "The text-books of God-intoxicated piety," and the inspiration of the preachers of his school, John Tauler (1300–1361), Suso (1300–1365), and Ruysbroeck (1293–1381).[89] The point of essential pertinence to our study and to all studies of the mythic imagery—not only of Christianity but of Judaism as well, and indeed, of all religions whatsoever—is the radical contrast that appears here between Eckhart's reading of the Christian symbols and that of Innocent III, as reproduced above (pp. 491–492). Eckhart's reading I would term poetic, and so, proper to the character and function of the symbol, which is not of value as a fact but as an awakener of the soul; for in more modern terms, symbols are energy-releasing and -directing signs: stimuli, which, if not effective, are of no more use than a battery gone dead. Whereas Innocent's reading of the Christian myth, I would term literal, rational, and improper to the character and function of the symbol, therefore dead, and to be enforced only by violence and (if I may say so) madness—which consists precisely in mistaking a visionary image for a fact.

In the words of Alan Watts in his brilliant volume, *Myth and Ritual in Christianity:*

Christianity has been expounded by an orthodox hierarchy which has consistently degraded the myth to a science and a history. . . . The living God has become the abstract God, and cannot deliver his creatures from the disease with which he himself is afflicted. . . . For when myth is confused with history, it ceases to apply to man's inner life. . . . The tragedy of Christian history is that it is a consistent failure to draw the life from the Christian myth and unlock its wisdom. . . .

Myth is only "revelation" so long as it is a message from heaven—that is, from the timeless and non-historical world—expressing not what *was* true once, but what *is* true always. Thus the Incarnation is without effect or significance for human beings living today if it is mere history; it is a "salvic truth" only if it is perennial, a revelation of a timeless event going on within man always.[90]

It is one of the great lessons of our study that for the vulgar, ill- or uninstructed mind, myths tend to become history and there ensues a type of attachment to the mere accidents of the local forms that, on the one hand, binds so-called believers into contending groups and, on the other hand, deprives them all of the substance of the message each believes itself alone to have received. All orthodoxies show this tendency in great or slight degree and they are consequently mutually opposed. Whereas when any of the great mythic imageries comes to be read as poetry, as art, as a vehicle not of empirical information but of experience—in other words: not as a newspaper—we find a message of accord, which, in brief, is that of the living God, who is not apart, but within all and of no definition. "God," as Eckhart declared, "is born in the empty soul by discovering himself to her in a new guise without guise, without light in divine light." [91]

The orthodox Christian notion that nature is corrupt and the Christian Church incorruptible can be said to represent an extreme statement of the implications of the Jewish myth of God apart from the world, creating, judging, condemning it, and then offering, as though from outside, to endow some particle of its immensity with the virtue of his particular attention—as by a Covenant, Koran, or Incarnation. Ironically, however, the very symbols used by the Church to teach of this supposed circumstance bore in themselves implicitly a contrary instruction, which of itself spoke to the open heart through the silence of their eloquent forms—and in Eckhart, as in Dante, as in the Grail and Tristan romances, the old lesson of eternal man awakened, within whom there dwell, and from whose heart there have been born, all the forms and experiences in all the world of both heaven and hell. The little image of Mary in Figures 31 and 32 tells first, that, as Eckhart knew, the Trinity is immanent in each of us and to be born by us in our knowledge; second, that, as the Cretans knew, the goddess is the mother womb, the ultimate

bound of all existence; and third, as all the world seems to have
known except our own authorized interpreters of the icons of our
common heritage: microcosm and macrocosm are in essence one
in God—who is by no means corrupt, corruptible, or to be mocked
by any definition of creed.

CONCLUSION

At the Close of an Age

A distinction must be drawn, through all our studies of mythology, between the attitudes toward divinities represented on one hand by the priest and his flock, and on the other by the creative poet, artist, or philosopher. The former tends to what I would call a positivistic reading of the imagery of his cult. Such a reading is fostered by the attitude of prayer, since in prayer it is extremely difficult to retain the balance between belief and disbelief that is proper to the contemplation of an image or idea of God. The poet, artist, and philosopher, on the other hand, being themselves fashioners of images and coiners of ideas, realize that all representation—whether in the visible matter of stone or in the mental matter of the word—is necessarily conditioned by the fallibility of the human organs. Overwhelmed by his own muse, a bad poet may imagine his visions to be supernatural facts and so fall into the posture of a prophet—whose utterances I would define as "poetry overdone," over-interpreted; wherefore he becomes the founder of a cult and a generator of priests. But so also a gifted priest may find his supernatural beings losing body, deepening into void, changing form, even dissolving: whereupon he will possibly become either a prophet or, if more greatly favored, a creative poet.

Three major metamorphoses of the motifs and themes of our subject, therefore, have to be recognized as fundamentally differing even though fundamentally related, namely: the true poetry of the poet, the poetry overdone of the prophet, and the poetry done to death of the priest. Whereas the history of religion is largely a record of the latter two, the history of mythology includes all three, and in doing so brings not only poetry but also religion into a fresh and healthily vivified relationship to the wellsprings of creative thought. For there is in poetry a tendency ("poetry underdone") to rest in the whimsies of personal surprise, joy, or anguish before the realities of life in a universe poets never made; whereas in religion the opposite tendency may prevail—that of rendering no personal experience whatsoever, but only authorized clichés.

In the long view of the history of mankind, four essential functions of mythology can be discerned. The first and most distinctive —vitalizing all—is that of eliciting and supporting a sense of awe before the mystery of being. Professor Rudolf Otto has termed this recognition of the *numinous* the characteristic mental state of all religions properly so called.[1] It antecedes and defies definition. It is, on the primitive level, demonic dread; on the highest, mystical rapture; and between there are many grades. Defined, it may be talked about and taught; but talk and teaching cannot produce it. Nor can authority enforce it. Only the accident of experience and the sign symbols of a living myth can elicit and support it; but such signs cannot be invented. They are found. Whereupon they function of themselves. And those who find them are the sensitized, creative, living minds that once were known as seers, but now as poets and creative artists. More important, more effective for the future of a culture than its statesmen or its armies are these masters of the spiritual breath by which the clay of man wakes to life.

The second function of mythology is to render a cosmology, an image of the universe that will support and be supported by this sense of awe before the mystery of a presence and the presence of a mystery. The cosmology has to correspond, however, to the actual experience, knowledge, and mentality of the culture folk involved. So we note that when the priestly watchers of the skies in ancient Sumer, c. 3500 B.C., learned of the order of the planets, the entire mythic system of the nuclear Near East stepped away from the simple primitive themes of the hunting and planting tribes. The grandiose vision of a mathematically impersonal temporal and

spatial order came into being, of which the world vision of the
Middle Ages—no less than that of ancient India, that of China,
and that of Yucatan—was but a late variant. Today that vision has
dissolved. And here we touch upon a crucial problem of the religions of our time; for the clergies, generally, still are preaching
themes from the first to fourth millenniums B.C.

No one of adult mind today would turn to the Book of Genesis to
learn of the origins of the earth, the plants, the beasts, and man.
There was no flood, no tower of Babel, no first couple in paradise,
and between the first known appearance of men on earth and the
first buildings of cities, not one generation (Adam to Cain) but a
good two million must have come into this world and passed along.
Today we turn to science for our imagery of the past and of the
structure of the world, and what the spinning demons of the atom
and the galaxies of the telescope's eye reveal is a wonder that
makes the babel of the Bible seem a toyland dream of the dear
childhood of our brain.

A third function of mythology is to support the current social
order, to integrate the individual organically with his group; and
here again, in the long view, we see that a gradual amplification of
the scope and content of the group has been the characteristic sign
of man's advance from the early tribal cluster to the modern post-
Alexandrian concept of a single world-society. Against the amplitude of this challenging larger concept numerous provinces still
stand out, as, for example, those of the various national, racial,
religious, or class mythologies, which may once have had their
reason but today are out of date.

The social function of a mythology and of the rites by which it is
rendered is to establish in every member of the group concerned
a "system of sentiments" that can be depended upon to link him
spontaneously to its ends. The "system of sentiments" proper to a
hunting tribe would be improper to an agricultural one; that proper
to a matriarchy is improper to a patriarchy; and that of any tribal
group is improper to this day of developed individuals crossing
paths from east to west and from north to south.

The older mythic orders gave authority to their symbols by attributing them to gods, to culture heroes, or to some such high impersonal force as the order of the universe; and the image of society itself, thus linked to the greater image of nature, became a vessel of religious awe. Today we know, for the most part, that our laws are not from God or from the universe, but from ourselves; are conventional, not absolute; and that in breaking them we offend not God but man. Neither animals nor plants, not the zodiac or its supposed maker, but our fellows have now become the masters of our fate and we of theirs. In the recent past it may have been possible for intelligent men of good will honestly to believe that their own society (whatever it happened to be) was the only good, that beyond its bounds were the enemies of God, and that they were called upon, consequently, to project the principle of hatred outward upon the world, while cultivating love within, toward those whose "system of sentiments" was of God. Today, however, there is no such outward. Enclaves of national, racial, religious, and class provincialism persist, but the physical facts have made closed horizons illusory. The old god is dead, with his little world and his little, closed society. The new focal center of belief and trust is mankind. And if the principle of love cannot be wakened actually within each—as it was mythologically in God—to master the principle of hate, the Waste Land alone can be our destiny and the masters of the world its fiends.

The fourth function of mythology is to initiate the individual into the order of realities of his own psyche, guiding him toward his own spiritual enrichment and realization. Formerly—but in archaic cultures still—the way was to subordinate all individual judgment, will, and capacities absolutely to the social order: the principle of ego (as we have seen in *Oriental Mythology*) was to be suppressed and, if possible, even erased; while the archetypes, the ideal roles, of the social order were impressed upon all inexorably, according to their social stations. In a world of static forms, such a massacre of the creative personality was acceptable, and where the archaic mind prevails today such patterning still goes on. One may take it as a point in evidence of the advanced position of Europe in the way of respect for the individual that, whereas Hitler's massacre of some 5,000,000 Jews evokes (and properly so) horror from all sides, Stalin's of 25,000,000 Russians passes almost without notice, and the present Chinese orgy is entirely overlooked. Both by the Orient and by the Occident such inhumanity is recognized as normal for the great East, whereas better things are expected of ourselves—and rightly so. For it was in Europe alone that the principle of individual judgment and responsibility was developed in relation not to a fixed order of supposed divine laws, but to a changing context of human actualities, rationally governed. The fostering in Europe, first among the Greeks, then the Romans, of the principle of ego—not as the mere "I will," "I want," of the nursery (Freud's "Pleasure Principle"), but as the informed, rational faculty of responsible judgment ("Reality Principle")[2]—has endowed us and our particular world with an order of spirituality and psychological problematic that is different in every way from that of the archaic Oriental mind. And this humanistic individualism has released powers of creativity that have brought about in a mere two centuries changes in the weal and woe of man such as no two millenniums before had ever worked. The result being that where the old patterns of morality are retained they no longer match the actualities even of the local, let alone the world, scene. The adventure of the Grail—the quest within for those creative values by which the Waste Land is redeemed—has become today for each the unavoidable task; for, as there is no more any fixed horizon, there is no more any fixed center, any Mecca, Rome, or Jerusalem. Our circle today is that announced, c. 1450, by Nicolaus Cusanus (1401–1464): whose circumference is nowhere and whose center is everywhere; the circle of infinite radius, which is also a straight line.

Hence it will be our charge in the volume next to come, *Creative Mythology*, to follow systematically from the period of the Table Round (where there was no one sitting at the head, but each was a champion paramount) to the present hour of the detonation of the atom, the long process of the Opening of the Eye of European man to a state that is no state but a becoming: and the vanishment thereby of all the earlier masks of God, which now are known to have been of developing man himself.

Some, perhaps, will desire to bow still to a mask, out of fear of nature. But if there is no divinity in nature, the nature that God created, how should there be in the idea of God, which the nature of man created?

"By my love and hope, I conjure thee," called Nietzsche's Zarathustra: "cast not away the hero in thy soul!"

REFERENCE NOTES
INDEX

REFERENCE NOTES

PART ONE: THE AGE OF THE GODDESS
INTRODUCTION: MYTH AND RITUAL: EAST AND WEST

1. *Kena Upaniṣad* 2.3.
2. *Tao Tê Ching* 56.
3. *Chāndogya Upaniṣad* 6.8.7.
4. Mumon, *The Gateless Gate*, translated by Nyogen Senzaki and Paul Reps, *Zen Flesh, Zen Bones* (New York: A Doubleday Anchor Book, 1961), p. 109.
5. *Prajñāpāramitā-hṛdaya Sūtra*.
6. Job 40:4.

CHAPTER 1: THE SERPENT'S BRIDE

1. William Hayes Ward, *The Seal Cylinders of Western Asia* (Washington, D.C.: The Carnegie Institution of Washington, 1910), p. 129, citing Léon Heuzey, *Catalogue des antiquités chaldéennes* (Paris: Imprimeries réunies, 1902), p. 281, Fig. 125.
2. Stephen Herbert Langdon, *Semitic Mythology*, The Mythology of All Races, Vol. V (Boston: Marshall Jones Company, 1931), p. 177, citing J. de Morgan, *Délégation en Perse. Mémoires* (Paris: E. Leroux, 1911), Vol. XII, p. 173, Fig. 288.
3. Henri Frankfort, "Sargonid Seals," *Iraq*, Vol. I, Part I (1934), p. 11, Fig. 2.
4. Ward, op. cit., p. 275.
5. *The Masks of God: Oriental Mythology*, pp. 15–21.
6. Ward, op. cit., p. 276.
7. Ibid., p. 139, citing Joachim Ménant, *Recherches sur la glyptique orientale* (Paris: Maisonneure & Cie, 1883–86), Part I, p. 191, Fig. 121.
8. Ward, op. cit., p. 138; also Ménant, op. cit., p. 189, Fig. 120.
9. The Fall theory was advanced by George Smith, *The Chaldean Account of Genesis* (New York: Scribner, Armstrong, & Co., 1876), and Langdon, op. cit., p.

179; rejected, however, by Ménant, op. cit., pp. 189–91, and Ward, op. cit., pp. 138–39.
10. Jane Ellen Harrison, *Themis* (Cambridge: The University Press, 2nd revised edition, 1927), p. 286; from Johannes A. Overbeck, *Atlas der griechischen Mythologie* (Leipzig: W. Engelmann, 1872), Vol. I, Plate XVI, 2.
11. Hesiod, *Theogony* 973–74; as cited to this figure by Jane Ellen Harrison, op. cit., p. 286.
12. *Jātaka* 1.74.26.
13. *Mahā-vagga* 1.3.1–3.
14. Genesis 3:22–24. I am quoting throughout the Revised Standard Version of the Bible.
15. Jane Ellen Harrison, *Prolegomena to the Study of Greek Religion* (Cambridge: Cambridge University Press, 1903; 3rd edition, 1922), p. 7.
16. Ibid., p. 19; citing Berlin Museum, *Beschreibung der Antiken Skulpturen*.
17. Ibid., p. 18.
18. Ibid., pp. 14–15, citing Lucian, *Icaro-Menippos* 24, scholiast ad loc.
19. Sir James George Frazer, *The Golden Bough* (New York: The Macmillan Company, one-volume edition, 1922), p. 1.
20. Aelian, *De natura animalium* XI.

2; following Harrison, *Themis,* p. 429.

21. Harrison, *Themis,* p. 431, Fig. 130.

22. Hesiod, *Theogony* 215.

23. Job 41:1–8. Compare Psalm 74: 13–14.

24. Hesiod, *Theogony* 823–880, abridged. Fig. 10 is from an early red-figured vase painting in the Munich Museum (c. 650 B.C.), in A. Furtwängler and K. Reichold, *Griechische Vasenmalerei* (Munich: F. Bruckmann, 1900–1932), No. 32.

25. *The Masks of God: Oriental Mythology,* pp. 182–84.

26. Ibid., pp. 184–89.

27. Harrison, *Themis,* p. 459.

28. Ovid, *Metamorphoses* 3.324–31.

29. *The Masks of God: Primitive Mythology,* p. 101.

30. From an early red-figured vase painting in Former National Museum, Berlin. Harrison, *Prolegomena,* p. 633, Fig. 168, citing Furtwängler and Reichold, op. cit.

31. Exodus 4:2–4.

32. Exodus 17:1–7.

33. Numbers 21:5–9.

34. II Kings 18:4.

35. Theophile James Meek, *Hebrew Origins* (New York: Harper Torchbook edition, 1960), p. 123.

36. Leo Frobenius, *Monumenta Terrarum: Der Geist über den Erdteilen,* Erlebte Erdteile, Bd. 7 (Frankfurt-am-Main: Forschungsinstitut für Kulturmorphologie, 2. Auflage, 1929), pp. 213–14.

37. Leo Frobenius, *Kulturgeschichte Africas* (Zurich: Phaidon-Verlag, 1933), pp. 103–104.

38. R. A. S. Macalister, *Ancient Ireland* (London: Methuen and Company, 1935), pp. 13–14.

39. R. A. S. Macalister, *The Archaeology of Ireland* (London: Methuen and Company, 2nd revised ed., 1949), p. 9.

40. Ibid., p. 15.

41. Macalister, *Ancient Ireland,* p. 131.

42. *The Book of Leinster* 54a, 11–18; following Standish Hayes O'Grady, in Eleanor Hull (ed.), *The Cuchullin Saga in Irish Literature* (London: David Nutt, 1898), pp. 111–13; and H. Zimmer, "Die kulturgeschichtliche Hintergrund in den Erzählungen der alten irischen Heldensage," *Sitzungsberichte der Königlich Preussischen Akademie der Wissenschaften,* Philosophisch-historische Classe, IX (1911), pp. 213–214.

43. Zimmer, op. cit., p. 217, citing *Ancient Laws of Wales* I.92.12.

44. Ibid., pp. 215–16.

45. Ibid., p. 218.

46. *The Book of Leinster* 54b; following Standish H. O'Grady, *Silva Gadelica* (London: Williams and Norgate, 1892), vol. 2, pp. 114–116, and Zimmer, op. cit., pp. 178–79.

47. W. B. Yeats, *Irish Fairy and Folk Tales* (New York: The Modern Library, no date), pp. 1–3.

Chapter 2: THE CONSORT OF THE BULL

1. Apuleius, *The Golden Ass,* translated by W. Adlington, Book XL; cited in *The Masks of God: Primitive Mythology,* p. 56.

2. For Krishna and the Gopis, see *The Masks of God: Oriental Mythology,* pp. 343–64.

3. *The Gospel of Sri Ramakrishna,* translation by Swami Nikhilananda (New York: Ramakrishna-Vivekananda Center, 1942), p. 371.

4. *The Masks of God: Primitive Mythology,* pp. 313–34.

5. Aspirations from the Litany of Loreto (15th century; sanctioned 1587).

6. *The Masks of God: Oriental Mythology,* pp. 155–72. Fig. 12 is from Sir Arthur John Evans, *British School at Athens, Annual,* Vol. VII (1900–1901), p. 29, Fig. 9.

7. Frazer, op. cit., p. 280. See also

529

Bedřich Hrozný, *Ancient History of Western Asia, India, and Crete* (New York: Philosophical Library, 1953), p. 198, note 1, and *The Masks of God: Primitive Mythology*, pp. 427–28.

8. Sir Arthur John Evans, *The Palace of Minos* (London: Macmillan and Company, Vol. I, 1921, to Vol. IV, Part II, 1935). Quotations and figures from *The Palace of Minos* are reproduced by permission of Mr. Wakeman-Long of Williams and James, Solicitors, Gray's Inn, London, Miss Susan Minet, and Mrs. Anne Ridler, Trustees of the copyright of the work.

9. Ibid., Vol. II, Part I, p. 277.

10. Martin P. Nilsson, *Geschichte der griechischen Religion*, 2 Vols. (Munich: C. H. Beck'sche Verlagsbuchhandlung, 2nd ed., 1955 and 1961).

11. Ibid., Vol. I, p. 298.

12. Michael Ventris, "Evidence for Greek Dialect in the Mycenaean Archives," *Journal of Hellenic Studies*, Vol. LXXIII (1953), pp. 84 ff.

13. Leonard R. Palmer, *Mycenaeans and Minoans* (New York: Alfred A. Knopf, 1962), p. 127, citing Paul Kretschmer, *Einleitung in die Geschichte der griechischen Sprache* (Göttingen: Vandenhoeck u. Ruprecht, 1896).

14. Michael Ventris and John Chadwick, *Documents in Mycenaean Greek* (Cambridge: The Cambridge University Press, 1956), p. 128.

15. Palmer, op. cit., pp. 123–24.

16. Ibid., pp. 82, 94.

17. *Odyssey* VI. 290; cited in this connection by Palmer, op. cit., p. 95.

18. National Museum, Athens.

19. Palmer, op. cit., pp. 124–25.

20. Harrison, *Prolegomena*, p. 555.

21. Palmer, op. cit., p. 124, and Harrison, *Prolegomena*, pp. 273, 555, 562 f., 609.

22. Harrison, *Prolegomena*, p. 273, citing O. Rubensohn, *Mittheilungen des Kaiserlichen Deutschen Archäologischen Instituts. Athenische Abteilung*, Vol. XXIV

(1899), Plate VII. From Former National Museum, Berlin.

23. Ibid., pp. 272–73.

24. Gorgias 497c.

25. Evans, op. cit., Vol. III, pp. 145–55, with parenthetical passage on the Sacral Ivy from Vol. II, Part II, pp. 482–83. See also Evans, in *Journal of Hellenic Studies*, Vol. XLIV (1925), p. 65, Fig. 55.

26. *The Masks of God: Oriental Mythology*, pp. 107–108, citing Samuel Noah Kramer, *From the Tablets of Sumer* (Indian Hills, Colo.: The Falcon's Wing Press, 1956), pp. 172–73, and Langdon, op. cit., pp. 194–95.

27. *Odyssey* IV. 563, from the S. H. Butcher and Andrew Lang translation; as cited by Evans, op. cit., Vol. III, pp. 155–56.

28. Nilsson, op. cit., Vol. I, p. 845.

29. *The Masks of God: Primitive Mythology*, pp. 406–407.

30. Robert H. Dyson, Jr., "Art of the Twin Rivers," *Natural History*, Vol. LXXI, No. 6, June–July 1962, p. 39.

31. *The Masks of God: Oriental Mythology*, pp. 108 and 111.

32. *The Masks of God: Primitive Mythology*, p. 85.

33. *The Masks of God: Oriental Mythology*, passim.

34. Isaiah 11:6–9.

35. Euripides, *Bacchae* 1017; trans., Harrison, *Prolegomena*, p. 433.

36. Michael Ventris and John Chadwick, *Documents in Mycenaean Greek* (Cambridge: The University Press, 1956), p. 127.

37. *The Masks of God: Oriental Mythology*, pp. 51–91.

38. Nilsson, op. cit., Vol. I, pp. 297 and 277, note 1.

39. Ibid., Vol. I, p. 303.

40. Evans, op. cit., Vol. II, Part I, p. 279.

41. James Mellaart, "Hacilar: A Neolithic Village Site," *Scientific American*, Vol. 205, No. 2, August 1961.

42. *The Masks of God: Primitive Mythology*, pp. 142–43.

43. *The Masks of God: Oriental Mythology*, pp. 37–41.

44. M. Untersteiner, *La fisiologia del mito* (Milan: Fratelli Bocca, 1946); Giovanni Patroni, *Com-*

mentari mediterranei all'Odissea di Omero (Milan: C. Marzorati, 1950).

45. Nilsson, op. cit., Vol. I, p. 257.
46. *The Masks of God: Oriental Mythology*, pp. 155–240.
47. R. J. C. Atkinson, *Stonehenge* (Harmondsworth and Baltimore: Pelican Books, 1960), pp. 148–50.
48. Ibid., pp. 151–53.
49. Macalister, *The Archaeology of Ireland*, p. 16.
50. *The Masks of God: Oriental Mythology*, p. 295.
51. Atkinson, op. cit., pp. 154–56 and 172.
52. Ibid., pp. 68, 101, 171–72.
53. *The Masks of God: Oriental Mythology*, pp. 462–63.
54. Atkinson, op. cit., p. 157.
55. Ibid., pp. 157–58, 173–74.
56. Ibid., p. 176.
57. Ibid., pp. 101, 158.
58. Ibid., pp. 161–65.
59. Ibid., pp. 68–69, 77–85, 88–92, 101, 165–67, 176–79.
60. Ibid., pp. 165–67.
61. Palmer, op. cit., pp. 229–47.
62. Marija Gimbutas, "Culture Change in Europe at the Start of the Second Millennium B.C.: A Contribution to the Indo-European Problem," *Selected Papers of the Fifth International Congress of Anthropological and Ethnological Sciences, Philadelphia, 1956* (Philadelphia: University of Pennsylvania Press, 1960), p. 544, Item 19.
63. Fig. 19 is from Evans, in *Journal of Hellenic Studies*, Vol. XXI (1901), p. 108, Fig. 4.
64. Leonard William King, *Chronicles Concerning Early Babylonian Kings* (London: Luzac and Co., 1907), Vol. II, pp. 87–91.
65. Otto Rank, *Der Mythus von der Geburt des Helden* (Leipzig and Vienna: Franz Deuticke Verlag, 2nd enlarged edition, 1922).
66. *The Masks of God: Oriental Mythology*, pp. 58–83.
67. Robert F. Harper, *The Code of Hammurabi, King of Babylon* (Chicago: University of Chicago Press, 1904); Bruno Meissner, *Babylon und Assyrian*, II (Heidelberg: C. Winter, 1920–1925), p. 46; O. E. Ravn, *Acta orientalia*, VII (1929), pp. 81–90: Alexander Heidel, *The Babylonian Genesis* (Chicago: University of Chicago Press, 2nd ed., 1951), p. 14.
68. *Tao Tê Ching* 6; translation, Arthur Waley, *The Way and Its Power* (London: George Allen and Unwin, Ltd., 1934), p. 149; quoted in *The Masks of Gods: Oriental Mythology*, p. 425.
69. *Enûma elish*, Tablets I to VI. 57, abridged; following various readings: Alexander Heidel, *The Babylonian Genesis* (Chicago: The University of Chicago Press, 2nd ed., 1951), pp. 18–48; E. A. Speiser, in James B. Pritchard, *The Ancient Near East* (Princeton: Princeton University Press, 1958), pp. 31–38; L. W. King, *Babylonian Religion and Mythology* (London: Kegan Paul, Trench, Trubner and Co., and New York: Henry Frowde, 1899), pp. 61–80.
70. Heidel, op. cit., p. 130.
71. Thorkild Jacobsen, *The Sumerian King List* (Chicago: University of Chicago Press, 1939), pp. 77–85.
72. William Foxwell Albright, *From the Stone Age to Christianity* (New York: Doubleday Anchor Books, 1957), p. 196.
73. *Ecclesiastes* 5:18; 8:15; 9:8–9.
74. Heidel, op. cit.; Speiser, op. cit.; King, op. cit.

PART TWO: THE AGE OF HEROES

CHAPTER 3: GODS AND HEROES OF THE LEVANT: 1500–500 B.C.

1. Wilhelm M. L. de Wette, *Beiträge zur Einleitung in das Alte Testament* (1806), translated by Theodore Parker, *A Critical and Historical Introduction to the Canonical Scriptures of the Old Testament* (Boston: C. C. Little and J. Brown, 1843, 2nd ed., 1858).
2. Following Eduard Meyer, *Ge-*

schichte des Altertums (Stuttgart-Berlin: J. G. Cotta'sche Buchhandlung Nachfolger, 2–5. Aufl. 1925–1937), Vol. II, Part 2, pp. 188–90.

3. II Kings, 22:3–11.
4. II Kings 22:3–23:25.
5. II Kings 23:32, 37; 24:9, 19.
6. II Kings 25:8–11.
7. *The Masks of God: Oriental Mythology*, pp. 107–11.
8. Genesis 2:4–4:16.
9. *The Masks of God: Primitive Mythology*, pp. 151–225.
10. S. N. Kramer, *Sumerian Mythology* (Philadelphia: The American Philosophical Society, 1944), pp. 102.
11. *Kena Upaniṣad* 1.3.
12. *Śvetāśvatara Upaniṣad* 4.20.
13. *Kena Upaniṣad* 2.5.
14. *Śvetāśvatara Upaniṣad* 6.12.
15. *Tao Tê Ching* 25; 35; 37. Translation, Arthur Waley, *The Way and Its Power* (London: George Allen and Unwin, Ltd., 1954), pp. 174, 186, 188.
16. From R. H. Blyth, *Haiku,* Vol. 1 (Kamakura: Kamakura Bunko, 1949), p. 203.
17. *Bṛhadāraṇyaka Upaniṣad* 1.4.10.
18. *Śvetāśvatara Upaniṣad* 4.4.
19. *Bṛhadāraṇyaka Upaniṣad* 1.4.7.
20. Blyth, op. cit., p. 197.
21. Swami Nikhilananda, *The Gospel of Sri Ramakrishna* (New York: Ramakrishna-Vivekananda Center, 1942), p. 627.
22. Stith Thompson, *Motif-Index of Folk Literature* (Bloomington, Ind.: Indiana University Studies, 1932), Motifs C 600–649.
23. For example, Washington Matthews, *Navaho Legends,* Memoirs of the American Folklore Society, Vol. V (New York: G. E. Stechert and Co., 1897), pp. 107 ff.
24. Gerald Vann, O.P., *The Paradise Tree* (New York: Sheed and Ward, 1959), p. 66.
25. Roman Catholic Missal, Holy Saturday, Blessing of the Paschal Candle; edition of Dom Gaspar Lefebure, *Daily Missal* (St. Paul: E. M. Lohmann, Co., 1934), p. 831.
26. Genesis 1:1–2:4a.

27. *The Masks of God: Oriental Mythology*, pp. 83–91.
28. *The Masks of God: Primitive Mythology*, p. 86.
29. *The Masks of God: Oriental Mythology*, pp. 121–30.
30. *The Masks of God: Oriental Mythology*, pp. 105–107.
31. Dr. J. H. Hertz, *The Pentateuch and Haftorahs* (London: Soncino Press, 5721 [1961]), pp. 196 & 200.
32. Genesis 12:1–4a.
33. *A Dictionary of the Holy Bible* (New York: American Tract Society, 1859), article, "Abraham," p. 10.
34. Genesis 11:27–32.
35. Alexander Scharff and Anton Moortgat, *Ägypten und Vorderasien im Altertum* (Munich: Verlag F. Bruckmann, 1950), pp. 269–71.
36. Ibid., pp. 281–82.
37. Hertz, op. cit., p. 200.
38. Gudea Cylinder A, following Scharff and Moortgat, op. cit., pp. 275–79, abridged.
39. Scharff and Moortgat, op. cit., p. 285.
40. See, for example, James Henry Breasted, *The Conquest of Civilization* (New York and London: Harper and Brothers, 1926), p. 145.
41. Meek, op. cit., p. 14.
42. Ibid., pp. 15–16.
43. *The Masks of God: Oriental Mythology*, pp. 391–96.
44. Kathleen M. Kenyon, *Archaeology in the Holy Land* (New York: Frederick A. Praeger, 1960), p. 194.
45. Genesis 12:10–13:1.
46. Genesis 20.
47. Genesis 26:1–17.
48. Kenyon, op. cit., p. 221; Scharff and Moortgat, op. cit., p. 385.
49. Sigmund Freud, *Moses and Monotheism,* translated by Katherine Jones (New York: Alfred A. Knopf, 1939), p. 109. Copyright, 1939 by Sigmund Freud. Reprinted by permission of Alfred A. Knopf, Inc. See also *Moses and Monotheism* in *The Complete Psychological Works of Sigmund Freud,* revised and edited by James Strachey (London: The Hogarth Press, 1953–   ), Vol. XXIV.

50. Ibid., p. 51.
51. Eduard Meyer, *Die Israeliten und ihre Nachbarstämme* (Halle: M. Niemeyer, 1906), p. 47; cited by Freud, op. cit., p. 51.
52. Freud, op. cit., p. 3.
53. I owe this observation to Mr. Edwin M. Wright, of Washington, D.C., to whose unpublished paper, *The "Image" of Moses*, the present discussion is greatly indebted.
54. Exodus 2:1–4.
55. Freud, op. cit., p. 15.
56. Meyer, *Geschichte des Altertums*, Vol. II, Part 2, p. 208.
57. Exodus 2:5–10.
58. Apollonios Rhodios 4. 1091; from Karl Kerényi, *The Heroes of the Greeks,* translated by H. J. Rose (New York: Grove Press, 1960), pp. 46–47 and 54.

59. Exodus 2:11–22.
60. Meek, op. cit., pp. 108–109.
61. Freud, op. cit., pp. 39–40.
62. See discussion of views in Meek, op. cit., pp. 7 ff. and 18 ff.
63. Josephus' theory. See Meek, op. cit., p. 18.
64. James W. Jack, *The Date of the Exodus in the Light of External Evidence* (Edinburgh: T. & T. Clark, 1925).
65. Thomas Mann, *Joseph in Egypt* (1936).
66. Freud, op. cit.
67. William Foxwell Albright, *From the Stone Age to Christianity* (New York: Doubleday Anchor Books, 1957), p. 13.
68. Scharff and Moortgat, op. cit., p. 165.
69. Meek, op. cit., p. 35.

CHAPTER 4: GODS AND HEROES OF THE EUROPEAN WEST: 1500–500 B.C.

1. N. G. L. Hammond, *A History of Greece to 322 B.C.* (Oxford: The Clarendon Press, 1959), pp. 36–37.
2. *The Masks of God: Oriental Mythology*, pp. 150–55.
3. Leo Frobenius, *Shicksalskunde im Sinne des Kulturwerdens* (Leipzig: R. Voigtländers Verlag, 1932), p. 99.
4. *The Masks of God: Primitive Mythology*, pp. 170–225.
5. *The Masks of God: Oriental Mythology*, p. 155.
6. Palmer, op. cit., p. 120; Hammond, op. cit., p. 74.
7. Nilsson, op. cit., Vol. I, p. 347. Figs. 20 and 21 are from statuettes in the Heraklion Museum, first reproduced by Evans.
8. K. Kerényi, *The Gods of the Greeks*, pp. 119–20, citing Hesiod, Pindar, Euripides, Homeric Hymn 28, Apollodorus Mythographus, and Chrysippus Stoicus.
9. Hammond, op. cit., p. 60.
10. Robert Graves, *The Greek Myths* (Harmondsworth and Baltimore: Penguin Books, 1955), Vol. I, pp. 17 and 244.
11. Hammond, op. cit., p. 39.
12. *The Masks of God: Oriental Mythology*, pp. 190–97.

13. *The Masks of God: Primitive Mythology*, pp. 170–202, 441–51.
14. Ibid., pp. 445 ff.
15. Palmer, op. cit., pp. 130–31.
16. Graves, loc. cit.
17. Frazer, op. cit., p. 5.
18. *The Masks of God: Primitive Mythology*, p. 161.
19. Aeschylus, Fragment 261; as cited by Kerényi, *The Heroes of the Greeks,* p. 51.
20. Kerényi, *The Gods of the Greeks,* pp. 48–49, with references; *The Heroes of the Greeks,* pp. 46–54, with references; also Graves, op. cit., Vol. I, pp. 237–45.
21. Sigmund Freud, *A General Introduction to Psychoanalysis* (New York: Garden City Publishing Company, 1935), p. 125.
22. Harrison, *Prolegomena*, p. 292.
23. Ibid., p. 298.
24. Carl G. Jung, *Two Essays on Analytical Psychology* (London: Bailliere, Tindall and Cox, 1928), pp. 188–89.
25. Ibid., p. 52.
26. Harrison, *Prolegomena*, p. 294. Fig. 22, from a Greco-Etruscan black-figured vase in the Louvre, was first discussed by Harrison in *Journal of Hellenic Studies*, Vol. VII (1886), p. 203.

27. Nilsson, op. cit., Vol. I, pp. 25–26.
28. Gilbert Murray, *The Rise of the Greek Epic* (Oxford: The Clarendon Press, 3rd ed. revised and enlarged, 1924), p. 211.
29. Ibid., pp. 211–12.
30. All my quotations from the *Odyssey* are from the translation of S. H. Butcher and A. Lang (London: Macmillan and Company, first edition, 1879).
31. *The Masks of God: Primitive Mythology*, pp. 183–90.
32. Sophocles, *Fragment* 837; A. C. Pearson, *The Fragments of Sophocles* (Cambridge: The University Press, 1917), Vol. III, p. 52; probably from his lost tragedy, *Triptolemus*.
33. *The Masks of God: Oriental Mythology*, pp. 197–206, especially pp. 201–202, citing *Chāndogya Upaniṣad* 5.3–10.
34. Ibid., pp. 204–205, citing *Kena Upaniṣad*, 3.1 to 4.1.
35. Ibid., pp. 211–40.
36. Karl Kerényi, "Vater Helios," *Eranos-Jahrbuch 1943* (Zurich:

Rhein-Verlag, 1944), p. 83.
37. Thucydides, *Peloponnesian War* II. 37–40, abridged. Translation by Benjamin Jowett.
38. H. D. F. Kitto, *The Greeks* (Harmondsworth and Baltimore: Penguin Books, revised, 1957), p. 11.
39. *The Masks of God: Oriental Mythology*, pp. 218–40, 249–52, 256–257; also Heinrich Zimmer, *Philosophies of India*, edited by Joseph Campbell, The Bollingen Series XXVI (New York: Pantheon Books, 1951), pp. 181 ff.
40. *The Masks of God: Primitive Mythology*, p. 101.
41. Euripides, Fragment 475, transl. Gilbert Murray, in Harrison, *Prolegomena*, p. 479.
42. *The Masks of God: Oriental Mythology*, pp. 137–44, 211–18.
43. Karl Kerényi, "Die orphische Kosmologie und der Ursprung der Orphik," *Eranos-Jahrbuch 1949* (Zurich: Rhein-Verlag, 1950), pp. 53–78.
44. Aristotle, *Metaphysics* A. 986a.

PART THREE: THE AGE OF THE GREAT CLASSICS

CHAPTER 5: THE PERSIAN PERIOD: 539–331 B.C.

1. L. H. Mills, *The Zend Avesta*, Part III, *Sacred Books of the East*, Vol. XXXI (Oxford: The Clarendon Press, 1887), pp. xxxiii–xxxvii.
2. Meyer, *Geschichte des Altertums*, Vol. III, p. 97.
3. Hans Heinrich Schaeder, *Der Mensch in Orient und Okzident* (Munich: R. Piper and Co., 1960), p. 103.
4. E.g. in Yasna 28:8; 46:14; 51:16 and 19; 53:2.
5. Ernst Herzfeld, *Zoroaster and His World* (Princeton: Princeton University Press, 1947), Vol. I, pp. 1–30; A. T. Olmstead, *History of the Persian Empire* (Chicago: University of Chicago Press, Phoenix Books, 1948, 1959), p. 94; R. C. Zaehner, *The Dawn and Twilight of Zoroastrianism* (New York: G. P. Putnam's Sons; London: Weidenfeld and Nicholson, 1961), pp. 33–36.

6. Meyer, *Geschichte des Altertums*, Vol. III, p. 110, n. 3.
7. Ibid., p. 97, n. 2.
8. Ibid.
9. *Vedāntasāra* 30.
10. Yasna 45:2–3; following, largely, L. H. Mills, op. cit. pp. 125–26.
11. Yasna 28:3; Mills, op. cit., p. 18.
12. Yasna 30:2; Mills, op. cit., p. 29.
13. Yasna 48:4; Mills, op. cit., p. 155.
14. *Artā-ī-Vīrāf Nāmak* IV, 7–33; following Martin Haug, Destur Hoshangji Jamaspji Asa, and E. W. West, *The Book of Arda Viraf* (London: Trübner and Co.; Bombay: Government Central Book Depot, 1872), pp. 154–55.
15. From ibid., abridged and summarized.
16. E. W. West, *Pahlavi Texts*, Part I: *The Bundahish, Bahman Yasht, and Shahyast La-shahyast; Sacred Books of the East*, Vol. V (Oxford: The Clarendon Press, 1880), pp. xlii, xliii.

17. James Darmesteter, *The Zend Avesta*, Part I: *The Vendidad; Sacred Books of the East*, Vol. IV (Oxford: The Clarendon Press, 1880), p. xii.

18. Yasna 30:3, 9; Mills, op. cit., pp. 29, 33–34.

19. *Bundahish* I–XV, abridged and with brief additions from XXIV, XXVII, and *Zat-sparam* II.6; V.1–2; VII.3–6; VIII.3–5; IX. 2–6; and X.3–4 (West, op. cit., pp. 3–58; 88; 99; 161–62; 167; 174; 176–77; 177–79; and 183).

20. *The Masks of God: Primitive Mythology*, pp. 174 ff.

21. Joseph Klausner, *The Messianic Idea in Israel*, transl. by W. F. Stinespring (London: George Allen and Unwin, Ltd., 1956), p. 59.

22. Ibid., pp. 65–66.

23. Ibid., p. 10.

24. Ibid., pp. 56–57 and note 8.

25. Yasht 19.2.11. James Darmesteter, *The Zend-Avesta*, Part II, *The Sirozahs, Yashts and Nyayis; Sacred Books of the East*, Vol. XXIII (Oxford: The Clarendon Press, 1883), p. 290.

26. Yasht 19.13.79–80. Darmesteter, *The Zend-Avesta*, Part II, pp. 304–305.

27. Yasht 13.93.

28. *Vendidad*, Fargard 19.1–2 (Darmesteter I, p. 204).

29. Yasht 5.7–15 (Darmesteter II, pp. 55–57).

30. Bundahish 32.8–9.

31. Yasht 13.141–42.

32. Bundahish 30.1–3.

33. Bundahish 30.4–33 abridged (West, op. cit., pp. 121–30).

34. Joshua 6:21.

35. Joshua 8:24.

36. Joshua 10:6–11:20.

37. Judges 1:27 ff.

38. Meyer, *Geschichte des Altertums*, Vol. III, pp. 6–8.

39. Ibid., pp. 11–12.

40. Amos 6:1–2.

41. Meyer, *Geschichte des Altertums*, Vol. III, p. 161.

42. Jeremiah 25:8–9.

43. Meyer, *Geschichte des Altertums*, Vol. III, p. 188.

44. Ezra 1:7–11.

45. Isaiah 45:1.

46. Isaiah 45:2–7.

47. G. Buchanan Gray, "The Foundation and Extension of the Persian Empire," in J. B. Bury, S. A. Cook, F. E. Adcock (eds.), *The Cambridge Ancient History*, Vol. IV (Cambridge: The University Press, 1939), Chapter I, p. 13, note 1; and for an extended study of Nabonidus's heresy, Sidney Smith, *Babylonian Historical Texts* (London: Methuen and Company, 1924), pp. 27–123.

48. Cyrus Cylinder, lines 6–36, in part; following F. H. Weissbach, *Die Keilinschriften der Achameniden* (Leipzig: J. C. Hinrich, 1911), pp. 2–7.

49. Meyer, *Geschichte des Altertums*, Vol. III, pp. 187–97.

50. Inscription of Behistun; the Great Inscription, paragraphs 1–15; Weissbach, op. cit., pp. 9–21.

51. Oswald Spengler, *Der Untergang des Abendlandes*, Vol. II (Munich: C. H. Beck, 1930), p. 285; translation from Charles Francis Atkinson, Oswald Spengler, *The Decline of the West* (London: Allen & Unwin, Ltd.; New York: Alfred A. Knopf, 1937), Vol. II, p. 235. Copyright, 1926, 1928 by Alfred A. Knopf, Inc. Renewed. Reprinted by permission of Alfred A. Knopf, Inc., and Allen & Unwin, Ltd.

52. Isaiah 10:20–23.

53. Ezra 1:2–4.

54. Ezra 2:64–65.

55. Nehemiah 1:11.

56. Nehemiah 2:11–17.

57. Ezra 9:1–3.

58. Ezra 10:1–17, 44.

59. Plato, *Symposium* 196c; Jowett translation.

60. Warner Fite, *The Platonic Legend* (New York and London: Charles Scribner's Sons, 1934), p. 153.

61. *The Masks of God: Primitive Mythology*, pp. 93–116.

62. Heinrich Zimmer, *The Art of Indian Asia*, completed and edited by Joseph Campbell, Bollingen Series XXXIX, (New York: Pantheon Books, 1955), Vol. I, p. 131.

63. Juvenal 6.324, as cited by Karl Kerényi, *The Religion of the Greeks and Romans* (New York:

E. P. Dutton and Co., 1962), p. 30.

64. Symposium 201d; translation by Michael Joyce, reprinted in Edith Hamilton and Huntington Cairns, *The Collected Dialogues of Plato,* Bollingen Series LXXI (New York: Pantheon Books, 1961), p. 553.

65. Symposium 210a–212a; translation by Michael Joyce, loc. cit.

66. Spengler, op. cit. Vol. I, 229–30

(English, Vol. I, pp. 176–77.)

67. *Theogony* 120–22; from the translation by Richmond Lattimore, *Hesiod* (Ann Arbor: The University of Michigan Press, 1961).

68. *The Masks of God: Primitive Mythology,* pp. 170–71.

69. *The Masks of God: Oriental Mythology,* pp. 81–83.

70. *The Masks of God: Oriental Mythology;* see index, under "sacrifice, human," and "suttee."

CHAPTER 6: HELLENISM: 331 B.C.–324 A.D.

1. Maximus of Tyre, Dissertation XXXVIII; translation from Gilbert Murray, *Five Stages of Greek Religion* (Garden City: Doubleday Anchor Books, no date), pp. 74–75, note 44; also in Thomas Taylor, *The Dissertations of Maximus Tyrius* (London: C. Whittingham, 1804), Vol. II, pp. 196–98.

2. Gilbert Murray, *Aeschylus* (Oxford: The Clarendon Press, 1940), p. 129.

3. Aeschylus, *The Persians,* lines 808–15 (translation, Gilbert Murray, *Aeschylus,* pp. 119–20.

4. Following Hammond, op. cit., pp. 212–44.

5. *The Masks of God: Primitive Mythology,* pp. 418 ff.

6. Alexander Pope, "The Universal Prayer," Stanzas 1, 7, 13.

7. Hermann Diels, *Die Fragmente der Vorsokratiker* (Berlin: Weidmann, 4th ed., 1922), Fragments 23, 24, 26, 14, 16, 11, 15.

8. Cited by Clement of Alexandria, *Exhortation to the Greeks,* p. 61P; as cited by F. M. Cornford, *Greek Religious Thought* (London: J. M. Dent and Sons, 1923), p. 237.

9. Aristotle, *Metaphysics* A. 986 b. 21.

10. H. Ritter and L. Preller, *Historia Philosophiae Graecae* (Gotha: F. R. Perthes, 1888) p. 83; Xenophanes, Fragment 90B.

11. *The Masks of God: Oriental Mythology,* pp. 422–29.

12. Matthew 19:21.

13. Matthew Arnold, "An Essay on

Marcus Aurelius," *Essays in Criticism: First Series* (London and Cambridge: Macmillan and Co.; Boston: Ticknor and Fields, 1st ed., 1865), p. 262.

14. Marcus Aurelius, translation by George Long (London: G. Routledge and Sons, 1862), Chapter IV, Paragraph 4.

15. Ibid., Chapter VII, Paragraph 55.

16. Ibid., Chapter VIII, Paragraph 59.

17. Ibid., Chapter V, Paragraph 6, in part.

18. Matthew 6:1–4.

19. Arnold, loc. cit.

20. Murray, *The Five Stages of Greek Religion,* Chapter IV.

21. W. W. Tarn, *Hellenistic Civilization,* revised by the author and G. T. Griffith (New York: Meridian Books, 1961), pp. 296–98.

22. Ibid., pp. 302–305.

23. Ibid., pp. 305–306.

24. See, for example, Joseph Needham's numerous comparisons of Greek and Chinese science in Joseph Needham and Wang Ling, *Science and Civilisation in China,* Vol. II (Cambridge: The University Press, 1956), pp. 216–345.

25. Arrian, *The Discourses of Epictetus,* iii.22.45–46; translation, Hastings Crossley, *The Golden Sayings of Epictetus* (London: Macmillan and Co., 1925), pp. 100–101.

26. Marcus Aurelius, Chapter XII, Paragraph 32; translation, George Long, *The Thoughts of Marcus Aurelius Antoninus* (London: G. Bell and Sons, 1919), pp. 215–16.

27. Tarn, op. cit., p. 330.

28. Seneca, *On Providence* II. 4.

29. Seneca, *Consolation of Helvia* VIII. 5.

30. Arrian, *Discourses* iii.20.12.

31. Ibid., i.16.15–18.

32. Ibid., ii.8.10–11.

33. *Bhagavad Gītā* 2:15.

34. Ibid., 3:19.

35. Arrian, op. cit., ii.8.2.

36. Jacob Hoschander, *The Priests and Prophets* (New York: The Jewish Theological Seminary of America, 1938), pp. 48 ff.

37. Isaiah 41–49.

38. Joseph Klausner, *From Jesus to Paul*, transl. by William F. Stinespring (Boston: Beacon Press edition, 1961), p. 185.

39. Ibid., p. 182.

40. H. Schenkl, *Epicteti Dissertationes* (Teubner, 1898), Fragment 17.

41. *The Masks of God: Oriental Mythology*, pp. 304, 492–93.

42. *The Masks of God: Oriental Mythology*, pp. 103–12.

43. Yasht 10.1; Darmesteter, *The Zend Avesta*, Part II, pp. 119–20.

44. Franz Cumont, *The Mysteries of Mithra*, translated by Thomas J. McCormack (London: Kegan Paul, Trench, Trubner and Co., 1903), p. 24. For the series of grades of initiation, ibid., pp. 152–64. Fig. 23 is from Cumont, *Textes et monuments figurés relatifs aux mystères de Mithra* (Brussels: H. Lamertin, 1896–99), Vol. II, p. 228, Fig. 59.

45. *The Masks of God: Primitive Mythology*, pp. 170–225.

46. William Blake, "Proverbs of Hell," from *The Marriage of Heaven and Hell* (etched about 1793).

47. Cumont, *The Mysteries of Mithra*, pp. 191–93.

48. Ibid., pp. 180–81.

49. Carl G. Jung, *Symbols of Transformation*, translated by R. F. C. Hull, The Bollingen Series XX (New York: Pantheon Books, 1956), pp. 200–201.

50. Jerome, *Adversus Jovinianum*, I. 7; as cited by Jung, *Symbols of Transformation*, p. 101, note 48.

51. Jung, *Symbols of Transformation*, p. 247.

52. Cumont, *The Mysteries of Mithra*, pp. 130–37.

53. Ibid., p. 105. Fig. 24 is from Cumont, *Textes et monuments figurés*, Vol. II, p. 238, Fig. 68.

54. Zimmer, *The Art of Indian Asia*, Vol. I, p. 194.

55. *The Masks of God: Oriental Mythology*, p. 487.

56. See L. de la Valée Poussin, "Tantrism (Buddhist)," in Hastings (ed.), *Encyclopaedia of Religion and Ethics*, Vol. XII, pp. 193–97.

57. *The Masks of God: Oriental Mythology*, pp. 303 ff.

58. Cumont, *The Mysteries of Mithra*, p. 151.

59. See *The Masks of God: Oriental Mythology*, pp. 177 and index, "Varuna."

60. *Śatapatha Brāhmaṇa* 4.1.4; as discussed by Ananda K. Coomaraswamy, *Spiritual Authority and Temporal Power in the Indian Theory of Government*, American Oriental Series, Volume 22 (New Haven: American Oriental Society, 1942), p. 6.

61. *Taittirīya Saṃhitā* 2.1.9.3; from Coomaraswamy, op. cit., note 22, pp. 28–29.

62. Coomaraswamy, op. cit., note 24, pp. 34–36.

63. Cumont, *The Mysteries of Mithra*, pp. 15 ff.

64. See, for example, Arthur Avalon (Sir John Woodroffe), *The Serpent Power* (Madras: Ganesh and Co., third revised edition, 1931), and Swami Nikhilananda (translator), *The Gospel of Sri Ramakrishna* (New York: Ramakrishna-Vivekananda Center, 1942), index, "Kundalini."

65. Cicero, *de Legibus* II.36.

66. Mark 13:3–37 (parallels in Matthew 24 and Luke 21; see also, II Thessalonians 2 and The Revelation to John).

67. I Maccabees 2:1–30.

68. Tarn, op. cit., pp. 217–26.

69. Erwin R. Goodenough, *Jewish Symbols in the Greco-Roman Period*, 8 volumes, The Bollingen Series XXXVII (New York: Pantheon Books, 1953–1958), Vol. 2, p. 216; discussion of the Anguipede, pp. 245–58. The figures

here reproduced are from Vol. III, Figs. 1083, 1094, 1097, 1104, 1109.

70. Ibid., Vol. 2, p. 248.
71. From the Greek Magical Papyri, Mithra Liturgy (Papyrus IV, lines 558–60), in Karl Lebrecht Preisendanz, *Papyri Graegae Magicae: Die Griechische Zauberpapyri* (Leipzig-Berlin: B. G. Teubner, Vol. I, 1928, Vol. II, 1931), Vol. I, p. 92, as cited by Goodenough, op. cit., Vol. 2, p. 270.
72. Josephus, *De Bello Judaico* 2.8.14 (paragraphs 162–63), translation by William Whiston, revised by D. S. Margoliouth, as published by Harper and Brothers, New York: Harper Torchbooks, 1960.
73. Ibid., 2.8.14 (paragraphs 164–165).
74. Ibid., 2.8.14 (paragraph 166).
75. Maccabees 2:45–48.
76. Ibid., 3:1–12 abridged.
77. Ibid., 8–9:23.
78. Ibid., 9:24–10:20.
79. Ibid., 14:38–43.
80. Josephus, op. cit., 1.2.4 (paragraphs 57–60).
81. Ibid., 1.2.8 (paragraph 67).
82. Ibid., 1.3.1. (paragraph 71).
83. Ibid., paragraph 70.
84. Ibid., 1.3.2–6 (paragraphs 72–84).
85. Ibid., 1.4.4 (paragraphs 91–92).
86. Ibid., 1.4.4–5 (paragraphs 92–95).
87. Ibid., 1.4.1–6 (paragraphs 85–97).
88. Duncan Howlett, *The Essenes and Christianity: An Interpretation of the Dead Sea Scrolls* (New York: Harper and Brothers, 1957), p. 14.
89. Translation from Millar Burrows, *The Dead Sea Scrolls* (New York: The Viking Press, 1955), pp. 392–93; from The War Scroll, columns iii and iv, abridged.
90. Howlett, op. cit., p. 22.
91. *Manual of Discipline*, section on

"The Two Spirits in Man," Burrows, op. cit., pp. 374–76, greatly abridged.
92. *The Masks of God: Oriental Mythology*, p. 292.
93. Rock Edict XII; Vincent A. Smith, *The Edicts of Achoka* (Broad Campden: Essex House Press, 1909), p. 20; cited in *The Masks of God: Oriental Mythology*, p. 294.
94. Howlett, op. cit., p. 18.
95. Burrows, op. cit., pp. 365–66.
96. Ibid., p. 365.
97. See Millar Burrows, *More Light on the Dead Sea Scrolls* (New York: The Viking Press, 1958), pp. 212 and 222, citing, among others, T. J. Milik and G. Vermes.
98. Frank Moore Cross, Jr., *The Ancient Library of Qumran and Modern Biblical Studies* (Garden City, New York: Doubleday and Company, 1958), pp. 101–16; discussed by Burrows, *More Light on the Dead Sea Scrolls*, p. 212.
99. Howlett, op. cit., pp. 48–58, and 66–67.
100. For the text, see Burrows, *More Light on the Dead Sea Scrolls*, p. 404, and for the identification with Jannaeus, Howlett, op. cit., pp. 68–78.
101. Howlett, op. cit., p. 76.
102. Burrows, *More Light on the Dead Sea Scrolls*, pp. 339–40.
103. Ibid., p. 341.
104. Cross, op. cit., p. 151.
105. Ibid., p. 151; the quoted phrase is from Rudolf Bultmann, *Theology of the New Testament*, translated by K. Grobel (New York: Scribner, 1951), Vol. I, p. 42.
106. Ibid., pp. 181–82; see also Bultmann, loc. cit.
107. Burrows, *The Dead Sea Scrolls*, p. 371.
108. Matthew 5:43–48.

Chapter 7: GREAT ROME: c. 500 B.C.–c. 500 A.D.

1. Mircea Eliade, *Forgerons et alchimists* (Paris: Flammarion, 1956), p. 24.
2. Ibid., p. 83.
3. Julius Caesar, *De Bello Gallico* 6.13–18. Translation by H. J. Ed-

wards, Loeb Classical Library (Cambridge, Mass.: Harvard University Press; London: William Heinemann), slightly modified.
4. For a survey of the Classical literature, see T. D. Kendrick, *The*

Druids (London: Methuen and Co., 1927), Chapter III.

5. Alfred Nutt, *The Voyage of Bran* (London: David Nutt, 1897), Vol. II, pp. 92–93, note 6.

6. John Arnott MacCulloch, *Celtic Mythology; The Mythology of All Races,* Vol. III (Boston: Marshall Jones Company, 1918), pp. 45–46.

7. Nutt, op. cit., Vol. II, pp. 91–96.

8. MacCulloch, op. cit., p. 43.

9. Nutt, op. cit., Vol. II, p. 92.

10. *The Masks of God: Primitive Mythology,* pp. 229–81.

11. Geoffrey Keating (c. 1570–1646), *History of Ireland,* translated by John O'Mahony (London: 1866), 105–106, as cited by J. A. MacCulloch, *The Religion of the Ancient Celts* (Edinburgh: T. and T. Clark, 1911), p. 50.

12. Keating 107; MacCulloch, *Religion,* pp. 50–51.

13. *The Masks of God: Primitive Mythology,* pp. 432–34.

14. Strabo 4.4.6; cited by Kendrick, op. cit., p. 139.

15. Mela, *Chorogr.* 3.6.48; Kendrick, op. cit., pp. 138–39.

16. *The Masks of God: Primitive Mythology,* pp. 183–90.

17. Kendrick, op. cit., pp. 139–40.

18. The Book of Leinster (*Leabhar Laignech*), 5; as cited by MacCulloch, *The Religion of the Ancient Celts,* pp. 50–51.

19. MacCulloch, *The Religion of the Ancient Celts,* p. 32.

20. Ibid., p. 69.

21. After Lady Gregory, *Gods and Fighting Men* (London: John Murray, 1904), pp. 51–52.

22. Texts from The Golden Book of Lecan, col. 648, lines 12 ff.; and Egerton, 1782, p. 148, as rendered by Ernst Windisch, *Irische Texte,* II Serie, 2 Heft, pp. 241 ff. Translation after Eleanor Hull, *The Cuchullin Saga in Irish Literature* (London: David Nutt, 1898), pp. 103–107.

23. H. D'Arbois de Jubainville, *Les Celtes depuis les temps les plus anciens jusqu'en 100 avant notre ère* (Paris: A. Fontemoing, 1904), pp. 63 ff.

24. MacCulloch, *The Religion of the Ancient Celts,* pp. 138–41.

25. Otto-Wilhelm von Vacano, *The Etruscans in the Ancient World,* translated by Sheila Ann Ogilvie (London: Edward Arnold Ltd.; New York: St. Martin's Press, 1960), pp. 57–58.

26. Ibid., p. 39.

27. Ibid., p. 40. Fig. 29. discussed by von Vacano, is from Eduard Gerhard, *Miroirs étrusques* (Berlin: 1841–67), Vol. II, Plate CLXXVI.

28. Horace Gregory, Ovid, *The Metamorphoses* (New York: The Viking Press, 1958), p. 214.

29. For the variants and sources, see K. Kerényi, *The Heroes of the Greeks* (New York: Grove Press, 1960), pp. 113–21 and appended notes.

30. Ibid., p. 171.

31. Seneca, *Quaestiones Naturales* II. 32, 41, 48; as cited by von Vacano, op. cit., p. 145.

32. Plutarch, *Romulus,* following the translation called Dryden's, as revised by A. H. Clough.

33. Ibid.

34. Luke 24:13–31.

35. Plutarch, op. cit.

36. Charlton T. Lewis and Charles Short, *A Latin Dictionary* (Oxford: The Clarendon Press, 1879), pp. 1224–25.

37. *The Masks of God: Oriental Mythology,* pp. 474–79.

38. Seneca, *Epist.* 41.3. Cited by Nilsson, op. cit., Vol. I, p. 286.

39. Ludwig Deubner, "Die Römer," in Chantepie de la Saussaye, *Lehrbuch der Religionsgeschichte* (Tübingen: J. C. B. Mohr, 4th revised edition, 1925), Vol. II, p. 443.

40. Ibid., pp. 438–42.

41. *The Masks of God: Primitive Mythology,* pp. 151–69.

42. Plutarch, *De Pythiae Oraculis;* as cited by H. C. O. Lanchester, "Sibylline Oracles," in Hastings (ed.), op. cit., Vol. XI, p. 497.

43. Servius, commentary on Virgil, Eclogue iv. 4; Georgius Thilo, *Servii Grammatici* (Hildesheim: Georg Olms, 1961), Vol. III, pp. 44–45.

44. Eclogue iv. Translation after J. W. Mackail.
45. Cicero, *De re publica* 6.9–26, greatly abridged, following the translation of Clinton Walker Keyes in the Loeb Classical Library, 1928 (Cambridge, Mass.: Harvard University Press; London: William Heinemann). Reprinted by permission of the publishers and the Loeb Classical Library.
46. Ibid., 6.13.
47. *The Masks of God: Oriental Mythology,* pp. 198–203.
48. Cicero, op. cit., 6.29.
49. *Aeneid* 6.790–807.
50. *Metamorphoses* 15.745–870.
51. Deubner, op. cit., pp. 469–71.
52. Ibid., p. 472.
53. I Corinthians 15:21–22 (date c. 54 A.D.)
54. Philippians 2:6–11. The identification of this passage as a traditional Christological hymn was made by Ernst Lohmeyer, "Kyrios Jesus," *Heidelberger Akademie der Wissenschaften. Sitzungsbericht. Philosophisch-historische Klasse, 1927–28.* 4 Abh., 1928. See Rudolf Bultmann, *Primitive Christianity in Its Contemporary Setting* (New York: Living Age Books, 1956), pp. 196–97.
55. Klausner, *The Messianic Idea in Israel,* p. 24.
56. Luke 1:26–35, 38.
57. Luke 2:1–20.
58. See Henri Corbin, "Terre céleste et corps de résurrection d'après quelques traditions iraniennes," *Eranos-Jahrbuch 1953* (Zurich: Rhein-Verlag, 1954), p. 109.
59. Matthew 2:1–12.
60. Epiphanius, *Penarion* 51, as cited by Kirsopp Lake, article, "Epiphany," in Hastings (ed.), op. cit., Vol. V, p. 332.
61. Kirsopp Lake, article, "Christmas," in Hastings (ed.), op. cit., Vol. III, p. 602.
62. Matthew 2:13–23.
63. Louis Ginzberg, *The Legends of the Jews,* translated by Henrietta Szold (Philadelphia: The Jewish Publication Society of America, 1913), Vol. I, pp. 186–89.
64. *Bhagavatā Puraṇa* 10.1.17–10.4. 14, greatly abridged.
65. *The Masks of God: Oriental Mythology,* pp. 347–50.
66. Hesiod, *Theogony* 453–506. Translation reprinted from *Hesiod,* by Richmond Lattimore, pp. 150–53, by permission of The University of Michigan Press. Copyright © by The University of Michigan 1959.
67. Charles Guignebert, *Jesus,* translated from the French by S. H. Hooke (New York: University Books, 1956), p. 43.
68. Mark 1:9–11.
69. Luke 3:22, *Western* text, Codex D; cited by Guignebert, op. cit., p. 108.
70. Josephus, *Antiquities* 18.5.2.
71. Mark 6:16–29.
72. Mark 1:4–8.
73. II Kings 1:8.
74. See the discussion of this point in Guignebert, op. cit., p. 149, who supplies, as for every question, a complete bibliography.
75. *The Masks of God: Oriental Mythology,* pp. 264–72.
76. Matthew 1:1–17; Luke 3:23–38.
77. Mark 1:12–13.
78. *The Masks of God: Oriental Mythology,* pp. 15–21 and 271–72.
79. Ibid., pp. 14–15.
80. Klausner, *The Messianic Idea in Israel,* pp. 9–10; italics Klausner's.
81. Mark 1:14–28.
82. Guignebert, op. cit., pp. 191–92.
83. Romans 13:11–12.
84. Mark 2:27.
85. Mark 2:22.
86. Mark 2:17.
87. Matthew 5:44.
88. Mark 12:28–31.
89. Matthew 16:13–23.
90. Mark 14:17–16:8.
91. Colossians 2:8–3:8, abridged.
92. Acts of John 88–89, translation following Montague Rhodes James, *The Apocryphal New Testament* (Oxford: The Clarendon Press, corrected edition, 1953), p. 251. Reprinted by permission of the Clarendon Press.
93. Acts of John 93; James, op. cit., pp. 252–53.
94. Vajracchedika 32; cited, *The*

Masks of God: Oriental Mythology, p. 319.

95. *The Tempest* IV.i.157–58.

96. *Corpus Hermeticum*, translated by Scott, Book XI (ii), 20b–22b; pp. 220–23. I owe the knowledge of this passage to the kindness and learning of Dr. Alan W. Watts and Mrs. Ananda K. Coomaraswamy.

97. *The Gospel According to Thomas*, Coptic text established and translated by A. Guillaumont, H.-Ch. Puech, G. Quispel, W. Till, and Yassah 'Abd al Masīh (Leiden: E. J. Brill; New York: Harper and Brothers, 1959), p. 43.

98. Thomas 80:14–19a; 99:13–18; 80:14b–81:4; op. cit., pp. 3 and 55, 57.

99. Luke 17:20–21.

100. Guignebert, op. cit., pp. 339–41.

101. Edward Gibbon; *The Decline and Fall of the Roman Empire*, from Chapters I and II.

102. Acts of John 94–96. Translation based on James, op. cit., pp. 253–54 and Max Pulver, "Jesus' Round Dance and Crucifixion," in Joseph Campbell (ed.), *The Mysteries*, The Bollingen Series XXX, Papers from the Eranos Yearbooks, Vol. 2, (New York: Pantheon Books, 1955), pp. 178–80.

103. Acts of John 97–102; James, op. cit., pp. 254–56, Pulver, op. cit., pp. 180–82.

104. Acts 1:6.

105. Isaiah 26:19.

106. Isaiah 65:17, 19.

107. Justin Martyr, First Apology 26; in Thomas B. Falls, *Writings of Saint Justin Martyr* (New York: Christian Heritage, 1949), p. 62.

108. R. M. Grant, *Gnosticism and Early Christianity* (New York: Columbia University Press, 1959), p. 185.

109. E. F. Scott, article "Gnosticism," in Hastings (ed.), op. cit., Vol. VI, p. 241.

110. Acts 7:58; 8:1, 3.

111. Galatians 3:13–14.

112. Galatians 3:24–25, 28–29.

113. I Corinthians 1:10; 5:9–13, abridged.

114. Ibid., 12:7, 12–13, 27–28.

115. Ibid., 11:3–10.

116. Ibid., 11:1.

117. Acts 8:1.

118. Acts 17:16–18:1.

119. Acts 21:30–36.

120. James Henry Breasted, *The Conquest of Civilization* (New York: Harper and Brothers, 1926), p. 673.

121. Eusebius of Caesarea, *Vita Constantini* (ed. I. A. Keikel, Berlin, 1902), translation, Nicene Library (ed. H. Wace and P. Schaff, Oxford, 1890 ff.).

122. *The Masks of God: Oriental Mythology*, pp. 293–94.

123. For a discussion of these controversies, see Adolf Harnack, *History of Dogma*, translated from the third German edition by Neil Buchanan (New York: Dover Publications, 1961), Vol. V, pp. 140–68 for the Donatist Controversy, and Vol. IV, Chapter I, for The Doctrine of the Homousia of the Son of God with God Himself.

124. John 18:36, in part.

125. H. M. Gwatkin, "Constantine and His City," in *The Cambridge Medieval History*, Vol. I, p. 3.

126. Translation from Gwatkin, "Arianism," in *The Cambridge Medieval History*, Vol. I, pp. 121–22.

127. Gibbon, op. cit., Chapter XXVIII, in part.

128. Augustine, *De Civitate Dei*, Book 22, Chapter 30.

PART FOUR: THE AGE OF THE GREAT BELIEFS

INTRODUCTION: THE DIALOGUE OF EUROPE AND THE LEVANT

1. Spengler, op. cit., Vol. I, p. 211 (English), p. 272 (German).

2. Ibid., Vol. I, p. 329 (English), p. 421 (German).

3. Ibid., Vol. I, p. 225 (English), p. 290 (German).
4. Ibid., Vol. I, p. 200 (English), p. 257 (German).
5. Ibid., Vol. II, p. 234 (English), Vol. II, page 283 (German).
6. Ibid., Vol. II, p. 189 (English), Vol. II, p. 227 (German).
7. Ibid., Vol. II, pp. 190–91 (English), pp. 228–29 (German).

CHAPTER 8: THE CROSS AND THE CRESCENT

1. *The Masks of God: Oriental Mythology*, pp. 296–98.
2. *Dēnkart* 412; from Zaehner, op. cit., pp. 175–76.
3. Ibid.
4. *Dēnkart* 413; Zaehner, op. cit., p. 176.
5. Zaehner, op. cit., p. 186.
6. Ibid., p. 187, citing *Shikand-Gumānīk Vichār* 10.70–71.
7. *Dēnkart* 413; Zaehner, op. cit., p. 176.
8. *Dēnkart* 414–15; Zaehner, op. cit., pp. 176–77.
9. Spengler, op. cit., Vol. II, pp. 235–36 (English), Vol. II, p. 285 (German).
10. Gwatkin, "Arianism," pp. 135–36.
11. Following Alice Gardner, "Religious Disunion in the Fifth Century," in *The Cambridge Medieval History*, Vol. I, pp. 494–503; and R. M. French, *The Eastern Orthodox Church* (London: Hutchinson's University Library, 1951), pp. 23–33.
12. Gibbon, op. cit., Chapter XXXVI, last paragraph.
13. Compare *The Masks of God: Oriental Mythology*, pp. 266–67.
14. For an introductory view of the temples, with photographs, see Imgard Bidder, *Lalibela: The Monolithic Churches of Ethiopia* (London: Thames and Hudson, 1959).
15. Cf. Ugo Monneret de Villard, *Aksum: Ricerche di Topografia Generale* (Rome: Pontificum Institutum Biblicum, 1938); Enno Littmann and Theodor von Lüpke, *Deutsche Aksum-Expedition*, 4 vols. (Berlin: Georg Reimer, 1913), "Legend of the Dragon King," Vol. I, p. 39.
16. Leo Frobenius, *Und Afrika Sprach. . . .* (Berlin: Vita Verlag, 1912), pp. 605–36.
17. Gardner, op. cit., pp. 510–11.
18. Adda B. Bozeman, *Politics and Culture in International History* (Princeton: Princeton University Press, 1960), p. 327.
19. Ibid., p. 322.
20. Robert Eisler, *Weltenmantel und Himmelszelt* (Munich: C. H. Beck'sche Verlagsbuchhandlung, 1910), Vol. I, p. 36, note 2, citing Liudprand of Cremona (d. c. 972), *Antapodosis* VI.5. Cf. translation by F. A. Wright, *The Works of Liudprand of Cremona* (London: George Routledge and Sons, 1930), pp. 207–208.
21. Norman H. Baynes, *The Byzantine Empire* (London: Williams and Norgate, Ltd., 1925), pp. 72–73; cited by Bozeman, *Politics and Culture in International History*, pp. 335–36.
22. Charles Diehl, "Justinian's Government in the East," in *The Cambridge Medieval History*, Vol. II, pp. 25–27, 45–49; French, op. cit., pp. 34–40.
23. E. W. Brooks, "The Successors of Heraclius to 717," in *The Cambridge Medieval History*, Vol. II, pp. 401–402.
24. French, op. cit., pp. 38–44.
25. Koran 1:1–7. Translation following Abdullah Yusuf Ali, *The Holy Qur-an: Text, Translation and Commentary* (New York: Hafner Publishing Company, no date), Vol. I, pp. 14–15. All the following Koranic quotations are based on this translation.
26. Koran 2:30–39.
27. Genesis 20:8–14.
28. Koran 2:127–28.
29. Koran 2:133.
30. Koran 2:140.
31. Koran 2:40–41.
32. Koran 2:87–88.
33. In this division I am following D. S. Margoliouth, "Muhammad," in Hastings (ed.), op. cit., Vol. VIII, p. 873.
34. Koran 96:1–5.

35. Abdullah Yusuf Ali, op. cit., Koranic Commentary 27–33, abridged, pp. 8–10.
36. Commentary 34, ibid., p. 10.
37. Koran 73:1–5.
38. Following the Commentary of Abdullah Yusuf Ali, op. cit., Vol. II, pp. 1633–40, notes 5754, 5755, 5778.
39. Koran 74:1–10.
40. A. A. Bevan, "Mahomet and Islām," in The Cambridge Medieval History, Vol. II, p. 306; and H. A. R. Gibb, Mohammedanism (New York: Oxford University Press, Galaxy Books, 1962), p. 38.
41. Koran 106.
42. Commentary 26, Abdullah Yusuf Ali, op. cit., p. 8.
43. Koran 9:40.
44. Gibb, op. cit., p. 29.
45. Bevan, op. cit., p. 325.
46. A. E. Crawley, article, "Kissing," in Hastings (ed.), op. cit., Vol. VII, p. 743.
47. Koran 44:38–59.
48. Jeremiah 10:2–3, 6–8, 10.
49. Koran 2:144.
50. Koran 3:85.
51. Isaiah 61:5–6.
52. Koran 50:37.
53. Gibb, op. cit., pp. 78–79.
54. Ibid., p. 94.
55. Spengler, op. cit., Vol. II, pp. 84–85 (German), pp. 72–73 (English).
56. Gibb, op. cit., pp. 95–98.
57. Ibid., p. 98.
58. Spengler, op. cit., Vol. II, pp. 85–86 (German), p. 73 (English).
59. Sir Mohammad Iqbal, translation by Arthur J. Arberry, The Mysteries of Selflessness (London: John Murray Ltd., 1953), p. xv; as cited by Bozeman, Politics and Culture in International History, p. 360, note 7.
60. Koran 74:49–50; 76:4–5 and 13–16.
61. Omar Khayyám, The Rubáiyát, E. H. Whinfield translation, stanzas 185; 244; 262.
62. Jalālu'ddīn Rūmī, Mathnawī I. 3360–95. Translation following Reynold A. Nicholson, The Mathnawí of Jalálu'ddín Rúmí, E. J. W.

63. Louis Massignon, "Die Ursprünge und die Bedeutung des Gnostizismus im Islam," Eranos-Jahrbuch 1937 (Zürich: Rhein-Verlag, 1938), p. 58, citing Moghira, Shahrastani, milal, II, 13–14.
64. Ibid., pp. 59–60, citing the Persian-Gnostic Omm-al-Kitāb and the doctrine of the Syrian Noseiri sect.
65. Ibid., pp. 64–65, citing Omm-al-Kitāb.
66. Ibid., p. 66.
67. Koran 97:1–5.
68. Koran 4:157.
69. Massignon, op. cit., pp. 69–70.
70. Ibid., p. 74, from Mansūr al-Hallāj, Kitāb al-Tawāsīn.
71. Koran 24:32.
72. Gibb, op. cit., p. 133.
73. Reynold A. Nicholson, article "Sufis," in Hastings (ed.), op. cit., Vol. XII, pp. 11–12.
74. Translation by R. A. Nicholson, article "Mysticism," in Sir Thomas Arnold (ed.), The Legacy of Islam (Oxford: The Clarendon Press, 1931), p. 211.
75. The Masks of God: Primitive Mythology, pp. 461–72.
76. Marion Morehouse and E. E. Cummings, Adventures in Value (New York: Harcourt, Brace and World, Inc., 1962), motto page.
77. Aṣṭavakra Saṁhitā 14–15, in part.
78. Nicholson, "Mysticism," p. 217.
79. Ibid., p. 215.
80. Koran 55:26–27.
81. Koran 50:16.
82. Koran 2:115.
83. Massignon, op. cit., pp. 74–75, citing Hallāj, op. cit.
84. Koran 2:26; see also 2:98.
85. Arabian Nights, Tale 155, "Hassan of Bassora and the King's Daughter of the Jinn." See Joseph Campbell (ed.) The Portable Arabian Nights (New York: The Viking Press, 1952, 1962), pp. 566–79.
86. Omar Khayyám, The Rubáiyát, stanza 491, Whinfield translation.
87. Spengler, op. cit., Vol. II, p. 278 (German), p. 237 (English).

Chapter 9: EUROPE RESURGENT

1. Standish H. O'Grady, *Silva Gadelica*, Vol. II (Translation and Notes), pp. 1–4.
2. O'Grady, op. cit., p. vi.
3. *The Masks of God: Oriental Mythology*, pp. 115–21, 129.
4. "The Lebar Brecc Homily on Saint Patrick," p. 24, col. 2; translation from Whitley Stokes, *The Tripartite Life of Patrick with Other Documents Relating to That Saint* (London: Eyre and Spottiswoode, 1887), Vol. II, p. 433.
5. Ibid., p. 26, col. 1; Stokes, op. cit., pp. 448–49.
6. *Bethu Phátraic Andso*, Egerton 93, fo. ca., in Stokes, op. cit., Vol. I, pp. 41–47, and *Lebar Brecc*, p. 27, col. i., in Vol. II, pp. 455–59.
7. Rawlinson B. 512, fo. 11 (Stokes, op. cit., Vol. I, pp. 91–93).
8. Optatus, *De schismate Donatistarum* 2.1. and 5.4; cited by Harnack, op. cit., Vol. V, pp. 44–45.
9. Following Harnack, op. cit., Vol. V, pp. 168–221.
10. Ibid., Chapter VI, note 1.
11. Following Henry Bett, *Joannes Scotus Erigena* (Cambridge: The University Press, 1928). The legend of Scotus's martyrdom is from William of Malmesbury.
12. Matthew 27:38. The Book of Kells is now in the library of Trinity College, Dublin.
13. Stokes, op. cit., Vol. I, p. clxi, citing *Lebar Brecc*, p. 257 a.
14. Sullivan, op. cit., p. 18.
15. T. G. E. Powell, *The Celts* (New York: Frederick A. Praeger, 1958), p. 61.
16. O'Grady, op. cit., pp. 103–104, 108, 137.
17. Tacitus, *Germania* 2–3, in part. Translation from H. Mattingly, *Tacitus on Britain and Germany* (Harmondsworth and Baltimore: The Penguin Classics, 1948), pp. 102–103.
18. Ibid., 7; Mattingly, op. cit., pp. 106–107.
19. Ibid., 9; Mattingly, op. cit., p. 108.
20. Ibid., 39–40, Mattingly, op. cit., pp. 132–34.
21. Ibid., 43; Mattingly, op. cit., p. 136.
22. Ibid., 45; Mattingly, op. cit., p. 138.
23. Ibid., 8; Mattingly, op. cit., pp. 107–108.
24. Ibid., 27; Mattingly, op. cit., pp. 122–23.
25. *The Masks of God: Primitive Mythology*, pp. 62–64.
26. *The Masks of God: Primitive Mythology*, pp. 74–75; 267–78.
27. Snorri Sturluson, *The Prose Edda*, Gylfaginning 48; translation following Arthur Gilchrist Brodeur, *The Prose Edda by Snorri Sturluson* (New York: The American-Scandinavian Foundation, 1929), pp. 68–70; and Lee M. Hollander, *The Skalds* (New York: The American-Scandinavian Foundation, 1947), pp. 28–30.
28. B. Phillpotts, "German Heathenism," in *The Cambridge Medieval History*, Vol. II, pp. 481–82, citing A.C. Haddon, *Magic and Fetishism* (London: 1906).
29. Phillpotts, op. cit., p. 481.
30. Otto von Friesen, article "Runes," in *Encyclopaedia Britannica*, 14th edition (1929), Vol. 19, p. 662, translating runes of the Bjorketorp Inscription and the Freilaubersheim Brooch.
31. Hovamol 139, 140, 142. Translation by Henry Adams Bellows, *The Poetic Edda* (New York: The American-Scandinavian Foundation, 1923), pp. 60–61.
32. Bellows, op. cit., p. xviii.
33. Holger Arbman, *The Vikings* (New York: Frederick A. Praeger, 1961), p. 90.
34. Eleanor Hull, *Early Christian Ireland* (London: David Nutt, 1905), pp. 167–68.
35. Arbman, op. cit., pp. 79–80, translating Ermentarius of Noirmoutier.
36. Hollander, op. cit., p. 56.
37. Grimnismol 23; Bellows, op. cit., p. 93.

38. Voluspo 45, 47, 48; Bellows, op. cit., pp. 19–21.

39. Voluspo 49–56; Bellows, op. cit., pp. 21–23.

40. Voluspo 57, 59, 62; Bellows, op. cit., pp. 24–25.

41. Sturluson, op. cit., Gylfaginning IV–IX; Brodeur, op. cit., pp. 16–22.

42. Sturluson, op. cit., Gylfaginning 20; Brodeur, op. cit., pp. 34–35.

43. Alexander Hamilton Thompson, "Medieval Doctrine to the Lateran Council of 1215," Cambridge Medieval History, Vol. VI, pp. 634–35.

44. Henry Charles Lea, A History of the Inquisition of the Middle Ages, in 3 volumes (New York: Russell and Russell, reprint edition, 1955), Vol. I, p. 5.

45. John 8:7.

46. Lea, op. cit., Vol. I, p. 14.

47. Ibid.

48. "La Gesta de Fra Peyre Cardinal," in François J. M. Raynouard, Lexique Roman (Paris: Silvestre, 1836–44), Vol. I, p. 464; translation from Lea, op. cit., Vol. I, p. 56.

49. Karl Pannier, Walthers von der Vogelweide Sämmtlich Gedichte (Leipzig: Philipp Reclam, 1876), p. 119, No. 110; cited by Lea, op. cit., Vol. I, p. 55.

50. S. Bernardi Sermones de Conversione, cap. 19, 20; as in Lea, op. cit., Vol., I, p. 52.

51. S. Hildegardae Revelat. Vis. X. cap. 16; as in Lea, op. cit., Vol. I, p. 53.

52. The Masks of God: Oriental Mythology, pp. 234–40.

53. Lea, op. cit., Vol. I, p. 104.

54. A. S. Turberville, "Heresies and the Inquisition in the Middle Ages, c. 1000–1305," Cambridge Medieval History, Vol. VI, pp. 701–702.

55. Lea, op. cit., Vol. I, pp. 104–105.

56. Ibid., pp. 119–20.

57. Ibid., pp. 123–24.

58. For a survey of these dance movements, see E. Louis Backman, Religious Dances in the Christian Church and in Popular Medicine, translated from the Swedish by E.

Classen (London: George Allen and Unwin, 1952), pp. 170 ff.

59. Ibid., pp. 161–70.

60. Matthew 6:6.

61. Lea, op. cit., Vol. I, pp. 129–61, where all references are supplied.

62. Lea, op. cit., Vol. III, pp. 90–119.

63. Dante, Paradiso XII.140–41.

64. Dante, Inferno XXVIII.55.

65. Dante, Convivio IV.4.120.

66. Ibid., IV.5.180.

67. Hilda Johnstone, "France: The Last Capetians," in The Cambridge Medieval History, Vol. VII, p. 314.

68. Ibid., p. 315.

69. Lea, op. cit., Vol. II, p. 491.

70. Ibid., Vol. II, pp. 467–93.

71. The Masks of God: Primitive Mythology, p. 402.

72. The Masks of God: Primitive Mythology, p. 231.

73. Franz Rolf Schröder, Die Parzivalfrage (Munich: C. H. Beck'sche Verlagsbuchhandlung, 1928).

74. See Jessie Weston, From Ritual to Romance (Cambridge: The University Press, 1920), pp. 11–22; also Roger Sherman Loomis, From Celtic Myth to Arthurian Romance (New York: Columbia University Press, 1927), pp. 250–70.

75. Wolfram von Eschenbach, Parzival 3.118.14–17 and 28; translated (in part) from Helen M. Mustard and Charles E. Passage (New York: Random House, Vintage Books, 1961), p. 67.

76. Ibid., 3.119.29–30.

77. J. Huizinga, The Waning of the Middle Ages (New York: Doubleday Anchor Books), p. 127.

78. Ibid., p. 107.

79. The Masks of God: Oriental Mythology, pp. 343–64.

80. Quoted from Lea, op. cit., Vol. II, p. 440.

81. Franz Pfeiffer, ed., Meister Eckhart, translation by C. de B. Evans (London: John M. Watkins, 1947), Vol. I, "Sermons and Collations," No. II, pp. 9–10.

82. Ibid., p. 10.

83. Ibid., p. 14.

84. Ibid., Vol. I, "Sermons and Collations," No. XXVI, pp. 76–77.

85. Ibid., Vol. I, "Sermons and Collations," No. LXIX, p. 171.

86. Ibid., Vol. I, "Sermons and Collations," No. LXXXVIII, pp. 221–22.

87. Ibid., Vol. II, "Sermons," No. I, p. 89.

88. Ibid., "Tractates," No. VII, Vol. I, pp. 334–36.

89. C. de B. Evans, in ibid., Vol. I, pp. xii–xiii.

90. Alan W. Watts, *Myth and Ritual in Christianity* (New York: The Vanguard Press, 1953), pp. 78–82.

91. Pfeiffer, op. cit., "Sermons and Collations," Vol. I, p. 46.

Conclusion: AT THE CLOSE OF AN AGE

1. *The Masks of God: Oriental Mythology*, pp. 35–36.

2. *The Masks of God: Oriental Mythology*, pp. 13–23.

INDEX

INDEX

INDEX

INDEX

INDEX

INDEX

INDEX

562